International Women's Rights, Equality, and Justice

Carolina Academic Press
Context and Practice Series
Michael Hunter Schwartz
Series Editor

Civil Procedure for All States
Benjamin V. Madison, III

Contracts
Michael Hunter Schwartz and Denise Riebe

Current Issues in Constitutional Litigation
Sarah E. Ricks, with contributions by Evelyn M. Tenenbaum

Employment Discrimination
Susan Grover, Sandra F. Sperino, and Jarod S. Gonzalez

International Women's Rights, Equality, and Justice
Christine M. Venter

Sales
Edith R. Warkentine

The Lawyer's Practice
Kris Franklin

International Women's Rights, Equality, and Justice

A Context and Practice Casebook

Christine M. Venter

Director of the Legal Writing Program,
Notre Dame Law School

Carolina Academic Press
Durham, North Carolina

ISBN: 978-1-59460-708-0
LCCN: 2012936949

Carolina Academic Press
700 Kent Street
Durham, North Carolina 27701
Telephone (919) 489-7486
Fax (919) 493-5668
www.cap-press.com

Printed in the United States of America

To Anré, Clea, William, Emma, Eli and Drew — with my love always

Contents

Series Editor's Preface

Welcome to a new type of casebook. Designed by leading experts in law school teaching and learning, Context and Practice casebooks assist law professors and their students to work together to learn, minimize stress, and prepare for the rigors and joys of practicing law. **Student learning and preparation for law practice are the guiding ethics of these books.**

Why would we depart from the tried and true? Why have we abandoned the legal education model by which we were trained? Because legal education can and must improve.

In Spring 2007, the Carnegie Foundation published *Educating Lawyers: Preparation for the Practice of Law* and the Clinical Legal Education Association published *Best Practices for Legal Education*. Both works reflect in-depth efforts to assess the effectiveness of modern legal education, and both conclude that legal education, as presently practiced, falls quite short of what it can and should be. Both works criticize law professors' rigid adherence to a single teaching technique, the inadequacies of law school assessment mechanisms, and the dearth of law school instruction aimed at teaching law practice skills and inculcating professional values. Finally, the authors of both books express concern that legal education may be harming law students. Recent studies show that law students, in comparison to all other graduate students, have the highest levels of depression, anxiety and substance abuse.

The problems with traditional law school instruction begin with the textbooks law teachers use. Law professors cannot implement *Educating Lawyers* and *Best Practices* using texts designed for the traditional model of legal education. Moreover, even though our understanding of how people learn has grown exponentially in the past 100 years, no law school text to date even purports to have been designed with educational research in mind.

The Context and Practice Series is an effort to offer a genuine alternative. Grounded in learning theory and instructional design and written with *Educating Lawyers* and *Best Practices* in mind, Context and Practice casebooks make it easy for law professors to change.

I welcome reactions, criticisms, and suggestions; my e-mail address is michael. schwartz@washburn.edu. Knowing the author(s) of these books, I know they, too, would appreciate your input; we share a common commitment to student learning. In fact, students, if your professor cares enough about your learning to have adopted this book, I bet s/he would welcome your input, too!

Professor Michael Hunter Schwartz, Series Designer and Editor
Co-Director, Institute for Law Teaching and Learning
Associate Dean for Faculty and Academic Development

Preface and Acknowledgments

As the Carnegie[1] and Stuckey[2] reports have pointed out, law schools are not doing an optimal job in preparing students for the practice of law. Among the deficiencies created by the traditional law school curriculum and teaching methods, are that students fail to fully comprehend the "rich complexity of actual situations that involve full-dimensional people."[3] Students also do not fully appreciate the "social consequences or ethical aspects"[4] of any legal conclusions that they might draw about the situations confronting those people. This book aims to expose students to that "rich complexity" and those consequences.

It also aims to expose students to different forms of advocacy and skills, and different research sources, aside from the traditional ones. Many of the problems illustrated in this book cannot be redressed by litigation alone. Advocacy must often take the form of education, activism, and negotiation, and the use of multi-faceted lawyering skills. Today's law students must also educate themselves broadly by looking beyond traditional legal research. Although, like any other traditional casebook, this book contains many cases, treaties and statutes, it also contains testimony from Senate hearings, reports of NGOs and international committees, and excerpts from briefs and newspaper articles. Law students need to learn that not all battles for justice and equality are conducted in courtrooms, and that sometimes working on a political, economic, and social level may be as, if not more, effective than litigation.

Women's International Rights — Course Objectives

This book has been designed to help students develop knowledge and skills in five areas:

1. To foster general knowledge about the Convention on the Elimination of All Forms of Discrimination against Women (CEDAW), and how that Convention works to implement equality and non discrimination.

2. To foster general knowledge about how the international legal system of treaty enforcement, the treaty reporting systems, and the complaint and investigation systems, all function.

3. To foster awareness about how women's rights fit within the general framework of international human rights.

---

1. William M. Sullivan, Anne Colby, Judith Welch Wegner, Lloyd Bond & Lee S. Schulman, EDUCATING LAWYERS: PREPARATION FOR THE PROFESSION E OF LAW (2007) (Hereafter CARNEGIE)
2. Roy Stuckey and Others, BEST PRACTICES FOR LEGAL EDUCATION (2007)
3. CARNEGIE fn 1 *supra* at p6.
4. *Id.*

4. To foster awareness about specific rights violations in particular areas of the world.

5. To expose students to the consequences for women when those rights are violated, and the various means of obtaining redress — including litigation, political advocacy, education, and working through NGOs.

Objectives Related to Expert Learning Skills

By the end of this text, students confronted with a particular context and issue involving women's rights, should be able to identify the particular treaties (both international and regional) that might regulate that context, as well as any jurisprudence (in the form of case law, Declarations, or Recommendations) from the treaty bodies that might be applicable. Students should also be able to identify any domestic or international government regulatory agencies that might be interested in the issue, as well as identify domestic law that might be relevant. Students should also be able to conduct research to establish whether any NGOs have conducted studies or issued reports in this area, that might be relied on to redress the situation. Students should also be able to assess the impact of their advocacy, whichever form it takes. They should be able to determine the likely consequences for the women involved, depending on the form of advocacy taken. They should also be able to identify who might oppose their efforts and why, and how to best accomplish the goals of equality and non discrimination.

Organization of the Text and of Each Chapter

The text begins with a brief history of women's rights and briefly traces the development of international human rights and regional human rights, post World War II. Thereafter, each chapter traces an important theme as it impacts women, and explores what the Convention on the Elimination of All Forms of Discrimination Against Women (CEDAW) has to say on that topic, as well as what both international and domestic case legislation and law has to teach us. Many chapters also contain excerpts from reports of NGOs, as well as newspapers or other sources that pertain to the topic.

Each chapter begins with a problem that poses a hypothetical situation that students should be able to address after completing the chapter readings, and pondering the questions that are interspersed throughout the chapter.

Most of the cases are excerpts, but links to the full cases are provided. In some of the cases, particularly those from Africa, some of the punctuation has been changed to conform to U.S. conventions. These changes are purely cosmetic, and have not altered the meaning in any way.

Acknowledgments

Thanks to my husband, Anré, for his love and support, and my children: Clea, Emma, Eli, and Drew. May they grow up with a love for justice. Thanks also to my family in London, Cape Town, and South Bend. And to Notre Dame (*Speculum Iustitiae*).

A special thank you to my research assistants: Chrissi Mark, Yara Sallam, Kim Williams, and Caitlin Sikes, for their patience and hard work. And to all of the Notre Dame students who have taken my gender class over the years, whose interest in, and commitment to justice, sustains me.

Thanks are also owed to Michael Schwartz for his advice, Sarah Ricks who persuaded me to do this, Sondra Byrnes for encouraging me along the way, and Rachel Smithson and Carolina Academic Press. I also salute all the women in Zimbabwe and South Africa, and all the women who work for women's rights, whose lives and courage continue to inspire me.

Introduction

Consider this:

- Women make up about 70% of the world's poor
- More women than men are illiterate; many more girls than boys are denied access to education merely because of their gender
- In many countries, women are denied access to economic resources
- In parts of Africa, women are not permitted to own land
- On average, women in the workforce earn 85% of men's salaries
- In some countries in Africa, women are not considered full legal adults, no matter their age
- An estimated 100–140 million women worldwide have undergone Female Genital Mutilation (FGM)
- Between 15% and 71% of women have reported physical or sexual violence by a husband or partner
- Many women said that their first sexual experience was not consensual (24% in rural Peru, 28% in Tanzania, 30% in rural Bangladesh, and 40% in South Africa)
- Worldwide, between 4% and 12% of women reported being physically abused during pregnancy
- Every year, about 5,000 women are murdered by family members in the name of honor
- Trafficking of women and girls for forced labor and sex is widespread, and often affects the most vulnerable
- Forced marriages and child marriages violate the human rights of women and girls, yet they are widely practiced in many countries in Asia, the Middle East, and sub-Saharan Africa

In 1979, the Convention on the Elimination of All Forms of Discrimination Against Women (CEDAW) was enacted, with the purpose of ending discrimination against women, as its title suggests. It entered into force in 1981. To date, 183 countries are parties to the Convention. Yet thirty years after CEDAW, rampant discrimination against women still persists. This book will explore the evolution of women's rights, the options available for victims of discrimination, and the impact of CEDAW on the lives and concerns of women.

International
Women's Rights,
Equality, and Justice

Chapter 1

A Brief History of the Origins of Women's Rights

Introduction

One may question why a context and practice casebook would start with a history of human rights, and the place of women's rights within that history. The short answer is that tracing the evolution of women's rights can provide us insight into contemporary problems. Consider the limited access to property rights that women were granted by the Magna Carta — note that some eight hundred years later, access to land and other resources is still a problem for women in some parts of the world. Note too, the concerns of Olympe de Gouges, Elizabeth Cady Stanton and others — namely: women's lack of access to public and political life; women's lack of access to resources and education; and women's subjugation in marriage. Now consider the issues faced by women in contemporary society — the concerns articulated by de Gouges and others are still prevalent today, and have not been sufficiently addressed by changes to legal systems.

Consider also that many of the limitations and forms of discrimination that women are forced to endure, take place within the domestic sphere, rather than the public one. The limitations of law to adequately address discrimination that takes place in the private sphere, is one of the central themes of this book.

Not only can women learn from the experiences of their forebearers, they can derive inspiration from them too. The inspiration that women today derive from the struggles of women who have gone before them is exemplified by the women of the Philippines, who, in 2010, canvassed for a women's rights bill, and named it the "Magna Carta of Women."

I. The History of Human Rights

The history of the enforcement of human rights, as least insofar as those rights are conceived of by means of international treaties and declarations, is relatively recent. The notion of human rights themselves is, however, much older. Natural Law, the *Magna Carta*,[1] the American Declaration of Independence, the French Revolution's rallying cry

---

1. Magna Carta art. 61 (1215), *quoted in* A. E. Dick Howard, Magna Carta: Text and Commentary 51 (1998).

of "liberty, equality, fraternity," all have contributed to our understanding of rights and dignity inuring to individuals or peoples, on the basis of their humanity. This understanding has been supplemented by philosophers such as Confucius, Montesquieu, Rousseau, Locke, Paine, Mill, Hume, and Blackstone, among others. In turn, our understanding of these concepts has also been broadened and challenged by ideas of communitarianism and complementarity from Africa and the East.

Originally, law concerned itself with governing relations between states and left it to domestic jurisdictions to guarantee the rights of individuals. That system began to change post World War II with the advent of the international human rights system and regional human rights systems such as the European, Inter-American, and African systems.

This book will trace the evolution of international human rights law, particularly with regard to women's rights. But human rights existed prior to their formal recognition by, and enshrinement in, international human rights law. Some theorists contend that the early history of human rights can trace its origins back to Natural Law and the Natural Law theory espoused by Cicero, Plato, and Thomas Aquinas.[2]

A. Natural Law

Robert George describes Natural Law as "the body of moral norms and other practical principles which provide reasons (including moral reasons) for action and restraint."[3] John Finnis claims a more universal application for Natural Law, asserting that:

> A sound 'natural law' theory has never been other than an appeal to public reasons — concerning kinds of choices consistent or incompatible with the real interests of all human persons — reasons that would command a universal consensus under ideal conditions of discourse, and meanwhile are available to, and could be accepted by anyone who is willing and able to give them fair and adequate attention, ...[4]

While Natural Law may provide a theoretical justification for rights, a more concrete articulation of those rights can be traced to the *Magna Carta*.

B. The *Magna Carta* (1215)

The *Magna Carta* (also called the *Magna Carta Libertatum* — the Great Charter of Freedom) is the famous document executed in 1215 after the Battle of Runnymede. It was signed by King John of England and a group of barons to "allay the discord"[5] that had arisen between them. It guaranteed certain liberties and due process of law, including the writ of habeas corpus. Although the Charter guaranteed the rights contained therein to "all freemen of our kingdom," certain of its provisions pertained to women, and these established some limited inheritance rights, property ownership, access to one's dowry,

---

2. *See* MARY ELLEN O'CONNELL, THE POWER AND PURPOSE OF INTERNATIONAL LAW (Oxford University Press 2008).

3. Robert P. George, *Natural Law Ethics* in Phillip L. Quinn and Charles Taliaferro (eds.) A COMPANION TO THE PHILOSOPHY OF RELIGION, (Oxford 1997) at 460.

4. John Finnis, *Natural Law and the Ethics of Discourse*, 12 RATIO JURIS Vol. 4, 354, 370 (1999).

5. Art. 61.

and marriage rights for women (matters that women were concerned with as far back as the 1200s). For example, Articles 7 and 8 provided that:

> (7) At her husband's death, a widow may have her marriage portion and inheritance at once and without trouble. She shall pay nothing for her dower, marriage portion, or any inheritance that she and her husband held jointly on the day of his death. She may remain in her husband's house for forty days after his death, and within this period her dower shall be assigned to her.

> (8) No widow shall be compelled to marry, so long as she wishes to remain without a husband. But she must give security that she will not marry without royal consent, if she holds her lands of the Crown, or without the consent of whatever other lord she may hold them of.

The Charter thus offered some limited protection to women and some limited recognition of autonomy for women. However, the Charter nowhere guaranteed equality for women. In fact, the reliability of women as witnesses was specifically called into question by Article 54 which provided that:

> (54) No one shall be arrested or imprisoned on the appeal of a woman for the death of any person except her husband.

It was in the wake of conflict that some recognition of limited rights for women was won. Yet, the next significant declaration of rights (which was also attained as a result of conflict) similarly did little to ameliorate the status of women. Nevertheless, the intellectual heritage of the *Magna Carta* cannot be underestimated. Consider what Eleanor Roosevelt said some 700 years later when unveiling the *Universal Declaration of Human Rights*:

> We stand today at the threshold of a great event both in the life of the United Nations and in the life of mankind. This declaration may well become the international Magna Carta for all men everywhere. We hope its proclamation by the General Assembly will be an event comparable to the proclamation in 1789 [of the French Declaration of the Rights of Man], the adoption of the Bill of Rights by the people of the U.S., and the adoption of comparable declarations at different times in other countries.[6]

C. The U.S. Declaration of Independence (1776)

The *Magna Carta* inspired the U.S. Declaration of Independence,[7] but the latter document reserved the rights articulated therein for white males. In professing that "all men are created equal," the Declaration really meant that white men were equal—women and slaves were not. Women were only given the right to vote in the United States on August 18, 1920.

---

6. Mary Ann Glendon, A World Made New: Eleanor Roosevelt and the Universal Declaration of Human Rights 166 (2001).

7. The Declaration was modeled on the Virginia Declaration of Rights. It also was undoubtedly influenced by the works of Thomas Paine who had written glowingly of the "illuminating and divine principle of the equal rights of man," Thomas Paine, Rights of Man: Being an Answer to Mr. Burke's Attack on the French Revolution 23 (Jordan 1792), as well as the writings of John Locke and Blackstone's *Commentaries*.

The same ideals that gave rise to the U.S. Declaration of Independence had also resonated in Europe, and there gave rise to the *Declaration of the Rights of Man*. That document too referred only to the masculine gender. Although predicated on the notion of *egalité* (equality), its provisions were not meant to extend to women.

D. The *Declaration of the Rights of Man* (1789)

The *Declaration* referred to the rights of man as "natural, unalienable, and sacred,"[8] and recognized both the "rights of man and of the citizen." It provided:

> 1. Men are born and remain free and equal in rights. Social distinctions may be founded only upon the general good.[9]

The male version of "citizen" (*citoyen*) as well as "man" (*homme*) was used in the Declaration, thereby implying that the rights contained therein did not extend to women. French citizenship was reserved for men at the time the *Declaration* was written; women were only accorded full citizenship rights in 1944.[10] Despite the references to "*egalité,*" the *Declaration* did not ameliorate the lives of women. This despite the fact that women were active during the French Revolution and fought alongside men on the barricades, as well as contributing to the intellectual platforms espoused during the Revolution and thereafter. Two years after the *Declaration of the Rights of Man* had been published, Olympe de Gouges, a butcher's daughter, penned the *Declaration of the Rights of Woman and the Female Citizen*—a direct challenge to the *Declaration of the Rights of Man*. De Gouges' *Declaration* paralleled the *Declaration of the Rights of Man*, but also supplied a critique and a call to arms. The women's *Declaration* exhorted women to "free yourselves, you only have to want to,"[11] and to participate in political and public life, pointing out that "[w]omen have the right to mount the scaffold; they must also have the right to mount the speaker's rostrum."[12] De Gouges went on to urge women to "discover your rights,"[13] thereby implying that rights were inherent, not bestowed. Many of de Gouges' concerns focused on the rights of women in marriage, certainly a contemporary concern that has not been fully addressed. She called on women to assert their rights to more equitable conjugal unions, arguing that "marriage is the tomb of love and trust."[14] De Gouges provided a standard form for a "social contract union" that women and men could enter into. She urged that laws be passed to "assist widows, and young girls deceived by the false promises of a man to whom they were attached."[15]

---

8. THE DECLARATION OF THE RIGHTS OF MAN AND OF THE CITIZEN, preamble (France 1789), *available at* http://www.constitution.org/fr/fr_drm.htm [hereinafter DECLARATION OF THE RIGHTS OF MAN].

9. DECLARATION OF THE RIGHTS OF MAN, art. 1.

10. Interestingly, women were active participants in the French Revolution, but it was only after their active role in the French Resistance during World War II that they were accorded the right to vote.

11. OLYMPE DE GOUGES, THE DECLARATION OF THE RIGHTS OF WOMAN AND OF THE FEMALE CITIZEN, postscript (France 1791) [hereinafter DECLARATION OF THE RIGHTS OF WOMAN].

12. DECLARATION OF THE RIGHTS OF WOMAN, art. 10.

13. DECLARATION OF THE RIGHTS OF WOMAN, postscript.

14. DECLARATION OF THE RIGHTS OF WOMAN, postscript.

15. DECLARATION OF THE RIGHTS OF WOMAN, Form for a Social Contract between Man and Woman.

II. A History of Women's Rights

A. *Declaration of the Rights of Woman and the Female Citizen* (1791)

Olympe de Gouges drafted this document based on the *Declaration of the Rights of Man* in 1791. Consider the central themes of her document, which are male tyranny, equal rights for women, and concerns not only about civil and political rights but also about a woman's economic dependence, especially as she ages. De Gouges was also concerned with the responsibilities placed on women when bearing a child. Compare de Gouges' *Declaration* to the *Declaration of the Rights of Man*, and note how the *Woman's Declaration* parallels the *Rights of Man* document. This practice of paralleling has been used on a number of occasions as will be illustrated in future chapters. The technique of paralleling asserts that if rights are innate as many rights documents assert, they should adhere to women as well.

For the National Assembly to decree in its last sessions, or in those of the next legislature:

Preamble

Mothers, daughters, sisters [and] representatives of the nation demand to be constituted into a national assembly. Believing that ignorance, omission, or scorn for the rights of woman are the only causes of public misfortunes and of the corruption of governments, [the women] have resolved to set forth a solemn declaration the natural, inalienable, and sacred rights of woman in order that this declaration, constantly exposed before all members of the society, will ceaselessly remind them of their rights and duties; in order that the authoritative acts of women and the authoritative acts of men may be at any moment compared with and respectful of the purpose of all political institutions; and in order that citizens' demands, henceforth based on simple and incontestable principles, will always support the constitution, good morals, and the happiness of all.

Consequently, the sex that is as superior in beauty as it is in courage during the sufferings of maternity recognizes and declares in the presence and under the auspices of the Supreme Being, the following Rights of Woman and of Female Citizens.

1. Comparison of the Declaration of the Rights of Man and the Rights of Woman

Rights of Man	Rights of Woman
1. Men are born and remain free and equal in rights. Social distinctions may be founded only upon the general good.	1. Woman is born free and lives equal to man in her rights. Social distinctions can be based only on the common utility.
2. The aim of all political association is the preservation of the natural and imprescriptible rights of man. These rights are liberty, property, security, and resistance to oppression.	2. The purpose of any political association is the conservation of the natural and imprescriptible rights of woman and man; these rights are liberty, property, security, and especially resistance to oppression.

3. The principle of all sovereignty resides essentially in the nation. Nobody nor individual may exercise any authority which does not proceed directly from the nation.

3. The principle of all sovereignty rests essentially with the nation, which is nothing but the union of woman and man; no body and no individual can exercise any authority which does not come expressly from the nation.

4. Liberty consists in the freedom to do everything which injures no one else; hence the exercise of the natural rights of each man has no limits except those which assure to the other members of the society the enjoyment of the same rights. These limits can only be determined by law.

4. Liberty and justice consist of restoring all that belongs to others; thus, the only limits on the exercise of the natural rights of woman are perpetual male tyranny; these limits are to be reformed by the laws of nature and reason.

5. Law can only prohibit such actions as are hurtful to society. Nothing may be prevented which is not forbidden by law, and no one may be forced to do anything not provided for by law.

5. Laws of nature and reason proscribe all acts harmful to society; everything which is not prohibited by these wise and divine laws cannot be prevented, and no one can be constrained to do what they do not command.

6. Law is the expression of the general will. Every citizen has a right to participate personally, or through his representative, in its foundation. It must be the same for all, whether it protects or punishes. All citizens, being equal in the eyes of the law, are equally eligible to all dignities and to all public positions and occupations, according to their abilities, and without distinction except that of their virtues and talents.

6. The law must be the expression of the general will; all female and male citizens must contribute either personally or through their representatives to its formation; it must be the same for all: male and female citizens, being equal in the eyes of the law, must be equally admitted to all honors, positions, and public employment according to their capacity and without other distinctions besides those of their virtues and talents.

7. No person shall be accused, arrested, or imprisoned except in the cases and according to the forms prescribed by law. Any one soliciting, transmitting, executing, or causing to be executed, any arbitrary order, shall be punished. But any citizen summoned or arrested in virtue of the law shall submit without delay, as resistance constitutes an offense.

7. No woman is an exception; she is accused, arrested, and detained in cases determined by law. Women, like men, obey this rigorous law.

8. The law shall provide for such punishments only as are strictly and obviously necessary, and no one shall suffer punishment except it be legally inflicted in virtue of a law passed and promulgated before the commission of the offense.

8. The law must establish only those penalties that are strictly and obviously necessary, and no one shall suffer punishment except it be legally inflicted in virtue of a law passed and promulgated before the commission of the offense.

9. As all persons are held innocent until they shall have been declared guilty, if arrest shall be deemed indispensable, all harshness not essential to the securing of the prisoner's person shall be severely repressed by law.

10. No one shall be disquieted on account of his opinions, including his religious views, provided their manifestation does not disturb the public order established by law.

11. The free communication of ideas and opinions is one of the most precious of the rights of man. Every citizen may, accordingly, speak, write, and print with freedom, but shall be responsible for such abuses of this freedom as shall be defined by law.

12. The security of the rights of man and of the citizen requires public military forces. These forces are, therefore, established for the good of all and not for the personal advantage of those to whom they shall be intrusted.

13. A common contribution is essential for the maintenance of the public forces and for the cost of administration. This should be equitably distributed among all the citizens in proportion to their means.

14. All the citizens have a right to decide, either personally or by their representatives, as to the necessity of the public contribution; to grant this freely; to know to what uses it is put; and to fix the proportion, the mode of assessment and of collection and the duration of the taxes.

9. Once any woman is declared guilty, complete rigor is exercised by law.

10. No one is to be disquieted for his very basic opinions; a woman has the right to mount the scaffold; she must equally have the right to mount the rostrum, provided that her demonstrations do not disturb the legally established public order.

11. The free communication of thoughts and opinions is one of the most precious rights of woman, since that liberty assures recognition of children by their fathers. Any female citizen thus may say freely, I am the mother of a child which belongs to you, without being forced by a barbarous prejudice to hide the truth; (an exception may be made) to respond to the abuse of this liberty in cases determined by law.

12. The guarantee of the rights of woman and the female citizen implies a major benefit; this guarantee must be instituted for the advantage of all, and not for the particular benefit of those to whom it is entrusted.

13. For the support of the public force and the expenses of administration, the contributions of woman and man are equal; she shares all the duties and all the painful tasks; therefore, she must have the same share in the distribution of positions, employment, offices, honors, and jobs.

14. Female and male citizens have the right to verify, either by themselves of through their representatives, the necessity of the public contribution. This can only apply to women if they are granted an equal share, not only of wealth, but also of public administration, and in the determination of the proportion, the base, the collection, and the duration of the tax.

15. Society has the right to require of every public agent an account of his administration.

15. The collectivity of women, joined for tax purposes to the aggregate of men, has the right to demand an accounting of his administration from any public agent.

16. A society in which the observance of the law is not assured, nor the separation of powers defined, has no constitution at all.

16. No society has a constitution without the guarantee of rights and the separation of powers; the constitution is null if the majority of individuals comprising the nation have not cooperated in drafting it.

17. Since property is an inviolable and sacred right, no one shall be deprived thereof except where public necessity, legally determined, shall clearly demand it, and then only on condition that the owner shall have been previously and equitably indemnified.

17. Property belongs to both sexes whether united or separate; for each it is an inviolable and sacred right; no one can be deprived of it, since it is the true patrimony of nature, unless the legally determined public need obviously dictates it, and then only with a just and prior indemnity.

2. Postscript

Women, wake up; the tocsin of reason sounds throughout the universe; recognize your rights. The powerful empire of nature is no longer surrounded by prejudice, fanaticism, superstition, and lies. The torch of truth has dispersed all the clouds of folly and usurpation. Enslaved man has multiplied his force and needs yours to break his chains. Having become free, he has become unjust toward his companion. Oh women! Women, when will you cease to be blind? What advantages have you gathered in the Revolution? A scorn more marked, a disdain more conspicuous. During the centuries of corruption you only reigned over the weakness of men. Your empire is destroyed; what is left to you then? Firm belief in the injustices of men. The reclaiming of your patrimony founded on the wise decrees of nature; why should you fear such a beautiful enterprise? ... Whatever the barriers set up against you, it is in your power to overcome them; you only have to want it. Let us pass now to the appalling account of what you have been in society; and since national education is an issue at this moment, let us see if our wise legislators will think sanely about the education of women.

The *Woman's Declaration* challenged several societal assumptions about women. It brought to the forefront not only property rights, but civil and political rights too (Article XVII — property rights, Article II — civil and political rights; Articles I and VI — formal equality). The Declaration also focused attention on a woman's role in public life (Articles X, XIII, XIV, XV), and challenged assumptions about the formerly private sphere of marriage and male/female relations (Articles IV, XI, and the Postscript).

De Gouges' success in promoting women's rights was at best extremely limited. France only accorded women the right to vote in 1944 during the Liberation.[16] On a personal

---

16. On April 21, 1944 by means of a proclamation issued by the Charles de Gaulle government (the Committee of National Liberation, *Comite Français de Liberation Nationale*), women were granted

level, de Gouges' views brought her only tragedy. She continued to loudly assert the rights of women and challenge the established social order. Ultimately her public position on women's rights, and her association with the Girondists[17] during the Revolutionary period, resulted in her being guillotined in November 1793 for her efforts. A report published at the time of her death noted that:

> Olympe de Gouges, born with an exalted imagination, mistook her delirium for an inspiration of nature. She wanted to be a man of state. She took up the projects of the perfidious people who want to divide France. It seems the law has punished this conspirator for having forgotten the virtues that belong to her sex.[18]

Her compatriots in the U.S. some fifty years later enjoyed scantly more success.

Questions for Discussion

1. *Do you think the development of women's rights has been impacted by the U.S. and French Declarations' failure to address even limited rights of women like the property rights established in the* Magna Carta? *How might this path have affected the development of our understanding of human rights as they pertain to women?*

2. *What kind of equality was contemplated in the* Woman's Declaration? *How does de Gouges view equality in the context of ownership of property? In the context of participation in law and public life? Contributions to society more generally? Employment? Contributions to military and civil service?*

3. *How is de Gouges' concept of natural rights, as they pertain to women, different from the philosophy referenced in the* Rights of Man? *How does this factor into the limits created by the "perpetual male tyranny"?*

4. *Why does freedom of "communications and thoughts" have a special importance for woman, according to de Gouges?*

5. *What do you think of the tactic of paralleling the* Women's Declaration *on the* Rights of Man — *a tactic later adopted by Lucretia Mott and Elizabeth Stanton (see below)? Is it effective? Why or why not?*

---

the right to vote—somewhat ironic considering the active role of women during the Resistance. *See e.g.,* Jytte Klausen & Charles S. Maier, Has Liberalism Failed Women?: Assuring Equal Representation in Europe and the United States 222 (2001); Joan Wallach Scott, Only Paradoxes to Offer: French Feminists and the Rights of Man 161 (1997).

17. The Girondists were a political faction that originally supported the Revolution, but later tried to curb its excesses. They prided themselves on their oratory. Many of the Girondists were denounced and executed during the Terror by Robespierre and his deputies.

18. Originally published in *La Feuille du Salut Public* and reprinted in *Le Moniteur Universel,* t. XVIII, 29 brumaire an II (Nov. 17, 1793), *quoted in* Catherine Montfort-Howard, Literate Women and the French Revolution of 1789, 58 (1994). *See also* Lisa Beckstrand, Deviant Women of the French Revolution and the Rise of Feminism 131 (2009); Bruce Burgett, Sentimental Bodies: Sex, Gender, and Citizenship in the Early Republic 104 (1998); Sophie Mousset, Women's Rights and the French Revolution: A Biography of Olympe de Gouges 97 (2007).

B. *Declaration of Sentiments* — Seneca Falls (1848)[19]

While Olympe de Gouges and others were demanding equal rights for women in France, in the United States, Lucretia Mott and Elizabeth Cady Stanton were opposed to oppression in any form, both being anti-slavery activists, as well as women's rights advocates. In 1848, they organized a convention at Seneca Falls, and Stanton drafted the *Declaration of Sentiments and Resolutions* based on the Declaration of Independence. She included eighteen "injuries and usurpations" — the same number as in the U.S. Declaration. The *Sentiments* document also borrowed Jefferson's language directly from the Declaration: "We hold these truths to be self-evident: that all men and women are created equal; that they are endowed by their Creator with certain inalienable rights; that among these are life, liberty, and the pursuit of happiness." Stanton also specifically acknowledged the influence of Blackstone's *Commentaries* in the opening lines of the Resolutions. Stanton was firm about including a woman's right to vote in the resolutions she drafted, despite the protests of Mott. Mott's reported reaction to the notion of suffrage was "Why, Lizzie, thee will make us ridiculous."[20] But Stanton later claimed "I persisted, for I saw clearly that the power to make the laws was the right through which all other rights could be secured."[21] Access to public and political life is still an issue for women today and will be discussed in detail in a later chapter. Like her forebearers, Stanton saw rights as inherent, and focused on the role that marriage played in the suppression of the rights of women. Her claims about lack of access to education, resources and property, and "different codes of morals for men and women" are still experienced by women in many parts of the world today.

C. The Seneca Declaration

When, in the course of human events, it becomes necessary for one portion of the family of man to assume among the people of the earth a position different from that which they have hitherto occupied, but one to which the laws of nature and of nature's God entitle them, a decent respect to the opinions of mankind requires that they should declare the causes that impel them to such a course.

We hold these truths to be self-evident: that all men and women are created equal; that they are endowed by their Creator with certain inalienable rights; that among these are life, liberty, and the pursuit of happiness; that to secure these rights governments are instituted, deriving their just powers from the consent of the governed. Whenever any form of government becomes destructive of these ends, it is the right of those who suffer from it to refuse allegiance to it, and to insist upon the institution of a new government, laying its foundation on such principles, and organizing its powers in such form, as to them shall seem most likely to effect their safety and happiness....

---

19. The DECLARATION OF SENTIMENTS in HISTORY OF WOMAN SUFFRAGE 70–71 (Elizabeth Cady Stanton et al. eds., 1889) [hereinafter DECLARATION OF SENTIMENTS].

20. ELIZABETH CADY STANTON, THEODORE STANTON & HARRIOT STANTON BLATCH, ELIZABETH CADY STANTON AS REVEALED IN HER LETTERS, DIARY AND REMINISCENCES 146 (1922).

21. *Id.*

[W]hen a long train of abuses and usurpations, pursuing invariably the same object, evinces a design to reduce them under absolute despotism, it is their duty to throw off such government and to provide new guards for their future security. Such has been the patient sufferance of the women under this government, and such is now the necessity which constrains them to demand the equal station to which they are entitled.

The history of mankind is a history of repeated injuries and usurpations on the part of man toward woman, having in direct object the establishment of an absolute tyranny over her. To prove this, let facts be submitted to a candid world.

He has never permitted her to exercise her inalienable right to the elective franchise.

He has compelled her to submit to law in the formation of which she had no voice.

He has withheld from her rights which are given to the most ignorant and degraded men, both natives and foreigners.

Having deprived her of this first right as a citizen, the elective franchise, thereby leaving her without representation in the halls of legislation, he has oppressed her on all sides.

He has made her, if married, in the eye of the law, civilly dead.

He has taken from her all right in property, even to the wages she earns.

He has made her morally, an irresponsible being, as she can commit many crimes with impunity, provided they be done in the presence of her husband. In the covenant of marriage, she is compelled to promise obedience to her husband, he becoming, to all intents and purposes, her master — the law giving him power to deprive her of her liberty and to administer chastisement.

He has so framed the laws of divorce, as to what shall be the proper causes and, in case of separation, to whom the guardianship of the children shall be given, as to be wholly regardless of the happiness of the women — the law, in all cases, going upon a false supposition of the supremacy of man and giving all power into his hands.

After depriving her of all rights as a married woman, if single and the owner of property, he has taxed her to support a government which recognizes her only when her property can be made profitable to it.

He has monopolized nearly all the profitable employments, and from those she is permitted to follow, she receives but a scanty remuneration. He closes against her all the avenues to wealth and distinction which he considers most honorable to himself. As a teacher of theology, medicine, or law, she is not known.

He has denied her the facilities for obtaining a thorough education, all colleges being closed against her.

He allows her in church, as well as state, but a subordinate position, claiming apostolic authority for her exclusion from the ministry, and, with some exceptions, from any public participation in the affairs of the church.

He has created a false public sentiment by giving to the world a different code of morals for men and women, by which moral delinquencies which exclude women from society are not only tolerated but deemed of little account in man.

He has usurped the prerogative of Jehovah himself, claiming it as his right to assign for her a sphere of action, when that belongs to her conscience and to her God.

He has endeavored, in every way that he could, to destroy her confidence in her own powers, to lessen her self-respect, and to make her willing to lead a dependent and abject life.

Now, in view of this entire disfranchisement of one-half the people of this country, their social and religious degradation, in view of the unjust laws above mentioned, and because women do feel themselves aggrieved, oppressed, and fraudulently deprived of their most sacred rights, we insist that they have immediate admission to all the rights and privileges which belong to them as citizens of the United States.

In entering upon the great work before us, we anticipate no small amount of misconception, misrepresentation, and ridicule; but we shall use every instrumentality within our power to effect our object. We shall employ agents, circulate tracts, petition the state and national legislatures, and endeavor to enlist the pulpit and the press in our behalf. We hope this Convention will be followed by a series of conventions embracing every part of the country.

Resolutions

Whereas, the great precept of nature is conceded to be that "man shall pursue his own true and substantial happiness." Blackstone in his *Commentaries* remarks that this law of nature, being coequal with mankind and dictated by God himself, is, of course, superior in obligation to any other. It is binding over all the globe, in all countries and at all times; no human laws are of any validity if contrary to this, and such of them as are valid derive all their force, and all their validity, and all their authority, mediately and immediately, from this original; therefore,

Resolved, that such laws as conflict, in any way, with the true and substantial happiness of woman, are contrary to the great precept of nature and of no validity, for this is "superior in obligation to any other."

Resolved, that all laws which prevent woman from occupying such a station in society as her conscience shall dictate, or which place her in a position inferior to that of man, are contrary to the great precept of nature and therefore of no force or authority.

Resolved, that woman is man's equal, was intended to be so by the Creator, and the highest good of the race demands that she should be recognized as such.

Resolved, that the women of this country ought to be enlightened in regard to the laws under which they live, that they may no longer publish their degradation by declaring themselves satisfied with their present position, nor their ignorance, by asserting that they have all the rights they want.

Resolved, that inasmuch as man, while claiming for himself intellectual superiority, does accord to woman moral superiority, it is preeminently his duty to encourage her to speak and teach, as she has an opportunity, in all religious assemblies.

Resolved, that the same amount of virtue, delicacy, and refinement of behavior that is required of woman in the social state also be required of man, and the same transgressions should be visited with equal severity on both man and woman.

Resolved, that the objection of indelicacy and impropriety, which is so often brought against woman when she addresses a public audience, comes with a very ill grace from those who encourage, by their attendance, her appearance on the stage, in the concert, or in feats of the circus.

Resolved, that woman has too long rested satisfied in the circumscribed limits which corrupt customs and a perverted application of the Scriptures have marked out for her, and that it is time she should move in the enlarged sphere which her great Creator has assigned her.

Resolved, that it is the duty of the women of this country to secure to themselves their sacred right to the elective franchise.

Resolved, that the equality of human rights results necessarily from the fact of the identity of the race in capabilities and responsibilities.

Resolved, that the speedy success of our cause depends upon the zealous and untiring efforts of both men and women for the overthrow of the monopoly of the pulpit, and for the securing to woman an equal participation with men in the various trades, professions, and commerce.

Resolved, therefore, that, being invested by the Creator with the same capabilities and same consciousness of responsibility for their exercise, it is demonstrably the right and duty of woman, equally with man, to promote every righteous cause by every righteous means; and especially in regard to the great subjects of morals and religion, it is self-evidently her right to participate with her brother in teaching them, both in private and in public, by writing and by speaking, by any instrumentalities proper to be used, and in any assemblies proper to be held; and this being a self-evident truth growing out of the divinely implanted principles of human nature, any custom or authority adverse to it, whether modern or wearing the hoary sanction of antiquity, is to be regarded as a self-evident falsehood, and at war with mankind.[22]

Questions for Discussion

1. *What philosophical basis does Stanton rest her belief in equality on?*

2. *One of Stanton's resolutions is that "the equality of human rights results necessarily from the fact of the identity of the race in capabilities and responsibilities." Has that been achieved today? Are women and men considered equally capable and responsible? Reconsider this question as you read the last chapter of this book which describes the Capabilities approach.*

---

22. Declaration of Sentiments, at 71–73.

Chapter 2

International Human Rights in the Modern Era — The Evolution of Women's Rights

Chapter Problem

The United States Senate Subcommittee on Human Rights and Law is considering sending a United Nations Convention relating to the rights of women to the United States Senate for a vote on ratification. This Convention (or treaty) is known as The Convention for the Elimination of All Forms of Discrimination Against Women or CEDAW. Under Article II Section 2 of the U.S. Constitution, the President may "make" a treaty, but for it to become law in the United States it must be ratified by two thirds of the Senate.[1] The Subcommittee on Human Rights and Law first reviews the treaty to determine if it is consistent with U.S. obligations and policy, and if it finds that it is, it may send the treaty to the Senate for its advice and consent on ratification. CEDAW was signed by President Jimmy Carter in 1979. It has been before the Subcommittee on several occasions, but has never been sent to the Senate for a vote. Before the Subcommittee would send CEDAW to the Senate for a vote, it would wish to know how this Convention fits against the backdrop of other international human rights treaties that the United States is a party to. Specifically, the Subcommittee would be interested in whether a treaty that focuses on specialized rights like women's rights is necessary, and whether this treaty is consistent with the United States' obligations under the UN Charter and other international human rights treaties. The Subcommittee would also wish to know how "enforceable" the treaty is, and what reporting requirements and complaint procedures are prescribed by the treaty. It would require information about how these reporting requirements differ from reporting and enforcement requirements under other treaties to which the U.S. is a party.

---

1. There is also the issue of whether a treaty is self-executing; *i.e.* whether it automatically becomes part of U.S. law, or whether some legislative action is required to implement the provisions of the treaty into U.S. law.

I. The History of Human Rights

A. The Evolution of Human Rights Treaties

Prior to the development of International Human Rights in the post World War II era, International Law had been primarily concerned with relationships between states. As we have seen from the previous chapter, the idea that individuals have inalienable rights was not a new concept, but the notion of individuals being able to enforce those rights in an international forum was a new idea. As Louis Henkin has noted:

> Human rights are rights which the individual has or should have in his society. If societies respected those rights adequately, there would be no need for international law and institutions to help protect them. International human rights law and institutions are designed to induce states to remedy the inadequacies of their national laws and institutions so that human rights will be respected and vindicated.[2]

This chapter will explore the evolution of human rights, and illustrate that as those rights developed, the international community has moved towards protecting specialized forms of rights, such as the right not to be discriminated against on the grounds of race, or protection against torture. Yet in this rights specialization, women's rights were not considered a priority. They were only addressed as late as 1979, with a comprehensive women's rights treaty (CEDAW) that entered into force in 1981. As we will see, CEDAW borrowed heavily from the treaties which preceded it, particularly with regard to many of the reporting and enforcement aspects of treaties like the Convention on the Elimination of All Forms of Racial Discrimination (CERD).

In 1941, President Franklin D. Roosevelt sowed the seeds for international human rights law when he delivered the famous "Four Freedoms" speech to Congress. Roosevelt envisioned a world "founded on four essential freedoms" that would create a "moral order."[3] He defined freedom as "the supremacy of human rights everywhere."[4]

B. The Four Freedoms (1941)

The first is freedom of speech and expression—everywhere in the world.

The second is freedom of every person to worship God in his own way—everywhere in the world.

The third is freedom from want—which, translated into world terms, means economic understandings which will secure to every nation a healthy peacetime life for its inhabitants—everywhere in the world.

The fourth is freedom from fear—which, translated into world terms, means a world-wide reduction of armaments to such a point and in such a thorough fashion that no nation will be in a position to commit an act of physical aggression against any neighbor—anywhere in the world.[5]

---

2. Louis Henkin, ed., The International Bill of Rights: The Covenant on Civil and Political Rights (1981) 13–16.

3. President Franklin D. Roosevelt, Message to Congress (Jan. 6, 1941) *in* 87 Cong. Rec. 44 (1941).

4. *Id.*

5. *Id.*

To guarantee the Four Freedoms, the world had to be united in creating and supporting this "new order." The idea for the modern United Nations which would more effectively protect against aggression, and foster a climate of human rights, emerged from conferences held by the Allied powers in Moscow (1941), Teheran (1943), and Washington DC (1944). At the Yalta Conference in 1945, post war reconstruction plans for Europe were drawn up, and these plans included plans for the United Nations to replace the old League of Nations.[6] On April 25, 1945, the United Nations Conference on International Organizations took place in San Francisco. The UN Charter was ratified on October 24, 1945. In its Preamble, the Charter acknowledged its desire to "reaffirm faith in fundamental human rights, in the dignity and worth of the human person."[7] The Preamble went on to specifically affirm "the equal rights of men and women."[8]

II. The United Nations (UN)

A. The UN System

Article 1(3) of the Charter describes one of the purposes of the UN as "encouraging respect for human rights and for fundamental freedoms for all without distinction as to race, sex, language, or religion." This was the first universal acknowledgment in a major public international law document of male and female equality.

The UN has developed both a Charter based system to generally promote human rights, and a treaty based system to protect specific rights, and to provide various *fora* within those treaty systems, for complaints about violations of those rights.[9] The objectives of the UN, as stated in Article 1 of its Charter, set the stage for the organization's human rights work. The language of the article reaffirms a commitment to human rights, equality and non-discrimination:

The Purposes of the United Nations are:

1. To maintain international peace and security ...

2. To develop friendly relations among nations based on respect for the principle of equal rights and self-determination of peoples ...

3. To achieve international cooperation ... in promoting and encouraging respect for human rights and for fundamental freedoms for all without distinction as to race, sex, language, or religion ...[10]

---

6. The League of Nations was primarily created to promote international cooperation, peace, and security. It was not designed to foster human rights, although Article 23 called on members to "endeavour to secure and maintain fair and humane conditions of labour for men, women, and children, both in their own countries and in all countries to which their commercial and industrial relations extend, and for that purpose will establish and maintain the necessary international organizations." LEAGUE OF NATIONS COVENANT (1919) *in* EDMUND JAN OSMACYZK, 2 ENCYCLOPEDIA OF THE UNITED NATIONS AND INTERNATIONAL AGREEMENTS 1303 (Anthony Mango, ed., 2003).

7. Charter of the United Nations, *available at* http://www.un.org/en/documents/charter/chapter1.shtml.

8. *Id.*

9. Many of these treaties create a Committee which member states must periodically report to. Groups and individuals may file complaints, and have them adjudicated by the Committee.

10. Art. 1.

There are several monitoring bodies that were created by the Charter, and others that were created under specific treaties or conventions to monitor the implementation of human rights.

1. The Charter Based System

Under the Charter based system, the three main UN organs concerned with human rights are the General Assembly, the Security Council—both of which may issues resolutions referring to human rights issues—and the Human Rights Council.

a. The Role and Functions of the Security Council

Under the Charter, the functions and powers of the Security Council are:

- to maintain international peace and security in accordance with the principles and purposes of the United Nations
- to investigate any dispute or situation which might lead to international friction
- to recommend methods of adjusting such disputes or the terms of settlement
- to formulate plans for the establishment of a system to regulate armaments
- to determine the existence of a threat to the peace or act of aggression and to recommend what action should be taken
- to call on Members to apply economic sanctions and other measures not involving the use of force to prevent or stop aggression
- to take military action against an aggressor
- to recommend the admission of new Members
- to exercise the trusteeship functions of the United Nations in "strategic areas"
- to recommend to the General Assembly the appointment of the Secretary-General and, together with the Assembly, to elect the Judges of the International Court of Justice.

b. The General Assembly

The General Assembly is the main deliberative organ of the UN. It makes decisions on important questions, such as those on peace and security, admission of new members and budgetary matters.

c. The Reporting and Complaint/Communication Procedure— The Human Rights Council

The Human Rights Council is comprised of representatives of forty seven member states who serve for a period of three years. It is responsible for strengthening the promotion and protection of human rights. In 2007, the Council adopted an "institution building package"[11] providing for the universal periodic review of human rights in all of the UN's

---

11. *Available at* http://ap.ohchr.org/documents/E/HRC/resolutions/A_HRC_RES_5_1.doc [last visited January 10, 2011].

192 member states. Under this procedure, the Council requires each member state to report to the Council every four years on actions taken to improve human rights situations in their countries, and generally on actions taken to fulfill their human rights obligations.

In response to country reports, the Council issues an official review and assessment of the report. The Council's review consists of a summary of the proceedings of the review process, conclusions and/or recommendations, and information regarding its dialogue with the state, as well as any commitments and undertakings made by the state under review. These reports, and the responses from the Committee, are important because they help to create a body of jurisprudence, that may be indicative of customary international law. Reports of the review sessions are available at: http://www.ohchr.org/EN/HRBodies/UPR/Pages/MeetingsHighlightsSession11.aspx.

The Council also established a complaint or communication procedure which is designed to be "impartial, objective, efficient, victims-oriented and conducted in a timely manner."[12] Complaints are referred to as communications. They are screened by a Working Group, to ensure that they are timely and appear well-founded. Two distinct working groups — the Working Group on Communications and the Working Group on Situations — were established with the mandate to examine the communications and bring to the attention of the Council "consistent patterns of gross and reliably attested violations of human rights and fundamental freedoms."[13]

The criteria for admissibility of a communication are as follows:

A communication related to a violation of human rights and fundamental freedoms is admissible, unless:

- It has manifestly political motivations and its object is not consistent with the UN Charter, the Universal Declaration of Human Rights and other applicable instruments in the field of human rights law; or

- It does not contain a factual description of the alleged violations, including the rights which are alleged to be violated; or

- Its language is abusive. However, such communication may be considered if it meets the other criteria for admissibility after deletion of the abusive language; or

- It is not submitted by a person or a group of persons claiming to be the victim of violations of human rights and fundamental freedoms or by any person or group of persons, including NGOs acting in good faith in accordance with the principles of human rights, not resorting to politically motivated stands contrary to the provisions of the UN Charter and claiming to have direct and reliable knowledge of those violations. Nonetheless, reliably attested communications shall not be inadmissible solely because the knowledge of the individual author is second hand, provided they are accompanied by clear evidence; or

- It is exclusively based on reports disseminated by mass media; or

- It refers to a case that appears to reveal a consistent pattern of gross and reliably attested violations of human rights already being dealt with by a special procedure, a treaty body or other United Nations or similar regional complaints procedure in the field of human rights; or

---

12. *See* http://www2.ohchr.org/english/bodies/chr/complaints.htm [last visited January 10, 2011].
13. *Id.*

- The domestic remedies have not been exhausted, unless it appears that such remedies would be ineffective or unreasonably prolonged.[14]

Delegates of the Human Rights Commission may also conduct country visits to investigate situations involving human rights in various countries. They have to seek the permission of the country to be visited, and if granted, may conduct fact finding missions on which they write follow-up reports.

The Human Rights Council may also appoint Special Rapporteurs. Their mandate is to "examine, monitor, advise and publicly report" on specific human rights issues. For example, Mr. Juan Mendez, the Special Rapporteur on torture and other cruel, inhuman or degrading treatment or punishment, issued a statement in August 2011, condemning the Syrian Government for its brutal repression of protestors. The UN Secretary General may also appoint "working groups" and "independent experts" to investigate human rights abuses.

d. The Office of the High Commissioner for Human Rights (OHCHR)

The High Commissioner for Human Rights is the principal human rights official of the UN. The High Commissioner supports the work of the Human Rights Council and the various treaty bodies, and works at the country and local levels to support human rights worldwide. The OHCHR has authority to establish offices in countries to support the development of human rights in those countries. The OHCHR then negotiates with the host government on issues pertaining to human rights protection and promotion. At the end of 2010 OHCHR had offices in Bolivia, Cambodia, Colombia, Guatemala, Guinea, Kosovo, Mauritania, Mexico, Nepal, the Occupied Palestinian Territories, Togo, and Uganda. Local offices of the OHCHR conduct monitoring, public reporting, provision of technical assistance, and the monitoring and development of long-term national capacities to address human rights issues. The High Commissioner may also make speeches and issue reports on human rights issues. The OHCHR may also send personnel to assist when a crisis develops, and conduct fact finding missions and form Commissions of Inquiry to investigate human rights abuses. The most recent and well known such fact finding commission was the Goldstone Commission which investigated human rights abuses by Israel and the Palestinian Authority in the Occupied Territories. There is no direct complaint procedure to the OHCHR.

e. The Economic and Social Council (ECOSOC)

The United Nations Charter also created the UN Economic and Social Council (ECOSOC) as one of its five principal organs,[15] to coordinate the economic and social work of various UN agencies and commissions. It serves as the central forum for formulating policy recommendations to member states on economic, social, educational and cultural issues. ECOSOC has the authority to conduct studies and issue reports on economic, social and cultural issues, and is also charged with inculcating respect for human rights. ECOSOC is also charged with furthering the *Millennium Development Goals* (MDGs), which are designed to reduce poverty by 50% by 2015, and will be discussed in a later

---

14. *See* http://www2.ohchr.org/english/bodies/chr/complaints.htm [last visited January 10, 2011].

15. In 1946, Ecosoc went on to create the Commission on Human Rights, which drafted the general Bill of Rights, which would come to be known as the Universal Declaration of Human Rights. This document will be discussed below under the treaty system.

chapter. In 2005, ECOSOC was authorized to assess progress made towards the *Millennium Development Goals* by means of the annual Ministerial Review.

f. The International Court of Justice (ICJ)

The ICJ is the "principal judicial organ of the United Nations." It has jurisdiction to decide inter-state cases and issue advisory opinions. Only a few cases involving human rights matters have come before the court.

g. Other Agencies

The UN also has specialized agencies which have addressed specific human rights. For example, the International Labor Organization (ILO), has drafted more than 180 conventions and has highly developed monitoring procedures. It is the oldest UN organization concerned with human rights. It focuses on rights related to employment, including "[working] conditions of freedom and dignity," trade union freedoms, freedom from forced labor, and freedom from child labor.

Additionally, the UN Educational, Scientific and Cultural Organization (UNESCO) has adopted conventions on educational and cultural rights, and it adopted the first international instrument to address the impact of biotechnology on human rights.

2. The Treaty System

The seven core human rights treaties set international standards for the promotion and protection of human rights. States become a party to these treaties by signing them (and, if necessary, ratifying them). Once a state has become a party it has an obligation to ensure that individuals living in that state enjoy the rights guaranteed by the treaty. The state also has reporting obligations under many of these treaties.

a. *The Universal Declaration of Human Rights* (1948)

Under the leadership of Chairperson Eleanor Roosevelt, the Human Rights Commission drafted the *Universal Declaration of Human Rights* (UDHR) which was adopted by the UN General Assembly on December 10, 1948. This *Declaration* reinforced the notion that rights were to be applied "universally"; that is, without distinctions based on "race, colour, sex, language, religion, political or other opinion, national or social origin, property, birth or other status."[16] Roosevelt's vision was to create an international *Magna Carta*, a new *Declaration of the Rights of Man*, a universal charter that would apply equally to men and women.[17] A supporter of women's rights, Roosevelt was mindful of the need for

---

16. Universal Declaration of Human Rights, G.A. Res. 217 (III) A, U.N. Doc. A/RES/217(III), art. 2 (Dec. 10, 1948), *available at* http://www.un.org/en/documents/udhr/ [last visited May 2, 2011]; [hereinafter *Universal Declaration*].

17. In her speech to the UN when she presented the Universal Declaration, Roosevelt proclaimed: "We stand today at the threshold of a great event both in the life of the United Nations and in the life of mankind. This declaration may well become the international Magna Carta for all men everywhere. We hope its proclamation by the General Assembly will be an event comparable to the proclamation in 1789 [of the French Declaration of the Rights of Man], the adoption of the Bill of Rights by the people of the U.S., and the adoption of comparable declarations at different times in other countries ..."

dignity and equality, not only on a grand scale in the public sphere, but also on a smaller scale in the private life of the individual. She later wrote:

> Where, after all, do universal human rights begin? In small places, close to home—so close and so small that they cannot be seen on any maps of the world. Yet they are the world of the individual person; the neighborhood he lives in; the school or college he attends; the factory, farm, or office where he works. Such are the places where every man, woman, and child seeks equal justice, equal opportunity, equal dignity without discrimination. Unless these rights have meaning there, they have little meaning anywhere. Without concerted citizen action to uphold them close to home, we shall look in vain for progress in the larger world.[18]

The UDHR was designed to foster the notion of the interdependence and indivisibility of human rights. It included both traditional civil and political rights such as access to a fair and impartial legal system,[19] freedom of speech,[20] religion,[21] and movement,[22] and socio-economic rights like the right to social security,[23] the right to work,[24] and the right to rest, leisure,[25] and an adequate standard of living.[26] The *Declaration* borrowed the general principles and wording of the *U.S. Declaration of Independence* noting in Article 1 that "All human beings are born free and equal in dignity and rights" but substituted the more gender neutral terminology of "human beings" for "men."

Contributing to the advancement of women's rights, the Declaration provided that: "No one shall be held in slavery or servitude; slavery and the slave trade shall be prohibited in all their forms."[27] Other noteworthy provisions were Article 6, which provided that "Everyone has the right to recognition everywhere as a person before the law;" and Article 16, which, recognizing that women were often forced into arranged marriages at young ages, guaranteed that:

> (1) Men and women of full age, without any limitation due to race, nationality or religion, have the right to marry and to found a family. They are entitled to equal rights as to marriage, during marriage and at its dissolution.

> (2) Marriage shall be entered into only with the free and full consent of the intending spouses.

The *Universal Declaration* was not without its critics. The very idea that there could be "universal" rights was contested by cultural relativists, who argued that no moral judgment is universally valid, and that rights should be culturally determined. The *Declaration* was seen as a western inspired document by some Islamic and African states. The clash between culture and human rights is played out in a variety of circumstances

---

Mary Ann Glendon, A World Made New: Eleanor Roosevelt and the Universal Declaration of Human Rights 166 (2001); *see also* Jussi M. Hanhimäki The United Nations: A Very Short Introduction 112 (2008).

18. Eleanor Roosevelt, Courage in a Dangerous World: The Political Writings of Eleanor Roosevelt (190; Allida M. Black, ed., 1999).
19. *Universal Declaration*, art. 10.
20. *Universal Declaration*, art. 19.
21. *Universal Declaration*, art. 18.
22. *Universal Declaration*, art. 13 & 20.
23. *Universal Declaration*, art. 22.
24. *Universal Declaration*, art. 23.
25. *Universal Declaration*, art. 24.
26. *Universal Declaration*, art. 25.
27. *Universal Declaration*, art. 4.

in the arena of women's rights. This clash, and its implications or women's rights are discussed in more detail in later chapters.

Additionally, supporters of the document pointed to the fact that it was merely a declaration, and thus had no binding force.[28] Other critics railed against various articles including Article 17 which called for the recognition of property rights, and Article 26 which called for compulsory education. Still other critics have pointed to the fact that there is no right to conscientious objection enshrined in the *Universal Declaration*.[29]

The fact that the Universal Declaration was a declaration, rather than a binding treaty, prompted the drafting and promulgation of several subsequent treaties, designed to delineate more precisely, the rights that had been articulated in the *Universal Declaration*. The new treaties also aimed to provide remedies for violations of those rights. Mindful of the mass atrocities that had been perpetrated against the Jewish people, the Romani, and the disabled by the Nazi regime, the first Convention to emerge after the *Declaration* was the Convention on the Prevention and Punishment of the Crime of Genocide in 1948, followed by the International Covenant on Civil and Political Rights (ICCPR), and the International Covenant on Economic, Social and Cultural Rights (ICESCR), both in 1966. These three documents are the constitutive documents of international human rights law and are collectively known as the International Bill of Rights. In addition, the Convention on the Elimination of All Forms of Racial Discrimination (CERD) entered into force in 1969.

Questions for Discussion

1. *Compare the description of fundamental rights and the concept of the human person that appeared in the UN Charter in 1945 with those that appeared in the* Magna Carta *and the eighteenth-century declarations. Do you think that the audience for whom each was written — individual nations, international or universal society — impacted the development of these documents?*

2. *Eleanor Roosevelt's idea of human rights in the small sphere, the private life of an individual, remains quite relevant. How do you think the concept of women's rights in the public sphere compares with the rights of women in their private lives today?*

3. *What were some of the early problems with the* Universal Declaration of Human Rights? *What does the development of other bodies and laws and the* Universal Declaration's *own increase in significance indicate about the development of human rights law? Of International Law?*

---

28. The *Universal Declaration* is now widely regarded as having become part of international customary law — legal principles which have attained the force of law because they are followed by states out of a sense of legal obligation (*opinio iuris*). According to Article 48 of the Statute of the International Court of Justice, customary international law is a source of law recognized and applied by the Court. Statute of the International Court of Justice art. 38(1)(b), June 26, 1945, 59 Stat. 1055 [hereinafter ICJ Statute].

29. *See generally* the report of the Special Rapporteur for Human Rights E/CN.4/1992/52, para. 185, where the Rapporteur noted that the right to freedom of thought, conscience, and religion referred to in Art. 18 of the Declaration would seem to legitimately convey the right to conscientious objection. *Available at* http://www2.ohchr.org/english/issues/religion/I3k.htm [last visited December 8, 2010].

b. The ICCPR (1966)[30]

The ICCPR, which was also drawn up by the UN Human Rights Commission, enshrined and expanded on the civil and political rights first articulated in the *Universal Declaration.* Signatories to the Convention, including the United States, undertook to "respect and ensure" to all individuals in their territories "the rights recognized in the present Covenant, without distinction of any kind, such as race, colour, sex, language, religion, political or other opinion, national or social origin, property, birth or other status."[31] The ICCPR further required those states to enact legislation to give effect to the rights contained in the Convention.[32] The ICCPR reiterated the equality and non discrimination rights referred to in the *Universal Declaration*, but did not define what it meant by the all important word "equality." As of 2010, 167 states have signed the Covenant, and all but 5 of these states have ratified it.[33]

Of particular interest to women are Articles 3, 16, 23, and 26, which provide:

(Article 3) The States Parties to the present Covenant undertake to ensure the equal right of men and women to the enjoyment of all civil and political rights set forth in the present Covenant.

(Article 16) Everyone shall have the right to recognition everywhere as a person before the law.

(Article 23) 1. The family is the natural and fundamental group unit of society and is entitled to protection by society and the State.

2. The right of men and women of marriageable age to marry and to found a family shall be recognized.

3. No marriage shall be entered into without the free and full consent of the intending spouses.

4. States Parties to the present Covenant shall take appropriate steps to ensure equality of rights and responsibilities of spouses as to marriage, during marriage and at its dissolution.

(Article 26) All persons are equal before the law and are entitled without any discrimination to the equal protection of the law. In this respect, the law shall prohibit any discrimination and guarantee to all persons equal and effective protection against discrimination on any ground such as race, colour, sex, language, religion, political or other opinion, national or social origin, property, birth or other status.

i. State Reporting Procedure under the ICCPR

Article 40 of the ICCPR requires party states to file a report within one year of ratifying the Covenant, and to file a report every four or five years thereafter, detailing the measures

---

30. International Covenant on Civil and Political Rights, G.A. Res. 2200A (XXI), U.N. Doc. A/RES/21/2200, art. 2 (Dec. 16, 1966), *available at* http://www2.ohchr.org/english/law/pdf/ccpr.pdf [hereinafter ICCPR].

31. ICCPR, art. 2(2).

32. ICCPR, art. 2(2).

33. U.N. TREATY COLLECTION, http://treaties.un.org/Pages/ViewDetails.aspx?src=TREATY&mtdsg_ no=IV-4&chapter=4&lang=en [last visited November 3, 2010].

adopted within the party state to give effect to the rights articulated in the Covenant. The Committee established by the ICCPR (known as the Human Rights Committee and consisting of experts on human rights from various countries) considers these reports and publishes "Concluding Observations" critiquing or praising the state and making suggestions and recommendations for improvement. The Committee publishes guidelines for states' reports in their Manual on Human Rights Reporting.[34]

Article 41 of the ICCPR provides for the Committee to consider inter-state complaints brought by one state party against another. This procedure has never been used.

ii. Enforceability—NGOs and Shadow Reports

It was recognized early on that states may choose to report only on matters and only in a manner that does not portray them in a negative light. The practice thus developed of "shadow reports" being filed by Non Governmental Organizations (NGOs). These shadow reports focus on areas of concern that the official state party report may have glossed over. The Human Rights Committee may use these reports in their "Concluding Observations" to a state party filing an official report. NGOs may register with the UN ECOSOC in order to be able to file shadow reports. The requisite instructions on how to apply for consultative status as an NGO are available at: http://esango.un.org/civilsociety/login.do.

NGOs generally have to have been in existence for two years to apply for accreditation.

iii. The Individual Complaint Procedure under the Optional Protocol[35]

It was soon recognized that the ICCPR would not be as effective without a more stringent means of enforcement. Thus, even while the ICCPR was being opened for signature, a First Optional Protocol with a complaint mechanism was being prepared. It entered into force in 1979 and currently 119 states are parties to it.[36] This procedure is only available if the state party is a signatory to the Optional Protocol, and the individual or individuals are direct victims of violations of their rights under the Covenant by the State Party. To bring a complaint before the Committee the following criteria must be met:

a.   Cases may only be taken by an individual who claims to be a victim of violations of the rights guaranteed under the Covenant;

b.   The alleged victim must have been subject to the jurisdiction of the State Party at the time of the alleged violation;

c.   The alleged violation must be a violation of rights set out in the ICCPR;

d.   The alleged violation must have occurred after the State Party acceded both to the Covenant and to the Optional Protocol;

e.   The State Party must not have *contracted out* of the specific provisions by means of a reservation or by a declaration under article 4;

f.   Cases may only be taken against a States Party. It is necessary to indicate culpability on the part of the State;

---

34. *Available at* http://www2.ohchr.org/english/bodies/hrc/index.htm [last visited December 28, 2010].

35. The Optional Protocol entered into force March 23, 1976. 21 U.N. GAOR Supp. (No. 16) at 59, U.N. Doc. A/6316 (1966), 999 U.N.T.S. 302 (1976).

36. There is also a Second Optional Protocol that deals with the death penalty.

g. Cases may not be taken which are subject to consideration by another redress mechanism; and

h. All relevant domestic redress procedures must have been exhausted. This requirement is waived if it can be shown that the pursuit of the local remedy would be ineffective.

When considering a complaint, the Council first determines whether it is admissible. If it is determined to be admissible, the matter is then considered on the merits. The Council consists of a body of eighteen experts who meet three times per year to consider such complaints.

Once a communication is received from an individual, the State party has 180 days to respond. If a state fails to respond or does not provide adequate redress, the state will be listed in the Committee's Annual Report. The Council may issue its "views" on complaints and issue recommendations to the state party concerned to take specific action.

Cases generally take between two and four years to go through the process before the Committee issues its view. However the Committee may request the state party to take interim measures to protect the victim. The Committee's view may address the matter in a broader context than just addressing the victim's injuries, by requesting that the state party address the situation for the benefit of all similarly situated potential and actual victims. NGOs may also make submissions to the Committee on behalf of individuals. The Council may request a report from the state party after six months to determine how the state party has implemented its views and recommendations.

iv. The Emergency Procedure under Article 40 of the ICCPR

Article 40 of the ICCPR permits the Committee to request a state to file a report on a matter of grave concern to the Committee. When this procedure is invoked, the state party is required to file a report or response on the issue within three months. If the Committee considers that the matter involves "grave human rights violations" it will bring the matter to the attention of the UN Secretary General, who may in turn bring it to the attention of the appropriate organs of the UN, including the Security Council.

c. The International Covenant on Economic, Social and Cultural Rights — ICESCR (1966)[37]

The ICESCR also confirmed that the rights guaranteed therein were to be "exercised without discrimination of any kind as to race, colour, sex, language, religion, political or other opinion, national or social origin, property, birth or other status."[38] Among obligations undertaken by signatories to the Convention was the obligation to "ensure the equal right of men and women to the enjoyment of all economic, social and cultural rights set forth in the present Covenant."[39] Among those rights are labor rights,[40] the right

---

37. International Covenant on Economic, Social and Cultural Rights, G.A. Res. 2200A (XXI), U.N. Doc. A/RES/21/2200, art. 2(2) (Dec. 16, 1966), *available at* http://www2.ohchr.org/english/law/cescr.htm [hereinafter ICESCR].

38. ICESCR, art. 2(2).

39. ICESCR, art. 3.

40. ICESCR, arts. 6 ("right to work"), 7 ("right of everyone to the enjoyment of just and favourable conditions of work"), and 8 ("right of everyone to form trade unions").

to social security,[41] family life,[42] housing,[43] the right to an adequate standard of living,[44] health,[45] education,[46] and the right to participate in cultural life.[47] Many of these rights could profoundly impact and ameliorate the lives of women. Girls often face discrimination in the area of education, where many families choose to educate boys over girls for cultural and financial reasons. As a result, girls have lower literacy rates than boys in every part of the world. Similarly, girls face discrimination in their nascent and married family life, often being forced into arranged marriages at early ages. The problem with these rights, as in many areas of international law, is the problem of enforcement which will be discussed in a later chapter.

The right to health has developed into one of the more controversial rights espoused in the IESCR, particularly as it applies to women's health. The language of Article 12 refers to both physical and mental health, and specifically calls on signatories to take steps for "the reduction of the stillbirth-rate and of infant mortality and for the healthy development of the child." This Article furthers the goal articulated in Article 10(2) which requires states to afford:

> Special protection … to mothers during a reasonable period before and after childbirth. During such period working mothers should be accorded paid leave or leave with adequate social security benefits.

In the context of women's rights, the right to health, and references to childbirth and maternity are often referred to as "reproductive rights." These rights are often considered controversial rights. They were given more context and specificity by the *Beijing Declaration* and *Platform for Action* which will be discussed in a later chapter.

Socio-economic and cultural rights have been described by some commentators as second generation rights, meaning they should be focused on only subsequent to civil and political rights being attained. Karel Vasek coined the taxonomy of "generations of rights."[48] The first generation: civil and political rights such as free speech, the right to vote, the right to a fair trial, etc. were derived from the French notion of *liberté*. The second, socio-economic rights, include the right to education, housing, health, employment and social security. The third generation of rights are solidarity rights or collective rights. They include the right to economic development, social harmony, and a clean environment.

A reporting procedure also exists for the ICESCR. The process is very similar to the ICCPR in that reports are made to a Committee, in this case the Committee on Economic, Social and Cultural Rights (CESCR). As the UN describes it:

> The CESCR is the body of independent experts that monitors implementation of the International Covenant on Economic, Social and Cultural Rights by its

---

41. ICESCR, art. 9.

42. ICESCR, art. 10.

43. ICESCR, art. 11 ("right of everyone … including adequate food, clothing and housing").

44. *Id.* ("right of everyone to an adequate standard of living").

45. ICESCR, art. 12.

46. ICESCR, arts. 13 ("right of everyone to education"); art. 14 (Each State Party … to work out and adopt a detailed plan of action for the progressive implementation, within a reasonable number of years, to be fixed in the plan, of the principle of compulsory education free of charge for all").

47. ICESCR, art. 15.

48. Karel Vasak, *Human Rights: A Thirty-Year Struggle: The Sustained Efforts to Give Force of Law to the Universal Declaration of Human Rights*, UNESCO COURIER 29–32 (Nov. 1977). *See also* ROGER NORMAND & SARAH ZAIDI, HUMAN RIGHTS AT THE UN: THE POLITICAL HISTORY OF UNIVERSAL JUSTICE 442, n. 64 (2008).

States parties. The Committee was established under ECOSOC Resolution 1985/17 of 28 May 1985 to carry out the monitoring functions. All States parties are obliged to submit regular reports to the Committee on how the rights are being implemented. States must report initially within two years of accepting the Covenant and thereafter every five years. The Committee examines each report and addresses its concerns and recommendations to the State party in the form of "concluding observations."

Individual communications or complaints are also permitted. The process is identical to the complaint procedure under the ICCPR.

With regard to individual complaints, on 10 December 2008, the General Assembly unanimously adopted an Optional Protocol (GA resolution A/RES/63/117) to the International Covenant on Economic, Social and Cultural Rights which provides the Committee competence to receive and consider communications. The General Assembly took note of the adoption by the Human Rights Council by its resolution 8/2 of 18 June 2008, of the Optional Protocol. The Optional Protocol was opened for signature at a signing ceremony in 2009. In addition to the Committee on Economic, Social and Cultural rights, other committees with competence can consider individual communications involving issues related to economic, social and cultural rights in the context of its treaty.[49]

d. The Convention on the Elimination of All Forms of Racial Discrimination — CERD

The Convention on the Elimination of All Forms of Racial Discrimination (CERD), entered into force in 1969. It reiterated principles of inherent human dignity, and equality and equal protection, while condemning any form of racial discrimination. It too created a Committee of experts to monitor treaty provisions, and has reporting requirements similar to the ICCPR and ICESCR.

Like the ICCPR and ICESCR, an individual may also file a complaint under CERD for a violation of his or her rights by a state party. Parties have the duty to exhaust domestic remedies before filing a claim, and any claim filed must be brought within six months of a decision being made on a domestic claim. The claims are heard by the CERD Committee, a body of eighteen experts which meets twice per year. A state party has to recognize the competence of the Committee in order for an individual to file a claim before that Committee. Claims may also be filed on behalf of a group of people similarly affected.

Of this treaty based system which comprises the Prevention and Punishment of the Crime of Genocide, the ICCPR, IESCR, CERD, CEDAW, the Convention on the Rights of the Child (CRC), and the Convention Against Torture and Other Cruel, Inhuman or Degrading Treatment or Punishment, Thomas Buergenthal has noted:[50]

Although the six treaty bodies in existence today are not judicial institutions, they have had to interpret and apply their respective conventions in reviewing

---

49. *See* http://www2.ohchr.org/english/bodies/cescr/ [last visited December 28, 2010].
50. Thomas Buergenthal, *The Evolving International Human Rights System*, 100 AMJIL 783, 789 (2006).

and commenting on the periodic reports the states parties must submit to them, and in dealing with the individual complaints that some treaty bodies are authorized to receive. This practice has produced a substantial body of international human rights law. While one can debate the question of the nature of this law and whether or not it is law at all, the fact remains that the normative findings of the treaty bodies have legal significance, as evidenced by references to them in international and domestic judicial decisions.

Over the years numerous states have ratified the human rights treaties the United Nations and its specialized agencies have adopted. These conventions not only have internationalized the subject of human rights as between the parties to them, but also to the same extent have internationalized the individual human rights these treaties guarantee. Since some of these treaties have been very widely ratified by member states of the international community, they may be viewed as creating an entire body of customary international human rights law. Non-states parties may therefore find it increasingly difficult to claim that the human rights guarantees these treaties proclaim, particularly those from which derogation is not permitted, impose no legal obligations on them.

Questions for Discussion

1. *What kind of tensions might arise between women's rights and the marriage and family rights contained in Article 23 of the ICCPR?*

2. *Can and should international treaties attempt to regulate family life? If so, what is the best way to disseminate information about these kinds of rights, and to enforce them?*

3. *Social, economic, and cultural rights like the ones covered in the ICESCR have been called "second generation" rights. What might be some problems with thinking of this system of rights as hierarchical?*

4. *For these treaties to function effectively, states must accept and give effect to all of the core provisions. Moreover, all of the respective treaty bodies need to present a cohesive and uniform approach to human rights and their implementation. Can you think of any situation where that has not been done?*

e. The Convention for the Elimination of All Forms of Discrimination against Women — CEDAW (1979)

i. History of CEDAW

As noted above, the period between the 1948 Universal Declaration and the drafting of CEDAW (also known as the Women's Convention), had seen several treaties that were designed to protect particular groups of people; many of these were drafted by the UN Human Rights Commission. The Convention on the Prevention and Punishment of the Crime of Genocide (1948) and the Convention on the Elimination of All Forms of Racial Discrimination or CERD (1969), are two such examples. Additionally several regional human rights treaties were drafted during this period. These include the European

Convention on Human Rights,[51] the Inter-American Convention on Human Rights,[52] and the African (Banjul) Charter.[53] These will be discussed in a later chapter.

In 1946, the Commission on the Status of Women had been established by ECOSOC pursuant to Resolution 11 (II), with the aim of preparing recommendations and reports to the Council on promoting women's rights in political, economic, civil, social and educational fields. During its first session, the Commission declared as one of its guiding principles:

> [t]o raise the status of women, irrespective of nationality, race, language or religion, to equality with men in all fields of human enterprise, and to eliminate all discrimination against women in the provisions of statutory law, in legal maxims or rules, or in interpretation of customary law.[54]

Before drafting CEDAW, the Commission embarked on a large research project to establish data documenting the lowly status of women. Member states and non-governmental organizations (NGOs) provided the Committee with statistics and reports on the political and legal status of women.[55] Consider that in 1945, only 22 of the member nations of the UN allowed women the right to vote. On December 20, 1952, the Convention on the Political Rights of Women, drafted by the Commission, was adopted by the General Assembly. This document, adopted by the UN in Resolution 640 (VII) provided for the rights of women to vote, run for any political office, and participate in political life on an equal basis with men. It was the first international document after the UDHR to explicitly provide for the equality of women in all aspects of political life.

Having dealt with discrimination against women in the political arena, the Commission, prompted by reports from Non Governmental Organizations (NGOs), turned its attention to discrimination in private life; specifically with regard to marriage and nationality. Many member states had laws providing that on marriage, a woman lost the right to transmit her nationality to her children. The Commission accordingly drafted the Convention on the Nationality of Married Women, which was adopted on January 29, 1957 by Resolution 1040 (XI). This was followed in 1962, by the Convention on Consent to Marriage, Minimum Age for Marriage and Registration of Marriages, adopted by the UN under Resolution 1763 A (XVII), and subsequently by the Recommendation on Consent to Marriage, Minimum Age for Marriage and Registration of Marriages which was adopted on November 1, 1965.

---

51. Convention for the Protection of Human Rights and Fundamental Freedoms, Nov. 4, 1950, 213 U.N.T.S. 221, *available at* http://www.hri.org/docs/ECHR50.html#Convention; http://www.echr.coe. int/nr/rdonlyres/D5CC24A7-DC13-4318-B457-5C9014916D7A/o/EnglishAnglais.pdf [hereinafter European Convention].

52. Organization of the American States, American Convention on Human Rights, Nov. 22, 1969, 1144 U.N.T.S. 123, *available at* http://www.cidh.oas.org/basicos/english/basic3.american%20 convention.htm [hereinafter Inter-American Convention].

53. African (Banjul) Charter on Human and Peoples' Rights, June 27, 1981, *available at* http://www.africa-union.org/official_documents/Treaties_%20Conventions_%20Protocols/Banjul%2 0Charter.pdf [hereinafter African Charter].

54. U.N. Commission on the Status of Women [CSW], Report of the CSW to ECOSOC on the First Session of the Commission, U.N. Doc. E/281/Rev.1, at 25 (Feb. 25, 1947); *see also* U.N. Commission on the Status of Women, *Short History of the Commission on the Status of Women*, http://www.un.org/womenwatch/daw/CSW60YRS/CSWbriefhistory.pdf [last visited November 4, 2010]. *See also* UNITED NATIONS, THE UNITED NATIONS AND THE ADVANCEMENT OF WOMEN 4 (1996).

55. UNITED NATIONS, THE UNITED NATIONS AND THE ADVANCEMENT OF WOMEN 4 (1996).

ii. CEDAW

Having prepared the groundwork for a comprehensive women's rights treaty, the Commission presented the *Declaration on the Elimination of All Forms of Discrimination Against Women* (DEDAW) to the UN on November 7, 1967. As the UN's own documented history of this period notes:

> Although the Declaration amounted only to a statement of moral and political intent, without the contractual force of a treaty, its drafting was none the less a difficult process. Article 6, concerning equality in marriage and the family, and article 10, relating to employment, proved to be particularly controversial, as did the question of whether the Declaration should call for the abolition of the customs and laws perpetuating discrimination or for their modification or change.[56]

The *Declaration* provided for a voluntary reporting system, whereby member states would report on the conditions of women in their countries. It soon became apparent that this was ineffective. Moreover, during this period, the UN was focusing on development, and soon realized that not only were women being left out of development issues, but current development policies were having an adverse impact on women, and were in fact contributing to what would be termed the *feminization of poverty*—women comprising the majority of the world's poor. Meanwhile, the women's movement and feminist theorists were focusing attention on women's rights, and women's economic participation, as well as cultural and social factors affecting women's participation in development. In 1970, a Special Rapporteur was appointed to head up the Status of Women and Family Planning Project. Another Special Rapporteur was appointed to look into ways of eliminating stereotypes of women and children in the media. In 1974, the Commission determined to prepare a treaty to combat discrimination against women in all of its forms. This culminated in the Convention for the Elimination of Discrimination Against Women (CEDAW) being adopted by the UN General Assembly in 1979[57] by 130 votes in favor, to 0 opposed, and 10 abstentions. The Convention provided that it would enter into force after the twentieth state had ratified it. On September 3, 1981, CEDAW entered into force. Currently, 186 states are parties to CEDAW, making it the most widely adopted human rights treaty. The United States signed the treaty in 1979 but has failed to ratify it. The fact that the U.S. has signed the treaty obliges it not to take any acts that would impede or defeat the object and purpose of the treaty but does not oblige it to actually enforce the treaty.

A full list of signatories may be found at: http://treaties.un.org/Pages/ViewDetails.aspx?src=TREATY&mtdsg_no=IV-8&chapter=4&lang=en.

One of the most important articles of the treaty is Article 1 which defines discrimination under CEDAW as:

---

56. Committee on the Elimination of Discrimination against Women, *Progress Achieved in the Implementation of the Convention on the Elimination of All Forms of Discrimination against Women*, U.N. Doc. A/CONF.177/7, 5 (June 21, 1995), *available at* http://www.un.org/esa/documents/ga/conf177/aconf177-7en.htm, quoted *in* U.N. Convention on the Elimination of All Forms of Discrimination against Women, *Short History of CEDAW Convention*, http://www.un.org/womenwatch/daw/cedaw/history.htm [last visited November 5, 2010].

57. The Convention was adopted by the General Assembly by Resolution 34/180.

For the purposes of the present Convention, the term "discrimination against women" shall mean any distinction, exclusion or restriction made on the basis of sex which has the effect or purpose of impairing or nullifying the recognition, enjoyment or exercise by women, irrespective of their marital status, on a basis of equality of men and women, of human rights and fundamental freedoms in the political, economic, social, cultural, civil or any other field.

This definition of discrimination is very similar to the one used in CERD,[58] where the "effect" and "purpose" of the discrimination on the equal rights of women is the determining factor. Thus, discriminatory intent need not be established, only the effect or impact is examined.

Article 2 went on to require states to:

condemn discrimination against women in all its forms, agree to pursue by all appropriate means and without delay a policy of eliminating discrimination against women and, to this end, undertake:

(a) To embody the principle of the equality of men and women in their national constitutions or other appropriate legislation if not yet incorporated therein and to ensure, through law and other appropriate means, the practical realization of this principle;

(b) To adopt appropriate legislative and other measures, including sanctions where appropriate, prohibiting all discrimination against women;

(c) To establish legal protection of the rights of women on an equal basis with men and to ensure through competent national tribunals and other public institutions the effective protection of women against any act of discrimination;

(d) To refrain from engaging in any act or practice of discrimination against women and to ensure that public authorities and institutions shall act in conformity with this obligation;

(e) To take all appropriate measures to eliminate discrimination against women by any person, organization or enterprise;

(f) To take all appropriate measures, including legislation, to modify or abolish existing laws, regulations, customs and practices which constitute discrimination against women;

(g) To repeal all national penal provisions which constitute discrimination against women.

Article 3

States Parties shall take in all fields, in particular in the political, social, economic and cultural fields, all appropriate measures, including legislation, to ensure the full development and advancement of women, for the purpose of guaranteeing them the exercise and enjoyment of human rights and fundamental freedoms on a basis of equality with men.

Article 4

1. Adoption by States Parties of temporary special measures aimed at accelerating de facto equality between men and women shall not be considered discrimination

---

58. The Convention on the Elimination of Racial Discrimination, *available at* http://www2.ohchr.org/english/law/cerd.htm [last visited December 8, 2010].

as defined in the present Convention, but shall in no way entail as a consequence the maintenance of unequal or separate standards; these measures shall be discontinued when the objectives of equality of opportunity and treatment have been achieved.

2. Adoption by States Parties of special measures, including those measures contained in the present Convention, aimed at protecting maternity shall not be considered discriminatory.

Article 5

States Parties shall take all appropriate measures:

(a) To modify the social and cultural patterns of conduct of men and women, with a view to achieving the elimination of prejudices and customary and all other practices which are based on the idea of the inferiority or the superiority of either of the sexes or on stereotyped roles for men and women;

(b) To ensure that family education includes a proper understanding of the role of maternity as a social function and the recognition of the common responsibility of men and women in the upbringing and development of their children, it being understood that the interest of the children is the primordial consideration in all cases.

Article 6

States Parties shall take all appropriate measures, including legislation, to suppress all forms of traffic in women and exploitation of prostitution of women.

PART II

Article 7

States Parties shall take all appropriate measures to eliminate discrimination against women in the political and public life of the country and, in particular, shall ensure to women, on equal terms with men, the right:

(a) To vote in all elections and public referenda and to be eligible for election to all publicly elected bodies;

(b) To participate in the formulation of government policy and the implementation thereof and to hold public office and perform all public functions at all levels of government;

(c) To participate in non-governmental organizations and associations concerned with the public and political life of the country.

Article 8

States Parties shall take all appropriate measures to ensure to women, on equal terms with men and without any discrimination, the opportunity to represent their Governments at the international level and to participate in the work of international organizations.

Article 9

1. States Parties shall grant women equal rights with men to acquire, change or retain their nationality. They shall ensure in particular that neither marriage to an alien nor change of nationality by the husband during marriage shall automatically change the nationality of the wife, render her stateless or force upon her the nationality of the husband.

2. States Parties shall grant women equal rights with men with respect to the nationality of their children.

PART III

Article 10

States Parties shall take all appropriate measures to eliminate discrimination against women in order to ensure to them equal rights with men in the field of education and in particular to ensure, on a basis of equality of men and women:

(a) The same conditions for career and vocational guidance, for access to studies and for the achievement of diplomas in educational establishments of all categories in rural as well as in urban areas; this equality shall be ensured in pre-school, general, technical, professional and higher technical education, as well as in all types of vocational training;

(b) Access to the same curricula, the same examinations, teaching staff with qualifications of the same standard and school premises and equipment of the same quality;

(c) The elimination of any stereotyped concept of the roles of men and women at all levels and in all forms of education by encouraging coeducation and other types of education which will help to achieve this aim and, in particular, by the revision of textbooks and school programmes and the adaptation of teaching methods;

(d) The same opportunities to benefit from scholarships and other study grants;

(e) The same opportunities for access to programmes of continuing education, including adult and functional literacy programmes, particularly those aimed at reducing, at the earliest possible time, any gap in education existing between men and women;

(f) The reduction of female student drop-out rates and the organization of programmes for girls and women who have left school prematurely;

(g) The same opportunities to participate actively in sports and physical education;

(h) Access to specific educational information to help to ensure the health and well-being of families, including information and advice on family planning.

Article 11

1. States Parties shall take all appropriate measures to eliminate discrimination against women in the field of employment in order to ensure, on a basis of equality of men and women, the same rights, in particular:

(a) The right to work as an inalienable right of all human beings;

(b) The right to the same employment opportunities, including the application of the same criteria for selection in matters of employment;

(c) The right to free choice of profession and employment, the right to promotion, job security and all benefits and conditions of service and the right to receive vocational training and retraining, including apprenticeships, advanced vocational training and recurrent training;

(d) The right to equal remuneration, including benefits, and to equal treatment in respect of work of equal value, as well as equality of treatment in the evaluation of the quality of work;

(e) The right to social security, particularly in cases of retirement, unemployment, sickness, invalidity and old age and other incapacity to work, as well as the right to paid leave;

(f) The right to protection of health and to safety in working conditions, including the safeguarding of the function of reproduction.

2. In order to prevent discrimination against women on the grounds of marriage or maternity and to ensure their effective right to work, States Parties shall take appropriate measures:

(a) To prohibit, subject to the imposition of sanctions, dismissal on the grounds of pregnancy or of maternity leave and discrimination in dismissals on the basis of marital status;

(b) To introduce maternity leave with pay or with comparable social benefits without loss of former employment, seniority or social allowances;

(c) To encourage the provision of the necessary supporting social services to enable parents to combine family obligations with work responsibilities and participation in public life, in particular through promoting the establishment and development of a network of child-care facilities;

(d) To provide special protection to women during pregnancy in types of work proved to be harmful to them.

3. Protective legislation relating to matters covered in this article shall be reviewed periodically in the light of scientific and technological knowledge and shall be revised, repealed or extended as necessary.

Article 12

States Parties shall take all appropriate measures to eliminate discrimination against women in the field of health care in order to ensure, on a basis of equality of men and women, access to health care services, including those related to family planning.

Notwithstanding the provisions of paragraph I of this article, States Parties shall ensure to women appropriate services in connection with pregnancy, confinement and the post-natal period, granting free services where necessary, as well as adequate nutrition during pregnancy and lactation.

Article 13

States Parties shall take all appropriate measures to eliminate discrimination against women in other areas of economic and social life in order to ensure, on a basis of equality of men and women, the same rights, in particular:

(a) The right to family benefits;

(b) The right to bank loans, mortgages and other forms of financial credit;

(c) The right to participate in recreational activities, sports and all aspects of cultural life.

Article 14

1. States Parties shall take into account the particular problems faced by rural women and the significant roles which rural women play in the economic survival of their families, including their work in the non-monetized sectors of the economy, and shall take all appropriate measures to ensure the application of the provisions of the present Convention to women in rural areas.

2. States Parties shall take all appropriate measures to eliminate discrimination against women in rural areas in order to ensure, on a basis of equality of men and women, that they participate in and benefit from rural development and, in particular, shall ensure to such women the right:

(a) To participate in the elaboration and implementation of development planning at all levels;

(b) To have access to adequate health care facilities, including information, counselling and services in family planning;

(c) To benefit directly from social security programmes;

(d) To obtain all types of training and education, formal and non-formal, including that relating to functional literacy, as well as, inter alia, the benefit of all community and extension services, in order to increase their technical proficiency;

(e) To organize self-help groups and co-operatives in order to obtain equal access to economic opportunities through employment or self employment;

(f) To participate in all community activities;

(g) To have access to agricultural credit and loans, marketing facilities, appropriate technology and equal treatment in land and agrarian reform as well as in land resettlement schemes;

(h) To enjoy adequate living conditions, particularly in relation to housing, sanitation, electricity and water supply, transport and communications.

PART IV

Article 15

1. States Parties shall accord to women equality with men before the law.

2. States Parties shall accord to women, in civil matters, a legal capacity identical to that of men and the same opportunities to exercise contracts and to administer property and shall treat them equally in all stages of procedure in courts and tribunals.

3. States Parties agree that all contracts and all other private instruments of any kind with a legal effect which is directed at restricting the legal capacity of women shall be deemed null and void.

4. States Parties shall accord to men and women the same rights with regard to the law relating to the movement of persons and the freedom to choose their residence and domicile.

Article 16

1. States Parties shall take all appropriate measures to eliminate discrimination against women in all matters relating to marriage and family relations and in particular shall ensure, on a basis of equality of men and women:

(a) The same right to enter into marriage;

(b) The same right freely to choose a spouse and to enter into marriage only with their free and full consent;

(c) The same rights and responsibilities during marriage and at its dissolution;

(d) The same rights and responsibilities as parents, irrespective of their marital status, in matters relating to their children; in all cases the interests of the children shall be paramount;

(e) The same rights to decide freely and responsibly on the number and spacing of their children and to have access to the information, education and means to enable them to exercise these rights;

(f) The same rights and responsibilities with regard to guardianship, wardship, trusteeship and adoption of children, or similar institutions where these concepts exist in national legislation; in all cases the interests of the children shall be paramount;

(g) The same personal rights as husband and wife, including the right to choose a family name, a profession and an occupation;

(h) The same rights for both spouses in respect of the ownership, acquisition, management, administration, enjoyment and disposition of property, whether free of charge or for a valuable consideration.

2. The betrothal and the marriage of a child shall have no legal effect, and all necessary action, including legislation, shall be taken to specify a minimum age for marriage and to make the registration of marriages in an official registry compulsory.

PART V

Article 17

1. For the purpose of considering the progress made in the implementation of the present Convention, there shall be established a Committee on the Elimination of Discrimination against Women (hereinafter referred to as the Committee) consisting, at the time of entry into force of the Convention, of eighteen and, after ratification of or accession to the Convention by the thirty-fifth State Party, of twenty-three experts of high moral standing and competence in the field covered by the Convention. The experts shall be elected by States Parties from among their nationals and shall serve in their personal capacity, consideration being given to equitable geographical distribution and to the representation of the different forms of civilization as well as the principal legal systems.

2. The members of the Committee shall be elected by secret ballot from a list of persons nominated by States Parties. Each State Party may nominate one person from among its own nationals.

3. The initial election shall be held six months after the date of the entry into force of the present Convention. At least three months before the date of each election the Secretary-General of the United Nations shall address a letter to the States Parties inviting them to submit their nominations within two months. The Secretary-General shall prepare a list in alphabetical order of all persons thus nominated, indicating the States Parties which have nominated them, and shall submit it to the States Parties.

4. Elections of the members of the Committee shall be held at a meeting of States Parties convened by the Secretary-General at United Nations Headquarters. At that meeting, for which two thirds of the States Parties shall constitute a quorum, the persons elected to the Committee shall be those nominees who obtain the largest number of votes and an absolute majority of the votes of the representatives of States Parties present and voting.

5. The members of the Committee shall be elected for a term of four years. However, the terms of nine of the members elected at the first election shall

expire at the end of two years; immediately after the first election the names of these nine members shall be chosen by lot by the Chairman of the Committee.

6. The election of the five additional members of the Committee shall be held in accordance with the provisions of paragraphs 2, 3 and 4 of this article, following the thirty-fifth ratification or accession. The terms of two of the additional members elected on this occasion shall expire at the end of two years, the names of these two members having been chosen by lot by the Chairman of the Committee.

7. For the filling of casual vacancies, the State Party whose expert has ceased to function as a member of the Committee shall appoint another expert from among its nationals, subject to the approval of the Committee.

8. The members of the Committee shall, with the approval of the General Assembly, receive emoluments from United Nations resources on such terms and conditions as the Assembly may decide, having regard to the importance of the Committee's responsibilities.

9. The Secretary-General of the United Nations shall provide the necessary staff and facilities for the effective performance of the functions of the Committee under the present Convention.

Article 18

1. States Parties undertake to submit to the Secretary-General of the United Nations, for consideration by the Committee, a report on the legislative, judicial, administrative or other measures which they have adopted to give effect to the provisions of the present Convention and on the progress made in this respect:

(a) Within one year after the entry into force for the State concerned;

(b) Thereafter at least every four years and further whenever the Committee so requests.

2. Reports may indicate factors and difficulties affecting the degree of fulfilment of obligations under the present Convention.

Articles 19 through 30 detail procedural requirements regarding reporting, disputes, and meetings of the CEDAW Committee. The full text of the Convention is available at: http://www.un.org/womenwatch/daw/cedaw/cedaw.htm.

iii. The CEDAW Committee

Like the ICCPR and ICESCR, CEDAW established a Committee to monitor the implementation of the treaty by party states. The Committee is made up of twenty three experts in the field of women's rights. Upon ratifying CEDAW, states are required to file an initial report with the Committee within a year on ratifying CEDAW. Thereafter they must submit a periodic report every four years on progress made in removing obstacles to equality. States parties that have fallen behind in their periodic reporting are encouraged to present consolidated reports (for example, second and third reports together). In 2008, the CEDAW Committee adopted new reporting guidelines specifically requiring that the reports consist of two documents: the treaty-specific report and a common core document (CCD). The CCD is an account of the State party's geography, economy, population, political system, and most importantly, describes the laws, policies, institutions, and remedies relating to human rights and specifically to discrimination. The treaty-specific report addresses the substantive articles of CEDAW and is required to describe the impact of policies to implement CEDAW. The guidelines for the CCD were endorsed by the Chairpersons of the Human Rights Treaty Bodies in 2006. They are available in the UN document, *Harmonized Guidelines on Reporting under the International Human Rights Treaties, Including Guidelines on a Common Core Document and Treaty-Specific Documents* (HRI/MC/2006/3).

The CEDAW Committee also encourages NGOs to file shadow reports or to make oral presentations at meetings of the CEDAW Committee. The CEDAW Committee meets each year in Geneva in at least two sessions of three weeks each. In 2009, the Committee will meet for two sessions, and from 2010, the Committee will meet three times every year. It is anticipated that one session per year will be at UN headquarters in New York. State party reports are considered approximately in the order in which they were submitted, with some variations to provide geographical balance as well as a balance of initial and periodic reports in each session. States parties are invited to be reviewed according to a list drawn up by the Committee at each session for future sessions. States parties do not have to accept the invitation to be reviewed in a particular session, and the Committee includes a number of "reserve" States to be invited if any on the initial list decline. Therefore the list may remain tentative until two or three months prior to the session.

States are not considered for review by the Committee until their report is submitted. The report backlog varies, and States may request a delay in their review, so they may be reviewed from one to two or more years after their reports are submitted. Also, states quite commonly delay filing their reports, sometimes for several years. Like the Human Rights Committee, the CEDAW Committee issues Concluding Observations on State parties' reports, and General Comments on matters of thematic concerns.

iv. CEDAW and Culture

CEDAW met cultural relativism head on by including culture as one of the fields that must be free from inequality and discrimination against women, and by requiring states to enact legislation to combat discrimination. *See* Articles 1 and 2. Additionally, Articles 3 and 5, respectively require states to "take all appropriate measures" "in all fields," and to "modify the social and cultural patterns of conduct of men and women, with a view to achieving the elimination of prejudices and customary and all other practices which are based on the idea of the inferiority or the superiority of either of the sexes or on stereotyped roles for men and women." Notably absent from the provisions of CEDAW, are articles specifically relating to violence, and to the role of religion in the subordination of women. These omissions will be discussed in later chapters. Several states have notably also filed reservations with regard to potential conflicts between Islamic law *(Shari'a),* and CEDAW. The impact of these reservations, and the potential and actual conflicts between CEDAW and *Shari'a* will be discussed in a later chapter.

v. CEDAW and the United States — The United States Senate Sub-Committee on Human Rights' Hearing on CEDAW

President Carter signed CEDAW in 1980 but CEDAW has never reached the House floor for a vote on ratification. On November 18, 2010, the U.S. Senate Subcommittee on Human Rights and the Law (part of the Senate Committee on the Judiciary) held a hearing on whether to ratify CEDAW. In his opening remarks, Chairman Durbin noted:

Why is CEDAW needed? Because the human rights of women and girls are violated at an alarming rate all over the world. To take just one example, violence against women is at epidemic levels. In South Asia, countless women and girls have been burned with acid, including Afghan girls attacked by the Taliban for the simple act of attending elementary school. And literally hundreds of thousands of women have been raped in the Democratic Republic of Congo and other conflict situations. This Subcommittee explored this horrible phenomenon in a 2008 hearing on rape as a weapon of war.

CEDAW is not a cure-all for these atrocities, but it has had a real impact in improving the lives of women and girls around the world. For example:

- CEDAW has led to the passage of laws prohibiting violence against women in countries like Afghanistan, Ghana, Mexico, and Sierra Leone
- It led to women being granted the right to vote in Kuwait
- It helped give women the right to inherit property in Kenya, Kyrgyzstan, and Tajikistan.

CEDAW has been ratified by 186 of 193 countries. Sadly, the United States is one of only seven countries in the world that has failed to ratify CEDAW, along with Iran, Somalia, and Sudan. CEDAW was transmitted to the Senate 30 years ago. Twice, in 1994 and 2002, a bipartisan majority in the Senate Foreign Relations Committee reported the treaty to the Senate floor, but the Senate has never voted on CEDAW.

Under Presidents Reagan, George H.W. Bush, and Clinton, the United States ratified similar agreements on genocide, torture, and race. It is time to renew this proud bipartisan tradition and join the rest of the world in demonstrating our commitment to women's rights.

Let's be clear. The United States does not need to ratify CEDAW to protect the rights of American women and girls. Women have fought a long and difficult struggle for equal rights in the United States, with many victories along the way To name just a few:

- The 19th Amendment, giving women the right to vote, in 1920
- Title IX, prohibiting discrimination in education, in 1972
- The Pregnancy Discrimination Act, in 1978
- The Violence Against Women Act, in 1994
- The election of the first woman Speaker of the U.S. House of Representatives in 2007
- Passage of the Lilly Ledbetter Fair Pay Act just last year.

Of course, the struggle for women's rights continues. Every year, millions of American women and girls are subjected to domestic violence, rape, and human trafficking. And women who work full-time still earn only 77 cents for every dollar that a man makes. That is why it is so unfortunate that the Paycheck Fairness Act failed to pass yesterday.

However, the robust women's rights protections in U.S. law in many ways exceed the requirements of CEDAW. Even opponents of CEDAW acknowledge that ratifying CEDAW wouldn't change U.S. law in any way.

So why should the United States ratify CEDAW? Because CEDAW will enhance our ability to advocate for women and girls around the world. Throughout our history, the United States has done more to advance human rights than any other country in the world. But now some are questioning our commitment to women's rights because we have failed to ratify CEDAW.

Yesterday I received a letter from retired Justice Sandra Day O'Connor, the first woman ever to serve on the Supreme Court. Justice O'Connor supports ratifying CEDAW and here is what she says:

> The Senate's failure to ratify CEDAW gives other countries a retort when U.S. officials raise issues about the treatment of women, and thus our non-ratification may hamper the effectiveness of the United States in achieving increased protection for women worldwide.

Justice O'Connor is right. We need to ratify CEDAW so that we can more effectively lead the fight for women's rights in corners of the globe where women and girls are subjected to the most extreme forms of violence and degradation simply for exercising their fundamental human rights.

CEDAW is about giving women all over the world the chance to enjoy the same freedoms and opportunities that American women have struggled long and hard to achieve. Women have been waiting for 30 years. The United States Senate should ratify this treaty without further delay.[59]

vi. Opposition to CEDAW

CEDAW faces strong opposition from various groups. Pro-life advocates see CEDAW as encouraging a right to abortion; some religious groups fear that CEDAW undermines the traditional roles of men and women in the family. Further, some education advocates see CEDAW as interfering in educational rights. Steven Groves of the Heritage Foundation, who testified at the Subcommittee hearing, argued that it was not in the United States' interests to ratify CEDAW, and that U.S. laws currently sufficiently protect women from discrimination. Mr. Groves moreover argued that the policies of the CEDAW Committee "do not comport with existing American legal and cultural norms and has encouraged the national governments of CEDAW members to engage in social engineering on a massive scale."[60] He noted that:

> The Committee appears to be particularly contemptuous of the role of women as mothers and caregivers. For example, in 1999 it determined that "the persistence of the emphasis on the role of women as mothers and caregivers [in Ireland] tends to perpetuate sex role stereotypes and constitutes a serious impediment to the full implementation of the Convention." In its report on Georgia, the Committee expressed concern over "the stereotyped roles of women ... based on patterns of behaviour and attitudes that overemphasize the role of women as mothers." In 2000, the Committee issued its now famous concluding observation to Belarus in which it referred to Mothers' Day as a stereotypical symbol and chided Belarus for "encouraging women's traditional roles."

---

59. *See* http://judiciary.senate.gov/hearings/testimony.cfm?id=4861&wit_id=747 [last visited January 4, 2011].

60. Testimony of Steven Groves *available at* http://judiciary.senate.gov/pdf/10-11-18%20 Groves%20Testimony.pdf [last visited January 4, 2011].

The CEDAW Committee has made other policy choices that are inconsistent with U.S. societal norms. Prostitution, in particular, has been treated by the Committee not as a crime that should be discouraged, but rather as a reality that should be tolerated and regulated. Indeed, the Committee appears to have little or no regard for the moral choices made by member states concerning whether they consider prostitution to be a criminal act that should be prohibited.[61]

These claims will be addressed in later chapters which specifically deal with reproductive rights, and trafficking and prostitution. Suffice it to say at this point that the CEDAW Committee is not as anti-motherhood and pro-prostitution as may appear to be the case from the comments above. The Committee does, however, oppose stereotyped roles for men and women, and it opposes singling women out to punish them for prostitution while not prosecuting the men who patronize them. The Committee has also noted on several occasions that many women are forced into prostitution; hence it may seem unduly harsh to prosecute them for an activity that they cannot escape.

vii. CEDAW and Intersectionality

Many women face multiple forms of discrimination because they are members of both the female sex, and minority or ethnic groups that often face discrimination on that basis too. Moreover, women because of their background, class, education, and other factors, do not all experience discrimination in the same way. Experiencing multiple forms of discrimination is known as intersectionality which has been described as follows:

a. *Project on a Mechanism to Address Laws that Discriminate against Women Commissioned by the Office of the High Commissioner for Human Rights* (2008)[62]

Linked to the issue of substantive equality must be the recognition that women are not a homogenous group. Their heterogeneity requires us to take into account the fact that women do not experience discrimination in the same way. Women are separated by age, caste, class, race, religion, disability, indigeneity, minority status including sexual orientation and multiple other factors. This demands that we take a holistic look at the way societies are organized and the differential impact of discrimination on the various groups within it. This last point has been termed "intersectionality"—a process by which one recognizes that certain groups may suffer multiple forms of discrimination simultaneously.

The consequences of discrimination are different for those who suffer single issue discrimination than for those who suffer from intersectional discrimination. There has over time been greater normative recognition given to the principle of intersectional discrimination. The Race Committee has in its *General Comment 25* on gender related dimensions of racial discrimination devised a four point "intersectionality questionnaire" which is helpful in considering how people are differentially impacted by gender based discrimination. It requires one to consider:

i) The form a violation takes;

ii) The circumstances in which a violation occurs;

---

61. *Id.* at 3.

62. The full text of the report is *available at* http://www.ohchr.org/Documents/Publications/laws_that_discriminate_against_women.pdf at 14 [last visited January 11, 2011]; (internal citations omitted).

iii) The consequences of a violation;

iv) The availability and accessibility of remedies and complaint mechanisms....[63]

A major challenge that is thrown up by intersectional discrimination is the perceived tension between rights of minorities and respect for culture and other human rights principles, not least non discrimination. Minorities or indigenous people may argue that they have the right to practise and to enjoy their right to culture without external interference. While, technically all rights are subject to the filter of non discrimination, the situation is more complex for as a UN official noted "Human rights mechanisms find it difficult to interfere with non State structures."

Notwithstanding what appear to be clear normative commitments to achieving equality between the sexes, the practice of States parties, indicates that there is still a equivocation over the principle of non-discrimination based on sex. States, and some academic writers, sometimes seek to invoke national, cultural, or religious justifications for the non-implementation of equality, claiming that the local interpretation of the norm is at variance with the international. Often this starts with a challenge to the notion of "sameness." During the drafting of CEDAW for example, the Moroccan representative argued for a change in the wording of the provision "men and women have the same rights and responsibilities during and after the dissolution of marriage" because as drafted the provision: "Failed to take account a fact which was a matter of common sense, namely, that men and women, in order to be truly equal, did not need to be treated as being the same, which would be contrary to nature." Preferred in some quarters is the equivalence or complementarity model which holds that men and women are "complements" of each other. Of this "dual sex" construction of sex difference, Nzegwu notes:

> In a dual-sex context, where individuals are valued for the skills they bring to community building and the role they play in developing the culture, gender identity is differently constructed. Identity is not abstractly construed in terms of sameness, but concretely defined in terms of the worth of social duties and responsibilities. Because gender equality implies comparable worth, women and men are complements, whose duties, though different, are socially comparable.

The difficulty of course is in the different economic and social value placed on the roles that men and women play. Additionally, sometimes both sexes are denied the opportunity to take on roles including in the domestic or public spheres that do not conform to the gender roles imposed upon them reinforcing stereotyping and denying them valuable opportunities to work.

State equivocation over the principle of equality can most clearly be seen when looking at the reservations entered to human rights instruments ...

Questions for Discussion

1. *One of the guiding principles of the Commission on the Status of Women was to "raise the status of women ... to equality with men." How might that concept of equality be limiting for the recognition of rights important to women? Is that disparity greater in realizing and enforcing rights of women regarding discrimination in private, rather than political, life?*

---

63. *CERD General Comment 25* on Gender Related Dimensions of Racial Discrimination, para. 5.

2. *What rights does CEDAW give women? In what ways do you think it has advanced women's rights and/or provided for future advancement of women's rights?*

3. *Do you think that requiring party states to file reports with the CEDAW Committee is an effective enforcement tool? Why or why not?*

4. *Which of the letters to the sub Committee (one in favor of signing CEDAW, and one opposed) sounded more persuasive to you? Why?*

5. *Does the United States lack moral authority to criticize other states regarding their treatment of women because it has not signed CEDAW?*

Chapter 3

Reservations, Understandings, and Declarations (RUDs)— Problems with Enforcement, and Post CEDAW Developments

Chapter Problem

Assume that the Subcommittee on Human Rights and the Law has read your memorandum on the United Nations' treaty system, and the various treaty reporting and enforcement mechanisms, with great interest. The Subcommittee has a mandate to consider whether to refer CEDAW to the full Senate for ratification. The Subcommittee recalls that in 1980, when then President Jimmy Carter signed CEDAW, the United States was considering entering several reservations to the treaty. In 2002, the U.S. Senate Committee on Foreign Relations, which was then reviewing CEDAW, attached some reservations, understandings and declarations (RUDs) to the treaty, and a majority of members voted to send the treaty to the Senate for a vote on ratification. The treaty was ultimately never sent to the Senate floor, but it appears that entering RUDs may help alleviate some of the concerns that some of the Committee's members have with regard to some of the provisions in CEDAW. Now the Subcommittee wants you to research the kinds of RUDs that have been entered with respect to CEDAW by other state parties. In particular, it seeks your guidance on the legal status of these RUDs, and how these RUDs impact CEDAW's applicability and enforceability. The Subcommittee also wishes to know if it should file the same RUDs that its predecessor Committee contemplated filing in 2002, or if there are other RUDs that it should enter. The Subcommittee also would like to you research how other states who are parties to CEDAW would respond to those RUDs, based on how they have responded to the RUDs filed by other signatories to CEDAW. The Subcommittee would also like you to research enforcement mechanisms under CEDAW.

I. CEDAW and Reservations

This chapter will explore the limitations of CEDAW by discussing the large number of reservations that have been filed to the Convention. We will also canvass the problem of enforceability that was created both by the large number of reservations, and also by the fact that, prior to the Optional Protocol, there was no forum before which complaints could be filed, nor any other meaningful enforcement mechanism.

A. Reservations, Understandings, and Declarations

When signing onto treaties, parties often file reservations, understandings, or declarations, along with their signatures. These documents, often referred to by the acronym RUDs, have murky legal status. As we will see below, reservations and declarations are permitted under international law. "Understandings" purport to be statements by the acceding state (the state becoming a party to the treaty) as to how it understands or interprets its obligations under the treaty or Convention.

The Vienna Convention on the Law of Treaties (1969)[1] permits states to file reservations and declarations to treaties. A reservation is defined by Article 2(d) as a:

> unilateral statement, however phrased or named, made by a State, when signing, ratifying, accepting, approving or acceding to a treaty, whereby it purports to exclude or to modify the legal effect of certain provisions of the treaty in their application to that State.

International Conventions and treaties themselves may regulate when and how a reservation may be filed. CEDAW contains express provisions with regard to the filing of reservations. These provisions are essentially the same as those contained in the Vienna Convention of the Law on Treaties and provide:

Article 28

1. The Secretary-General of the United Nations shall receive and circulate to all States the text of reservations made by States at the time of ratification or accession.

2. A reservation incompatible with the object and purpose of the present Convention shall not be permitted.

3. Reservations may be withdrawn at any time by notification to this effect addressed to the Secretary-General of the United Nations, who shall then inform all States thereof. Such notification shall take effect on the date on which it is received.

However, as Jennifer Riddle has noted,[2] the Convention "allows reservations that do not conflict with the 'object and purpose' of the treaty, but it contains no objective criteria to determine if this requirement has been met, nor does the Convention establish an independent committee to deal specifically with reservations. Because no independent body evaluates reservations, objections tend to be haphazard and subjective."

In addition to reservations, a common practice has developed whereby states would file Declarations of Interpretation or Understanding alongside their reservations. For example, Chile filed the following declaration on signing CEDAW:

---

1. *Available at* http://untreaty.un.org/ilc/texts/instruments/english/conventions/1_1_1969.pdf [last visited July 1, 2011].

2. Jennifer Riddle, *Making CEDAW Universal: A Critique of CEDAW's Reservation Regime under Article 28 and the Effectiveness of the Reporting Process*, 34 Geo. Wash. Int'l L. Rev. 605, 614 (2002).

The Government of Chile has signed this Convention on the Elimination of All Forms of Discrimination Against Women, mindful of the important step which this document represents, not only in terms of the elimination of all forms of discrimination against women, but also in terms of their full and permanent integration into society in conditions of equality.

The Government is obliged to state, however, that some of the provisions of the Convention are not entirely compatible with current Chilean legislation.

At the same time, it reports the establishment of a Commission for the Study and Reform of the Civil Code, which now has before it various proposals to amend, *inter alia*, those provisions which are not fully consistent with the terms of the Convention.

The legal impact of such declarations is not entirely clear. Presumably this declaration means that Chile is attempting to bring its national legislation in line with the provisions of CEDAW, but the filing of such statements makes the implementation and enforcement of CEDAW rather difficult. The International Law Commission (ILC) appointed a Special Rapporteur in 1994 to look at the issue of reservations to treaties, and whether declarations of understanding or interpretation should be treated as reservations. Certainly the declaration filed by Morocco reads like a reservation:

1. Declarations of Morocco

1. With regard to article 2:

The Government of the Kingdom of Morocco express its readiness to apply the provisions of this article provided that:

They are without prejudice to the constitutional requirement that regulate the rules of succession to the throne of the Kingdom of Morocco;

They do not conflict with the provisions of the Islamic *Shariah*. It should be noted that certain of the provisions contained in the Moroccan Code of Personal Status according women rights that differ from the rights conferred on men may not be infringed upon or abrogated because they derive primarily from the Islamic *Shariah*, which strives, among its other objectives, to strike a balance between the spouses in order to preserve the coherence of family life.

Yet, Morocco also filed a specific reservation in respect of Article 9(2)'s nationality provisions, and termed that a reservation, not a declaration or understanding.

The Rapporteur also examined whether the various Vienna Conventions[3] were sufficiently clear and specific on this issue. The International Law Commission (ILC) has issued several reports on the topic,[4] based on the recommendations of the Special Rapporteur. The ILC noted that it is still problematic that states may file reservations to a treaty, which other state parties find unacceptable. Since treaties are generally documents based on consensus, there are no clear guidelines on what the objecting state should do if it finds

---

3. The Vienna Conventions include the 1969 Vienna Convention on the Law of Treaties, the 1978 Vienna Convention on the Succession of States with Respect to Treaties, and the 1986 Vienna Convention on the Law of Treaties between States and International Organizations or between International Organizations.

4. *See* INTERNATIONAL LAW COMMISSION ANALYTICAL GUIDE: RESERVATIONS TO TREATIES, *available at* http://untreaty.un.org/ilc/guide/1_8.htm [last visited May 6, 2010].

a reservation inadmissible. Many of the objections filed to CEDAW relate to potential conflicts between the rights articulated in CEDAW and the *Shari'a* (Islamic law). These conflicts will be explored in a later chapter.

Disturbingly, many countries who have signed onto CEDAW have filed reservations to Article 2, the general equality provision of CEDAW, which, along with Article 16, is considered a core provision. Core provisions are supposed to be non derogable. Article 2 calls on states to condemn and eliminate discrimination against women. This means that no reservation to those Articles may be entered because such a reservation would be impermissible under Article 28 of CEDAW which prohibits reservations incompatible with the "object and purpose of the Convention."[5]

Most treaties specifically articulate their object and purpose by means of a preamble or in some other declaratory form. In attempting to interpret a treaty or ascertain its purpose, one may look to the *travaux preparatoires,* the preparatory documents that are similar to legislative history in domestic legislation.

2. Reservation Filed by the Bahamas

An example of a reservation to a core provision is the reservation filed by the Bahamas, which noted reservations, to not one but two core provisions as follows:

Reservations:

The Government of the Commonwealth of the Bahamas does not consider itself bound by the provisions of article 2(a), ... article 9, paragraph 2, ... article 16(h), ... [and] article 29, paragraph 1, of the Convention.[6]

Whether one may file a reservation to Article 2, and still not be said to be frustrating the object of CEDAW seems inconsistent with the Vienna Convention, but has not been definitively resolved. As discussed below, the Committee has been working to encourage states to withdraw such reservations, and other states parties have in fact objected to the filing of these kinds of reservations. However, CEDAW has the unfortunate distinction of being known as the treaty to which the most reservations and declarations have been filed. Most of the reservations filed by states at the time that they became a party to the treaty, remain in effect and have not been withdrawn despite some objections from other member states.

3. Reservations, Understandings, and Declarations to CEDAW Proposed by the United States in 2002

Private Conduct

The Constitution and laws of the United States establish extensive protections against discrimination reaching all forms of governmental activity as well as significant areas of non-governmental activity. However individual privacy and freedom from governmental interference in private conduct are also recognized as among the fundamental values of our free and democratic society.

The United States understands that by its terms the Convention requires broad regulation of private conduct, in particular under Articles 2, 3, and 5. The United

---

5. As will be discussed, many states have nevertheless entered reservations to Article 2.

6. *Available at* http://www.un.org/womenwatch/daw/cedaw/reservations-country.htm [last visited May 5, 2010].

States does not accept any obligation under the Convention to enact legislation or to take any other action with respect to private conduct except as mandated by the Constitution of and law of the United States.

Combat Assignments

Under current U.S. law and practice women are permitted to volunteer for military service without restriction and women in fact serve in all U.S. armed services, including in combat positions. However the United States does not accept an obligation under the Convention to assign women to all military units and positions which may require engagement in direct combat.

Comparable Worth

U.S. law provides strong protections against gender discrimination in the area of remuneration, including the right to equal pay for equal work in jobs that are substantially similar. However, the United States does not accept any obligation under this Convention to enact legislation establishing the doctrine of comparable worth as that term is understood in U.S. practice.

Paid Maternity Leave

Current U.S. law contains substantial provisions for maternity leave in many employment situations but does not require paid maternity leave. Therefore the United States does not accept an obligation under Article 11(2)(b) to introduce maternity leave with pay or with comparable social benefits without loss of former employment, seniority, or social allowances.

2. Understandings

Federal State Implementations

The United States understands that this Convention shall be implemented by the Federal Government to the extent that it exercises jurisdiction over the matters covered therein and otherwise by the state and local governments. To the extent that state and local governments exercise jurisdiction over such matters, the Federal Government shall as necessary take appropriate measures to ensure the fulfillment of this Convention.

Freedom of Speech, Expression and Association

"The Constitution and laws of the United States contain extensive protections of individual freedom of speech, expression and association, Accordingly the United States does not accept any obligation under this Convention, in particular under Articles 5, 7, 8 and 13, to restrict those rights, through the adoption of legislation or any other measures, to the extent that they are protected by the Constitution and laws of the United States.

Free Health Care Services

The United States understands that Article 12 permits States Parties to determine which health care services are appropriate in connection with family planning, pregnancy, confinement and the post-natal period, as well as when the provision of free services is necessary and does not mandate the provision of particular services on a cost-free basis.

3. Declarations

Non Self Executing

The United States declares that, for purposes of its domestic law, the provisions of the Convention are non self executing.

Dispute Settlement

With reference to Article 29(2), the United States declares that it does not consider itself bound by the provisions of Article 29(1). The specific consent of the United States to the jurisdiction of the International Court of Justice concerning disputes over the interpretation or application of this Convention is required on a case-by-case basis.

B. *The International Court of Justice Advisory Opinion on the Convention on the Prevention and Punishment of the Crime of Genocide*

This advisory opinion[7] is often looked to as authority for when reservations may validly be entered. In answering three questions referred to the Court by the UN General Assembly, the Court held as follows:

On Question I:

A State which has made and maintained a reservation which has been objected to by one or more of the parties to the Convention but not by others, can be regarded as being a party to the Convention if the reservation is compatible with the object and purpose of the Convention; otherwise, that State cannot be regarded as being a party to the Convention.

On Question II:

(a) if a party to the Convention objects to a reservation which it considers to be incompatible with the object and purpose of the Convention, it can in fact consider that the reserving State is not a party to the Convention;

(b) if, on the other hand, a party accept the reservation as being compatible with the object and purpose of the Convention, it can in fact consider that the reserving State is a party to the Convention;

On Question III:

(a) an objection to a reservation made by a signatory State which has not yet ratified the Convention can have the legal effect indicated in the reply to Question I only upon ratification. Until that moment it merely serves as a notice to the other State of the eventual attitude of the signatory State;

(b) an objection to a reservation made by a State which is entitled to sign or accede but which has not yet done so is without legal effect.

Questions for Discussion

1. *Given the high number of reservations that have been filed with respect to CEDAW, what does this tell us about the willingness of countries to enforce women's rights?*

---

7. Opinion handed down May 1951. *Available at* http://www.icj-cij.org/docket/index.php?sum=276&code=ppcg&p1=3&p2=4&case=12&k=90&p3=5 [last visited January 11, 2011].

2. *How should the Secretary General of the UN handle reservations that seem to subvert the purpose of CEDAW?*

3. *How should other countries respond when a new country signs onto CEDAW, but enters a reservation that seems incompatible with the purpose of CEDAW?*

4. *Is it worth having a country sign onto the treaty to bring them into the fold, even if that country does not have a good record on women's rights?*

C. The Response of States Parties to Reservations Filed by Other States Parties

At the time that state party accedes to a treaty, other states parties may file Objections to the reservations filed by the newly acceding state party. These objections do not necessarily have any legal impact, nor do they prevent the newly acceding state party from becoming a party to the treaty. Below you will find an example of these kinds of Objections, filed by Austria when first Maldives, then Pakistan became parties to CEDAW.

1. Austria

26 October 1994

With regard to the reservations made by Maldives upon accession:

The reservation made by the Maldives is incompatible with the object and purpose of the Convention and is therefore inadmissible under article 19 (c) of the Vienna Convention on the Law of Treaties and shall not be permitted, in accordance with article 28 (2) of the Convention on the Elimination of All Forms of Discrimination Against Women. Austria therefore states that this reservation cannot alter or modify in any respect the obligations arising from the Convention for any State Party thereto.

5 June 1997

With regard to the declaration made by Pakistan upon accession:

Austria is of the view that a reservation by which a State limits its responsibilities under the Convention in a general and unspecified manner by invoking internal law creates doubts as to the commitment of the Islamic Republic of Pakistan with its obligations under the Convention, essential for the fulfillment of its object and purpose.

It is in the common interests of States that treaties to which they have chosen to become Parties are respected, as to their object and purpose, by all Parties and that States are prepared to undertake any legislative changes necessary to comply with their obligations under the treaties.

Austria is further of the view that a general reservation of the kind made by the Government of the Islamic Republic of Pakistan, which does not clearly specify the provisions of the Convention to which it applies and the extent of the derogation therefrom, contributes to undermining the basis of international treaty law.

Given the general character of this reservation a final assessment as to its admissibility under international law cannot be made without further clarification.

According to international law a reservation is inadmissible to the extent as its application negatively affects the compliance by a State with its obligations under the Convention essential for the fulfillment of its object and purpose.

Therefore, Austria cannot consider the reservation made by the Government of the Islamic Republic of Pakistan as admissible unless the Government of the Islamic Republic of Pakistan, by providing additional information or through subsequent practice, ensures that the reservation is compatible with the provisions essential for the implementation of the object and purpose of the Convention.

D. The CEDAW Committee and Reservations

As described in Chapter 2, the CEDAW Committee was established by Article 17. In response to the number of reservations filed and the objections to those reservations, the Committee has noted that:

Some States parties that enter reservations to the Convention do not enter reservations to analogous provisions in other human rights treaties. A number of States enter reservations to particular articles on the ground that national law, tradition, religion or culture are not congruent with Convention principles, and purport to justify the reservation on that basis. Some States enter a reservation to article 2, although their national constitutions or laws prohibit discrimination. There is therefore an inherent conflict between the provisions of the State's constitution and its reservation to the Convention. Some reservations are drawn so widely that their effect cannot be limited to specific provisions in the Convention.

Although the Convention does not prohibit the entering of reservations, those which challenge the central principles of the Convention are contrary to the provisions of the Convention and to general international law. As such they may be challenged by other States parties.

Articles 2 and 16 are considered by the Committee to be core provisions of the Convention. Although some States parties have withdrawn reservations to those articles, the Committee is particularly concerned at the number and extent of reservations entered to those articles.

The Committee holds the view that article 2 is central to the objects and purpose of the Convention. States parties which ratify the Convention do so because they agree that discrimination against women in all its forms should be condemned and that the strategies set out in article 2, subparagraphs (a) to (g), should be implemented by States parties to eliminate it.

Neither traditional, religious or cultural practice nor incompatible domestic laws and policies can justify violations of the Convention. The Committee also remains convinced that reservations to article 16, whether lodged for national, traditional, religious or cultural reasons, are incompatible with the Convention and therefore impermissible and should be reviewed and modified or withdrawn.

Removing reservations

The Committee considers that those States parties which have entered reservations to the Convention have certain options open to them. According to the Special Rapporteur appointed by the International Law Commission to report on the law and practice relating to reservations to treaties a State party may:

(a) After having examined the finding in good faith, maintain its reservation;

(b) Withdraw its reservation;

(c) "Regularize" its situation by replacing its impermissible reservation with a permissible reservation;

(d) Renounce being a party to the Treaty.

To date, few reservations to article 2 have been withdrawn or modified by any State party and that reservations to article 16 are rarely withdrawn.

The role of the Committee

The Committee has certain responsibilities as the body of experts charged with the consideration of periodic reports submitted to it. The Committee, in its examination of States' reports, enters into constructive dialogue with the State party and makes concluding comments routinely expressing concern at the entry of reservations, in particular to articles 2 and 16, or the failure of States parties to withdraw or modify them.

The Special Rapporteur considers that control of the permissibility of reservations is the primary responsibility of the States parties. However, the Committee again wishes to draw to the attention of States parties its grave concern at the number and extent of impermissible reservations. It also expresses concern that, even when States object to such reservations there appears to be a reluctance on the part of the States concerned to remove and modify them and thereby comply with general principles of international law....

Several States parties have entered interpretative declarations to the Convention on ratification or accession. While it is not always easy to distinguish a declaration from a reservation, any statement, irrespective of its title, which seeks to modify the legal effect of the Convention in respect of a State party, will be considered by the Committee to be a reservation. The Committee has noted, in this regard, that a number of States parties have entered general declarations which constitute, in fact, general reservations.[8]

II. After CEDAW — Moving Forward

A. *The Nairobi Forward Looking Strategy*

The large number of reservations filed to CEDAW gave rise to some dissent about how best to move forward in advancing women's rights. The United Nations designated

---

8. *Available at* http://www.un.org/womenwatch/daw/cedaw/reports/18report.pdf [last visited January 4, 2011]. UN A/53/38/Rev.1.

1990–2000 the "Decade of Women," and a conference was planned for Beijing in 1995. In 1985, representatives of member states and from a number of NGOs, and women's rights organizations, met in Nairobi, Kenya to share their various concerns and strategize about how best to advance women's rights. They drafted the *Nairobi Forward Looking Strategy* which pinpointed three areas of focus: equality, development, and peace. The representatives set a goal of coming up with strategies to advance equality, development and peace for women at a regional, national and international level.

Given the large number of reservations that had been filed with regard to Article 2 (the equality article) of CEDAW, the *Nairobi Forward Looking Strategy* attempted to provide some clarification about what was meant by "equality." The clarification provided:

> Equality is both a goal and a means whereby individuals are accorded equal treatment under the law and equal opportunities to enjoy their rights and to develop their potential talents and skills so that they can participate in national political, economic, social and cultural development and can benefit from its results. For women in particular, equality means the realization of rights that have been denied as a result of cultural, institutional, behavioral and attitudinal discrimination.

This equality definition further clarified that signatories to CEDAW should focus on obtaining equality for women rather than equity, and that culture would no longer be regarded as a justification for denying women equal rights.

The *Forward Looking Strategy* also focused on development and economic issues. Stagnating or under-developed economies, failure to eradicate diseases like malaria, and the oil crisis of the 1970s and 1980s, had detrimentally impacted the ability of many poorer nations in the developing world to pay back the debt owed to wealthy countries and institutions like the World Bank and International Monetary Fund (IMF). The 1980s also marked the beginning of the AIDS epidemic, and the devastating impact that it had on peoples' health and lives. Moreover, the detrimental impact of environmental degradation, was beginning to be felt by women in particular, as women often work in the fields growing food for their families. The participants at the Nairobi Conference all realized that impeded development had a direct effect on women. With debt servicing and interest payments amounting to around 40% of the GDP of many highly indebted countries, the governments of those countries had little to spend on education, health, maternal mortality prevention, child mortality rates and other areas that directly impacted women's lives. Poor agricultural practices and drought also disproportionately affected women and children. In 1984–8 approximately one million people died in Ethiopia as a result of the famine that followed a prolonged drought. The organizers of the Nairobi Conference, recognizing the interrelationship of development and equality, issued the following statement on development:

> The role of women in development is directly related to the goal of comprehensive social and economic development and is fundamental to the development of all societies. Development means total development, including development in the political, economic, social, cultural and other dimensions of human life, as well as the development of the economic and other material resources and the physical, moral, intellectual and cultural growth of human beings. It should be conducive to providing women, particularly those who are poor or destitute, with the necessary means for increasingly claiming, achieving, enjoying and utilizing equality of opportunity. More directly, the increasingly successful participation of each woman in societal activities as a legally independent agent will contribute to further recognition in practice of her right to equality.

Despite the fact that thirty years have elapsed since the recognition of the impact that development has on the lives of women, debt relief and cancellation remains an ongoing issue. In 2000 (the so-called Jubilee year), many organizations called on developed countries to cancel the debts owed by highly impoverished poor countries—HIPCs. Development issues are also being addressed through the *Millennium Development Goals* which will be discussed in a later chapter.

With respect to peace, the *Nairobi Forward Looking Strategy* reminded member states that:

> Peace includes not only the absence of war, violence and hostilities at the national and international levels but also the enjoyment of economic and social justice, equality and the entire range of human rights and fundamental freedoms within society. It depends upon respect for ... international covenants and ... upon mutual co-operation and understanding among all States irrespective of their social political and economic systems and upon the effective implementation by States of the fundamental human rights standards to which their citizens are entitled.

> Peace is promoted by equality of the sexes, economic equality and the universal enjoyment of basic human rights and fundamental freedoms. Its enjoyment by all requires that women be enabled to exercise their right to participate on an equal footing with men in all spheres of the political, economic and social life of their respective countries ...

The *Forward Looking Strategies* also focused on inequality in access to education, inequality in health services, violence against women, power and decision making at all levels and managing natural resources. This book will canvass these themes in later chapters.

B. The Beijing Conference—The Fourth World Conference on Women (1995)

The Beijing Conference reemphasized the themes of advancing equality, development and peace, and reiterated the commitment of the international community and NGOs to human rights documents, such as CEDAW, the UN Charter, and the Universal Declaration of Human Rights.

Attendees at the Conference drafted a *Declaration* and *Platform for Action* which was adopted by the United Nations General Assembly.

1. The *Beijing Declaration*

The *Beijing Declaration* reaffirmed the commitment of the delegates to:

> 8. The equal rights and inherent human dignity of women and men and other purposes and principles enshrined in the Charter of the United Nations, to the Universal Declaration of Human Rights and other international human rights instruments, in particular the Convention on the Elimination of All Forms of Discrimination against Women and the Convention on the Rights of the Child, as well as the Declaration on the Elimination of Violence against Women and the Declaration on the Right to Development;

9. Ensure the full implementation of the human rights of women and of the girl child as an inalienable, integral and indivisible part of all human rights and fundamental freedoms;...

The delegates also adopted a *Platform for Action* designed to "ensur[e] that a gender perspective is reflected in all our policies and programmes."

2. The *Beijing Platform for Action*[9]

The *Beijing Platform for Action* identified various critical areas of concern, namely: women and poverty; education; health; violence; armed conflict; the economy; women in power and decision-making; institutional mechanisms for the advancement of women; human rights; the media; the environment; and the girl child. The *Platform for Action* noted that:

> Women's empowerment and their full participation on the basis of equality in all spheres of society, including participation in the decision-making process and access to power, are fundamental for the achievement of equality, development and peace;

> Women's rights are human rights;

> Equal rights, opportunities and access to resources, equal sharing of responsibilities for the family by men and women, and a harmonious partnership between them are critical to their well-being and that of their families as well as to the consolidation of democracy.

One of the most contentious issues arising out of the *Beijing Platform for Action* was the issue of reproductive rights. Article 17 of the *Beijing Platform for Action* noted that "[t]he explicit recognition and reaffirmation of the right of all women to control all aspects of their health, in particular their own fertility, is basic to their empowerment." This explicit recognition did not sit well with all delegates to the Conference, particularly those from African countries. Reproductive rights will be discussed in more detail in a later chapter.

The *Platform for Action* also noted delegates' "determination to ensure women's equal access to economic resources, including land, credit, science and technology ..."[10] and reaffirmed their commitment to "enhance [women's] role in the development process."[11] Since Beijing, women's access to economic resources and their participation in the development process has increased, in part due to the *Millennium Development Goals* which are described in more detail in the final chapter. However progress towards attaining these goals has been uneven, as will be discussed in Chapter 20.

C. *The Beijing +5 Reviews*

Five years after the Beijing Conference, the United Nations General Assembly held a special session on *Beijing +5 Reviews*. The session was called *Women 2000: Gender Equality, Development and Peace for the Twenty-First Century.* Countries which had participated in the Beijing Conference were invited to share reports on actions and initiatives taken to

---

9. *Available at* http://www.un.org/womenwatch/daw/beijing/pdf/BDPfA%20E.pdf [last visited July 1, 2011].

10. Art. 35.

11. Art. 34.

implement the *Beijing Platform for Action*. At the session the General Assembly adopted a *Political Declaration* and outcome document entitled *Further Actions and Initiatives to Implement the Beijing Declaration and Platform for Action*. Among other issues it was noted:

> Despite much progress, responses from Member States indicate that much more work needs to be done with regard to implementation of the Platform for Action. Two major areas—violence and poverty—continue to be major obstacles to gender equality worldwide. Globalization has added new dimensions to both areas, creating new challenges for the implementation of the Platform, such as trafficking in women and girls, changing nature of armed conflict, growing gap between nations and genders, the detachment of macroeconomic policy from social protection concerns.

> Overall, the analysis of the national reports on the implementation of the *Platform for Action* revealed that there had been no major breakthrough with regard to equal sharing of decision making in political structures at national and international levels. In most countries of the world, representation of women remains low. Even in countries where a "critical mass" in decision-making positions within the public sector has been achieved, there are few women on boards of directors of major business corporations. There is need for more careful monitoring of progress in ensuring women's equal participation in these positions of economic power.

In his comments, the Secretary General noted:

> much still remained to be done, including addressing new challenges such as HIV/AIDS and increased armed conflict. While women entered the labour market in unprecedented numbers, the gender divide still persisted, women earned less, and were involved in informal and unpaid work. There has been no breakthrough in women's participation in decision making processes and little progress in the legislation in favour of women's rights to own land and other property. In his statement, the Secretary-General focused on the importance of education, stressing that it was both the entry point into the global economy and the best defense against its pitfalls. Once they were educated and integrated into the workforce, women would have more choices and be able to provide better nutrition, health care and education for their children.

Each five year period the General Assembly and the UN Commission on the status of women undertake a review of the progress made towards attaining and implementing the *Beijing Platform for Action*. They may focus on specific areas of concern, such as the plight of women in Palestine and Afghanistan, or more general matters affecting women. These special sessions are known as *Beijing +5*, *Beijing +10*, and *Beijing +15*. In the most recent session (*Beijing +15*) which took place in March 2010, emphasis was placed on the sharing of experiences and good practices to overcome obstacles faced by women. Much attention was also placed on the implementation of the *Millennium Development Goals* which will be discussed in a later chapter. Details of the *Beijing+15* session are available at: http://www.un.org/womenwatch/daw/beijing15/index.html.

D. CEDAW and Enforceability Issues

The record number of reservations to CEDAW, and the late filing, failure to file, and significant omissions in country reports, all contributed to CEDAW being widely viewed as an aspirational document rather than an enforceable treaty. Moreover, if a member state was not complying with some core aspect of CEDAW, but failed to address this issue in its report, no consequences attached to the state's failure or omission. NGOs therefore developed the practice of filing "shadow reports" because of the member states' failures to point out and address their own failures to promote equality and non-discrimination. Despite these shadow reports, enforcement of women's rights was, and is still is, a problem. For example, under article 29 of CEDAW, two or more State parties can refer disputes about the interpretation and implementation of CEDAW to arbitration, and if the dispute is not settled, it can be referred to the International Court of Justice. This procedure is subject to a large number of reservations and has never been used. It was realized very early on that CEDAW needed more stringent enforcement procedures in addition to the reporting procedures.

In creating a communications procedure, activists looked to the other human rights treaties as a model. The First Optional Protocol to the ICCPR permits individuals whose rights have been violated to file a communication with the UN Human Rights Committee, if they have exhausted domestic remedies. CERD, and the Convention against Torture also offer complaint or communication procedures. These procedures offered a blueprint whereby CEDAW could have more teeth, and individuals could bring their specific grievances before the CEDAW Committee. In October, 1999 the UN adopted the Optional Protocol to CEDAW, and it entered into force on December 22, 2000.

E. The Optional Protocol to CEDAW[12]

The Optional Protocol provides a complaint procedure whereby "communications" or complaints may be filed by individuals or NGOs, or other organizations, with the CEDAW Committee. The Committee may reach a finding on the merits of a communication and transmit this to the State party concerned. The Optional Protocol also creates a procedure under Article 8 whereby the Committee may launch an "inquiry" into "grave and systematic violations" of the Protocol. Importantly, the Protocol is only binding on those states which sign and ratify it.

The States Parties to the present Protocol,

Noting that the Charter of the United Nations reaffirms faith in fundamental human rights, in the dignity and worth of the human person and in the equal rights of men and women,

Also noting that the Universal Declaration of Human Rights proclaims that all human beings are born free and equal in dignity and rights and that everyone is entitled to all the rights and freedoms set forth therein, without distinction of any kind, including distinction based on sex,

Recalling that the International Covenants on Human Rights and other international human rights instruments prohibit discrimination on the basis of sex,

Also recalling the Convention on the Elimination of All Forms of Discrimination against Women ("the Convention"), in which the States Parties thereto condemn discrimination against women in all its forms and agree to pursue by all appropriate means and without delay a policy of eliminating discrimination against women.

---

12. UN Doc. A/RES/54/4 (1999).

Reaffirming their determination to ensure the full and equal enjoyment by women of all human rights and fundamental freedoms and to take effective action to prevent violations of these rights and freedoms, *Have agreed as follows:*

Article 1

A State Party to the present Protocol ("State Party") recognizes the competence of the Committee on the Elimination of Discrimination against Women ("the Committee") to receive and consider communications submitted in accordance with article 2.

Article 2

Communications may be submitted by or on behalf of individuals or groups of individuals, under the jurisdiction of a State Party, claiming to be victims of a violation of any of the rights set forth in the Convention by that State Party. Where a communication is submitted on behalf of individuals or groups of individuals, this shall be with their consent unless the author can justify acting on their behalf without such consent.

Article 3

Communications shall be in writing and shall not be anonymous. No communication shall be received by the Committee if it concerns a State Party to the Convention that is not a party to the present Protocol.

Article 4

1. The Committee shall not consider a communication unless it has ascertained that all available domestic remedies have been exhausted unless the application of such remedies is unreasonably prolonged or unlikely to bring effective relief.

2. The Committee shall declare a communication inadmissible where:

(*a*) The same matter has already been examined by the Committee or has been or is being examined under another procedure of international investigation or settlement;

(*b*) It is incompatible with the provisions of the Convention;

(*c*) It is manifestly ill-founded or not sufficiently substantiated;

(*d*) It is an abuse of the right to submit a communication;

(*e*) The facts that are the subject of the communication occurred prior to the entry into force of the present Protocol for the State Party concerned unless those facts continued after that date.

Article 5

1. At any time after the receipt of a communication and before a determination on the merits has been reached, the Committee may transmit to the State Party concerned for its urgent consideration a request that the State Party take such interim measures as may be necessary to avoid possible irreparable damage to the victim or victims of the alleged violation.

2. Where the Committee exercises its discretion under paragraph 1 of the present article, this does not imply a determination on admissibility or on the merits of the communication.

Article 6

1. Unless the Committee considers a communication inadmissible without reference to the State Party concerned, and provided that the individual or

individuals consent to the disclosure of their identity to that State Party, the Committee shall bring any communication submitted to it under the present Protocol confidentially to the attention of the State Party concerned.

2. Within six months, the receiving State Party shall submit to the Committee written explanations or statements clarifying the matter and the remedy, if any, that may have been provided by that State Party.

Article 7

1. The Committee shall consider communications received under the present Protocol in the light of all information made available to it by or on behalf of individuals or groups of individuals and by the State Party concerned, provided that this information is transmitted to the parties concerned.

2. The Committee shall hold closed meetings when examining communications under the present Protocol.

3. After examining a communication, the Committee shall transmit its views on the communication, together with its recommendations, if any, to the parties concerned.

4. The State Party shall give due consideration to the views of the Committee, together with its recommendations, if any, and shall submit to the Committee, within six months, a written response, including information on any action taken in the light of the views and recommendations of the Committee.

5. The Committee may invite the State Party to submit further information about any measures the State Party has taken in response to its views or recommendations, if any, including as deemed appropriate by the Committee, in the State Party's subsequent reports under article 18 of the Convention.

Article 8

1. If the Committee receives reliable information indicating grave or systematic violations by a State Party of rights set forth in the Convention, the Committee shall invite that State Party to cooperate in the examination of the information and to this end to submit observations with regard to the information concerned.

2. Taking into account any observations that may have been submitted by the State Party concerned as well as any other reliable information available to it, the Committee may designate one or more of its members to conduct an inquiry and to report urgently to the Committee. Where warranted and with the consent of the State Party, the inquiry may include a visit to its territory.

3. After examining the findings of such an inquiry, the Committee shall transmit these findings to the State Party concerned together with any comments and recommendations.

4. The State Party concerned shall, within six months of receiving the findings, comments and recommendations transmitted by the Committee, submit its observations to the Committee.

5. Such an inquiry shall be conducted confidentially and the cooperation of the State Party shall be sought at all stages of the proceedings.

Article 9

1. The Committee may invite the State Party concerned to include in its report under article 18 of the Convention details of any measures taken in response to an inquiry conducted under article 8 of the present Protocol.

2. The Committee may, if necessary, after the end of the period of six months referred to in article 8.4, invite the State Party concerned to inform it of the measures taken in response to such an inquiry.

Article 10

1. Each State Party may, at the time of signature or ratification of the present Protocol or accession thereto, declare that it does not recognize the competence of the Committee provided for in articles 8 and 9.

2. Any State Party having made a declaration in accordance with paragraph 1 of the present article may, at any time, withdraw this declaration by notification to the Secretary-General.

Article 11

A State Party shall take all appropriate steps to ensure that individuals under its jurisdiction are not subjected to ill treatment or intimidation as a consequence of communicating with the Committee pursuant to the present Protocol.

Article 12

The Committee shall include in its annual report under article 21 of the Convention a summary of its activities under the present Protocol.

Article 13

Each State Party undertakes to make widely known and to give publicity to the Convention and the present Protocol and to facilitate access to information about the views and recommendations of the Committee, in particular, on matters involving that State Party.

Article 14

The Committee shall develop its own rules of procedure to be followed when exercising the functions conferred on it by the present Protocol.

Article 15

1. The present Protocol shall be open for signature by any State that has signed, ratified or acceded to the Convention.

2. The present Protocol shall be subject to ratification by any State that has ratified or acceded to the Convention. Instruments of ratification shall be deposited with the Secretary-General of the United Nations.

3. The present Protocol shall be open to accession by any State that has ratified or acceded to the Convention.

4. Accession shall be effected by the deposit of an instrument of accession with the Secretary-General of the United Nations.

Article 16

1. The present Protocol shall enter into force three months after the date of the deposit with the Secretary-General of the United Nations of the tenth instrument of ratification or accession.

2. For each State ratifying the present Protocol or acceding to it after its entry into force, the present Protocol shall enter into force three months after the date of the deposit of its own instrument of ratification or accession.

Article 17

No reservations to the present Protocol shall be permitted.

Article 18

1. Any State Party may propose an amendment to the present Protocol and file it with the Secretary-General of the United Nations. The Secretary-General shall thereupon communicate any proposed amendments to the States Parties with a request that they notify her or him whether they favour a conference of States Parties for the purpose of considering and voting on the proposal. In the event that at least one third of the States Parties favour such a conference, the Secretary-General shall convene the conference under the auspices of the United Nations. Any amendment adopted by a majority of the States Parties present and voting at the conference shall be submitted to the General Assembly of the United Nations for approval.

2. Amendments shall come into force when they have been approved by the General Assembly of the United Nations and accepted by a two-thirds majority of the States Parties to the present Protocol in accordance with their respective constitutional processes.

3. When amendments come into force, they shall be binding on those States Parties that have accepted them, other States Parties still being bound by the provisions of the present Protocol and any earlier amendments that they have accepted.

Article 19

1. Any State Party may denounce the present Protocol at any time by written notification addressed to the Secretary-General of the United Nations. Denunciation shall take effect six months after the date of receipt of the notification by the Secretary-General.

2. Denunciation shall be without prejudice to the continued application of the provisions of the present Protocol to any communication submitted under article 2 or any inquiry initiated under article 8 before the effective date of denunciation.

Article 20

The Secretary-General of the United Nations shall inform all States of:

(*a*) Signatures, ratifications and accessions under the present Protocol;

(*b*) The date of entry into force of the present Protocol and of any amendment under article 18;

(*c*) Any denunciation under article 19.

Article 21

1. The present Protocol, of which the Arabic, Chinese, English, French, Russian and Spanish texts are equally authentic, shall be deposited in the archives of the United Nations.

2. The Secretary-General of the United Nations shall transmit certified copies of the present Protocol to all States referred to in article 25 of the Convention.

The Optional Protocol is an extremely important document because it finally provided the opportunity for redress that had been lacking in CEDAW. Complaints, or communications, as they are known, may be filed either by the party herself, or by representatives on her behalf. Notably, the first complaint and subsequent complaints have been filed on behalf of affected women by Non Governmental Organizations (NGOs). The communication procedure is straightforward and easy to complete, as befits a procedure designed to be able to be completed by the complainant. The decisions rendered by the Committee are also much more accessible and easy to follow when compared to any other court decision. They are notably shorter, use very few legal terms, state the facts in a clear straightforward way and apply the law to the facts in a readily comprehensible manner.

Before the Committee will consider the merits of any communication, they first determine if it is admissible by examining, among other criteria, whether domestic remedies have been exhausted. The Committee will not dismiss a complaint for failure to exhaust domestic remedies if pursuing those remedies would be ineffective. The Committee also determines whether the alleged violation occurred subsequent to the state party signing the Optional Protocol. Only once those criteria have been met, does the Committee move to a consideration of the merits. Even if the Committee issues a decision and recommendations finding in favor of the complainant, the Committee is powerless to enforce its decisions. Presumably, by becoming a party to the Optional Protocol, states signal their commitment to the process, and their intention to abide by the Committee's decisions. However, there is no real enforcement mechanism. The Committee may order the state to compensate the complainant financially, but lacks any police power to enforce that decision.

F. The Complaint Procedure — Model Form

MODEL FORM
FOR SUBMISSION OF COMMUNICATIONS TO THE
COMMITTEE ON THE ELIMINATION OF DISCRIMINATION AGAINST
WOMEN UNDER THE OPTIONAL PROTOCOL OF THE CONVENTION

The Optional Protocol to the Convention on the Elimination of All Forms of Discrimination against Women entered into force on 22 December, 2000. It entitles the Committee on the Elimination of Discrimination against Women, a body of 23 independent experts, to receive and consider communications(petitions) from, or on behalf of, individuals or a group of individuals who claim to be victims of violations of the rights protected by the Convention.

To be considered by the Committee, a communication:

- must be in writing;
- may not be anonymous;
- must refer to a State which is a party to both the Convention on the Elimination of All Forms of Discrimination against Women and the Optional Protocol;
- must be submitted by, or on behalf of, an individual or a group of individuals under the jurisdiction of a State which is a party to the Convention and the Optional Protocol. In cases where a communication is submitted on behalf of an individual or a group of individuals, their consent is necessary unless the person submitting the communication can justify acting on their behalf without such consent.

A communication will *not* normally be considered by the Committee:

- unless all available domestic remedies have been exhausted

- where the same matter is being or has already been examined by the Committee or another international procedure
- if it concerns an alleged violation occurring before the entry into force of the Optional Protocol for the State.

In order for a communication to be considered, the victim or victims must agree to disclose her/their identity to the State against which the violation is alleged. The communication, if admissible, will be brought confidentially to the attention of the State party concerned.

* * *

If you wish to submit a communication, please follow the guidelines below as closely as possible. Also, please submit any relevant information which becomes available *after* you have submitted this form.

Further information on the Convention on the Elimination of All Forms of Discrimination against Women and its Optional Protocol, as well as the rules of procedure of the Committee can be found at: http://www.un.org/womenwatch/daw/cedaw/index.html.

Guidelines for submission

The following questionnaire provides a guideline for those who wish to submit a communication for consideration by the Committee on the Elimination of Discrimination against Women under the Optional Protocol to the Convention on the Elimination of All Forms of Discrimination against Women. Please provide as much information as available in response to the items listed below.

Send your communication to:

Committee on the Elimination of Discrimination against Women
c/o Division for the Advancement of Women, Department of Economic and Social Affairs
United Nations Secretariat
2 United Nations Plaza
DC-2/12th Floor
New York, NY 10017
United States of America
Fax: 1-212-963-3463

1. Information concerning the author(s) of the communication

- Family name
- First name
- Date and place of birth
- Nationality/citizenship
- Passport/identity card number (if available)
- Sex
- Marital status/children
- Profession
- Ethnic background, religious affiliation, social group (if relevant)
- Present address
- Mailing address for confidential correspondence (if other than present address)

- Fax/telephone/e-mail
- Indicate whether you are submitting the communication as:
  — Alleged victim(s). If there is a group of individuals alleged to be victims, provide basic information about each individual.
  — On behalf of the alleged victim(s). Provide evidence showing the consent of the victim(s), or reasons that justify submitting the communication without such consent.

2. Information concerning the alleged victim(s) (if other than the author)

- Family name
- First name
- Date and place of birth
- Nationality/citizenship
- Passport/identity card number (if available)
- Sex
- Marital status/children
- Profession
- Ethnic background, religious affiliation, social group (if relevant)
- Present address
- Mailing address for confidential correspondence (if other than present address)
- Fax/telephone/e-mail.

3. Information on the State party concerned

- Name of the State party (country).

4. Nature of the alleged violation(s)

Provide detailed information to substantiate your claim, including:

- Description of alleged violation(s) and alleged perpetrator(s)
- Date(s)
- Place(s)
- Provisions of the Convention on the Elimination of All Forms of Discrimination against Women that were allegedly violated. If the communication refers to more than one provision, describe each issue separately.

5. Steps taken to exhaust domestic remedies

Describe the action taken to exhaust domestic remedies; for example, attempts to obtain legal, administrative, legislative, policy or programme remedies, including:

- Type(s) of remedy sought
- Date(s)
- Place(s)
- Who initiated the action
- Which authority or body was addressed
- Name of court hearing the case (if any)

- If domestic remedies have not been exhausted, explain why.

Please note: Enclose copies of all relevant documentation.

6. Other international procedures

Has the same matter already been examined or is it being examined under another procedure of international investigation or settlement? If yes, explain:

- Type of procedure(s)
- Date(s)
- Place(s)
- Results (if any).

Please note: Enclose copies of all relevant documentation.

7. Date and signature

Date/place: _____

Signature of author(s) and/or victim(s):

_____

8. List of documents attached (do *not* send originals, only copies).

_____

The Optional Protocol also contains a provision whereby the Committee may investigate a state for grave and systematic violations of human rights. This procedure, which has only been used once, will be discussed in a later chapter.

Questions for Discussion

1. *Only 100 countries are parties to CEDAW's Optional Protocol—compared to about 183 signatories to CEDAW itself. What does this tell us about how serious countries are about actually enforcing CEDAW?*

2. *The CEDAW Committee has thus far decided fourteen cases under the Optional Protocol. It does not appear that many individuals are making use of the procedure. Why might this be the case? Do you think the procedure is sufficiently well known and accessible?*

3. *Look at the length, organization, style of writing and language of some of the CEDAW decisions. Are they accessible to the layperson?*

4. *Are the instructions for filing a complaint with the CEDAW Committee sufficiently clear and not unduly burdensome?*

5. *How might the requirement of exhausting domestic procedures impact the kind and number of CEDAW complaints?*

Chapter 4

International and Regional Protection of Human Rights

Chapter Problem

Thanks to your Memorandum, the Subcommittee now has a clearer picture of how CEDAW fits into the overall UN treaty system. It understands the RUD system, and has a general idea of the RUDs filed by other states parties, and the responses to those RUDs from other states. Should the Subcommittee choose to transmit CEDAW to the Senate for a vote on ratification it also understands its reporting obligations under CEDAW and the enforcement process whereby a complaint may be filed with the CEDAW Committee. What the Subcommittee now needs to know, is how CEDAW fits within other regional human rights systems. Is it consistent with the United States' obligations under the Inter-American system, or does it conflict with any provisions, for example? Does it duplicate protections offered to women under any other regional system such as the European or African systems? The Subcommittee would like a Memorandum that offers an overview of the regional human rights systems and their enforcement bodies and mechanisms.

I. The UN System and Regional Human Rights Systems

While the UN was crafting human rights treaties and enforcement procedures during 1940s–1990s and beyond, regional bodies were also negotiating and implementing their own regional accords. Many of these systems came into existence in the wake of the adoption of the *Universal Declaration of Human Rights* in 1948, and many of the Conventions were modeled on this document. There is thus considerable overlap among the various systems.

This chapter will outline the major regional human rights treaties and enforcement procedures, as well as special courts created by the United Nations. The trend in regional systems is similar to the one that took place in the UN system — namely a move towards permitting individuals to file complaints, and a move toward a more stringent enforcement procedure than the reporting system.

As Thomas Buergenthal has noted:[1]

---

1. Thomas Buergenthal, *The Evolving International Human Rights System*, 100 AMJIL 783, 789 (2006).

The European Convention on Human Rights ushered in the first regional system for the protection of human rights. It was followed by the inter-American and African systems. All three of the existing systems seek in one form or another to supplement the human rights efforts of the United Nations by providing protective mechanisms suited to their regions. In addition to guaranteeing many of the human rights that various UN instruments proclaim, each regional system also codifies those rights to which the region attaches particular importance because of its political and legal traditions, its history and culture.

A. The Inter-American System

The Inter-American system was created by the Organization of American States (OAS) in 1948. In that year the member states of the OAS adopted the *American Declaration on the Rights and Duties of Man*, a document which paralleled the *Universal Declaration of Human Rights*. The *American Declaration* introduced the notion of duties owed by the individual to the community and the nation.

1. The American Convention on Human Rights

In 1969 the *Declaration* was codified into the American Convention on Human Rights wherein the parties recognized that:

> the essential rights of man are not derived from one's being a national of a certain state, but are based upon attributes of the human personality, and that they therefore justify international protection in the form of a convention reinforcing or complementing the protection provided by the domestic law of the American states;

Article 1 of the Convention prohibits discrimination on the basis of sex by providing that:

> 1. The States Parties to this Convention undertake to respect the rights and freedoms recognized herein and to ensure to all persons subject to their jurisdiction the free and full exercise of those rights and freedoms, without any discrimination for reasons of race, color, sex, language, religion, political or other opinion, national or social origin, economic status, birth, or any other social condition.
>
> 2. For the purposes of this Convention, "person" means every human being.

Article 17 moreover provides for gender equality during marriage:

Article 17. Rights of the Family

> 1. The family is the natural and fundamental group unit of society and is entitled to protection by society and the state.
>
> 2. The right of men and women of marriageable age to marry and to raise a family shall be recognized, if they meet the conditions required by domestic laws, insofar as such conditions do not affect the principle of nondiscrimination established in this Convention.
>
> 3. No marriage shall be entered into without the free and full consent of the intending spouses.
>
> 4. The States Parties shall take appropriate steps to ensure the equality of rights and the adequate balancing of responsibilities of the spouses as to marriage,

during marriage, and in the event of its dissolution. In case of dissolution, provision shall be made for the necessary protection of any children solely on the basis of their own best interests.

5. The law shall recognize equal rights for children born out of wedlock and those born in wedlock.

The Convention also created a Commission charged under Article 41 with the responsibility:

a. to develop an awareness of human rights among the peoples of America;

b. to make recommendations to the governments of the member states, when it considers such action advisable, for the adoption of progressive measures in favor of human rights within the framework of their domestic law and constitutional provisions as well as appropriate measures to further the observance of those rights;

c. to prepare such studies or reports as it considers advisable in the performance of its duties;

d. to request the governments of the member states to supply it with information on the measures adopted by them in matters of human rights;

e. to respond, through the General Secretariat of the Organization of American States, to inquiries made by the member states on matters related to human rights and, within the limits of its possibilities, to provide those states with the advisory services they request;

f. to take action on petitions and other communications pursuant to its authority under the provisions of Articles 44 through 51 of this Convention; and

g. to submit an annual report to the General Assembly of the Organization of American States.

The Convention created a procedure whereby any "person or group of persons, or any nongovernmental entity legally recognized in one or more member states of the Organization, may lodge petitions with the Commission containing denunciations or complaints of violation of this Convention by a State Party."[2] The procedure to be followed by the Commission is prescribed by Article 48, and may only be invoked on condition that domestic law remedies have been exhausted. The Commission consists of seven independent experts elected by the General Assembly of the OAS.

Article 52 of the Convention created the Inter-American Court of Human Rights which pursuant to Article 61 may hear complaints only from member States or those referred to it by the Commission. It consists of seven judges. Only state parties to the Convention may nominate and elect judges to the Court.

The rights contained in the American Convention on Human Rights are largely based on the ICCPR, but the Convention also contains rights that reflect the Catholic nature of many of its signatory states. One of those rights significantly and explicitly guaranteed the right to life, requiring that this right "shall be protected by law and, in general, from the moment of conception."[3]

---

2. Art. 44.
3. Art. 4.

In 1970 the Protocol of Buenos Aires[4] amended the OAS Charter and transformed the Commission into a Charter organ whose "principal function shall be to promote the observance and protection of human rights and to serve as a consultative organ of the Organization in these matters."[5] The Commission prepared reports on human rights situations in various countries based on their onsite visits and filed petitions. The Commission's first country reports in the 1960s dealt with the human rights situations in Cuba, Haiti, and the Dominican Republic. The Commission also undertook a country visit of the Dominican Republic to investigate the human rights situation there. It subsequently undertook an in-country investigation of the disappearances in Argentina. As Buergenthal has noted,[6] "[t]he publication of its report on the Argentine situation had a highly beneficial impact on conditions in that country." Widespread human rights violations in several Latin American countries meant that the Commission wrote many critical country reports from the 1970s–1990s.

By ratifying the American Convention, states are automatically considered to have accepted the jurisdiction of the Commission to hear cases brought against them by individuals. Interstate complaints can be heard by the Commission only if the applicant and respondent states have each filed a separate declaration accepting the Commission's jurisdiction to receive such complaints. If the Commission does not refer the matter before it to the Inter American Court, the Commission may examine the merits of a case before it. The matter may be referred to the Court by the Commission itself or by an interested state party, with the proviso that the party who is the subject matter of the complaint must have accepted the Court's jurisdiction. Individuals may not refer matters to the Court but may appear before the Court in the event that a matter is referred to the Court. Since 2001, the Commission commonly refers cases of non-compliance to the Court, pursuant to new Rules of Procedure.

The U.S. and Canada still have not ratified the Convention. However, the Convention itself permits OAS member states, whether or not they have ratified the Convention, to request advisory opinions from the Court, seeking the interpretation of the Convention or of other human rights treaties of the inter-American system. Member states and OAS organs may also seek Advisory Opinions on the compatibility with the Convention of national legislation.

2. The Convention of Belém Do Pará

Additionally, in 1994, the OAS drafted the Convention on the Eradication, Punishment and Prevention of Violence Against Women, otherwise known as the Convention of Belém do Pará, to protect the rights of women. Women in the region had been agitating for a convention specifically addressing women's rights as far back as 1923, when a general report was prepared for the International Conference of American States about the status of women in the Americas. As the Inter-American Commission's web site describes it:

> Women from all the American nations came to Havana in 1928 demanding that they be allowed to participate in the Sixth International Conference of American States and that the members of the conference ratify an Equal Rights Treaty. Drafted by Alice Paul of the National Women's Party in the United States,

---

4. *Available at* http://www1.umn.edu/humanrts/oasinstr/buenosaires.html [last visited January 12, 2011].

5. Art. 112.

6. Thomas Buergenthal, *The Evolving International Human Rights System*, 100 AmJIL 783, 789 (2006).

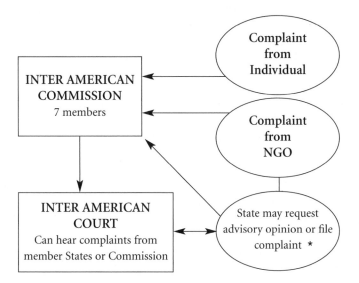

* After a decision by the Commission
The Inter-American Commission has created a form and handbook to assist Petitioners in filing claims. That information is available at: https://www.cidh.oas.org/cidh_apps/manual_pdf/MANUAL2002_ E.pdf. Instructions and a complaint form are available at: https://www.cidh.oas.org/cidh_apps/ instructions.asp?gc_language=E.

the treaty would have moved the consideration of women's rights into political debates throughout the hemisphere. In spite of the expectations raised in 1923, not one woman was included in the delegation of any country. Representatives of twenty-one member nations argued that only they were allowed to speak on the floor and that the meeting's agenda had no room for discussion of a treaty on equal rights.

After a month of protests and active campaigning, the women were finally allowed a voice at the conference. For the first time women officially spoke at a plenary and public session of a Pan American conference. To hear the first speeches, "more than a thousand women filled the galleries, staircases, and the conference floor of the University of Havana's great hall." Although the Treaty for Equal Rights was not ratified, the decision was taken to create the Inter-American Commission of Women (CIM) and to charge it with conducting a study of the legal status of women in the Americas, which would be presented to the next International Conference of American States.[7]

The demand for specific acknowledgment of, and protection for women's rights resulted in the following conventions being drafted: The Convention on the Nationality of Women (Montevideo, Uruguay, 1933); the Inter-American Convention on the Granting of Civil Rights to Women (Bogota, Columbia, 1948); the Inter-American Convention on the Granting of Political Rights to Women 1948, and finally the Inter-American Convention on the Prevention, Punishment and Eradication of Violence Against Women (Belém do Pará).

Specifically articulated rights in Belém do Pará include:

---

7. History of the Inter-American Commission of Women; *available at* http://www.oas.org/cim/ english/History2.htm [last visited January 5, 2011].

Article 3

Every woman has the right to be free from violence in both the public and private spheres.[8]

Article 4

Every woman has the right to the recognition, enjoyment, exercise and protection of all human rights and freedoms embodied in regional and international human rights instruments. These rights include, among others:

a. The right to have her life respected;

b. The right to have her physical, mental and moral integrity respected;

c. The right to personal liberty and security;

d. The right not to be subjected to torture;

e. The right to have the inherent dignity of her person respected and her family protected;

f. The right to equal protection before the law and of the law;

g. The right to simple and prompt recourse to a competent court for protection against acts that violate her rights;

h. The right to associate freely;

i. The right of freedom to profess her religion and beliefs within the law; and

j. The right to have equal access to the public service of her country and to take part in the conduct of public affairs, including decision-making.

Article 5

Every woman is entitled to the free and full exercise of her civil, political, economic, social and cultural rights, and may rely on the full protection of those rights as embodied in regional and international instruments on human rights. The States Parties recognize that violence against women prevents and nullifies the exercise of these rights.

Article 6

The right of every woman to be free from violence includes, among others:

a. The right of women to be free from all forms of discrimination; and

b. The right of women to be valued and educated free of stereotyped patterns of behavior and social and cultural practices based on concepts of inferiority or subordination.

States are required to include information on measures taken to protect women from violence in their reports to the Inter-American Commission. Additionally, individuals and NGOs may file complaints against a state party with the Inter-American Commission. An example of the utilization of this mechanism will be discussed in Chapter 7.

---

8. This obligation of states to protect women in both the public and private spheres will be discussed in more detail in a later chapter.

3. The Inter-American Commission on Women and the Special Rapporteur on the Rights of Women

The Inter-American Commission on Women (CIM) was established in 1928 to fight for the civil and political rights of women in the Americas. It was instrumental in the creation of the Convention on the Nationality of Women (Uruguay 1933) and the Convention of Belém do Pará. In 1998, Delegates of the CIM adopted the *Declaration of Santo Domingo*[9] which recognizes the rights of women throughout their entire life cycle as an inalienable, integral, and indivisible part of universal human rights. The *Declaration* reaffirmed the importance of protecting women's human rights and eliminating all forms of discrimination against women.

The Inter-American Commission on Human Rights (IACHR) established its Rapporteurship on the Rights of Women in 1994, to renew its commitment that the rights of women are fully respected and ensured in each member State. While the constitutions of each member State formally guarantee equality, the Commission's examination of national legal systems and practices had increasingly revealed the persistence of discrimination based on gender.[10] The Rapporteur conducts in-country visits and writes reports that are included in the Inter-American Commission's comments on country reports.

Questions for Discussion

1. *Why do you think that the Inter-American system has been such a proactive system in the field of human rights? Could the history of autocratic and violent regimes have impacted the development of this regional human rights system?*

2. *The Commission on Women was established in 1928. Do you think that this early outward commitment to women's rights has influenced the jurisprudence of the Inter-American Commission?*

3. *The United States has not recognized the jurisdiction of the Inter-American Court. Is that likely to cause a divergence in the jurisprudence of the United States Supreme Court and the Inter-American system?*

B. The European System

The European Convention for the Protection of Human Rights and Fundamental Freedoms (1950) was also inspired by the *Universal Declaration of Human Rights*, and thus contains many of the same provisions as that document. It is often referred to simply as the European Convention on Human Rights (ECHR), and was the first international human rights treaty with enforcement mechanisms. Only member states of the Council

---

9. CIM/RES.195(XXIX-O/98).
10. *See* http://www.cidh.oas.org/women/mandate.htm [last visited January 12, 2011].

of Europe (COE) can become a party to the ECHR.[11] The Convention mainly focused on civil and political rights and did not specifically prohibit discrimination. Buergenthal notes that:

> The list of these rights has grown significantly over the years with the adoption of additional protocols that have expanded the Convention's catalog of rights. In the meantime, these rights have been extensively interpreted by the Convention institutions and the national courts of the member states. In the process, the meaning and scope of these rights also have increasingly come to reflect the contemporary needs of European society. The result is a modern body of human rights law to which other international, regional, and national institutions frequently look when interpreting and applying their own human rights instruments.[12]

1. The European Court of Human Rights

Article 19 of the Convention created the European Court of Human Rights which sits in Committees of 3 judges, Chambers of 7 judges or the Grand Chamber which consists of 17 judges.[13] The jurisdiction of the Court extends to all matters concerning the interpretation and application of the Convention and the protocols thereto.

Article 33 — Inter-State cases

Any High Contracting Party may refer to the Court any alleged breach of the provisions of the Convention and the protocols thereto by another High Contracting Party.

Article 34 — Individual applications

The Court may receive applications from any person, non-governmental organisation or group of individuals claiming to be the victim of a violation by one of the High Contracting Parties of the rights set forth in the Convention or the protocols thereto. The High Contracting Parties undertake not to hinder in any way the effective exercise of this right.

Article 35 — Admissibility criteria

The Court may only deal with the matter after all domestic remedies have been exhausted, according to the generally recognised rules of international law, and within a period of six months from the date on which the final decision was taken.

The Court shall not deal with any application submitted under Article 34 that:

is anonymous; or

is substantially the same as a matter that has already been examined by the Court or has already been submitted to another procedure of international investigation or settlement and contains no relevant new information.

The Court shall declare inadmissible any individual application submitted under Article 34 which it considers incompatible with the provisions of the Convention or the protocols thereto, manifestly ill-founded, or an abuse of the right of application.

---

11. There are 47 members of the Council of Europe.
12. Thomas Buergenthal, *The Evolving International Human Rights System*, 100 Amjil 783, 789 (2006).
13. Art 27.

The Court shall reject any application which it considers inadmissible under this Article. It may do so at any stage of the proceedings.

Buergenthal[14] considers the European system to be "the most effective international system for the protection of individual human rights to date." It originally started out as a dual system with a Commission and a Court like the Inter-American system but this system was abolished by Protocol 11 which came into force in 1998. This Protocol also gave individuals direct access to the Court.

Buergenthal claims[15] that the Court has "become Europe's constitutional court in matters of civil and political rights. Its judgments are routinely followed by the national courts of the states parties to the Convention, their legislatures, and their national governments." Moreover, the Convention itself has acquired the status of domestic law in most of the states parties and can be invoked as such in their courts.

The Court's controversial opinion on abortion rights for an Irish woman will be discussed in a later chapter.

2. The European Court of Justice

The European Court of Justice is the judicial arm of the European Union. This court's purpose is to ensure that European Union (EU) legislation is interpreted and applied in the same way in all European countries. It settles disputes between EU member states, EU institutions, business and individuals.

Questions for Discussion

1. *Why do you think that the European Court has been so influential?*

2. *Does it make sense to have such a multiplicity of systems — the Inter-American system, the UN system, the African system, and the European system — all with their own conventions and courts? Isn't this likely to lead to conflicting or inconsistent decisions?*

3. *Does having regional human rights systems alongside the UN treaty based system lead to a risk of forum shopping?*

4. *Should regional systems be able to represent the needs of a particular region and embody cultural mores, even if these have the potential to conflict with portions of the UN treaty system?*

C. The African System

In 2000, the African Union (AU) replaced the previous Organization of African Unity (OAU), which had been formed in 1980. Like its American counterparts, the African

---

14. Thomas Buergenthal, *The Evolving International Human Rights System*, 100 AMJIL 783, 789 (2006).

15. *Id.*

system originally created a Commission — the African Commission on Human and Peoples' Rights that reviewed claims of violations of human rights. Unlike the Inter-American system, however, the African system did not originally have a court. In 2004, by means of a protocol, the African Court of Human and Peoples' Rights came into existence. The Court was formally inaugurated in 2006. Thus far the Court has yet to hear any women's rights cases.

The African Charter proclaims not only rights but also duties, and it guarantees both individual and peoples' rights. In addition to civil and political rights, it also provides for economic and social rights. African historical traditions and customs are also reflected in some provisions of the Charter, particularly those dealing with duties of individuals and family matters. These duties and obligations often may conflict with women's rights, as will be discussed in a later chapter. Moreover, State parties may limit the rights guaranteed by the Charter.

1. The African Commission on Human Right and Peoples' Rights

The Commission's mandate is "to promote human and peoples' rights and ensure their protection in Africa." It is composed of eleven elected members who serve in their individual capacities. The Commission may make recommendations to governments, calling on them to address human rights problems It also issues recommendations based on reports submitted by countries, and may conduct in-country visits. The Commission may also issue advisory opinions when requested by State parties, the African Union or duly accredited NGOs. It may also hear interstate and individual complaints. Individual complaints are limited to those cases which reveal the existence of a series of "serious or massive violations of human and peoples' rights." Thus allegations of less serious individual violations would not be permitted.

In rendering an opinion, Article 60 provides that:

> The Commission shall draw inspiration from international law on human and peoples' rights, particularly from the provisions of various African instruments on human and peoples' rights, the Charter of the United Nations, the Charter of the [African Union], the Universal Declaration of Human Rights, other instruments adopted by the United Nations and by African countries in the field of human and peoples' rights as well as from the provisions of various instruments adopted within the Specialized Agencies of the United Nations of which the parties to the present Charter are members.

Article 61 moreover provides that:

> The Commission shall also take into consideration, as subsidiary measures to determine the principles of law, other general or special international conventions, laying down rules expressly recognized by member states of the [African Union], African practices consistent with international norms on human and peoples' rights, customs generally accepted as law, general principles of law recognized by African states as well as legal precedents and doctrine.

2. The African Court of Human Rights

The Court has the competence to take final and binding decisions on human rights violations perpetrated by AU member states. It also may issue advisory opinions when requested by a member state, an organ of the AU or any African organization. To date only 25 of the AU's 56 member states have ratified the Court's Protocol. The Court further has jurisdiction over disputes arising not only under the Charter and the Protocol establishing the Court, but also "under any other relevant Human Rights instrument ratified by the States concerned." On its face, this broad language would permit the Court to adjudicate disputes between African states even with regard to non-African human rights instruments to which they are parties.

3. The African Women's Protocol

In 2005, the Protocol on the Rights of Women in Africa entered into force after receiving its fifteenth ratification. This Protocol explicitly guarantees the reproductive right of women to medical abortion, when pregnancy results from rape or incest, or when the continuation of pregnancy endangers the health or life of the mother. In another first, the Protocol explicitly calls for the legal prohibition of female genital mutilation, and prohibits the abuse of women in advertising and pornography. The Protocol sets forth a broad range of economic and social welfare rights for women. The rights of particularly vulnerable groups of women, including widows, elderly women, disabled women and "women in distress," which includes poor women, women from marginalized populations groups, and pregnant or nursing women in detention. In the Protocol, discrimination is defined as:

> any distinction, exclusion or restriction or any differential treatment based on sex and whose objectives or effects compromise or destroy the recognition, enjoyment or the exercise by women, regardless of their marital status, of human rights and fundamental freedoms in all spheres of life;[16]

Violence is defined as:

> "Violence against women" means all acts perpetrated against women which cause or could cause them physical, sexual, psychological, and economic harm, including the threat to take such acts; or to undertake the imposition of arbitrary restrictions on or deprivation of fundamental freedoms in private or public life in peace time and during situations of armed conflicts or of war.[17]

4. The SADC Tribunal

African leaders from Angola, Botswana, Democratic Republic of Congo (DRC), Lesotho, Madagascar, Malawi, Mauritius, Mozambique, Namibia, Seychelles, South Africa, Swaziland, United Republic of Tanzania, Zambia, and Zimbabwe concluded the Southern African Development Community (SADC) Treaty in 1992. The representatives pledged economic cooperation and committed themselves to good governance, peace and security. In 2005, the SADC Tribunal came into existence, with a mandate to resolve conflicts over SADC among its members, to hear labor disputes and to hear matters alleging a violation of SADC law by SADC members. Complaints may be filed by party states or individuals. The parties must have exhausted domestic remedies before filing a complaint with the SADC Tribunal.

---

16. Art. 1.
17. Art. 1.

Questions for Discussion

1. *Why do you think that the African system has taken so long to create a Court system?*

2. *Does the creation of tribunals like the SADC tribunal, create the risk of forum shopping or inconsistent jurisprudence among the African Court and tribunal?*

3. *Look at the protection afforded women's rights in the African system's treaties. Why do you think that the rights protection language is strong but enforcement is weak?*

4. *The African system is one of the few systems to speak to an individual's duties as well as rights. What impact might this have on the enforcement of rights under the African system?*

II. Other Courts and Tribunals

A. International Criminal Tribunals

Although the UN's primary judicial organ is the International Court of Justice (ICJ), that court only adjudges matters between states—individuals are not parties to the proceedings. Until the UN established the International Criminal Court (ICC) by means of the Treaty of Rome in 2002, no permanent criminal court existed. A need for such court was made apparent by the multiple mass violations of human rights that took place during the twentieth century. The killing fields perpetrated by Pol Pot and the Khmer Rouge in Cambodia, the multiple wars in the former Yugoslavia, and the genocides in Rwanda, Sudan and the Democratic Republic of Congo (DRC), and the atrocities in Sierra Leone all pointed to the need for a permanent criminal court. The UN Security Council responded by first creating various tribunals designed to deal with particular crimes committed in each situation. The International Criminal Tribunal for the Former Yugoslavia (ICTY), the International Criminal Tribunal for Rwanda (ICTR), the Extraordinary Chambers in the Courts of Cambodia, and the Special Court for Sierra Leone, are all examples of special UN tribunals created to try individuals charged with violations of the laws of war, international humanitarian law and human rights violations. Notably the ICTR and ICTY have crafted some groundbreaking jurisprudence regarding rape, and the crime of genocidal rape. Their contributions to women's rights will be discussed in a later chapter.

B. The International Criminal Court (ICC)

The ad hoc nature of the various tribunals described above, illustrates the need for a permanent court. The International Criminal was created by the Rome Statute, and came into being in 2002. Today, some hundred and nineteen states are parties to the Rome

Statute.[18] The Court has its seat in The Hague, Netherlands. It is an independent organization and not part of the UN system. Its mandate includes the ability to investigate and charge individuals for genocide, crimes against humanity, and war crimes. The Prosecutor may also conduct investigations into situations where such crimes may have been committed.

Among the individuals currently being tried by the ICC, is Congolese rebel leader Jean Pierre Bemba, who is charged with three counts of war crimes (including murder, mass rape, and pillaging) and two counts of crimes against humanity (again including mass rape). The ICC also investigated the situation in Darfur (including the mass rapes that occurred there) and has issued arrest warrants for Ali Kushayb and Ahmad Harun, charging them with crimes against humanity and war crimes.[19] Cases that are currently being tried include cases regarding the situations in the DRC, the Central African Republic, and Uganda respectively.

Questions for Discussion

1. *One of the criticisms levied against the ICC is that its focus seems to be almost exclusively on African countries. Is that a legitimate criticism? Might it impact the Court's legitimacy, and its ability to get countries to respect and enforce arrest warrants for example?*

2. *Does the United States' refusal to sign the Treaty of Rome impact the Court's legitimacy at all?*

III. Human Rights in Domestic Legal Orders — Thomas Buergenthal[20]

The proliferation of human rights treaties and the emergence of international and regional human rights tribunals with jurisdiction to interpret and apply these treaties have prompted an increasing number of states to accord human rights treaties a special status in their national constitutions. That status facilitates the domestic implementation of the decisions of these tribunals. It also contributes to a legal and political climate in the countries concerned that enables their judiciaries and legislatures to take international and regional human rights obligations into account without having to face some of the constitutional obstacles that have traditionally impeded effective domestic compliance with international judicial and quasi-judicial decisions. Various countries in Europe and the Americas have pioneered these constitutional changes, influenced in part by their past

---

18. The Statute of Rome is *available at* http://www.icc-cpi.int/NR/rdonlyres/EA9AEFF7-5752-4F84-BE94-0A655EB30E16/0/Rome_Statute_English.pdf [last visited January 17, 2011].

19. The arrest warrant for these individuals who are still at large, is *available at* http://www.icc-cpi.int/iccdocs/doc/doc279813.PDF [last visited January 17, 2011].

20. Thomas Buergenthal, *The Evolving International Human Rights System*, 100 AMJIL 783, 789 (2006).

experience with dictatorial regimes and the emergence in those regions of strong human rights systems, which were created in part to prevent the return to power of such regimes. One of the most interesting constitutional provisions in this regard is Article 10(2) of the Spanish Constitution of 1978, which reads as follows: "The norms relative to basic rights and liberties which are recognized by the Constitution shall be interpreted in conformity with the Universal Declaration of Human Rights and the international treaties and agreements on those matters ratified by Spain." In complying with this provision, Spanish courts have looked not only to the language of the Universal Declaration and the human rights treaties to which Spain is a party, but also to the case law of international tribunals interpreting these treaties, in particular the judgments of the European Court of Human Rights. As a practical matter, this approach has had the effect of transforming the European Court's judgments into Spanish constitutional jurisprudence. Other countries, among them Argentina, have conferred constitutional rank on human rights treaties. Argentina did so when it amended its Constitution in 1994 and adopted a new Article 75(22). That provision confers constitutional rank on various international human rights instruments, including the American Convention on Human Rights and the two International Covenants on Human Rights. Also included in that list are the Universal Declaration of Human Rights and the American Declaration of the Rights and Duties of Man. The reference to the latter two instruments, both adopted in the form of nonbinding resolutions, no doubt reflects the view of some states that these declarations have acquired a normative character. Another constitutional development worth noting is the amendment by Costa Rica of its Constitution in 1989, which established a constitutional chamber within the Supreme Court. The legislation implementing the amendment granted the new chamber the power, inter alia, to issue writs of habeas corpus and *amparo* to protect individuals claiming the denial of rights guaranteed them under both the Costa Rican Constitution and any human rights treaty ratified by that state. In this regard, it is also noteworthy that the Austrian law ratifying the European Convention on Human Rights declared the treaty to have the normative rank of a constitutional law. A large number of countries, particularly in Europe and Latin America, consider many provisions of various human rights treaties, especially those guaranteeing civil and political rights such as the European and American Conventions and the International Covenant on Civil and Political Rights to be self-executing in character. As such, they become directly applicable domestic law. In other countries, incorporating legislation is required to make a treaty provision directly applicable. The United Kingdom, for example, promulgated such a law in 1998 with respect to the European Convention on Human Rights. Some other countries have adopted similar measures.

Chapter 5

Gender Equality and Discrimination against Women: Litigating Equality Based Claims in Domestic Jurisdictions

Chapter Problem

Suppose that you are a staff attorney working or the newly established United States Office of Global Women's Issues.[1] *The Office was established by the Obama Administration, which also created the position of Ambassador-at-Large for Global Women's Issues; a position currently held by Melanne Verveer. The Office of Global Women's Issues works for the political, social, and economic empowerment of women. Ambassador Verveer's goal is to "mobilize concrete support for women's rights and political and economic empowerment through initiatives and programs designed to increase women's and girls' access to education and health care, to combat violence against women and girls in all its forms, and to ensure that women's rights are fully integrated with human rights in the development of U.S. foreign policy." The Office of Global Women's Issues reports to the Secretary of State, Hillary Clinton.*

The Secretary of State operates a fund called the International Fund for Women and Girls, which seeks to empower women. As the Secretary's website puts it, the Fund invests in efficient and innovative solutions to combat violence, improve health and education, promote climate change solutions, and create economic and political opportunities for women and girls.[2] *The Fund provides grants for NGOs working to advance women's rights. The Fund has received a grant application from an NGO working to promote the equality of women in legal systems worldwide. The Office of Global Women's Issues has been requested to review the grant application, and comment on its merits. However, the Office is finding that the term "equality" is a difficult term to define. Before it can comment on the merits of the grant application, the Office is seeking some clarity about what the term "equality" connotes. It has therefore requested that you research and write a Memorandum on how equality for women is perceived in various jurisdictions, including the United States.*

---

1. *See* the Office's website *available at* http://www.state.gov/s/gwi/ [last visited May 14, 2011].
2. *See* the Fund's website *available at* http://www.state.gov/s/gwi/womensfund/index.htm [last visited July 1, 2011].

I. Gender Equality Jurisprudence in CEDAW

As we will see in this chapter, many countries were developing a gender equality jurisprudence in their domestic courts during the 1980s and '90s. Some of these countries (Canada for example) had ratified CEDAW, and were influenced by its provisions in their domestic jurisprudence. Other countries, like the U.S., had not ratified CEDAW, and its Supreme Court did not openly acknowledge the influence of CEDAW in its equality decisions (although on occasion amici attempted to bring CEDAW to the Court's attention in briefs).

Equality is a term that is often bandied around without full awareness of its implications; similarly the term "non discrimination." By focusing attention on the equality of women, CEDAW helped focus attention on the issue of equality, and how best to implement and achieve equality for women. Domestic courts were grappling with this same issue. In this Chapter we will consider the provisions of CEDAW that directly relate to equality and non discrimination, and the CEDAW Committee's Recommendations about equality. Then we will look at how some party and some non party states were interpreting equality and developing their own jurisprudence in this area. These domestic decisions are important, because not only are parties required to exhaust domestic remedies before filing a claim in regional or international *fora*, but moreover CEDAW had no enforcement mechanisms until 2001, so filing a claim in one's domestic jurisdiction was the first (and sometimes only) stage in the quest for equality.

A. CEDAW's Equality and Non-Discrimination Provisions

Article 1 of CEDAW defines discrimination as:

any distinction, exclusion or restriction made on the basis of sex which has the effect or purpose of impairing or nullifying the recognition, enjoyment or exercise by women, irrespective of their marital status, on a basis of equality of men and women, of human rights and fundamental freedoms in the political, economic, social, cultural, civil or any other field.

Article 2 of CEDAW is the so-called equality provision and requires that:

States Parties condemn discrimination against women in all its forms, agree to pursue by all appropriate means and without delay a policy of eliminating discrimination against women and, to this end, undertake:

a. to embody the principle of the equality of men and women in their national constitutions or other appropriate legislation if not yet incorporated therein and to ensure, through law and other appropriate means, the practical realization of this principle;

b. to adopt appropriate legislative and other measures, including sanctions where appropriate, prohibiting all discrimination against women;

c. to establish legal protection of the rights of women on an equal basis with men and to ensure through competent national tribunals and other public institutions the effective protection of women against any act of discrimination;

d. to refrain from engaging in any act or practice of discrimination against women and to ensure that public authorities and institutions shall act in conformity with this obligation;

e. to take all appropriate measures to eliminate discrimination against women by any person, organization or enterprise;

f. to take all appropriate measures, including legislation, to modify or abolish existing laws, regulations, customs and practices which constitute discrimination against women;

g. to repeal all national penal provisions which constitute discrimination against women.

B. CEDAW and the ICCPR Committee's Comments on Equality and Non-Discrimination

The CEDAW Committee has taken the view that equality for women is the crux of the Convention, and has urged party states to "embody the principle of equality in their Constitutions or national legislation."[3] The CEDAW Committee has also noted that it considered Articles 2 and 16 (equality before the law) to be "core provisions,"[4] which are "central to the objects and purpose of the Convention."[5] Thus it is important that member states have a common understanding of how to interpret and provide for "equality." The IESCR and the ICCPR both contain similar "equality" and "non-discrimination" language as Article 2 of CEDAW. The phrase "by all appropriate means" that appears in Article 2 has been interpreted by the ICESCR Committee as encompassing administrative, social, legislative, judicial and financial means.[6]

In 2005, the Human Rights Committee (the body that adjudicates the ICCPR) commented extensively in its *General Comment 16 on Equality and Non Discrimination*. With regard to equality, it noted that "[t]he equal right of men and women to the enjoyment of all human rights is one of the fundamental principles recognized under international law and enshrined in the main international human rights instruments."[7] It further provided that "the same rights should be expressly recognized for men and women on an equal footing and suitable measures should be taken to ensure that women had the opportunity to exercise their rights […]"[8] The Committee also noted:

7. The enjoyment of human rights on the basis of equality between men and women must be understood comprehensively. Guarantees of non-discrimination and equality in international human rights treaties mandate both de facto and de jure equality. De jure (or formal) equality and de facto (or substantive) equality

---

3. Art. 2 CEDAW.

4. *See* http://www.un.org/womenwatch/daw/cedaw/reservations.htm [last visited July 28, 2010].

5. *Id.*

6. Committee on Economic, Social and Cultural Rights, GENERAL COMMENT 16, Art. 3: THE EQUAL RIGHT OF MEN AND WOMEN TO THE ENJOYMENT OF ALL ECONOMIC, SOCIAL AND CULTURAL RIGHTS (Thirty-fourth session, 2005), UN Doc. E/C.12/2005/3 (2005).

7. *General Comment No. 16* at 1. Committee on Economic, Social and Cultural Rights, GENERAL COMMENT 16, Art. 3: THE EQUAL RIGHT OF MEN AND WOMEN TO THE ENJOYMENT OF ALL ECONOMIC, SOCIAL AND CULTURAL RIGHTS (Thirty-fourth session, 2005), UN Doc. E/C.12/2005/3 (2005).

8. *Id.*

are different but interconnected concepts. Formal equality assumes that equality is achieved if a law or policy treats men and women in a neutral manner. Substantive equality is concerned, in addition, with the effects of laws, policies and practices and with ensuring that they do not maintain, but rather alleviate, the inherent disadvantage that particular groups experience.

8. Substantive equality for men and women will not be achieved simply through the enactment of laws or the adoption of policies that are gender-neutral on their face. In implementing Article 3, States parties should take into account that such laws, policies and practice can fail to address or even perpetuate inequality between men and women, because they do not take account of existing economic, social and cultural inequalities, particularly those experienced by women.[9]

With regard to non-discrimination, the Committee interpreted this as being:

10. [T]he corollary of the principle of equality. Subject to what is stated in Paragraph 15 on temporary special measures, it prohibits differential treatment of a person or group of persons based on his/her or their particular status or situation, such as race, colour, sex, language, religion, political and other opinion, national or social origin, property, birth, or other status, such as age, ethnicity, disability, marital, refugee or migrant status.

11. Discrimination against women is "any distinction, exclusion or restriction made on the basis of sex which has the effect or purpose of impairing or nullifying the recognition, enjoyment or exercise by women, irrespective of their marital status, on a basis of equality of men and women, of human rights and fundamental freedoms in the political, economic, social, cultural, civil or any other field." Discrimination on the basis of sex may be based on the differential treatment of women because of their biology, such as refusal to hire women because they could become pregnant; or stereotypical assumptions, such as tracking women into low-level jobs on the assumption that they are unwilling to commit as much time to their work as men.

12. Direct discrimination occurs when a difference in treatment relies directly and explicitly on distinctions based exclusively on sex and characteristics of men or of women, which cannot be justified objectively.

13. Indirect discrimination occurs when a law, policy or programme does not appear to be discriminatory on its face, but has a discriminatory effect when implemented. This can occur, for example, when women are disadvantaged compared to men with respect to the enjoyment of a particular opportunity or benefit due to pre-existing inequalities. Applying a gender-neutral law may leave the existing inequality in place, or exacerbate it.

14. Gender affects the equal right of men and women to the enjoyment of their rights. Gender refers to cultural expectations and assumptions about the behavior, attitudes, personality traits, and physical and intellectual capacities of men and women, based solely on their identity as men or women. Gender-based assumptions and expectations generally place women at a disadvantage with respect to substantive enjoyment of rights, such as freedom to act and to be recognized as autonomous, fully capable adults, to participate fully in economic, social and political development, and to make decisions concerning their cir-

---

9. *Id.*

cumstances and conditions. Gender-based assumptions about economic, social and cultural roles preclude the sharing of responsibility between men and women in all spheres that is necessary to equality.

The CEDAW Committee has likewise affirmed that equality for women must be substantive rather than purely formal, noting that:

> In the Committee's view, a purely formal legal or programmatic approach is not sufficient to achieve women's *de facto* equality with men ... In addition, the Convention requires that women be given an equal start and that they be empowered by an enabling environment to achieve equality of results. It is not enough to guarantee women treatment that is identical to that of men. Rather, biological as well as socially and culturally constructed differences between men and women must be taken into account. Under certain circumstances, non-identical treatment of women and men will be required in order to address such differences. Pursuit of the goal of substantive equality also calls for an effective strategy aimed at overcoming under-representation of women and a redistribution of resources and power between men and women.

> Substantive equality demands that consideration be given to the ways in which the different roles and position of men and women in society, generally known as gender, impact upon women's ability to claim and enjoy their human rights. It also requires States: "to monitor, through measurable indicators, the impact of laws, policies and action plans and to evaluate progress achieved towards the practical realization of women's substantive equality with men."[10]

C. CEDAW and Stereotyping

The CEDAW Committee has also issued several comments on stereotyping in its responses to reports filed by member states. CEDAW itself calls upon state parties to eliminate stereotyping of men and women, and in particular to eliminate stereotyped roles for men and women. Their comments in this area have resulted in criticism. In particular, many conservative groups in the United States have pointed to CEDAW's comments on motherhood as evidence that CEDAW is anti family. Some of the most criticized of the Concluding Observations made by the CEDAW Committee were the Observations made to Belarus in 2000. Below is an excerpt from Belarus' report and the Comments of the Committee on the Report.

1. Committee on the Elimination of Discrimination against Women, Concluding Observations Belarus (2000)

Introduction by the State party

...335. In introducing the third report, the representative of Belarus noted that since the submission of the second periodic report in 1992 significant changes had occurred for women in Belarus in the context of economic and social transition. She emphasized the positive impact in Belarus of the outcome of the Fourth World Conference on Women

---

10. *General Comment No. 25.*

and her country's elaboration and implementation of a national action plan for the period 1996–2000. She also noted the importance of implementing the Convention and other international documents and events addressing issues of equality between women and men and indicated that the Government intended to sign the Optional Protocol to the Convention. Particular attention had been given to the areas of labour, decision-making, family and social protection, health, education, prevailing gender stereotypes and violence against women. Nonetheless, many obstacles related to the transition, and the insufficient understanding of gender issues by society had hampered efforts to achieve full equality between women and men and the implementation of the Convention.

336. Many legislative and policy changes had occurred and new alliances had been forged or strengthened between the Government, local authorities, the Parliament, women's groups, civil society and international organizations. Centres offering training and curricula in gender and women's studies had been created. The collection of gender-sensitive information and data had improved and numerous publications, awareness-raising campaigns and seminars had contributed to greater visibility and better understanding of gender equality issues by the public.

337. Violence against women had been recognized as a social problem. The 1997 Penal Code addressed violence against women in all its forms and included provisions relating to the protection of victims, witnesses and their families. In 1998, the first women's crisis centre had been established and awareness-raising campaigns, the provision of information and the publication of studies had been initiated. A forthcoming criminal code would strengthen regulations and penalties in cases of trafficking in persons, violations of equal rights of citizens and all forms of exploitation, including sexual exploitation and direct and indirect violence.

338. The representative stated that women's political participation at the highest de-cision-making levels remained low, with 4.5 per cent women in the national Parliament, only one woman cabinet minister and two women ambassadors, despite the attention given to the issue by policy makers. She noted that women's participation at the higher levels of administration, management, the judiciary and in local parliaments had increased, with the number of women reaching 37 per cent on average.

339. The representative noted that the difficulties of transition, including declining living standards and increasing daily workloads, as well as the aftermath of the disaster in Chernobyl, had had a negative impact on the health status of women and children. However, health care and medical institutions in all areas had been strengthened, with particular attention being given to prenatal, childbirth and childcare-related services and the provision of medication. Advice to mothers, including awareness campaigns to promote breastfeeding, was also provided. A national plan focusing on reproductive health, including family planning, was being developed. Special legal regulations, policies and programmes had been instituted to provide assistance to the victims of the Chernobyl disaster, including medical advice to pregnant women and mothers.

340. The restructuring of the economy, changes in the labour market and budgetary cuts in the social sphere, combined with the prevailing unequal distribution of domestic tasks between women and men, had been having a negative impact on women, who were among the most vulnerable social groups. There were cases when women were the first to be fired and the last to be hired in the changing labour market. Living standards, in particular for single mothers, women in low-income families, women with disabilities and elderly women had decreased. Training courses in non-traditional areas such as management, marketing and auditing had been introduced to redress

these factors and women also received financial and in-kind assistance. Newly created jobs often included quotas for women and vulnerable groups and women occupied more than half of the 20,000 work places created in 1999. Special protective provisions were in place for pregnant women workers, women with children below 3 years of age and single mothers with children between the ages of 3 and 14. Cases of discrimination against female workers and of non-compliance with labour regulations by employers had been addressed through conciliatory means, or — in one third of the cases — in the courts.

341. The economic and social transition had been particularly difficult for rural women, whose living conditions, in general, were more difficult than those of women living in urban areas. Rural women's share of unremunerated work at home and on the farm was higher. Despite efforts to modernize agriculture and village infrastructures and to ensure proper educational, health and social services to women, progress remained insufficient.

342. Increased attention had been paid to women's roles as mothers and to the family and its needs, so as to increase its protection. Changes in legislation had brought assistance to families, in particular to single mothers with children. These included: additional financial resources for single mothers with a child below 18 months of age or a disabled child below 16 years; and assistance in kind to families with children with special needs, families with numerous children and children with HIV/AIDS. In view of the high rate of divorce affecting one family in two the diminishing number of marriages and high number of orphans, legislative and policy measures had also addressed the needs of young families, education for family life, reconciliation of work and family life, social support services, human rights, including women's and children's rights, and the situation of orphans. Family-oriented policies, however, had been criticized by some feminist groups on the grounds that they overemphasized women's traditional roles in the family and weakened their position in the labour market, rather than supporting equal division of responsibilities between women and men in all spheres of life....

Concluding Comments by the Committee

Positive aspects

347. The Committee commends the Government for the adoption, in 1996, of a national plan of action to improve the situation of women for the period 1996–2000 and of a national programme entitled "Women of the Republic of Belarus"....

349. The Committee commends the Government for recognizing violence against women as a societal problem and for initiating legislation, establishing a crisis centre for victims of sexual and domestic violence and starting awareness-raising activities. It also commends the Government for recognizing trafficking in women as an emerging problem, requiring sustained attention....

351. The Committee commends the Government for recognizing the difficult economic situation women face in Belarus, in particular with regard to women's employment and the incidence of poverty among women. It also commends the efforts undertaken by the Government to alleviate the situation....

Factors and difficulties affecting the implementation of the Convention

354. The Committee considers that the negative effects of the ongoing transition of the country to a market-based economy and the resulting levels of women's unemployment and poverty are major impediments to the full implementation of the Convention.

Principal areas of concern and recommendations

355. The Committee is concerned that the absence of an enabling environment in the country prevents women from fully participating in all aspects of public life in accordance with articles 3, 7 and 8 of the Convention. The Committee is in particular concerned at the small number of women holding political and decision-making positions.

356. The Committee recommends that the Government take all necessary steps to ensure an open and enabling environment where women have equal opportunity to express their opinions and to participate equally in all aspects of the political process and in civil society organizations. The Committee notes that such an environment is necessary for the advancement of women and the full implementation of the Convention.

357. The Committee expresses its concern that no unified State policy is in place to eliminate discrimination against women and achieve equality between women and men. In particular, the Committee notes with concern that the Government predominantly uses an approach of service delivery to women rather than a human rights approach when implementing the Convention. In addition, such an approach emphasizes the protection of and the delivery of services to women mainly as mothers and members of families, thus perpetuating stereotypical attitudes concerning the roles and responsibilities of women....

359. The Committee expresses its concern that the country's legislation, in particular with regard to women's role in the labour market, appears to be overly protective of women as mothers and thus creates further obstacles to women's participation in the labour market....

361. The Committee is concerned by the continuing prevalence of sex-role stereotypes and by the reintroduction of such symbols as a Mothers' Day and a Mothers' Award, which it sees as encouraging women's traditional roles. It is also concerned whether the introduction of human rights and gender education aimed at countering such stereotyping is being effectively implemented....

365. The Committee is concerned at the economic situation of women, which is characterized by poverty and unemployment, displacement of women from the labour market and even from sectors previously dominated by women. The Committee also notes with concern that re-employed women hold positions below their levels of education and skills. The Committee is also concerned that women are employed predominantly in low paying jobs and that a wage gap between women and men persists. The Committee expresses its concern at the economic situation of particularly vulnerable groups of women, such as those with sole responsibility for families, older women and women with disabilities.

366. The Committee urges the Government to establish a legislative basis that ensures women equal access to the labour market and equal opportunities to work and to create protection against direct and indirect discrimination with regard to access and opportunities. It calls on the Government to implement unemployment policies targeted at women. In particular, it recommends measures to facilitate women's entry into growth sectors of the economy rather than into traditionally female-dominated employment. It calls on the Government to support women's entrepreneurship through the creation of a conducive legislative and regulatory environment and access to loans and credit.

367. The Committee is concerned that poverty is widespread among women ...

While the Committee's comments about Mother's Day may seem surprising, and may be used by those opposed to the U.S. ratification of CEDAW to support their opposition to ratification of the Convention, the Committee's concern has a context. Mother's Day in Belarus was originally celebrated on March 8. Under the Soviet regime it evolved into International Women's Day, a celebration of women generally, rather than one limited to mothers. The new regime in Belarus reintroduced Mother's Day on October 14. It was intended to celebrate a more traditional view of mothers. Given the high rate of poverty among women in Belarus, their lack of access to employment, and the disproportionate amount of work they were required to do in the home, as documented in the report above, the Committee feared that celebrating traditional motherhood was a guise to keep women from the workforce and maintain their stereotyped role in the home. It is interesting to read a letter from the President of Belarus to mothers on Mother's Day printed below. Note that even nine years after the Committee's comments, President Lukashenko still refers to women's "main calling" as being "hearth keepers," although he does acknowledge women's "professional activities" too.

2. President Congratulates Women on Mother's Day[11]

Dear women,

Please accept my hearty congratulations on Mother's Day.

On this day our hearts are filled with the feeling of immense gratitude to our dearest people on Earth, our mothers. Your unconditional love and devotion envelope a person from the moment of their birth, serve as reliable support in difficult situations, give self-confidence, help achieve success and victories.

Today we have a good reason to express to you the words of sincere admiration and gratitude for your remarkable ability to combine professional activities with your main calling, which is to be hearth keepers, the keepers of traditional moral values and principles, to give birth to and raise your sons and daughters. To apologise to you for not being attentive enough to you sometimes.

Dear mothers, the state values highly your tireless, everyday work. Protection of motherhood and childhood, comprehensive support of young and large families are critical areas of the social policy in our country.

May your children grow intelligent, strong and talented, live up to their parents' expectations, give you their love and care.

I wish for your strong health, consent, wellbeing and prosperity at home, happiness and love.

Alexander Lukashenko

3. The Origins of Mother's Day

Recall too, that Mother's Day was originally created by Julia Ward Howe as part of a pacifist movement in response to the carnage of the American Civil War and the Franco Prussian War. Howe urged[12] in her *Mother's Day Proclamation* that women from all different nations come together to affirm that they:

---

11. *Available at* http://www.president.gov.by/en/press84286.html#doc [last visited January 17, 2011].

12. *Available at* http://womenshistory.about.com/od/howejwriting/a/mothers_day.htm [last visited July 1, 2011].

[W]ill not have great questions decided by irrelevant agencies,

Our husbands will not come to us, reeking with carnage, for caresses and applause.

Our sons shall not be taken from us to unlearn all that we have been able to teach them of charity, mercy and patience.

We, the women of one country, will be too tender of those of another country to allow our sons to be trained to injure theirs . . .

Howe concluded:

In the name of womanhood and humanity, I earnestly ask

That a general congress of women without limit of nationality

May be appointed and held at someplace deemed most convenient

And at the earliest period consistent with its objects,

To promote the alliance of the different nationalities,

The amicable settlement of international questions,

The great and general interests of peace.

II. Interpretations of Equality in Domestic Courts

Aristotle posited that "equality consists in the same treatment for equal persons,"[13] but as the CEDAW Committee and the Human Rights Committee have noted, equal treatment does not always result in substantive equality for women. Particularly with regard to women's access to education, employment, political power, and health, just to name a few areas, women are not on equal terms, nor can they be considered "equal persons." Because of women's reproductive functions and past inequalities, a strict form of equality is not always possible. In this section we will look at how the concepts of "equality" and "non discrimination" have been applied in some major cases from various jurisdictions. This is an important exercise because, before bringing a claim before a regional or international forum, claimants are required to exhaust domestic remedies. Thus it is important to determine how one's domestic jurisdiction might adjudicate the claim.

A. The United States' Equality Jurisprudence

Although the United States is not a party to CEDAW,[14] similar to developments in international *fora*, one may trace a shift from formal, or *de jure* equality, to more substantive equality, in the equality jurisprudence of the United States Supreme Court. In the U.S.,

---

13. ARISTOTLE, THE POLITICS (Benjamin Jowett, trans., Random House 1943) at 307.
14. CEDAW was signed by President Jimmy Carter in 1980 but has not yet been ratified by the United States Senate.

equal protection of the law is guaranteed by the Fifth and Fourteenth Amendments, and it was the equal protection issue that came before the Court in the famous case of *Brown v. Board of Education*,[15] albeit in the form of racial as opposed to gender equality. In that case the U.S. Supreme Court rejected the concept of "separate but equal" that had been established in *Plessy v. Fergusson*.[16] In *Brown*, the Court did not examine the equality of "tangible factors,"[17] as *Plessy* had, but rather analyzed whether the "effect" of the system was to deprive Petitioner of the "equal protection of the law." The Court found that segregating the races "is usually interpreted as denoting the inferiority of the negro group"[18] and that "[s]eparate education facilities are inherently unequal."[19]

Note that the United States has failed to ratify the Equal Rights Amendment (ERA), written in 1923 by Alice Paul, suffragist leader and founder of the National Women's Party. The ERA was introduced into every session of Congress between 1923 and 1972 when it was passed and sent to the states for ratification. To date only thirty five of the thirty eight states necessary for ratification have passed the ERA. The ERA provides that:

> Section 1. Equality of rights under the law shall not be denied or abridged by the United States or by any state on account of sex.
>
> Section 2. The Congress shall have the power to enforce, by appropriate legislation, the provisions of this article
>
> Section 3. This amendment shall take effect two years after the date of ratification.

Although the ERA failed to pass, in 1964 Congress passed the Civil Rights Act. The prohibition against discrimination on the basis of sex was added as a last minute amendment. Its implications were therefore somewhat unclear, which made the courts' job of interpreting and applying it more challenging. As Justice Rehnquist later noted in *Meritor Savings Bank v. Vinson*[20] "[t]he prohibition against discrimination based on sex was added to Title VII at the last minute on the floor of the House of Representatives ... the bill quickly passed as amended, and we are left with little legislative history to guide us in interpreting the Act's prohibition against discrimination based on 'sex.'"

1. *Reed v. Reed*[21]

The U.S. Supreme Court's first opportunity to confront the equality issue with regard to gender came in the 1971 case of *Reed v. Reed* where Sally and Richard Reed, the divorced parents of a deceased sixteen year old, both sought to be appointed the executor of his estate. Sally Reed challenged an Idaho statute that afforded preference to men as administrators of estates. The Idaho Supreme Court ruled against Ms. Reed, finding that in enacting the statute in question, the legislature may have reasonably concluded that "men are better qualified to act as [administrators] than are women."[22] The court also

---

15. 347 U.S. 483 (1954). In many countries early equality jurisprudence focused on racial equality. This development is also mirrored in the international community where the Convention on All Forms of Racial Discrimination (CERD) came into existence some 15 years before CEDAW.

16. 163 U.S. 567 (1896).

17. In *Brown*, these factors included buildings, curricula, and qualifications and salaries of teachers.

18. *Id*. at 492.

19. *Id*.

20. 477 U.S. 57, at 63–64.

21. 404 U.S. 71 (1971).

22. 465 P.2d 635, 638 (Idaho 1970).

went on to find that the preference for men served the legitimate purpose of "curtailing litigation over the appointment of administrators."[23] The U.S. Supreme Court came to a very different conclusion, finding that the statute violated the Equal Protection clause, and holding that "[t]o give a mandatory preference to members of either sex over the other, merely to accomplish the elimination of hearings on the merits is to make the very kind of arbitrary legislative choice forbidden by the equal protection Clause of the Fourteenth Amendment."[24]

Reed is a notable case for a number of reasons, chief among them is obviously the Court's explicit rejection of assigned gender preferences. Another noteworthy aspect of the case is the fact that Sally Reed was ably represented by (among others) a young volunteer attorney for the ACLU, who was then teaching at Rutgers Law School — Ruth Bader Ginsburg. In her brief, Ginsburg urged the Court to find gender a "suspect class" and thus subject the law to the "strict scrutiny" standard. Ginsburg devoted forty six pages of her brief to this argument, and only seven pages to the fallback argument that the Court should subject the law to a "rational basis" level of scrutiny. The Summary of the Argument from the ACLU brief appears below:

a. Brief of Appellant[25]

Summary of Argument

I

Idaho Code, Sec. 15-314, which provides that as between persons "equally entitled to administer [a decedent's estate], males must be preferred to females," denies appellant, an "equally entitled" woman, the equal protection of the laws.

The sex line drawn by Sec. 15-314, mandating subordination of women to men without regard to individual capacity, creates a "suspect classification" requiring close judicial scrutiny. Although the legislature may distinguish between individuals on the basis of their need or ability, it is presumptively impermissible to distinguish on the basis of an unalterable identifying trait over which the individual has no control and for which he or she should not be disadvantaged by the law. Legislative discrimination grounded on sex, for purposes unrelated to any biological difference between the sexes, ranks with legislative discrimination based on race, another congenital, unalterable trait of birth, and merits no greater judicial deference.

The distance to equal opportunity for women in the United States remains considerable in face of the pervasive social, cultural and legal roots of sex-based discrimination. As other groups that have been assisted toward full equality before the law via the "suspect classification" doctrine, women are sparsely represented in legislative and policy-making chambers and lack political power to remedy the discriminatory treatment they are accorded in the law and in society generally. Absent firm constitutional foundation for equal treatment of men and women by the law, women seeking to be judged on their individual merits will continue to encounter law-sanctioned obstacles.

Prior decisions of this Court have contributed to the separate and unequal status of women in the United States. But the national conscience has been awakened to the some-

---

23. *Id.*
24. 404 U.S. at 76.
25. 1971 WL 133596.

times subtle assignment of inferior status to women by the dominant male culture. In very recent years, both federal and state courts have expressed sharp criticism of lines drawn or sanctioned by governmental authority on the basis of sex. With some notable exceptions, for example, the case at bar, these lines have not survived judicial scrutiny. The time is ripe for this Court to repudiate the premise that, with minimal justification, the legislature may draw "a sharp line between the sexes," just as this Court has repudiated once settled law that differential treatment of the races is constitutionally permissible. At the very least the Court should reverse the presumption of rationality when sex-based discrimination is implicated and, rather than requiring the party attacking a statute to show that the classification is irrational, should require the statute's proponent to prove it rational.

Biological differences between the sexes bear no relation-ship to the duties performed by an administrator. Idaho's interest in administrative convenience, served by excluding women who would compete with men for appointment as an administrator, falls far short of a compelling state interest when appraised in light of the interest of the class against which the statute discriminates—an interest in treatment by the law as full human personalities. If sex is a "suspect classification," a state interest in avoiding a hearing cannot justify rank discrimination against a person solely on the ground that she is a female.

II

The sex line drawn by sec. 15-314, arbitrarily ranking the woman as inferior to the man by directing that the probate court take no account of the respective qualifications of the individuals involved, lacks a fair and substantial relation to a permissible legislative purpose. The judgment that "in general men are better qualified to act as an administrator than are women" rests on totally unfounded assumptions of differences in mental capacity or experience relevant to the office of administrator. To eliminate a woman who shares an eligibility category with a man when there is no basis in fact to assume that women are less competent to administer than are men, is patently unreasonable and constitutionally impermissible.

Ginsburg was arguing for sex, like race, to be considered a suspect class which would require the Court to subject the statute in question to strict scrutiny. Despite these impassioned arguments, the Court chose to subject the Idaho statute to the "rational basis" test, without outright rejecting the notion of classifying gender as a "suspect class."

2. *Frontiero v. Richardson*[26]

The next major U.S. case to deal with sex discrimination was *Frontiero v. Richardson*, where Sharron Frontiero, an air force lieutenant, sued the Secretary of Defense after being denied an increased housing allowance and medical benefits for her husband, a veteran, who was also a full-time college student. Frontiero contended that a federal law, which entitled the wives of active members of the armed forces to such benefits was discriminatory, because male spouses had to prove that they were dependant on their wives for more than one half of their support before being entitled to the benefits; wives of service members, on the other hand, did not have to meet any such requirement. Counsel for the Frontiers argued that the "dissimilar treatment for men and women who are similarly situated,"

---

26. 411 U.S. 677 (1973).

constituted a violation of the Due Process Clause. Ruth Bader Ginsburg, as counsel for the Frontieros, again addressed the issue of the level of scrutiny in oral argument before the Court, cogently pleading for the Court to apply strict scrutiny. Justice Brennan could not muster a majority opinion on the Court to find that strict scrutiny was the appropriate standard. Instead he was forced to settle for a plurality opinion ruling that sex should be considered a "suspect classification" and therefore subject to strict scrutiny. On this basis the federal law was invalidated.

Brennan J.[27]

> There can be no doubt that our Nation has had a long and unfortunate history of sex discrimination. Traditionally, such discrimination was rationalized by an attitude of 'romantic paternalism' which, in practical effect, put women, not on a pedestal, but in a cage. Indeed, this paternalistic attitude became so firmly rooted in our national consciousness that, 100 years ago, a distinguished Member of this Court was able to proclaim:

>> Man is, or should be, women's protector and defender. The natural and proper timidity and delicacy which belongs to the female sex evidently unfits it for many of the occupations of civil life. The constitution of the family organization, which is founded in the divine ordinance, as well as in the nature of things, indicates the domestic sphere as that which properly belongs to the domain and functions of womanhood. The harmony, not to say identity, of interests and views which belong, or should belong, to the family institution is repugnant to the idea of a woman adopting a distinct and independent career from that of her husband....

> The paramount destiny and mission of woman are to fulfil the noble and benign offices of wife and mother. This is the law of the Creator.' Bradwell v. State of Illinois, 16 Wall. 130, 141, 21 L.Ed.2d 442 (1873) (Bradley, J., concurring).

> As a result of notions such as these, our statute books gradually became laden with gross, stereotyped distinctions between the sexes and, indeed, throughout much of the 19th century the position of women in our society was, in many respects, comparable to that of blacks under the pre-Civil War slave codes. Neither slaves nor women could hold office, serve on juries, or bring suit in their own names, and married women traditionally were denied the legal capacity to hold or convey property or to serve as legal guardians of their own children.

> It is true, of course, that the position of women in America has improved markedly in recent decades. Nevertheless, it can hardly be doubted that, in part because of the high visibility of the sex characteristic, women still face pervasive, although at times more subtle, discrimination in our educational institutions, in the job market and, perhaps most conspicuously, in the political arena.... Moreover, since sex, like race and national origin, is an immutable characteristic determined solely by the accident of birth, the imposition of special disabilities upon the members of a particular sex because of their sex would seem to violate 'the basic concept of our system that legal burdens should bear some relationship to individual responsibility....' Weber v. Aetna Casualty & Surety Co., 406 U.S. 164, 175, 92 S.Ct. 1400, 1407, 31 L.Ed.2d 768 (1972).

> And what differentiates sex from such non-suspect statuses as intelligence or physical disability, and aligns it with the recognized suspect criteria, is that the

---

27. *Id.* at 684–8.

sex characteristic frequently bears no relation to ability to perform or contribute to society. As a result, statutory distinctions between the sexes often have the effect of invidiously relegating the entire class of females to inferior legal status without regard to the actual capabilities of its individual members. The sole basis of the classification established in the challenged statutes is the sex of the individuals involved. Thus, under 37 U.S.C. §§ 401, 403, and 10 U.S.C. §§ 2072, 2076, a female member of the uniformed services seeking to obtain housing and medical benefits for her spouse must prove his dependency in fact, whereas no such burden is imposed upon male members. In addition, the statutes operate so as to deny benefits to a female member, such as appellant Sharron Frontiero, who provides less than one-half of her spouse's support, while at the same time granting such benefits to a male member who likewise provides less than one-half of his spouse's support. Thus, to this extent at least, it may fairly be said that these statutes command 'dissimilar treatment for men and women who are … similarly situated.' Reed v. Reed, 404 U.S., at 77, 92 S.Ct., at 254.

Moreover, the Government concedes that the differential treatment accorded men and women under these statutes serves no purpose other than mere 'administrative convenience.' In essence, the Government maintains that, as an empirical matter, wives in our society frequently are dependent upon their husbands, while husbands rarely are dependent upon their wives. Thus, the Government argues that Congress might reasonably have concluded that it would be both cheaper and easier simply conclusively to presume that wives of male members are financially dependent upon their husbands, while burdening female members with the task of establishing dependency in fact.

The concurring opinion signed by Chief Justice Burger, and Justices Blackmun and Powell noted that it was "unnecessary for the Court in this case to characterize sex as a suspect classification, with all of the far-reaching implications of such a holding."[28]

Questions for Discussion

1. *Listen to the oral argument of Frontiero v. Richardson — available at:*

   http://www.oyez.org/cases/1970-1979/1972/1972_71_1694/

   Note how Counsel for the Frontieros starts his argument with a recitation of the facts. Was that a persuasive device — why or why not? What do you think the Frontieros' attorney was trying to accomplish by doing this?

2. *Listen also to Ruth Bader Ginsburg's arguments about the standard of scrutiny and the classification of gender as a suspect criterion. Was it worth insisting on that classification?*

3. *Was it important for the Court to add sex to the list of suspect classifications? Why or why not?*

4. *What is the impact of a plurality as opposed to a majority opinion? How does this type of decision impact the development of the law in the area of gender equality?*

---

28. *Id.* at 691–9.

3. *United States v. Virginia*[29]

The most recent major iteration of the Court's sex equality jurisprudence came in the case of *United States v. Virginia*. There, a student who had been denied admission to Virginia Military Institute (VMI) complained to the Justice Department that VMI's male only admission policy constituted a denial of equal protection. The Justice Department sued the Commonwealth of Virginia and VMI on the basis that discrimination on the basis of sex violated Constitution's Equal Protection Clause. The District Court ruled in VMI's favor.[30] On appeal, the Fourth Circuit vacated the decision and questioned why Virginia made this type of education only available to men. The Fourth Circuit further found that the Commonwealth had failed to articulate "an important objective which supports the provision of this unique educational opportunity to men only."[31] After the Fourth Circuit remanded the case back to the District Court, VMI and the Commonwealth had three options: admit women to VMI; establish parallel institutions or programs; or abandon state support, leaving VMI free to pursue its policies as a private institution.

The Commonwealth chose to create a supposed parallel program for women, which was called the Virginia Women's Institute for Leadership (VWIL). The 4 year, state sponsored undergraduate program was located at Mary Baldwin College, a private liberal arts school for women, and would start off by enrolling about thirty women. VMI would remain all male. The District Court accepted this plan and ruled that it met the requirements of the Equal Protection Clause finding that "[T]he VMI methodology could be used to educate women and, in fact, some women ... may prefer the VMI methodology to the VWIL methodology."[32] The District Court further found that the Commonwealth was not required "to provide a mirror image VMI for women" and that the two schools would "achieve substantially similar outcomes."[33] It concluded: "If VMI marches to the beat of a drum, then Mary Baldwin marches to the melody of a fife and when the march is over, both will have arrived at the same destination."[34]

The Justice Department appealed this decision to the Fourth Circuit. This time the Court of Appeals found in favor of VMI, finding that the two parallel single sex options would provide "substantially comparable benefits."[35] The Justice Department then appealed to the Supreme Court which, per Ginsburg J.'s majority opinion, rejected the "comparable quality" of the women's program at Mary Baldwin.

———————

Ginsburg J.[36]

> The average combined SAT score of entrants at Mary Baldwin is about 100 points lower than the score for VMI freshmen. See *id.*, at 501. Mary Baldwin's faculty holds "significantly fewer Ph.D.'s than the faculty at VMI," *id.*, at 502, and receives significantly lower salaries, see Tr. 158 (testimony of James Lott, Dean of Mary Baldwin College), ... While VMI offers degrees in liberal arts, the sciences, and engineering, Mary Baldwin, at the time of trial, offered only bachelor of arts degrees. See 852 F. Supp., at 503. A VWIL student seeking to earn an engineering

———————

29. 518 U.S. 515 (1996).
30. United States v. Virginia, 766 F.Supp. 1407 (W.D. Va. 1991).
31. United States v. Virginia, 976 F.2d 890, 892 (4th Cir. 1992).
32. United States v. Virginia, 852 F.Supp.471 (W.D. Va. 1994).
33. *Id.* at 481.
34. *Id.* at 484.
35. United States v. Virginia, 44 F.3d 1229 (4th Cir. 1995).
36. United States v. Virginia, 518 U.S. 515, 526 (1996).

degree could gain one, without public support, by attending Washington University in St. Louis, Missouri, for two years, paying the required private tuition....

[T]he VWIL House would not have a military format, ... and VWIL would not require its students to eat meals together or to wear uniforms during the school day, ... In lieu of VMI's adversative method, the VWIL Task Force favored "a cooperative method which reinforces self esteem." ...

The cross petitions in this case present two ultimate issues. First, does Virginia's exclusion of women from the educational opportunities provided by VMI—extraordinary opportunities for military training and civilian leadership development—deny to women "capable of all of the individual activities required of VMI cadets," ... the equal protection of the laws guaranteed by the Fourteenth Amendment? Second, if VMI's "unique" situation, ... —as Virginia's sole single sex public institution of higher education—offends the Constitution's equal protection principle, what is the remedial requirement?

Today's skeptical scrutiny of official action denying rights or opportunities based on sex responds to volumes of history. As a plurality of this Court acknowledged a generation ago, "our Nation has had a long and unfortunate history of sex discrimination." *Frontiero* v. *Richardson*, 411 U.S. 677, 684 (1973). Through a century plus three decades and more of that history, women did not count among voters composing "We the People" not until 1920 did women gain a constitutional right to the franchise.... And for a half century thereafter, it remained the prevailing doctrine that government, both federal and state, could withhold from women opportunities accorded men so long as any "basis in reason" could be conceived for the discrimination. *See, e.g., Goesaert* v. *Cleary*, 335 U.S. 464, 467 (1948) (rejecting challenge of female tavern owner and her daughter to Michigan law denying bartender licenses to females—except for wives and daughters of male tavern owners;

In 1971, for the first time in our Nation's history, this Court ruled in favor of a woman who complained that her State had denied her the equal protection of its laws. *Reed* v. *Reed*, 404 U.S. 71, 73 (holding unconstitutional Idaho Code prescription that, among " 'several persons claiming and equally entitled to administer [a decedent's estate], males must be preferred to females' "). Since *Reed*, the Court has repeatedly recognized that neither federal nor state government acts compatibly with the equal protection principle when a law or official policy denies to women, simply because they are women, full citizenship stature— equal opportunity to aspire, achieve, participate in and contribute to society based on their individual talents and capacities. See, *e.g., Kirchberg* v. *Feenstra*, 450 U.S. 455, 462–463 (1981) (affirming invalidity of Louisiana law that made husband "head and master" of property jointly owned with his wife, giving him unilateral right to dispose of such property without his wife's consent); *Stanton* v. *Stanton*, 421 U.S. 7 (1975) (invalidating Utah requirement that parents support boys until age 21, girls only until age 18) ...

Focusing on the differential treatment or denial of opportunity for which relief is sought, the reviewing court must determine whether the proffered justification is "exceedingly persuasive." The burden of justification is demanding and it rests entirely on the State. See *Mississippi Univ. for Women*, 458 U.S., at 724. The State must show "at least that the [challenged] classification serves 'important governmental objectives and that the discriminatory means employed' are 'substantially related to the achievement of those objectives.'" ... The justification must be genuine, not hypothesized or invented *post hoc* in response to litigation. And it must not rely on overbroad generalizations about the different talents, capacities, or preferences of males and females ...

Sex classifications may be used to compensate women "for particular economic disabilities [they have] suffered," *Califano* v. *Webster*, 430 U.S. 313, 320 (1977) *(per curiam)*, to "promot[e] equal employment opportunity," see *California Federal Sav. & Loan Assn.* v. *Guerra*, 479 U.S. 272, 289 (1987), to advance full development of the talent and capacities of our Nation's people. But such classifications may not be used, as they once were, see *Goesaert*, 335 U.S., at 467, to create or perpetuate the legal, social, and economic inferiority of women.

Measuring the record in this case against the review standard just described, we conclude that Virginia has shown no "exceedingly persuasive justification" for excluding all women from the citizen soldier training afforded by VMI. We therefore affirm the Fourth Circuit's initial judgment, which held that Virginia had violated the Fourteenth Amendment's Equal Protection Clause. Because the remedy proffered by Virginia—the Mary Baldwin VWIL program—does not cure the constitutional violation, *i.e.*, it does not provide equal opportunity, we reverse the Fourth Circuit's final judgment in this case.

———

Justice Ginsburg therefore found that the Court would not endorse a program which "denies to women, simply because they are women, full citizenship stature—equal opportunity to aspire, achieve, participate in and contribute to society."[37] Ginsburg wrote that while "Virginia serves the state's sons, it makes no provision whatever for her daughters. That is not equal protection."[38]

a. Justice Scalia's Dissent

Justice Scalia filed the sole dissent in the case, noting that:[39]

Much of the Court's opinion is devoted to deprecating the closed mindedness of our forebears with regard to women's education, and even with regard to the treatment of women in areas that have nothing to do with education. Closed minded they were—as every age is, including our own, with regard to matters it cannot guess, because it simply does not consider them debatable. The virtue of a democratic system with a First Amendment is that it readily enables the people, over time, to be persuaded that what they took for granted is not so, and to change their laws accordingly. That system is destroyed if the smug assurances of each age are removed from the democratic process and written into the Constitution.

It is my view that "when a practice not expressly prohibited by the text of the Bill of Rights bears the endorsement of a long tradition of open, widespread, and unchallenged use that dates back to the beginning of the Republic, we have no proper basis for striking it down." *Rutan* v. *Republican Party of Ill.*, 497 U.S. 62, 95 (1990) (Scalia, J., dissenting). The same applies, *mutatis mutandis,* to a practice asserted to be in violation of the post-Civil War Fourteenth Amendment ...

———

37. *Id.* at 528 *et seq.*
38. *Id.*
39. Justice Clarence Thomas recused himself because his son was attending VMI.

The all male constitution of VMI comes squarely within such a governing tradition. Founded by the Commonwealth of Virginia in 1839 and continuously maintained by it since, VMI has always admitted only men. And in that regard it has not been unusual ... And all the federal military colleges — West Point, the Naval Academy at Annapolis, and even the Air Force Academy, which was not established until 1954 — admitted only males for most of their history. Their admission of women in 1976 (upon which the Court today relies, see ...), came not by court decree, but because the people, through their elected representatives, decreed a change ... In other words, the tradition of having government funded military schools for men is as well rooted in the traditions of this country as the tradition of sending only men into military combat. The people may decide to change the one tradition, like the other, through democratic processes; but the assertion that either tradition has been unconstitutional through the centuries is not law, but politics smuggled into law.

Justice Scalia also took issue with the Court's use of the phrase "exceedingly persuasive justification" as the test for determining whether the State had demonstrated sufficient that the discriminatory means were substantially related to important governmental objectives finding that:[40]

Only the amorphous "exceedingly persuasive justification" phrase, and not the standard elaboration of intermediate scrutiny, can be made to yield this conclusion that VMI's single sex composition is unconstitutional because there exist several women (or, one would have to conclude under the Court's reasoning, a single woman) willing and able to undertake VMI's program. Intermediate scrutiny has never required a least restrictive means analysis, but only a "substantial relation" between the classification and the state interests that it serves. Thus, in *Califano v. Webster*, 430 U.S. 313 (1977) *(per curiam)*, we upheld a congressional statute that provided higher Social Security benefits for women than for men. We reasoned that "women ... as such have been unfairly hindered from earning as much as men," but we did not require proof that each woman so benefited had suffered discrimination or that each disadvantaged man had not; it was sufficient that even under the former congressional scheme "women *on the average* received lower retirement benefits than men." ... The reasoning in our other intermediate scrutiny cases has similarly required only a substantial relation between end and means, not a perfect fit....

The brief filed on behalf of the United States did not reference CEDAW at all; not surprisingly since the U.S. has not ratified the Convention. Moreover, several members of the Court are not known to find International Law persuasive. The point headings for the brief on the merits filed on behalf of the United States appear below:

b. Brief of Petitioner, the United States — Summary of the Argument[41]

Since its founding in 1839, the Virginia Military Institute has not admitted women. That practice has correctly been held to violate the Equal Protection Clause, and the question before the court in this case is how that violation should be remedied. Respondents have argued that the value to men of a men-only VMI is an absolute barrier to women's admission. The remedy they chose continues to maintain VMI exclusively for men, and

---

40. *Id.* at 573.
41. 1995 WL 703403.

offers an alternative for women that is admittedly separate, different, and unequal. They defend that plan on the basis of harmful sex-role stereotypes, and continue to resist the determination of liability. The program for women that they sponsored-itself a constitutionally inadequate remedy-in their view provides women more than they constitutionally deserve.

Women are entitled to equal access to all the benefits that VMI seeks to provide exclusively to men. Women who, but for their sex, are qualified for VMI and want to go to VMI are entitled to an equal opportunity to attend the program they find more valuable; they cannot be relegated to a separate and substantially different education. The only adequate redress for women's unconstitutional exclusion from VMI is to order that VMI's men-only admissions policy be ended.

I.A. Traditional remedial principles demand a remedy that closely fits the violation. Once a constitutional violation is identified, the court's remedial order must eradicate, to the greatest extent possible, the harm caused by the unconstitutional conduct. Application of that principle makes it evident that an order enjoining VMI's men-only admission policy is the only adequate remedy in this case, and that the remedy approved by the court of appeals falls far short of the goal of providing complete relief.

VMI's men-only admissions policy has caused and continues to cause both tangible and intangible harms. It has deprived women of the VMI educational experience, which is unlike the experience at any other college in Virginia. VMI has an intensive, highly structured military-style educational program that challenges students to achieve more than they might otherwise have accomplished, and that has been remarkably successful in producing leaders in male-dominated careers. Women barred from VMI are also excluded from membership in the circle of VMI's powerful alumni and from the particular prestige carried by a VMI degree. Finally, VMI's admissions policy has communicated a message that, in the eyes of the Commonwealth, women do not possess the qualities of self-discipline, ability to withstand stress, and respect for hierarchy that are widely associated with VMI. The only way to offer women the benefits of VMI, and to cure the stigma imposed on women by their historical exclusion, is to prohibit its men-only admissions policy.

B. The court of appeals viewed the prospect of women's admission to VMI as presenting a "Catch 22" for women, because, in its view, women's admission would "destroy" the very opportunity women seek to share. Under that theory, respondents' interest in preserving VMI's benefits exclusively for men outweighs women's right to equal treatment. That theory is, not surprisingly, completely without support in modern equal protection doctrine. Preserving a benefit for one sex is not an adequate reason for denying it to the other; sex discrimination is not self-justifying.

Respondents have not, in any event, shown that integration of women at VMI would be impossible, or even that the changes that might be required at VMI when women are admitted would have a substantial or significant negative impact on the character or the effectiveness of VMI's educational program. Accommodations necessary to preserve privacy or account for physical differences would not change the fundamental nature of the program. The court of appeals' concern that the "decency that still permeates the relationship between the sexes" would suffer as a result of women's admission to VMI is constitutionally invalid; it is another example in a long history of official discriminations against and exclusions of women in the name of protecting them. The experience of co-education at the federal military service academies also shows that the admission of women into a rigorous, military-style educational program does not impair any governmental interest in producing military personnel, let alone "citizen-soldiers."

II. A. The court of appeals approved a remedy that is itself unconstitutional. It would be appropriate for the Court to review that remedy under strict scrutiny, because differences in treatment based solely on sex are inherently suspect. The long history of discrimination against women, the general irrelevance of sex as a ground for official decision-making, and women's continuing underrepresentation in government, all support the application of strict scrutiny here.

B. The constitutional violation in this case is, however, plain even under intermediate scrutiny. The approved remedy was designed, defended, and approved through the use of impermissible sex-stereotypes and overgeneralizations about the capacities and aspirations of "most" men and "most" women. Equal protection precludes reliance on such stereotypes and generalizations to foreclose individual opportunity. The inequality of treatment caused by the substantial differences between the sex-segregated VMI and VWIL programs is invalid under intermediate scrutiny.

Respondents' asserted interest in providing single-sex education cannot support the VWIL remedy. Respondents have shown no real interest in providing single-sex education, but have asserted it post hoc, in order to reserve VMI for men only. An interest in providing single-sex education would, in any event, not validate a program that offers substantially different programs and benefits to men and women and that bases those differences on invalid assumptions about the limited abilities of women.

———————

The Petitioner's brief argued both the strict scrutiny and the intermediate scrutiny standard. Most of the briefs filed by amici focused on the strict scrutiny standard, arguing that sex like race should be considered a suspect classification. One passing mention of international law and standards may be found in the brief of the ACLU's National Women's Law Center, which referred to Trends and Statistics regarding women on page 25 of their brief.[42] Another notable citation in their brief was a citation to an article written by Ruth Bader Ginsburg in the 1976 Human Rights Journal. The article was entitled "*Women as Full Members of the Club: An Evolving American Ideal.*"[43]

c. Brief Filed by Amici American Association of University Professors, the Center for Women Policy Studies and Others— Summary of the Argument

Virginia Military Institute, a state-supported all-male school, excludes otherwise qualified female students solely because of their sex. The question before this Court on cross-petitions for a writ of certiorari is whether that admissions policy violates the Equal Protection Clause and, if so, whether the violation can be cured by the creation of a separate single-sex program for women.

VMI has sought to justify its single-sex status by relying on purportedly scientific evidence relating to alleged physiological and psychological differences between the sexes and the purported benefits to males from single-sex education at VMI. Even if these claims were accurate, however, they would be insufficient as a matter of law, because sex-based

———————

42. The cite appears on p. 25 of the brief and refers generally to the work on the United Nations (United Nations, The World's Women: 1995 Trends and Statistics 152 (1995). CEDAW itself does not merit a point heading or even sub point heading in the brief.

43. Ruth Bader Ginsburg, *Women as Full Members of the Club: An Evolving American Ideal*, 6 Hum. Rts. 1 (1976–77).

classifications that rely on stereotypes violate equal protection even if some statistical support "can be conjured up." *J.E.B. v. Alabama ex rel. T.B.*, 114 S. Ct. 1419, 1427 n.11 (1994). Likewise, in defense of the remedial plan, VMI offers "'the very stereotype the law condemns.'" *Id.* at 1426. None of the interests asserted by VMI provides the "exceedingly persuasive" rationale necessary to justify a policy that explicitly relies on stereotypes and perpetuates historical patterns of discrimination: it is not relevant if "the benefited class profits from the classification," nor can there be a legitimate interest in providing men with a college "composed of members of a particular ... gender." *Mississippi Univ. for Women v. Hogan,* 458 U.S. 718, 731 n.17 (1982); *J.E.B.,* 114 S. Ct. at 1430 (O'Connor, J. concurring), 1434 (Kennedy, J. concurring).

To avoid the plain import of the law, the lower courts relied on tenuous theories about alleged sex-based differences and the purported benefits of single-sex education for men. These propositions were often advanced by witnesses with no apparent expertise, whose testimony lacks necessary indicia of scientific validity and evidentiary reliability. See Fed. R. Evid. 702–703, 28 U.S.C.A.; *Daubert v. Merrell Dow Pharmaceuticals*, 113 S. Ct. 2786 (1993). The record oversimplifies highly complex areas of research and misinterprets scholarly research, including that of Carol Gilligan and Valerie Lee, amici curiae herein. Such "proofs" are clearly inadequate to justify discrimination, both in themselves and as a matter of law.

The only explicit citation to CEDAW is found in the amicus brief of the Employment Law Center and others,[44] and that cite comes only in a footnote on page 28 of the brief, justifying programs intended to remedy past discrimination. CEDAW has thus not played a large role in addressing discrimination against women in the United States.

Some amici were concerned that if the Court found VMI in violation of the Equal Protection clause, that it would mean the end of single sex education in the United States. Several supporters of single sex education argue that such education can be very beneficial for girls, and they were concerned about the impact of the decision on women's colleges. Yet, twenty five women's colleges filed a brief in support of the Petitioner,[45] arguing that "*A Single-Gender Public College May Not Rely on Stereotyped Generalizations about Men and Women in Justifying Its Admissions Policy,*" and that even if the Court found in favor of the Petitioner, that would not undermine or threaten the maintenance of women's colleges.

One theme that strongly emerged from this case was the concept of stereotyping based on gender. Many of the briefs are replete with references to gender stereotyping, and indeed, the testimony of several of the witnesses for VMI at the trial level stage of this litigation provide classic examples of gender stereotyping. Consider the following testimony of Dean Heather Wilson of the VWIL program at Mary Baldwin College, who was explaining why the VWIL program did not model itself on the VMI program.

---

44. Brief of the Employment Law Center, A Project of the Legal Aid Society of San Francisco, Equal Rights Advocates, Inc., Chinese for Affirmative Action, National Economic Development and Law Center, Human Rights Advocates, Women's Employment Rights Clinic (Golden Gate University School of Law), Professor Maria Blanco, Professor Connie De La Vega, Professor Marci Seville, and Professor Stephanie Wildman as Amici Curiae in Support of Petitioner.

45. 1995 WL 702837.

d. Testimony of Dean Heather Wilson of the VWIL Program at Mary Baldwin College

The VMI model wasn't adopted [for VWIL] because young men and young women of 18 come to college, having had different experiences in their lives. I can't even tell you when it starts except that I know that a friend of mine is [a] clinical psychologist [and] has a four year old daughter who she is trying to raise very carefully.... Her four year old's favorite movie is Aladdin ... In the movie Aladdin, and this is representative of what young children are taking in, the princess, even though she has a large tiger at her command, has to wait to be rescued by Aladdin.

Children[s'] stories are filled with things like this.... [W]omen internalize these messages; they should take the passive role not the active role ...[46]

[Y]oung men [in fraternities] will paddle their pledges; they will brand them; they will make them consume alcohol and will make them eat disgusting things ... Young women [in sororities] will give flowers, write poems ...[47]

Among the generalizations and stereotypes offered by another witness for VMI, David Riesman, were the following:

e. Testimony of David Riesman for VMI

[W]omen at the present so often flounder [with regard to] [s]patial things, geometric things, topology, math and physics, and leadership itself ...

When the boys have a chance to run on the school track, [t]hey run and they run and they run and they run ...

When girls have a chance to go up on the track, they don't stick at it long ...

One reason I suspect [women] don't do as well in verbal tests, they don't read as many sports stories as boys do ...

In the rat system [at VMI] one has one's buddies to endure it with one, and one is being what boys are supposed to be, brave, physically hardy, unafraid.[48]

Eliminating gender based stereotypes is one of the primary focuses of CEDAW. Had the United States been a party to the Convention, perhaps Petitioner could have argued among other arguments, a violation of Article 5 which requires state parties to:

take all appropriate measures:

(a) To modify the social and cultural patterns of conduct of men and women, with a view to achieving the elimination of prejudices and customary and all other practices which are based on the idea of the inferiority or the superiority of either of the sexes or on stereotyped roles for men and women;

---

46. Testimony at 595–9.
47. *Id.* at 599.
48. *Id.* at 684–85 and Tr.II at 538, 546.

Questions for Discussion

1. *Do you think gender should be classified as a "suspect class" thus meriting a "strict scrutiny" approach? Why or why not?*

2. *Would it be possible to create a "separate but equal" facility for women or has this decision ruled out that possibility?*

3. *Some social science research seems to show that girls do better in single sex classes during high school. What ramifications, if any, does this decision have for publicly funded high schools that try to create single sex classes?*

B. Canada's Equality Jurisprudence

1. *Andrews v. Law Society of British Columbia*[49]

Like the U.S.' equality jurisprudence, Canada's equality jurisprudence first evolved outside of the gender context. Canada's Bill of Rights guarantees equality and equal protection of law under Section 1[50] and Section 15(1) of the Canadian Charter of Rights and Freedoms.[51] In *Andrews v. Law Society of British Columbia*, a British citizen who otherwise met all qualifications for admission to the Bar in Canada was denied admission to the Bar because he was not a Canadian citizen. Andrews sued, alleging a violation of § 15(1) of the Charter. The Court, per Dickson C.J. and McIntyre, Lamer, Wilson and L'Heureux-Dube, held that:[52]

> The "similarly situated should be similarly treated" approach will not necessarily result in equality nor will every distinction or differentiation in treatment necessarily result in inequality. The words "without discrimination" in § 15 are crucial.

> Discrimination is a distinction which, whether intentional or not but based on grounds relating to personal characteristics of the individual or group, has an effect which imposes disadvantages not imposed upon others or which withholds or limits access to advantages available to other members of society. Distinctions based on personal characteristics attributed to an individual solely on the basis of association with a group will rarely escape the charge of discrimination, while those based on an individual's merits and capacities will rarely be so classed ...

---

49. [1989] 1 S.C.R. 143.

50. Section 1 of the Canadian Bill of Rights provides that:

1. (a) It is hereby recognized and declared that in Canada there have existed and shall continue to exist without discrimination by reason of race, national origin, colour, religion or sex, the following human rights and fundamental freedoms, namely,

(b) the right of the individual to equality before the law and the protection of the law ...

51. Section 15(1) provides that: 15(1) Every individual is equal before and under the law and has the right to the equal protection and equal benefit of the law without discrimination and, in particular, without discrimination based on race, national or ethnic origin, colour, religion, sex, age or mental or physical disability.

52. *Id.* at 146 *et seq.*

[T]he Charter requires a two-step approach to § 15(1). The first step is to determine whether or not an infringement of a guaranteed right has occurred. The second step is to determine whether, if there has been an infringement, it can be justified under § 1. The two steps must be kept analytically distinct because of the different attribution of the burden of proof; the citizen must establish the infringement of his or her Charter right and the state must justify the infringement.

The grounds of discrimination enumerated in § 15(1) are not exhaustive ...

The words "without discrimination" require more than a mere finding of distinction between the treatment of groups or individuals. These words are a form of qualifier built into § 15 itself and limit those distinctions which are forbidden by the section to those which involve prejudice or disadvantage. The effect of the impugned distinction or classification on the complainant must be considered. Given that not all distinctions and differentiations created by law are discriminatory, a complainant under § 15(1) must show not only that he or she is not receiving equal treatment before and under the law or that the law has a differential impact on him or her in the protection or benefit of the law but must show in addition that the law is discriminatory.

A rule which bars an entire class of persons from certain forms of employment, solely on the grounds of a lack of citizenship status and without consideration of educational and professional qualifications or the other attributes or merits of individuals in the group, infringes § 15 equality rights.

The Court went on to hold that Andrews' denial of admission to the Bar on the grounds of citizenship was not justified.

2. *Symes v. Canada*

The Canadian Supreme Court's consideration of equality in a gender related context arose in the case of *Symes v. Canada*,[53] where a female attorney appealed the decision of the tax authority to disallow her claiming childcare expenses as a business rather than a personal deduction. In finding that the tax authority had properly characterized these deductions as personal rather than business deductions, the Supreme Court held that:

There has been no violation of § 15(1) of the *Charter* in this case. Since § 63 constitutes a complete code with respect to child care expenses, it is the proper focus of the *Charter* argument. The appellant has not demonstrated a violation of § 15(1) of the *Charter* with respect to § 63 as she has not proved that § 63 draws a distinction based upon the personal characteristic of sex. While it is clear that women disproportionately bear the burden of child care in society, it has not been shown that women disproportionately incur child care expenses. Although the appellant has overwhelmingly demonstrated how the issue of child care negatively affects women in employment terms, proof that women incur social costs is not sufficient proof that they incur child care expenses.

L'Heureux-Dubé J. dissenting:

As my colleague asserts, child care expenses have traditionally been viewed as expenses that were not incurred for the purpose of gaining or producing income,

---

53. [1993] 4 S.C.R. 695 (internal citations omitted).

as they were considered personal in nature and, accordingly, could not be regarded as commercial. My colleague is of the view (at pp. 742–43) that: ...

[T]here *is* value in the traditional tax law test which seeks to identify those expenses which simply make a taxpayer available to the business, and which proceeds to classify such expenses as "personal" for the reason that a "personal need" is being fulfilled. [Emphasis in original.]

In my view, such a test serves no purpose. The rationale of availability to the business is neither objective nor determinative. To be available for the business is the first requirement of doing business, otherwise, there can be no business. In this regard, it would be unthinkable for a businessperson's special needs, for example those associated with a disability, to be ineligible for deduction because they satisfy a "personal need". A woman's need for child care in order to do business is no different. One's personal needs can simply not be objectively determined, they are by their very definition subjective.

Courts in the past, and the Court of Appeal in this case, have also always assumed that commercial needs were an objectively neutral set of needs. As a consequence, they did not examine the close relationship between child care and women's business income. It is crucial, in my view, to examine the link between child care and the generation of income from business, as did Cullen J. After consideration of the evidence of the expert witness Dr. Armstrong, the trial judge went on to say (at p. 72): ...

[T]here has been a significant social change in the late 1970s and into the 1980s, in terms of the influx of women of child-bearing age into business and into the workplace.

Dr. Armstrong testified that dramatic and fundamental changes have been taking place in both the labour market and the family structure over the past 40 years. In 1951, only 24 percent of Canadian women participated in the labour force. By 1987, this number had risen to 56 percent.

Further, the increase was most dramatic for women in their childbearing years, with nearly three-quarters of women between the ages of 16 and 44 being counted as members of the labour force, particularly in the 1980s. Today, a majority of women, even those with very young children, are now in the labour force. Fully 70 percent of employed mothers with children younger than six years old work *full time*, as do 75 percent of employed mothers with school-age children (6 to 15 years). Current forecasts suggest that by the year 2000, fully 88 percent of women aged 25 to 34 years will be in the work force. This increasing trend is particularly noteworthy, since women aged 25 to 34 years are the group most likely to have young children at home, thus requiring child care. It is evident that for most Canadian families, the issue of child care is of crucial importance.

It is with these statistics and expert testimony in mind that we must consider whether child care expenses can be accommodated within the definition of a business expense. In this regard, I agree with Cullen J.'s thoughtful and thorough analysis of the complex issues in this case, which recognizes the evolution of our societal structure and mandates that the interpretation of statutes be done in context, not in a vacuum ...

Our Court has, in the past, altered its interpretation of legislation in a number of cases to conform with our changing social framework ... Furthermore, the respect of *Charter* values must be at the forefront of statutory interpretation ...

Human rights legislation is intended to give rise, amongst other things, to individual rights of vital importance, rights capable of enforcement, in the final analysis, in a court of law. I recognize that in the construction of such legislation the words of the Act must be given their plain meaning, but it is equally important that the rights enunciated be given their full recognition and effect. We should not search for ways and means to minimize those rights and to enfeeble their proper impact....

In my view, this approach is equally apposite in the case at hand. The provision for deduction pursuant to §9(1) should also be given a "fair, large and liberal interpretation".

In the past, the scope of deductible business disbursements has been expanded constantly. It has been held to include a wide array of expenditures, such as club dues, meals and entertainment expenses, car expenses, home office expenses, legal and accounting fees, to name only a few....

There is no dispute that salaries paid to employees are deductible as business expenses, provided they are laid out to earn income and are reasonable. Further, under certain circumstances, wages or salaries paid to spouses or children are also deductible as business expenses. If this is so, the plaintiff contends, why shouldn't the wages paid to the plaintiff's nanny be deductible as a business expense? Certainly, if the plaintiff hired a junior lawyer or articling student whose duties also included looking after the partner's children (if perhaps a daycare service was provided by the firm), there would be no dispute that the wages of the junior or the articling student would be deductible as a business expense....

The multiplicity of tests, in my view, leaves it open for one to conclude that any legitimate expense incurred in relation to a business may be deducted as a business expense. In fact, in this regard, Brooks confirms that a judge's personal experience may strongly influence the conclusion that he or she may reach as to whether a particular disbursement may be classified as a business expense. He writes (at p. 259):

> Judges know on the basis of their own experience that an expense incurred under certain circumstances would be incurred by them for a personal purpose; they infer, therefore, that it is probable that some other person, under similar circumstances, would incur the expense for the same purpose.

When we look at the case law concerning the interpretation of "business expense", it is clear that this area of law is premised on the traditional view of business as a male enterprise and that the concept of a business expense has itself been constructed on the basis of the needs of business*men*. This is neither a surprising nor a sinister realization, as the evidence well illustrates that it has only been in fairly recent years that women have increasingly moved into the world of business as into other fields, such as law and medicine. The definition of "business expense" was shaped to reflect the experience of business*men*, and the ways in which they engaged in business ... As a consequence, the male standard now frames the backdrop of assumptions against which expenses are determined to be, or not to be, legitimate business expenses. Against this backdrop, it is hardly surprising that child care was seen as irrelevant to the end of gaining or producing income from business but rather as a personal non-deductible expense.

As Cullen J. recognized, the world of yesterday is not the world of today. In 1993, the world of business is increasingly populated by both men *and* women and the meaning of "business expense" must account for the experiences of all participants in the field. This fact is enhanced by expert evidence which indicates that the practices and requirements of businesswomen may, in fact, differ from those of businessmen. When we look at the current situation, it becomes clear that one of the critical differences in the needs of businessmen and businesswomen is the importance of child care for business people with children, particularly women. Cullen J., as confirmed by the expert evidence before him, recognized that child care is vital to women's ability to earn an income. In this regard, I am wholly in agreement with Cullen J.'s conclusion that it made "good business sense" for Ms. Symes to hire child care and that this expense should come within the calculation of profit. In my view, Ms. Symes' child care expenses come within the definition of "the purpose of gaining or producing income" and, as a result, are not prevented by the wording of § 18(1)(*a*) from deduction under § 9(1)....

If we survey the experience of many men, it is apparent why it may seem intuitively obvious to some of them that child care is clearly within the personal realm. This conclusion may, in many ways, reflect many men's experience of child care responsibilities. In fact, the evidence before the Court indicates that, for most men, the responsibility of children does not impact on the number of hours they work, nor does it affect their ability to work. Further, very few men indicated that they made any work-related decisions on the basis of child-raising responsibilities. The same simply cannot currently be said for women. For women, business and family life are not so distinct and, in many ways, any such distinction is completely unreal, since a woman's ability to even participate in the work force may be completely contingent on her ability to acquire child care. The decision to retain child care is an inextricable part of the decision to work, in business or otherwise.

Child care ... is an expense ... which necessarily arises only when both parents are employed ... A working mother's provision for child care is a nondiscretionary expense directly related to the fact of her employment.

One of the main causes of discrimination against women lawyers is the culture that surrounds work in the legal profession. That culture has been shaped by and for male lawyers. It is predicated on historical work patterns that assume that lawyers do not have significant family responsibilities. The "hidden gender" of the current arrangements for legal work manifests itself in many ways, including: the extremely long and irregular hours of work; assumptions about the availability of domestic labour to support a lawyer's activities at work; promotion within law firms which is incompatible with the child bearing and child rearing cycles of most women's lives; and the perceived conflict between allegiances owed to work and family.

Particularly with respect to child care responsibilities, provincial surveys provided clear evidence that women lawyers bear by far a greater responsibility for child care than do their male counterparts ...

The proportion of responsibility borne by women lawyers for their children is almost double that borne by male lawyers.

The Saskatchewan survey revealed that women assume primary responsibility for child care in all areas broken down by activity. For example, 59% of women report they care for children when the latter are ill compared to only 4% of men....

Although both male and female lawyers have experienced stress as a result of competing demands of career and child care responsibilities, women reported negative material effects in the form of loss of income or reduced career opportunities to a degree not reported by men....

As a consequence, one must ask whether the many business deductions available, for cars, for club dues and fees, for lavish entertainment and the wining and dining of clients and customers, and for substantial charitable donations, are so obviously business expenses rather than personal ones. Although potentially personal, each one of these expenses has been accepted as a legitimate business expense and, as each reflects a real cost incurred by certain kinds of business people to produce income from business, a deduction has been allowed. The real costs incurred by businesswomen with children are no less real, no less worthy of consideration and no less incurred in order to gain or produce income from business ...

The decision to have children is not like any other "consumption" decision. To describe the raising of children in comparable terms to "choosing" to purchase a certain kind of automobile or live in a certain dwelling is simply untenable. As well, the many complexities surrounding child care make it inappropriate to adopt the language of voluntary assumption of costs, where those costs may, in fact, be allocated in a discriminatory fashion — the burden falling primarily on women.

In conclusion, to the question of whether child care expenses are precluded from being deducted as a business expense under § 9(1) by the interplay of either § 18(1)(*a*) or § 18(1)(*h*) of the *Act*, I answer that child care may be held to be a business expense deductible pursuant to §§ 9(1), 18(1)(*a*) and 18(1)(*h*) of the *Act*, all other criteria being respected. This result leads me to the most crucial consideration in this appeal, that is whether § 63 of the *Act* precludes the deduction of child care expenses as a business expense. Here, I part company with my colleague since, in my view, § 63 of the *Act*, properly interpreted, is no such bar.

Questions for Discussion

1. *Do you agree with this judge's dissenting view that "the definition of 'business expense' was shaped to reflect the experience of business**men**, and the ways in which they engaged in business"? Should and could the Court have taken judicial notice of that?*

2. *What about the contention that "Judges know on the basis of their own experience that an expense incurred under certain circumstances would be incurred by them for a personal purpose; they infer, therefore, that it is probable that some other person, under similar circumstances, would incur the expense for the same purpose." Does that mean that we should ensure that there are equal numbers of male and female judges on the bench so that litigants' experiences will resonate with at least some of the judges?*

3. The Women's Court of Canada

Outraged with some of the decisions of the Canadian Supreme Court, a group of Canadian feminists and academics got together in 2004, to create the Women's Court of Canada. The Court is not an official body, but rather a group of academics and lawyers who take a feminist approach to Canada's jurisprudence, and take it upon themselves to rewrite many of the major decisions of the Canadian Supreme Court. The Women's Court rewrites the decisions from the perspective of women,[54] and with the notion of equality in mind. They publish their decisions on their website on the internet. Consider their version of *Symes:*[55]

> Ms. Symes's claim is at once simple and complex. She asks this Court to confirm that childcare costs that she incurred to allow her to engage in her business activities are deductible as business expenses under the Income Tax Act (ITA), R.S.C. 1952, c. 148. At one level, this claim is a relatively simple issue relating to statutory interpretation of the proper treatment of childcare expenses under the ITA. At another level, it raises complex issues regarding the role of equality rights and women's status within Canadian society. As in all equality claims, a resolution of the issues requires a deep appreciation of the full political, social, and economic context.... The Canadian Constitution, and, in particular, the fundamental constitutional principle of substantive equality, demands an ongoing process of scrutiny of the underlying norms that shape laws and policies in order to reveal any embedded structures of inequality and to contribute to the overreaching goal of substantive equality. Societal responsibility for childcare and its impact on women's equality is as vitally important an issue today, in 2006 before this court, as it was when this claim was decided by the Supreme Court of Canada in 1993. The failure to challenge the long-standing social norms associated with gender roles and the division of labour in the household as well as the lack of recognition for the public good of caring for children continue to cast a long shadow on the struggle for women's equality. To the detriment of children, women, and Canadian society as a whole, only minimal progress has been made in acknowledging and acting upon the collective responsibility for childcare in the intervening years.

> 4. The tax rules engaged in Ms. Symes's claim afford only a narrow opportunity to recognize the important connection between women's inequality and society's continued failure to ensure that women do not bear unfair burdens as an incident of motherhood. Her claim does not give rise to a comprehensive solution to the urgent need for publicly funded, high-quality childcare. Nor does it acknowledge or rectify the undervaluing of the work of childcare providers, the majority of whom are particularly vulnerable to experiencing poor working conditions and discriminatory pay due to their status as recent immigrants and/or racialized minorities. Lack of comprehensiveness cannot be used as an excuse to ignore an existing inequality. By failing to address the substantive equality concerns in this case, the courts missed an important opening to press for reconstruction of the

---

54. *Available at* http://womenscourt.ca [last visited July 22, 2011].
55. *Available at* http://womenscourt.ca/wp-content/uploads/2009/07/Symes.pdf [last visited July 22, 2011].

tax system so that it begins to fully reflect women's realities as well as men's. This omission must be rectified ...

Substantive equality, by contrast to formal equality, posits that:—equality is not a matter of sameness and difference, but rather a matter of dominance, subordination, and material disparities between groups;—the effects of laws, policies, and practices, not the absence or presence of facial neutrality, determine whether laws or actions are discriminatory;—remedying inequality between groups requires government action;

—the so-called "private" realms of the family and the marketplace cannot be set outside the boundaries of equality inquiry or obligation, because they are key sites of inequality;

—neither liberty nor equality for individuals can be achieved unless equality is achieved for disadvantaged groups;—it is essential to be conscious of patterns of advantage and disadvantage associated with group membership; and—the test of equality is not whether an individual is like the members of a group that is treated more favourably by a law, policy, or practice; rather, the test is whether the members of a group that has historically been disadvantaged enjoy equality in real conditions, including economic conditions (at 46–7). It is important to repudiate the conception of choice as it relates to women's decisions with respect to childbearing, child rearing, and work outside of the home. The social assignment of caregiving responsibility to women seriously circumscribes women's choices and places the primary financial and other burdens on women. There are multiple and persistent difficulties in having and affording outside childcare, and these difficulties translate into barriers to women participating in the paid workforce or business. "Family choices" are made within the constrained circumstances established by these barriers and the structural inequalities that inform them. To analyze these issues within the framework of "family choice" is to ignore the reality that sex-based inequality is perpetuated at all levels of social relations from within families to communities to broader public policy. Rather than falling into the trap of "family choice," the role of equality analysis is to expose these underlying false assumptions. Parental responsibilities have a unique and significant negative impact on mothers' participation in the workforce. However, there is no comparable detrimental impact on father's participation in the workforce. For example, statistics show that, within the legal profession, fathers are the highest income group, earning more than men without children, women without children, and mothers ...

One of the main causes of discrimination against women lawyers is the culture that surrounds work in the legal profession. That culture has been shaped by and for male lawyers. It is predicated on historical work patterns that assume that lawyers do not have significant family responsibilities. The "hidden gender" of the current arrangements for legal work manifests itself in many ways, including: the extremely long and irregular hours of work; assumptions about the availability of domestic labour to support a lawyer's activities at work; promotion within law firms which is incompatible with the child bearing and child rearing cycles of most women's lives; and the perceived conflict between allegiances owed to work and family.

For more information about the Women's Court of Canada, see: http://www.facebook.com/group.php?gid=26905885010, http://www.lawyersweekly.ca/index.php?section=article&articleid=1224.

C. South Africa's Equality Jurisprudence

The South African Constitutional Court also found itself confronting the stereotype of the role of women as child caregivers early in its democracy. This was a particularly problematic case for the court given its commitment to equality and non discrimination in the post apartheid era. In *Hugo v. President of the Republic of South Africa,* the Constitutional Court grappled with the issue of whether a Presidential Act that the Court found to be discriminatory on the basis of sex, could pass constitutional muster if the discrimination that it perpetuated was not "unfair discrimination." The Court also had to contend with the fact that the Act, although designed to benefit mothers of young children (and their children), actually perpetuated gender stereotypes of women as primary caregivers to children.

1. *The President of the Republic of South Africa v. Hugo* (The South African Constitutional Court)[56]

GOLDSTONE J:

[1]   This matter comes before us on appeal against a judgment of Magid J. in the Durban and Coast Local Division of the Supreme Court.[57] The applicant in the court below (now respondent) is a prisoner who, on 6 December, 1991, commenced serving an effective sentence of fifteen and a half years. Some nine years prior to his incarceration, the respondent married and a child was born of that marriage on 11, December 1982. The respondent's wife died in 1987.

[2]   On 27 June 1994, acting pursuant to his powers under section 82(1)(k) of the interim Constitution,[58] the President (first appellant) and the two Executive Deputy Presidents signed a document styled Presidential Act No. 17 (the "Presidential Act"), in terms of which special remission of sentences was granted to certain categories of prisoners. The category of direct relevance to these proceedings was *"all mothers in prison on 10 May 1994, with minor children under the age of twelve (12) years".* It is common cause that the respondent would have qualified for remission, but for the fact that he was the father (and not the mother) of his son who was under the age of twelve years at the relevant date ...

The respondent alleged that the Presidential Act was in violation of the provisions of section 8(1) and (2) of the interim Constitution in as much as it unfairly discriminated against him on the ground of sex or gender and indirectly against his son in terms of section 8(2) because his incarcerated parent was not a female ...

[3]   In the present case we are asked to decide whether rights of male prisoners have been violated by the manner in which the President exercised his power to pardon or reprieve prisoners in the impugned part of the Presidential Act. Here the President did not exercise his power of pardon or reprieve in a single case. He exercised it "wholesale" as it were—in general terms. That is the only way in which such a power can be exercised

---

56. Constitutional Court of South Africa Case CCT 11/96; *available at* http://www.saflii.org/za/cases/ZACC/1997/4.html [last visited July 1, 2011].

57. *Hugo v. President of the Republic of South Africa and Another* 1996 (4) SA 1012 (D). (internal citations omitted).

58. Act 200 of 1993.

in a case such as the instant one, where the head of state wishes to confer a benefit upon groups of prisoners to mark an important event in the life of the nation. The relevant date chosen in the Presidential Act was 10, May 1994, the date on which the President was inaugurated. For the first time in its history, South Africa had a head of state and a head of the executive chosen as the result of a democratic constitutional process, and representing the whole nation.

[4]   Where the power of pardon or reprieve is used in general terms and there is an "amnesty" accorded to a category or categories of prisoners, discrimination is inherent. The line has to be drawn somewhere, and there will always be people on one side of the line who do not benefit and whose positions are not significantly different to those of persons on the other side of the line who do benefit. For instance there may be no meaningful difference between prisoners whose birthday was shortly before the cut off date identified by the President, and who were eighteen when the decision took effect, and those whose birthday was shortly after the cut off date and were under eighteen at the effective date. Indeed, there might well have been prisoners in the first category who, if assessed individually, might have been considered to be more deserving of a remission of sentence than persons in the latter category.

[5]   The respondent argued that the Presidential Act was in conflict with section 8 of the interim Constitution in that by releasing all mothers whose children were under the age of twelve, it discriminated against fathers of children of a similar age. Section 8 of the interim Constitution provides as follows:

(1) Every person shall have the right to equality before the law and to equal protection of the law.

(2) No person shall be unfairly discriminated against, directly or indirectly, and, without derogating from the generality of this provision, on one or more of the following grounds in particular: race, gender, sex, ethnic or social origin, colour, sexual orientation, age, disability, religion, conscience, belief, culture or language.

(3) (a) This section shall not preclude measures designed to achieve the adequate protection and advancement of persons or groups or categories of persons disadvantaged by unfair discrimination, in order to enable their full and equal enjoyment of all rights and freedoms.

(b) ...

(4) *Prima facie* proof of discrimination on any of the grounds specified in subsection (2) shall be presumed to be sufficient proof of unfair discrimination as contemplated in that subsection, until the contrary is established.

[6]   The respondent argues that in releasing mothers of small children but not fathers, the President discriminated on the grounds of sex. The advantage that was afforded mothers was not afforded to fathers of small children and that failure is sufficient to establish discrimination within the context of section 8(2) of the interim Constitution. The Presidential Act, in fact, discriminates on a combined basis, sex coupled with parenthood of children below the age of twelve. Only women who are parents of such children were released: women without children were not. In *Brink v Kitshoff NO*, this Court held that it is sufficient if the discrimination is substantially based on one of the listed grounds in section 8(2). Accordingly, it is clear that the Presidential Act *prima facie* discriminates on one of the grounds listed in section 8(2). As such, section 8(4) requires us to presume that the discrimination is unfair, until the contrary is proved.

[7]   The appellants rely on an affidavit of the President to which is attached a supporting affidavit of Ms. Helen Starke, the National Director of the South African National Council for Child and Family Welfare. Those affidavits were filed in a similar application which came before the Transvaal Provincial Division of the Supreme Court in *Kruger and Another v Minister of Correctional Services and Others....* In his affidavit, the President stated that in regard to the special remission of all mothers of minor children, he

> was motivated predominantly by a concern for children who had been deprived of the nurturing and care which their mothers would ordinarily have provided. Having spent many years in prison myself, I am well aware of the hardship which flows from incarceration. I am also well aware that imprisonment inevitably has harsh consequences for the family of the prisoner.

> Account was taken of the special role I believe that mothers play in the care and nurturing of younger children. In this regard I refer to the affidavit of HELEN STARKE ... respectfully draw attention to the fact that the well-being of young children has been of particular concern to me and was an important factor in identifying two of the three categories in the Presidential Act....

> I have had an on-going concern about the general plight of young children in South Africa. There have been many occasions upon which I have expressed this concern publicly.

In her affidavit, Ms. Starke stated in relation to the special remission of mothers of minor children:

> In my opinion, the identification of this special category for remission of sentence is rationally and reasonably explicable as being in the best interests of the children concerned. It is generally accepted that children bond with their mothers at a very early age and that mothers are the primary nurturers and care givers of young children ...

> Although it could be argued that fathers play a more significant role in the lives of older children, the primary bonding with the mother and the role of mothers as the primary nurturers and care givers extends well into childhood.

> The reasons for this are partly historical and the role of the socialisation of women who are socialised to fulfil the role of primary nurturers and care givers of children, especially pre-adolescent children and are perceived by society as such (sic) ...

> In my experience, there are only a minority of fathers who are actively involved in nurturing and caring for their children, particularly their pre-adolescent children. There are, of course, exceptions to this generalisation, but the *de facto* situation in South Africa today is that mothers are the major custodians and the primary nurturers and care givers of our nation's children."

[8]   The reason given by the President for the special remission of sentence of mothers with small children is that it will serve the interests of children. To support this, he relies upon the evidence of Ms. Starke that mothers are, generally speaking, primarily responsible for the care of small children in our society. Although no statistical or survey evidence was produced to establish this fact, I see no reason to doubt the assertion that mothers, as a matter of fact, bear more responsibilities for child-rearing in our society than do fathers. This statement, of course, is a generalisation. There will, doubtless, be particular instances where fathers bear more responsibilities than mothers for the care of children. In addition, there will also be many cases where a natural mother is not the primary care

giver, but some other woman fulfils that role, whether she be the grandmother, stepmother, sister, or aunt of the child concerned. However, although it may generally be true that mothers bear an unequal share of the burden of child rearing in our society as compared to the burden borne by fathers, it cannot be said that it will ordinarily be *fair* to discriminate between women and men on that basis.

[9]   For all that it is a privilege and the source of enormous human satisfaction and pleasure, there can be no doubt that the task of rearing children is a burdensome one. It requires time, money and emotional energy. For women without skills or financial resources, its challenges are particularly acute. For many South African women, the difficulties of being responsible for the social and economic burdens of child rearing, in circumstances where they have few skills and scant financial resources are immense. The failure by fathers to shoulder their share of the financial and social burden of child rearing is a primary cause of this hardship. The result of being responsible for children makes it more difficult for women to compete in the labour market and is one of the causes of the deep inequalities experienced by women in employment. The generalisation upon which the President relied is therefore a fact which is one of the root causes of women's inequality in our society. That parenting may have emotional and personal rewards for women should not blind us to the tremendous burden it imposes at the same time. It is unlikely that we will achieve a more egalitarian society until responsibilities for child rearing are more equally shared.

[10]   The fact, therefore, that the generalisation upon which the appellants rely is true, does not answer the question of whether the discrimination concerned is fair. Indeed, it will often be unfair for discrimination to be based on that particular generalisation. Women's responsibilities in the home for housekeeping and child rearing have historically been given as reasons for excluding them from other spheres of life. To use the generalisation that women bear a greater proportion of the burdens of child rearing for justifying treatment that deprives women of benefits or advantages or imposes disadvantages upon them would clearly, therefore, be unfair.

[11]   That, however, has not happened in this case. The President has afforded an opportunity to mothers, on the basis of the generalisation, that he has not afforded to fathers. In my view, the fact that the individuals who were discriminated against by a particular action, such as the one under consideration, were not individuals who belonged to a class who had historically been disadvantaged does not necessarily mean that the discrimination is fair.

[12]   The prohibition on unfair discrimination in the interim Constitution seeks not only to avoid discrimination against people who are members of disadvantaged groups. It seeks more than that. At the heart of the prohibition of unfair discrimination lies a recognition that the purpose of our new constitutional and democratic order is the establishment of a society in which all human beings will be accorded equal dignity and respect regardless of their membership of particular groups. The achievement of such a society in the context of our deeply inegalitarian past will not be easy, but that that is the goal of the Constitution should not be forgotten or overlooked ...

The considerations mentioned here would well nigh have made it impossible for the President to release all fathers who were in prison as well as mothers. Male prisoners outnumber female prisoners almost fiftyfold. A release of all fathers would have meant that a very large number of men prisoners would have gained their release. As many fathers play only a secondary role in child rearing, the release of male prisoners would not have contributed as significantly to the achievement of the President's purpose as the release of mothers. In addition, the release of a large number of male prisoners in the current circumstances where crime has reached alarming levels would almost certainly have led to considerable public outcry. In the circumstances it must be accepted that it would have been very difficult, if not impossible, for the President to have released fathers on the same basis as mothers. Were he obliged to release fathers on the same terms as mothers, the result may have been that no parents would have been released at all.

[13] In this case, two groups of people have been affected by the Presidential Act: mothers of young children have been afforded an advantage: an early release from prison; and fathers have been denied that advantage. The President released three groups of prisoners as an act of mercy. The three groups—disabled prisoners, young people and mothers of young children—are all groups who are particularly vulnerable in our society, and in the case particularly of the disabled and mothers of young children, groups who have been the victims of discrimination in the past. The release of mothers will in many cases have been of real benefit to children which was the primary purpose of their release. The impact of the remission on those prisoners was to give them an advantage. As mentioned, the occasion the President chose for this act of mercy was 10, May 1994, the date of his inauguration as the first democratically elected President of this country. It is true that fathers of young children in prison were not afforded early release from prison. But although that does, without doubt, constitute a disadvantage, it did not restrict or limit their rights or obligations as fathers in any permanent manner. It cannot be said, for example, that the effect of the discrimination was to deny or limit their freedom, for their freedom was curtailed as a result of their conviction, not as a result of the Presidential Act . . .

Per Kriegler J. dissenting:

The importance of equality in the constitutional scheme bears repetition. The South African Constitution is primarily and emphatically an egalitarian constitution. The supreme laws of comparable constitutional states may underscore other principles and rights. But in the light of our own particular history, and our vision for the future, a constitution was written with equality at its centre. Equality is our Constitution's focus and organising principle. The importance of equality rights in the Constitution, and the role of the right to equality in our emerging democracy, must both be understood in order to analyse properly whether a violation of the right has occurred.

The importance of equality is demonstrated by the Constitution's insistence that discrimination on a specified s 8(2) basis be presumed unfair until the contrary is established. The insistence on such rebuttal is not new to this Court. A burden of "justification" was placed on the President by s 8(4) read with s 8(2). The latter states that

> [n]o person shall be unfairly discriminated against, directly or indirectly, and, without derogating from the generality of this provision, on one or more of the following grounds in particular: race, gender, sex, ethnic or social origin, colour, sexual orientation, age, disability, religion, conscience, belief, culture or language.

One can accept for the sake of argument that the President's belief is empirically confirmed. The question then is whether the fact that in South Africa mothers are the primary care givers can establish fairness under s 8(4). In this regard I agree with the majority judgment that the fact that women generally "bear an unequal share of the burden of child rearing" cannot render it ordinarily "fair to discriminate between women and men on that basis". What I cannot endorse, is the majority's conclusion that although the discrimination inherent in the Act was based on that very stereotyping, it is nevertheless vindicated. In my view the notion relied upon by the President, namely that women are to be regarded as the primary care givers of young children, is a root cause of women's inequality in our society. It is both a result and a cause of prejudice; a societal attitude which relegates women to a subservient, occupationally inferior yet unceasingly onerous role. It is a relic and a feature of the patriarchy which the Constitution so vehemently condemns. Section 8 and the other provisions mentioned above outlawing gender or sex discrimination were designed to undermine and not to perpetuate patterns of discrimination of this kind. Indeed I find it startling that the appellants could have placed this fact before the Court in order to establish that their conduct does not constitute unfair discrimination. I would have thought that this is precisely the kind of motive that the respondent might have attempted to divine in the appellant's conduct in order to condemn it. It hardly has justificatory power. One of the ways in which one accords equal dignity and respect to persons is by seeking to protect the basic choices they make about their own identities. Reliance on the generalisation that women are the primary care givers is harmful in its tendency to cramp and stunt the efforts of both men and women to form their identities freely.

I am prepared to accept without deciding, that in very narrow circumstances a generalisation—although reflecting a discriminatory reality—could be vindicated if its ultimate implications were equalising. But I would suggest that at least two criteria would have to be satisfied for this to be the case. First, there would have to be a strong indication that the advantages flowing from the perpetuation of a stereotype compensate for obvious and profoundly troubling disadvantages. Second, the context would have to be one in which discriminatory benefits were apposite ... [T]he benefits in this case are to a small group of women—the 440 released from prison—and the detriment is to all South African women who must continue to labour under the social view that their place is in the home. In addition, men must continue to accept that they can have only a secondary/surrogate role in the care of their children. The limited benefit in this case cannot justify the reinforcement of a view that is a root cause of women's inequality in our society. In truth there is no advantage to women qua women in the President's conduct, merely a favour to perceived child minders ...

Mokgoro J. [an African woman] dissenting:

Section 8 of our Constitution gives us the opportunity to move away from gender stereotyping. Society should no longer be bound by the notions that a woman's place is in the home, (and conversely, not in the public sphere), and that fathers do not have a significant role to play in the rearing of their young children. Those notions have for too long deprived women of a fair opportunity to participate in public life, and deprived society of the valuable contribution women can make. Women have been prevented from gaining economic self-sufficiency, or forging identities for themselves independent of their roles as wives and mothers. By the same token, society has denied fathers the opportunity to participate in child rearing, which is detrimental both to fathers and their children. As recognized by this Court in *Fraser v Children's Court, Pretoria North and Others*, fathers have a meaningful contribution to make in child rearing, and I am concerned that this Court may be perceived as retreating from the valuable principles laid down in that case. It is important that those principles be adhered to, so that they may begin to benefit all mothers, fathers and their children ...

Questions for Discussion

1. Consider the gender of the judges that have written opinions in some of these decisions. Does a judge's gender impact her decision? Should it?

2. *Should judges receive training on gender sensitization?*

3. *Was there a way to uphold the constitutionality of this provision or should it have been held to discriminate on the basis of gender?*

4. *Should the Court have taken into account the reaction of the public if men had been released? Doesn't including that as a consideration involve gender stereotyping about men?*

5. *Does a decision like this reinforce stereotyping of women and reinforce traditional gender roles? How could the Court have decided this case differently?*

Chapter 6

Ending Discrimination—
Special Temporary Measures

Chapter Problem

In Chapter 5, you were informed about an NGO that applied for a grant from the Secretary of State's International Fund for Women and Girls. This NGO also mentioned in its grant application that, along with promoting equality for women, it plans to assess whether affirmative action may play a role in advancing women's equality. The Administrators of the Secretary's Fund for Women and Girls have read your memorandum on equality, and now would like you to write a memorandum on affirmative action. They want to know how the concept of affirmative action affects the notion of equality, if at all. Affirmative action has become a fairly controversial topic in the United States, and the administrators would like to know if it is still an accepted practice in other countries, and if CEDAW and the CEDAW Committee take a position on it.

They also want to know if affirmative action is an effective policy; specifically, they have questions about whether affirmative action is still necessary, and whether it promotes differential treatment and inequality.

I. CEDAW and Affirmative Action

CEDAW calls on party states not only to promote equality but to end discrimination. To end discrimination, state parties sometimes find themselves having to remedy past inequalities in order to fulfill women's rights. As the United Nations itself has noted:

> States parties have the three-fold obligation to respect, protect and fulfil women's human rights. To "respect," the State must abstain from any conduct or activity of its own that violates human rights. To "protect," the State must prevent violations by non-state actors, including individuals, groups, institutions and corporations. And to "fulfil," the State must take whatever measures are needed to move towards the full realization of women's human rights.[1]

---

1. *See* http://www.unifem.org/cedaw30/about_cedaw/ [last visited July 2, 2011].

A. Special Measures in CERD

The concept of affirmative action was first enshrined in the Convention on the Elimination of All Forms of Racial Discrimination (CERD). Article 1(4) permits states to impose measures:

> taken for the sole purpose of securing adequate advancement of certain racial or ethnic groups or individuals requiring such protection as may be necessary in order to ensure such groups or individuals equal enjoyment or exercise of human rights and fundamental freedoms ... provided, however, that such measures do not, as a consequence, lead to the maintenance of separate rights for different racial groups and that they shall not be continued after the objectives for which they were taken have been achieved

Similarly, Article 2.2 permits and encourages states to:

> [W]hen the circumstances so warrant, take, in the social, economic, cultural and other fields, special and concrete measures to ensure the adequate development and protection of certain racial groups or individuals belonging to them, for the purpose of guaranteeing them the full and equal enjoyment of human rights and fundamental freedoms. These measures shall in no case entail as a consequence the maintenance of unequal or separate rights for different racial groups after the objectives for which they were taken have been achieved.

These measures, sometimes referred to as affirmative action, have not been uncontroversial. In fact, the Human Rights Committee (the reporting body of CERD) devoted its *General Recommendation No. 32* in 2001 to the meaning and scope of these special measures. The Committee pointed out that:

> *General Recommendation 30* of the Committee observed that differential treatment will 'constitute discrimination if the criteria for such differentiation, judged in the light of the objectives and purposes of the Convention, are not applied pursuant to a legitimate aim, and are not proportional to the achievement of this aim.'[2] As a logical corollary of this principle, *General Recommendation 14* observes that 'differentiation of treatment will not constitute discrimination if the criteria for such differentiation, judged against the objectives and purposes of the Convention, are legitimate.'[3] The term 'non-discrimination' does not signify the necessity of uniform treatment when there are significant differences in situation between one person or group and another, or, in other words, if there is an objective and reasonable justification for differential treatment. To treat in an equal manner persons or groups whose situations are objectively different will constitute discrimination in effect, as will the unequal treatment of persons whose situations are objectively the same. The Committee has also observed that the application of the principle of non-discrimination requires that the characteristics of groups be taken into consideration.

---

2. *General Recommendation No. 30*, paragraph 4.
3. A/48/18, chapter VIII B.

The Recommendation thus appears to establish a test of objective and reasonable justification for differential treatment.

B. Special Temporary Measures in CEDAW

Special temporary measures, sometimes called affirmative action, are permitted and even encouraged under Article 4 of CEDAW which provides:

> Article 4 (1). Adoption by States Parties of temporary special measures aimed at accelerating de facto equality between men and women shall not be considered discrimination as defined in the present Convention, but shall in no way entail as a consequence the maintenance of unequal or separate standards; these measures shall be discontinued when the objectives of equality of opportunity and treatment have been achieved.

> 2. Adoption by States Parties of special measures, including those measures contained in the present Convention, aimed at protecting maternity shall not be considered discriminatory.

In particular, the CEDAW Committee has spoken approvingly of affirmative action measures being adopted with regard to promoting equality in the public and political spheres.

C. The CEDAW Committee's *General Recommendations on Special Measures*

As early as 1988, the CEDAW Committee referred to the need for special temporary measures in its *General Comments Nos. 5 and 8. General Recommendation No. 23 of 1997* also addressed the need for women's political participation, and discussed discrimination against women in political and public life. The CEDAW Committee specifically requested that states parties undertake special recruiting efforts; financial assistance for women and the training of women candidates; amending electoral procedures; campaigns aimed at ensuring equal participation; targeting women for appointment to public positions; and setting numerical goals and quotas.

1. *General Recommendation No. 5*

> Taking note that the reports, the introductory remarks and the replies by States parties reveal that while significant progress has been achieved in regard to repealing or modifying discriminatory laws, there is still a need for action to be taken to implement fully the Convention by introducing measures to promote de facto equality between men and women,

> Recalling Article 4.1 of the Convention,

> Recommends that States parties make more use of temporary special measures such as positive action, preferential treatment or quota systems to advance women's integration into education, the economy, politics and employment.

2. *General Recommendation No. 25*

General Recommendation No. 25 was devoted to special temporary measures; the Committee there stated:

> One of the ways advanced for mitigating inequality or accelerating women's equality is by using temporary special measures, provided for in article 4 of CEDAW. Human rights law provides for the principle of non-discrimination to be derogated from in the use of such measures. This is on the understanding that the measures will be dismantled once the position between men and women has been achieved. In order to avoid a reversal of gains made, it is equally important that temporary special measures are not dismantled prematurely ...[4]

The CEDAW Committee has found that:

> Article 1 of CEDAW includes both direct and indirect discrimination and requires States parties to ensure equality of opportunity and result, thus taking it beyond the formal (liberal) model of equality which Mackinnon argues simply requires a reversal and comparison of the sexes. Mackinnon argues that by relying on a false premise, namely that the playing field is level for both men and women, a formal model of equality fails to take into account socio-structural inequalities which result in women not being able to enjoy their rights on an equal basis with men. True equality is not simply about reversing the sexes and comparing, nor is it simply about passing laws that appear on the face of them to be gender neutral. ...
>
> The principle of non-discrimination on the basis of sex is an immediate and not a progressive obligation. The Human Rights Committee has noted that the principle should be guaranteed, including during states of emergency while any public emergency derogations should show that they are non discriminatory.

The Committee went on to stress that temporary special measures are not discriminatory when their application is aimed at accelerating the attainment of de facto equality.

> In the Committee's view, a purely formal legal or programmatic approach is not sufficient to achieve women's de facto equality with men, which the Committee interprets as substantive equality. In addition, the Convention requires that women be given an equal start and that they be empowered by an enabling environment to achieve equality of results. It is not enough to guarantee women treatment that is identical to that of men. Rather, biological as well as socially and culturally constructed differences between women and men must be taken into account. Under certain circumstances, non-identical treatment of women and men will be required in order to address such differences. Pursuit of the goal of substantive equality also calls for an effective strategy aimed at overcoming underrepresentation of women and a redistribution of resources and power between men and women ...
>
> Certain groups of women, in addition to suffering from discrimination directed against them as women, may also suffer from multiple forms of discrimination based on additional grounds such as race, ethnic or religious identity, disability, age, class, caste or other factors. Such discrimination may affect these groups of

---

4. *General Recommendation No. 25*; *available at* http://www.un.org/womenwatch/daw/cedaw/recommendations/General%20recommendation%2025%20(English).pdf [last visited January 25, 2011].

women primarily, or to a different degree or in different ways than men. States parties may need to take specific temporary special measures to eliminate such multiple forms of discrimination against women and its compounded negative impact on them....

The Convention, targets discriminatory dimensions of past and current societal and cultural contexts which impede women's enjoyment of their human rights and fundamental freedoms. It aims at the elimination of all forms of discrimination against women, including the elimination of the causes and consequences of their de facto or substantive inequality. Therefore, the application of temporary special measures in accordance with the Convention is one of the means to realize de facto or substantive equality for women, rather than an exception to the norms of non-discrimination and equality.[5]

The Committee also noted that it has "encouraged states to include in their reports information about the measures that they have taken to advance the rights of women, and in particular to detail information regarding special temporary measures."[6] The Committee itself has issued no guidelines on the content of these measures, primarily because they are context specific. The measures are often challenged on the basis that they discriminate against other parties who are not beneficiaries of the measures. However, both the CEDAW Committee and the ICCPR's Human Rights Committee have consistently noted that these measures are corollaries to the principles of equality and non discrimination.

3. *The Beijing Platform for Action* and Special Temporary Measures

At the World Conference for Women held in 1995 in Beijing, the delegates drafted a *Platform for Action*, which would advance women's rights. There special temporary measures were again reaffirmed, and delegates were encouraged to:

Commit themselves to establishing the goal of gender balance in governmental bodies and committees, as well as in public administrative entities, and in the judiciary, including, inter alia, setting specific targets and implementing measures to substantially increase the number of women with a view to achieving equal representation of women and men, if necessary through positive action, in all governmental and public administration positions.[7]

No cases involving affirmative action have been before the CEDAW Committee. Because special temporary measures may be context specific, it is helpful to look to other domestic jurisdictions to see how they have applied the concept of special temporary measures.

4. Terminology

The CEDAW Committee has noted that no consistent terminology had been used with regard to these measures.

The *travaux préparatoires* of the Convention use different terms to describe the "temporary special measures" included in article 4, Paragraph 1. The Committee

---

5. *Id.* at paras. 1–12.

6. *Id.* at para. 25.

7. United Nations. 2001. *Beijing Declaration and Platform for Action with the Beijing+5 Political Declaration and Outcome Document.* New York: United Nations. pp. 111–13 (in particular, paragraphs 190 (a and b)).

itself, in its previous general recommendations, used various terms. States parties often equate "special measures" in its corrective, compensatory and promotional sense with the terms "affirmative action", "positive action", "positive measures", "reverse discrimination", and "positive discrimination". These terms emerge from the discussions and varied practices found in different national contexts. In the present general recommendation, and in accordance with its practice in the consideration of reports of States parties, the Committee uses solely the term "temporary special measures", as called for in article 4, Paragraph 1.[8]

That terminology can be important. In the United States for example, opponents of such measures often refer to them as "reverse discrimination"; proponents describe them as "affirmative action." Currently, narrowly tailored affirmative action is constitutionally permissible under certain circumstances in education in the United States, according to the Supreme Court's decision in *Grutter v. Bollinger*,[9] while "quotas" are generally disallowed.

Questions for Discussion

1. *The CEDAW Committee seems to envision that affirmative action should be ended when equality is achieved. How will a state party know when the appropriate time has come to end affirmative action?*

2. *Is terminology important both with regard to consistency, and with regard to how affirmative action is perceived by the public? Is the term "temporary special measures" more effective at conveying the idea that these measures are not intended to be long term?*

II. Affirmative Action in the United States

A. Presidential Executive Orders

The term "affirmative action" was first officially used by President John F. Kennedy in his Executive Order No. 10925 of 1961, which required federal contractors to "take affirmative action to ensure that applicants are employed, and that employees are treated during employment, without regard to their race, creed, color, or national origin." President Johnson also used the term in his 1965 Executive Order No. 11246, and in his 1967 Order which expanded affirmative action to include women. The Order prohibits federal contractors and federally-assisted construction contractors and subcontractors, who do over $10,000 in Government business in one year from discriminating in employment decisions on the basis of race, color, religion, sex, or national origin. It also requires Government contractors to take affirmative action to insure that equal opportunity is provided in all aspects of their employment. The Order applies to government contractors with 50 or more employees and $50,000 or more in government contracts, and requires them to

---

8. *Id.* at paras. 16–17.
9. 539 U.S. 306 (2003).

develop a written affirmative action program (AAP) for each of its establishments. This requirement is intended to help "the contractor identify and analyze potential problems in the participation and utilization of women and minorities in the contractor's workforce." The contractor is also required to specify in its AAP the specific procedures it will follow and the good faith efforts it will make to provide equal employment opportunity in the event that problems arise. These provisions are designed to "help members of the protected groups compete for jobs on equal footing with other applicants and employees."

Several states such as California and Michigan have passed propositions outlawing the use of affirmative action in state funded universities. Michigan amended its Constitution to ban affirmative action in education after Michigan voters passed Proposition 2 outlawing it in 2006. Article 26 of the Michigan Constitution now provides:

> The University of Michigan, Michigan State University, Wayne State University, and any other public college or university, community college, or school district shall not discriminate against, or grant preferential treatment to, any individual or group on the basis of race, sex, color, ethnicity, or national origin in the operation of public employment, public education, or public contracting.

However, in a recent decision, *Coalition to Defend Affirmative Action v. Regents of the Univ. of Michigan*, handed down on July 1, 2011, the Sixth Circuit Court of Appeals found Article 26 to be a violation of the Equal Protection clause holding:

> Ensuring a fair political process is nowhere more important than in education. Education is the bedrock of equal opportunity and "the very foundation of good citizenship." Safeguarding the guarantee "that public institutions are open and available to all segments of American society, including people of all races and ethnicities, represents a paramount government objective." "Moreover, universities, and in particular, law schools, represent the training ground for a large number of our Nation's leaders.... [T]o cultivate a set of leaders with legitimacy in the eyes of the citizenry, it is necessary that the path to leadership be visibly open to talented and qualified individuals of every race and ethnicity." Therefore, in the context of education, we must apply the "political process" protection with the utmost rigor given the high stakes.[10]

B. The 1964 Civil Rights Act

The Act was passed to counter pervasive racial discrimination, but Title VII also addressed discrimination on the grounds of gender. It has been amended by the Civil Rights Act of 1991 and by the Lily Ledbetter Fair Pay Act which will be discussed in a later chapter.

The purpose of the Civil Rights Act is stated as:

> To enforce the constitutional right to vote, to confer jurisdiction upon the district courts of the United States to provide injunctive relief against discrimination in public accommodations, to authorize the Attorney General to institute suits to protect constitutional rights in public facilities and public education, to extend the Commission on Civil Rights, to prevent discrimination in federally assisted programs, to establish a Commission on Equal Employment Opportunity, and for other purposes.

---

10. Case Nos. 08-1387/1389/1534; 09-1111; as yet unpublished opinion, at 9–10 (internal citations omitted).

Unlawful employment practices are defined as:

It shall be an unlawful employment practice for an employer—

(1) to fail or refuse to hire or to discharge any individual, or otherwise to discriminate against any individual with respect to his compensation, terms, conditions, or privileges of employment, because of such individual's race, color, religion, sex, or national origin; or

(2) to limit, segregate, or classify his employees or applicants for employment in any way which would deprive or tend to deprive any individual of employment opportunities or otherwise adversely affect his status as an employee, because of such individual's race, color, religion, sex, or national origin.

(b) Employment agency practices

It shall be an unlawful employment practice for an employment agency to fail or refuse to refer for employment, or otherwise to discriminate against, any individual because of his race, color, religion, sex, or national origin, or to classify or refer for employment any individual on the basis of his race, color, religion, sex, or national origin.

(c) Labor organization practices

It shall be an unlawful employment practice for a labor organization:

(1) to exclude or to expel from its membership, or otherwise to discriminate against, any individual because of his race, color, religion, sex, or national origin;

(2) to limit, segregate, or classify its membership or applicants for membership, or to classify or fail or refuse to refer for employment any individual, in any way which would deprive or tend to deprive any individual of employment opportunities, or would limit such employment opportunities or otherwise adversely affect his status as an employee or as an applicant for employment, because of such individual's race, color, religion, sex, or national origin; or

(3) to cause or attempt to cause an employer to discriminate against an individual in violation of this section.

(j) Preferential treatment not to be granted on account of existing number or percentage imbalance

Nothing contained in this subchapter shall be interpreted to require any employer, employment agency, labor organization, or joint labor-management committee subject to this subchapter to grant preferential treatment to any individual or to any group because of the race, color, religion, sex, or national origin of such individual or group on account of an imbalance which may exist with respect to the total number or percentage of persons of any race, color, religion, sex, or national origin employed by any employer, referred or classified for employment by any employment agency or labor organization, admitted to membership or classified by any labor organization, or admitted to, or employed in, any apprenticeship or other training program, in comparison with the total number or percentage of persons of such race, color, religion, sex, or national origin in any community, State, section, or other area, or in the available work force in any community, State, section, or other area.

No Government contract, or portion thereof, with any employer, shall be denied, withheld, terminated, or suspended, by any agency or officer of the United States under any equal employment opportunity law or order, where such employer has an affirmative action plan which has previously been accepted by the Government for the same facility within the past twelve months without first according such employer full hearing and adjudication under the provisions of section 554 of Title 5 [*United States Code*], and the following pertinent sections: Provided, That if such employer has deviated substantially from such previously agreed to affirmative action plan, this section shall not apply: Provided further, That for the purposes of this section an affirmative action plan shall be deemed to have been accepted by the Government at the time the appropriate compliance agency has accepted such plan unless within forty-five days thereafter the Office of Federal Contract Compliance has disapproved such plan.

(g) Injunctions; appropriate affirmative action; equitable relief; accrual of back pay; reduction of back pay; limitations on judicial orders

(1) If the court finds that the respondent has intentionally engaged in or is intentionally engaging in an unlawful employment practice charged in the complaint, the court may enjoin the respondent from engaging in such unlawful employment practice, and order such affirmative action as may be appropriate, which may include, but is not limited to, reinstatement or hiring of employees, with or without back pay (payable by the employer, employment agency, or labor organization, as the case may be, responsible for the unlawful employment practice), or any other equitable relief as the court deems appropriate. Back pay liability shall not accrue from a date more than two years prior to the filing of a charge with the Commission. Interim earnings or amounts earnable with reasonable diligence by the person or persons discriminated against shall operate to reduce the back pay otherwise allowable.

Questions for Discussion

1. *The Presidential Orders mandating affirmative action in government contracting were passed in the 1960s. Are they still relevant in today's society, especially given that many voters seem opposed to them?*

2. *Should each state be allowed to decide the question of affirmative action for itself—or is affirmative action a basic civil and human right?*

III. Affirmative Action Directives in National Constitutions and Legislation

A. The South African Constitution and Legislation

Section 9 of the South African Constitution provides that:

1. Everyone is equal before the law and has the right to equal protection and benefit of the law.

2. Equality includes the full and equal enjoyment of all rights and freedoms. To promote the achievement of equality, legislative and other measures designed to

protect or advance persons, or categories of persons, disadvantaged by unfair discrimination may be taken.

Note that one of the purposes of the South African Constitution was to transform a society formerly divided by race. It seems particularly appropriate for South Africa to undertake affirmative action to compensate for the extreme form of racial discrimination that was known as apartheid. Consistent with the interpretation of the ICCPR, such measures in South Africa are seen as not seen as an exception to the requirement of equality, but a means by which equality may be brought about.

Two South African laws, in addition to the Constitution, support the use of affirmative action on behalf of previously disadvantaged groups. The Promotion of Equality and Prevention of Unfair Discrimination Act recognizes the constitutional requirement of equality and notes that:

> This implies the advancement, by special legal and other measures, of historically disadvantaged individuals, communities and social groups who were dispossessed of their land and resources, deprived of their human dignity and who continue to endure the consequences.

At the same time, the Employment Equity Act aims to:

achieve equity in the workplace by:

> a) promoting equal opportunity and fair treatment in employment through the elimination of unfair discrimination; and

> b) implementing affirmative action measures to redress the disadvantages in employment experienced by designated groups, in order to ensure their equitable representation in all occupational categories and levels in the workforce.

The Employment Equity Act requires, among other things, that "Every designated employer must, in order to achieve employment equity, implement affirmative action measures for people from designated groups in terms of this Act." According to Article 15 of this Act:

> 1. Affirmative action measures are measures designed to ensure that suitably qualified people from designated groups have equal employment opportunities and are equitably represented in all occupational categories and levels in the workforce of a designated employer.

> 2. Affirmative action measures implemented by a designated employer must include:

> a. measures to identify and eliminate employment barriers, including unfair discrimination, which adversely affect people from designated groups;...

Designated groups include "black people, women, and people with disabilities." To date, the affirmative action cases that have gone before the South African Constitutional Court involve issues of race rather than gender. Several cases based on gender have gone before the Labour Court; many of those cases were settled. South Africa has also ratified the ICCPR, the IESCR and CEDAW.

B. The Indian Constitution

The Indian Constitution guarantees equality for all citizens by providing that "[t]he State shall not deny to any person equality before the law or the equal protection of the laws within the territory of India." At the same time, it explicitly allows for affirmative action by providing that "[n]othing ... shall prevent the State from making any special provision for the advancement of any socially and educationally backward classes of citizens or for the Scheduled Castes and the Scheduled Tribes."[11] Affirmative action or special measures are thus generally implemented on the basis of caste, class and education, not gender. In the field of public employment, the Constitution mandates that "[n]othing in this article shall prevent the State from making any provision for the reservation of appointments or posts in favor of any backward class of citizens which, in the opinion of the State, is not adequately represented in the services under the State." Part XVI of the Constitution specifically lays out in detail the affirmative action, or "reservation," program for Scheduled Castes and Scheduled Tribes. Because the Indian Constitution explicitly charges the government with implementing affirmative action programs for backward classes, no cases challenging the concept of affirmative action have been filed. However, there have been some challenges regarding who qualified as a member of a "backward class." Several Commissions have been appointed to determine this, and their findings have not always enjoyed popular support.[12] Nevertheless, India's affirmative action program is credited with allowing some upward mobility for lower caste and lower class members of Indian society. Recently India introduced legislation to reserve seats in their legislative bodies for women. Similar measures reserving seats for lower castes have already been implemented. This legislation will be discussed in a later chapter. In addition to its domestic measures, India has ratified CERD, the ICCPR, the ICESCR, and CEDAW.

C. The Canadian Constitution

Affirmative action or special temporary measures are generally referred to in Canada as employment equity.

Canada's constitution guarantees equality among citizens, providing that:

> Every individual is equal before and under the law and has the right to the equal protection and equal benefit of the law without discrimination and, in particular, without discrimination based on race, national or ethnic origin, color, religion, sex, age or mental or physical disability.

The Constitution also makes clear however, that affirmative action is permissible by stating that the above guarantee:

> does not preclude any law, program or activity that has as its object the amelioration of conditions of disadvantaged individuals or groups including those that are disadvantaged because of race, national or ethnic origin, color, religion, sex, age or mental or physical disability.

Canada's Employment Equity Act has the goal of effecting equality in the workplace in order to:

> correct the conditions of disadvantage in employment experienced by women, aboriginal peoples, persons with disabilities and members of visible minorities by giving effect to the principle that employment equity means more than treating

---

11. INDIAN CONST. OF 1950 as amended.
12. *See e.g.*, Indira Sawhney v. Union of India, 80 A.I.R. 1993 S.C. 477, 558–60.

persons in the same way but also requires special measures and the accommodation of differences.[13]

The Act applies to employers in the public sector, and large employers in the private sector, specifically those with more than 100 employees. Among other things, the Employment Equity Act requires employers to take positive steps to ensure that people in the designated groups are represented in the workplace in proportion to their representation in the Canadian workforce, or the sector of the Canadian workforce from which the employer can be expected to hire. Employers must analyze their organizational practices to determine whether designated groups are underrepresented, and develop employment equity plans to lay out remedial policies where needed. A finding that certain groups are underrepresented should lead to the use of "short term numerical goals for the hiring and promotion of persons in designated groups in order to increase their representation in each occupational group in the workforce."[14]

The Canadian Human Rights Commission, established under section 26 of the Canadian Human Rights Act, is charged with enforcing the Employment Equity Act. Employers are required to report annually to the Commission, detailing breakdown of their employees. The Commission may also audit employers. Tribunals may be convened to review allegations of non noncompliance; if an employer is found to have violated the Act it may be fined.

Canada's requirement that analysis must be conducted to determine if certain groups are underrepresented is a sound one, and one that highlights some of the problems inherent in implementing special measures. In many countries, comprehensive and reliable data is not always available to determine how underrepresented certain groups are. Thus, it is difficult to determine if affirmative action is necessary and appropriate, or once it has been implemented, whether it has been effective.

Questions for Discussion

1. *Given the legacy of apartheid in South Africa, is affirmative action an appropriate form of redress for those who were excluded from many positions by apartheid laws? Is the South African terminology, which refers to "previously disadvantaged" groups, helpful in persuading people of the merits of affirmative action?*

2. *Is affirmative action only appropriate in countries where gross disparities exist among sections of the population? How would one go about determining whether sufficient disparities were present to justify affirmative action? How would one determine when conditions were such that affirmative action was no longer necessary?*

3. *It has been estimated that women earn 85 cents for every dollar earned by a man in the U.S. Does this justify affirmative action on the basis of gender?*

---

13. *See* EMPLOYMENT EQUITY ACT, Art. 2 (S.C. 1995 c. 44). "Aboriginal peoples" means persons who are Indians, Inuit, or Métis … at Art. 3. "Members of visible minorities" means persons, other than aboriginal peoples, who are non-Caucasian in race or non-white in color."

14. *See* EMPLOYMENT EQUITY ACT OF CANADA (S.C. 1995, c. 44).

IV. Affirmative Action Jurisprudence in the European Court of Justice

The European Union has met with only limited success in promoting affirmative action. As far back as 1976, in an attempt to promote equal treatment for women, the European Community issued a *Council Directive on the Implementation of Equal Treatment for Men and Women as Regards Access to Employment, Vocational Training and Promotion and Working Conditions* (the *Equal Treatment Directive*).[15] Article 1(1) of the *Equal Treatment Directive* states that "the purpose of this Directive is to put into effect in the Member States the principle of equal treatment for men and women as regards access to employment, including promotion, and to vocational training and as regards working conditions...."[16] Article 2(1) defines "equal treatment" to "mean that there shall be no discrimination whatsoever on grounds of sex either directly or indirectly by reference in particular to marital or family status." Article 2(4) provides that "this Directive shall be without prejudice to measures to promote equal opportunity for men and women, in particular by removing existing inequalities that affect women's opportunities in the areas referred to in Article 1(1)." This Directive has given rise to litigation regarding affirmative action in Europe.

A. *Kalanke v. Freie Hansestadt Bremen*[17] (European Court of Justice)

The case originated in Germany and involved the Bremen Law on Equal Treatment for Men and Women in the Public Service (the Bremen Law) (which had been issued to conform with a European Equal Treatment Directive described above).[18] Article 4 of the Bremen Law in question provided that:

Appointment, assignment to an official post and promotion:

(1) In the case of an appointment (including establishment as a civil servant or judge) which is not made for training purposes, women who have the same qualifications as men applying for the same post are to be given priority in sectors where they are under-represented.

(2) In the case of an assignment to a position in a higher pay, remuneration and salary bracket, women who have the same qualifications as men applying for the same post are to be given priority if they are under-represented. This also applies in the case of assignment to a different official post and promotion....

(5) There is under-representation if women do not make up at least half of the staff in the individual pay, remuneration and salary brackets in the relevant

---

15. Council Directive 76/207/EEC of 9 February 1976.

16. *Id.*

17. Case C-450/93 (1995) IRLR 660. *Available at* http://eur-lex.europa.eu/LexUriServ/LexUriServ.do? uri=CELEX:61993J0450:EN:HTML [last visited July 3, 2011].

18. The Directive in question was Council Directive 76/207/EEC of 9 February 1976 on the implementation of the principle of equal treatment for men and women.

personnel group within a department. This also applies to the function levels provided for in the organization chart.

Kalanke, the male plaintiff, and a horticultural employee in the Parks Department, applied for a promotion but was denied the post because a woman, Glissman, had applied for it. Both Kalanke and the female employee had diplomas in horticulture; Kalanke had worked for the Parks Department since 1973; Glissman had been employed since 1975, but women were underrepresented in the Parks Department. The case first went to arbitration where the ruling favored Kalanke. An appeal was taken to the Staff Committee (which decision was binding on the employer). This Committee found that the two candidates were equally qualified and that the priority should therefore be given to the woman, Glissman. Kalanke then filed a claim with the Labor Court, claiming to be better qualified than the female candidate, and asserting that the Bremen Law was inconsistent with the Constitution because it was effectively a quota system. Kalanke lost, but appealed, and the matter ended up before the German Bundesarbeitsgericht. That Court preliminarily found that the Bremen Law did not appear to be a strict quota system, but it stayed the proceedings and sought a preliminary ruling from the European Court of Justice seeking clarification on the scope of derogation permitted from the principle of equal treatment. The German Court pointed out that:

> a quota system such as that in issue may help to overcome in the future the disadvantages which women currently face and which perpetuate past inequalities, inasmuch as it accustoms people to seeing women also filling certain more senior posts. The traditional assignment of certain tasks to women and the concentration of women at the lower end of the scale are contrary to the equal rights criteria applicable today. In that connection, the national court cites figures illustrating the low proportion of women in the higher career brackets among city employees in Bremen, ...

The European Court of Justice was not persuaded by this argument, finding that:

> The purpose of the Directive is, as stated in Article 1(1), to put into effect in the Member States the principle of equal treatment for men and women as regards, inter alia, access to employment, including promotion. Article 2(1) states that the principle of equal treatment means that "there shall be no discrimination whatsoever on grounds of sex either directly or indirectly".

> A national rule that, where men and women who are candidates for the same promotion are equally qualified, women are automatically to be given priority in sectors where they are under-represented, involves discrimination on grounds of sex.[19]

The ECJ then went on to consider whether the Bremen Law was permissible because it sought to "remov[e] existing inequalities which affect women's opportunities." It ultimately found that:

> National rules which guarantee women absolute and unconditional priority for appointment or promotion go beyond promoting equal opportunities and overstep the limits of the exception in Article 2(4) of the Directive.

> Furthermore, in so far as it seeks to achieve equal representation of men and women in all grades and levels within a department, such a system substitutes for equality of opportunity as envisaged in Article 2(4) the result which is only to be arrived at by providing such equality of opportunity.

---

19. Case C-450/93 at paras 14–15.

The answer to the national court's questions must therefore be that Article 2(1) and (4) of the Directive precludes national rules such as those in the present case which, where candidates of different sexes shortlisted for promotion are equally qualified, automatically give priority to women in sectors where they are under-represented, under-representation being deemed to exist when women do not make up at least half of the staff in the individual pay brackets in the relevant personnel group or in the function levels provided for in the organization chart.[20]

The European Court of Justice had another opportunity to consider affirmative action in the case of *Marschall v. Land Nordrhein-Westfalen.*[21]

B. *Marschall v. Land Nordrhein-Westfalen* (European Court of Justice)

In this case, Marschall, a school teacher, was denied promotion in favor of a woman, pursuant to a regulation which afforded women preference when:

> in the sector of the authority responsible for promotion, there are fewer women than men in the particular higher grade post in the career bracket, women are to be given priority for promotion in the event of equal suitability, competence and professional performance, unless reasons specific to an individual [male] candidate tilt the balance in his favour. (emphasis added)

The German Court opined that the provision constituted impermissible discrimination under Article 2(1) of the European Equal Treatment Directive, which calls for equal treatment of men and women with respect to employment and promotion. As in *Kalanke*, it again sought a preliminary ruling from the European Court of Justice. Various countries intervened in the case and made representations to the Court. France and the United Kingdom sided with the decision of the German Court, averring that the law went further than promoting equality of opportunity, but rather aimed at promoting equality of result. Austria, Finland, Spain, Sweden and Norway took the opposite position, arguing that promoting women preferentially helped to attain gender equality in labor markets that were "still broadly partitioned on the basis of gender in that they concentrate female labour in lower positions in the occupational hierarchy."[22] Finland added that "past experience shows in particular that action limited to providing occupational training and guidance for women or to influencing the sharing of occupational and family responsibilities is not sufficient to put an end to this partitioning of labour markets."[23]

The European Court agreed with those who supported the measure, finding that:

> even where male and female candidates are equally qualified, male candidates tend to be promoted in preference to female candidates particularly because of prejudices and stereotypes concerning the role and capacities of women in working life and the fear, for example, that women will interrupt their careers more frequently, that owing to household and family duties they will be less flexible

---

20. *Id.* at para. 24.
21. Case No. C-409/95 (1997) ECE I-6363.
22. *Id.* at paras. 14 & 16.
23. *Id.*

in their working hours, or that they will be absent from work more frequently because of pregnancy, childbirth and breastfeeding.[24]

The Court also went on to find that the last clause of the law constituted a "savings clause" that distinguished the law from that in *Kalanke*. The Court concluded that a law that contains a savings clause was permissible:

> If in each individual case, the rule provides for male candidates who are equally as qualified as the female candidates a guarantee that the candidatures will be the subject of an objective assessment which will take account of all criteria specific to the individual candidates and will override the priority accorded to female candidates where one or more of those criteria tilts the balance in favour of the male candidate.[25]

The Court concluded by pointing out that "the mere fact that a male and female candidate are equally qualified does not mean that they have the same chances."[26]

Giving priority to women who were as qualified for a job as their male rivals could be a legitimate way, the Court held, to "counteract the prejudicial effects on female candidates of the attitudes and behaviour described above and thus reduce actual instances of inequality which may exist in the real world."[27]

Questions for Discussion

1. *Do you agree that men benefit from "deep rooted prejudices and stereotypes"? What might some of those prejudices and stereotypes be? Are they, as the Court suggested, "Men as bread winners and providers for the family"?*

2. *How does one work to overcome those stereotypes? Has CEDAW been effective in this regard?*

3. *How does one determine when the balance has been restored? In the absence of concrete data that shows that women with the same qualifications as male candidates are promoted less frequently, is affirmative action justified?*

4. *Should affirmative action aim to promote "equality of result" or only "equality of opportunity"?*

C. Subsequent European Council Directives

Recent European Council Directives have continued to affirm the validity of special measures. For example, in 2000 the European Council subsequently passed Directive 2000/78/EC (Nov. 27, 2000)[28] which establishes equal treatment in employment and oc-

---

24. *Id.* at para. 29.
25. *Id.* at para. 35.
26. *Id.* at para. 30.
27. *Id.* at para. 31.
28. *Available at* http://eur-lex.europa.eu/LexUriServ/LexUriServ.do?uri=OJ:L:2000:303:0016: 0022:en:PDF [last visited July 1, 2011].

cupation and also precludes discrimination, without prejudice to "measures intended to prevent or compensate for disadvantages suffered by a group of persons ... where their main object is the promotion of the special needs of those persons."

Similarly, in 2006 the Council passed Directive No. 2006/54/EC of the European Parliament and of the Council, which provides:

> (21) The prohibition of discrimination should be without prejudice to the maintenance or adoption of measures intended to prevent or compensate for disadvantages suffered by a group of persons of one sex. Such measures permit organisations of persons of one sex where their main object is the promotion of the special needs of those persons and the promotion of equality between men and women.[29]

V. Affirmative Action in Other Regional Organizations and Conventions

A. The International Labor Organization (ILO) Employment and Occupation Convention No. 111[30]

The International Labor Organization's (ILO) Discrimination Convention also decisively precludes discrimination and endorses affirmative action. The Convention defines discrimination in two ways. First, it is "any distinction, exclusion or preference made on the basis of race, colour, sex, religion, political opinion, national extraction, or social origin, which has the effect of nullifying or impairing equality of opportunity or treatment in employment or occupation."[31] Second it is any "other distinction, exclusion or preference which has the effect of nullifying or impairing equality of opportunity or treatment in employment or occupation.[32] The Convention also commits all state parties to formulate and implement national policies to promote equal opportunity in employment, to eliminate discrimination in this area, and to strive to achieve cooperation between industry and labor, as well as among other relevant organizations. The Convention also mandates that:

> [E]ach Member for which this Convention is in force undertakes to declare and pursue a national policy designed to promote, by methods appropriate to national conditions and practice, equality of opportunity and treatment in respect of employment and occupation, with a view to eliminating any discrimination in respect thereof.[33]

---

29. *Available at* http://eur-lex.europa.eu/LexUriServ/LexUriServ.do?uri=OJ:L:2006:204:0023:0036:en:PDF [last visited February 1, 2001].
30. I.L.O. No. 111, 362 U.N.T.S. entered into force June 15, 1960.
31. Art. 1(a).
32. Art. 1(b).
33. Art. 2.

To this end, Article 5 expressly authorizes "special measures of protection or assistance" oriented toward satisfying particular needs of people who, for reasons of sex, age, disability, family obligations, social, or cultural background, require it. The Convention moreover provides that such measures shall not be deemed to constitute discrimination.

B. African Provisions on Special Temporary Measures

1. *The Banjul Charter*

The 1981 *Banjul Charter on Human and Peoples' Rights* does not have a specific gender based affirmative action or special measures clause, although it contains the traditional equality and non discrimination clauses. The only special form of protection it offers is to the aged, and disabled, noting in Article 18 that:

1. The family shall be the natural unit and basis of society. It shall be protected by the State which shall take care of its physical health and moral.

2. The State shall have the duty to assist the family which is the custodian of morals and traditional values recognized by the community.

3. The State shall ensure the elimination of every discrimination against women and also ensure the protection of the rights of the woman and the child as stipulated in international declarations and conventions.

4. The aged and the disabled shall also have the right to special measures of protection in keeping with their physical or moral needs.

2. The Protocol to the African Charter on Human and Peoples Rights on the Rights of Women in Africa

In 2005, the Protocol to the African Charter on Human and Peoples Rights on the Rights of Women in Africa entered into force after receiving its fifteenth ratification. This Protocol does specifically provide for special measures in Article 1, which mandates that:

1. States Parties shall combat all forms of discrimination against women through appropriate legislative, institutional and other measures. In this regard they shall:

a) include in their national constitutions and other legislative instruments, if not already done, the principle of equality between women and men and ensure its effective application;

b) enact and effectively implement appropriate legislative or regulatory measures, including those prohibiting and curbing all forms of discrimination particularly those harmful practices which endanger the health and general well-being of women;

c) integrate a gender perspective in their policy decisions, legislation, development plans, programmes and activities and in all other spheres of life;

d) take corrective and positive action in those areas where discrimination against women in law and in fact continues to exist;

e) support the local, national, regional and continental initiatives directed at eradicating all forms of discrimination against women.

Claims about violation of the *Protocol* are to be taken to the African Court, although the African Commission had jurisdiction over matters pertaining to the Protocol, while the African Court was being set up. The African Court began functioning in 2006, but has yet to hear any case involving special temporary measures.

3. The SADC Protocol

The SADC Community consists of the following states: Angola, Botswana, The Democratic Republic of Congo, Lesotho, Madagascar, Malawi, Mauritius, Mozambique, Namibia, Seychelles, South Africa, Swaziland, Tanzania, Zambia, and Zimbabwe. In 2008, the SADC member states signed the SADC Protocol on Gender and Development. It specifically uses the term "affirmative action," and defines it in Article 1 as:

> "affirmative action" means a policy programme or measure that seeks to redress past discrimination through active measures to ensure equal opportunity and positive outcomes in all spheres of life.

Equality is defined as a:

> State of being equal in terms of enjoyment of rights, treatment, quantity or value, access to opportunities and outcomes, including resources.

Gender equity is:

> the equal enjoyment of rights and the access to opportunities and outcomes, including resources, by women, men, girls and boys.

Note that substantive equality is the standard in this document.

The affirmative action provision is contained in Article 2.2 and is broadly written, requiring states to:

> [A]dopt the necessary policies, strategies and programmes such as affirmative action to facilitate the implementation of this Protocol. Affirmative action measures shall be put in place with particular reference to women and girls, in order to eliminate all barriers which prevent them from participating meaningfully in all spheres of life.

The Protocol is still too recent to evaluate its implementation. State parties are required to submit reports every two years on the progress they have made in implementing the Protocol. Any dispute over the Protocol which cannot be resolved amicably may be referred to the SADC Tribunal. To date no such cases have been referred.

C. The Work of NGOs

As noted previously, the CEDAW Committee has welcomed the work of NGOs and has encouraged them to work with the governments of States parties to implement CEDAW and the Optional Protocol. At its 45th session, the Committee issued a statement on its relationship with non-governmental organizations.[34] The Committee acknowledged that its review of a State party's implementation of CEDAW would be guided not only by the

---

34. Statement by the Committee on the Elimination of Discrimination against Women on its relationship with non-governmental organizations; *available at* http://www.egyptiancedawcoalition.org/uploads/CEDAW%20With%20NGO's.pdf [last visited January 25, 2011].

State's official report, but also by the "shadow" or "alternative" reports that NGOs are encouraged to file.[35] States parties are also encouraged by the Committee's *General Recommendation No. 25* to include information about special temporary measures in their reports, as NGOs are encouraged to do in their shadow reports. The Committee reminded states to include in their state reports:

> 29. [A]dequate explanations with regard to any failure to adopt temporary special measures. Such failures may not be justified simply by averring powerlessness, or by explaining inaction through predominant market or political forces, such as those inherent in the private sector, private organizations, or political parties. States parties are reminded that article 2 of the Convention, which needs to be read in conjunction with all other articles, imposes accountability on the State party for action by these actors....

> The Committee reiterates its general recommendations 5, 8 and 23, wherein it recommended the application of temporary special measures in the fields of education, the economy, politics and employment, in the area of women representing their Governments at the international level and participating in the work of international organizations, and in the area of political and public life.

In its 2008 shadow report the Nigeria NGO Coalition wrote the following with regard to the implementation of affirmative action in Nigeria:

> The National Gender Policy adopted in 2006 incorporates the principles of CEDAW and other global and regional frameworks that support gender equality and women empowerment in the country's laws, legislative processes, judicial and administrative systems.

> Two out of 36 states have passed Gender and Equal Opportunities Laws (Lmo and Anambra 2006). The laws also incorporate and enforce certain aspects of CEDAW. They provide for the adoption of temporary special measures aimed at accelerating de facto equality between men and women, such measures shall not be considered discrimination.

> 4.3 GAPS AND CHALLENGES

> The National Gender Policy on Affirmative Action is yet to be operationalized and translated into action.

> Policy statements by Ministries of Women Affairs in Nigeria are difficult to implement as a result of the failure to legislate on Affirmative Action or adopt a legal framework for gender mainstreaming.

> Lack of gender disaggregated data is a major constraint to the achievement of equality of women and men before the law, depriving gender actors' evidence to argue for affirmative action and gender specific concessions and interventions as a strategy for attaining gender equality. There is need to have useful data on the prevalence and pattern of violence against women and discriminatory practices in the various parts of the country.

> The political climate is still not gender friendly. Women are not able to compete favourably with men, thus making it difficult to accelerate equality in political participation and governance in general.

This report illustrates two things. First, for affirmative action or special temporary measures to be effectively implemented, there must be reliable data which demonstrates

---

35. *Id.* at para. 7.

areas in which women are underrepresented. Moreover, supporters of such measures have to combat the opposition of those who regard such measures as reverse discrimination.

D. Special Temporary Measures under CEDAW in U.S. Cities

Although the U.S. has not ratified CEDAW, some cities have incorporated legislation directly based on CEDAW. For example, In 1998, San Francisco became the first city to enact a city ordinance implementing the principles underlying CEDAW.

> The ordinance requires the city [San Francisco] to take measures to eliminate discrimination against women and girls in employment and economic opportunities, to prevent and redress sexual and domestic violence, and to eliminate discrimination in the healthcare field to ensure access to adequate care. The Commission on the Status of Women is required to conduct gender analyses on selected city departments and to develop an Action Plan that contains specific recommendations on how deficiencies in these departments will be rectified. The ordinance also creates a Task Force to advise the Mayor and others about the implementation of CEDAW. Since the enactment of this ordinance, the San Francisco Commission on the Status of Women has also advocated for national ratification of CEDAW.

> While few cities have enacted ordinances like that in San Francisco, many states, cities, and counties have passed resolutions urging national ratification of the treaty. Los Angeles passed a resolution on March 15, 2000, which stated that "the principles of CEDAW [would] be adopted and included as a part of the city's ongoing federal and state legislative program," that the city would "not discriminate against women and girls in the areas of employment practices, allocation of funding, and delivery of direct and indirect services," and that the city urged the United States Senate to ratify CEDAW. In New York City, women's rights activists and lawyers are developing a New York City Human Rights Initiative, a model ordinance that would draw on aspects of CEDAW and the Convention on the Elimination of All Forms of Racial Discrimination (CERD). This initiative would set forth local human rights principles drawn from CERD and CEDAW as goals the city aspires to achieve, and would define processes the city would have to follow to integrate human rights principles into all of its programs, policies, and budget considerations. The ordinance would require the city to train personnel in human rights, to undertake a Local Human Rights Analysis of the operations of each department, program and entity, and to create Human Rights Action Plans. It would also present "an opportunity for community organizing and public education about human rights principles."

E. Ruth Bader Ginsburg—*Affirmative Action as an International Human Rights Dialogue: Considered Opinion*[36]

A 1995 United Nations report estimated that white Americans, if ranked as a separate nation, would lead the world in well-being, a measure that combines life expectancy, educational achievement, and income. African Americans, in contrast, would rank a depressing twenty-seventh, while Hispanic Americans would rank even lower at thirty-second. The authors of the UN report observed: "full equality still is a distant prospect in the United States, despite affirmative action policies and market opportunities."

The words affirmative action do not appear in the 1948 *Universal Declaration of Human Rights*, the foundation document for contemporary human rights discourse. The declaration does, however, contain two intellectual anchors for affirmative action. First, the declaration repeatedly endorses the principle of human equality. Second, it declares that everyone has the right to work, to an adequate standard of living, and to education. The declaration does not command that all will share equally, but it does suggest strongly that there are minimum levels of employment, education, and subsistence that all should share. If a nation finds that citizens of one race or sex or religion endure a markedly inadequate standard of living, then, the declaration suggests, it has an obligation to uncover the cause of, and respond to, that endurance.

If we take seriously the promises of employment, education, and sustenance made in the *Universal Declaration of Human Rights,* the discrepancies in racial well-being in the United States noted by the United Nations report demand affirmative government attention. It seems implausible that such marked differences would occur with no discrimination lurking in the background.

---

36. Brookings Institution Considered Opinion; *available at* www.brookings.edu/articles/2000/winter_politics_ginsburg.aspx [last visited March 9, 2012].

Chapter 7

State Responsibility to Protect Women from Violence

Chapter Problem

Imagine that you have a client who has been the victim of repeated domestic violence by her partner. She has obtained restraining orders against him in the past, but local law enforcement officers are often slow to enforce them, and occasionally do not respond to her calls. When she files complaints about this at her local police station, the officers on duty do not seem that concerned. You want to work towards not only helping this individual client, but to effect change in how domestic violence is treated in your jurisdiction. You conduct some research and find that the Department of Justice has created an Office on Violence Against Women (OVW). The mission of that office is to provide federal leadership in developing the nation's capacity to reduce violence against women and administer justice for, and strengthen services to, victims of domestic violence, dating violence, sexual assault, and stalking. The OVW provides funding to local and state and tribal governments, courts, non-profit organizations, community-based organizations, institutes of higher education, and state and tribal coalitions to help them work toward developing more effective responses to violence against women. Their activities include direct services, crisis intervention, transitional housing, legal assistance to victims, court improvement, and training for law enforcement and courts. The OVW also has an Advisory Committee.[1] The Committee helps the OVW fulfill its mission, and provides specific recommendation to the Department of Justice on how to best protect women who are victims of domestic violence.

To bring attention not only to your client's plight, but also to the plight of other women in similar situations whose abuse is not being taken seriously by local authorities, you and your client determine that the best course of action is to have your client testify before the OVW's Advisory Committee. What references and statistics would you bring to the attention of the Advisory Committee to lay the groundwork before your client testifies and tells her story? Would CEDAW be of use to you and your client in helping to make the case that domestic violence is a serious international human rights violation that the state has to respond to? What other sources might you rely on to make this case?

---

1. The Committee is known as the National Advisory Committee on Violence Against Women (NAC).

I. Defining Domestic Violence

The OVW website offers the following definition of domestic violence:

Domestic violence can be defined as a pattern of abusive behavior that is used by an intimate partner to gain or maintain power and control over the other intimate partner. Domestic violence can be physical, sexual, emotional, economic, or psychological actions or threats of actions that influence another person. This includes any behaviors that intimidate, manipulate, humiliate, isolate, frighten, terrorize, coerce, threaten, blame, hurt, injure, or wound someone.

A. CEDAW and Violence against Women

One of the most striking omissions from CEDAW was any provision specifically relating to violence. Domestic violence is one of the most common forms of discrimination faced by women, yet CEDAW was silent on issues of violence.

While CEDAW may have omitted any reference to domestic violence, feminists have not been silent on this subject. Many feminist authors and activists have worked to make the state, and other domestic and international institutions take responsibility for what has traditionally been considered a private family matter. In fact, one of the main contributions of feminist jurisprudence has been to work to erode the distinction between the public and private spheres. Traditionally international human rights law has focused on the public sector—protecting the individual from acts of the state. However, feminists asserted that individuals need protection in the domestic sphere from acts of private individuals too. Since many women spend their lives largely interacting in the domestic sphere where they are unlikely to encounter the coercive power of the state, international human rights does not offer sufficient protection if it does extend into the private sphere. One of the more recent developments of international human rights law is that it now does address private violations of another individual's human rights.

This chapter deals with the issue of state responsibility for acts of private individuals that violate the human rights of another individual. The general principle is that states are responsible if they fail to act with "due diligence." Not all legal systems have embraced this concept. In fact, the U.S. legal system seems to reject it outright, while some other regional systems have embraced it. We will compare the approach adopted by various systems to illustrate that the forum does matter in terms of obtaining redress for violations of human rights. We will also explore the effectiveness of the communications procedure under the Optional Protocol to CEDAW.

B. Feminist Jurisprudence— The Public/Private Distinction

One of the most original contributions made by feminist jurisprudence is to point out that failure of law to afford protection to individuals in the private sphere left women particularly vulnerable. For many women, the majority of their lives and interactions are lived and conducted in the private sphere—in their homes with their families and loved ones. The home is also the place where most violence takes place. Yet many international treaties and documents such as the ICCPR and the Convention on the Rights of the Child acknowledge the role of the family and call on the state to enshrine the right to privacy in the family. Feminist scholars have pointed out that the decision to regard the lives people live in the home as "private" while regarding the lives led in the community as "public" is a gendered decision, with more economic and social value being accorded to public lives, and less to domestic ones. This distinction places women at great disadvantage, as less protection is offered in the private domain.

Until quite recently, human rights were considered to be vertical; that is, states would guarantee to observe, promote and protect the rights of subject individuals, and that no action would be taken by the state or its officials that violated the rights of individuals, or the state would be liable for such action.

Feminist scholars, among others, have suggested that in fact human rights should be seen as horizontal. That is the state should also be liable for actions taken by an individual against another individual if the state failed to exercise "due diligence" in protecting the victim, or prosecuting the perpetrator. This approach has not been widely adopted in the U.S.

C. *CEDAW Committee General Recommendation No. 19*

One of the early Recommendations issued by the CEDAW Committee addressed the issue of state responsibility for private acts that violate human rights. In *General Recommendation No. 19*, part (9)[2] addressing the issue of violence against women, the Committee emphasized that:

> discrimination under the Convention is not restricted to action by or on behalf of Governments (see articles 2(e), 2(f) and 5). For example, under article 2(e) the Convention calls on States parties to take all appropriate measures to eliminate discrimination against women by any person, organization or enterprise. Under general international law and specific human rights covenants, States may also be responsible for private acts if they fail to act with due diligence to prevent violations of rights or to investigate and punish acts of violence, and for providing compensation.

D. *General Recommendation No. 25*

This Recommendation left no doubt that states should consider themselves responsible for acts of violence that occur in "private," pointing out:

> The Convention makes very clear that these responsibilities extend to private life as well as public life. Historically, one of the biggest obstacles to realizing women's rights in many countries has been the perception that the State should not interfere in the "private" realm of family relations. The Convention recognizes that unequal

---

2. *General Recommendation No. 19* (11th session 1992). *Available at* www.un.org/womenwatch/daw/cedaw/recommendations/recomm.htm [last visited June 1, 2011].

power relations within the private sphere contribute very significantly to gender inequality in all aspects of women's lives, and directs States to take measures that will correct this power imbalance.[3]

As the statistics below show, violence against women is an endemic problem, and for CEDAW an impact on the lives of women, it has to address acts of violence that occur in domains hitherto considered "private."

The failure of the CEDAW Convention itself to specifically address and eliminate violence was a marked omission that the UN attempted to remedy through its promulgation of the Declaration on the Elimination of Violence against Women.[4]

E. Declaration on the Elimination of Violence against Women

The General Assembly,

Recognizing the urgent need for the universal application to women of the rights and principles with regard to equality, security, liberty, integrity and dignity of all human beings, …

Recognizing that effective implementation of the Convention on the Elimination of All Forms of Discrimination against Women would contribute to the elimination of violence against women and that the Declaration on the Elimination of Violence against Women, set forth in the present resolution, will strengthen and complement that process,

Concerned that violence against women is an obstacle to the achievement of equality, development and peace, as recognized in the Nairobi Forward-looking Strategies for the Advancement of Women, in which a set of measures to combat violence against women was recommended, and to the full implementation of the Convention on the Elimination of All Forms of Discrimination against Women,

Affirming that violence against women constitutes a violation of the rights and fundamental freedoms of women and impairs or nullifies their enjoyment of those rights and freedoms, and concerned about the long-standing failure to protect and promote those rights and freedoms in the case of violence against women,

Recognizing that violence against women is a manifestation of historically unequal power relations between men and women, which have led to domination over and discrimination against women by men and to the prevention of the full advancement of women, and that violence against women is one of the crucial social mechanisms by which women are forced into a subordinate position compared with men,

Concerned that some groups of women, such as women belonging to minority groups, indigenous women, refugee women, migrant women, women living in rural or remote communities, destitute women, women in institutions or in detention, female children, women with disabilities, elderly women and women in situations of armed conflict, are especially vulnerable to violence,

Recalling the conclusion in Paragraph 23 of the annex to Economic and Social Council resolution 1990/15 of 24 May 1990 that the recognition that violence against women in

---

3. *Available at* http://www.unifem.org/cedaw30/about_cedaw/ [last visited May 6, 2010].
4. Proclaimed by General Assembly Resolution 48/104 of 20 December 1993; *available at* http://www2.ohchr.org/english/law/eliminationvaw.htm [last visited November 28, 2010].

the family and society was pervasive and cut across lines of income, class and culture had to be matched by urgent and effective steps to eliminate its incidence, ...

Welcoming the role that women's movements are playing in drawing increasing attention to the nature, severity and magnitude of the problem of violence against women,

Alarmed that opportunities for women to achieve legal, social, political and economic equality in society are limited, inter alia, by continuing and endemic violence,

Convinced that in the light of the above there is a need for a clear and comprehensive definition of violence against women, a clear statement of the rights to be applied to ensure the elimination of violence against women in all its forms, a commitment by States in respect of their responsibilities, and a commitment by the international community at large to the elimination of violence against women,

Solemnly proclaims the following Declaration on the Elimination of Violence against Women and urges that every effort be made so that it becomes generally known and re-spected:

Article 1

For the purposes of this Declaration, the term "violence against women" means any act of gender-based violence that results in, or is likely to result in, physical, sexual or psychological harm or suffering to women, including threats of such acts, coercion or arbitrary deprivation of liberty, whether occurring in public or in private life.

Article 2

Violence against women shall be understood to encompass, but not be limited to, the following:

(a) Physical, sexual and psychological violence occurring in the family, including battering, sexual abuse of female children in the household, dowry-related violence, marital rape, female genital mutilation and other traditional practices harmful to women, non-spousal violence and violence related to exploitation;

(b) Physical, sexual and psychological violence occurring within the general community, including rape, sexual abuse, sexual harassment and intimidation at work, in educational institutions and elsewhere, trafficking in women and forced prostitu-tion;

(c) Physical, sexual and psychological violence perpetrated or condoned by the State, wherever it occurs.

Article 3

Women are entitled to the equal enjoyment and protection of all human rights and fundamental freedoms in the political, economic, social, cultural, civil or any other field. These rights include, inter alia:

(a) The right to life;

(b) The right to equality;

(c) The right to liberty and security of person;

(d) The right to equal protection under the law;

(e) The right to be free from all forms of discrimination;

(f) The right to the highest standard attainable of physical and mental health;

(g) The right to just and favourable conditions of work;

(h) The right not to be subjected to torture, or other cruel, inhuman or degrading treatment or punishment.

Article 4

States should condemn violence against women and should not invoke any custom, tradition or religious consideration to avoid their obligations with respect to its elimination. States should pursue by all appropriate means and without delay a policy of eliminating violence against women and, to this end, should:

(a) Consider, where they have not yet done so, ratifying or acceding to the Convention on the Elimination of All Forms of Discrimination against Women or withdrawing reservations to that Convention;

(b) Refrain from engaging in violence against women;

(c) Exercise due diligence to prevent, investigate and, in accordance with national legislation, punish acts of violence against women, whether those acts are perpetrated by the State or by private persons;

(d) Develop penal, civil, labour and administrative sanctions in domestic legislation to punish and redress the wrongs caused to women who are subjected to violence; women who are subjected to violence should be provided with access to the mechanisms of justice and, as provided for by national legislation, to just and effective remedies for the harm that they have suffered; States should also inform women of their rights in seeking redress through such mechanisms;

(e) Consider the possibility of developing national plans of action to promote the protection of women against any form of violence, or to include provisions for that purpose in plans already existing, taking into account, as appropriate, such cooperation as can be provided by non-governmental organizations, particularly those concerned with the issue of violence against women;

(f) Develop, in a comprehensive way, preventive approaches and all those measures of a legal, political, administrative and cultural nature that promote the protection of women against any form of violence, and ensure that the re-victimization of women does not occur because of laws insensitive to gender considerations, enforcement practices or other interventions;

(g) Work to ensure, to the maximum extent feasible in the light of their available resources and, where needed, within the framework of international cooperation, that women subjected to violence and, where appropriate, their children have specialized assistance, such as rehabilitation, assistance in child care and maintenance, treatment, counselling, and health and social services, facilities and programmes, as well as support structures, and should take all other appropriate measures to promote their safety and physical and psychological rehabilitation;

(h) Include in government budgets adequate resources for their activities related to the elimination of violence against women;

(i) Take measures to ensure that law enforcement officers and public officials responsible for implementing policies to prevent, investigate and punish violence against women receive training to sensitize them to the needs of women;

(j) Adopt all appropriate measures, especially in the field of education, to modify the social and cultural patterns of conduct of men and women and to eliminate prejudices, customary practices and all other practices based on the idea of the inferiority or superiority of either of the sexes and on stereotyped roles for men and women;

(k) Promote research, collect data and compile statistics, especially concerning domestic violence, relating to the prevalence of different forms of violence against women and encourage research on the causes, nature, seriousness and consequences of violence against women and on the effectiveness of measures implemented to prevent and redress violence against women; those statistics and findings of the research will be made public;

(l) Adopt measures directed towards the elimination of violence against women who are especially vulnerable to violence;

(m) Include, in submitting reports as required under relevant human rights instruments of the United Nations, information pertaining to violence against women and measures taken to implement the present Declaration;

(n) Encourage the development of appropriate guidelines to assist in the implementation of the principles set forth in the present Declaration;

(o) Recognize the important role of the women's movement and non-governmental organizations world wide in raising awareness and alleviating the problem of violence against women;

(p) Facilitate and enhance the work of the women's movement and non-governmental organizations and cooperate with them at local, national and regional levels;

(q) Encourage intergovernmental regional organizations of which they are members to include the elimination of violence against women in their programmes, as appropriate.

Article 5

The organs and specialized agencies of the United Nations system should, within their respective fields of competence, contribute to the recognition and realization of the rights and the principles set forth in the present Declaration and, to this end, should, inter alia:

(a) Foster international and regional cooperation with a view to defining regional strategies for combating violence, exchanging experiences and financing programmes relating to the elimination of violence against women;

(b) Promote meetings and seminars with the aim of creating and raising awareness among all persons of the issue of the elimination of violence against women;

(c) Foster coordination and exchange within the United Nations system between human rights treaty bodies to address the issue of violence against women effectively;

(d) Include in analyses prepared by organizations and bodies of the United Nations system of social trends and problems, such as the periodic reports on the world social situation, examination of trends in violence against women;

(e) Encourage coordination between organizations and bodies of the United Nations system to incorporate the issue of violence against women into ongoing programmes, especially with reference to groups of women particularly vulnerable to violence;

(f) Promote the formulation of guidelines or manuals relating to violence against women, taking into account the measures referred to in the present Declaration;

(g) Consider the issue of the elimination of violence against women, as appropriate, in fulfilling their mandates with respect to the implementation of human rights instruments;

(h) Cooperate with non-governmental organizations in addressing the issue of violence against women.

Article 6

Nothing in the present Declaration shall affect any provision that is more conducive to the elimination of violence against women that may be contained in the legislation of a State or in any international convention, treaty or other instrument in force in a State.

II. Litigating Domestic Violence— The CEDAW Committee and Domestic Violence under the Optional Protocol

A. *A.T. v. Hungary*

The first domestic violence case brought under CEDAW's Optional Protocol involved a claim of domestic violence by a Hungarian woman—Ms. A.T. In affirming the position that a state party may be liable for the acts of a private individual, the Committee noted that:

> The author, Ms. "A.T.," alleges that she and her two children, one of whom is severely brain-damaged, have been subjected to constant and severe domestic violence by her common law husband and father of her two children, "L.F." Despite this, A.T. is unable to move into an appropriate shelter since there is no shelter in Hungary able to adequately provide and care for a disabled child, her mother, and sister. There are also no protection orders or restraining orders available under the laws of Hungary either.

> Subsequently, L.F. moved out of their family home to live with another female partner. For three years, he refused to pay for child support. He added this financial abuse to his continuing threats of physical abuse and even threatened A.T. that he would rape their two children. The foregoing events forced the author to change the locks of their apartment but L.F., through the use of force and violence, eventually forced his way into the apartment. L.F. has consistently physically abused and battered A.T. resulting in her hospitalization. She has ten medical certificates to prove his physical violence, abuse and battery.

> A.T. has instituted civil proceedings against L.F., praying for possession of their apartment but the court ruled that L.F. is equally entitled to the use and possession of the apartment and that A.T.'s claim of battery is unsubstantiated. Further proceedings about the property's division have been suspended. She has also filed two criminal proceedings against L.F. concerning his assault and battery (that resulted in her hospitalization). However, L.F. has never been detained throughout these proceedings and the Hungarian authorities have informed the author that there is hardly anything that they can legally do to help in these kinds of situations. As such, A.T. feared for her life and for her children.

> The author sought justice through the intervention of the CEDAW Committee on the ground that she is a victim of Hungary's violations of its positive obligations

under the CEDAW. She alleged that Hungary's failure to provide for sufficient legal and actual protection from L.F. constitutes a violation of articles 2 (a), (b) and (e), 5 (a) and 16 of the CEDAW.

Held: The *Committee's General Recommendation (GR) No. 19* on violence against women states that the definition of discrimination is inclusive of gender-based violence and that "[G]ender-based violence may breach specific provisions of the Convention, regardless of whether those provisions expressly mention violence." The GR also poses the question of whether States Parties can be held accountable for the conduct of non-State actors. The GR states that:

"[U]nder general international law and specific human rights covenants, States may also be responsible for private acts if they fail to act with due diligence to prevent violations of rights or to investigate and punish acts of violence, and for providing compensation."

Although the Committee appreciates Hungary's current efforts to improve the women's situation and uphold their rights, these efforts are presently unable to sufficiently address the needs and provide the necessary assistance to women victims of domestic violence, such as A.T. The court proceedings are far too long and the laws fail to give adequate protection to the victims during such proceedings. Women's rights, as well as cases involving their rights, are not given a high priority in Hungarian courts. A woman's basic right to life and to physical and mental integrity cannot and should not be subordinate to mere property and privacy rights. Sadly, the State-Party has not provided any alternative measure which A.T. could have taken, in order to attain justice and protection for herself and her children.

[The Committee chastised Hungary for failing to provide remedies for Ms. A.T., noting that:]

[T]he Committee is concerned about the prevalence of violence against women and girls, including domestic violence. It is particularly concerned that no specific legislation has been enacted to combat domestic violence and sexual harassment and that no protection or exclusion orders or shelters exist for the immediate protection of women victims of domestic violence." Bearing this in mind, the Committee concludes that the obligations of the State Party set out in article 2 (a), (b) and (e) of the Convention extend to the prevention of and protection from violence against women, which obligations in the present case, remain un-fulfilled and constitute a violation of the author's human rights and fundamental freedoms, particularly her right to security of person.

For four years and continuing to the present day, the author has felt threatened by her former common law husband, the father of her two children. The author has been battered by this same man, her former common law husband. She has been unsuccessful, either through civil or criminal proceedings, to temporarily or permanently bar L.F. from the apartment where she and her children have continued to reside. The author could not have asked for a restraining or protection order, since neither option currently exists in the State Party. She has been unable to flee to a shelter because none are equipped to accept her together with her children, one of whom is fully disabled. None of these facts have been disputed by the State Party and, considered together, they indicate that the rights of the author under articles 5 (a) and 16 of the Convention have been violated.

B. *Goekce v. Austria*; *Yildirim v. Austria* (CEDAW Committee Communications 2005)

In 2005, two cases were brought against Austria for failing to protect women from domestic violence perpetrated by their abusive spouses. Each victim was murdered by her spouse despite having sought protection from the state. Although Austria, unlike Hungary, had some laws and procedures in place to protect women from domestic violence, local police and prosecutors tended not to enforce these laws. In *Goekce v. Austria*[5] the Vienna Intervention Centre Against Domestic Violence filed a complaint on behalf of the surviving children of the victim, Sahide Goekce, alleging that Goekce was the:

> victim of a violation by the State party of articles 1, 2, 3 and 5 of the Convention on the Elimination of All Forms of Discrimination against Women because the State party did not actively take all appropriate measures to protect Şahide Goekce's right to personal security and life. The State party failed to treat Mustafa Goekce as an extremely violent and dangerous offender in accordance with criminal law. The authors claim that the Federal Act for the Protection against Violence within the Family (Bundesgesetz zum Schutz vor Gewalt in der Familie) does not provide the means to protect women from highly violent persons, especially in cases of repeated, severe violence and death threats. Instead, the authors insist that detention is necessary. The authors also allege that had the communication between the police and Public Prosecutor been better and faster, the Public Prosecutor would have known about the ongoing violence and death threats and may have found that he had sufficient reason to prosecute Mustafa Goekce. The authors further contend that the State party also failed to fulfil its obligations stipulated in the general recommendations Nos. 12, 19 and 21 of the Committee on the Elimination of Discrimination against Women, the United Nations Declaration on the Elimination of Violence against Women, the concluding comments of the Committee (June 2000) on the combined third and fourth periodic report and the fifth periodic report of Austria, the United Nations Resolution on Crime Prevention and Criminal Justice Measures to Eliminate Violence against Women, several provisions of the outcome document of the twenty-third special session of the General Assembly, article 3 of the United Nations Universal Declaration of Human Rights, articles 6 and 9 of the International Covenant on Civil and Political Rights, several provisions of other international instruments, and the Austrian Constitution.

> In its response to the complaint filed by Goekce's heirs, the state party detailed how Goecke had filed complaints against her husband and subsequently withdrawn them, and how she had had her husband removed from the apartment by authorities and then subsequently let him back in.

> The State party summarizes its position by asserting that Şahide Goekce could not be guaranteed effective protection because she had not been prepared to cooperate with the Austrian authorities. In light of the information available to the public authorities, any further interference by the State in the fundamental rights and freedoms of Mustafa Goekce would not have been permissible under the Constitution.

---

5. Communication No. 5/2005 CEDAW; *available at* http://www.un.org/ga/search/view_doc.asp?symbol=CEDAW/C/39/D/5/2005 [last visited November 28, 2010].

In the instant case, the Committee notes that during the three-year period starting with the violent episode that was reported to the police on 3 December 1999 and ending with the shooting of Şahide Goekce on 7 December 2002, the frequency of calls to the police about disturbances and disputes and/or battering increased; the police issued prohibition to return orders on three separate occasions and twice requested the Public Prosecutor to order that Mustafa Goekce be detained; and a three-month interim injunction was in effect at the time of her death that prohibited Mustafa Goekce from returning to the family apartment and its immediate environs and from contacting Şahide Goekce or the children. The Committee notes that Mustafa Goekce shot Şahide Goekce dead with a handgun that he had purchased three weeks earlier, despite a valid weapons prohibition against him as well as the uncontested contention by the authors that the police had received information about the weapon from the brother of Mustafa Goekce. In addition, the Committee notes the unchallenged fact that Şahide Goekce called the emergency call service a few hours before she was killed, yet no patrol car was sent to the scene of the crime.

The Committee considers that given this combination of factors, the police knew or should have known that Şahide Goekce was in serious danger; they should have treated the last call from her as an emergency, in particular because Mustafa Goekce had shown that he had the potential to be a very dangerous and violent criminal. The Committee considers that in light of the long record of earlier disturbances and battering, by not responding to the call immediately, the police are accountable for failing to exercise due diligence to protect Şahide Goekce.

Acting under article 7, Paragraph 3, of the Optional Protocol to the Convention on the Elimination of All Forms of Discrimination against Women, the Committee on the Elimination of Discrimination against Women is of the view that the facts before it reveal a violation of the rights of the deceased Şahide Goekce to life and physical and mental integrity under article 2 (a) and (c) through (f), and article 3 of the Convention read in conjunction with article 1 of the Convention and general recommendation 19 of the Committee and makes the following recommendations to the State party:

(a) Strengthen implementation and monitoring of the Federal Act for the Protection against Violence within the Family and related criminal law, by acting with due diligence to prevent and respond to such violence against women and adequately providing for sanctions for the failure to do so;

(b) Vigilantly and in a speedy manner prosecute perpetrators of domestic violence in order to convey to offenders and the public that society condemns domestic violence as well as ensure that criminal and civil remedies are utilized ...

(c) Ensure enhanced coordination among law enforcement and judicial officers and also ensure that all levels of the criminal justice system (police, public prosecutors, judges) routinely cooperate with non-governmental organizations that work to protect and support women victims of gender-based violence;

(d) Strengthen training programmes and education on domestic violence for judges, lawyers and law enforcement officials, including on the Convention on the Elimination of All Forms of Discrimination against Women, general Recommendation 19 of the Committee, and the Optional Protocol thereto.

Like Sahide Goekce, Fatma Yildirim was also murdered by her husband. She too had filed domestic violence charges against him and had him ordered removed from their apartment. Her subsequent requests to the Public Prosecutor that he be detained were denied. Despite the restraining order that Fatma Yildirim had obtained against her husband, he fatally stabbed her on her way home from work. In this case the Committee too found violations of Fatma Yildirim's right to life and to physical and mental integrity.[6]

Questions for Discussion

1. *Do you think that CEDAW's failure to address violence in the Convention itself has been adequately addressed by General Recommendations 19 and 25? Has the Declaration on the Elimination of Violence against Women addressed that deficit?*

2. *Is violence against women generally recognized as a form of discrimination?*

3. *Consider the CEDAW Committee's Recommendation that states bear responsibility for acts committed by private individuals if they fail to act with "due diligence." Is it sufficiently clear what is required of a state in order to meet the standard of due diligence?*

4. *The CEDAW Committee and others have posited that government intrusion into the private sphere is required because many episodes of violence take place in that sphere. Might people concerned about privacy and personal liberty feel the intrusion is unjustified? Do they have a valid argument?*

5. *Consider that three of the Communications heard by the CEDAW Committee have been cases involving domestic violence. What does that tell us about the effectiveness of the Declaration on the Elimination of Violence against Women? What does it tell us about the commitment of state governments to protect women from violence?*

III. The Scope of the Problem — Violence against Women

In a 10-country study on women's health and domestic violence conducted by the World Health Organization (WHO) in 2005, the organization found:

- Between 15% and 71% of women reported physical or sexual violence by a husband or partner;

---

6. *Available at* http://www.un.org/ga/search/view_doc.asp?symbol=CEDAW/C/39/D/6/2005 [last visited November 26, 2010].

- Many women said that their first sexual experience was not consensual (24% in rural Peru, 28% in Tanzania, 30% in rural Bangladesh, and 40% in South Africa);

- Between 4% and 12% of women reported being physically abused during pregnancy;

- Every year, about 5,000 women worldwide are murdered by family members in the name of honour;

- Trafficking of women and girls for forced labor and sex is widespread and often affects the most vulnerable;

- Forced marriages and child marriages violate the human rights of women and girls, yet they are widely practiced in many countries in Asia, the Middle East and sub-Saharan Africa;

- Worldwide, up to one in five women and one in 10 men report experiencing sexual abuse as children. Children subjected to sexual abuse are much more likely to encounter other forms of abuse later in life.

The same study found significant health effects on women, including:

- **Injuries:** Physical and sexual abuse by a partner is closely associated with injuries. Violence by an intimate partner is the leading cause of non-fatal injuries to women in the USA;

- **Death:** Deaths from violence against women include honor killings (by families for cultural reasons); suicide; female infanticide (murder of infant girls); and maternal death from unsafe abortion;

- **Sexual and reproductive health:** Violence against women is associated with sexually transmitted infections such as HIV/AIDS, unintended pregnancies, gynaecological problems, induced abortions, and adverse pregnancy outcomes, including miscarriage, low birth weight and fetal death;

- **Risky behaviors:** Sexual abuse as a child is associated with higher rates of sexual risk-taking (such as first sex at an early age, multiple partners and unprotected sex), substance use, and additional victimization. Each of these behaviors increases risks of health problems;

- **Mental health:** Violence and abuse increase risk of depression, post-traumatic stress disorder, sleep difficulties, eating disorders and emotional distress;

- **Physical health:** Abuse can result in many health problems, including headaches, back pain, abdominal pain, fibromyalgia, gastrointestinal disorders, limited mobility, and poor overall health.

IV. Addressing the Problem in Regional Systems — The Inter-American System

The Inter-American system (which has been discussed in an earlier chapter), has been at the forefront of developing jurisprudence on the importance of extending human rights protection into the private sphere. It was also one of the earliest regional human rights systems to develop a Convention to eliminate violence against women.

A. Convention of Belém Do Pará

THE STATES PARTIES TO THIS CONVENTION,

RECOGNIZING that full respect for human rights has been enshrined in the American Declaration of the Rights and Duties of Man and the Universal Declaration of Human Rights, and reaffirmed in other international and regional instruments;

AFFIRMING that violence against women constitutes a violation of their human rights and fundamental freedoms, and impairs or nullifies the observance, enjoyment and exercise of such rights and freedoms;

CONCERNED that violence against women is an offense against human dignity and a manifestation of the historically unequal power relations between women and men;

RECALLING the Declaration on the Elimination of Violence against Women, adopted by the Twenty-fifth Assembly of Delegates of the Inter-American Commission of Women, and affirming that violence against women pervades every sector of society regardless of class, race or ethnic group, income, culture, level of education, age or religion and strikes at its very foundations:

CONVINCED that the elimination of violence against women is essential for their individual and social development and their full and equal participation in all walks of life; and

CONVINCED that the adoption of a convention on the prevention, punishment and eradication of all forms of violence against women within the framework of the Organization of American States is a positive contribution to protecting the rights of women and eliminating violence against them,

HAVE AGREED to the following:

CHAPTER I
DEFINITION AND SCOPE OF APPLICATION

Article 1

For the purposes of this Convention, violence against women shall be understood as any act or conduct, based on gender, which causes death or physical, sexual or psychological harm or suffering to women, whether in the public or the private sphere.

Article 2

Violence against women shall be understood to include physical, sexual and psychological violence:

a. that occurs within the family or domestic unit or within any other interpersonal relationship, whether or not the perpetrator shares or has shared the same residence with the woman, including, among others, rape, battery and sexual abuse;

b. that occurs in the community and is perpetrated by any person, including, among others, rape, sexual abuse, torture, trafficking in persons, forced prostitution, kidnapping and sexual harassment in the workplace, as well as in educational institutions, health facilities or any other place; and

c. that is perpetrated or condoned by the state or its agents regardless of where it occurs.

CHAPTER II
RIGHTS PROTECTED

Article 3

Every woman has the right to be free from violence in both the public and private spheres.

Article 4

Every woman has the right to the recognition, enjoyment, exercise and protection of all human rights and freedoms embodied in regional and international human rights instruments. These rights include, among others:

a. The right to have her life respected;

b. The right to have her physical, mental and moral integrity respected;

c. The right to personal liberty and security;

d. The right not to be subjected to torture;

e. The rights to have the inherent dignity of her person respected and her family protected;

f. The right to equal protection before the law and of the law;

g. The right to simple and prompt recourse to a competent court for protection against acts that violate her rights;

h. The right to associate freely;

i. The right of freedom to profess her religion and beliefs within the law; and

j. The right to have equal access to the public service of her country and to take part in the conduct of public affairs, including decision-making.

Article 5

Every woman is entitled to the free and full exercise of her civil, political, economic, social and cultural rights, and may rely on the full protection of those rights as embodied in regional and international instruments on human rights. The States Parties recognize that violence against women prevents and nullifies the exercise of these rights.

Article 6

The right of every woman to be free from violence includes, among others:

a. The right of women to be free from all forms of discrimination; and

b. The right of women to be valued and educated free of stereotyped patterns of behavior and social and cultural practices based on concepts of inferiority or subordination.

CHAPTER III
DUTIES OF THE STATES

Article 7

The States Parties condemn all forms of violence against women and agree to pursue, by all appropriate means and without delay, policies to prevent, punish and eradicate such violence and undertake to:

a.   refrain from engaging in any act or practice of violence against women and to ensure that their authorities, officials, personnel, agents, and institutions act in conformity with this obligation;

b.   apply due diligence to prevent, investigate and impose penalties for violence against women;

c.   include in their domestic legislation penal, civil, administrative and any other type of provisions that may be needed to prevent, punish and eradicate violence against women and to adopt appropriate administrative measures where necessary;

d.   adopt legal measures to require the perpetrator to refrain from harassing, intimidating or threatening the woman or using any method that harms or endangers her life or integrity, or damages her property;

e.   take all appropriate measures, including legislative measures, to amend or repeal existing laws and regulations or to modify legal or customary practices which sustain the persistence and tolerance of violence against women;

f.   establish fair and effective legal procedures for women who have been subjected to violence which include, among others, protective measures, a timely hearing and effective access to such procedures;

g.   establish the necessary legal and administrative mechanisms to ensure that women subjected to violence have effective access to restitution, reparations or other just and effective remedies; and

h.   adopt such legislative or other measures as may be necessary to give effect to this Convention.

Article 8

The States Parties agree to undertake progressively specific measures, including programs:

a.   to promote awareness and observance of the right of women to be free from violence, and the right of women to have their human rights respected and protected;

b.   to modify social and cultural patterns of conduct of men and women, including the development of formal and informal educational programs appropriate to every level of the educational process, to counteract prejudices, customs and all other practices which are based on the idea of the inferiority or superiority of either of the sexes or on the stereotyped roles for men and women which legitimize or exacerbate violence against women;

c.   to promote the education and training of all those involved in the administration of justice, police and other law enforcement officers as well as other personnel responsible for implementing policies for the prevention, punishment and eradication of violence against women;

d.   to provide appropriate specialized services for women who have been subjected to violence, through public and private sector agencies, including shelters, counseling services for all family members where appropriate, and care and custody of the affected children;

e.   to promote and support governmental and private sector education designed to raise the awareness of the public with respect to the problems of and remedies for violence against women;

f. to provide women who are subjected to violence access to effective readjustment and training programs to enable them to fully participate in public, private and social life;

g. to encourage the communications media to develop appropriate media guidelines in order to contribute to the eradication of violence against women in all its forms, and to enhance respect for the dignity of women;

h. to ensure research and the gathering of statistics and other relevant information relating to the causes, consequences and frequency of violence against women, in order to assess the effectiveness of measures to prevent, punish and eradicate violence against women and to formulate and implement the necessary changes; and

i. to foster international cooperation for the exchange of ideas and experiences and the execution of programs aimed at protecting women who are subjected to violence.

Article 9

With respect to the adoption of the measures in this Chapter, the States Parties shall take special account of the vulnerability of women to violence by reason of, among others, their race or ethnic background or their status as migrants, refugees or displaced persons. Similar consideration shall be given to women subjected to violence while pregnant or who are disabled, of minor age, elderly, socioeconomically disadvantaged, affected by armed conflict or deprived of their freedom.

Questions for Discussion

1. *Does the Belém do Pará Convention give more context to the concept of due diligence by specifying the duties of a state in Article 7?*

2. *Although the Declaration on the Elimination of Violence against Women and the Belém do Pará Convention reject the idea that custom or culture may be used to justify violence, might there be cultural differences as to whether a cultural practice constitutes violence? Can you think of any such practices?*

3. *How should we respond to these kinds of practices?*

While the Inter-American system has been proactive in proclaiming its intolerance of violence in any sphere, its Court has also been consistent about extending the right to be free from violence into the private sphere.

B. *Velasquez Rodriguez v. Honduras*[7]

In submitting the case, the Commission invoked Articles 50 and 51 of the American Convention on Human Rights (hereinafter "the Convention" or "the American Convention") and requested that the Court determine whether the State in question had

---

7. Judgment of July 29, 1988, Inter-Am.Ct.H.R. (Ser. C) No. 4 (1988).

violated Articles 4 (Right to Life), 5 (Right to Humane Treatment) and 7 (Right to Personal Liberty) of the Convention in the case of Angel Manfredo Velásquez Rodríguez (also known as Manfredo Velásquez). In addition, the Commission asked the Court to rule that "the consequences of the situation that constituted the breach of such right or freedom be remedied and that fair compensation be paid to the injured party or parties." According to the petition filed with the Commission, and the supplementary information received subsequently, Manfredo Velasquez, a student at the National Autonomous University of Honduras, "was violently detained without a warrant for his arrest by members of the National Office of Investigations (DNI) and G-2 of the Armed Forces of Honduras." The detention took place in Tegucigalpa on the afternoon of September 12, 1981. According to the petitioners, several eyewitnesses reported that Manfredo Velasquez and others were detained and taken to the cells of Public Security Forces Station No. 2 located in the Barrio E1 Manchen of Tegucigalpa, where he was "accused of alleged political crimes and subjected to harsh interrogation and cruel torture." The petition added that on September 17, 1981, Manfredo Velásquez was moved to the First Infantry Battalion, where the interrogation continued, but that the police and security forces denied that he had been detained.

[...] The Commission presented testimony and documentary evidence to show that there were many kidnappings and disappearances in Honduras from 1981 to 1984 and that those acts were attributable to the Armed Forces of Honduras (hereinafter "Armed Forces"), which was able to rely at least on the tolerance of the Government. Three officers of the Armed Forces testified on this subject at the request of the Court.

Based on the above, the Court finds that the following facts have been proven in this proceeding: ...

(1) a practice of disappearances carried out or tolerated by Honduran officials existed between 1981 and 1984;

(2) Manfredo Velásquez disappeared at the hands of or with the acquiescence of those officials within the framework of that practice; and

(3) the Government of Honduras failed to guarantee the human rights affected by that practice.... The practice of disappearances, in addition to directly violating many provisions of the Convention, such as those noted above, constitutes a radical breach of the treaty in that it shows a crass abandonment of the values which emanate from the concept of human dignity and of the most basic principles of the inter-American system and the Convention. The existence of this practice, moreover, evinces a disregard of the duty to organize the State in such a manner as to guarantee the rights recognized in the Convention, as set out below ...

Article 1(1) is essential in determining whether a violation of the human rights recognized by the Convention can be imputed to a State Party. In effect, that article charges the States Parties with the fundamental duty to respect and guarantee the rights recognized in the Convention. Any impairment of those rights which can be attributed under the rules of international law to the action or omission of any public authority constitutes an act imputable to the State, which assumes responsibility in the terms provided by the Convention.

The first obligation assumed by the States Parties under Article 1(1) is "to respect the rights and freedoms" recognized by the Convention. The exercise of public authority has certain limits which derive from the fact that human rights are inherent attributes of human dignity and are, therefore, superior to the power of the State. On another occasion, this Court stated:

> The protection of human rights, particularly the civil and political rights set forth in the Convention, is in effect based on the affirmation of the existence of certain inviolable attributes of the individual that cannot be legitimately restricted through the exercise of governmental power. These are individual domains that are beyond the reach of the State or to which the State has but limited access. Thus, the protection of human rights must necessarily comprise the concept of the restriction of the exercise of state power ...

Thus, in principle, any violation of rights recognized by the Convention carried out by an act of public authority or by persons who use their position of authority is imputable to the State. However, this does not define all the circumstances in which a State is obligated to prevent, investigate and punish human rights violations, nor all the cases in which the State might be found responsible for an infringement of those rights.

An illegal act which violates human rights and which is initially not directly imputable to a State (for example, because it is the act of a private person or because the person responsible has not yet been identified) can lead to international responsibility of the State, not because of the act itself, but because of the lack of due diligence to prevent the violation or to respond to it as required by the Convention ...

Violations of the Convention cannot be founded upon rules that take psychological factors into account in establishing individual culpability. For the purposes of analysis, the intent or motivation of the agent who has violated the rights recognized by the Convention is irrelevant — the violation can be established even if the identity of the individual perpetrator is unknown. What is decisive is whether a violation of the rights recognized by the Convention has occurred with the support or the acquiescence of the government, or whether the State has allowed the act to take place without taking measures to prevent it or to punish those responsible. Thus, the Court's task is to determine whether the violation is the result of a State's failure to fulfill its duty to respect and guarantee those rights, as required by Article 1(1) of the Convention.

174. The State has a legal duty to take reasonable steps to prevent human rights violations and to use the means at its disposal to carry out a serious investigation of violations committed within its jurisdiction, to identify those responsible, to impose the appropriate punishment and to ensure the victim adequate compensation.

175. This duty to prevent includes all those means of a legal, political, administrative and cultural nature that promote the protection of human rights and ensure that any violations are considered and treated as illegal acts, which, as such, may lead to the punishment of those responsible and the obligation to indemnify the victims for damages. It is not possible to make a detailed list of all such measures, since they vary with the law and the conditions of each State Party. Of course, while the State is obligated to prevent human rights abuses, the existence of a particular violation does not, in itself, prove the failure to take preventive measures

176. The State is obligated to investigate every situation involving a violation of the rights protected by the Convention. If the State apparatus acts in such a way that the violation goes unpunished and the victim's full enjoyment of such rights is not restored as soon as possible, the State has failed to comply with its duty to ensure the free and full exercise of those rights to the persons within its jurisdiction. The same is true when the State allows private persons or groups to act freely and with impunity to the detriment of the rights recognized by the Convention.

177. In certain circumstances, it may be difficult to investigate acts that violate an individual's rights. The duty to investigate, like the duty to prevent, is not breached merely

because the investigation does not produce a satisfactory result. Nevertheless, it must be undertaken in a serious manner and not as a mere formality preordained to be ineffective. An investigation must have an objective and be assumed by the State as its own legal duty, not as a step taken by private interests that depends upon the initiative of the victim or his family or upon their offer of proof, without an effective search for the truth by the government. This is true regardless of what agent is eventually found responsible for the violation. Where the acts of private parties that violate the Convention are not seriously investigated, those parties are aided in a sense by the government, thereby making the State responsible on the international plane.

178. In the instant case, the evidence shows a complete inability of the procedures of the State of Honduras, which were theoretically adequate, to carry out an investigation into the disappearance of Manfredo Velásquez, and of the fulfillment of its duties to pay compensation and punish those responsible, as set out in Article 1(1) of the Convention ...

The Court, therefore, concludes that the facts found in this proceeding show that the State of Honduras is responsible for the involuntary disappearance of Angel Manfredo Velásquez Rodríguez. Thus, Honduras has violated Articles 7, 5 and 4 of the Convention.

The *Velasquez Rodriguez* case was the first regional human rights court decision to establish the liability of the state for non-state actors. The Inter-American Court has reaffirmed this proposition several times; once specifically in a case involving domestic violence, *Maria da Penha Maia Fernandes v. Brazil,* and most recently in the so called *"Cotton Field"* case that addressed the claims of the families of some of the victims in Ciudad Juarez. This case will be described in a subsequent chapter.

C. *Maria da Penha Maia Fernandes v. Brazil*[8]

The petition states that on May 29, 1983, Mrs. María da Penha Maia Fernandes, a pharmacist, was the victim of attempted murder by her then husband, Marco Antônio Heredia Viveiros, an economist, at her home in Fortaleza, Ceará State. He shot her while she was asleep, bringing to a climax a series of acts of aggression carried out over the course of their married life. As a result of this aggression of her spouse, Mrs. Fernandes sustained serious injuries, had to undergo numerous operations, and suffered irreversible paraplegia and other physical and psychological trauma.

The petitioners state that Mr. Heredia Viveiros was an aggressive and violent person, and that he would assault his wife and three daughters during his marriage. According to the victim, the situation became unbearable but she was too afraid to take steps to obtain a separation. They maintain that the husband tried to cover up the attack by reporting it as an attempted robbery and the work of thieves who had fled. Two weeks after Mrs. Fernandes returned from the hospital and was recovering from the attempt on her life on May 29, 1983, Mr. Heredia Viveiros again attempted to kill her by allegedly trying to electrocute her while she was bathing. At that point, she decided to seek a legal separation from him.

---

8. Inter-American Court Case 12.051, Report No. 54/01, OEA/Ser.L/V/II.111 Doc. 20 rev. at 704 (2000).

They maintain that Mr. Viveiros acted with premeditation, since the week before the attack he had tried to convince his wife to make him the beneficiary of a life insurance policy, and five days before attacking her, he tried to force her to sign a document for the sale of her car that provided no indication of the name of the purchaser. They state that Mrs. Fernandes learned subsequently that Mr. Viveiros had a criminal record, that he was bigamous, and that he had a child in Colombia, information that he had concealed from her.

They add that because of the resulting paraplegia, the victim had to undergo extensive physical therapy, and, because of her loss of independence, required constant assistance from nurses in order to move around. The ongoing need for medication and physical therapy is expensive and Mrs. Maria da Penha receives no financial assistance from her ex-husband to cover her expenses. Also, he is not paying the alimony stipulated in the separation order.

The petitioners maintain that during the judicial investigation, which was launched a few days after the June 6, 1983 assault, statements were taken establishing that Mr. Heredia Viveiros was responsible for the assault, and that despite this, he maintained that it was the work of thieves who were trying to enter their home. During the judicial proceedings, evidence was presented demonstrating that Mr. Heredia Viveiros intended to kill her, and a rifle owned by him was found in the house, contradicting his claim that he did not own any firearms. Subsequent analyses indicated that this was the weapon used in the assault. Based on all of the above, the Office of the Public Prosecutor filed charges against Mr. Heredia Viveiros on September 28, 1984, leading to public criminal proceedings in the First District Court of Fortaleza, in Ceara State.

The petitioners indicate that despite the clear nature of the charges and preponderance of the evidence the case languished for eight years before the jury found Mr. Viveiros guilty on May 4, 1991, sentencing him to 15 years in prison for assault and attempted murder, which was reduced to ten years because he had no prior convictions.

They state that on that same day, that is, May 4, 1991, the defense filed an appeal against the decision handed down by the Jury. According to Article 479 of the Brazilian Code of Criminal Procedure, this appeal was time-barred, since it could only be filed during rather than after the proceedings, a matter that has been borne out repeatedly by Brazilian case law and, in the case at hand, by the Office of the Public Prosecutor.

Another three years went by. On May 4, 1994, the Appeal Court ruled on the appeal. In that decision, it accepted the time-barred appeal, and, using as a basis the argument of the defense that the formulation of questions to the jury was flawed, threw out its decision.

They allege that at the same time, other legal action was being taken to appeal the indictment [*pronuncia*] (first judicial decision by means of which the judge identifies signs pointing to a perpetrator that warrant a trial by jury). This appeal was also time-barred and the judge handed down a ruling to that effect. That decision was also appealed in the Ceará State court, which agreed to hear the appeal and issued an unfavorable ruling, upholding the indictment on April 3, 1995, maintaining once more that there was sufficient evidence pointing to a perpetrator.

In the petition providing an account of legal ineptitude and delays, it is further stated that two years after the guilty sentence of the first jury was thrown out, a second trial by jury took place on March 15, 1996, in which Mr. Viveiros was condemned to ten years and six months in prison.

The petitioners claim that the Court again agreed to hear a second appeal filed by the defense, in which it was maintained that the accused was convicted without consideration being given to the evidence contained in the court file. Since April 22, 1997, a decision has been pending in the second instance appeal to the Ceará State Court. As of the date of submission of the petition to the Commission, no decision had been handed down regarding the appeal.

The petitioners maintain that as of the date of the petition, the Brazilian justice system had dragged its feet for more than 15 years without handing down a final ruling against the ex-husband of Mrs. Fernandes, who has been free during that entire period, despite the serious nature of the charges, the mountain of evidence against him, and the serious nature of the crime committed against Mrs. Fernandes. The judicial system of Ceará and the Brazilian State have thus been ineffective, as seen in their failure to conduct proceedings in a prompt and efficient manner, thereby creating a great risk of impunity, since punishment in this case will be barred by the statute of limitations twenty years after the occurrence of these events, a date that is approaching. They maintain that the primary aim of the Brazilian State ought to have been to ensure compensation for the suffering of Maria da Penha, by guaranteeing her a fair trial within a reasonable time period.

They maintain that this complaint does not represent an isolated situation in Brazil; rather, it is an example of a pattern of impunity in cases of domestic violence against women in Brazil, since the majority of complaints filed do not lead to criminal prosecution and in the few cases where they do, the perpetrators are convicted in only a small number of cases. We note the comments of this Commission in its report on Brazil:

The crimes which fall within the heading of violence against women constitute human rights violations under the American Convention, as well as under the more specific terms of the Convention of Belém do Pará. When committed by state agents, the use of violence against the physical and/or mental integrity of an individual gives rise to the direct responsibility of the State. Additionally, the State has an obligation under Article 1(1) of the American Convention and Article 7.b of the Convention of Belém do Pará to exercise due diligence to prevent human rights violations. This means that, even where conduct may not initially be directly imputable to a state (for example, because the actor is unidentified or not a state agent), a violative act may lead to state responsibility "not because of the act itself, but because of the lack of due diligence to prevent the violation or respond to it as the Convention requires.

Compared to men, women are the victims of domestic violence in disproportionate numbers. A study done by the National Movement for Human Rights in Brazil compares the incidence of domestic violence against women and men and shows that in terms of murders, women are 30 times more likely to be killed by their husbands than husbands by their wives. In its special report on Brazil in 1997, the Commission found that there was clear discrimination against women who were attacked, resulting from the inefficiency of the Brazilian judicial system and inadequate application of national and international rules, including those arising from the case law of the Brazilian Supreme Court. In its 1997 Report on the Situation of Human Rights, the Commission stated:

Moreover, even where these specialized stations exist, it remains frequently the case that complaints are not fully investigated or prosecuted. In some cases, resource limitations hinder efforts to respond to these crimes. In other cases, women refrain from pressing formal charges. In practice, legal and other limitations often expose women to situations where they feel constrained to act. By law, women have to register their complaint at a police station, and explain what happened so the delegate can write up an "incident report." Delegates who have not received sufficient training may be unable to provide the required services, and some reportedly continue to respond to victims in ways that make them feel shame and humiliation. For certain crimes, such as rape, victims must present themselves at an Institute of Forensic Medicine (*Instituto Médico Legal*), which has the exclusive competence to perform the examinations required by law to process a charge. Some women are not aware of this requirement, or do not have access to such a facility in the timely manner necessary to obtain the required evidence. These Institutes tend to be located in urban areas, and, where available, are often understaffed. Moreover, even when women take the steps necessary to denounce the use of criminal violence, there is no guarantee that the crime will be investigated and prosecuted.

Although the Supreme Court of Brazil struck down the archaic "honor defense" as a jus-tification for wife-killing in 1991, many courts remain reluctant to prosecute and punish the perpetrators of domestic violence. In some areas of the country, use of the "honor defense" persists, and in some areas the conduct of the victim continues to be a focal point within the judicial process to prosecute a sexual crime. Rather than focusing on the existence of the legal elements of the crime in question, the practices of some defense lawyers—sustained in turn by some courts—have the effect of requiring the victim to demonstrate the sanctity of her reputation and her moral blamelessness in order to exercise the remedies legally required to be available to her. The initiatives taken by the public and private sector to confront violence against women have begun to combat the silence which customarily has concealed it, but have yet to surmount the social, legal and other barriers which contribute to the impunity in which these crimes too often languish

The impunity that the ex-husband of Mrs. Fernandes has enjoyed and continues to enjoy is at odds with the international commitment voluntarily assumed by the State when it ratified the Convention of Belém do Pará. The failure to prosecute and convict the perpetrator under these circumstances is an indication that the State condones the violence suffered by Maria da Penha, and this failure by the Brazilian courts to take action is exacerbating the direct consequences of the aggression by her ex-husband. Furthermore, as has been demonstrated earlier, that tolerance by the State organs is not limited to this case; rather, it is a pattern. The condoning of this situation by the entire system only serves to perpetuate the psychological, social, and historical roots and factors that sustain and encourage violence against women.

Article 7

The States Parties condemn all forms of violence against women and agree to pursue, by all appropriate means and without delay, policies to prevent, punish and eradicate such violence and undertake to:

    a.   refrain from engaging in any act or practice of violence against women and to ensure that their authorities, officials, personnel, agents, and institutions act in conformity with this obligation;

    b.   apply due diligence to prevent, investigate and impose penalties for violence against women;

    c.   include in their domestic legislation penal, civil, administrative and any other type of provisions that may be needed to prevent, punish and eradicate violence against women and to adopt appropriate administrative measures where necessary;

    d.   adopt legal measures to require the perpetrator to refrain from harassing, in-timidating or threatening the woman or using any method that harms or endangers her life or integrity, or damages her property;

e.   take all appropriate measures, including legislative measures, to amend or repeal existing laws and regulations or to modify legal or customary practices which sustain the persistence and tolerance of violence against women;

f.   establish fair and effective legal procedures for women who have been subjected to violence which include, among others, protective measures, a timely hearing and effective access to such procedures;

g.   establish the necessary legal and administrative mechanisms to ensure that women subjected to violence have effective access to restitution, reparations or other just and effective remedies; and

h.   adopt such legislative or other measures as may be necessary to give effect to this Convention.

56.   Given the fact that the violence suffered by Maria da Penha is part of a general pattern of negligence and lack of effective action by the State in prosecuting and convicting aggressors, it is the view of the Commission that this case involves not only failure to fulfill the obligation with respect to prosecute and convict, but also the obligation to prevent these degrading practices. That general and discriminatory judicial ineffectiveness also creates a climate that is conducive to domestic violence, since society sees no evidence of willingness by the State, as the representative of the society, to take effective action to sanction such acts.

57.   The Commission must consider, in relation to Articles 7(c) and (h), the measures taken by the State to eliminate the condoning of domestic violence. The Commission notes the positive measures taken by the current administration towards that objective, in particular the establishment of special police stations, shelters for battered women, and others. However, in this case, which represents the tip of the iceberg, ineffective judicial action, impunity, and the inability of victims to obtain compensation provide an example of the lack of commitment to take appropriate action to address domestic violence. Article 7 of the Convention of Belém do Pará seems to represent a list of commitments that the Brazilian State has failed to meet in such cases.

58.   In light of the foregoing, the Commission holds the view that this case meets the conditions for domestic violence and tolerance on the part of the State, defined in the Convention of Belém do Pará, and that the State is liable for failing to perform its duties set forth in Articles 7(b), (d), (e), (f), and (g) of that Convention in relation to rights protected therein, among them, the right to a life free of violence (Article 3), the right of a woman to have her life, her physical, mental, and moral integrity, her personal safety, and personal dignity respected, to equal protection before and of the law, and to simple and prompt recourse to a competent court for protection against acts that violate her rights (Articles 4(a), (b), (c), (d), (e), (f), and (g).

Questions for Discussion

1. *Do you agree with the Court that: "The condoning of this situation by the entire system only serves to perpetuate the psychological, social, and historical roots and factors that sustain and encourage violence against women"?*

2. *In this case the court found that: "Ineffective judicial action, impunity, and the inability of victims to obtain compensation provide an example of the lack of commitment to take appropriate action to address domestic violence." Keep that*

standard in mind as you read the DeShaney and Gonzales cases described below. Does the U.S. appear to subscribe to these principles?

V. Domestic Violence in the United States

A. *DeShaney v. Winnebago County Dept. of Social Services*[9]

Petitioner is a child who was subjected to a series of beatings by his father, with whom he lived. Respondents, a county department of social services and several of its social workers, received complaints that petitioner was being abused by his father and took various steps to protect him; they did not, however, act to remove petitioner from his father's custody. Petitioner's father finally beat him so severely that he suffered permanent brain damage and was rendered profoundly retarded. Petitioner and his mother sued respondents under 42 U.S.C. § 1983, alleging that respondents had deprived petitioner of his liberty interest in bodily integrity, in violation of his rights under the substantive component of the Fourteenth Amendment's Due Process Clause, by failing to intervene to protect him against his father's violence. The District Court granted summary judgment for respondents, and the Court of Appeals affirmed.

[The Court, per Rehnquist C.J. held that:]

(a) A State's failure to protect an individual against private violence generally does not constitute a violation of the Due Process Clause, because the Clause imposes no duty on the State to provide members of the general public with adequate protective services. The Clause is phrased as a limitation on the State's power to act, not as a guarantee of certain minimal levels of safety and security; while it forbids the State itself to deprive individuals of life, liberty, and property without due process of law, its language cannot fairly be read to impose an affirmative obligation on the State to ensure that those interests do not come to harm through other means.[10]

(b) There is no merit to petitioner's contention that the State's knowledge of his danger and expressions of willingness to protect him against that danger established a "special relationship" giving rise to an affirmative constitutional duty to protect. While certain "special relationships" created or assumed by the State with respect to particular individuals may give rise to an affirmative duty, enforceable through the Due Process Clause, to provide adequate protection, see *Estelle v. Gamble,* 429 U.S. 97, 97 S.Ct. 285, 50 L.Ed.2d 251; *Youngberg v. Romeo,* 457 U.S. 307, 102 S.Ct. 2452, 73 L.Ed.2d 28, the affirmative duty to protect arises not from the State's knowledge of the individual's predicament or from its expressions of intent to help him, but from the limitations which it has imposed on his freedom to act on his own behalf, through imprisonment, institutionalization, or other similar restraint of personal liberty. No such duty existed here, for the harms petitioner suffered occurred not while the State was holding him in its custody, but while

---

9. 489 U.S. 189 (1989).
10. *Id.* at 189.

he was in the custody of his natural father, who was in no sense a state actor. While the State may have been aware of the dangers that he faced, it played no part in their creation, nor did it do anything to render him more vulnerable to them. Under these circumstances, the Due Process Clause did not impose upon the State an affirmative duty to provide petitioner with adequate protection.[11]

(c) It may well be that by voluntarily undertaking to provide petitioner with protection against a danger it played no part in creating, the State acquired a duty under state tort law to provide him with adequate protection against that danger. But the Due Process Clause does not transform every tort committed by a state actor into a constitutional violation.[12]

Brennan J. dissenting:

As the Court today reminds us, "the Due Process Clause of the Fourteenth Amendment was intended to prevent government 'from abusing [its] power, or employing it as an instrument of oppression.'" *Ante*, at 1003, quoting *Davidson, supra*, at 348, 106 S.Ct., at 670. My disagreement with the Court arises from its failure to see that inaction can be every bit as abusive of power as action, that oppression can result when a State undertakes a vital duty and then ignores it. Today's opinion construes the Due Process Clause to permit a State to displace private sources of protection and then, at the critical moment, to shrug its shoulders and turn away from the harm that it has promised to try to prevent. Because I cannot agree that our Constitution is indifferent to such indifference, I respectfully dissent.[13]

Blackmun J. dissenting:

Poor Joshua! Victim of repeated attacks by an irresponsible, bullying, cowardly, and intemperate father, and abandoned by respondents who placed him in a dangerous predicament and who knew or learned what was going on, and yet did essentially nothing except, as the Court revealingly observes, *ante*, at 1001, "dutifully recorded these incidents in [their] files." It is a sad commentary upon American life, and constitutional principles— so full of late of patriotic fervor and proud proclamations about "liberty and justice for all"—that this child, Joshua DeShaney, now is assigned to live out the remainder of his life profoundly retarded. Joshua and his mother, as petitioners here, deserve—but now are denied by this Court—the opportunity to have the facts of their case considered in the light of the constitutional protection that 42 U.S.C. § 1983 is meant to provide.[14]

———————

When given another opportunity to find the state liable for the violent acts of a third party, the U.S. Supreme Court again declined to do so in the case of *Town of Castle Rock, Colo v. Gonzales.*[15]

B. *Town of Castle Rock, Colo v. Gonzales*[16]

Respondent [Jessica Gonzales] allege[d] that petitioner, the town of Castle Rock, Colorado, violated the Due Process Clause of the Fourteenth Amendment to the United States Constitution when its police officers, acting pursuant to official policy or custom,

———————

11. *Id.* at 189–90.
12. *Id.* at 190.
13. *Id.* at 211–12.
14. *Id.* at 212–13.
15. 545 U.S. 748 (2005).
16. 545 U.S. 748 (2005).

failed to respond properly to her repeated reports that her estranged husband was violating the terms of a restraining order ...

According to the complaint, at about 5 or 5:30 p.m. on Tuesday, June 22, 1999, respondent's husband took the three daughters while they were playing outside the family home. No advance arrangements had been made for him to see the daughters that evening. When respondent noticed the children were missing, she suspected her husband had taken them. At about 7:30 p.m., she called the Castle Rock Police Department, which dispatched two officers. The complaint continues: "When [the officers] arrived..., she showed them a copy of the TRO and requested that it be enforced and the three children be returned to her immediately. [The officers] stated that there was nothing they could do about the TRO and suggested that [respondent] call the Police Department again if the three children did not return home by 10:00 p.m." ...

At approximately 8:30 p.m., respondent talked to her husband on his cellular telephone. He told her "he had the three children [at an] amusement park in Denver." *Ibid.* She called the police again and asked them to "have someone check for" her husband or his vehicle at the amusement park and "put out an [all points bulletin]" for her husband, but the officer with whom she spoke "refused to do so," again telling her to "wait until 10:00 p.m. and see if" her husband returned the girls.

At approximately 10:10 p.m., respondent called the police and said her children were still missing, but she was now told to wait until midnight. She called at midnight and told the dispatcher her children were still missing. She went to her husband's apartment and, finding nobody there, called the police at 12:10 a.m.; she was told to wait for an officer to arrive. When none came, she went to the police station at 12:50 a.m. and submitted an incident report. The officer who took the report "made no reasonable effort to enforce the TRO or locate the three children. Instead, he went to dinner." [...]

At approximately 3:20 a.m., respondent's husband arrived at the police station and opened fire with a semiautomatic handgun he had purchased earlier that evening. Police shot back, killing him. Inside the cab of his pickup truck, they found the bodies of all three daughters, whom he had already murdered.

On the basis of the foregoing factual allegations, respondent brought an action under Rev. Stat. § 1979, 42 U.S.C. § 1983, claiming that the town violated the Due Process Clause because its police department had "an official policy or custom of failing to respond properly to complaints of restraining order violations" and "tolerate[d] the non-enforcement of restraining orders by its police officers." App. to Pet. for Cert. 129a. The complaint also alleged that the town's actions "were taken either willfully, recklessly or with such gross negligence as to indicate wanton disregard and deliberate indifference to" respondent's civil rights. *Ibid.*

As the Court of Appeals recognized, we left a similar question unanswered in *DeShaney v. Winnebago County Dept. of Social Servs.*, 489 U.S. 189, 109 S.Ct. 998, 103 L.Ed.2d 249 (1989), another case with "undeniably tragic" facts: Local child-protection officials had failed to protect a young boy from beatings by his father that left him severely brain damaged. *Id.*, at 191–193, 109 S.Ct. 998. We held that the so-called "substantive" component of the Due Process Clause does not "requir[e] the State to protect the life, liberty, and property of its citizens against invasion by private actors." *Id.*, at 195, 109 S.Ct. 998. We noted, however, that the petitioner had not properly preserved the argument that—and we thus "decline[d] to consider" whether—state "child protection statutes gave [him] an 'entitlement' to receive protective services in accordance with the terms of the statute, an entitlement which would enjoy due process protection." *Id.*, at 195, n. 2, 109 S.Ct. 998.

The procedural component of the Due Process Clause does not protect everything that might be described as a "benefit": "To have a property interest in a benefit, a person clearly must have more than an abstract need or desire" and "more than a unilateral expectation of it. He must, instead, have a legitimate claim of entitlement to it." *Board of Regents of State Colleges v. Roth*, 408 U.S. 564, 577, 92 S.Ct. 2701, 33 L.Ed.2d 548 (1972). Such entitlements are, "'of course, … not created by the Constitution. Rather, they are created and their dimensions are defined by existing rules or understandings that stem from an independent source such as state law.'" *Paul v. Davis*, 424 U.S. 693, 709, 96 S.Ct. 1155, 47 L.Ed.2d 405 (1976) (quoting *Roth, supra*, at 577, 92 S.Ct. 2701); …

[The Court went on to consider whether the restraining order that Ms. Gonzales had obtained against her husband constituted an "entitlement." In so doing, the Court looked to the language on the back of the restraining order which was directed to law enforcement personnel and which provided that:]

> (a) Whenever a restraining order is issued, the protected person shall be provided with a copy of such order. *A peace officer shall use every reasonable means to enforce a restraining order.*

> (b) *A peace officer shall arrest, or, if an arrest would be impractical under the circumstances, seek a warrant for the arrest of a restrained person* when the peace officer has information amounting to probable cause that:

> > (I) The restrained person has violated or attempted to violate any provision of a restraining order; and

> > (II) The restrained person has been properly served with a copy of the restraining order or the restrained person has received actual notice of the existence and substance of such order.

> (c) In making the probable cause determination described in Paragraph (b) of this subsection (3), a peace officer shall assume that the information received from the registry is accurate. *A peace officer shall enforce a valid restraining order whether or not there is a record of the restraining order in the registry.*" Colo.Rev.Stat. § 18-6-803.5(3) (Lexis 1999) (emphases added).

The Supreme Court also noted that the Tenth Circuit in its decision had looked to the legislative history of the Colorado statute and found that it established the Colorado Legislature's clear intent "to alter the fact that the police were not enforcing domestic abuse restraining orders," and thus its intent "that the recipient of a domestic abuse restraining order have an entitlement to its enforcement."[17] Any other result, it said, "would render domestic abuse restraining orders utterly valueless."[18]

The Supreme Court disagreed that the language and legislative history rendered the enforcement of the restraining order mandatory, holding:

> We do not believe that these provisions of Colorado law truly made enforcement of restraining orders *mandatory*. A well established tradition of police discretion has long coexisted with apparently mandatory arrest statutes.

> In each and every state there are long-standing statutes that, by their terms, seem to preclude nonenforcement by the police … However, for a number of reasons,

---

17. 366 F.3d. at 1108.
18. *Id.* at 1109.

including their legislative history, insufficient resources, and sheer physical impossibility, it has been recognized that such statutes cannot be interpreted
literally ... [T]hey clearly do not mean that a police officer may not lawfully
decline to ... make an arrest. As to third parties in these states, the full-enforcement
statutes simply have no effect, and their significance is further diminished." The
deep-rooted nature of law-enforcement discretion, even in the presence of
seemingly mandatory legislative commands, is illustrated by *Chicago v. Morales,*
527 U.S. 41, 119 S.Ct. 1849, 144 L.Ed.2d 67 (1999), which involved an ordinance
that said a police officer " 'shall order' " persons to disperse in certain circumstances,
id., at 47, n. 2, 119 S.Ct. 1849. This Court rejected out of hand the possibility
that "the mandatory language of the ordinance ... afford[ed] the police *no*
discretion." *Id.,* at 62, n. 32, 119 S.Ct. 1849. It is, the Court proclaimed, simply
"common sense that *all* police officers must use some discretion in deciding when
and where to enforce city ordinances." *Ibid.* (emphasis added).

Against that backdrop, a true mandate of police action would require some
stronger indication from the Colorado Legislature than "shall use every reasonable
means to enforce a restraining order" (or even "shall arrest ... or ... seek a
warrant"), §§ 18-6-803.5(3)(a), (b). That language is not perceptibly more mandatory than the Colorado statute which has long told municipal chiefs of police
that they "shall pursue and arrest any person fleeing from justice in any part of
the state" and that they "shall apprehend any person in the act of committing
any offense ... and, forthwith and without any warrant, bring such person before
a ... competent authority for examination and trial." Colo.Rev.Stat. § 31-4-112
(Lexis 2004). It is hard to imagine that a Colorado peace officer would not have
some discretion to determine that—despite probable cause to believe a restraining
order has been violated—the circumstances of the violation or the competing
duties of that officer or his agency counsel decisively against enforcement in a
particular instance. The practical necessity for discretion is particularly apparent
in a case such as this one, where the suspected violator is not actually present
and his whereabouts are unknown.

[The Court appeared to place great emphasis on the fact that the duty of the police to
arrest Ms. Gonzales' husband was diminished by the fact that he was not in the home,
finding that:]

[T]here will be situations when no arrest is possible, *such as when the alleged
abuser is not in the home." Donaldson,* 65 Wash.App., at 674, 831 P.2d, at 1105
(emphasis added). That case held that Washington's mandatory-arrest statute
required an arrest only in "cases where the offender is on the scene," and that it
"d[id] not create an on-going mandatory duty to conduct an investigation" to
locate the offender. *Id.,* at 675, 831 P.2d, at 1105. Colorado's restraining-order
statute appears to contemplate a similar distinction, providing that when arrest
is "impractical"—which was likely the case when the whereabouts of respondent's
husband were unknown—the officers' statutory duty is to "seek a warrant" rather
than "arrest." § 18-6-803.5(3)(b).

Respondent does not specify the precise means of enforcement that the Colorado
restraining-order statute assertedly mandated—whether her interest lay in having
police arrest her husband, having them seek a warrant for his arrest, or having
them "use every reasonable means, up to and including arrest, to enforce the
order's terms," Brief for Respondent 29–30 Such indeterminacy is not the hallmark
of a duty that is mandatory. Nor can someone be safely deemed "entitled" to

something when the identity of the alleged entitlement is vague. See *Roth,* 408 U.S., at 577.

[The Court also went on to find that Gonzales did not have a property entitlement to having the restraining order enforced, holding that:]

[I]t is by no means clear that an individual entitlement to enforcement of a re-straining order could constitute a "property" interest for purposes of the Due Process Clause. Such a right would not, of course, resemble any traditional conception of property. Although that alone does not disqualify it from due process protection, as *Roth* and its progeny show, the right to have a restraining order enforced does not "have some ascertainable monetary value," as even our "*Roth*-type property-as-entitlement" cases have implicitly required. Merrill, The Landscape of Constitutional Property, 86 Va. L.Rev. 885, 964 (2000). Perhaps most radically, the alleged property interest here arises *incidentally,* not out of some new species of government benefit or service, but out of a function that government actors have always performed — to wit, arresting people who they have probable cause to believe have committed a criminal of-fense ...

We conclude, therefore, that respondent did not, for purposes of the Due Process Clause, have a property interest in police enforcement of the restraining order against her husband. It is accordingly unnecessary to address the Court of Appeals' determination (366 F.3d, at 1110–1117) that the town's custom or policy prevented the police from giving her due process when they deprived her of that alleged interest.

Stevens J. dissenting:

The Court similarly errs in speculating that the Colorado Legislature may have mandated police enforcement of restraining orders for "various legitimate ends other than the conferral of a benefit on a specific class of people," *ante,* at 2808; see also *ibid.* (noting that the "serving of public rather than private ends is the normal course of the criminal law"). While the Court's concern would have some bite were we faced with a broadly drawn statute directing, for example, that the police "*shall suppress* all riots," there is little doubt that the statute at issue in this case conferred a benefit "on a specific class of people" — namely, recipients of domestic restraining orders. Here, respondent applied for and was granted a re-straining order from a Colorado trial judge, who found a risk of "irreparable injury" and found that "physical or emotional harm" would result if the husband were not excluded from the family home. 366 F.3d, at 1143 (appendix to dissent of O'Brien, J.). As noted earlier, the restraining order required that the husband not "molest or disturb" the peace of respondent and the daughters, and it ordered (with limited exceptions) that the husband stay at least 100 yards away from the family home. It also directed the police to "use every reasonable means to enforce this ... order," and to arrest or seek a warrant upon probable cause of a violation. *Id.,* at 1144. Under the terms of the statute, when the order issued, respondent and her daughters became "'protected person[s].'" § 18-6-803.5(1.5)(a) ("'Protected person' means the person or persons identified in the restraining order as the person or persons for whose benefit the restraining order was issued") The statute criminalized the knowing violation of the restraining order, § 18-6-803.5(1), and, as already discussed, the statute (as well as the order itself) mandated police enforcement, §§ 18-6-803.5(3)(a)–(b) ...

Because the statute's guarantee of police enforcement is triggered by, and operates only in reference to, a judge's granting of a restraining order in favor of an identified "'protected person,'" there is simply no room to suggest that such a person has received merely an "'incidental'" or "'indirect'" benefit, see *ante*, at 2810. As one state court put it, domestic restraining order statutes "identify with precision when, to whom, and under what circumstances police protection must be afforded. The legislative purpose in requiring the police to enforce individual restraining orders clearly is to protect the named persons for whose protection the order is issued, not to protect the community at large by general law enforcement activity."[...]

Given that Colorado law has quite clearly eliminated the police's discretion to deny enforcement, respondent is correct that she had much more than a "unilateral expectation" that the restraining order would be enforced; rather, she had a "legitimate claim of entitlement" to enforcement ... Police enforcement of a restraining order is a government service that is no less concrete and no less valuable than other government services, such as education ... Surely, if respondent had contracted with a private security firm to provide her and her daughters with protection from her husband, it would be apparent that she possessed a property interest in such a contract. Here, Colorado undertook a comparable obligation, and respondent — with restraining order in hand — justifiably relied on that undertaking. Respondent's claim of entitlement to this promised service is no less legitimate than the other claims our cases have upheld, and no less concrete than a hypothetical agreement with a private firm. The fact that it is based on a statutory enactment and a judicial order entered for her special protection, rather than on a formal contract, does not provide a principled basis for refusing to consider it "property" worthy of constitutional protection ... Because respondent had a property interest in the enforcement of the restraining order, state officials could not deprive her of that interest without observing fair procedures. Her description of the police behavior in this case and the department's callous policy of failing to respond properly to reports of restraining order violations clearly alleges a due process violation. At the very least, due process requires that the relevant state decisionmaker *listen* to the claimant and then *apply the relevant criteria* in reaching his decision.

Interestingly, despite the Inter-American court decisions of *Velasquez-Rodrigues* and *Fernandes v. Brazil*, Gonzales' attorneys chose not to raise any international law arguments in their brief, choosing to focus instead on Gonzales' entitlement to police protection under U.S. domestic law, the plain language of the statute and restraining order itself, and the intent of the Colorado legislature. They tried to focus the issues very narrowly and distinguish this case from *DeShaney*. If one looks at the Supreme Court brief, one sees only U.S. domestic legal cases cited. Consider the Summary of the Argument contained in the Reply Brief on the Merits filed by Ms. Gonzales' counsel:[19]

---

19. *Available at* http://web2.westlaw.com/result/previewcontroller.aspx?TF=756&TC=4&serial num=2006237306&rp=%2ffind%2fdefault.wl&sv=Split&rs=WLW11.04&tc=-1&tf=-1&findtype=Y&fn= _top&mt=208&vr=2.0&pbc=55AA8BF6&ordoc=2006858594&RP=/find/default.wl&bLinkViewer=true [last visited July 1, 2011].

1. Respondent Gonzales' Brief on the Merits

SUMMARY OF THE ARGUMENT

The issue before this Court is distinct from the substantive due process claim addressed by this Court in *DeShaney v. Winnebago County Dep't of Soc. Servs.*, 489 U.S. 189 (1989). This Court is not being asked to address whether Ms. Gonzales had a substantive right under the Constitution to receive government protection that could not be denied without a reasonable justification in the service of a legitimate government objective. Rather, this Court must determine whether the state of Colorado created for Ms. Gonzales an entitlement that cannot be taken away from her without procedural due process, and if so, whether Castle Rock's arbitrary denial of that entitlement was procedurally unfair under the well-pleaded facts of Ms. Gonzales' complaint.

The state court's issuance of the restraining order to Ms. Gonzales, containing mandatory language and specific objective criteria curtailing the decisionmaking discretion of police officers, clearly commanded that the domestic abuse restraining order be enforced. The mandatory statute, its legislative history, and the grant of immunity to officers for the erroneous enforcement of restraining orders provides added weight to this conclusion. For this Court to hold otherwise would render domestic abuse restraining orders utterly valueless and law enforcement agencies completely unaccountable to the legislative or judicial branches of government.

"It is a purpose of the ancient institution of property to protect those claims upon which people rely in their daily lives, reliance that must not be arbitrarily undermined." *Board of Regents of State Colleges v. Roth*, 408 U.S. 564, 577 (1972). There can be no doubt Ms. Gonzales and her daughters relied on the State's promises of enforcement of the restraining order to go about their daily lives. Nor can there be any doubt, based upon the factual allegations contained in Ms. Gonzales' complaint (which must be taken as true at this stage of the proceedings), that their reliance was arbitrarily undermined by the failure of the Castle Rock police to enforce the restraining order, resulting in an unspeakably tragic outcome.

The process set up in Colorado's statutory scheme was that the police must, in a timely fashion, consider the merits of any request to enforce a restraining order and, if such a consideration reveals probable cause, the police must enforce the order. Here, Ms. Gonzales alleges that due to the city's policy and custom of failing to properly respond to complaints of restraining order violations, she was denied the process laid out in the statute. The police did not consider her request in a timely fashion, but instead repeatedly required her to call the station over several hours. The statute promised a process by which her restraining order would be given vitality through careful and prompt consideration of an enforcement request, and the Constitution requires no less. Denial of that process drained all of the value from her property interest in the restraining order.

If one considers the Constitutional process to include a right to be heard, Ms. Gonzales was deprived of that process because, according to her allegations, the police never "heard" nor seriously entertained her request to enforce and protect her interests in the restraining order. Alternatively, if one considers that the process to which she was entitled was a bona fide consideration by the police of a request to enforce a restraining order, she was denied that process as well. According to Ms. Gonzales' allegations, the police never engaged in a bona fide consideration of whether there was probable cause to enforce the restraining order. Their response, in other words, was meaningless, which rendered her property interest in the restraining order a nullity.

Based on the well-pleaded facts of Ms. Gonzales' complaint, she has adequately stated a procedural due process claim upon which relief can be granted. She had a property interest in the enforcement of the restraining order which was allegedly taken from her without due process of law. Her § 1983 action should therefore proceed in the trial court.

2. Amicus Brief of International Law Scholars and Women's Civil Rights and Human Rights Organizations

Contrast the amicus brief filed by International Law Scholars and Women's, Civil Rights and Human Rights Organizations, which sought to remind the United States of its obligations under international and regional human rights law.[20]

The authors of that brief cited cases not only from the Inter-American Commission and Court, but also from the European Court of Human Rights, as well as the South African Constitutional Court, and the Indian and Canadian Supreme Courts.

Their Table of Authorities included:

Airey v. Ireland, 32 Eur. Ct. H.R. (Ser. A) (1979)

M.C. v. Bulgaria, 2003-I Eur. Ct. H.R. 646 (2004)

M.Z. v. Bolivia, in Annual Report of the Inter-American Commission of Human Rights, Case No. 12.350, Inter-Am. C.H.R. 121 (Oct. 10, 2001)

Maria da Penha Maia Fernandes v. Brazil, in Annual Report of the Inter-American Commission on Human Rights, Case No. 12.051, Inter-Am. C.H.R. 704 (Apr. 16, 2001)

R. v. Ewanchuk, [1999] 1 S.C.R. 330 (Can.)

State v. Baloyi, 2000 (1) BCLR 86 (CC) (S. Afr.)

Vishaka v. State of Rajasthan, [1997] 6 (India)

Consider and contrast their Summary of the Argument:

SUMMARY OF ARGUMENT

Ms. Gonzales' brief explains that the police failure to accord her due process in the enforcement of the protective order violated her constitutional right to due process of law. We concur in, but do not address, the legal arguments she makes. Rather, we explain that the principles expressed in the evolved international customary norm of protection from and remedies for domestic violence, as well as our obligations as a State Party to the International Covenant on Civil and Political Rights ("ICCPR"), should inform this Court's consideration of the due process question at hand so as to grant Ms. Gonzales a federal remedy against the Town of Castle Rock.

This Court has repeatedly acknowledged that international and comparative law may be persuasive sources of authority for questions arising under our own Constitution. As it did in *Lawrence v. Texas,* 539 U.S. 558 (2003), this Court may appropriately consider

---

20. 2005 WL 328200. *Available at* http://web2.westlaw.com/result/previewcontroller.aspx?TF= 756&TC=4&serialnum=2006210368&rp=%2ffind%2fdefault.wl&sv=Split&rs=WLW11.04&tc=-1&tf= -1&findtype=Y&fn=_top&mt=208&vr=2.0&pbc=55AA8BF6&ordoc=2006858594&RP=/find/default. wl&bLinkViewer=true [last visited July 1, 2011].

the opinions of foreign jurisdictions in determining the scope of the Due Process Clause, and should also give due weight to other international sources of law. *Infra* Point I.

International human rights developments in recent decades have resulted in the emergence of a worldwide consensus that women and children have a fundamental human right to be protected from family violence, and to have effective remedies when such protection fails. This consensus is so powerful that it represents an evolved norm of customary international law—a norm that provides additional persuasive authority to support a determination by this Court that Ms. Gonzales' due process rights were violated. *Infra* Point II.

Finally, the United States has ratified the ICCPR, a treaty whose terms are now recognized to encompass States Parties' obligations to ensure persons, particularly women and children, the right to freedom from domestic violence. Recognizing Ms. Gonzales' right of action under 42 U.S.C. § 1983 is both consistent with the federal obligations undertaken by ratifying that treaty and with the federalism understanding that accompanied it. *Infra* Point III.

For these additional reasons, the decision of the Tenth Circuit Court of Appeals should be affirmed.

In reaching its decision in favor of the Town of Castle Rock, the Supreme Court did not cite to any international or foreign case law.

3. *Gonzales v. USA* (Inter-American Commission)[21]

In 2007, dissatisfied with the finding of the U.S. Supreme Court, Jessica Gonzales filed a petition with the Inter-American Commission.[22] The ACLU and Columbia Law School's Human Rights Clinic and represented her. The Commission found that:

> The petition alleges that the preventable deaths of Ms. Gonzales' children and the harm she suffered violated their rights to life and personal security under Article I, their right to protection of private and family life under Article V, their right to protection of the family under Article VI, their right to special protection for mothers and children under Article VII, and their right to the inviolability of the home under Article IX of the American Declaration on the Rights and Duties of Man (hereinafter "the American Declaration"). Petitioners further allege that the United States' failure to investigate Ms Gonzales' complaint and provide her with a remedy violated her right to resort to the courts under Article XVIII, and her right to obtain a prompt decision from the authorities under Article XXIV. Finally, the petition claims that the United States' failure to ensure the substantive rights under the above articles violated Ms. Gonzales' right to equality under Article II. In response to the petition, the State argues that the Petitioners' claims are inadmissible because the alleged victim has failed to exhaust domestic remedies.

[In finding the Petition admissible and that the Petitioner had exhausted domestic remedies as required, the Commission noted that:]

---

21. INTER-AMERICAN COMMISSION ON HUMAN RIGHTS: Jessica Gonzales, *in her individual capacity and on behalf of her deceased daughters,* Katheryn, Rebecca, and Leslie Gonzales v. The United States of America. Case No. 12.626 Observations & Responses Concerning the October 22, 2008 Hearing Before the Commission, March 2, 2009.

22. A copy of the Commission's Admissibility determination is *available at* http://www.cidh.oas.org/annualrep/2007eng/USA1490.05eng.htm [last visited November 26, 2010].

The Petitioners highlight that domestic violence is a widespread and tolerated phenomenon in the United States that has a disproportionate impact on women and has negative repercussions on their children. The petitioners also stress that even though the prevalence, persistence and gravity of the issue are recognized at the state and federal levels and legislative measures have been adopted to confront the problem, the response of police officers is to treat it as a family and private matter of low priority, as compared to other crimes. This perception influences negatively the response of the police in the implementation of protection orders.

21. Regarding the right to equality before the law, the Petitioners allege that the lack of State response to Ms. Gonzales' reports was based on negative stereotypes embraced by some police officers and a facially neutral police department policy of assigning lower priority to reports of domestic violence incidents, a policy that affects women disproportionately. According to the Petitioners, this attitude from state authorities has a particularly alarming effect on women pertaining to different racial, ethnic, and lower-income groups ...

Finally, the Petitioners stress that Supreme Court interpretation of the Constitution prevents victims of domestic violence from obtaining legal remedies, and from holding the police legally accountable for failure to protect victims from acts of domestic violence. Therefore, negative stereotypes affecting women are perpetuated, and structures sustaining domestic violence are strengthened. The petition indicates that in 2000, the Supreme Court struck down a federal law which had created a cause of action to sue perpetrators of domestic violence by holding that Congress at the federal level did not have the constitutional authority to adopt such law. The Supreme Court also allegedly held in another decision that the government is under no substantive obligation to protect an individual from violence committed by a non-State actor. The Petitioners finally allege that the Supreme Court again denied legal remedy to victims of domestic violence in the case involving Ms. Gonzales, stating that an individual was not constitutionally entitled to the enforcement of a restraining order ...

54. In their allegations, the Petitioners raise three main claims of violations of Ms. Gonzales' rights under the American Declaration:

55. The State opposes these claims on the ground that the Petitioners have not cited any provision of the American Declaration that imposes an affirmative duty on States to actually prevent the commission of individual crimes by private parties such as the tragic criminal murders by Mr. Simon Gonzales of his three daughters. The State claims that no other provision of the Declaration contains language that even addresses implementation of the enumerated rights, let alone imposes an affirmative duty to prevent crimes such as those at issue in this case.

With regard to the Petitioners' claims, after carefully reviewing the information and arguments provided by the Petitioners and the State outlined by the Commission in Part III of this Report, the Commission considers that the facts alleged by the Petitioners in respect to these claims could tend to establish violations of Articles I, V, VI, VII, XVIII and XXIV of the rights of Ms. Gonzales and her daughters under the American Declaration and warrant an analysis on the merits of the complaint ...

58. Furthermore, it considers that the alleged facts would constitute possible violations to Article II of the American Declaration. The IACHR observes that the Petitioners allege that the police authorities engage in a systematic and widespread

practice of treating domestic violence as a low-priority crime, belonging to the private sphere, as a result of discriminatory stereotypes about the victims. These stereotypes influence negatively the police response to the implementation of restraining orders. The failures in the police response affect women disproportionately since they constitute the majority of victims of domestic violence. The deficiencies in the state response allegedly have a particularly alarming effect on women that pertain to racial and ethnic minorities, and lower-income groups.

The Inter-American Commission recently affirmed this decision on the merits.

Questions for Discussion

1. *Why do you think that the United States has been so reluctant to embrace the view that in the absence of due diligence the state is responsible for acts of violence by private individuals against another private individual?*

2. *Given the wording of the restraining order, do you agree with the Supreme Court's conclusion in the Gonzales case that the police had discretion to enforce the order?*

3. *Could the Supreme Court have concluded on the basis of the language of the restraining order, and the statute under which the restraining order was issued, that the police were liable for not enforcing the order, without adopting the doctrine of state responsibility for acts of violence by private individuals in the absence of due diligence?*

4. *The Inter-American Commission found that domestic violence is treated as a low priority crime in the United States. In your opinion is that an accurate reflection of the situation in the U.S.?*

VI. The African Position on Violence against Women

As will be discussed in a later chapter, some African cultural practices like Female Genital Mutilation are considered a form of violence against women. The African regional system has addressed violence against women in the African Protocol on Women's Rights.

A. The African Protocol on Women's Rights

Article 1 Definitions

"Violence against women" means all acts perpetrated against women which cause or could cause them physical, sexual, psychological, and economic harm, including the threat to take such acts; or to undertake the imposition of arbitrary restrictions on or deprivation of fundamental freedoms in private or public life in peace time and during situations of armed conflicts or of war; …

Article 3 Right to Dignity

States Parties shall adopt and implement appropriate measures to ensure the protection of every woman's right to respect for her dignity and protection of women from all forms of violence, particularly sexual and verbal violence.

Article 4 The Rights to Life, Integrity and Security of the Person

Every woman shall be entitled to respect for her life and the integrity and security of her person. All forms of exploitation, cruel, inhuman or degrading punishment and treatment shall be prohibited.

States Parties shall take appropriate and effective measures to:

enact and enforce laws to prohibit all forms of violence against women including unwanted or forced sex whether the violence takes place in private or public;

adopt such other legislative, administrative, social and economic measures as may be necessary to ensure the prevention, punishment and eradication of all forms of violence against women;

identify the causes and consequences of violence against women and take appropriate measures to prevent and eliminate such violence;

actively promote peace education through curricula and social communication in order to eradicate elements in traditional and cultural beliefs, practices and stereotypes which legitimise and exacerbate the persistence and tolerance of violence against women;

punish the perpetrators of violence against women and implement programmes for the rehabilitation of women victims;

establish mechanisms and accessible services for effective information, rehabilitation and reparation for victims of violence against women;

prevent and condemn trafficking in women, prosecute the perpetrators of such trafficking and protect those women most at risk;

prohibit all medical or scientific experiments on women without their informed consent;

provide adequate budgetary and other resources for the implementation and monitoring of actions aimed at preventing and eradicating violence against women;

ensure that, in those countries where the death penalty still exists, not to carry out death sentences on pregnant or nursing women;

ensure that women and men enjoy equal rights in terms of access to refugee status, determination procedures and that women refugees are accorded the full protection and benefits guaranteed under international refugee law, including their own identity and other documents; ...

Article 11 Protection of Women in Armed Conflicts

States Parties undertake to respect and ensure respect for the rules of international humanitarian law applicable in armed conflict situations which affect the population, particularly women.

States Parties shall, in accordance with the obligations incumbent upon them under the international humanitarian law, protect civilians including women, irrespective of the population to which they belong, in the event of armed conflict. States Parties undertake to protect asylum seeking women, refugees, returnees and internally displaced persons, against all forms of violence, rape and other forms of sexual exploitation, and to ensure that such acts are considered war crimes, genocide and/or crimes against humanity and that their perpetrators are brought to justice before a competent criminal jurisdiction.

States Parties shall take all necessary measures to ensure that no child, especially girls under 18 years of age, take a direct part in hostilities and that no child is recruited as a soldier.

This Protocol is not as explicit as the Convention of Belém do Pará about the responsibility of the state for private acts of violence in the absence of due diligence. Prior to the Protocol entering into force in 2003, the African Commission had never heard a case involving women's rights. With the entering into force of the Protocol, and the establishment of the African Court, that may change.

B. Constitutional Protection against Violence in the South African Constitution

In its Constitution, South Africa has explicitly incorporated the principle that an individual has the right to be free not only from public acts of violence, but also private acts of violence.

Art 12. Freedom and security of the person

1. Everyone has the right to freedom and security of the person, which includes the right

     a. not to be deprived of freedom arbitrarily or without just cause;

     b. not to be detained without trial;

     c. to be *free from all forms of violence from either public or private sources*; (emphasis added);

     d. not to be tortured in any way; and

     e. not to be treated or punished in a cruel, inhuman or degrading way.

VII. The Response to Domestic Violence by the European Court of Human Rights

A. *Opuz v. Turkey*[23]

In this case Ms. Opuz sued Turkey for failing to protect her and her mother from the domestic violence of her husband. The Court found:[24]

The Court reiterates that the first sentence of Article 2 § 1 enjoins the State not only to refrain from the intentional and unlawful taking of life, but also to take

---

23. 33401-02 E.Ct.H.R (2009); *available at* http://www.unhcr.org/refworld/docid/4a2f84392.html [last visited July 17, 2011].

24. At para. 128.

appropriate steps to safeguard the lives of those within its jurisdiction ... This involves a primary duty on the State to secure the right to life by putting in place effective criminal-law provisions to deter the commission of offences against the person backed up by law-enforcement machinery for the prevention, suppression and punishment of breaches of such provisions. It also extends in appropriate circumstances to a positive obligation on the authorities to take preventive operational measures to protect an individual whose life is at risk from the criminal acts of another individual ... Bearing in mind the difficulties in policing modern societies, the unpredictability of human conduct and the operational choices which must be made in terms of priorities and resources, the scope of the positive obligation must be interpreted in a way which does not impose an impossible or disproportionate burden on the authorities. Not every claimed risk to life, therefore, can entail for the authorities a Convention requirement to take operational measures to prevent that risk from materialising.

For a positive obligation to arise, it must be established that the authorities knew or ought to have known at the time of the existence of a real and immediate risk to the life of an identified individual from the criminal acts of a third party and that they failed to take measures within the scope of their powers which, judged reasonably, might have been expected to avoid that risk.

Another relevant consideration is the need to ensure that the police exercise their powers to control and prevent crime in a manner which fully respects the due process and other guarantees which legitimately place restraints on the scope of their action to investigate crime and bring offenders to justice, including the guarantees contained in Articles 5 and 8 of the Convention.

In the opinion of the Court, where there is an allegation that the authorities have violated their positive obligation to protect the right to life in the context of their above-mentioned duty to prevent and suppress offences against the person, it must be established to its satisfaction that the authorities knew or ought to have known at the time of the existence of a real and immediate risk to the life of an identified individual or individuals from the criminal acts of a third party and that they failed to take measures within the scope of their powers which, judged reasonably, might have been expected to avoid that risk. Furthermore, having regard to the nature of the right protected by Article 2, a right fundamental in the scheme of the Convention, it is sufficient for an applicant to show that the authorities did not do all that could be reasonably expected of them to avoid a real and immediate risk to life of which they have or ought to have knowledge. This is a question which can only be answered in the light of all the circumstances of any particular case ...

[I]t appears that there was an escalating violence against the applicant and her mother by H.O. The crimes committed by H.O. were sufficiently serious to warrant preventive measures and there was a continuing threat to the health and safety of the victims. When examining the history of the relationship, it was obvious that the perpetrator had a record of domestic violence and there was therefore a significant risk of further violence.

Furthermore, the victims' situations were also known to the authorities and the mother had submitted a petition to the Diyarbakır Chief Public Prosecutor's Office, stating that her life was in immediate danger and requesting the police to take action against H.O. However, the authorities' reaction to the applicant's mother's request was limited to taking statements from H.O. about the mother's allegations. Approximately two weeks after this request, on 11 March 2002, he killed the applicant's mother (see Paragraph 54).

Having regard to the foregoing, the Court finds that the local authorities could have foreseen a lethal attack by H.O. While the Court cannot conclude with certainty that matters would have turned out differently and that the killing would not have occurred if the authorities had acted otherwise, it recalls that a failure to take reasonable measures which could have had a real prospect of altering the outcome or mitigating the harm is sufficient to engage the responsibility of the State.

As regards the Government's argument that any further interference by the national authorities would have amounted to a breach of the victims' rights under Article 8 of the Convention, the Court recalls its ruling in a similar case of domestic violence (see *Bevacqua and S. v. Bulgaria*, no. 71127/01, § 83, 12 June 2008), where it held that the authorities' view that no assistance was required as the dispute concerned a "private matter" was incompatible with their positive obligations to secure the enjoyment of the applicants' rights. Moreover, the Court reiterates that, in some instances, the national authorities' interference with the private or family life of the individuals might be necessary in order to protect the health and rights of others or to prevent commission of criminal acts ... The seriousness of the risk to the applicant's mother rendered such intervention by the authorities necessary in the present case.

Questions for Discussion

1. *Consider the approach offered by the European Court of Human Rights in* Opuz. *The crucial test articulated by the Court appears to be:*

   For a positive obligation to arise, it must be established that the authorities knew or ought to have known at the time of the existence of a real and immediate risk to the life of an identified individual from the criminal acts of a third party and that they failed to take measures within the scope of their powers which, judged reasonably, might have been expected to avoid that risk.

   Is this a reasonable test? Might U.S. courts be persuaded to adopt such a test?

2. *Is this the same test as the due diligence standard used by the Inter-American court?*

Chapter 8

Grave and Systematic Violations under Article 8 of the Optional Protocol—The CEDAW Committee's Investigation of the Murders in Ciudad Juarez, Mexico

Chapter Problem

Article 8 of the Optional Protocol to CEDAW gives the Committee the right to initiate an investigation to determine if there is an ongoing "grave and systematic" violation of the rights guaranteed under CEDAW, occurring in the territory of a state party. To date only one such investigation has been brought, and it is described below. Engaging in this type of investigation involves a serious commitment of resources on the part of the Committee, and it places the Committee in a potentially awkward position vis-a-vis the state party concerned. The violations concerned must also be both "grave" and "systematic"—difficult terms to define when no prior investigations have taken place, and the Committee has no jurisprudence to rely on.[1]

Imagine that you work for an NGO, and that you are attending a conference, along with other NGOs, to brainstorm which human rights violations you might bring to the attention of the CEDAW Committee so that it might pursue an investigation under Article 8. Each NGO has a particular situation in mind that it is lobbying for the Committee to investigate. Which situation would you request the Committee to investigate, and why would you choose that particular situation? What evidence would you bring to the Committee's attention to support the claim? Would bringing the Committee's attention to this situation be likely to be effective, and to result in any redress for the victims of the violations? Besides requesting the Committee to pursue an investigation, what other remedies might you choose to pursue?

---

1. The CEDAW Committee recently agreed to launch an investigation under Article 8 into the disappearances and murders of Native American women in Canada.

I. Article 8 of the Optional Protocol to CEDAW

Article 8:

1. If the Committee receives reliable information indicating grave or systematic violations by a State Party of rights set forth in the Convention, the Committee shall invite that State Party to cooperate in the examination of the information and to this end to submit observations with regard to the information concerned.

2. Taking into account any observations that may have been submitted by the State Party concerned as well as any other reliable information available to it, the Committee may designate one or more of its members to conduct an inquiry and to report urgently to the Committee. Where warranted and with the consent of the State Party, the inquiry may include a visit to its territory.

3. After examining the findings of such an inquiry, the Committee shall transmit these findings to the State Party concerned together with any comments and recommendations....

Article 8 of the Optional Protocol to CEDAW thus gives the CEDAW Committee the right to initiate an investigation on the basis of credible evidence, to determine if there is a grave and systematic violation of the Convention. Thus far the Committee has undertaken only one inquiry—that was into the killing of women in Ciudad Juarez, Mexico.

A. The Femicides in Ciudad Juarez

Ciudad Juarez is a border town which, in the wake of NAFTA, has seen the rapid expansion of *maquiladoras* (foreign owned factories), and an influx of workers to staff those factories. Many of the workers are young women between the ages of sixteen and twenty-five. Between 1993 and 2004, approximately 400 bodies of young girls turned up, primarily in the desert areas or vacant lots surrounding the town. Some 4000 more girls have been reported missing. Most of the murdered girls were *maquiladora* workers. Many of them had been brutally raped, tortured, and mutilated. Many had had their breasts cut off, or their head removed from their torso. Despite the fact that family members would report the disappearance of a daughter or sister to the police, little or no action would be taken by the police and days later the girl's body would be found. The police also demonstrated little interest in, or ability to, apprehend the murderers. When pressed police and prosecutors blamed the victims for being promiscuous or for going to the local bars. Two non-governmental organizations (NGOs), Equality Now and Casa Amiga, urged the CEDAW Committee to bring an inquiry. With the permission of the Mexican government, the Committee sent a team to Mexico in October 2003, and issued a report in 2005.

B. The Report of the CEDAW Committee on the Femicides in Ciudad Juarez

The overall situation has led to a range of criminal behaviours, including organized crime, drug trafficking, trafficking in women, undocumented migration, money-laundering, pornography, procuring, and the exploitation of prostitution ...

25. In addition, the situation created by the establishment of the maquilas and the creation of jobs mainly for women, without the creation of enough alternatives for men, has changed the traditional dynamic of relations between the sexes, which was characterized by gender inequality. This gives rise to a situation of conflict towards the women—especially the youngest—employed in the maquilas. This social change in women's roles has not been accompanied by a change in traditionally patriarchal attitudes and mentalities, and thus the stereotyped view of men's and women's social roles has been perpetuated.

26. Within this context, a culture of impunity has taken root which facilitates and encourages terrible violations of human rights. Violence against women has also taken root, and has developed specific characteristics marked by hatred and misogyny. There have been widespread kidnappings, disappearances, rapes, mutilations and murders, especially over the past decade ...

34. There is a gradual realization of the extent of the problem, as a phenomenon that goes beyond isolated cases in a structurally violent society. Under these circumstances, focusing solely on the murders and disappearances as isolated cases would not appear to be the answer in terms of resolving the underlying sociocultural problem. Along with combating crime, resolving the individual cases of murders and disappearances, finding and punishing those who are guilty, and providing support to the victims' families, the root causes of gender violence in its structural dimension and in all its forms—whether domestic and intra-family violence or sexual violence and abuse, murders, kidnappings, and disappearances must be combated, specific policies on gender equality adopted and a gender perspective integrated into all public policies. This concept does appear to be on the political agenda, especially at the Federal level, but the authorities have been too slow in coming to terms with it, and it remains unclear whether such a process has occurred at all levels of authority ...

63. Generally speaking, the victims of crimes of sexual violence are pretty, very young women, including adolescents, living in conditions of poverty and vulnerability; most of them are workers in maquilas or at other jobs or are students.

64. For many years, these victims disappeared while on their way to or from their homes since they had to cross deserted, unlit areas at night or in the early morning. Now, these disappearances take place in broad daylight in the city centre, escaping police notice and with no one reporting having seen anything unusual.

65. As far as we know, the method of these sexual crimes begins with the victims' abduction through deception or by force. They are held captive and subjected to sexual abuse, including rape and, in some cases, torture until they are murdered; their bodies are then abandoned in some deserted spot.

66. As stated above, they are murdered because they are women and because they are poor. Since these are gender-based crimes, they have been tolerated for years by the authorities with total indifference. It is also alarming to learn that the problem is spreading under similar conditions to other cities in Mexico.

67. Some high-level officials of Chihuahua state and Ciudad Juárez have gone so far as to publicly blame the victims themselves for their fate, attributing it to

their manner of dress, the place in which they worked, their conduct, the fact that they were walking alone, or parental neglect; this has provoked justifiable indignation and highly vocal criticism ...

73. It is impossible even to guess how many women have actually disappeared in Ciudad Juárez during the past decade; the current estimate varies from the 44 acknowledged by the State authorities to the 400 mentioned by NGOs and the 4,500 reported by the National Human Rights Commission.

The report found a "serious lapse" by Mexico with regard to its obligations under CEDAW, and urged Mexican authorities to investigate, prosecute, train police, preserve evidence, and interact more effectively with victims' families. Specifically, the Committee found:

263. The Committee considers that there have been serious lapses in compliance with the commitments made by Mexico through its ratification of the Convention on the Elimination of All Forms of Discrimination against Women, as evidenced by the persistence and tolerance of violations of women's human rights. This is shown by the continuation of very widespread and systematic violence against women and by the crimes of murder and disappearance of women as one of its most brutal manifestations. The Committee therefore makes the following recommendation:

264. Comply with all obligations assumed under the Convention on the Elimination of All Forms of Discrimination against Women. Recall, in particular, that the obligation to eliminate discrimination against women refers not only to actions or omissions by the State at all levels, but also to the need to take all appropriate measures to eliminate discrimination against women by any person, organization or enterprise.

II. Regional, International, and NGO Responses to the Situation in Ciudad Juarez

In 2003 the Special Rapporteur from the Inter-American Commission on Human Rights also visited Mexico to investigate the situation, and to urge Mexico to uphold its obligations under the Convention of Belém do Pará. Additionally, in 2003, Amnesty International issued a report on the murders,[1] and in 2006, the U.S. Congress passed a resolution condemning the killings.[2] In August 2007, the U.S. House of Representatives sent a letter to President Felipe Calderon urging him to bring those responsible to justice.[3]

---

1. *See* Amnesty International, *Intolerable Killings: 10 Years of Abductions and Murders of Women in Ciudad Juarez and Chihuahua* (2003); *available at* http://www.amnesty.org/en/library/info/AMR41/026/2003 [last visited November 21, 2011].

2. H. Con. Res. 90.

3. *Available at* http://www.votesmart.org/speech_detail.php?sc_id=312394&keyword=&phrase=&contain= [last visited July 3, 2011].

A. The Amnesty International Report—*Intolerable Killings: 10 Years of Abductions and Murders of Women in Ciudad Juárez and Chihuahua*

Amnesty International conducted an investigation into the killings of women in Ciudad Juarez and published a report based on their findings in 2003. The report opens with this chilling story:

> It is 10.15 on the night of 19 February, 2001. People living near waste ground close to a maquila (an assembly plant) in Ciudad Juárez dial 060, the number of the municipal police emergency services, to inform them that an apparently naked young woman is being beaten and raped by two men in a car.

> No patrol car is dispatched in response to the first call. Following a second call, a police unit is sent out but does not arrive until 11.25pm, too late to intervene. The car has already left.

> Four days earlier, the mother of Lilia Alejandra García reported her 17-year-old daughter missing to the Unidad de Atención a Víctimas de Delitos Sexuales y Contra de la Familia, Unit for the Care of Victims of Sexual Offences and Offences against the Family.

> Lilia Alejandra, the mother of a baby and a three-year old boy, was working at a maquila called Servicios Plásticos y Ensambles. At 7.30pm on the previous night, her colleagues saw her walking towards an unlit area of waste ground near the factory. Lilia Alejandra used to cross it every day to catch the bus home. But that night she never reached her destination.

> On 21 February the body of a young woman was found on the waste ground near to where the emergency call had been made. It was wrapped in a blanket and showed signs of physical and sexual violence. The cause of death was found to be asphyxia resulting from strangulation. The body of the young woman was identified by the parents as being that of Lilia Alejandra. The forensic report concluded that she had died a day and a half earlier and that she had spent at least five days in captivity prior to her death.

> A Municipal Police report taken at 11.15 pm on 19 February simply states "nothing to report" ("reporte sin novedad"). The identity of the woman attacked that day was never established and no attempt was made to investigate whether there was any connection between the incident and the abduction of Lilia Alejandra or any other case. The authorities never investigated the lack of response on the part of the 060 Emergency Services in Ciudad Juárez. There is still no lighting on the waste ground near the maquiladora. A small cross commemorates the place where the body was found.

Irene Khan, then President of Amnesty International, traveled to Mexico in 2003 to present the report to Mexican Authorities, and relatives of the victims. President Vincente Fox acknowledged that the killings were "serious" but noted that they were "isolated instances." Among the recommendations called for in the report were:

1. The federal authorities should immediately intervene to ensure that justice is done in Ciudad Juárez and Chihuahua and the state authorities should cooperate fully in investigating the cases in question.

2. An independent judicial mechanism should be set up to review the cases of all those detained in connection with the abductions and murders and the

extensive reforms required at the state level in the public security sphere and criminal justice system should be implemented.

3. Respect for the dignity of the relatives and organizations working for women's rights should be demonstrated by publicly recognizing the legitimacy of their struggle for justice and condemning any acts of intimidation or harassment against them.

B. Draft Congressional Resolution Proposed by U.S. Representative Hilda Solis (H.Con. Res. 90 2006)

Resolved by the House of Representatives (the Senate concurring), That Congress—

(1) condemns the ongoing abductions and murders of young women in Ciudad Juarez and the city of Chihuahua in the State of Chihuahua, Mexico, since 1993;

(2) expresses its sincerest condolences and deepest sympathy to the families of the victims of these murders;

(3) recognizes the courageous struggle of the victims' families in seeking justice for the victims;

(4) urges the President and Secretary of State to incorporate the investigative and preventative efforts of the Mexican Government in the bilateral agenda between the Governments of Mexico and the United States and to continue to express concern over these abductions and murders to the Government of Mexico;

(5) urges the President and Secretary of State to continue to express support for the efforts of the victims' families to seek justice for the victims, to express concern relating to the continued harassment of these families and the human rights defenders with whom they work, and to express concern with respect to impediments in the ability of the families to receive prompt and accurate information in their cases;

(6) supports ongoing efforts to identify unknown victims through forensic analysis, including DNA testing, conducted by independent, impartial experts who are sensitive to the special needs and concerns of the victims' families, as well as efforts to make these services available to any families who have doubts about the results of prior forensic testing;

(7) condemns the use of torture as a means of investigation into these crimes;

(8) encourages the Secretary of State to continue to include in the annual Country Report on Human Rights of the Department of State all instances of improper investigatory methods, threats against human rights activists, and the use of torture with respect to cases involving the murder and abduction of young women in the State of Chihuahua;

(9) encourages the Secretary of State to urge the Government of Mexico and the State of Chihuahua to review the cases of murdered women in which those accused or convicted of murder have credibly alleged they were tortured or forced by a state agent to confess to the crime; ...

Questions for Discussion

1. Note the coordination of a number of different organizations in spotlighting the failure of the Mexican government to address the violent murders of women in

Ciudad Juarez. Did all of the evidence gathered by these various NGOs help to show that these were not isolated incidents, but rather "grave and systematic" violations?

2. *Is it a weakness of Article 8 that the Committee may only visit a state to conduct an inquiry with the government's permission?*

3. *Consider all of the different forms of pressure that were brought to bear on the Mexican government. What does this teach us about human rights advocacy?*

C. The Inter-American Court — *The Cotton Field Case*[4]

In 2001, the bodies of three young women were found in a cotton field in Ciudad Juarez. The parents of these murdered women filed a complaint with the Inter-American Commission, which in turn brought a complaint on behalf of the parents to the Inter-American Court. The case was filed against Mexico requesting that:

3. The Commission asked that the Court declare the State responsible for the violation of the rights embodied in Articles 4 (Right to Life), 5 (Right to Humane Treatment), 8 (Right to a Fair Trial), 19 (Rights of the Child) and 25 (Right to Judicial Protection) of the Convention, in relation to the obligations established in Articles 1(1) (Obligation to Respect Rights) and 2 (Domestic Legal Effects) thereof, together with failure to comply with the obligations arising from Article 7 of the Convention on the Prevention, Punishment and Eradication of Violence against Women (hereinafter "the Convention of Belém do Pará") ...

133. Various reports agree that, although there are different motives for the murders in Ciudad Juárez and different perpetrators, many cases relate to gender violence that occurs in a context of systematic discrimination against women. According to Amnesty International, the characteristics shared by many of the cases reveal that the victim's gender appears to have been a significant factor in the crime, "influencing both the motive and the context of the crime, and also the type of violence to which the women were subjected." The report of the IACHR Rapporteur indicates that the violence against women in Ciudad Juárez "has its roots in concepts of the inferiority and subordination of women." In turn, CEDAW stressed that gender-based violence, including the murders, kidnappings, disappearances and the domestic violence "are not isolated, sporadic or episodic cases of violence; rather they represent a structural situation and a social and cultural phenomenon deeply rooted in customs and mindsets" and that these situations of violence are founded "in a culture of violence and discrimination."

134. The United Nations Rapporteur on violence against women explained that the violence against women in Mexico can only be understood in the context of "socially entrenched gender inequality." The Rapporteur referred to "forces of change [that] challenge the very basis of the *machismo*" including the incorporation of women into the workforce, which gives them economic independence and

---

4. Case of González *et al.* ("*Cotton Field*") *v.* Mexico, Judgment of November 16, 2009; *available at* http://www.corteidh.or.cr/docs/casos/articulos/seriec_205_ing.pdf [last visited July 2, 2011].

offers new opportunities for education and training. While ultimately empowering women to overcome structural discrimination, these factors may exacerbate violence and hardship in the short-run. The inability of men to fulfill traditional *machista* roles as providers causes family abandonment, unstable relationships or alcoholism, which in turn may increase the risk of violence. Even cases of rape and murder, may be understood as desperate attempts to uphold discriminatory norms that are outpaced by changing socio-economic conditions and the advance of human rights.

The Court's conclusions

164. Based on the foregoing, the Court concludes that, since 1993, there has been an increase in the murders of women, with at least 264 victims up until 2001, and 379 up to 2005. However, besides these figures, which the Tribunal notes are unreliable, it is a matter of concern that some of these crimes appear to have involved extreme levels of violence, including sexual violence and that, in general, they have been influenced, as the State has accepted, by a culture of gender-based discrimination which, according to various probative sources, has had an impact on both the motives and the method of the crimes, as well as on the response of the authorities. In this regard, the ineffective responses and the indifferent attitudes that have been documented in relation to the investigation of these crimes should be noted, since they appear to have permitted the perpetuation of the violence against women in Ciudad Juárez. The Court finds that, up until 2005, most of the crimes had not been resolved, and murders with characteristics of sexual violence present higher levels of impunity ...

194. Although the State alleges that it began the search for the victims immediately, according to the case file, the only measures it took before the remains were found were registering the disappearances and preparing the posters reporting them, taking statements, and sending an official letter to the Judicial Police. There is no evidence in the case file that the authorities circulated the posters or made more extensive inquiries into reasonably relevant facts provided by the 20 or more statements taken.

195. In addition, the Court finds that these facts can be considered within a general context documented in the case file. Indeed, in January 2006, the United Nations Rapporteur on violence against women indicated that "[r]eportedly, the municipal police of Ciudad Juárez does not routinely initiate search actions or other preventive measures as soon as it receives a report about a missing woman. Inexplicably, the police often wait for confirmation that a crime has actually been committed." The Tribunal considers that, in the instant case, the comments made by officials that the victims had gone off with a boyfriend or that they led a disreputable life, and the use of questions about the sexual preference of the victims constitute stereotyping. In addition, both the attitude and statements of the officials reveal that, at the very least, they were indifferent towards the next of kin of the victims and their complaints ...

Obligation to guarantee

243. The Tribunal reiterates that the States should not merely abstain from violating rights, but must adopt positive measures to be determined based on the specific needs of protection of the subject of law, either because of his or her personal situation or because of the specific circumstances in which he or she finds himself ...

253. The Convention of Belém do Pará defines violence against women (*supra* Para. 226) and its Article 7(b) obliges the States Parties to use due diligence to prevent, punish and eliminate this violence.

254. Since 1992, CEDAW established that "States may also be responsible for private acts if they fail to act with due diligence to prevent violations of rights or to investigate and punish acts of violence, and for providing compensation." The 1993 Declaration on the Elimination of Violence against Women of the General Assembly of the United Nations urged the States to "[e]xercise due diligence to prevent, investigate and, in accordance with national legislation, punish acts of violence against women, whether those acts are perpetrated by the State or by private persons" and so did the Platform for Action of the Beijing World Conference on Women. In 2006, the U.N. Special Rapporteur on violence against women stated that "[b]ased on practice and the *opinio juris* […] it may be concluded that there is a norm of customary international law that obliges States to prevent and respond with due diligence to acts of violence against women."

255. In the case of *Maria Da Penha v. Brazil* (2000), presented by a victim of domestic violence, the Inter-American Commission applied the Convention of Belém do Pará for the first time and decided that the State had violated its obligation to exercise due diligence to prevent, punish and eliminate domestic violence, by failing to convict and punish the perpetrator for 15 years, despite all the complaints opportunely submitted. The Commission concluded that, since the violation was part of a "general pattern of negligence and lack of effectiveness of the State," not only had the obligation to prosecute and convict been violated, but also the obligation to prevent this degrading practice.

256. In addition, the U.N. Special Rapporteur on violence against women has provided guidelines on the measures that States should take to comply with their international obligations of due diligence with regard to prevention, namely: ratification of the international human rights instruments; constitutional guarantees on equality for women; existence of national legislation and administrative sanctions providing adequate redress for women victims of violence; executive policies or plans of action that attempt to deal with the question of violence against women; sensitization of the criminal justice system and the police to gender issues; availability and accessibility of support services; existence of measures in the field of education and the media to raise awareness and modify practices that discriminate against women, and collection of data and statistics on violence against women....

258. The foregoing reveals that States should adopt comprehensive measures to comply with due diligence in cases of violence against women. In particular, they should have an appropriate legal framework for protection that is enforced effectively, and prevention policies and practices that allow effective measures to be taken in response to the respective complaints. The prevention strategy should also be comprehensive; in other words, it should prevent the risk factors and, at the same time, strengthen the institutions that can provide an effective response in cases of violence against women. Furthermore, the State should adopt preventive measures in specific cases in which it is evident that certain women and girls may be victims of violence. This should take into account that, in cases of violence against women, the States also have the general obligation established in the American Convention, an obligation reinforced since the Convention of Belém do Pará came into force. Even though the State was fully aware

of the danger faced by these women of being subjected to violence, it has not shown that, prior to November 2001, it had adopted effective measures of prevention that would have reduced the risk factors for the women. Although the obligation of prevention is one of means and not of results (*supra* para. 251), the State has not demonstrated that the creation of the FEIHM and some additions to its legislative framework, although necessary and revealing a commitment by the State, were sufficient and effective to prevent the serious manifestations of violence against women that occurred in Ciudad Juárez at the time of this case ...

280. Nevertheless, according to the Court's jurisprudence, it is evident that a State cannot be held responsible for any human rights violation committed between private individuals within its jurisdiction. Indeed, a State's obligation of guarantee under the Convention does not imply its unlimited responsibility for any act or deed of private individuals, because its obligation to adopt measures of prevention and protection for private individuals in their relations with each other is conditional on its awareness of a situation of real and imminent danger for a specific individual or group of individuals and the reasonable possibility of preventing or avoiding that danger. In other words, even though the juridical consequence of an act or omission of a private individual is the violation of certain human rights of another private individual, this cannot be attributed automatically to the State, because the specific circumstances of the case and the discharge of such obligation to guarantee must be taken into account.

281. In this case, there are two crucial moments in which the obligation of prevention must be examined. The first is prior to the disappearance of the victims and the second is before the discovery of their bodies.

282. Regarding the first moment — before the disappearance of the victims — the Tribunal finds that the failure to prevent the disappearance does not *per se* result in the State's international responsibility because, even though the State was aware of the situation of risk for women in Ciudad Juárez, it has not been established that it knew of a real and imminent danger for the victims in this case. Even though the context of this case and the State's international obligations impose on it a greater responsibility with regard to the protection of women in Ciudad Juárez, who are in a vulnerable situation, particularly young women from humble backgrounds, these factors do not impose unlimited responsibility for any unlawful act against such women. Moreover, the Court can only note that the absence of a general policy which could have been initiated at least in 1998 — when the CNDH warned of the pattern of violence against women in Ciudad Juárez — is a failure of the State to comply in general with its obligation of prevention.

283. With regard to the second moment — before the discovery of the bodies — given the context of the case, the State was aware that there was a real and imminent risk that the victims would be sexually abused, subjected to ill-treatment and killed. The Tribunal finds that, in this context, an obligation of strict due diligence arises in regard to reports of missing women, with respect to search operations during the first hours and days. Since this obligation of means is more rigorous, it requires that exhaustive search activities be conducted. Above all, it is essential that police authorities, prosecutors and judicial officials take prompt immediate action by ordering, without delay, the necessary measures to determine the whereabouts of the victims or the place where they may have been retained. Adequate procedures should exist for reporting disappearances, which should

result in an immediate effective investigation. The authorities should presume that the disappeared person has been deprived of liberty and is still alive until there is no longer any uncertainty about her fate.

284. Mexico did not prove that it had adopted reasonable measures, according to the circumstances surrounding these cases, to find the victims alive. The State did not act promptly during the first hours and days following the reports of the disappearances, losing valuable time. In the period between the reports and the discovery of the victims' bodies, the State merely carried out formalities and took statements that, although important, lost their value when they failed to lead to specific search actions. In addition, the attitude of the officials towards the victims' next of kin, suggesting that the missing persons' reports should not be dealt with urgently and immediately, leads the Court to conclude reasonably that there were unjustified delays following the filing of these reports. The foregoing reveals that the State did not act with the required due diligence to prevent the death and abuse suffered by the victims adequately and did not act, as could reasonably be expected, in accordance with the circumstances of the case, to end their deprivation of liberty. This failure to comply with the obligation to guarantee is particularly serious owing to the context of which the State was aware—which placed women in a particularly vulnerable situation—and of the even greater obligations imposed in cases of violence against women by Article 7(b) of the Convention of Belém do Pará.

285. In addition, the Tribunal finds that the State did not prove that it had adopted norms or implemented the necessary measures, pursuant to Article 2 of the American Convention and Article 7(c) of the Convention of Belém do Pará, that would have allowed the authorities to provide an immediate and effective response to the reports of disappearance and to adequately prevent the violence against women. Furthermore, it did not prove that it had adopted norms or taken measures to ensure that the officials in charge of receiving the missing reports had the capacity and the sensitivity to understand the seriousness of the phenomenon of violence against women and the willingness to act immediately.

286. Based on the foregoing, the Court finds that the State violated the rights to life, personal integrity and personal liberty recognized in Articles 4(1), 5(1), 5(2) and 7(1) of the American Convention, in relation to the general obligation to guarantee contained in Article 1(1) and the obligation to adopt domestic legal provisions contained in Article 2 thereof, as well as the obligations established in Article 7(b) and 7(c) of the Convention of Belém do Pará, to the detriment of Claudia Ivette González, Laura Berenice Ramos Monárrez and Esmeralda Herrera Monreal.

The court further ruled that the Mexican government must publicly acknowledge its responsibility, pay compensation to the families of the victims, publish the sentence in official government records, and build a monument in memory of the victims. Authorities must also investigate the murders and bring those responsible for the slayings to justice.

Questions for Discussion

1. *Compare the remedies that the Court and the CEDAW Committee were able to order. Is it more likely that Mexico will comply with the Court's order rather than the Committee's? Does this indicate the enforceability problems with CEDAW despite the entering into force of the Optional Protocol?*

2. *Note that the Court ordered Mexico to publicly acknowledge its responsibility for its failure to bring the killers to justice. Do remedies like these help to reinforce the concept that states that fail to act with due diligence to protect women are responsible for acts of private violence?*

3. *The CEDAW Committee is planning an Article 8 investigation into the "stolen sisters" in Canada. The investigation will involve ascertaining whether Canada has violated CEDAW by failing to properly investigate and prosecute the disappearances and murder of at least 600 Native American women.*

Chapter 9

Trafficking—Modern Day Slavery

Chapter Problem

The United States State Department has taken the lead internationally with regard to efforts to combat trafficking in persons. The Trafficking Victims Protection Act (TVPA) is coming up for reauthorization, and you have been asked to prepare a memorandum for the Subcommittee which is reviewing the TVPA. One of the questions that has been raised by the Subcommittee relates to the relationship, if any, between trafficking and prostitution. The Subcommittee has previously heard evidence that around the time of large sporting events trafficking seems to spike. This phenomenon was recently recognized when the South African government, which hosted World Cup Soccer in 2010, considered legalizing and regulating prostitution (at least temporarily) to better monitor whether women were being trafficked into the country, or whether they were voluntarily engaging in prostitution. It was also argued by the Police Commissioner that legalizing prostitution and requiring prostitutes to apply for licenses would diminish the spread of HIV/AIDs.

The Subcommittee would like you to research international instruments designed to protect women from being trafficked. The Subcommittee would like to know whether current methods are effective, or whether more could be done. The Subcommittee would also like you to explore the relationship between trafficking and prostitution, and consider whether the Subcommittee's efforts to end trafficking should also encompass a particular approach towards prostitution.

I. CEDAW on Trafficking and Prostitution

Article 6 of CEDAW provides that:

> States Parties shall take all appropriate measures, including legislation, to suppress all forms of traffic in women and exploitation of prostitution of women.

Another form of violence that is commonly perpetrated against women is human trafficking. Poverty, lack of education, and lack of economic opportunity make women and young girls particularly vulnerable to human trafficking. Some women who live in patriarchal societies may be sold by their families to discharge debts, while others may be tricked into applying for what they believe are legitimate paying jobs abroad, only to find that they have been trafficked into sexual or some other form of slavery. While trafficking for the purpose of prostitution is common, trafficking is not limited to the sex trade. Women and girls are often trafficked into forced labor as domestic servants, workers in so called sweat shops, as well as forced marriages. Women and men are also trafficked for organs.

II. Early Forms of Trafficking and Sexual Slavery

A. The Comfort Women — Japan

Trafficking is not a new problem. During the days of the slave trade, human beings were predominantly trafficked from Africa to the Americas and Europe to become slaves. After the slave trade was outlawed, various forms of forced labor still continued to exist, including forced prostitution. An example of forced prostitution on a large scale was the so-called comfort women. These were primarily Korean women who were forced by the Japanese army during World War II to accompany the Japanese troops and provide sexual services to them. They have been variously referred to as "comfort women," "military sex slaves," "military comfort women," or, in Japanese — "*jugun ianfu*." It is difficult to ascertain how many women were forced to become comfort women. Estimates range from 50,000 to 200,000. Japanese military leaders were not prosecuted for their abuse of comfort women during the Tokyo War Crimes Tribunal, but one war crimes tribunal headed by the Dutch in Jakarta prosecuted Japanese officers for the crime of "forced prostitution" of thirty-five Dutch women.

In 1992, the UN launched an investigation into the forced prostitution endured by the comfort women and, in 1998, the UN Human Rights Commission issued a report urging Japan to accept legal responsibility for the comfort women, apologize to them and compensate them, and educate the public about the history of the comfort women. EU member states also urged Japan to formally apologize. Japan has not yet fully acknowledged responsibility for this shameful part of its history. As recently as 2007, then Prime Minister Abe denied that women had been coerced into servicing the troops. Japan's indifference to the plight of the comfort women led the U.S. Congress to draft a resolution calling on Japan to accept responsibility for its actions with regard to the comfort women, which the Bill referred to as a "crime against humanity."[1]

III. International Attempts to Limit Trafficking

As far back as the early 1900s, trafficking, or "white slave traffic," as it was then often referred to, was recognized as a problem. In 1902, the International Agreement for the Suppression of the White Slave Traffic was drafted. In 1910, the United States passed the Mann Act which prohibited "the procuration of women and girls for immoral purposes

---

1. House Resolution 759 (109th Congress). Although the Bill passed out of Committee it never went to the House floor for a vote.

abroad." Yet, the slave trade and trafficking continued, which led the League of Nations to draft the 1926 Slavery Convention. In 1949, this was supplanted by the Convention for the Suppression of the Traffic in Persons and of the Exploitation of the Prostitution of Others; followed by the 1956 Supplementary Convention on the Abolition of Slavery, the Slave Trade, and Institutions and Practices Similar to Slavery. In 2000, the United Nations, recognizing the increasing involvement of organized crime in serious crimes including trafficking, drafted the Convention Against Transnational Organized Crime.[2] Although this Convention does not specifically refer to trafficking, it calls for international cooperation in combating "serious crimes."[3] Despite the existence of all of these international conventions, trafficking has continued to flourish. Efforts to end the practice are frustrated by the facts that it can be an extremely profitable business, women are vulnerable to being trafficked, and to prevent it, there must be strict enforcement of borders, international intolerance of trafficking, as well as strict and uniform adherence to and enforcement of these protocols. Thus far, trafficking has proven to be extremely difficult to suppress.

A. The CEDAW Committee's Concluding Observations to China (2006)[4]

The CEDAW Committee has been criticized for what has been referred to as its support for the decriminalization of prostitution. This is one of the reasons cited by opponents of CEDAW in the United States as a reason why the U.S. should not ratify the treaty. In fact, the Committee has rebuked party states which prosecute prostitutes, while allowing those who patronize them to remain unscathed. An example of this approach is contained in the Committee's Concluding Observations to China in 2006:

19. While recognizing the efforts made by the State party to address trafficking in women and girls, including cross-border and international cooperation, the Committee is concerned that the definition of trafficking in the Penal Code is limited to the purpose of exploitation of prostitution and is therefore not in line with international standards. The Committee also expresses concern that the continued criminalization of prostitution disproportionately impacts on prostitutes rather than on the prosecution and punishment of pimps and traffickers. It is also concerned that prostitutes may be kept in administrative detention without due process of law.

Moreover, the Committee is concerned about the insufficient data and statistical information about the extent of trafficking, in particular internal trafficking.

20. The Committee recommends that the State party increase its efforts to combat all forms of trafficking in women and girls. It urges the State party to bring its domestic legislation in line with international standards and to speedily complete, adopt and implement the draft national programme of action against human trafficking. It requests the State party to enhance enforcement of the law against trafficking so as to ensure that those who traffic and sexually exploit women and

---

2. Adopted by the General Assembly by UN Resolution 55/25 of 2000. The Convention entered into force in 2003.

3. Serious crimes are defined in Art. 1, and include corruption and money laundering.

4. *Available at* http://www.un.org/womenwatch/daw/cedaw/cedaw36/cc/CHINA_advance%20 unedited.pdf [last visited July 14, 2011].

girls are prosecuted and punished, and to provide all necessary assistance to the victims of trafficking. The Committee also urges the State party to take measures aimed at the rehabilitation and reintegration of women in prostitution into society, to enhance other livelihood opportunities for women to leave prostitution, provide support for them to do so and to prevent any detention of women without due legal process. It calls upon the State party to systematically compile detailed data on cross-border and internal trafficking, reflecting the age and ethnic background of the victims. The Committee requests the State party to provide in its next report comprehensive information and data on the trafficking of women and girls as well as on the impact of measures taken and results achieved in this regard.

Questions for Discussion

1. *The Committee's position appears to be that pimps and traffickers should be prosecuted rather than the prostitutes themselves. Do you think this would be an effective approach?*

2. *If prostitution were to be totally decriminalized, what do you think the effect would be?*

B. The Protocol to Prevent, Suppress and Punish Trafficking in Persons, Especially Women and Children[5]

The Protocol to Prevent, Suppress and Punish Trafficking in Persons, Especially Women and Children, is one of the Protocols to the Convention Against Transnational Organized Crime, and is to be read and interpreted in conjunction with that Convention. It entered into force in 2003.[6] It is also sometimes referred to as the Palermo Protocol. Its purpose is to

(*a*) To prevent and combat trafficking in persons, paying particular attention to women and children;

(*b*) To protect and assist the victims of such trafficking, with full respect for their human rights; and

(*c*) To promote cooperation among States Parties in order to meet those objectives.[7]

It defines trafficking in Article 3(a) as:

"Trafficking in persons" shall mean the recruitment, transportation, transfer, harbouring or receipt of persons, by means of the threat or use of force or other

---

5. The full title of the Convention is Protocol to Prevent, Suppress and Punish Trafficking in Persons, Especially Women and Children, Supplementing the United Nations Convention Against Transnational Organized Crime.

6. It was adopted by General Assembly Resolution 55/25.

7. Art. 2.

forms of coercion, of abduction, of fraud, of deception, of the abuse of power or of a position of vulnerability or of the giving or receiving of payments or benefits to achieve the consent of a person having control over another person, for the purpose of exploitation. Exploitation shall include, at a minimum, the exploitation of the prostitution of others or other forms of sexual exploitation, forced labour or services, slavery or practices similar to slavery, servitude or the removal of organs.[8]

It also notes that the "consent of a victim of trafficking in persons to the intended exploitation set forth in sub-paragraph *(a)* of this article shall be irrelevant where any of the means set forth in sub-paragraph *(a)* have been used."

The Protocol goes on to call on states parties to establish trafficking as a criminal offence,[9] and to offer assistance and protection to victims of trafficking.[10] Among the forms of assistance that states parties should offer to victims are:

(a) Information on relevant court and administrative proceedings;

(b) Assistance to enable their views and concerns to be presented and considered at appropriate stages of criminal proceedings against offenders, in a manner not prejudicial to the rights of the defence.

3. Each State Party shall consider implementing measures to provide for the physical, psychological and social recovery of victims of trafficking in persons, including, in appropriate cases, in cooperation with non-governmental organizations, other relevant organizations and other elements of civil society, and, in particular, the provision of:

(a) Appropriate housing;

(b) Counselling and information, in particular as regards their legal rights, in a language that the victims of trafficking in persons can understand;

(c) Medical, psychological and material assistance; and

(d) Employment, educational and training opportunities.

4. Each State Party shall take into account, in applying the provisions of this article, the age, gender and special needs of victims of trafficking in persons, in particular the special needs of children, including appropriate housing, education and care.

5. Each State Party shall endeavour to provide for the physical safety of victims of trafficking in persons while they are within its territory.

6. Each State Party shall ensure that its domestic legal system contains measures that offer victims of trafficking in persons the possibility of obtaining compensation for damage suffered.[11]

Article 7 suggests that states parties consider adopting measures to permit trafficking victims to stay either temporarily or permanently in the country they have been trafficked to.

---

8. Art. 3.
9. Art. 5.
10. Art. 6.
11. Art. 6.

C. Efforts by the United States to Combat Trafficking — The Trafficking Victims Protection Act (TVPA)

Under the presidency of George W. Bush, the United States has played a leadership role in efforts to combat trafficking. In 2000, Congress passed the Trafficking Victims Protection Act.[12] Its purpose was to combat trafficking in persons, and it focused on the three goals of prevention, punishing traffickers, and protecting victims of trafficking. It noted that "at least 700,000 persons annually, primarily women and children, are trafficked within or across international borders. Approximately 50,000 women and children are trafficked into the United States each year."[13] The Act acknowledges that people are trafficked not only for sexual purposes, but also for forced labor. Congress found that:

> Traffickers primarily target women and girls, who are disproportionately affected by poverty, the lack of access to education, chronic unemployment, discrimination, and the lack of economic opportunities in countries of origin. Traffickers lure women and girls into their networks through false promises of decent working conditions at relatively good pay as nannies, maids, dancers, factory workers, restaurant workers, sales clerks, or models. Traffickers also buy children from poor families and sell them into prostitution or into various types of forced or bonded labor.
>
> (5) Traffickers often transport victims from their home communities to unfamiliar destinations, including foreign countries away from family and friends, religious institutions, and other sources of protection and support, leaving the victims defenseless and vulnerable.
>
> (6) Victims are often forced through physical violence to engage in sex acts or perform slavery-like labor. Such force includes rape and other forms of sexual abuse, torture, starvation, imprisonment, threats, psychological abuse, and coercion.
>
> (7) Traffickers often make representations to their victims that physical harm may occur to them or others should the victim escape or attempt to escape.[14]

The statute refers to trafficking as an "evil" and notes that the right to be free from slavery and servitude is one of the unalienable rights articulated in the Declaration of Independence. It goes on to provide that like slavery:

> Current practices of sexual slavery and trafficking of women and children are similarly abhorrent to the principles upon which the United States was founded.
>
> (23) The United States and the international community agree that trafficking in persons involves grave violations of human rights and is a matter of pressing international concern.[15]

That statute also acknowledges that:

> (17) Existing laws often fail to protect victims of trafficking, and because victims are often illegal immigrants in the destination country, they are repeatedly punished more harshly than the traffickers themselves.

---

12. Public Law 106-386 Oct. 2000.
13. Section 102.
14. Section 102 (b).
15. Section 102 (22).

(18) Additionally, adequate services and facilities do not exist to meet victims' needs regarding health care, housing, education, and legal assistance, which safely reintegrate trafficking victims into their home countries.

(19) Victims of severe forms of trafficking should not be inappropriately incarcerated, fined, or otherwise penalized solely for unlawful acts committed as a direct result of being trafficked, such as using false documents, entering the country without documentation, or working without documentation.

(20) Because victims of trafficking are frequently unfamiliar with the laws, cultures, and languages of the countries into which they have been trafficked, because they are often subjected to coercion and intimidation including physical detention and debt bondage, and because they often fear retribution and forcible removal to countries in which they will face retribution or other hardship, these victims often find it difficult or impossible to report the crimes committed against them or to assist in the investigation and prosecution of such crimes.

(21) Trafficking of persons is an evil requiring concerted and vigorous action by countries of origin, transit or destination, and by international organizations.

The statute also creates T-visas which are visas issued to non U.S. resident victims of human trafficking, and which permit those victims to remain in the United States. To apply for a T-visa, applicant must complete form I-914 along with a personal statement and supporting evidence. T-visas may also be available for family members of victims who may qualify as indirect victims. Forms are available at the U.S. Citizenship and Immigration Services website.

D. The Trafficking in Persons Report (TIP)

The United States also created an Office to Monitor and Combat Trafficking in Persons, and each year issues a Trafficking in Persons (TIP) report, which classifies countries into one of three tiers. According to the Department of State's website,[16] a Tier 1 ranking indicates that a government has acknowledged the existence of human trafficking, has made efforts to address the problem, and meets the TVPA's minimum standards. Tier 2 countries are those whose governments do not fully comply with the TVPA's minimum standards but are making significant efforts to bring themselves into compliance with those standards, while Tier 3 consists of countries whose governments do not fully comply with the minimum standards, and are not making significant efforts to do so. The TVPA has been reauthorized and renamed the William Wilberforce Trafficking Victims Protection Reauthorization Act of 2008, in honor of Wilberforce the great slave abolitionist.

The State Department notes that:

The TVPA lists three factors by which to determine whether a country should be on Tier 2 (or Tier 2 Watch List) versus Tier 3: (1) the extent to which the country is a country of origin, transit, or destination for severe forms of trafficking; (2) the extent to which the country's government does not comply with the TVPA's minimum standards and, in particular, the extent to which officials or government employees have been complicit in severe forms of trafficking; and (3) what measures are reasonable to bring the government into compliance with

---

16. *Available at* http://www.state.gov/g/tip/rls/tiprpt/2010/142749.htm [last visited July 1, 2011].

the minimum standards in light of the government's resources and capabilities to address and eliminate severe forms of trafficking in persons.

As a result of amendments made by the William Wilberforce Trafficking Victims Protection Reauthorization Act of 2008 (TVPRA of 2008), any country that has been ranked Tier 2 Watch List for two consecutive years (beginning from the time of the 2009 report) and that would otherwise be ranked Tier 2 Watch List for the next year will instead be ranked Tier 3 for the next year, unless the president waives application of this provision based on a determination that, among other things, the government has a written plan for meeting the TVPA's minimum standards.[17]

There are penalties for countries which fall into Tier 3, whereby the U.S. government may withhold non humanitarian, non trade related, foreign assistance. In fact, in September 2010, the President released his determination with regard to Burma, Zimbabwe, North Korea, Cuba, Democratic Republic of Congo, Dominican Republic, Kuwait, Congo, Eritrea, Iran, Mauritania, Papua New Guinea, Saudi Arabia, and Sudan that the U.S. government would not provide certain assistance to these countries until they comply with minimum standards or make "significant efforts to bring themselves into compliance."[18]

E. Tier Rankings under TIP[19]

Afghanistan	2WL	Greece	2	Oman	2
Albania	2	Guatemala	2WL	Pakistan	2
Algeria	2WL	Guinea	2WL	Palau	2
Angola	2WL	Guinea-Bissau	2WL	Panama	2WL
Antigua & Barbuda	2	Guyana	2WL	Papua New Guinea	3
Argentina	2	Honduras	2	Paraguay	2
Armenia	2	Hong Kong	2	Peru	2
Australia	1	Hungary	2	Philippines	2WL
Austria	1	Iceland	2	Poland	1
Azerbaijan	2WL	India	2WL	Portugal	2
The Bahamas	2	Indonesia	2	Qatar	2WL
Bahrain	2	Iran	3	Romania	2
Bangladesh	2WL	Iraq	2WL	Russia	2WL
Barbados	2WL	Ireland	1	Rwanda	2
Belarus	2	Israel	2	St. Vincent & The Gren.	2WL
Belgium	1	Italy	1	Saudi Arabia	3
Belize	2WL	Jamaica	2	Senegal	2WL
Benin	2	Japan	2	Serbia	2
Bolivia	2	Jordan	2	Sierra Leone	2
Bosnia & Herzegovina	1	Kazakhstan	2WL	Singapore	2WL

---

17. *See* http://www.state.gov/g/tip/rls/other/2010/147148.htm [last visited February 3, 2011].
18. *See* http://www.state.gov/g/tip/rls/other/2010/147148.htm [last visited February 3, 2011].
19. *Id.* Note that the letters WL denote those countries that are on the U.S.' Watch List.

Botswana	2	Kenya	2	Slovak Republic	2
Brazil	2	Kiribati	2WL	Slovenia	1
Brunei	2WL	Korea, North	3	South Africa	2
Bulgaria	2	Korea, South	1	Spain	1
Burkina Faso	2	Kosovo	2	Sri Lanka	2WL
Burma	3	Kuwait	3	Sudan	3
Burundi	2	Kyrgyz Republic	2	Suriname	2
Cambodia	2	Laos	2WL	Swaziland	2WL
Cameroon	2WL	Latvia	2	Sweden	1
Canada	1	Lebanon	2WL	Switzerland	2
Central African Rep.	2WL	Lesotho	2WL	Syria	2WL
Chad	2WL	Liberia	2	Taiwan	1
Chile	2	Libya	2WL	Tajikistan	2WL
China (PRC)	2WL	Lithuania	1	Tanzania	2WL
Colombia	1	Luxembourg	1	Thailand	2WL
Congo (DRC)	3	Macau	2	Timor-Leste	2
Congo (ROC)	2WL	Macedonia	2	Togo	2
Costa Rica	2	Madagascar	2WL	Trinidad & Tobago	2WL
Cote d'Ivoire	2WL	Malawi	2	Tunisia	2WL
Croatia	1	Malaysia	2WL	Turkey	2
Cuba	3	Maldives	2WL	Turkmenistan	2WL
Cyprus	2	Mali	2WL	Uganda	2
Czech Republic	1	Malta	2WL	Ukraine	2
Denmark	1	Mauritania	3	United Arab Emirates	2
Djibouti	2	Mauritius	1	United Kingdom	1
Dominican Republic	3	Mexico	2	United States of America	1
Ecuador	2	Micronesia	2WL	Uruguay	2
Egypt	2	Moldova	2WL	Uzbekistan	2WL
El Salvador	2	Mongolia	2	Venezuela	2WL
Equatorial Guinea	2WL	Montenegro	2	Vietnam	2WL
Eritrea	3	Morocco	2	Yemen	2WL
Estonia	2	Mozambique	2WL	Zambia	2
Ethiopia	2	Namibia	2	Zimbabwe	3
Fiji	2WL	Nepal	2	Haiti	SC
Finland	1	Netherlands	1	Somalia	SC
France	1	Neth. Antilles*	2		
Gabon	2WL	New Zealand	1		
The Gambia	2	Nicaragua	2WL		
Georgia	1	Niger	2WL		
Germany	1	Nigeria	1		
Ghana	2	Norway	1		

Questions for Discussion

1. One of the goals of the TIP list seems to be public naming and shaming. How effective do you think such a tactic might be?

2. Many of the countries on the watch list or lower tiers seem to be developing countries. Many of these countries might lack resources to track and prosecute traffickers. Is withholding aid from such countries an effective measure to ensure that those countries become more proactive in prosecuting traffickers?

F. Trafficking and the Sex Trade

The whole issue of trafficking calls into question the role of the sex trade. The new TVPA includes a section specifically prohibiting sex tourism. Yet, it has been noted recently that trafficking often spikes during world sporting or cultural events, as women are often trafficked into the host country to provide sexual services for tourists at the event. This phenomenon is so widely known that recently when South Africa hosted the 2010 World Cup for soccer, the South African Police Commissioner Jackie Selebi suggested legalizing prostitution, so that the police could control matters and minimize trafficking and the spread of AIDs.[20] (Note too, that during the World Cup the French National team was involved in a scandal over entertaining prostitutes.) This proposal, which was ultimately defeated, was not the first time that South Africa had considered legalizing prostitution.

G. Legalizing Prostitution — *Jordan and ano. v. The State* (South African Constitutional Court)

On 20 August 1996 a police officer entered a brothel owned by the first appellant in Pretoria, paid R250 to the second appellant, a salaried employee, and received a pelvic massage from the third appellant, a prostitute or sex worker. The three appellants admitted in the Magistrate's Court that they had contravened the Sexual Offences Act 23 of 1957, which criminalises providing sex for reward and brothel-keeping, but claimed that the relevant provisions of the Act were unconstitutional and should be declared invalid ...

[1] After being found guilty and sentenced by the magistrate, they appealed to the Pretoria High Court to have the provisions set aside. In a judgment handed down on 2 August 2001, the High Court held that section 20(1)(aA) of the Act, which penalised sex for reward, was unconstitutional. That section reads:

20. Persons living on earnings of prostitution or committing or assisting in commission of indecent acts. —

(1) Any person who ...

---

20. *See* http://soccerlens.com/legalizing-prostitution-for-world-cup-2010/5660/ [last visited February 3, 2011].

> (aA) has unlawful carnal intercourse, or commits an act of indecency, with any other person for reward; ... shall be guilty of an offence."

"Unlawful carnal intercourse" is in turn defined in the same section as "carnal intercourse otherwise than between husband and wife". The High Court held that section 2 was a measure to restrict the commercial exploitation of prostitutes, which it described as "trading in the body of a human being", and added that a third party managing a prostitute or prostitutes with their consent amounts to trafficking in human beings. The High Court concluded that public abhorrence at this kind of exploitation permitted the state to limit the individual rights of the third parties to freedom of trade, occupation and profession, by regulating and prohibiting such practices. The declaration of invalidity of the section dealing with sex for reward was referred to this Court [the Constitutional Court] for confirmation ... The state relied on a substantial body of affidavit evidence, which included testimony by the Minister of Justice, in support of upholding the law as it stands. Much of this evidence was contested by the appellants who also filed voluminous affidavits. In addition, a number of amici curiae were admitted and permitted to make written and oral submissions in support of confirmation of the order of invalidity and upholding the appeal. They were the Sex Worker Education and Advocacy Taskforce (SWEAT); the Centre for Applied Legal Studies (CALS) ... the differences in position adopted by the experts and other deponents related not so much to empirical facts as to how to characterise the activities concerned and what conclusions should be drawn from them ... The High Court held that to the extent that section 20(1)(aA) criminalised only the prostitute or sex worker and not the client, it amounted to unfair discrimination. The High Court also held that to the extent that the provision criminalised any sexual intercourse between consenting adults where some favour or consideration was given by one party to the other, it was in breach of the Constitution.... we must decide whether it was correct in concluding that the provision criminalised only the prostitute and not the client, and that it criminalised any non-marital sexual intercourse, where one party gives another party a present or benefit that could be construed as "for reward" in the context of the section and not only commercial sex ...

[2] It has generally been accepted in our law that section 20(1)(aA) criminalises only the conduct of the prostitute and not that of the client. So Burchell and Milton state:

> It is noteworthy that the section does not penalize the person who gives the reward in return for the sexual intercourse. In short, the prohibition is directed only at prostitutes and not their customers. This feature of the section reflects a form of discrimination against prostitutes. The discrimination lies in the fact that the customer's role in the act is not penalized while that of the prostitute is.

[3] Not a single case of a prosecution of a customer since 1988 (when section 20(1)(aA) was introduced into the statute) was brought to our attention, and the state did not seek to challenge the assertion that in practice only the prostitutes were charged in terms of the section.... Counsel for the state argued that the broader interpretation of the section should be preferred because if the section criminalises both the conduct of the prostitute and the client, it would have no discriminatory effect. However, extending the definition of a crime, even to avoid what may otherwise constitute unfair discrimination, is something that a

Court should only do, if ever, in exceptional circumstances.... The question in the present matter, then, is whether the section is reasonably capable of a restrictive interpretation which would narrow its ambit and bring it within constitutional limits, such interpretation being achieved without undue strain. The question is whether the phrase "unlawful sexual intercourse or indecent act for reward" is capable of being read to include only activity ordinarily understood as prostitution. In other words, is the phrase reasonably capable of being read so as to cover only commercial sex, that is, sex where the body is made available for sexual stimulation on a paid basis? We think there are strong contextual pointers in favour of the more restrictive reading....

The heading to the section includes the words: "persons living on the earnings of prostitution". In *President of the Republic of South Africa v. Hugo*, this Court held that it was legitimate for a court interpreting a statute to have regard to the heading of a legislative provision. In this case, the heading of section 20 makes it clear that the section is dealing with persons living on the earnings of prostitution ... If one reads the criminal prohibition contained in section 20(1)(aA) in the light of the heading, one would attribute a meaning to the section which renders criminal the conduct of those who earn their living from prostitution, or commercial sex ...

The constitutionality of section 20(1)(aA)

[4] Counsel for the appellants and the amici contended that the criminalisation of prostitution limits the following fundamental constitutional rights of those concerned:

8. Equality

   (1) Every person shall have the right to equality before the law and to equal protection of the law.

   (2) No person shall be unfairly discriminated against, directly or indirectly, and, without derogating from the generality of this provision, on one or more of the following grounds in particular: race, gender, sex, ethnic or social origin, colour, sexual orientation, age, disability, religion, conscience, belief, culture or language.

10. Human dignity

   Every person shall have the right to respect for and protection of his or her dignity.

11. Freedom and security of the person

   (1) Every person shall have the right to freedom and security of person, which shall include the right not to be detained without trial.

13. Privacy

   Every person shall have the right to his or her personal privacy, which shall include the right not to be subject to searches of his or her person, home or property, the seizure of private possessions or the violation of private communications."

26. Economic activity

   (1) Every person shall have the right to freely engage in economic activity and to pursue a livelihood anywhere in the national territory.

(2) Subsection (1) shall not preclude measures designed to promote the protection or the improvement of the quality of life, economic growth, human development, social justice, basic conditions of employment, fair labour practices or equal opportunity for all, provided such measures are justifiable in an open and democratic society based on freedom and equality ...

[T]he question [remains] whether this right could be claimed only in respect of lawful economic activity....

[T]he state is not precluded from taking measures under section 26(2) of the Constitution "designed to promote the protection or the improvement of the quality of life"....

The state argued that section 20(1)(aA) is aimed at improving the quality of life. In our view, whether one considers that prostitution should be tolerated, regulated or prohibited, there can be no doubt that it does have an impact on the quality of life. The Legislature is therefore entitled to take the steps it considers appropriate to regulate prostitution in terms of section 26(2) so long as it does not limit other fundamental rights in a way that would not be justifiable in an open and democratic society.

The appellants argued that to the extent that section 20(1)(aA) criminalises only the conduct of the prostitutes and not that of the client, it is in breach of section 8 of the Constitution ...

There are two enquiries: the first is to consider whether the impugned provision differentiates between people or categories of people and if it does, whether it does so rationally. The second is to consider whether a differentiation is made, directly or indirectly on a ground which could be said to have the potential to impair human dignity or to affect people adversely in a comparably serious manner. If the differentiation is on such a ground, the question that then arises is whether it is unfair or not ...

The differentiation in this case is between prostitutes and patrons. The conduct of one group is rendered criminal by the section, that of the other, not. It cannot be said that it is irrational for the Legislature to criminalise the conduct of only one group and not the other. The legislative purpose may be to target the purveyors of sex for reward, rather than the purchasers. In each case the question at this stage is the narrow one of whether it is rational for the law to punish only one side of the bargain. In our view, in this case it cannot be said that rendering criminal the conduct of the prostitute and not that of the client is so lacking in any plausible foundation as to be irrational ...

It was accordingly submitted that because prostitutes are overwhelmingly (though not exclusively) female, and patrons are overwhelmingly (though not exclusively) male, the effect of section 20(1)(aA), to the extent that it criminalises only the conduct of prostitutes and not that of patrons, is indirectly discriminatory on the grounds of sex ...

Moreover, the effect of making the prostitute the primary offender directly reinforces a pattern of sexual stereotyping which is itself in conflict with the principle of gender equality ...

The differential impact between prostitute and client is therefore directly linked to a pattern of gender disadvantage which our Constitution is committed to eradicating. In all these circumstances, we are satisfied that, ... this is a case where an apparently neutral differentiating criterion producing a markedly differential impact on a listed ground results in indirect discrimination on that ground ...

This distinction is, indeed, one which for years has been espoused both as a matter of law and social practice. The female prostitute has been the social outcast, the male patron has been accepted or ignored. She is visible and denounced, her existence tainted by her activity. He is faceless, a mere ingredient in her offence rather than a criminal in his own right, who returns to respectability after the encounter. In terms of the sexual double standards prevalent in our society, he has often been regarded either as having given in to temptation, or as having done the sort of thing that men do. Thus, a man visiting a prostitute is not considered by many to have acted in a morally reprehensible fashion. A woman who is a prostitute is considered by most to be beyond the pale. The difference in social stigma tracks a pattern of applying different standards to the sexuality of men and women.

H. Catherine MacKinnon on Prostitution

Catherine MacKinnon, a noted feminist author, strongly believes that prostitution is not an activity that many women engage in voluntarily, and contends it is a violation of women's civil rights.

1. MacKinnon — *Trafficking, Prostitution and Inequality*[21]

ROMEO

[F]amine is in thy cheeks,

Need and oppression starveth in thine eyes,

Contempt and beggary hangs upon thy back;

The world is not thy friend nor the world's law;

The world affords no law to make thee rich;

Then be not poor, but break it, and take this.

APOTHECARY

My poverty, but not my will, consents.

ROMEO

I pay thy poverty, and not thy will.[22]

No one defends trafficking. There is no pro-sex-trafficking position any more than there is a public pro-slavery position for labor these days. The only issue is defining these terms so nothing anyone wants to defend is covered. It is hard to find overt defenders of inequality either, even as its legal definition is also largely shaped by existing practices the powerful want to keep. Prostitution is not like this. Some people are for it; they affirmatively

---

21. Catherine MacKinnon, *Trafficking, Prostitution and Inequality*, 46 HARV. C.R.-C.L. L.REV. 271—280 (2011).
22. William Shakespeare, ROMEO & JULIET, Act 5, sc. 1.

support it. Many more regard it as politically correct to tolerate and oppose doing anything effective about it. Most assume that, if not exactly desirable, prostitution is necessary or inevitable and harmless. These views of prostitution lie beneath and surround any debate on sex trafficking, whether prostitution is distinguished from trafficking or seen as indistinguishable from it, whether seen as a form of sexual freedom or understood as its ultimate denial. The debate on the underlying reality, and its relation to inequality, intensifies whenever doing anything effective about either prostitution or trafficking is considered.

Wherever you are in the world, the debate, and usually the law as well, is organized by five underlying moral distinctions that divide the really bad from the not-so-bad. Adult is distinguished from child prostitution, indoor from outdoor, legal from illegal, voluntary from forced, and prostitution from trafficking. Child prostitution is always bad for children; adult prostitution is not always bad for adults. Outdoor prostitution can be rough; indoor prostitution is less so. Illegal prostitution has problems that legal prostitution solves. Forced prostitution is bad; voluntary prostitution can be not-so-bad. Trafficking is really, really bad. Prostitution—if, say, voluntary, indoor, legal, adult—can be a tolerable life for some people. Measured against known facts of the sex trade, these purported distinctions emerge as largely illusory, occupying instead points of emphasis on common continua with convergence and overlap among the dimensions. These moral distinctions are revealed as ideological, with consequences for law, policy, and culture that are real.

Within or across nations, the fundamental positions in this debate—to polarize somewhat, but this debate is remarkably polarized—are the sex work model and the sexual exploitation approach.[23] When prostitution is termed "sex work," it is usually understood as the oldest profession, a cultural universal, consensual because paid, stigmatized because illegal, a job like any other denied that recognition, love in public, a form of sexual liberation.[24] Sex workers are expressing what its academic advocates term

---

23. Proponents of the sex work position include the Sex Worker Education and Advocacy Taskforce ("SWEAT") in South Africa; Durbar Mahila Samanwaya Committee ("DMSC") in India; the New Zealand Prostitutes Collective ("NZPC") in New Zealand; Call Off Your Old Tired Ethics ("COYOTE") in the United States; the Initiative Against Trafficking in Persons, also based in the U.S.; and the international Network of Sex Work Projects ("NSWP"), founded in 1991. The sexual exploitation approach is exemplified internationally by the Coalition Against Trafficking in Women ("CATW") and Equality Now, as well as by Apne Aap in India, Embrace Dignity in Cape Town, South Africa, and similar organizations worldwide. Some U.S. groups pursuing this work are Girls Educational & Mentoring Services ("GEMS"), New York; End Demand Illinois, a campaign of the Chicago Alliance Against Sexual Exploitation ("CAASE"); Council for Prostitution Alternatives ("CPA"), Portland, Or.; Breaking Free, Minneapolis, Minn.

24. Carol Leigh, who also calls herself "Scarlot Harlot," says she coined the term "sex work" in its contemporary usage. *See* Carol Leigh, *Inventing Sex Work,* in WHORES AND OTHER FEMINISTS 223 (Jill Nagel ed., 1997). Representative influential exponents of various facets of this view—among them activists, policymakers, and academics in a voluminous literature—are listed chronologically. *See, e.g.,* Lars O. Ericsson, *Charges Against Prostitution: An Attempt at a Philosophical Assessment,* 90 ETHICS 335 (1980); David A.J. Richards, *Commercial Sex and the Rights of the Person: A Moral Argument for the Decriminalization of Prostitution,* 127 U. PA. L. REV. 1195 (1979); Gayle Rubin, THINKING SEX: NOTES FOR A RADICAL THEORY OF THE POLITICS OF SEXUALITY, IN PLEASURE AND DANGER: EXPLORING FEMALE SEXUALITY 267 (Carole S. Vance ed., 1992); Margo St. James, *THE RECLAMATION OF WHORES,* in GOOD GIRLS/BAD GIRLS: FEMINISTS AND SEX TRADE WORKERS FACE TO FACE 81 (Laurie Bell ed., 1987); Valerie Jenness, *From Sex as Sin to Sex as Work: COYOTE and the Reorganization of Prostitution as a Social Problem,* 37 SOC. PROBS. 403 (1990); Gail Pheterson, THE PROSTITUTION PRISM (1996); Priscilla Alexander, *Bathhouses and Brothels: Symbolic Sites in Discourse and Practice,* in POLICING PUBLIC SEX: QUEER POLITICS AND THE FUTURE OF AIDS ACTIVISM 221 (Ephen Glenn Colter ed., 1996); Priscilla Alexander, *MAKING A LIVING: WOMEN WHO GO OUT,* in WOMEN'S EXPERIENCES WITH

their "agency." Of the many meanings of this slippery piece of jargon that no one seems to think they have to define, agency here appears to mean freely choosing, actively empowering, deciding among life chances, asserting oneself in a feisty fashion, fighting back against forces of femininity, resisting moralistic stereotypes. Some who take this view see prostitution as an expression of agency, sometimes as potentially if not always actually a model of sex equality. The agentic actors, sex workers, most of them women, control the sexual interaction, are compensated for what is usually expected from women for free, and have independent lives and anonymous sex with many partners—behaviors usually monopolized by men, hence liberating for women. Some women graduate to the higher masculine role of selling other women to men for sex—which strains sisterhood, if perhaps less than women who have never been and never will be part of the sex industry effectively defending pimping does.

By contrast, the sexual exploitation approach sees prostitution as the oldest oppression, as widespread as the institutionalized sex inequality of which it is analyzed as a cornerstone. Prostitute, the noun, is seen to misleadingly and denigratingly equate who these people are with what is being done to them; the past participle verb form, by contrast, highlights the other people and social forces who are acting upon them. Based on information from the women themselves,[25] women in prostitution are observed to be prostitut*ed* through choices precluded, options restricted, possibilities denied.

HIV/AIDS: An International Perspective 75 (Lynellyn D. Long & E. Maxine Ankrah eds., 1996); Priscilla Alexander, *Feminism, Sex Workers and Human Rights,* in Whores and Other Feminists, *supra,* at 83; Ann D. Jordan, *Commercial Sex Workers in Asia: A Blind Spot in Human Rights Law,* in 2 Women and International Human Rights Law 525 (Kelly D. Askin & Doreen M. Koenig eds., 2000); Carol Leigh, Unrepentant Whore: Collected Works of Scarlot Harlot (2004); Carole Vance, *Innocence and Experience: Melodramatic Narratives of Sex Trafficking and Their Consequences for Health and Human Rights* (2004) (unpublished paper delivered as part of a panel on Sex Slaves and Media at Columbia University, New York, N.Y.) (on file with author); Belinda Brooks-Gordon, *Clients and Commercial Sex: Reflections on Paying the Price: AConsultation Paper on Prostitution,* Crim. L. Rev. 425 (2005); Ronald Weitzer, *The Growing Moral Panic over Prostitution and Sex Trafficking,* 30 Criminologist 1 (2005); Belinda Brooks-Gordon, The Price of Sex: Prostitution, Policy and Society (2006); Laura Maria Agustín, Sex at the Margins: Migration, Labour Markets and the Rescue Industry (2007); Prabha Kotiswaran, *Born unto Brothels—Toward a Legal Ethnography of Sex Work in an Indian Red-Light Area,* 33 Law & Soc. Inquiry 579 (2008); Marlise Richter, *Sex Work, Reform Initiatives and HIV/AIDS in Inner-City Johannesburg,* 7 Afr. J. AIDS Res. 323 (2008); Marlise Richter, *Pimp My Ride for 2010: Sex Work, Legal Reform and HIV/AIDS,* 7 Gender & Media Diversity J. 80 (2009); Jo Doezema, Sex Slaves and Discourse Masters (2010); Ronald Weitzer, *The Movement to Criminalize Sex Work in the United States,* 37 J.L. & Soc'y 61 (2010); Ronald Weitzer, *The Mythology of Prostitution: Advocacy Research and Public Policy,* 7 Sexuality Res. & Soc. Pol'y 15 (2010). Pro-prostitution writings have also been collected in several anthologies, including A Vindication of the Rights of Whores (Gail Pheterson ed., 1989); Sex Work: Writings by Women in the Sex Industry (Frédérique Delacoste & Priscilla Alexander eds., 2d ed. 1998); Global Sex Workers: Rights, Resistance, and Redefinition (Kamala Kempadoo & Jo Doezema eds., 1998); Whores and Other Feminists, *supra;* Sex for Sale: Prostitution, Pornography, and the Sex Industry (Ronald Weitzer ed., 2d ed. 2010). For an analysis taking this perspective on New Zealand, *see* Taking the Crime Out of Sex Work: 'New Zealand Sex Workers' Fight for Decriminalisation (Gillian Abel et al. eds., 2010), and on Africa, *see* Chi Mgbaka & Laura A. Smith, *Sex Work and Human Rights in Africa,* 33 Fordham Int'l L.J. 1178 (2010).

25. Melissa Farley of Prostitution Research & Education in San Francisco, California, has conducted authoritative studies with colleagues worldwide based largely on the testimony of prostituted people. *See, e.g.,* Melissa Farley, Prostitution and Trafficking in Nevada: Making the Connections (2007) [hereinafter Farley, Nevada]; Melissa Farley et al., *Prostitution and Trafficking in Nine Countries: An Update on Violence and Posttraumatic Stress Disorder,* 2 J. Trauma Practice 33 (2003) [hereinafter Farley et al., *Nine Countries*]; Melissa Farley et al., *Prostitution in Five Countries: Violence and Posttraumatic Stress* Disorder, 8 Feminism & Psychol. 405 (1998) [hereinafter Farley et al., *Five*

Although the full scope and prevalence of prostitution's arrangements, with all its varieties of transactional sex, is not known, use of this term reflects an evaluation of considerable information on the sex industry, not an *a priori* attribution of victim status. Prostitution here is observed to be a product of lack of choice, the resort of those with the fewest choices, or none at all when all else fails. The coercion behind it, physical and otherwise, produces an economic sector of sexual abuse, the lion's share of the profits of which goes to others. In these transactions, the money coerces the sex rather than guaranteeing consent to it, making prostitution a practice of serial rape. In this analysis, there is, and can be, nothing equal about it. Prostituted people pay for paid sex. The buyers do not pay for what they take or get. It is this, not its illegality, that largely accounts for prostitution's stigma. People in prostitution, in this view, are wrongly saddled with a stigma that properly belongs to their exploiters.

Each account has a corresponding legal approach. The sex work approach favors across-the-board decriminalization with various forms of legalization, usually with some state regulation, sometimes beginning with unionization. Its goal is to remove criminal sanctions from all actors in the sex industry so that prostitution becomes as legitimate as any other mode of livelihood. The Netherlands, Germany, New Zealand, Victoria in Australia, as well as ten counties in Nevada, United States, have adopted versions of this approach, although some are retreating from it.[26]

Countries]. This methodology is also used, for example, by Evelina Giobbe, *Prostitution: Buying the Right to Rape,* in RAPE AND SEXUAL ASSAULT III: A RESEARCH HANDBOOK 143 (Ann Wolbert Burgess ed., 1991) and Susan Kay Hunter, *Prostitution is Cruelty and Abuse to Women and Children,* 1 MICH. J. GENDER & L. 91 (1993).

26. For the Netherlands, *see* Staatsblad van het Koninkrijk der Nederlanden 464, Wet van 28 oktober 1999 tot wijziging van het Wetboek van Strafrecht, enige andere wetboeken en enige wetten (opheffing algemeen bordeelverbod) (Neth.); *see also* Working Group on the Legal Regulation of the Purchase of Sexual Services, *Purchasing Sexual Services in Sweden and the Netherlands: Legal Regulation and Experiences* 27-29 (2004) [hereinafter Working Group, Purchasing Sexual Services]. On the recent shift toward stricter regulation of licensed brothels, *see* Julie Bindel & Liz Kelly, *A Critical Examination of Prostitution* in FOUR COUNTRIES: VICTORIA, AUSTRALIA; IRELAND; THE NETHERLANDS; AND SWEDEN 13 (2003) (quoting Mayor of Amsterdam, "it appeared impossible to create a safe and controllable zone for women that was not open to abuse by organised crime"). Prior research showed that 80% of women engaged in window prostitution in the Netherlands were illegal immigrants, possibly supporting strictures that resulted in a 35% decline in commercial sex establishments. *See* S. African Law Reform Comm'n, *Sexual Offenses: Adult Prostitution* 128 (2009) [hereinafter SALRC, Sexual Offenses]. Similar concerns underlay Amsterdam's municipal act—"Wet BIBOB"—authorizing local law enforcement to investigate businesses suspected of illegal activities, notably trafficking and money laundering, and to refuse to license dubious establishments, thereby leading to the closure of a number of Amsterdam's window brothels. *See* Wet bevordering integriteitsbeoordelingen door het openbaar bestuur [Act to Encourage Integrity Judgments by the Public Authorities] (2002) (Amsterdam, Neth.). A bill was introduced in 2010 in the Dutch Parliament to create a national framework for regulating prostitution. Wet regulering prostitutie enbestrijding misstanden seksbranche (voorstel van wet hangende onder dossiernummer 32 211) [Draft Bill for the Regulation of Prostitution and the Reduction of Abuses in the Sex Industry, pending under file number 32 211]. In Germany, an act effective January 1, 2002, deemed prostitution a legitimate occupation, legalizing promotion of sex for sale, pimping, and brothel operation. Gesetz zur Regelung der Rechtsverhältnisse der Prostituierten (Prostitutions-gesetz—ProstG) [Act Regulating the Legal Situation of Prostitutes] (Jan. 1, 2002) (F.R.G.). For signs of retreat from this policy, *see* Joachim Renzikowski, REGLEMENTIERUNG VON PROSTITUTION: ZIELE UND PROBLEME (2007). Prostitution was decriminalized in New Zealand by the Prostitution Reform Act (2003), available at http://www.legislation.govt.nz/act/public/2003/0028/latest/DLM197815. html. In Victoria, Australia, the Prostitution Control Act of 1994 legalized brothels and escort agencies. In Nevada, as of 1971, in unincorporated towns and cities, a county license board can grant licenses to individuals and businesses to maintain and work in legal brothels. *See* Nev. Rev. Stat. § 244.345 (2009). Except when licensed, prostitution is a misdemeanor in the state. *See id.* § 201.354.

The sexual exploitation approach seeks to abolish prostitution. The best way to end this industry is debated. But criminalizing the buyers—the demand—as well as the sellers (pimps and traffickers), while eliminating any criminal status for prostituted people—the sold—and providing them services and job training they say they want, is the approach being pioneered in Sweden,[27] Iceland,[28] and Norway,[29] and recent changes in the U.K. that point in this direction.[30] Movements in South Africa, which like South Korea[31] recently expressly criminalized buyers,[32] a bill in Israel,[33] and debate in the Scottish Parliament[34] involve steps along similar lines. For the Swedish model, at least as crucial as criminalizing the buyers and enforcing that prohibition is decriminalizing prostituted people, which seems even more difficult to achieve.[35] In a growing list of jurisdictions, the Swedish model is one initiative that, having shown promise, is increasingly favored by abolitionists at the principled and practical forefront of this movement.

Each person who confronts this issue decides which approach best reflects the reality known and experienced and best promotes the world one wants to live in. But apart from preferences, commitments, values, and politics, each position can be measured against

---

27. *See* Lag om förbud mot köp av sexuella tjänster 405 (1998) ("A person who obtains casual sexual relations in exchange for payment shall be sentenced—unless the act is punishable under the Swedish Penal Code—for the purchase of sexual services to a fine or imprisonment for at most six months."). For the origin of the idea, *see* Catharine A. MacKinnon, *On Sex and Violence: Introducing the Antipornography Civil Rights Law in Sweden*, in ARE WOMEN HUMAN? AND OTHER INTERNATIONAL DIALOGUES 91 (2006), and Andrea Dworkin, *Against the Male Flood: Censorship, Pornography, and Equality*, in LETTERS FROM A WAR ZONE 253 (1988). For subsequent modifications in the Swedish law, *see infra* notes 105-12 and accompanying text.

28. Iceland made the purchase of sexual services illegal in 2009. *See* Lög um breytingu á almennum hegningarlögum, nr. 19/1940, me sí ari breytingum [Icelandic Law No. 54 of 2009] (2009) (Ice.).

29. As of January 1, 2009, citizens of Norway were prohibited from paying for sex domestically or abroad. *See* Law Amending the Penal Code and Criminal Procedure Act of 1902, No. 104 (2008) (Nor.), available at http:// www.lovdata.no/cgi-wift/ldles?doc=/all/nl-20081212-104.html.

30. The U.K.'s new Policing and Crime Act (2009), amending the 2003 Sexual Offenses Act, prohibits buying any sex that is forced under its heading, Art. 14(1), the substance of the provision operatively defining any form of pimping, and including "any other form of coercion." Policing and Crime Act, 2009, c. 26 § 14 (Eng. & Wales).

31. South Korea's laws of March 22, 2004, are Act on the Prevention of Prostitution and Protection of Victims Thereof, Statutes of South Korea, Act No. 7212; and Act on the Punishment of Procuring Prostitution and Associated Acts, Statutes of South Korea, Act No. 7196 (criminalizing at article 21(1) "[a]nyone who sells sex or buys sex" while exempting "victims of prostitution" from punishment, at article 6(1)).

32. *See* Criminal Law (Sexual Offences and Related Matters) Amendment Act 32 of 2007 § 11 (S. Afr.) (criminalizing purchase of sex from persons 18 years of age and older).

33. See Rebecca Anna Stoil, *Knesset Bill Seeks to Ban Hiring a Prostitute*, JERUSALEM POST, Dec. 21, 2009, at 4

34. Scottish Parliament, Justice Committee, Official Report of 20 April 2010 (Scot.), at cols. 2919, 2937, available at http:// www.scottish.parliament.uk/s3/committees/justice/or-10/ju10-1302.htm. Ireland may consider the Swedish model, *see, e.g., Call to Follow Sweden on Vice Law Reform*, INDEPENDENT, Feb. 7, 2011, available at http:// www.independent.ie/national-news/call-to-follow-sweden-on-vice-law-reform-2528518.html, as may France, *France May Make Buying Sex Illegal*, Radio France Internationale (Mar. 31,2011), http://www.english.rfi.fr/france/20110331-france-may-make-buying-sex-illegal. ("There is no such thing as prostitution which is freely chosen and consenting," [Social Affairs Minister Roselyne] Bachelot declared. "The sale of sexual acts means that women's bodies are made available, for men, independently of the wishes of those women.").

35. New York State, for example, moved towards the Swedish model in 2007 by legislating penalties for buyers higher than for prostituted people, by creating the class B felony for "sex trafficking," and by excluding victims from accomplice liability for trafficking. *See* N.Y. Penal Law §§ 230.34, 230.36 (2010). But the sold remained criminals. *See id.* § 230.00 (deeming "Prostitution" a class B misdemeanor).

evidence of what is known about the sex industry, including conditions of entrance, realities of treatment, and possibilities for exit.

Everywhere, prostituted people are overwhelmingly poor, indeed normally destitute. There is no disagreement on this fact. Urgent financial need is the most frequent reason mentioned by people in prostitution for being in the sex trade.[36] Having gotten in because of poverty, almost no one gets out of poverty through prostituting.[37] They are lucky to get out with their lives, given the mortality figures.[38] It is not unusual for the women in the industry to get further into poverty, deeper in debt. In India, not only do they have few if any options to start with, landlords who keep them in houses charge exorbitant rent, take chunks of their earnings, and refuse to let them leave the house or do anything else, although they would make and keep more money pumping gas.

Disproportionately, people in prostitution are members of socially disadvantaged racial groups or lower castes.[39] In Vancouver, prostituted women are First Nations women in

36. *See* Mike Dottridge, Kids as Commodities? Child Trafficking and What To Do About It 28 (2004) ("The principal reason why children, as well as adults, from particular communities end up being trafficked is the lack of alternative ways of earning a living for them and their families."); Chandré Gould & Nicolé Fick, *Report to the South African Law Reform Commission: Preliminary Research Findings of Relevance to the Draft Legislation to Combat Trafficking in Persons and Legislation Pertaining to Adult Prostitution* 12 (2007) (relating from focus group discussions with people in prostitution that "[i]n all cases financial responsibilities, or expectations from families or dependents led to entry into the industry"); SALRC, Sexual Offenses, *supra* note 4, at 27 ("'None of us are doing this for pleasure. We are doing this for survival.'"); Special Comm. on Pornography & Prostitution in Can., 2 Pornography and Prostitution in Canada 376-77 (1985) ("Overwhelmingly, prostitutes cite economic causes as the reason they are on the streets.") [hereinafter 2 Fraser Report]; Farley et al., *Nine Countries*, *supra* note 25, at 34, 56, 65; Amber Hollibaugh, *On the Street Where We Live*, 5 Women's Rev. of Books 1, 1 (Jan. 1988) ("The bottom line for any woman in the sex trades is economics. However a woman feels when she finally gets into the life, it always begins as survival— the rent, the kids, the drugs, pregnancy, financing an abortion, running away from home, being un-documented, having a 'bad' reputation, incest—it always starts at trying to get by.").

37. *See, e.g.*, Dorchen Leidholdt, *Prostitution: A Violation of Women's Human Rights*, 1 Cardozo Women's L.J. 133, 142 (1993) ("In the vast majority of cases, prostitution enables a woman at best to eke out a subsistence living."); Cynthia Mayer, *The Last Trick: Prostitutes Who Want to Get Out Find That Someone Does Care*, Chi. Trib., May 30, 1993, at 12 ("It's a myth that women get rich doing this ... I know of no one who is retired with a pension, sitting by a pool.").

38. A Canadian study estimated a mortality rate as high as forty times the national average for prostituted women. *See* 2 Fraser Report, *supra* note 36, at 350 (1985). Homicide of women in prostitution vastly exceeds that of any other cohort in the United States. *See* Hilary Kinnell, *Murder Made Easy: The Final Solution to Prostitution?*, in Sex Work Now 141 (Rosie Campbell & Maggie O'Neill eds., 2006); Devon D. Brewer et al., *Extent, Trends, and Perpetrators of Prostitution-Related Homicide in the United States*, 51 J. Forensic Sci. 1101, 1101, 1107 (2006) (estimating conservatively that 2.7% of female homicide victims in the United States between 1982 and 2000 were prostitutes— the highest rate of victimization for any set of women ever studied); John J. Potterat et al., *Mortality in a Long-term Open Cohort of Prostitute Women*, 159 Am. J. Epidemiology 778, 783 (2004) (concluding, based on a study of prostituted women in Colorado Springs, Colo., that "[t]o our knowledge, no population of women studied previously has had a crude mortality rate, standardized mortality ratio, or percentage of deaths due to murder even approximating those observed in our cohort"); Jonathan Adam Dudek, When Silenced Voices Speak: An Exploratory Study of Prostitute Homicide (2002) (unpublished Ph.D. dissertation, Hahnemann University) (on file with author).

39. Research throughout the U.S. shows that African American women and girls are overrepresented in the sex trade. *See, e.g.*, Jennifer James, Entrance into Juvenile Prostitution: Final Report 17, 19 (1980) (finding African American girls, 4.2% of the population in the geographic area of the study, were 25% of sample of prostituted girls interviewed in Seattle area (n = 136)). Interviews conducted with over 3000 "streetwalking prostitutes" for an outreach project in New York City found approximately half were African American, a quarter Hispanic, and the remaining quarter white. Barbara Goldsmith, *Women on the Edge*, New Yorker, Apr. 26, 1993, at 64, 65. A survivor activist

numbers that far exceed their proportion of the population.[40] In India, although caste is illegal, there are still prostitute castes. Women members of the Nat caste, for example, are selected to prostitute by men in their families; men of this caste are supposed to prostitute women to higher caste men.[41] As this example suggests, the structure of who is in prostitution often derives from colonialism and persists after it.[42]

No one chooses to be born into poverty or to stay in prostitution in order to stay poor. No one chooses the racial group or caste one is born into. No country freely chooses to be colonized or the post-colonial social pathologies that so often organize this industry. These circumstances, from the uncontested evidence of who the prostituted

---

states that "20 to 30% of prostitutes are women of color" in conditions exacerbated by racism and poverty. Carol Leigh, BLACK WOMEN AND PROSTITUTION, I Gauntlet 113, 113 (1994); *see also* Vednita Nelson, *Prostitution: Where Racism and Sexism Intersect*, 1 MICH. J. GENDER & L. 81, 83 (1993) ("Racism makes Black women and girls especially vulnerable to sexual exploitation and keeps them trapped in the sex industry.").

40. *See* Melissa Farley et al., *Prostitution in Vancouver: Violence and Colonization of First Nations Women*, 42 TRANSCULTURAL PSYCHIATRY 242, 242, 249 [hereinafter Farley et al., Vancouver] (finding 52% of 100 prostituted women in Vancouver, British Columbia, of First Nations descent, a group constituting 1.7-7% of the population); 2 Fraser Report, *supra* note 25, at 347 (stating most prostitutes on prairies "are young native women"); *see also* Aboriginal Women's Action Network, Statement Opposing Legalized Prostitution & Total Decriminalization of Prostitution (Dec. 2007) (opposing proposed legal brothels for 2010 Vancouver Olympics), available at http:// www.prostitutionresearch.com/ racism/000153.html#more. Similar conditions prevail among American Indian and Native Alaskan women in the United States. *See* Sarah Deer, *Relocation Revisited: Sex Trafficking of Native Women in the United States*, 36 WM. MITCHELL L. REV. 621, 621 (2010); Suzanne Koepplinger, YPERLINK"http:// www.westlaw.com/Find/Default.wl?rs=dfa1.0&vr=2.0&DB=182912&FindType=Y&ReferencePosition-Type=S&SerialNum=0345562516&ReferencePosition=129"*Sex Trafficking of American Indian Women and Girls in Minnesota*, 6 U. ST. THOMAS L.J. 129, 129 (2008), and Maori in New Zealand, *see* Miriam Saphira & Averil Herbert, THE INVOLVEMENT OF CHILDREN IN COMMERCIAL SEXUAL ACTIVITY 8 (2004); Libby Plumridge & Gillian Abel, *A 'Segmented' Sex Industry in New Zealand: Sexual and Personal Safety of Female Sex Workers*, 25 AUSTL. & N.Z. J. PUB. HEALTH 78, 79 (2001). Trafficking from less developed nations has been observed to focus "particularly on indigenous and aboriginal women who are from remote tribal communities...." Kathleen Barry, THE PROSTITUTION OF SEXUALITY: THE GLOBAL EXPLOITATION OF WOMEN 178 (1995). Sex traffickers worldwide are known to target women and girls from ethnically disadvantaged populations. *See, e.g.*, National Criminal Police (Swed.), *Trafficking in Human Beings for Sexual Purposes: Situation Report No. 8*, January 1- December 31, 2005, at 18 (2006) [hereinafter Situation Report No. 8] ("Information about girls and women from Rumania and Slovakia indicates that they are gypsies....").

41. The vulnerability of Nat women and girls to compulsory prostitution through caste-based family networks is documented in K.K. Mukherjee & Sutapa Mukherjee, GIRLS/WOMEN IN PROSTITUTION IN INDIA: A NATIONAL STUDY 25-26, 73, 95-96, 97, 141-42, 144-45, 275-76 (2004); Moni Nag, SEX WORKERS OF INDIA: DIVERSITY IN PRACTICE OF PROSTITUTION AND WAYS OF LIFE 131, 230-33 (2006); Christine Joffres et al., *Sexual Slavery Without Borders: Trafficking for Commercial Sexual Exploitation in India*, 7 INT'L J. FOR EQUITY IN HEALTH 22, 24 (2008); R.C. Swarankar, *Ethnographic Study of Community-Based Sex Work Among Nats*, in PROSTITUTION AND BEYOND: AN ANALYSIS OF SEX WORK IN INDIA 118 (Rohini Sahni et al. eds., 2008); Ramesh Chand Swarankar, *Traditional Female Sex Workers of Rajasthan, India: An Ethnographic Study of the Nat Community*, in UNPACKING GLOBALIZATION: MARKETS, GENDER, AND WORK 155 (Linda E. Lucas ed., 2007); Mohammad Kalam, *Hindu and Muslim Nutts are Equally Marginalized*, 1 RED LIGHT DESPATCH 1 (2007), available at http://www.apneaap.org/redlight_ despatch/?q=node/39; Ruchira Gupta & Apne Aap Team, *Thrice Oppressed: Prostitution of Nat Women in Bihar and Rajasthan* (Feb. 15, 2009) (privately printed paper) (on file with author); Whitney Russell, *The Nat of Khasmati, Rajasthan* (Feb. 2009) (unpublished paper) (on file with author

42. This point is analyzed by Deer, *supra* note 40.

disproportionately are, most powerfully determine who is used in this industry. These circumstances are not chosen by any of them.

Another global commonality of prostitution—another that no one contests—is that people typically enter prostitution when they are young, often well below the age of majority.[43] And the age of entry may be dropping.[44] Most of the women and girls I met in India were first prostituted at age ten. This is not a time when you are fully empowered to make a choice about the rest of your life. It is not a time when, if you decide not to let family members or other adults do something to you, you have much power to stop them. In most countries where prostituted people have been studied in any depth, sexual abuse in childhood prior to entry into prostitution is a major precondition.[45] In many places,

---

43. *See, e.g.,* Debra Boyer et al., SURVIVAL SEX IN KING COUNTY: HELPING WOMEN OUT 3 (1993) (reporting 15 of 16 subjects interviewed entered prostitution between ages 12 and 14); Comm. on Sexual Offenses Against Children, 2 *Sexual Offenses Against Children: Report of the Committee on Sexual Offenses Against Children* 229, 991 (1984) [hereinafter 2 Badgley Report] (conducting in-depth interviews with 229 sexually exploited youth in Canada recounting turning first trick between ages 8 and 19—most were 15 or 16, many aged 13 or 14); Cecilie Hóigard & Liv Finstad, BACKSTREETS: PROSTITUTION, MONEY, AND LOVE 76 (1992) (calculating 15.5 as the mean age of first prostitution in sample of 26 women in commercial sex in Oslo, Norway); James, *supra* note 17, at 17 (describing sample of 136 prostituted girls in Seattle area whose mean age of entry was 15, with 36% being 14 or younger); Mimi H. Silbert et al., *Sexual Assault of Prostitutes: Phase One Final Report* 39 (1980) [hereinafter Silbert et al., Sexual Assault Final Report] (presenting study of 200 women presently and formerly involved in prostitution in San Francisco Bay area showing 78% started on the streets as minors (here defined as under 18), 62% at 16 or younger); Chris Bagley & Loretta Young, *Juvenile Prostitution and Child Sexual Abuse: A Controlled Study,* 6 CANADIAN J. COMMUNITY MENTAL HEALTH 5, 11, 17-19 (1987) (studying 45 Canadian women formerly involved in prostitution of whom 51.1% began at age 15 or younger); Farley et al., NINE COUNTRIES, *supra* note 25, at 39-41 (reporting 47% (n = 353) of a sample of prostituted women in nine countries entered the sex trade before age 18); Diana Gray, *Turning Out: A Study of Teenage Prostitution,* 1 J. CONTEMP. ETHNOGRAPHY 401, 404, 412 (1973) (interviewing 17 teenage girls engaged in commercial sex in Seattle, Washington, among whom the average age at first prostitution was 14.7); Susan M. Nadon et al., *Antecedents to Prostitution: Childhood Victimization,* 13 J. INTERPERSONAL VIOLENCE 206, 213 (1998) (finding average age of entry of 14.1 years in a sample of prostituted adolescents); Mimi H. Silbert & Ayala M. Pines, *Entrance into Prostitution,* 13 YOUTH & SOC'Y 471, 483 (1982) (analyzing 200 women presently and formerly in prostitution of whom 62% began before age 16, 78% before age 18, with "[a] number under 9, 10, 11, and 12"); Herbst, *Male Sex Workers in Pretoria: An Occupational Health Perspective* 167 (June 2002) (unpublished Ph.D. dissertation) (on file with University of South Africa) (indicating all participants in study of males in Pretoria, South Africa's commercial sex industry were first prostituted between ages 10 and 16, most commencing at 12). For analysis of the issues raised by these numbers, *See* Michelle Stransky & David Finkelhor, *Fact Sheet: How Many Juveniles Are Involved in Prostitution in the U.S.?* (2008), available at http://www.unh.edu/ccrc/prostitution/Juvenile_ Prostitution_factsheet.pdf.

44. The United Nations Office on Drugs and Crime ("UNOCD") and the United Nations Interregional Crime Research Institute ("UNICRI") report on trafficking victims in the Czech Republic and Poland states, "[c]hanges in the profile of victims were characterized by the experts as follows: the age of victims is decreasing; the emphasis is particularly on young girls living in socially and economically disadvantaged conditions...." Ivana Trávníèková et al., TRAFFICKING IN WOMEN: THE CZECH REPUBLIC PERSPECTIVE 81 (2004). If adequate longitudinal studies of age cohort samples do not yet exist to substantiate this trend in other settings, the sexualization of girls at ever younger ages, *see generally* Am. Psychological Ass'n, *Task Force on the Sexualization of Girls, Report of the APA Task Force on the Sexualization of Girls* (2007), available at http:// www.apa.org/pi/women/programs/girls/report.aspx; GETTING REAL: CHALLENGING THE SEXUALISATION OF GIRLS (Melinda Tankard Reist ed., 2009); Sharna Olfman, THE SEXUALIZATION OF CHILDHOOD (2009); Patrice A. Oppliger, GIRLS GONE SKANK: THE SEXUALIZATION OF GIRLS IN AMERICAN CULTURE (2008).

45. Numerous studies have documented the pervasiveness of child sexual abuse in the life histories of prostituted women. *See, e.g.,* Boyer et al., *supra* note 43, at 3 (reporting from interviews with

including the United States, you only very rarely meet a woman in prostitution who was not sexually or physically[46] abused before, frequently in her intimate circle. In India, the women told me that their first sexual abuse — their first sexual experience period — occurred in prostitution, mind you at age 10. If they resisted then or later, they said they were gang-raped and tortured.

Depending, it seems, upon social and cultural circumstances — we really do not know what causes cultural variance in prevalence and incidence of sexual abuse in childhood, or even for certain if it does vary — children can be sexually abused prior to prostitution, or it can simply be socially assumed that a life of sexual use is your destiny. In this connection, caste functions in India like sexual abuse in childhood does in other places where it is documented: *it tells you what you are for.*[47]

---

currently and recently prostituted women in Washington State, 100% (n = 16) stated they had been sexually abused as girls); ENABLERS, INC., JUVENILE PROSTITUTION MINNESOTA 22-23 (1978) [hereinafter Enablers, Juvenile Prostitution]; James, *supra* note 17, at 29; Saphira & Herbert, *supra* note 18, at 4 (presenting study of 47 prostituted people in New Zealand of whom 59% disclosed childhood sexual abuse); Silbert et al., *Sexual Assault Final Report, supra* note 24, at 26 (stating 60% of subjects (n = 200) "were sexually exploited as juveniles by an average of two people each"); Bagley & Young, *supra* note 21, at 5, 11-13 (concluding 73% of 45 Canadian women formerly involved in sex trade had prior sexual abuse histories); Farley et al., Nine Countries, *supra* note 3, at 42-44, 57 (finding 63% of currently prostituted interviewees acknowledged being victims of child sexual abuse, positing comparatively low number (rates ordinarily fall between 65% and 95%) reflects patterns of denial and minimization common with ongoing traumatization); Farley et al., Vancouver *supra* note 18, at 242, 249, 255 (finding 82% of prostituted women surveyed had been sexually abused in childhood by an average of 4 perpetrators); Evelina Giobbe, *Confronting the Liberal Lies About Prostitution,* in The SEXUAL LIBERALS AND THE ATTACK ON FEMINISM 67, 73 (Dorchen Leidholdt & Janis Raymond eds., 1990) (stating that 74% of participants in the WHISPER Oral History Project said they had been sexually abused between ages 3 and 14); Mimi H. Silbert & Ayala M. Pines, *Early Sexual Exploitation as an Influence in Prostitution,* 28 SOC. WORK 285, 286 (1983) (interviewing 200 street prostitutes of whom 60% identified sexual abuse as girls as a precursor to prostitution in adulthood); Mimi H. Silbert & Ayala M. Pines, *Sexual Child Abuse as an Antecedent to Prostitution,* 5 CHILD ABUSE & NEGLECT 407, 407, 409 (1981); Ronald L. Simons & Les B. Whitbeck, *Sexual Abuse as a Precursor to Prostitution and Victimization Among Adolescent and Adult Homeless Women,* 12 J. FAM. ISSUES 361, 375 (1991) (concluding that "child sexual abuse increases the probability of involvement in prostitution irrespective of any influence exerted through other variables"); Cathy Spatz Widom & Joseph B. Kuhns, *Childhood Victimization and Subsequent Risk for Promiscuity, Prostitution, and Teenage Pregnancy: A Prospective Study,* 86 AM. J. PUB. HEALTH 1607, 1607, 1609 (1996) (identifying strong correlation between sexual abuse of girls and subsequent female prostitution). As one survivor participating in a focus group in 1993 put it, "[w]e've all been molested. Over and over, and raped. We were all molested and sexually abused as children...." Boyer et al., *supra* note 21, at 16.

46. Prior physical abuse of women in prostitution is documented across populations by diverse methodologies. *See* Farley et al., NINE COUNTRIES, *supra* note 3, at 42, 43 (reporting 59% of prostituted respondents in nine countries beaten to the point of injury by caregivers as children); ENABLERS, JUVENILE PROSTITUTION, *supra* note 43, at 22, 29; James, *supra* note 39, at 29; Silbert et al., *Sexual Assault Final Report, supra* note 44, at 20; Bagley & Young, JUVENILE PROSTITUTION AND CHILD SEXUAL ABUSE, *supra* note 21, at 11, 12-13 (1987); Giobbe, *supra* note 23, at 73 (discussing oral histories conducted with prostituted women of whom 90% recalled being battered as children); Hunter, *supra* note 25, at 99 (finding 90% of subjects acknowledged physical abuse in childhood); Widom & Kuhns, *supra* note 25, at 1607, 1609 (finding early history of physical abuse alone or with neglect "a significant predictor of prostitution for females").

47. A strikingly convergent observation is made by Vednita Nelson concerning the role of zoning in largely black neighborhoods in encouraging the perception that black women and girls are available for purchase, in particular by white men: "[W]e got the message growing up, just like our daughters are getting it today, that this is how it is, this is who we are, this is what we are for." Nelson, *supra* note 39, at 84.

Questions for Discussion

1. *Compare MacKinnon's approach to the arguments made by the sex worker organization, SWEAT, in the* Jordan *case in South Africa. Can prostitution be a legitimate form of work, an exercise of one's right to economic activity? Or is MacKinnon correct in asserting that "to be a prostitute is to be a legal non person in the ways that matter"?*

2. *Does prostitution reinforce the notion of women as property?*

I. The Second Optional Protocol on the Rights of the Child

Article 1

States Parties shall prohibit the sale of children, child prostitution and child pornography as provided for by the present Protocol.

Article 2

For the purposes of the present Protocol:

(a) Sale of children means any act or transaction whereby a child is transferred by any person or group of persons to another for remuneration or any other consideration;

(b) Child prostitution means the use of a child in sexual activities for remuneration or any other form of consideration;

(c) Child pornography means any representation, by whatever means, of a child engaged in real or simulated explicit sexual activities or any representation of the sexual parts of a child for primarily sexual purposes.

Article 3

1. Each State Party shall ensure that, as a minimum, the following acts and activities are fully covered under its criminal or penal law, whether such offences are committed domestically or transnationally or on an individual or organized basis:

(a) In the context of sale of children as defined in article 2:

(i) Offering, delivering or accepting, by whatever means, a child for the purpose of:

a. Sexual exploitation of the child;

b. Transfer of organs of the child for profit;

c. Engagement of the child in forced labour;

(ii) Improperly inducing consent, as an intermediary, for the adoption of a child in violation of applicable international legal instruments on adoption; ...

(b) Offering, obtaining, procuring or providing a child for child prostitution, as defined in article 2;

(c) Producing, distributing, disseminating, importing, exporting, offering, selling or possessing for the above purposes child pornography as defined in article 2.

2. Subject to the provisions of the national law of a State Party, the same shall apply to an attempt to commit any of the said acts and to complicity or participation in any of the said acts.

3. Each State Party shall make such offences punishable by appropriate penalties that take into account their grave nature.

4. Subject to the provisions of its national law, each State Party shall take measures, where appropriate, to establish the liability of legal persons for offences established in Paragraph 1 of the present article. Subject to the legal principles of the State Party, such liability of legal persons may be criminal, civil or administrative.

5. States Parties shall take all appropriate legal and administrative measures to ensure that all persons involved in the adoption of a child act in conformity with applicable international legal instruments ...

Article 5

1. The offences referred to in article 3, Paragraph 1, shall be deemed to be included as extraditable offences in any extradition treaty existing between States Parties and shall be included as extraditable offences in every extradition treaty subsequently concluded between them, in accordance with the conditions set forth in such treaties ...

Article 7

States Parties shall, subject to the provisions of their national law:

(a) Take measures to provide for the seizure and confiscation, as appropriate, of:

(i) Goods, such as materials, assets and other instrumentalities used to commit or facilitate offences under the present protocol;

(ii) Proceeds derived from such offences;

(b) Execute requests from another State Party for seizure or confiscation of goods or proceeds referred to in sub-paragraph (a);

(c) Take measures aimed at closing, on a temporary or definitive basis, premises used to commit such offences.

Article 8

1. States Parties shall adopt appropriate measures to protect the rights and interests of child victims of the practices prohibited under the present Protocol at all stages of the criminal justice process, in particular by:

(a) Recognizing the vulnerability of child victims and adapting procedures to recognize their special needs, including their special needs as witnesses;

(b) Informing child victims of their rights, their role and the scope, timing and progress of the proceedings and of the disposition of their cases;

(c) Allowing the views, needs and concerns of child victims to be presented and considered in proceedings where their personal interests are affected, in a manner consistent with the procedural rules of national law;

(d) Providing appropriate support services to child victims throughout the legal process;

(e) Protecting, as appropriate, the privacy and identity of child victims and taking measures in accordance with national law to avoid the inappropriate dissemination of information that could lead to the identification of child victims;

(f) Providing, in appropriate cases, for the safety of child victims, as well as that of their families and witnesses on their behalf, from intimidation and retaliation;

(g) Avoiding unnecessary delay in the disposition of cases and the execution of orders or decrees granting compensation to child victims.

2. States Parties shall ensure that uncertainty as to the actual age of the victim shall not prevent the initiation of criminal investigations, including investigations aimed at establishing the age of the victim.

3. States Parties shall ensure that, in the treatment by the criminal justice system of children who are victims of the offences described in the present Protocol, the best interest of the child shall be a primary consideration.

4. States Parties shall take measures to ensure appropriate training, in particular legal and psychological training, for the persons who work with victims of the offences prohibited under the present Protocol.

5. States Parties shall, in appropriate cases, adopt measures in order to protect the safety and integrity of those persons and/or organizations involved in the prevention and/or protection and rehabilition of victims of such offences.

6. Nothing in the present article shall be construed to be prejudicial to or inconsistent with the rights of the accused to a fair and impartial trial.

J. Child Soldiers

1. Optional Protocol to the Convention on the Rights of the Child on the Involvement of Children in Armed Conflict (entered into force 2002)

The Protocol was designed to prohibit the use of child soldiers and encourage party states to demobilize and reintegrate children under 18 who had been part of the armed forces. The Protocol itself does not specifically refer to girl child soldiers.

However, as has been documented by the UN High Commissioner for Refugees (UNHCR) in countries like Liberia, Sierra Leone, Chad and Sudan, girls have often been forcibly conscripted to serve as "wives" and sex slaves for rebel forces. Only recently have these girls been regarded as child soldiers. It is important to designate them in this way, as this makes them eligible for demobilization and rehabilitation programs. Currently, Thomas Lubanga is being prosecuted in the ICC, for, among other crimes, using female child soldiers as sex slaves.[48]

2. The United States Child Soldiers Prevention Act of 2008 (CSPA)[49]

The Child Soldiers Prevention Act of 2008 (CSPA) was signed into law on December 23, 2008 and became effective on June 21, 2009. The CSPA requires publication in the annual TIP Report of a list of foreign governments identified during the previous year as hosting governmental armed forces or government supported armed groups that recruit and use child soldiers, as defined in the Act. According to the CSPA, and generally consistent

---

48. *See* http://www.icc-cpi.int/Menus/ICC/Structure+of+the+Court/Office+of+the+Prosecutor/Reports+and+Statements/Press+Releases/Press+Releases+2006/Child+soldier+charges+in+the+first+International+Criminal+Court+case.htm [last visited July 17, 2011].

49. Title IV of Pub. L. 110-457.

with the provisions of the Optional Protocol to the Convention on the Rights of the Child on the Involvement of Children in Armed Conflict, the term "child soldier" means:

(i) any person under 18 year of age who takes a direct part in hostilities as a member of governmental armed forces;

(ii) any person under 18 years of age who has been compulsorily recruited into governmental armed forces;

(iii) any person under 15 years of age who has been voluntarily recruited into governmental armed forces; or,

(iv) any person under 18 years of age who has been recruited or used in hostilities by armed forces distinct from the armed forces of a state.

The term "child soldier" includes any person described in clauses (ii), (iii), or (iv) "who is serving in any capacity, including in a support role such as a cook, porter, messenger, medic, guard, or sex slave."

Distinct from the Optional Protocol on the Involvement of Children in Armed Conflict, Sub section (iv) thus specifically acknowledges as a child soldier a child who has been used as a sex slave in an armed force.

The Act creates a list of countries known to tolerate child soldiers. The CSPA prohibits the following forms of assistance to governments identified on the list: international military education and training, foreign military financing, excess defense articles, section 1206 assistance, and the issuance of licenses for direct commercial sales of military equipment.

The 2010 CSPA list consists of governments in the following countries:

1. Burma

2. Chad

3. Democratic Republic of the Congo

4. Somalia

5. Sudan

6. Yemen

Chapter 10

Rape and Other Gender Based Crimes during Armed Conflict

Chapter Problem

You are working as a research associate to the Special Advisor on Gender Issues[1] at the International Criminal Court (ICC). The Court is aware that there have been many recent developments with regard to prosecuting the crime of rape in the international law of armed conflict. Members of the Court have asked you to prepare a Memorandum detailing these developments. In particular they would like you to focus on recent jurisprudence regarding the definition of rape, the types of act that constitute rape, issues of consent and intent, and the various options with regard to prosecuting the crime of rape, when the crime occurs during an armed conflict. The recent developments come from a variety of sources, and the Special Advisor has requested that you write a Memorandum that synthesizes international human rights jurisprudence in this area.

"In many . . . conflict zones, it is more dangerous to be a civilian woman or girl than it is to be a soldier or other combatant."[2]

I. CEDAW and Rape

A. *General Recommendation No. 19*

As noted earlier, CEDAW had omitted any reference to the obligations of a state to protect women from violence, including sexual or gender based violence. However, *General Recommendation No. 19* provides that:

States parties should ensure that laws against family violence and abuse, rape, sexual assault and other gender-based violence give adequate protection to all women, and respect their integrity and dignity.

---

1. Catherine MacKinnon is currently the Advisor on Gender Issues to the ICC.
2. Stephen J. Rapp, Ambassador-at-Large for War Crimes Issues, U.S. Department of State. *Available at* http://www.peacewomen.org/news_article.php?id=654&type=news [last visited July 15, 2010].

II. International Responses to Gender Based Violence during Armed Conflict

According to the World Health Organization (WHO), one in five women will experience rape or attempted rape in her lifetime. The chances of being raped during times of armed conflict are exponentially increased, as the estimated 500,000 rapes that took place during the Rwandan genocide attest.[3] Approximately ninety percent of current war victims are civilians, mostly women and children, compared to a century ago when ninety percent of those who died were military personnel.[4] Yet, rape and violence against women during times of conflict is not a new phenomenon. Rape was fairly widespread during World War I, and some of the Allied Powers, specifically France, believed that mass rapes should be prosecuted. Yet there appeared to be little support for that view.

In 1937, during the Nanking Massacre, it is estimated that between twenty thousand to as many as eighty thousand women were raped by Japanese troops during the Sino/Japanese War. During the Second World War, around two hundred thousand Korean and Filipino, so-called "comfort women" were forcibly conscripted or abducted by the Japanese army, who raped and sexually abused these women, and made them accompany and provide sexual services for the troops. The Nuremburg Tribunal did not prosecute rape as a war crime despite some evidence of mass rape of French and Belgian women. The International Military Tribunal for the Far East (Tokyo War Crimes Trial) did find Japanese leaders guilty of "violations of the laws and customs of war" in respect of the Rape of Nanking.

A. The Charter of the International Military Tribunal for the Far East (1946)

Article 5 — Jurisdiction over persons and offences

The Tribunal shall have the power to try and punish Far Eastern war criminals who as individuals or as members of organizations are charged with offences which include Crimes against Peace.

The following acts, or any of them, are crimes coming within the jurisdiction of the Tribunal for which there shall be individual responsibility:

   a. *Crimes against Peace:* Namely, the planning, preparation, initiation or waging of a declared or undeclared war of aggression, or a war in violation of international law, treaties, agreements or assurances, or participation in a common plan or conspiracy for the accomplishment of any of the foregoing;

   b. *Conventional War Crimes:* Namely, violations of the laws or customs of war;

   c. *Crimes against Humanity:* Namely, murder, extermination, enslavement, deportation, and other inhumane acts committed against any civilian population,

---

3. The genocide in Rwanda took place in 1994 over a hundred day period.

4. Women 2000: Gender Equality, Development and Peace for the Twenty-First Century, Fact Sheet No. 5, Women and Armed Conflict; *available at* http:// www.un.org/womenwatch/daw/ followup/session/presskit/fs5.htm [last visited February 11, 2008].

before or during the war, or persecutions on political or racial grounds in execution of or in connection with any crime within the jurisdiction of the Tribunal, whether or not in violation of the domestic law of the country where perpetrated. Leaders, organizers, instigators and accomplices participating in the formulation or execution of a common plan or conspiracy to commit any of the foregoing crimes are responsible for all acts performed by any person in execution of such plan.

B. The Fourth Geneva Convention—"Attack on Honor"

Although the Fourth Geneva Convention of 1949, enacted in the wake of World War II, provides that "women shall be protected against any attack on their honor, in particular against rape, enforced prostitution, or any form of indecent assault,"[5] rape during times of conflict has, until recently, been seen more as a crime committed by individual soldiers than as a strategy of war. Rape was also not expressly designated a "grave breach" under the Geneva Conventions, but was treated rather as an act that individual states should prosecute.[6] Perhaps this approach stems from the attitude that women were seen as the property of men, and the historical linking of rape and pillaging illustrates the idea that in both cases property is being despoiled.

It was only when the mass rapes and sexual torture came to light during the war in the former Yugoslavia, that the International Tribunal created to prosecute those responsible for these crimes, was forced to reevaluate the crime of rape during times of armed conflict. The statute of the International Criminal Tribunal for the Former Yugoslavia (ICTY)[7] did not originally designate acts of sexual violence as war crimes, although it did designate specifically rape as a crime against humanity.[8]

C. The Statute of the International Criminal Tribunal for the Former Yugoslavia (ICTY)

Article 1 Competence of the International Tribunal

The International Tribunal shall have the power to prosecute persons responsible for serious violations of international humanitarian law committed in the territory of the former Yugoslavia since 1991 in accordance with the provisions of the present Statute.

Article 2 Grave breaches of the Geneva Conventions of 1949

The International Tribunal shall have the power to prosecute persons committing or ordering to be committed grave breaches of the Geneva Conventions of 12 August 1949,

---

5. Art. 27 of the Fourth Geneva Convention of 1949.

6. It should be noted that pursuant to Article 147 of the Fourth Geneva Convention, grave breaches include "torture, inhuman treatment or willfully causing great suffering or injury to body or health." These crimes would seem to encompass rape and thus arguably give rise to universal jurisdiction.

7. Adopted by the UN Security Council May 27, 1993 pursuant to Resolution 827.

8. Moreover, under Article 4(2)(b) rape could arguably be considered a form of genocide, although it is not specifically thus designated.

namely the following acts against persons or property protected under the provisions of the relevant Geneva Convention:

(a) wilful killing;

(b) torture or inhuman treatment, including biological experiments;

(c) wilfully causing great suffering or serious injury to body or health;

(d) extensive destruction and appropriation of property, not justified by military necessity and carried out unlawfully and wantonly;

(e) compelling a prisoner of war or a civilian to serve in the forces of a hostile power;

(f) wilfully depriving a prisoner of war or a civilian of the rights of fair and regular trial;

(g) unlawful deportation or transfer or unlawful confinement of a civilian;

(h) taking civilians as hostages.

Article 3 Violations of the laws or customs of war

The International Tribunal shall have the power to prosecute persons violating the laws or customs of war. Such violations shall include, but not be limited to:

(a) employment of poisonous weapons or other weapons calculated to cause unnecessary suffering;

(b) wanton destruction of cities, towns or villages, or devastation not justified by military necessity;

(c) attack, or bombardment, by whatever means, of undefended towns, villages, dwellings, or buildings;

(d) seizure of, destruction or wilful damage done to institutions dedicated to religion, charity and education, the arts and sciences, historic monuments and works of art and science;

(e) plunder of public or private property.

Article 4 Genocide

1. The International Tribunal shall have the power to prosecute persons committing genocide as defined in Paragraph 2 of this article or of committing any of the other acts enumerated in Paragraph 3 of this article.

2. Genocide means any of the following acts committed with intent to destroy, in whole or in part, a national, ethnical, racial or religious group, as such:

(a) killing members of the group;

(b) causing serious bodily or mental harm to members of the group;

(c) deliberately inflicting on the group conditions of life calculated to bring about its physical destruction in whole or in part;

(d) imposing measures intended to prevent births within the group;

(e) forcibly transferring children of the group to another group.

3. The following acts shall be punishable:

(a) genocide;

(b) conspiracy to commit genocide;

(c) direct and public incitement to commit genocide;

(d) attempt to commit genocide;

(e) complicity in genocide.

Article 5 Crimes against humanity

The International Tribunal shall have the power to prosecute persons responsible for the following crimes when committed in armed conflict, whether international or internal in character, and directed against any civilian population:

(a) murder;

(b) extermination;

(c) enslavement;

(d) deportation;

(e) imprisonment;

(f) torture;

(g) rape;

(h) persecutions on political, racial and religious grounds;

(i) other inhumane acts.

Questions for Discussion

1. *Compare the offences listed in the Tokyo War Crimes Tribunal's Charter with that of the ICTY. Note how detailed the list of violations of the laws and customs of war is in Article 3 of the ICTY Statute. Note too, that Article 5 of the ICTY Statute—Crimes against Humanity—is more detailed than the Tokyo Tribunal's list. Why might this be so? Is it better to have a more detailed list of crimes over which the tribunal has jurisdiction?*

2. *Note also that the ICTY has jurisdiction under Article 4 to prosecute the crime of genocide—this option was not available to the Tokyo Tribunal. Might the Rape of Nanking have met the criteria for genocide or genocide related crimes?*

D. Gender Based Crimes in the Former Yugoslavia

The crimes committed in the former Yugoslavia gave rise to the term "genocidal rape," and introduced the world to the concept of rape as a form of ethnic cleansing. Approximately 50,000 women were raped during the four separate wars in the region.[9] The UN appointed a Commission to investigate the breaches of the Geneva Conventions that occurred during these conflicts.

---

9. The four wars are the War in Slovenia (1991), the Croatian War of Independence (1991–1995), the Bosnian War (1992–1995), and the Kosovo War (1996–1999).

1. United Nations Commission Report on Breaches of Geneva Law in Former Yugoslavia

250. Common threads run through the cases reported whether within or outside the detention context:

(a) Rapes seem to occur in conjunction with efforts to displace the targeted ethnic group from the region. This may involve heightened shame and humiliation by raping victims in front of adult and minor family members, in front of other detainees or in public places, or by forcing family members to rape each other. Young women and virgins are targeted for rape, along with prominent members of the community and educated women;

(b) Many reports states that perpetrators said they were ordered to rape, or that the aim was to ensure that the victims and their families would never return to the area. Perpetrators tell female victims that they will bear children of the perpetrator's ethnicity, that they must become pregnant, and then hold them in custody until it is too late for the victims to get an abortion. Victims are threatened that if they ever tell anyone, or anyone discovers what has happened, the perpetrators will hunt them down and kill them;

(c) Large groups of perpetrators subject victims to multiple rapes and sexual assault. In detention, perpetrators go through the detention centres with flashlights at night selecting women and return them the next morning, while camp commanders often know about, and sometimes participate in, the sexual assaults;

(d) Victims may be sexually abused with foreign objects like broken glass bottles, guns and truncheons. Castrations are performed through crude means such as forcing other internees to bite off a prisoner's testicles.

251. Rape has been reported to have been committed by all sides to the conflict. However, the largest number of reported victims have been Bosnian Muslims, and the largest number of alleged perpetrators have been Bosnian Serbs. There are few reports of rape and sexual assault between members of the same ethnic group.

252. In Bosnia, some of the reported rape and sexual assault cases committed by Serbs, mostly against Muslims, are clearly the result of individual or small group conduct without evidence of command direction or an overall policy. However, many more seem to be a part of an overall pattern whose characteristics include: similarities among practices in non-contiguous geographic areas; simultaneous commission of other international humanitarian law violations; simultaneous military activity; simultaneous activity to displace civilian populations; common elements in the commission of rape, maximizing shame and humiliation to not only the victim, by also the victim's community; and the timing of the rapes. One factor in particular that leads to this conclusion is the large number of rapes which occurred in places of detention. These rapes in detention do not appear to be random, and they indicate at least a policy of encouraging rape supported by the deliberate failure of camp commanders and local authorities to exercise command and control over the personnel under their authority.

253. These patterns strongly suggest that a systematic rape policy existed [*sic*] in certain areas, but it remains to be proven whether such an overall policy existed

[*sic*] which was to apply to all non-Serbs. It is clear that some level of organization and group activity was required to carry out many alleged rapes.[10]

To date, the ICTY has charged about 160 accused with crimes committed between 1991 and 2001. Thus far about 60 people have been convicted and approximately 40 are currently in various stages of trial. Some accused remain at large. The ICTY has contributed to international jurisprudence regarding rape as genocide, and rape as a war crime and a crime against humanity, primarily through the *Furundzija, Kunarac,* and *Tadic* cases. In its Rules of Procedure, the ICTY provides the following with regard to evidence pertaining to sexual assault charges:

2. Rules of Procedure of the ICTY

Rule 96 — Evidence in Cases of Sexual Assault[11]

In cases of sexual assault:

(i) no corroboration of the victim's testimony shall be required;

(ii) consent shall not be allowed as a defence if the victim

(a) has been subjected to or threatened with or has had reason to fear violence, duress, detention or psychological oppression, or

(b) reasonably believed that if the victim did not submit, another might be so subjected, threatened or put in fear;

(iii) before evidence of the victim's consent is admitted, the accused shall satisfy the Trial Chamber in camera that the evidence is relevant and credible;

(iv) prior sexual conduct of the victim shall not be admitted in evidence.

E. Prosecuting Rape after the Rwandan Genocide — The International Criminal Tribunal for Rwanda (ICTR)

The ICTR has pioneered groundbreaking jurisprudence on prosecuting rape in international law. The opportunity to do so came in the *Akayesu* case in the wake of the Rwandan genocide. In a period of one hundred days commencing in April 1994, over 800,000 Tutsis were killed by the majority Hutu population. Countless women were raped, and rape was used as a form of ethnic cleansing to eliminate the Tutsis as an ethnic group. As several authors have noted, "rape was the rule, its absence the exception."

1. The *Akayesu Case* in the ICTR

In April 1993, Mr. Jean-Paul Akayesu was elected bourgmestre, or mayor, of Taba Commune in Rwanda. He was bourgmestre for a period of a little over a year from

---

10. (S/25274) United Nations Commission Report on Breaches of Geneva Law in Former Yugoslavia (1992).

11. Adopted February 11, 1994.

1993–1994, and exerted significant influence in the community. According to later testimony, "His advice would generally be followed, and he was considered a father-figure or parent of the commune, to whom people would also come for informal advice." During the period of the genocide, Akayesu was actively involved in ordering the deaths of many Tutsis in his Commune. In 1995, he was charged by the ICTR with 15 counts including genocide, crimes against humanity and violations of the Geneva Convention. At his trial, as the prosecutors were calling their final witnesses in May 1997, Witnesses J and H spontaneously testified about rapes that they had personally experienced or witnessed, including the gang rape of Witness J's six-year-old daughter. As a result of this evidence on 16 June, 1997, the Prosecution requested, and was granted by the Chamber, leave to amend the indictment to include three new charges against Akayesu: rape and inhumane acts as crimes against humanity, outrages upon personal dignity as a war crime, and genocide. The proceedings were suspended to provide the Parties with time to prepare their cases concerning the new charges. Four months later, on 23 October 1997, the Prosecution reopened its case and presented six additional witnesses who testified about how Akayesu encouraged, by his words or by his presence, brutal rapes and acts of gender violence, including sexual mutilation and forced nudity.

The Amended Indictment alleged the following facts in support of the new charges:

12A. Between April 7 and the end of June 1994, hundreds of civilians (hereinafter "displaced civilians") sought refuge at the bureau communal. The majority of these displaced civilians were Tutsi. While seeking refuge at the bureau communal, female displaced civilians were regularly taken by armed local militia and/or communal police and subjected to sexual violence, and/or beaten on or near the bureau communal premises.... Many women were forced to endure multiple acts of sexual violence which were at times committed by more than one assailant. These acts of sexual violence were generally accompanied by explicit threats of death or bodily harm. The female displaced civilians lived in constant fear and their physical and psychological health deteriorated as a result of the sexual violence and beatings and killings.

12B. Jean Paul Akayesu knew that the acts of sexual violence, beatings and murders were being committed and was at times present during their commission. Jean Paul Akayesu facilitated the commission of the sexual violence, beatings and murders by allowing the sexual violence and beatings and murders to occur on or near the bureau communal premises. By virtue of his presence during the commission of the sexual violence, beatings and murders and by failing to prevent the sexual violence, beatings and murder, Jean Paul Akayesu encouraged these activities.

Genocide, pursuant to Article 2 of the ICTR Statute:

means any of the following acts committed with intent to destroy, in whole or in part, a national, ethnical, racial or religious group, as such:

(a) Killing members of the group;

(b) Causing serious bodily or mental harm to members of the group;

(c) Deliberately inflicting on the group conditions of life calculated to bring about its physical destruction in whole or in part;

(d) Imposing measures intended to prevent births within the group;

(e) Forcibly transferring children of the group to another group.

7.7. Count 13 (rape) and Count 14 (other inhumane acts) — Crimes against Humanity ...

[The Court went on to hear evidence about the forced impregnations that occurred in the Commune, which the prosecution alleged were done with the intent to destroy the Tutsis as an ethnic group. The Court found:]

> [I]n patriarchal societies, where membership of a group is determined by the identity of the father, an example of a measure intended to prevent births within a group is the case where, during rape, a women of the said group is deliberately impregnated by a man of another group, with the intent to have her give birth to a child who will consequently not belong to its mother's group.

685. In the light of its factual findings with regard to the allegations of sexual violence set forth in Paragraphs 12A and 12B of the Indictment, the Tribunal considers the criminal responsibility of the Accused on Count 13, crimes against humanity (rape), punishable by Article 3(g) of the Statute of the Tribunal and Count 14, crimes against humanity (other inhumane acts), punishable by Article 3(i) of the Statute.

686. In considering the extent to which acts of sexual violence constitute crimes against humanity under Article 3(g) of its Statute, the Tribunal must define rape, as there is no commonly accepted definition of the term in international law. The Tribunal notes that many of the witnesses have used the term "rape" in their testimony. At times, the Prosecution and the Defence have also tried to elicit an explicit description of what happened in physical terms, to document what the witnesses mean by the term "rape." The Tribunal notes that while rape has been historically defined in national jurisdictions as non-consensual sexual intercourse, variations on the form of rape may include acts which involve the insertion of objects and/or the use of bodily orifices not considered to be intrinsically sexual. An act such as that described by Witness KK in her testimony — the Interahamwes thrusting a piece of wood into the sexual organs of a woman as she lay dying — constitutes rape in the Tribunal's view.

687. The Tribunal considers that rape is a form of aggression and that the central elements of the crime of rape cannot be captured in a mechanical description of objects and body parts. The Tribunal also notes the cultural sensitivities involved in public discussion of intimate matters and recalls the painful reluctance and inability of witnesses to disclose graphic anatomical details of sexual violence they endured. The United Nations Convention Against Torture and Other Cruel, Inhuman and Degrading Treatment or Punishment does not catalogue specific acts in its definition of torture, focusing rather on the conceptual framework of state-sanctioned violence. The Tribunal finds this approach more useful in the context of international law. Like torture, rape is used for such purposes as intimidation, degradation, humiliation, discrimination, punishment, control or destruction of a person. Like torture, rape is a violation of personal dignity, and rape in fact constitutes torture when it is inflicted by or at the instigation of or with the consent or acquiescence of a public official or other person acting in an official capacity.

688. The Tribunal defines rape as a physical invasion of a sexual nature, committed on a person under circumstances which are coercive. The Tribunal considers sexual violence, which includes rape, as any act of a sexual nature which is committed on a person under circumstances which are coercive. Sexual violence is not limited to physical invasion of the human body and may include acts which do not involve penetration or even physical contact. The incident described by

Witness KK in which the Accused ordered the Interhamwe to undress a student and force her to do gymnastics naked in the public courtyard of the bureau communal, in front of a crowd, constitutes sexual violence. The Tribunal notes in this context that coercive circumstances need not be evidenced by a show of physical force. Threats, intimidation, extortion and other forms of duress which prey on fear or desperation may constitute coercion, and coercion may be inherent in certain circumstances, such as armed conflict or the military presence of Interhamwe among refugee Tutsi women at the bureau communal. Sexual violence falls within the scope of "other inhumane acts," set forth Article 3(i) of the Tribunal's Statute, "outrages upon personal dignity," set forth in Article 4(e) of the Statute, and "serious bodily or mental harm," set forth in Article 2(2)(b) of the Statute.

689. The Tribunal notes that as set forth by the Prosecution, Counts 13–15 are drawn on the basis of acts as described in Paragraphs 12(A) and 12(B) of the Indictment. The allegations in these Paragraphs of the Indictment are limited to events which took place "on or near the bureau communal premises." Many of the beatings, rapes and murders established by the evidence presented took place away from the bureau communal premises, and therefore the Tribunal does not make any legal findings with respect to these incidents pursuant to Counts 13, 14 and 15.

690. The Tribunal also notes that on the basis of acts described in Paragraphs 12(A) and 12(B), the Accused is charged only pursuant to Article 3(g) (rape) and 3(i) (other inhumane acts) of its Statute, but not Article 3(a) (murder) or Article 3(f) (torture). Similarly, on the basis of acts described in Paragraphs 12(A) and 12(B), the Accused is charged only pursuant to Article 4(e) (outrages upon personal dignity) of its Statute, and not Article 4(a) (violence to life, health and physical or mental well-being of persons, in particular murder as well as cruel treatment such as torture, mutilation or any form of corporal punishment). As these Paragraphs are not referenced elsewhere in the Indictment in connection with these other relevant Articles of the Statute of the Tribunal, the Tribunal concludes that the Accused has not been charged with the beatings and killings which have been established as Crimes Against Humanity or Violations of Article 3 Common to the Geneva Conventions. The Tribunal notes, however, that Paragraphs 12(A) and 12(B) are referenced in Counts 1–3, Genocide and it considers the beatings and killings, as well as sexual violence, in connection with those counts.

691. The Tribunal has found that the Accused had reason to know and in fact knew that acts of sexual violence were occurring on or near the premises of the bureau communal and that he took no measures to prevent these acts or punish the perpetrators of them. The Tribunal notes that it is only in consideration of Counts 13, 14 and 15 that the Accused is charged with individual criminal responsibility under Section 6(3) of its Statute. As set forth in the Indictment, under Article 6(3) "an individual is criminally responsible as a superior for the acts of a subordinate if he or she knew or had reason to know that the subordinate was about to commit such acts or had done so and the superior failed to take the necessary and reasonable measures to prevent such acts or punish the perpetrators thereof." Although the evidence supports a finding that a superior/subordinate relationship existed between the Accused and the Interhamwe who were at the bureau communal, the Tribunal notes that there is no allegation in

the Indictment that the Interhamwe, who are referred to as "armed local militia," were subordinates of the Accused. This relationship is a fundamental element of the criminal offence set forth in Article 6(3). The amendment of the Indictment with additional charges pursuant to Article 6(3) could arguably be interpreted as implying an allegation of the command responsibility required by Article 6(3). In fairness to the Accused, the Tribunal will not make this inference. Therefore, the Tribunal finds that it cannot consider the criminal responsibility of the Accused under Article 6(3).

692. The Tribunal finds, under Article 6(1) of its Statute, that the Accused, by his own words, specifically ordered, instigated, aided and abetted the following acts of sexual violence:

> (i) the multiple acts of rape of ten girls and women, including Witness JJ, by numerous Interhamwe in the cultural center of the bureau communal;

> (ii) the rape of Witness OO by an Interhamwe named Antoine in a field near the bureau communal;

> (iii) the forced undressing and public marching of Chantal naked at the bureau communal.

693. The Tribunal finds, under Article 6(1) of its Statute, that the Accused aided and abetted the following acts of sexual violence, by allowing them to take place on or near the premises of the bureau communal, while he was present on the premises in respect of (i) and in his presence in respect of (ii) and (iii), and by facilitating the commission of these acts through his words of encouragement in other acts of sexual violence, which, by virtue of his authority, sent a clear signal of official tolerance for sexual violence, without which these acts would not have taken place:

> (i) the multiple acts of rape of fifteen girls and women, including Witness JJ, by numerous Interhamwe in the cultural center of the bureau communal;

> (ii) the rape of a woman by Interhamwe in between two buildings of the bureau communal, witnessed by Witness NN;

> (iii) the forced undressing of the wife of Tharcisse after making her sit in the mud outside the bureau communal, as witnessed by Witness KK;

694. The Tribunal finds, under Article 6(1) of its Statute, that the Accused, having had reason to know that sexual violence was occurring, aided and abetted the following acts of sexual violence, by allowing them to take place on or near the premises of the bureau communal and by facilitating the commission of such sexual violence through his words of encouragement in other acts of sexual violence which, by virtue of his authority, sent a clear signal of official tolerance for sexual violence, without which these acts would not have taken place:

> (i) the rape of Witness JJ by an Interhamwe who took her from outside the bureau communal and raped her in a nearby forest;

> (ii) the rape of the younger sister of Witness NN by an Interhamwe at the bureau communal;

> (iii) the multiple rapes of Alexia, wife of Ntereye, and her two nieces Louise and Nishimwe by Interhamwe near the bureau communal;

> (iv) the forced undressing of Alexia, wife of Ntereye, and her two nieces Louise and Nishimwe, and the forcing of the women to perform exercises naked in public near the bureau communal.

695. The Tribunal has established that a widespread and systematic attack against the civilian ethnic population of Tutsis took place in Taba, and more generally in Rwanda, between April 7 and the end of June, 1994. The Tribunal finds that the rape and other inhumane acts which took place on or near the bureau communal premises of Taba were committed as part of this attack.

COUNT 13

696. The Accused is judged criminally responsible under Article 3(g) of the Statute for the following incidents of rape:

(i) the rape of Witness JJ by an Interhamwe who took her from outside the bureau communal and raped her in a nearby forest;

(ii) the multiple acts of rape of fifteen girls and women, including Witness JJ, by numerous Interhamwe in the cultural center of the bureau communal;

(iii) the multiple acts of rape of ten girls and women, including Witness JJ, by numerous Interhamwe in the cultural center of the bureau communal;

(iv) the rape of Witness OO by an Interhamwe named Antoine in a field near the bureau communal;

(v) the rape of a woman by Interhamwe in between two buildings of the bureau communal, witnessed by Witness NN;

(vi) the rape of the younger sister of Witness NN by an Interhamwe at the bureau communal;

(vii) the multiple rapes of Alexia, wife of Ntereye, and her two nieces Louise and Nishimwe by Interhamwe near the bureau communal.

COUNT 14

697. The Accused is judged criminally responsible under Article 3(i) of the Statute for the following other inhumane acts:

(i) the forced undressing of the wife of Tharcisse outside the bureau communal, after making her sit in the mud, as witnessed by Witness KK;

(ii) the forced undressing and public marching of Chantal naked at the bureau communal;

(iii) the forced undressing of Alexia, wife of Ntereye, and her two nieces Louise and Nishimwe, and the forcing of the women to perform exercises naked in public near the bureau communal.

7.8. Count 1 — Genocide, Count 2 — Complicity in Genocide

698. Count 1 relates to all the events described in the Indictment. The Prosecutor submits that by his acts alleged in Paragraphs 12 to 23 of the Indictment, Akayesu committed the crime of genocide, punishable under Article 2(3)(a) of the Statute.

699. Count 2 also relates to all the acts alleged in Paragraphs 12 to 23 of the Indictment. The Prosecutor alleges that, by the said acts, the accused committed the crime of complicity in genocide, punishable under Article 2(3)(e) of the Statute.

700. In its findings on the applicable law, the Chamber indicated *supra* that, in its opinion, the crime of genocide and that of complicity in genocide were two distinct crimes, and that the same person could certainly not be both the principal perpetrator of, and accomplice to, the same offence. Given that genocide and

complicity in genocide are mutually exclusive by definition, the accused cannot obviously be found guilty of both these crimes for the same act. However, since the Prosecutor has charged the accused with both genocide and complicity in genocide for each of the alleged acts, the Chamber deems it necessary, in the instant case, to rule on counts 1 and 2 simultaneously, so as to determine, as far as each proven fact is concerned, whether it constituted genocide or complicity in genocide.

701. Hence the question to be addressed is against which group the genocide was allegedly committed. Although the Prosecutor did not specifically state so in the Indictment, it is obvious, in the light of the context in which the alleged acts were committed, the testimonies presented and the Prosecutor's closing statement, that the genocide was committed against the Tutsi group. Article 2(2) of the Statute, like the Genocide Convention, provides that genocide may be committed against a national, ethnical, racial or religious group. In its findings on the law applicable to the crime of genocide *supra*, the Chamber considered whether the protected groups should be limited to only the four groups specifically mentioned or whether any group, similar to the four groups in terms of its stability and permanence, should also be included. The Chamber found that it was necessary, above all, to respect the intent of the drafters of the Genocide Convention which, according to the *travaux préparatoires*, was clearly to protect any stable and permanent group.

702. In the light of the facts brought to its attention during the trial, the Chamber is of the opinion that, in Rwanda in 1994, the Tutsi constituted a group referred to as "ethnic" in official classifications. Thus, the identity cards at the time included a reference to *"ubwoko"* in Kinyarwanda or *"ethnie"* (ethnic group) in French which, depending on the case, referred to the designation Hutu or Tutsi, for example. The Chamber further noted that all the Rwandan witnesses who appeared before it invariably answered spontaneously and without hesitation the questions of the Prosecutor regarding their ethnic identity. Accordingly, the Chamber finds that, in any case, at the time of the alleged events, the Tutsi did indeed constitute a stable and permanent group and were identified as such by all.

703. In the light of the foregoing, with respect to each of the acts alleged in the Indictment, the Chamber is satisfied beyond reasonable doubt, based on the factual findings it has rendered regarding each of the events described in Paragraphs 12 to 23 of the Indictment, of the following:

704. The Chamber finds that, as pertains to the acts alleged in Paragraph 12, it has been established that, throughout the period covered in the Indictment, Akayesu, in his capacity as bourgmestre, was responsible for maintaining law and public order in the commune of Taba and that he had effective authority over the communal police. Moreover, as "leader" of Taba commune, of which he was one of the most prominent figures, the inhabitants respected him and followed his orders. Akayesu himself admitted before the Chamber that he had the power to assemble the population and that they obeyed his instructions. It has also been proven that a very large number of Tutsi were killed in Taba between 7 April and the end of June 1994, while Akayesu was bourgmestre of the Commune. Knowing of such killings, he opposed them and attempted to prevent them only until 18 April 1994, date after which he not only stopped trying to maintain law and order in his commune, but was also present during the acts of violence and killings, and sometimes even gave orders himself for bodily or

mental harm to be caused to certain Tutsi, and endorsed and even ordered the killing of several Tutsi.

705. In the opinion of the Chamber, the said acts indeed incur the individual criminal responsibility of Akayesu for having ordered, committed, or otherwise aided and abetted in the preparation or execution of the killing of and causing serious bodily or mental harm to members of the Tutsi group. Indeed, the Chamber holds that the fact that Akayesu, as a local authority, failed to oppose such killings and serious bodily or mental harm constituted a form of tacit encouragement, which was compounded by being present to such criminal acts.

706. With regard to the acts alleged in Paragraphs 12 (A) and 12 (B) of the Indictment, the Prosecutor has shown beyond a reasonable doubt that between 7 April and the end of June 1994, numerous Tutsi who sought refuge at the Taba Bureau communal were frequently beaten by members of the Interhamwe on or near the premises of the Bureau communal. Some of them were killed. Numerous Tutsi women were forced to endure acts of sexual violence, mutilations and rape, often repeatedly, often publicly and often by more than one assailant. Tutsi women were systematically raped, as one female victim testified to by saying that "each time that you met assailants, they raped you". Numerous incidents of such rape and sexual violence against Tutsi women occurred inside or near the Bureau communal. It has been proven that some communal policemen armed with guns and the accused himself were present while some of these rapes and sexual violence were being committed. Furthermore, it is proven that on several occasions, by his presence, his attitude and his utterances, Akayesu encouraged such acts, one particular witness testifying that Akayesu, addressed the Interhamwe who were committing the rapes and said that "never ask me again what a Tutsi woman tastes like" In the opinion of the Chamber, this constitutes tacit encouragement to the rapes that were being committed.

707. In the opinion of the Chamber, the above-mentioned acts with which Akayesu is charged indeed render him individually criminally responsible for having abetted in the preparation or execution of the killings of members of the Tutsi group and the infliction of serious bodily and mental harm on members of said group.

708. The Chamber found *supra*, with regard to the facts alleged in Paragraph 13 of the Indictment, that the Prosecutor failed to demonstrate beyond reasonable doubt that they are established.

709. As regards the facts alleged in Paragraphs 14 and 15 of the Indictment, it is established that in the early hours of 19 April 1994, Akayesu joined a gathering in Gishyeshye and took this opportunity to address the public; he led the meeting and conducted the proceedings. He then called on the population to unite in order to eliminate what he referred to as the sole enemy: the accomplices of the Inkotanyi; and the population understood that he was thus urging them to kill the Tutsi. Indeed, Akayesu himself knew of the impact of his statements on the crowd and of the fact that his call to fight against the accomplices of the Inkotanyi would be understood as exhortations to kill the Tutsi in general. Akayesu who had received from the Interhamwe documents containing lists of names did, in the course of the said gathering, summarize the contents of same to the crowd by pointing out in particular that the names were those of RPF accomplices. He specifically indicated to the participants that Ephrem Karangwa's name was one

of the lists. Akayesu admitted before the Chamber that during the period in question, that to publicly label someone as an accomplice of the RPF would put such a person in danger. The statements thus made by Akayesu at that gathering immediately led to widespread killings of Tutsi in Taba.

710. Concerning the acts with which Akayesu is charged in Paragraphs 14 and 15 of the Indictment, the Chamber recalls that it has found *supra* that they constitute direct and public incitement to commit genocide, a crime punishable under Article 2(3)(c) of the Statute as distinct from the crime of genocide …

730. Furthermore, the Chamber has already established that genocide was committed against the Tutsi group in Rwanda in 1994, throughout the period covering the events alleged in the Indictment. Owing to the very high number of atrocities committed against the Tutsi, their widespread nature not only in the commune of Taba, but also throughout Rwanda, and to the fact that the victims were systematically and deliberately selected because they belonged to the Tutsi group, with persons belonging to other groups being excluded, the Chamber is also able to infer, beyond reasonable doubt, the genocidal intent of the accused in the commission of the above-mentioned crimes.

731. With regard, particularly, to the acts described in Paragraphs 12(A) and 12(B) of the Indictment, that is, rape and sexual violence, the Chamber wishes to underscore the fact that in its opinion, they constitute genocide in the same way as any other act as long as they were committed with the specific intent to destroy, in whole or in part, a particular group, targeted as such. Indeed, rape and sexual violence certainly constitute infliction of serious bodily and mental harm on the victims and are even, according to the Chamber, one of the worst ways of inflict harm on the victim as he or she suffers both bodily and mental harm. In light of all the evidence before it, the Chamber is satisfied that the acts of rape and sexual violence described above, were committed solely against Tutsi women, many of whom were subjected to the worst public humiliation, mutilated, and raped several times, often in public, in the Bureau Communal premises or in other public places, and often by more than one assailant. These rapes resulted in physical and psychological destruction of Tutsi women, their families and their communities. Sexual violence was an integral part of the process of destruction, specifically targeting Tutsi women and specifically contributing to their destruction and to the destruction of the Tutsi group as a whole.

732. The rape of Tutsi women was systematic and was perpetrated against all Tutsi women and solely against them. A Tutsi woman, married to a Hutu, testified before the Chamber that she was not raped because her ethnic background was unknown. As part of the propaganda campaign geared to mobilizing the Hutu against the Tutsi, the Tutsi women were presented as sexual objects. Indeed, the Chamber was told, for an example, that before being raped and killed, Alexia, who was the wife of the Professor, Ntereye, and her two nieces, were forced by the Interhamwe to undress and ordered to run and do exercises "in order to display the thighs of Tutsi women". The Interhamwe who raped Alexia said, as he threw her on the ground and got on top of her, "let us now see what the vagina of a Tutsi woman takes (*sic*) like". As stated above, Akayesu himself, speaking to the Interahamwe who were committing the rapes, said to them: "don't ever ask again what a Tutsi woman tastes like". This sexualized representation of ethnic identity graphically illustrates that tutsi women were subjected to sexual violence because they were Tutsi. Sexual violence was a step in the process of destruction

of the tutsi group—destruction of the spirit, of the will to live, and of life it-self.

733. On the basis of the substantial testimonies brought before it, the Chamber finds that in most cases, the rapes of Tutsi women in Taba, were accompanied with the intent to kill those women. Many rapes were perpetrated near mass graves where the women were taken to be killed. A victim testified that Tutsi women caught could be taken away by peasants and men with the promise that they would be collected later to be executed. Following an act of gang rape, a witness heard Akayesu say "tomorrow they will be killed" and they were actually killed. In this respect, it appears clearly to the Chamber that the acts of rape and sexual violence, as other acts of serious bodily and mental harm committed against the Tutsi, reflected the determination to make Tutsi women suffer and to mutilate them even before killing them, the intent being to destroy the Tutsi group while inflicting acute suffering on its members in the process.

734. In light of the foregoing, the Chamber finds firstly that the acts described *supra* are indeed acts as enumerated in Article 2 (2) of the Statute, which constitute the factual elements of the crime of genocide, namely the killings of Tutsi or the serious bodily and mental harm inflicted on the Tutsi. The Chamber is further satisfied beyond reasonable doubt that these various acts were committed by Akayesu with the specific intent to destroy the Tutsi group, as such. Consequently, the Chamber is of the opinion that the acts alleged in Paragraphs 12, 12A, 12B, 16, 18, 19, 20, 22 and 23 of the Indictment and proven above, constitute the crime of genocide, but not the crime of complicity; hence, the Chamber finds Akayesu individually criminally responsible for genocide.

FOR THE FOREGOING REASONS, having considered all of the evidence and the arguments,

THE CHAMBER unanimously finds as follows:

Count 1: Guilty of Genocide

Count 2: Not guilty of Complicity in Genocide

Count 3: Guilty of Crime against Humanity (Extermination)

Count 4: Guilty of Direct and Public Incitement to Commit Genocide

Count 5: Guilty of Crime against Humanity (Murder)

Count 6: Not guilty of Violation of Article 3 common to the Geneva Conventions (Murder)

Count 7: Guilty of Crime against Humanity (Murder)

Count 8: Not guilty of Violation of Article 3 common to the Geneva Conventions (Murder)

Count 9: Guilty of Crime against Humanity (Murder)

Count 10: Not guilty of Violation of Article 3 common to the Geneva Conventions (Murder)

Count 11: Guilty of Crime against Humanity (Torture)

Count 12: Not guilty of Violation of Article 3 common to the Geneva Conventions (Cruel Treatment)

Count 13: Guilty of Crime against Humanity (Rape)

Count 14: Guilty of Crime against Humanity (Other Inhumane Acts)

Count 15: Not guilty of Violation of Article 3 common to the Geneva Conventions and of Article 4(2)(e) of Additional Protocol II (Outrage upon personal dignity, in particular Rape, Degrading and Humiliating Treatment and Indecent Assault).

Questions for Discussion

1. *The judge who stopped the proceedings when the witnesses began to testify about rape was a South African woman judge, Navanethem Pillay. Judge Pillay has been a pioneer in the field of women's rights in many respects — she was the first woman in her province in apartheid South Africa to open her own law office; she was the first woman of color to be appointed acting judge of South Africa's Supreme Court; she is currently serving as a judge on the International Criminal Court (ICC). One can only assume that Judge Pillay's background, experience, and commitment to women's rights made her more attuned to the violations that the witnesses were describing. Given this, should we offer gender sensitivity training for all judges, particularly judges in international tribunals? Should prosecutors get more training on gender issues and rape in particular?*

2. *Is it appropriate for a judge to play such an active role in the court proceedings?*

F. Prosecuting Rape in the Former Yugoslavia

1. *Prosecutor v. Furundzija* — Defining the *Actus Reus* and *Mens Rea* of Rape

In *Furundzija*, the accused, a member of militant special unit known as the Jokers, was charged with several counts of violations of the Geneva Convention, as well as torture, torture and inhumane treatment, and outrages against personal dignity, including rape. The charges pertained to the following acts:

Count 13: On or about 15 May 1993, at the Jokers Headquarters in Nadioci (the "Bungalow"), Anto FURUNDZIJA the local commander of the Jokers, [REDACTED] and another soldier interrogated Witness A. While being questioned by FURUNDZIJA, [REDACTED] rubbed his knife against Witness A's inner thigh and lower stomach and threatened to put his knife inside Witness A's vagina should she not tell the truth.

Count 15: Then Witness A and Victim B, a Bosnian Croat who had previously assisted Witness A's family, were taken to another room in the "Bungalow". Victim B had been badly beaten prior to this time. While FURUNDZIJA continued to interrogate Witness A and Victim B, [REDACTED] beat Witness A and Victim B on the feet with a baton. Then [REDACTED] forced Witness A to have oral and vaginal sexual intercourse with him. FURUNDZIJA was present during this entire incident and did nothing to stop or curtail [REDACTED] actions.

The Trial Chamber could find no definition of rape in international law. It therefore looked to other sources, such as the decision in ICTR case *Prosecutor v. Akayesu*. In *Akayesu*, that Trial Chamber concluded that the elements of rape "cannot be captured in a mechanical description of objects or body parts."[12] The Chamber in *Akayesu* went on to describe it as "a physical invasion of a sexual nature, committed on a person under circumstances which are coercive."[13]

The Trial Chamber in *Furundzija* also looked at the criminal laws common to major legal systems of the world to find a standard definition of rape. Although there were some discrepancies, the Chamber found that the general consensus tended to be that rape is the "forcible sexual penetration of the human body by the penis or the forcible insertion of any other object into either the vagina or the anus."[14] While some national legislatures do not classify forced oral sex as rape, the Trial Chamber in *Furundzija* found that it should be so classified. The Tribunal found that the extreme humiliation and degradation which accompanies such an act, coupled with the overarching goal of shielding human beings from outrages upon their personal dignity which underpins international human rights law, mandated that forced oral penetration should be classified as rape.

The ICTY therefore defined the actus reus of rape as consisting of:

i) the sexual penetration, however slight;

a) of the vagina or anus of the victim by the penis of the perpetrator or any other object used by the perpetrator; or

b) by the mouth of the victim by the penis of the perpetrator;

ii) by coercion or force or threat of force against the victim or a third person.[15]

Regarding the *mens rea* necessary to satisfy a conviction on aiding and abetting, the Trial Chamber concluded that the accomplice need not share the *mens rea* of the principal, he need only have knowledge that his actions aid the perpetrator in committing the crime. It is not even necessary that the accomplice knows the exact crime intended by the principal, only that some crime or another will probably will be committed, and that one of those crimes contemplated is in fact committed.

The Trial Chamber found that the Defendant had reason to know that sexual violence was taking place and that he aided and abetted these acts by allowing them to take place and by previously issuing words of encouragement in other acts of sexual violence. The Chamber held that due to the defendant's position of authority, these acts sent the message that such sexual violence was tolerated and without such tolerance, these acts would not have happened.

2. *Prosecutor v. Kunarac* — Rape as a Crime against Humanity

Subsequent to *Furundzija*, the ICTY decided *Kunarac*,[16] the first case where the ICTY's prosecutor successfully convicted the defendants of rape as a crime against humanity.

---

12. Prosecutor v. Akayesu, ICTR-96-4-T, para. 597.

13. *Id.*

14. Prosecutor v. Furundzija, Case No. IT-95-17/1-T, para. 181 (Dec. 10, 1998).

15. *Id.* at para. 185.

16. Prosecutor v. Kunarac, Kovac and Vukovic, Case No. IT-96-23-T & IT-96-23/1-T, Trial Chamber Judgment (Feb. 22, 2001).

Rape was redefined as a "non consensual or non voluntary sexual act" rather than necessarily an act of coercion or force. The Tribunal found that rape would be considered non consensual or non voluntary when the victim suffered from:

> an incapacity of an enduring or qualitative nature (e.g., mental or physical illness, or the age of minority) or of a temporary or circumstantial nature (e.g., being subjected to psychological pressure or otherwise in a state of inability to resist).[17] [T]he actus reus of the crime of rape in international law is constituted by: the sexual penetration, however slight: (a) of the vagina or anus of the victim by the penis of the perpetrator or any other object used by the perpetrator; or

> (b) of the mouth of the victim by the penis of the perpetrator; where such sexual penetration occurs without the consent of the victim. Consent for this purpose must be consent given voluntarily, as a result of the victim's free will, assessed in the context of the surrounding circumstances. The mens rea is the intention to effect this sexual penetration, and the knowledge that it occurs without the consent of the victim.[18]

Questions for Discussion

1. *What do you think of the Tribunal's* actus reus *requirement for rape? Does defining rape more broadly offer more protection for victims?*

2. *The Tribunal stressed that "consent ... must be ... given voluntarily, as a result of the victim's free will, assessed in the context of the surrounding circumstances." When the "surrounding circumstances" are an armed conflict and detention facilities, would it be feasible to show consent?*

3. *The Tribunal seems to be acknowledging in many of these cases that it is often not possible for the victim to resist, particularly in such coercive surroundings. Do you think that rape prosecutions before domestic courts have recognized that principle? Should they?*

4. *In a recent European Court of Human Rights case,* MC v. Bulgaria, *a young woman who had been raped sued Bulgaria for failing to prosecute her case because of a finding that she had not resisted.[19] The Court held that many victims respond to rape with "frozen fright"—where the terrorized victim submits passively out of fear. The Court found further that there was a positive obligation under articles 3 and 8 of the European Convention requiring Bulgaria to enact criminal law proceedings which effectively punished rape regardless of the behavior of the victim. It was the absence of consent on the part of the victim that was crucial in prosecuting rape, not the failure to resist the assault. Do you think these cases represent an evolving jurisprudence on consent in rape cases?*

---

17. *Id.* at para. 442.
18. *Id.* at para. 460.
19. MC v. Bulgaria, Judgment of the European Court of Human Rights, 3972/98 (December 4, 2003).

III. Other Developments in the International Prosecution of Rape

A. The Convention against Torture (CAT)

Recent prosecutions of rape before international tribunals have recognized that rape can be a form of torture. Consider the definition of torture from the Convention against Torture:

> For the purposes of this Convention, torture means any act by which severe pain or suffering, whether physical or mental, is intentionally inflicted on a person for such purposes as obtaining from him or a third person information or a confession, punishing him for an act he or a third person has committed or is suspected of having committed, or intimidating or coercing him or a third person, or for any reason based on discrimination of any kind, when such pain or suffering is inflicted by or at the instigation of or with the consent or acquiescence of a public official or other person acting in an official capacity. It does not include pain or suffering arising only from, inherent in or incidental to lawful sanctions.

B. The International Criminal Court (ICC) and the Rome Statute

The Rome Statute of the ICC and its Elements of Crimes are the first international instruments to codify the elements of rape. The Elements of Crimes for the crime against humanity of rape under the Rome Statute are as follows:

> (1) The perpetrator invaded the body of a person by conduct resulting in penetration, however slight, of any part of the body of the victim or of the perpetrator with a sexual organ, or of the anal or genital opening of the victim with any object or any other part of the body.

> (2) The invasion was committed by force, or by threat of force or coercion, such as that caused by fear of violence, duress, detention, psychological oppression or abuse of power, against such person or another person, or by taking advantage of a coercive environment, or the invasion was committed against a person incapable of giving genuine consent.

> (3) The conduct was committed as part of a widespread or systematic attack directed against a civilian population.

> (4) The perpetrator knew that the conduct was part of or intended the conduct to be part of a widespread or systematic attack directed against a civilian population. The elements for the war crime of rape can be found at Art. 8(2)(b)(xxii)-1 for international conflicts, and 8(2)(e)(vi)-1 for non-international conflicts. Paragraphs (1) and (2) are identical to rape as a crime against humanity, but the elements then vary because of the nature of the crime: (3) The conduct took place in the context of and was associated with an international [or non-

international] armed conflict; and (4) The perpetrator was aware of factual circumstances that established the existence of an armed conflict.

C. UN Security Council Resolution 1820

In 2008, the UN Security Council passed UN Security Resolution 1820 which provides as follows:

Reaffirming also the resolve expressed in the 2005 World Summit Outcome Document to eliminate all forms of violence against women and girls, including by ending impunity and by ensuring the protection of civilians, in particular women and girls, during and after armed conflicts, in accordance with the obligations States have undertaken under international humanitarian law and international human rights law; ...

Reaffirming also the obligations of States Parties to the Convention on the Elimination of All Forms of Discrimination against Women, the Optional Protocol thereto, the Convention on the Rights of the Child and the Optional Protocols thereto, and *urging* states that have not yet done so to consider ratifying or acceding to them, ...

1. *Stresses* that sexual violence, when used or commissioned as a tactic of war in order to deliberately target civilians or as a part of a widespread or systematic attack against civilian populations, can significantly exacerbate situations of armed conflict and may impede the restoration of international peace and security, *affirms* in this regard that effective steps to prevent and respond to such acts of sexual violence can significantly contribute to the maintenance of international peace and security, and *expresses its readiness*, when considering situations on the agenda of the Council, to, where necessary, adopt appropriate steps to address widespread or systematic sexual violence;

2. *Demands* the immediate and complete cessation by all parties to armed conflict of all acts of sexual violence against civilians with immediate effect;

3. *Demands* that all parties to armed conflict immediately take appropriate measures to protect civilians, including women and girls, from all forms of sexual violence, which could include, inter alia, enforcing appropriate military disciplinary measures and upholding the principle of command responsibility, training troops on the categorical prohibition of all forms of sexual violence against civilians, debunking myths that fuel sexual violence, vetting armed and security forces to take into account past actions of rape and other forms of sexual violence, and evacuation of women and children under imminent threat of sexual violence to safety; and *requests* the Secretary-General, where appropriate, to encourage dialogue to address this issue in the context of broader discussions of conflict resolution between appropriate UN officials and the parties to the conflict, taking into account, inter alia, the views expressed by women of affected local communities;

4. *Notes* that rape and other forms of sexual violence can constitute a war crime, a crime against humanity, or a constitutive act with respect to genocide, *stresses the need for* the exclusion of sexual violence crimes from amnesty provisions in the context of conflict resolution processes, and *calls upon* Member States to comply with their obligations for prosecuting persons responsible for such acts, to ensure that all victims of sexual violence, particularly women and girls, have

equal protection under the law and equal access to justice, and *stresses* the importance of ending impunity for such acts as part of a comprehensive approach to seeking sustainable peace, justice, truth, and national reconciliation;

5. *Affirms its intention*, when establishing and renewing state-specific sanctions regimes, to take into consideration the appropriateness of targeted and graduated measures against parties to situations of armed conflict who commit rape and other forms of sexual violence against women and girls in situations of armed conflict;

6. *Requests* the Secretary-General, in consultation with the Security Council, the Special Committee on Peacekeeping Operations and its Working Group and relevant States, as appropriate, to develop and implement appropriate training programs for all peacekeeping and humanitarian personnel deployed by the United Nations in the context of missions as mandated by the Council to help them better prevent, recognize and respond to sexual violence and other forms of violence against civilians; ...

12. *Urges* the Secretary-General and his Special Envoys to invite women to participate in discussions pertinent to the prevention and resolution of conflict, the maintenance of peace and security, and post-conflict peacebuilding, and encourages all parties to such talks to facilitate the equal and full participation of women at decision-making levels; ...

D. Testimony of Dr. Kelly Dawn Askin before the U.S. Senate Judiciary Committee— *Rape as a Weapon of War*[20]

In 2004, the Bush Administration set up the Darfur Atrocities Documentation Project in which the U.S. State Department and the Coalition for International Justice assembled dozens of investigators to interview over 1100 victims and witnesses in Chad about the crimes committed against them in Darfur. As a result of the testimonies, then-Secretary of State Colin Powell termed the Darfur crimes a genocide. I collaborated with this project, and at refugee camps and in makeshift huts on the border of Darfur, I met with camp leaders and women survivors who told heart-wrenching and consistent stories of gang rape, sexual slavery, and other crimes committed by the government of Sudan and their Janjaweed puppets. Earlier this year, I spent a couple of weeks in the eastern provinces of the Democratic Republic of Congo, where I met more survivors who told terrible stories of their own sexual abuse, as well as the rape of babies from eleven months old to 86-year-old women. I travel frequently to Rwanda, Uganda, and Sierra Leone, where sexual violence has been committed in epidemic proportions, affecting millions of lives. Rarely are these crimes prosecuted, particularly when government leaders are architects of the crimes. Rape is exceedingly common during armed conflict.

But make no mistake about it: sexual violence, including wartime sexual violence, is not just an African problem, it is a problem of enormous magnitude in every region of

---

20. Dr. Kelly Askin, *Rape as a Weapon of War: Accountability for Sexual Violence in Conflict*, Testimony before the Subcommittee on Human Rights and the Law Committee on the Judiciary, United States Senate. April 1, 2008. *Available at* http://www.judiciary.senate.gov/hearings/testimony. cfm?id=e655f9e2809e5476862f735da137076a&wit_id=e655f9e2809e5476862f735da137076a-1-3 [last visited July 3, 2011].

the globe. I have worked with each of the international and hybrid courts set up in the past fifteen years and have traveled to dozens of conflict and post-conflict zones. During the course of my work on international crimes and gender justice, I have had the opportunity to speak with rape and sexual slavery survivors of World War II from Europe and Asia, with women from Burma who have been subjected to rape campaigns by the Burmese military, with Cambodian women who were forced into marriage to Khmer Rouge soldiers in the late 1970s, with Bangladeshi/Bengali women raped during the war with Pakistan, with Haitian women who had their gang rapes amnestied, with women in East Timor who were held as sex slaves by Indonesian forces, with Iraqi and Kurdish women leaders who have shared stories of the sexual violence inflicted under the Saddam regime, with men and women from Chechnya who were raped with foreign objects, with women from Bosnia, Croatia, Serbia, and Kosovo who survived repeated or systematic rape, with Afghani girls who were sold into sexual slavery, and with women from Colombia, Guatemala, Argentina and Peru who were gang raped repeatedly during years of war and oppression. And their stories, like those of the women and girls in Africa, and those of some men, are strikingly similar. They were used and abused by men with weapons, often attacking in gangs, often committing the crimes in public, often in front of cheering crowds or before the victim's own families. They were often left naked, bleeding, and publicly displayed as a terrifying and very real threat to others as to what might happen to them — or their daughters, wives, mothers, or sisters — soon ...

The Historical Treatment of Wartime Rape

My research found that wartime rape had indeed been outlawed for centuries, but the prohibition was rarely and only selectively enforced. Further, many of the laws were couched in obscure or antiquated terms, such as violating "family honour and rights" or committing "attacks against honor," "outrages upon personal dignity," or "indecent assault." In 1863 the United States codified customary international law in its U.S. Army regulation on the laws of land warfare. This code-known as the Lieber Code or General Orders No. 100 — formed the cornerstone of subsequent codified humanitarian law and served as the foundation for military codes in many other countries. Article 44 explicitly declared that "all rape ... is prohibited under the penalty of death" and Article 47 dictated that "[c]rimes punishable by all penal codes, such as ... rape ... are not only punishable as at home, but in all cases in which death in not inflicted, the severer punishment shall be preferred."1 Regrettably, the United States is no longer on the forefront of criminalizing and protecting against wartime sexual violence and the many different forms the crimes take in contemporary wars. It has been and remains one of the leaders however in establishing international accountability for atrocity crimes.

The United States played the lead role in setting up the landmark International Military Tribunals at Nuremberg and Tokyo to prosecute war crimes, crimes against humanity, and crimes against peace committed during World War II.... At these trials of the chief architects of the war and the atrocities committed against millions of innocent civilians, rape and other forms of sexual violence were implicitly, and to some degree explicitly, prosecuted. They were also prosecuted in some of the subsequent war crimes trials of so-called 'lesser' war criminals held in Germany and Japan. After reviewing tens of thousands of pages of transcripts of the postwar trials, it became clear to me that vast amounts of various forms of sexual violence had been documented and entered into evidence during trials, and that the sexual atrocities were subsumed within the judgments even if they were not highlighted or explicitly mentioned in them.

While a variety of gender related crimes — including rape, enforced prostitution, forced sterilization, forced miscarriage, and forced nudity — were prosecuted at the Nuremberg and Tokyo trials, countless sex crimes were ignored. Let me mention just two examples: First, the sexual slavery to which the Japanese military subjected some 200,000 so-called "comfort women" was not prosecuted at the Tokyo tribunal, and to this day the survivors of these sex crimes have received no substantial legal redress. Second, as the Russian army advanced through eastern Europe towards Germany "an estimated two million women were sexually abused with Stalin's blessing."

After the postwar trials, and in large part due to the Cold War, there were scant efforts to enforce the legal principles established at Nuremberg and Tokyo. For five decades, dictators, despots, and war lords around the world waged war on innocent civilians without facing a legal reckoning.

Gender Jurisprudence of Contemporary War Crimes Tribunals

The crimes committed during the 1990s conflicts in the former Yugoslavia finally snapped the international community out of its complacency. Around the world people were horrified as stories of ethnic cleansing, murder, and mass rape camps emerged. In Bosnia-Herzegovina, it was reported that women and girls were repeatedly raped until they became pregnant and detained until they gave birth. Horror story after horror story continued until televised images of emaciated detainees behind barbed wire fences demonstrated that horrific crimes were again happening on European soil, evoking reminders of promises after the Holocaust that 'never again' would such acts be allowed to happen, much less go unpunished. A UN Commission of Experts investigated and reported that crimes, including sex crimes, were rampant.

As a result, the United Nations Security Council established the International Criminal Tribunal for the former Yugoslavia (ICTY) in 1993. The Statute of the ICTY authorized prosecution of genocide, crimes against humanity and war crimes (grave breaches and violations of the laws or customs of war, including Common Article 3 to the Geneva Conventions). Rape was specifically listed as a crime against humanity in the Statute. The United States provided extraordinary leadership in establishing, supporting, and even staffing the ICTY, particularly in its formative years.

Less than a year after the Security Council established the ICTY, a genocide raged through Rwanda, with as many as 700,000 people massacred and hundreds of thousands of others maimed, raped, and otherwise brutalized during 100 days — the swiftest killing and raping spree in recorded history. By the end of 1994, the Security Council also set up the International Criminal Tribunal for Rwanda (ICTR) to prosecute war crimes, crimes against humanity, and genocide committed there.

The Yugoslavia and Rwanda Tribunals have been unparalleled in their treatment of gender-related crimes, and this has had and will continue to have a major impact on other international or hybrid courts (courts having a mixture of international and national judges, prosecutors, and defense counsel and applying both domestic and international laws), namely the Special Court for Sierra Leone, the Serious Crimes Panels in East Timor, the Kosovo Regulation 61 Panels, the Bosnian War Crimes Chamber, and the Extraordinary Chambers in the Courts of Cambodia, as well as the permanent International Criminal Court.

Case law from these contemporary courts stands in marked contrast to the textual silence of the Nuremberg Tribunal when it came to crimes of sexual violence....

AFRC Judgment

In 2007, the Special Court for Sierra Leone (SCSL) rendered the AFRC Judgment, finding the accused guilty of rape and sexual slavery as crimes against humanity. The case was upheld and amended in part by the SCSL Appeals Chamber in February 2008. In this case, three leaders of the Armed Forces Revolutionary Council (AFRC) were charged with 14 counts, including the crimes against humanity of rape, sexual slavery, and other inhumane acts ('forced marriage'). This was the first verdict of the Special Court for Sierra Leone and it represented the first time the charge of "sexual slavery" was formally prosecuted by an internationalized tribunal. The prosecution disappointingly charged 'forced marriage' as an inhumane act instead of as 'other forms of sexual violence,' which would have recognized it as a distinct crime and indicated the sexual nature of the crime. Nevertheless, this charge was used for when a woman or girl was forced to provide sexual services solely to one man as well as look after his household, doing cooking and cleaning and other chores. 'Forced marriage' is essentially a more exclusive form of sexual slavery where the victims are treated as 'wives,' but unlike sexual slavery victims, the victims of 'forced marriage' are typically rejected by their community as collaborators with the enemy. Therefore, the victims are essentially denied victim status by their community, and further victimized by their banishment.

While all of these cases represented a major advance, progress is neither foregone nor absolute. It took the extraordinary confluence of circumstances, including the presence of women judges and major pressure by non-governmental organizations, to achieve these results. It should also be emphasized that while enormous progress has been made in investigating, charging, prosecuting, and rendering judgment on various forms of sexual violence, the cases tried represent a miniscule percentage of the sex crimes actually committed and for the tens of thousands of other cases there will likely be wholesale and absolute impunity. Holding leaders responsible, then, for the policies and practices of sexual violence in conflict greatly increases the number of victims who are vindicated far beyond that addressed by prosecuting individual perpetrators.

Expanded Articulation of Sex Crimes

The *Akayesu*, *Celebici*, and *Furundzija* cases were ongoing during deliberations in Rome in 1998 to draft the Statute for the International Criminal Court (ICC) and the cases left an indelible footprint on the gender provisions of the Statute. The U.S. delegation in Rome played a monumental role in ensuring that gender crimes were prominently featured and adequately covered in the Statute, including by explicitly enumerating rape, sexual slavery, enforced prostitution, forced pregnancy, and enforced sterilization as both crimes against humanity and war crimes. The U.S. team played a leading role in the legally and symbolically significant effort to de-link sex crimes from the misguided language of 'outrages upon personal dignity' or violations of honor, thus acknowledging rape as a crime of violence, not a crime against dignity or honor. They also played an important role in adding into the Statute language stressing the importance of gender equity on the court and expertise in gender crimes. The sex crimes in the Rome Statute, like the other crimes, have been deemed amongst the most serious crimes of international concern, threatening peace and security when committed in large numbers and with impunity. Of the nine individuals currently indicted by the ICC for crimes committed in Uganda, the Democratic Republic of Congo, and Darfur, eight are charged with crimes against humanity, including rape and sexual slavery. Only the first trial, that of D.R. Congo's Thomas Lubanga, focuses exclusively on the war crime of conscripting child soldiers.

The United States has been a driving force in the field of international justice and in establishing courts to try individuals most responsible for atrocity crimes. The Clinton and Bush Administrations have played key roles in establishing, supporting, and funding international and hybrid war crimes tribunals. Providing justice to victims, including victims of sexual violence, through both international and domestic trials has been strongly supported by Republicans and Democrats alike. The specific acts that make up war crimes, crimes against humanity, and genocide, including the sexual atrocities, are crimes in every jurisdiction, and have been since at least the Second World War. Under international law these crimes are not subject to statutes of limitation.

The Need for Gender Justice and Reversing Harmful Stereotypes

Criminal prosecution of sex crimes is absolutely critical in order to punish the crime and highlight its gravity. Rape and other forms of sexual violence are frequent crimes in virtually every domestic jurisdiction. If they are common in so-called peacetime, the frequency and savagery multiplies when there is a war and atmosphere of violence, chaos, and oppression. In virtually all wars, there is opportunistic rape, rape committed because the atmosphere of violence, the prevalence of weapons, and the breakdown of law and order present the opportunity. But over the last couple of decades, we have witnessed a trend toward using women's bodies as the battlefield in a calculated and concerted effort to harm the whole community through physical, mental, and sexual violence inflicted on the women and girls, the bearers of future generations. In most war-torn countries, the legal system is in shambles and there is little or no means to secure accountability for the crimes.

Another common theme that runs throughout survivors from Asia, Africa, Latin America, and Europe, one that shines a bright spot on human beings and gives hope for the future, is one of the extraordinary strength, resilience, creativity, perseverance, and goodness of survivors. Most survivors, though extremely traumatized and angry, have not sought revenge or retribution, although they do want justice and reparation. They have survived despite not only the sexual violence committed against them, but also often the loss of family members, their homes, land, possessions and jobs, sometimes even the loss of their country if they have been forced to flee or forcibly evacuated. Their extraordinary courage and tenacity in the face of such cruelty and hardship is truly amazing. They have lost so much yet they remain ever ready to share their meager possessions, provide hospitality to strangers, and to struggle for a better future for their children and others in their community. They need the full protection of the law and for it to be rigorously enforced. The survivors want, need, and deserve justice. They also need support for trauma counseling, rehabilitation, medical services, and economic survival.

In the past decade, there has been a growing movement to make crimes against humanity the central charge in most of the war crime tribunals, as this crime does not carry the onerous intent proof requirement that genocide requires, but it captures the widespread or systematic nature of the crimes which war crimes fail to portray. The Yugoslavia Tribunal, Rwanda Tribunal, and the Special Court for Sierra Leone in particular have shown that using crimes against humanity to prosecute rape and other forms of sexual violence can be powerful and successful—it is not necessary to prove, for example, that rape itself was widespread or systematic in order for there to be a conviction, although rape is itself often both widespread and systematic. But to render a conviction (in addition to linking the crimes to the accused), the prosecution must simply prove that the attack was widespread or systematic, and that rape formed part of the attack. And as more leaders are being charged with both individual and superior responsibility for their role in ignoring, facilitating, or ordering crimes, including sex crimes, crimes against humanity allows for a larger victim pool to be covered by a conviction.

The Tribunals have unequivocally established that rape is not a mere "spoil of war" or incidental byproduct of war, but is instead one of the most serious and violent crimes committed during armed conflict. For greater justice, peace, and security, it is especially crucial to go after the leaders, the policy makers, the authorities who order, encourage, allow, or ignore the use of rape as a weapon of war, terror, and destruction....

In addition to prosecuting rape crimes, the United States and other countries must also pour resources and effort into redressing gender stereotypes that serve to perpetuate sex crimes. The shame and stigma attached to sex crimes must be reversed before it has significant deterrent effect and before it is reported in closer proportion to the crimes actually committed. I use the term "reversed" instead of "deconstructed" or "rejected" quite intentionally. One of the reasons rape has been such a potent weapon of terror and destruction is because the shame and stigma wrongfully attached to the victims makes the crime more attractive to perpetrators seeking to inflict maximum harm on all members of the enemy group.

Women and girls are often rejected by their families and communities if they suffer a sexual assault, but not if they are shot in the arm or knifed in the back, as there is no stigma typically attached to non-sexual crimes. Women and girls are considered the vessels of family honor by their sexual purity or faithfulness, but such attributes rarely attach to the male, who can in some religions even have several wives lawfully. As the bearers of children, women's sexual lives are rigorously monitored in most societies, and males are blamed for failing to maintain or protect the sexual purity or exclusivity of their daughters, wives, sisters, or mothers. Many crimes evoke paralyzing terror, and rape is one of the most common, attacking one of the most private and intimate parts of a person's body. But the shame and stigma attached to sex crimes causes harm-plus.

With sexual violence, terror as well as physical and psychological harm are frequently only the beginning of a terrible sequence of consequences visited upon the victim. These are all the more destructive because, as the perpetrator well knows, many emanate from the victim's own support network of family and friends. Sex crime victims face possible rejection from their family or community; plus a strong possibility that she will never marry because she's considered "spoiled goods" or she rejects all contact with men after her assault; plus a possibility that HIV/AIDS or other diseases will be caught and can be passed on; plus a possibility that the damage caused from the rape(s) will destroy her reproductive capacity; plus a probability that violence inflicted upon pregnant women will result in miscarriage; plus a likelihood that the woman or girl will get pregnant from the rapes and they will be forced to either abort or bear the child of the rapist; plus a possible jail term or public whipping for the victim in societies where sex outside of a marital context is a crime if the victim cannot prove rape by producing four male witnesses; plus a re-victimization by the justice system in most countries where the presumption is often that the victim "asked for" or otherwise is responsible for the attack. These additional forms of pain and suffering caused by sex crimes distinguish them from other crimes that also evoke sheer, unbridled terror. Therefore, a key method of providing protections against sex crimes is reversing the shame and stigma, and placing it squarely on the shoulders of the perpetrators and others responsible for the crime: the weak cowards who prey on vulnerable portions of the population-people typically without guns or other weapons and those forced to look after children, the sick, and the elderly or to venture far from the beaten path to scrounge for firewood or food during armed conflict situations.

The majority of rapes committed during wartime are committed publicly, and in gangs, with no fear of legal — much less societal or moral — repercussion. If instead of the victims, it is the perpetrators who are outcast, ostracized and rejected by their communities, including by their armed forces/militia groups and their own families, and treated as pathetic and cowardly, I am confident that the numbers of these crimes and their strategic use as a tool of destruction would be reduced. The United States can provide effective and desperately needed leadership in this area ...

Questions for Discussion

1. *Much of the evolving jurisprudence on rape seems to be developing on an ad hoc basis. Do you think this is problematic?*

2. *Has the ad hoc nature of crimes of sexual violence been resolved by the Statute of the International Criminal Court?*

3. *On June 24, 2011, the ICTR convicted the former Minister for Women's Development, Pauline Nyiramasuhuko, a woman, on charges of genocide and crimes against humanity including rape, in the Butare case. The evidence showed that she ordered rape and aided and abetted it. This is the first time a woman has been convicted of rape in an international tribunal. What does this conviction tell us about how the jurisprudence of rape has evolved?*

4. *The ongoing ICC case of the* Prosecutor v. Thomas Lubanga Dyilo *has been widely criticized over the Court's decision not to allow the Prosecutor to add the charges of sexual slavery, violations of dignity, and cruel and inhuman treatment to the charges of conscripting children as soldiers and rape that Mr. Lubanga was already facing. Should the Prosecutor be permitted to amend the charges against the accused mid-trial based on testimony provided by the witnesses? What would have happened in the* Akayesu *case if additional charges had not been permitted?*

E. CEDAW Committee Rape Case — *Vertido v. The Phillipines*

2.1   The author is a Filipino woman who is now unemployed. She served as Executive Director of the Davao City Chamber of Commerce and Industry ("the Chamber") in Davao City, the Philippines, when J. B. C. ("the accused"), at that time a former 60-year-old President of the Chamber, raped her. The rape took place on 29 March 1996.

2.2   The accused offered to take the author home, together with one of his friends, after a meeting of the Chamber on the night of 29 March 1996. When the author realized that Mr. C. intended to drop off his friend first, she told him that she would rather take a taxi because she was in a hurry to get home. Mr. C., however, did not allow her to take a taxi and sped away. Shortly after the accused dropped off his friend, he suddenly grabbed the author's breast. This action caused her to lose her balance. While trying to regain her balance, the author felt something in the accused's left-hand pocket that she thought was a gun. She tried to stop him from driving her anywhere other than to her home, but he very quickly drove the vehicle into a motel garage. The author refused to leave the car but the accused dragged her towards a room, at which point he let her go in order to unlock the door (the car was only three to four metres away from the motel room). The author ran inside to look for another exit, but found only a bathroom. She locked herself in the bathroom for a while in order to regain her composure and, as she could hear no sounds or movements outside, she went out to look for a telephone or another exit. She went back towards the room, hoping that the accused had left, but then saw him standing in the doorway, almost naked, with his back to her and apparently talking to someone. The accused felt her presence behind him, so he suddenly shut the door and turned towards her. The author became afraid that the accused was reaching for his gun. The accused pushed her onto the bed and forcibly pinned her down using his weight. The author could hardly breathe and pleaded with the accused to let her go. While pinned down, the author lost consciousness. When she regained consciousness, the accused was raping her. She tried to push him ..., while continuing to beg him to stop. But the accused persisted.... She finally succeeded in pushing him away.... After washing and dressing, the author took advantage of the accused's state of undress to run out of the room towards the car, but could not manage to open it. The accused ran after her and told her that he would bring her home. He also told her to calm down.

2.3   On 30 March 1996, within 24 hours of being raped, the author underwent a medical and legal examination at the Davao City Medical Centre ...

2.4   Within 48 hours of being raped, the author reported the incident to the police. On 1 April 1996, she filed a complaint in which she accused J. B. C. of raping her.

2.5   The case was initially dismissed for lack of probable cause ... The author filed an appeal ... the Secretary of the Department of Justice, ... reversed the dismissal and, on 24 October 1996, ordered that the accused be charged with rape ...

2.6   The information was filed in court on 7 November 1996 and the Court issued an arrest warrant for J. B. C. that same day. He was arrested more than 80 days later, after the chief of the Philippine National Police issued an order on national television directing the police to make the arrest within 72 hours.

2.7   The case remained at the trial court level from 1997 to 2005....

2.9   On 26 April 2005, the Regional Court of Davao City, presided by Judge Virginia Hofileña-Europa, issued a verdict acquitting J. B. C. In her decision, Judge Hofileña-Europa was guided by the following three principles, derived from previous case law of the Supreme Court: (a) it is easy to make an accusation of rape; it is difficult to prove but more difficult for the person accused, though innocent, to disprove; (b) in view of the intrinsic nature of the crime of rape, in which only two persons are usually involved, the testimony of the complainant must be scrutinized with extreme caution; and (c) the evidence for the prosecution must stand or fall on its own merits and cannot be allowed to draw strength from the weakness of the evidence of the defence. The Court challenged the credibility of the author's testimony. Although the Court allegedly took into account a Supreme Court ruling according to which "the failure of the victim to try to escape does not negate the existence of rape", it concluded that that ruling could not apply in this case, as the Court did not understand why the author had not escaped when she allegedly appeared to have had so many opportunities to do so.... [T]he Court concluded that should the author really have fought off the accused when she had regained consciousness and when he was raping her, ... [T]he Court therefore declared itself unconvinced that there existed sufficient evidence to erase all reasonable doubts that the accused committed the offence with which he was charged and acquitted him ...

3.1   The author argues that she suffered revictimization by the State party after she was raped. She refers to article 1 of the Convention in relation to general recommendation No. 19 of the Committee on the Elimination of Discrimination against Women. She claims that by acquitting the perpetrator, the State party violated her right to non-discrimination and failed in its legal obligation to respect, protect, promote and fulfil that right.... She submits that this shows the State party's failure to comply with its obligation to address gender-based stereotypes that affect women, in particular those working in the legal system and in legal institutions. She further submits that the acquittal is also evidence of the failure of the State party to exercise due diligence in punishing acts of violence against women, in particular, rape ...

3.3   The author submits that the decision of acquittal is discriminatory within the meaning of article 1 of the Convention in relation to general recommendation No. 19, in that the decision was grounded in gender-based myths and misconceptions about rape and rape victims, and that it was rendered in bad faith, without basis in law or in fact ...

8.2   The Committee will consider the author's allegations that gender-based myths and misconceptions about rape and rape victims were relied on by Judge Hofileña-Europa ...

The Committee notes the undisputed fact that the case remained at the trial court level from 1997 to 2005. It considers that for a remedy to be effective, adjudication of a case involving rape and sexual offenses claims should be dealt with in a fair, impartial, timely and expeditious manner.

8.4   The Committee further reaffirms that the Convention places obligations on all State organs and that States parties can be responsible for judicial decisions which violate the provisions of the Convention.... The Committee further recalls its general recommendation No. 19 on violence against women. This general recommendation addresses the question of whether States parties can be held accountable for the conduct of non-State actors in stating that "[...] discrimination under the Convention is not restricted to action by or on behalf of Governments ..." and that "under general international law and specific human rights covenants, States may also be responsible for private acts if they fail to act with due diligence to prevent violations of rights or to investigate and punish acts of violence, and for providing compensation". In the particular case, the compliance of the State party's due diligence obligation to banish gender stereotypes on the grounds of articles 2 (f) and 5 (a) needs to be assessed in the light of the level of gender sensitivity applied in the judicial handling of the author's case.

8.5   The Committee notes that, ... the Court referred to guiding principles derived from judicial precedents.... At the outset of the judgement, the Committee notes a reference in the judgement to three general guiding principles ... The Committee finds that one of them, in particular, according to which "an accusation for rape can be made with facility", reveals in itself a gender bias.... [T]he judgement refers to principles such as that physical resistance is not an element to establish a case of rape, that people react differently under emotional stress, that the failure of the victim to try to escape does not negate the existence of the rape as well as to the fact that "in any case, the law does not impose upon a rape victim the burden of proving resistance". The decision shows, however, that the judge did not apply these principles in evaluating the author's credibility against expectations about how the author should have reacted before, during and after the rape owing to the circumstances and her character and personality. The judgement reveals that the judge came to the conclusion that the author had a contradictory attitude by reacting both with resistance at one time and submission at another time, and saw this as being a problem. The Committee notes that the Court did not apply the principle that "the failure of the victim to try and escape does not negate the existence of rape" and instead expected a certain behaviour from the author, who was perceived by the court as being not "a timid woman who could easily be cowed". It is clear from the judgement that the assessment of the credibility of the author's version of events was influenced by a number of stereotypes, the author in this situation not having followed what was expected from a rational and "ideal victim" or what the judge considered to be the rational and ideal response of a woman in a rape situation ...

[T]he Committee finds that to expect the author to have resisted in the situation at stake reinforces in a particular manner the myth that women must physically resist the sexual assault. In this regard, the Committee stresses that there should be no assumption in law or in practice that a woman gives her consent because she has not physically resisted the unwanted sexual conduct, regardless of whether the perpetrator threatened to use or used physical violence.

8.6   Further misconceptions are to be found in the decision of the Court, which contains several references to stereotypes about male and female sexuality being more supportive for the credibility of the alleged perpetrator than for the credibility of the victim....

8.7   With regard to the definition of rape, the Committee notes that the lack of consent is not an essential element of the definition of rape in the Philippines Revised Penal Code.[21] [...] [T]he Committee has clarified time and again that rape constitutes a violation of women's right to personal security and bodily integrity, and that its essential element was lack of consent....

Questions for Discussion

1. *What other kinds of stereotypes are imposed on rape victims?*

2. *How does one go about overcoming those stereotypes?*

3. *What role do judges play in negating or reinforcing those stereotypes?*

---

21. Article 266-A of the Revised Penal Code of the Philippines. Rape: When and How Committed. Rape is committed:
    1. By a man who shall have carnal knowledge of a woman under any of the following circumstances:
        (a) Through force, threat, or intimidation;
        (b) When the offended party is deprived of reason or otherwise unconscious;
        (c) By means of fraudulent machination or grave abuse of authority; and
        (d) When the offended party is under 12 years of age or is demented, even though none of the circumstances mentioned above be present.
    2. By any person who, under any of the circumstances mentioned in paragraph 1 hereof, shall commit an act of sexual assault by inserting his penis into another person's mouth or anal orifice, or any instrument or object, into the genital or anal orifice of another person.

Chapter 11

Cultural Practices and Women's Rights

Chapter Problem

Your client, an NGO, wants to begin a campaign to raise awareness of women's rights, and also wants to focus on educating the community to eliminate cultural practices that may be harming women. The NGO has sought your advice in identifying some of those harmful practices, and identifying international treaties that might be relevant. The NGO understands that international law also recognizes the right to one's culture, and the importance of cultural practices. It understands that there may be an apparent conflict between gender rights and cultural practices. It wants you to help it make the argument that gender rights have to be respected, despite cultural practices.

The NGO understands, moreover, that the first step in eradicating harmful practices is to raise awareness about such practices. It has asked you to write a Memorandum identifying some of the most prevalent and harmful cultural practices, and the international human rights documents and other data that could be used to advocate against such practices.

I. CEDAW and Cultural Practices

Article 2

States Parties condemn discrimination against women in all its forms, agree to pursue by all appropriate means and without delay a policy of eliminating discrimination against women and, to this end, undertake ...

(f) To take all appropriate measures, including legislation, to modify or abolish existing laws, regulations, customs and practices which constitute discrimination against women;

A. Female Genital Mutilation (FGM)

1. Statistics from the WHO

According to the World Health Organization's Fact sheet on FGM:[1]

- FGM includes procedures that intentionally alter or injure female genital organs for non-medical reasons;
- The procedure has no health benefits for girls or women;
- Procedures can cause severe bleeding and problems urinating, and later, potential childbirth complications and newborn deaths;
- An estimated 100 to 140 million girls and women worldwide are currently living with the consequences of FGM;
- It is mostly carried out on young girls sometime between infancy and age 15 years;
- In Africa an estimated 92 million girls from 10 years of age and above have undergone FGM.

Procedures

Female genital mutilation is classified into four major types:

- Clitoridectomy: partial or total removal of the clitoris (a small, sensitive and erectile part of the female genitals) and, in very rare cases, only the prepuce (the fold of skin surrounding the clitoris);
- Excision: partial or total removal of the clitoris and the labia minora, with or without excision of the labia majora (the labia are "the lips" that surround the vagina);
- Infibulation: narrowing of the vaginal opening through the creation of a covering seal. The seal is formed by cutting and repositioning the inner, or outer, labia, with or without removal of the clitoris;
- Other: all other harmful procedures to the female genitalia for non-medical purposes, e.g., pricking, piercing, incising, scraping and cauterizing the genital area.

Who is at risk?

Procedures are mostly carried out on young girls sometime between infancy and age 15, and occasionally on adult women. In Africa, about three million girls are at risk for FGM annually.

No health benefits, only harm

FGM has no health benefits, and it harms girls and women in many ways. It involves removing and damaging healthy and normal female genital tissue, and interferes with the natural functions of girls' and women's bodies.

Immediate complications can include severe pain, shock, haemorrhage (bleeding), tetanus or sepsis (bacterial infection), urine retention, open sores in the genital region and injury to nearby genital tissue.

---

1. *See* http://www.who.int/mediacentre/factsheets/fs241/en/ [last visited May 2, 2011].

Long-term consequences can include:

- recurrent bladder and urinary tract infections;
- cysts;
- infertility;
- an increased risk of childbirth complications and newborn deaths;
- the need for later surgeries. For example, the FGM procedure that seals or narrows a vaginal opening (type 3 above) needs to be cut open later to allow for sexual intercourse and childbirth. Sometimes it is stitched again several times, including after childbirth; hence the woman goes through repeated opening and closing procedures, further increasing and repeated both immediate and long-term risks.

2. The CEDAW Committee's *General Recommendation 14 on FGM* (1990)[2]

Concerned about the continuation of the practice of female circumcision and other traditional practices harmful to the health of women,

Noting with satisfaction that Governments, where such practices exist, national women's organizations, non-governmental organizations, and bodies of the United Nations system, such as the World Health Organization and the United Nations Children's Fund, as well as the Commission on Human Rights and its Sub-Commission on Prevention of Discrimination and Protection of Minorities, remain seized of the issue having particularly recognized that such traditional practices as female circumcision have serious health and other consequences for women and children,

Taking note with interest the study of the Special Rapporteur on Traditional Practices Affecting the Health of Women and Children, and of the study of the Special Working Group on Traditional Practices,

Recognizing that women are taking important action themselves to identify and to combat practices that are prejudicial to the health and well-being of women and children,

Convinced that the important action that is being taken by women and by all interested groups needs to be supported and encourage by Governments,

Noting with grave concern that there are continuing cultural, traditional and economic pressures which help to perpetuate harmful practices, such as female circumcision,

Recommends that States parties:

(a) Take appropriate and effective measures with a view to eradicating the practice of female circumcision. Such measures could include:

(i) The collection and dissemination by universities, medical or nursing associations, national women's organizations or other bodies of basic data about such traditional practices;

---

2. *Available at* http://www.un.org/womenwatch/daw/cedaw/recommendations/recomm.htm [last visited May 2, 2011].

(ii) The support of women's organizations at the national and local levels working for the elimination of female circumcision and other practices harmful to women;

(iii) The encouragement of politicians, professionals, religious and community leaders at all levels, including the media and the arts, to co-operate in influencing attitudes towards the eradication of female circumcision;

(iv) The introduction of appropriate educational and training programmes and seminars based on research findings about the problems arising from female circumcision;

(b) Include in their national health policies appropriate strategies aimed at eradicating female circumcision in public health care. Such strategies could include the special responsibility of health personnel, including traditional birth attendants, to explain the harmful effects of female circumcision;

(c) Invite assistance, information and advice from the appropriate organizations of the United Nations system to support and assist efforts being deployed to eliminate harmful traditional practices;

(d) Include in their reports to the Committee under articles 10 and 12 of the Convention on the Elimination of All Forms of Discrimination against Women information about measures taken to eliminate female circumcision.

3. The CEDAW Committee's *General Recommendation 24 on FGM* (1999)

[…] (b) Socio-economic factors that vary for women in general and some groups of women in particular. For example, unequal power relationships between women and men in the home and workplace may negatively affect women's nutrition and health. They may also be exposed to different forms of violence which can affect their health. Girl children and adolescent girls are often vulnerable to sexual abuse by older men and family members, placing them at risk of physical and psychological harm and unwanted and early pregnancy. Some cultural or traditional practices such as female genital mutilation also carry a high risk of death and disability.

4. *The Beijing Declaration and Platform for Action*

Eradicate Violence Against the Girl Child

Actions to be taken

283. By Governments and, as appropriate, international and non-governmental organizations:

(d) Enact and enforce legislation protecting girls from all forms of violence, including female infanticide and prenatal sex selection, genital mutilation, incest, sexual abuse, sexual exploitation, child prostitution and child pornography, and develop age-appropriate safe and confidential programmes and medical, social and psychological support services to assist girls who are subjected to violence.

5. *The Cairo Declaration for the Elimination of FGM* (2003)

1. Governments, in consultation with civil society, should adopt specific legislation addressing FGM in order to affirm their commitment to stopping the practice and to ensure women's and Girl's human rights. Where politically feasible, a prohibition on FGM should be integrated into broader legislation addressing other issues, such as:

- gender equality
- protection from all forms of violence against women and children
- women's reproductive health and rights

2. The use of law should be one component of a multi-disciplinary approach to stopping the practice of FGM. Depending on the national context, outreach efforts by civil society and governments aimed at changing perceptions and attitudes regarding FGM should precede or accompany legislation on FGM. These activities should reach as many members of the public as possible and should include the participation of both elected officials and other government actors and members of civil society, including advocates, religious leaders, traditional leaders, medical providers, teachers, youth, social workers, and the all forms of media including electronic media. In particular, men must be targets of outreach, as well as family members, including grandmothers, mothers-in-law, etc. Means of outreach should take as many forms as available in each country, including community gatherings, media (radio, theatre) and other creative means of communication.

3. The work of NGOs is at the heart of social change. NGOs and governments should work together to support an ongoing process of social change leading to the adoption of legislation against FGM. A long-term, multi-strategy approach shaping attitudes and perceptions about women's status and human rights should lead in the long-run to the criminalization of FGM.

Governments and international donors should provide financial resources to empower national NGOs in their struggle to stop FGM. In addition, governments must ensure that national NGOs are able to pursue their activities freely.

4. The legal definition of FGM, which should encompass all forms of FGM, should be formulated by national legislatures on the basis of the World Health Organization definition and in consultation with civil society, including the medical community. However, depending on the national context, it may be desirable to provide for a period of sensitization to precede enforcement of the prohibition as it applies to parents and family members.

5. Governments should formulate time-bound objectives, strategies, plans of action, and programmes, backed by adequate national resources, whereby FGM laws will be enforced, taking into account that legislation condemning FGM has a moral force and an educational impact that could dissuade many individuals from submitting girls to the practice.

6. If existing criminal sanctions are enforced in the absence of specific legislation on FGM, governments should work with civil society to undertake a major information campaign to ensure that all members of society, particularly those who practice FGM, are aware that the existing law will be enforced.

7. In adopting a law, religious leaders, civil society organizations, including women's and community-based organizations, and health care providers, among others, should be part of the consultative process. Efforts to end FGM must be focused on empowering women to make choices impacting their health and lives.

8. Religious leaders should be sensitized to the negative impact of FGM on women's reproductive and sexual health. Religious leaders who support ending FGM should be incorporated into outreach strategies.

9. Once legislation prohibiting FGM has been adopted, whoever performs FGM, including health professionals and traditional circumcisers, should be put on immediate notice that performing FGM gives rise to legal and professional sanctions.

10. Licensed medical practitioners should be subject to the maximum available criminal penalties. Professional associations should adopt clear standards condemning the practice of FGM and apply strict sanctions to practitioners who violate those standards. Practitioners may be suspended or lose their licenses to practice. In addition, they should face civil liability for malpractice or unauthorized practice of medicine. Appropriate ethical guidelines against FGM should be incorporated into medical education and training curricula.

11. Provided sufficient outreach and sensitization has taken place, members of the community with knowledge of cases of FGM should be held criminally liable for failure to report such cases.

6. General Assembly Resolution on Traditional or Customary Practices Affecting the Health of Women and Girls[3]

[...] 3. *Calls upon* all States:

(*a*) To ratify or accede to, if they have not yet done so, the relevant human rights treaties, in particular the Convention on the Elimination of All Forms of Discrimination against Women and the Convention on the Rights of the Child, to consider signing and ratifying or acceding to the Optional Protocol to the Convention on the Elimination of All Forms of Discrimination against Women and to respect and implement fully their obligations under any such treaties to which they are parties;[...]

(*g*) To address specifically in the training of health and other relevant personnel traditional or customary practices affecting the health of women and girls, also addressing the increased vulnerability of women and girls to HIV/AIDS and other sexually transmitted infections due to such practices;

(*h*) To take all necessary measures to empower women and strengthen their economic independence and protect and promote the full enjoyment of all human rights and fundamental freedoms in order to allow women and girls better to protect themselves from, inter alia, traditional or customary practices affecting the health of women and girls;

(*i*) To intensify efforts to raise awareness of and to mobilize international and national public opinion concerning the harmful effects of traditional or

---

3. Resolution adopted by the General Assembly on the Report of the Third Committee (A/56/576)] 56/128.

customary practices affecting the health of women and girls, including female genital mutilation, inter alia, by involving public opinion leaders, educators, religious leaders, chiefs, traditional leaders, medical practitioners, teachers, women's health and family planning organizations, social workers, childcare agencies, relevant non-governmental organizations, the arts and the media in awareness-raising campaigns, in order to achieve the total elimination of those practices;

(*j*) To address traditional or customary practices affecting the health of women and girls in education curricula, as appropriate;

(*k*) To promote men's understanding of their roles and responsibilities with regard to promoting the elimination of harmful practices, such as female genital mutilation;

(*l*) To continue to take specific measures to increase the capacity of communities, including immigrant and refugee communities, in which female genital mutilation is practised, to engage in activities aimed at preventing and eliminating such practices;

(*m*) To explore, through consultations with communities and religious and cultural groups and their leaders, alternatives to harmful traditional or customary practices, in particular where those practices form part of a ritual ceremony or rite of passage, as well as through alternative training and education possibilities for traditional practitioners;

(*n*) To cooperate closely with the Special Rapporteur of the Subcommission on the Promotion and Protection of Human Rights on traditional practices affecting the health of women and the girl child, in particular by supplying all necessary information requested by her and by giving serious consideration to inviting her to visit their countries;

(*o*) To cooperate closely with relevant specialized agencies and United Nations funds and programmes, as well as with regional intergovernmental organizations, as appropriate, and relevant community and non-governmental organizations, including women's organizations, in a joint effort to eradicate traditional or customary practices affecting the health of women and girls;

(*p*) To include in their reports to the Committee on the Elimination of Discrimination against Women, the Committee on the Rights of the Child and other relevant treaty bodies specific information on measures taken to eliminate traditional or customary practices affecting the health of women and girls, including female genital mutilation, and to prosecute the perpetrators of such practices; …

7. Report of the Special Rapporteur on Violence against Women — Cultural Practices in the Family That Are Violent towards Women[4]

[F]emale genital mutilation (FGM), a deeply rooted traditional practice, is believed to have started in Egypt some 2,000 years ago. It is estimated that more

---

4. Ms. Radhika Coomaraswamy, submitted in accordance with Commission on Human Rights Resolution 2001/49; E/CN.4/2002/83.

than 135 million girls and women in the world have undergone FGM and 2 million girls a year are at risk of mutilation.

FGM is practised in many African countries including Chad, Côte d'Ivoire, Ethiopia, Kenya, Mali, Nigeria, Sierra Leone, the Sudan, Uganda and the United Republic of Tanzania. In the Middle East, FGM is practised in Egypt, Oman, the United Arab Emirates and Yemen. It has also been reported in Asian countries such as India, Indonesia, Malaysia and Sri Lanka.

Immigrants from these countries perform FGM in Australia, Canada, Denmark, France, Italy, the Netherlands, Sweden, the United Kingdom and the United States of America. It is suspected that FGM is performed among some indigenous groups in Central and South America.

13. The methods and types of mutilation differ according to each country and ethnic group. But, FGM may be broadly classified into four groups:

(i) Circumcision, or cutting of the prepuce or hood of the clitoris, known in Muslim countries as *sunna* (tradition). This is the mildest form, of FGM and affects only a small proportion of women. It is the only form of mutilation to be correctly termed circumcision, but there has been a tendency to group all kinds of mutilations under the misleading term "female circumcision."

(ii) Excision, meaning the cutting of the clitoris and all or part of the labia minora.

(iii) Infibulation, the cutting of the clitoris, labia minora and at least the anterior two thirds and often the whole of the labia majora. The two sides of the vulva are then pinned together by silk or catgut sutures, or with thorns, leaving a small opening for the passage of urine or menstrual blood. These "operations" are done with special knives, razor blades, scissors or pieces of glass and stone. The girl's legs are then bound together from hip to ankle and she is kept immobile for up to 40 days to permit the formation of scar tissue.

(iv) Intermediate, meaning the removal of the clitoris and some or all of the labia minora. Sometimes, slices of the labia majora are removed. The practice varies according to the demands of the girl's relatives.

14. The main reasons given for the continuation of this practice are custom and tradition. In societies where FGM is practised, a girl is not considered an adult or a complete woman until she goes through the "operation." Some societies believe that all persons are hermaphroditic and the removal of the clitoris makes the female a "pure woman." It is said also to test a woman's ability to bear pain and defines her future roles in life and marriage while preparing her for the pain of childbirth. FGM is also a result of the patriarchal power structures which legitimize the need to control women's lives. It arises from the stereotypical perception of women as the principal guardians of sexual morality, but with uncontrolled sexual urges. FGM reduces a woman's desire for sex, reduces the chances of sex outside marriage and thus promotes virginity.

It is also deemed necessary by society to enhance her husband's sexual pleasure. A husband may reject a woman who has not gone through the "operation." Health reasons are also put forward as justifications for FGM. Unmutilated women are considered unclean. It is believed that FGM enhances fertility. It is considered that the clitoris is poisonous and that it could prick the man or kill a baby at childbirth. In some FGM-practising societies, there is a belief that the clitoris could grow and become like a man's penis. Even though FGM pre-dates Islam, religious reasons are given for the continuation of FGM in some societies.

15. Despite such justifications, the reality is that FGM is a practice that has many negative consequences. Owing to the unhygienic circumstances in which it is carried out, there are many short-term and long-term health hazards connected with it. Short-term complications include local and systematic infections, abscesses, ulcers, delayed healing, septicaemia, tetanus, gangrene, severe pain and haemorrhage that can lead to shock, damage to the bladder or rectum and other organs, or even death. Long-term complications include urine retention, resulting in repeated urinary infections; obstruction of menstrual flow, leading to frequent reproductive tract infections and infertility; prolonged and obstructed labour leading to fistula formation which results in dribbling urine; severe pain during intercourse; extremely painful menstruation; and psychological problems such as chronic anxiety and depression. The cycle of pain continues when cutting and restitching is carried out to accommodate sexual intimacy and childbirth. [...]

19. In many countries in Africa, there now exist strong indigenous movements aimed at stopping the practice of female genital mutilation. In Kenya there now exists a ceremony called "circumcision with words," celebrating a young girl's entry into womanhood but with words rather than through genital cutting. In Senegal, religious leaders have gone on village-to-village pilgrimages to stop the practice. It is only with enthusiastic support from the local community that this practice can eventually be eliminated....

8. Other International Instruments Condemning FGM

The Maputo Protocol and *Declaration on the Elimination of Violence Against Women* also specifically condemn FGM. Article 7 of the Council of Europe Resolution 1247 (2001), specifically describes FGM as "inhuman and degrading treatment within the meaning of Article 3 of the European Convention on Human Rights, even if carried out under hygienic conditions by competent personnel."

9. The Convention against Torture (CAT) and FGM

According to the *2008 Report of the UN Special Rapporteur on Torture and Other Cruel, Inhuman or Degrading Treatment or Punishment,* FGM "can amount to torture if States fail to act with due diligence" to prevent it occurring. The Report further stated that "even if a law authorizes the practice, any act of FGM would amount to torture and the existence of the law by itself would constitute consent or acquiescence by the State."

Questions for Discussion

1. *There are multiple documents condemning FGM and denouncing it as a human rights violation. Yet, the practice persists in large numbers. What else could be done to eliminate FGM if legislation and punishment are not effective?*

2. *Will practices like FGM ever be eradicated as long as societies are so invested in women's sexuality?*

II. Other Cultural Practices Harmful to Women

A. Dowry and Bride Burnings in India and Pakistan

In India, Pakistan, and Bangladesh, dowries are often paid by the father of the bride to her future husband and his family. In those countries, the woman, once married, often leaves her home and moves in with her in-laws. Marriages are often arranged between families, and one of the purposes of the dowry is to compensate the husband's family for taking on the new bride as an economic burden. Dowry has long been legally prohibited in India, but is still commonly practiced. Moreover, dowry is often seen as necessary under Islamic Law, so in countries like Pakistan and Bangladesh with large Islamic populations, many families feel compelled to scrape together a dowry for the daughters in their family. This often causes a woman's family great hardship, and is one of the reasons why "son preference" is a common phenomenon in India—resulting in many baby girls being aborted. It has been estimated that over 5000 women die each year in India as a result of being burned by their husband's family, because of inability to pay the dowry to the husband's family in full. Some women commit suicide rather than face the constant pressure from their in-laws to pay the dowry. Hospitals have had to establish special burn units to deal with the number of women who either self-immolate or are burned by their husband's families.

According to the *Say No to Dowry* Campaign[5]

> Dowry is closely interlinked to many crimes committed against women—female infanticide, domestic violence, neglect of the girl child, denial of educational and career opportunities to daughters, rape, extortion, homicide, and discrimination against women to name a few. Some these crimes can be directly traced to the inability of the bride's family to meet the demands of the groom and his family.

> World Bank Gender Statistics (1999) reveals the following about India: Female population as % of total: 49.4% (testimony to declining sex ratio). Adult illiteracy rate: Male—29%; Female—48% ... Youth illiteracy rate: Male—19%, Female—31%. Female labor force as % of total: 38%. These statistics reveal gender inequality in all aspects of human development.

> In 1995, the National Crime Bureau of the Government of India reported about 6,000 dowry deaths during the year. A more recent police report stated that by 1997 dowry deaths had risen by 170 percent in the decade. All of these official figures are considered to be gross understatements of the real situation. Unofficial estimates cited in a 1999 article by Himendra Thakur *"Are our sisters and daughters for sale?"* put the number of deaths at 25,000 women a year, with many more left maimed and scarred as a result of attempts on their lives.

1. Dowry Prohibition Act of 1961 (India)

> Penalty for giving or taking dowry—If any person, after the commencement of this Act, gives or takes or abets the giving or taking of dowry, he shall be punishable

---

5. *Available at* http://www.indiatogether.org/women/dowry/pledge.htm [last visited July 3, 2011].

with imprisonment for a term which shall not be less than five years, and with fine which shall not be less than fifteen thousand rupees or the amount of the value of such dowry, whichever is more.

Provided that the Court may, for adequate and special reasons to be recorded in the judgment, impose a sentence of imprisonment for a term of less than five years.

Penalty for demanding dowry—If any person demands, directly or indirectly, from the parents or other relatives or guardian of a bride or bridegroom, as the case may be, any dowry, he shall be punishable with imprisonment for a term which shall not be less than six months, but which may extend to two years and with fine which may extend to ten thousand rupees.

2. Indian Penal Code 304(B)

(1) Where the death of a woman is caused by any burns or bodily injury or occurs otherwise than under normal circumstances within seven years of her marriage and it is shown that soon before her death she was subjected to cruelty or harassment by her husband or any relative of her husband for, or in connection with, any demand for dowry, such death shall be called "dowry death", and such husband or relative shall be deemed to have caused her death.

———————

Despite these statutes, dowry remains a common practice, and more than 5000 dowry deaths occur each year.

B. Other Harmful Marriage-Related Practices

1. Honor Killings—Report of the Special Rapporteur on Violence against Women[6]

[…]21. Honour killings in Pakistan (originally a Baloch and Pashtun tribal custom) have recently received international attention. Honour killings are now reported not only in Balochistan, the North-West Frontier Province and Upper Sind, but in Punjab province, as well. They are also reported in Turkey (eastern and south-eastern Turkey but also in Istanbul and Izmir in western Turkey), Jordan, Syria, Egypt, Lebanon, Iran, Yemen, Morocco and other Mediterranean and Gulf countries. It also takes place in countries such as Germany, France and the United Kingdom within the migrant communities.

22. Honour killings are carried out by husbands, fathers, brothers or uncles, sometimes on behalf of tribal councils. The killing is mainly carried out by under-aged males of the family to reduce the punishment. They are then treated as heroes. The action is further endorsed by their fellow inmates in prison, if they are sent there, who wash these young boys' feet and tell them that they are now "complete" men. The act is regarded as a rite of passage into manhood. Ironically,

———————

6. E/CN.4/2002/83 (2002); *Available at* http://www2.ohchr.org/english/issues/women/rapporteur/annual.htm [last visited July 13, 2011].

it is not unheard of for female relatives to either carry out the murder or be an accomplice to it.

23. It should be stated here that it is extremely difficult to collect accurate statistical data on honour killings in any given community. As honour killings often remain a private family affair, there are no official statistics on practice or frequency and the real number of such killings is vastly greater than those reported. The Washington Post Foreign Service reports that 278 murders were reported in Punjab in 1999, (8 May 2000). The Special Task Force for Sindh of the Human Rights Commission of Pakistan received reports of 196 cases of honour killings in 1998 and more than 300 in 1999. Every year more than 1,000 women are killed in the name of honour in Pakistan alone. During the summer of 1997, Khaled Al-Qudra, then Attorney-General in the Palestinian National Authority stated that he suspected that 70 percent of all murders in Gaza and the West Bank were honour killings. They are usually attributed to natural causes. In Lebanon, 36 honour crimes were reported between 1996 and 1998, in Jordan 20 honour killings in 1998 and in Egypt 52 similar crimes in 1997. In Iraq more than 4000 women have been killed since 1991. The same report stated that between 1996 and 1998 in Bangladesh, about 200 women were attacked with acid by husbands or close relatives, but the number of deaths is unknown. In the West there are honour killings among immigrant communities. In the United Kingdom, IN-TERIGHTS has a special project that documents forced marriage cases and the threat of honour killings to British women who come from immigrant communities.

24. In a frequently cited case, a teenager's throat was slit in a town square in Turkey because a love ballad was dedicated to her over the radio. Other reasons include bringing food late, answering back, undertaking forbidden family visits etc. These women's lives are circumscribed by traditions which enforce extreme seclusion and submission to men. Male relatives virtually own them and punish contraventions of their proprietorship with violence.

25. It is not necessarily for love, shame, jealousy or social pressure that these crimes are committed. Economic and social issues also contribute to the rise in honour killings. Amnesty International claims that factors such as the progressive brutalization of society due to conflict and war, increased access to heavy weapons, economic decline and social frustration also lead to increased resort to the honour killing system.

26. Cleansing one's honour of shame is typically handled by shedding the blood of a loved one; the person being murdered is typically a female, the murderer is typically a male relative, and the punishment of the male is typically minimal. Most significantly, the murderer is revered and respected as a true man ...

But what masquerades as "honour" is really men's need to control women's sexuality and their freedom. These murders are not based on religious beliefs but, rather, deeply rooted cultural ones. Family status depends on honour. In patriarchal and patrilineal societies maintaining the honour of the family is a woman's responsibility. In these societies, the concept of women as commodities and not as human beings endowed with dignity and rights equal to those of men is deeply embedded. Women are seen as the property of men and they have to be obedient and passive, not assertive and active. Their assertion is considered as an element which would result in an imbalance of power relations within the parameters of the family unit.

28. Women are seen to embody the honour of the men to whom they "belong". As such they must guard their virginity and chastity. […]

34. Honour crimes are not confined to Muslim communities only. They occur in various parts of the world. In Brazil, men who kill their spouse after the wife's alleged adultery are able to obtain an acquittal based on the theory that the killing was justified to defend the man's "honour". Enormous pressure by women's groups resulted in the honour defence being removed from the books or judges' instructions to juries. However, juries continue to acquit men whom they feel have killed their wives for reasons of honour …

Questions for Discussion

1. *Given that some of these cultural practices are so entrenched and long standing, what is the best way to overcome them?*

2. *The sexuality and fertility of girls is often closely tied to cultural practices and concepts such as "honor." Is there any way to disentangle girls' sexuality from cultural practices?*

3. *International human rights documents enshrine respect for culture in conventions like the International Covenant on Economic, Social and Cultural Rights (ICESCR). When does a cultural practice become one that violates human rights, rather than one that is protected by international human rights?*

4. *One of the criticism levied against the UN is that it is biased in favor of the west, and not sensitive enough to the cultural practices and differences of non-western countries. How could the UN combat this criticism and still critique cultural practices it considers harmful?*

C. The Report on the Situation Regarding the Elimination of Traditional Practices Affecting the Health of Women and the Girl Child[7]

1. Son Preference

[…]66. In various studies, the historical roots of the phenomenon are attributed to the existence of patriarchal systems. Furthermore, participants at both seminars felt that economic considerations, such as the traditional role of men in agriculture and as property owners, underlay this type of discrimination against women. Whereas in Africa it was recognized that religion or an erroneous interpretation of religion might also be one of the causes of the practice (because, for example, women were not allowed to perform certain religious functions and ceremonies),

---

7. Report by Ms. Halima Embarek Warzazi for the Economic and Social Council E/CN.4/Sub.2/2005/36 11 July 2005.

it is interesting to note that in Asia it was clearly stated that the practice was not based on religion....

67. Son preference frequently takes the form of a preference for sons over daughters in nutritional matters. The physical and psychological consequences for girls are often disastrous, especially if we remember that girls are married off at a very early age and become pregnant far too early. Maternal mortality and morbidity rates remain high in countries where this phenomenon is particularly common.

68. Preference for male children can even give rise to criminal behaviour, inducing parents to dispose of their daughters at birth. The use of modern techniques to guarantee the birth of a boy allows parents to find out the unborn child's sex and to practise prenatal selection. The Special Rapporteur notes with regret the misuse of these modern techniques, which were supposed to improve the quality of life for all, particularly women, and to help reduce risks during pregnancy and childbirth.

2. Harmful Marriage Practices

69. These practices range from forced marriage to early—and also often forced— marriage, crimes and violence relating to dowries or the inferior status accorded to the wife and sexual and all other forms of exploitation within marriage. [...]

[I]n the Asian region both marriage and motherhood were mandatory. Women were generally required to marry at a very young age and were frequently subjected to virginity tests. Early marriage and resulting early maternity adversely affected the health, nutrition, education, and employment opportunities of women and lowered their life expectancy. As a result, maternal and child mortality rates were extremely high in the region, with South Asia recording the highest maternal mortality rate of 650 maternal deaths per 100,000 births.

71. At the seminar, it was stated that marriage and procreation were affected by religious, social and economic factors such as unequal access to education and training; however, economic security for women was cited as one of the main reasons why the practices were condoned.

72. As mentioned above, son preference, which is widespread in Africa, also frequently leads to early marriages. Although in Africa harmful traditional marriage practices were not as prevalent as in Asia, in some countries, notably in East Africa, the number of girls married at an early age was increasing, as young virgins were less likely to be infected with HIV/AIDS and, therefore, were seen as fit and healthy brides.

73. The Special Rapporteur has been informed that in some regions of Ethiopia the abduction of girls is a cultural practice whereby a man who wishes to marry a girl has her kidnapped and then rapes her in order to force the parents to agree to the marriage. Under the Criminal Code in force until July 2004, anyone who committed such a crime would elude prosecution by marrying his victim. However, after many years of negotiations, the Ethiopian Parliament has amended the Criminal Code and introduced harsher penalties for rape of a girl, whether or not the act is followed by marriage.

Questions for Discussion

1. *The practice of son preference seems to be linked to a variety of other practices that discriminate against girls and women, such as land ownership and inheritance. How can we best address these types of practices that intersect with other discriminatory practices?*

2. *If we consider that men generally earn more than women and are generally more economically advantaged, doesn't son preference make sense, especially in societies that lack social security networks, and where parents rely on children to support them in their old age? How then do we go about persuading people that son preference should be eradicated?*

D. *Sati*

Sati or *"suthee"* literally means "virtuous woman" in Hindi. However, the phrase has come to refer to the Hindu practice of a woman self-immolating on her husband's funeral pyre. It is a practice that has persisted in some parts of India since the fourth century, despite attempts by the British and Indian leaders to outlaw it. Dorothy Stein claims that "*sati* was an expression of the perceived superfluity of women who were considered unmarriageable in a social context where marriage was the only approved status for women."[8]

The issue of *sati* was brought to the public's attention in 1987, when a young widow, Roop Kanwar, committed *sati* on her husband's funeral pyre. Many suspected that Kanwar had been forced to commit *sati* by the crowd or her in-laws. Eleven people were prosecuted for inciting *sati* and for murder. In 2004, all eleven were acquitted for lack of evidence. *Sati* is a crime in India.

1. The Commission of *Sati* Prevention Act[9]

[…]Whereas *sati* or the burning or burying alive of widows or women is revolting to the feelings of human nature and nowhere enjoined by any of the religions of India as an imperative duty;

And whereas it is necessary to take more effective measure to prevent the commission of *sati* and its glorification;

(b) "glorification" in relation to *sati*, whether such *sati*, was committed before or after the commencement of this Act, includes, among other things—

(i) the observance of any ceremony or the taking out of a procession in connection with the commission of *sati*; or

---

8. D. Stein, *Women to Burn: Suttee as a Normative Institution*, in J. Sharma, ed., INDIVIDUALS AND IDEAS IN MODERN INDIA (Calcutta: Firma KLM, 1982).

9. Act No. 3 of 1988. *Available at* http://wcd.nic.in/commissionofsatiprevention.htm [last visited July 23, 2011].

(ii) the supporting, justifying or propagating the practice of *sati* in any manner; or

(iii) the arranging of any function to eulogise the person who has committed *sati*; or

(iv) the creation of a trust, or the collection of funds, or the construction of temple or other structure or the carrying on of any form of worship or the performance of any ceremony thereat, with a view to perpetuate the honour of, or to preserve the memory of, a person who has committed *sati*; …

(c) "*sati*" means the burning or burying alive of—

(i) any widow along with the body of her deceased husband or any other relative or with any article, object or thing associated with the husband or such relative; or

(ii) any woman along with the body of any of her relatives, irrespective of whether such burning or burying is claimed to be voluntary on the part of the widow or the women or other-wise; …

[W]hoever attempts to commit *sati* and does any act towards such commission shall be punishable with imprisonment for a term which may extend to one year or with fine or with both …

Questions for Discussion

1. *India seems to have taken steps to prohibit practices like dowry killings and* sati *by enacting legislation prohibiting them. Yet, these practices still continue. What else could India do to eradicate these practices?*

2. *What roles could NGOs play in helping to eradicate harmful practices?*

E. The Treatment of Widows in India

One of the reasons that women may be driven to commit *sati* is the lowly position occupied by widows in India, who are often dependent on the goodwill of their in-laws for survival.

1. *India's Unwanted 30 Million Widows*[10]

CUDDALORE, India—Even before the tsunami ripped away her husband, Vallatha was the subject of gossip and derision, through no fault of her own.

Because her eyes are a stunning shade of green, an unusual twist of genetics in a country of brown-eyed people, she was considered evil. Behind her back, villagers call her the "cat-eyed woman."

---

10. DEBORAH HASTINGS, NEW YORK TIMES, Published: Monday, January 31, 2005 at A 5. (Used with permission.)

Adding to her reputation was the fact she married her husband because she loved him. That is not a valued reason to wed in this seaside village. Here, marriages are arranged by parents based on similarities of social status and the size of the bride's dowry. Worse, after 15 years of marriage, her husband recently took up with the woman next door. To save face among disapproving neighbors, he took that woman as his second wife, which violates Hindu custom. Vallatha was shamed.

Now she sits on the floor of her mother-in-law's stone house. The tsunami, which killed five men in this poor village of 200 families, has left her penniless, homeless and a new member of one of the lowest rungs of Indian society: widowhood.

For the rest of her life, she must depend on the continued good graces of her in-laws. Without them, she could lose her children and her place in this tight-knit community. She can never remarry.

In India, for all of its recent modernization and openness to foreign cultures, being a widow remains one of the worst stigmas a woman can endure, and women are far from equal here. When her husband dies, the widow often becomes a pariah, excluded from family gatherings for fear the mere fall of her shadow will bring bad luck and tragedy.

In the North, many journey to the holy cities of Vrindavan and Varanasi, where they beg, and are paid a pittance to recite prayers in the temple. The ruby dots on their foreheads, which denote a married Hindu woman, will be replaced with a smear of chalky white. They can be forced to shave their heads and dress only in white so that they will not induce carnal urges in another man.

There are an estimated 30 million widows in India, the most in any country. Despite the continued work of women's rights groups and an abundance of political rhetoric decrying such treatment, the degradation continues, steeped in cultural rules thousands of years old.

The practice of *suttee*, in which a woman throws herself, or is sometimes pushed, onto the funeral pyre of her husband, has been forbidden by law for more than a century. But it has happened since then. In 1996, nine years after Roop Kanwar was burnt along with her husband's body, a trial court in Neem Ka Thana acquitted her accused in-laws.

A recent study by the Guild of Service, an Indian rights group, described widowhood this way: "Her life is socially, culturally and emotionally dead. Widowed women are harassed, abused, and denied land and livelihood."

Vallatha has no knowledge of such studies. But she knows, with a heavy heart, what she must do. She must keep peace in her mother-in-law's house, where she now lives with her two children, a daughter, 13, and a son, 11. She must sleep in the same room with her husband's second wife, Vanaroja, who sits in the shadows, just behind Vallatha, watching with downcast eyes.

"I am dependent on my mother-in-law to take care of me," Vallatha says carefully, casting a wary look at her husband's mother, who scrutinizes Vallatha's every word …

Vanaroja, wife No. 2, has secondary status behind Vallatha. She is 25, and was living with another woman in the village when she began her affair with Rul. She is asked how she will survive in this cramped two-room house with four new occupants. "Even if there are problems, I will have to live with them," she says. "I don't have any parents. I am confident these people will not throw me out," she says, beaming a hopeful smile at her mother-in-law.

F. Witch Hunting — Report of the Special Rapporteur on Violence against Women[11]

[...] 45. Another cultural practice that is found mainly in Asian and African communities is witch hunting or witch burning. This practice is common in societies where there is a belief in superstition and the evil spirit. Sixteenth and seventeenth century England abounded with witches. Epileptic fits, illness and death were thought to be connected with witchcraft. Women branded as "witches" were tortured to confess. They were beaten and put on the racks and even burnt alive. The practice was brutal and directed against women.

46. The South African regions of Northern Transvaal and especially Venda report incidents of witch burning even today. The women branded as witches are stoned or beaten to death before being burnt. There is a belief that the body of the "witch" along with her magic paraphernalia must be completely destroyed to get rid of the effect of the "witch". While both men and women are accused of being witches, statistics show that women are twice as more likely to be so accused. Although the Witchcraft Suppression Act helps people who are accused of being witches, many people who take violent action against "witches" are not prosecuted under the Act. There are many reasons why women are likely to be branded as witches. Jealousy has a big role to play in such accusations. This could be because of having more property, having healthier children or being better skilled at something. There is a saying in Venda that "all women are the same and all women are witches". It is believed that women have supernatural powers because of their ability to bear children. In some rural African societies no causal link is made between sexual intercourse and the conception of children. So, a woman falling pregnant can only be explained by supernatural occurrence. Like in some gypsy communities, women of Venda are considered impure because of their menstrual cycle. This concept is closely linked to the beliefs in witchcraft. Older women are more likely to be accused of being witches in Venda. Their inability to defend themselves and the physical appearance of old women often lend themselves to accusations of being witches. In Tanzania, an estimated 500 women are murdered every year and many others are harassed after being accused of witchcraft. In Sierra Leone, if a woman giving birth to a child suffers from obstructed labour in spite of all magical and medicinal attempts, she is labelled a witch. She suffers rejection by her husband and by society. She is forced to confess her sin of having been the cause of all misfortunes that have befallen the community. Her death is believed to be a punishment for her crimes.

47. In India, the West Bengal region reports many such incidents. When people suffer from illnesses, or if there is a lack of drinking water, or if there is a death in the family, or cattle die, or if there is a crop failure, or even if there is a natural calamity, the local magic doctor is approached. His orders are accepted unques-

---

11. E/CN.4/2002/83 (2002); *available at* http://www2.ohchr.org/english/issues/women/rapporteur/annual.htm [last visited July 13, 2011]

tioningly. He usually declares a woman or women to be witches or "dayans" and suggests their elimination through death, to be rid of the evil spirit that is causing the problems. The magic doctor is paid a large sum of money for his services. In many cases, people who will inherit property by the death of the "witch" usually pay the magic doctor. Some people believe that the death will bring rewards in terms of property and some others truly believe in the evil spirit. The women declared to be witches are then killed or ostracized from the community. Most of the deaths are caused by stabbing, slugging or burning.

48. Nepal, too, reports cases of women being branded as witches. While different communities have different reasons for women being branded and killed as witches, some feminists argue that the entire concept of witches or witchcraft is a manifestation of a sexist, male-dominated society. According to some scholars, the women who are accused of being witches are in most cases economically independent or without a male partner. In a male dominated society both factors are considered as potential threats.

Questions for Discussion

1. *England and the United States used to have problems with "witch hunting." How was this practice ended in those countries? Might those techniques work in parts of Africa and Asia where witch hunting is still prevalent?*

2. *What do practices like witch hunting or the shunning of widows as "unlucky" tell us about how women are viewed in society?*

Chapter 12

Women's Rights in Parallel Legal Systems — African Customary Law

Chapter Problem

Your client has sought your advice about her impending marriage to an indigenous South African man. Her future husband has suggested that the marriage take place in South Africa, and that they enter into marriage in accordance with African Customary Law, rather than South Africa's common law legal system (which is also known as Roman Dutch law). Your client knows very little about Customary Law, and she has questions about the consequences of marrying in accordance with African Customary Law — specifically about the proprietary consequences of her marriage. Since her husband owns property in several southern African countries, including Botswana and Zimbabwe, your client wants to know if African Customary Law is the same in all of those countries, and if it (rather than the common law), would govern devolution of those properties on divorce, or the death of one of the parties to the marriage. She has also heard that some African marriages are polygamous, and wants to know if her husband is permitted (with or without her permission) to take another wife or wives and enter into a polygamous marriage.

I. CEDAW and Customary Law (Marriage)

Article 16

1. States Parties shall take all appropriate measures to eliminate discrimination against women in all matters relating to marriage and family relations and in particular shall ensure, on a basis of equality of men and women:

   a. the same right to enter into marriage;

   b. the same right freely to choose a spouse and to enter into marriage only with their free and full consent;

   c. the same rights and responsibilities during marriage and at its dissolution;

   d. the same rights and responsibilities as parents, irrespective of their marital status, in matters relating to their children; in all cases the interests of the children shall be paramount;

e. the same rights to decide freely and responsibly on the number and spacing of their children and to have access to the information, education and means to enable them to exercise these rights;

f. the same rights and responsibilities with regard to guardianship, wardship, trusteeship and adoption of children, or similar institutions where these concepts exist in national legislation; in all cases the interests of the children shall be paramount;

g. the same personal rights as husband and wife, including the right to choose a family name, a profession and an occupation;

h. the same rights for both spouses in respect of the ownership, acquisition, management, administration, enjoyment and disposition of property, whether free of charge or for a valuable consideration.

II. Recognition of African Customary Law by Colonial Rulers

African Customary Law is generally understood to be the system of tribal law practiced by African communities. T.W. Bennett describes it as "the law of small scale communities."[1] It was the existing legal system that colonial powers like Britain and France found to be in place among the indigenous people when they colonized Africa. Although many of the colonial powers had originally anticipated imposing the law of their home nation on indigenous occupants of the colonies, that task proved to be more challenging than they had thought, particularly in rural areas. Limited resources and manpower, as well as the challenges of introducing a foreign legal system to an indigenous people who already had their own functioning legal system, meant that colonial powers found themselves tolerating Customary Law.

Moreover, because Customary Law generally functioned quite adequately, and African people governed their lives in accordance with its dictates in the areas of marriage, succession/inheritance and property ownership, colonial rulers permitted Customary Law to continue functioning as the *de facto* legal system for African people—at least as far as personal law was concerned. Many colonial governments imposed the additional restriction that they would recognize and enforce Customary Law as long as it was not "*contra bonos mores*" or "repugnant to natural justice." This rule of recognition came to be known as the "repugnancy" rule. Basically it meant that Customary Law would be enforced and applied as long as colonial rulers did not consider it to be offensive to western morals or sensibilities. This approach led to uneven application of Customary Law, but it is nevertheless often the approach taken to customary law today in Africa. Customary Law is explicitly recognized as a valid parallel legal system by many African countries, including South Africa, Botswana, and Zimbabwe in their constitutions.[2]

---

1. T.W. BENNETT, A SOURCEBOOK OF AFRICAN CUSTOMARY LAW FOR SOUTHERN AFRICA (Juta 1991) at 1.

2. *See* Article 211(3) of the Constitution of South Africa, Article 15(4) of the Constitution of Botswana, and Article 89 of the Constitution of Zimbabwe.

III. The Current Application of Customary Law

A. General Characteristics of African Customary Law

African Customary Law is a community based legal system. T.R. Nhlapo describes it as: "the system of norms which governs the lives of millions of African people, particularly (but not exclusively) in the rural areas."[3] Like culture, Customary Law is dynamic and changes based on social, economic, and legal developments.[4] Customary Law is largely unwritten, although in some South African provinces,[5] colonial rulers codified their understanding of Customary Law. Even today, largely in the rural areas, (and to a limited degree in urban areas) indigenous African people are familiar with the precepts of Customary Law, and many still govern their lives in accordance with those precepts, particularly in the area of family law.

The focus of Customary Law is on the group, rather than the individual, and the goal of on maintaining and restoring harmony in the community is paramount. Professor Dlamini describes African Customary Law as:

> A creative response of the people to the environment in which they found themselves ... African Customary Law embodied the common moral code of the people. There was no sharp distinction between what ordinary members of society regarded as proper conduct and what the official organs of society decreed as law ... Most interactions took place in small areas, with permanent relationships serving a variety of purposes ... African definitions of human rights differed in important respects from those prevalent in the West. The context of family, clan, and ethnic solidarity or the kinship network provided the framework within which individuals exercised their economic, political and social liberties and abilities, and provided restraints upon arbitrary official action that might otherwise have prevailed.... The rights of individuals however, have, often been limited by the rights of the communities of which the holders formed part. There has been no emphasis on the individual as such because society has been pervaded by a communitarian ethic. Many rights have to be exercised in a group context. In traditional African society in particular, family units often functioned as corporate legal entities.[6]

Efforts by newly independent African states to integrate Customary Law into a western rights-based system have not been consistent nor easy. In Customary Law, because rights

---

3. Thandabantu Nhlapo, *Indigenous Law and Gender in South Africa: Taking Human Rights and Cultural Diversity Seriously*, 1994–95 THIRD WORLD LEGAL STUD. 49, 53.

4. *See generally* Abdullah A. An-Na'im, *Toward a Cross-Cultural Approach to Defining International Standards of Human Rights: The Meaning of Cruel, Inhuman, or Degrading Treatment or Punishment*, in HUMAN RIGHTS IN CROSS-CULTURAL PERSPECTIVES: A QUEST FOR CONSENSUS 19, 23 Abdullahi Ahmed An-Na'im ed., (1992).

5. KwaZulu-Natal is one area where Customary Law was codified by the British.

6. C.R. Dlamini, *The Role of Customary Law in Meeting Social Needs*, ACTA JURIDICA (1991) at 72–7.

vest in the community rather than the individual, there is no emphasis on equality. Moreover, in Customary Law one person had to represent the community and exercise rights on behalf of the community or family group—that person is always a male. The fact that the "rights-bearer" is always male has had a profound and deleterious impact on the lives of women in African society.

Women may not own real property. They generally may not marry without the consent of their male guardian, since marriage was regarded as a union between families and not just individuals. Women generally may not enter into contractual relationships on their own—even if the common law legal system legislates to the contrary. Women are generally subjected to the guardianship of a male throughout their lives, whether they are married or not.[7]

Customary Law courts continue to operate throughout many African countries as a valid parallel legal system. The tribal or chiefs' courts are staffed by local chiefs or headmen, all of whom are male. In any disputes involving a woman, she would be represented by her male guardian. The jurisdiction of the courts is largely confined to minor civil matters, and their emphasis is on restoring harmony in the community. Justice tends to be informal with few or no rules of evidence, and more restorative, rather than focusing on a vindication of rights. In many African countries, appeals may be taken from chiefs' courts to the common law courts.

The common law courts have encountered many challenges when applying Customary Law. Once most African countries became independent they embraced constitutionally adjudicable, individual rights based Bills of Rights that guarantee equality for all citizens. However, the constitutions of many of these newly formed democracies also guarantee the right to culture, and acknowledge a role for Customary Law, while recognizing the validity of the chiefs' courts. These two different legal systems sometimes find themselves in conflict.

Many judges in the common law courts find themselves in the unenviable position of trying to harmonize a communitarian-based rights system (Customary Law) which vests rights in a male rights-bearer, with an individual-rights based system that guarantees equality to women. The problem is compounded by the fact that judges in these courts are often not trained in Customary Law, so their application of Customary Law is predicated on what their understanding of Customary Law is, or was, since Customary Law is not necessarily a fixed and static system. Yet, once a judge in a common law legal system enters a decision, it becomes enshrined into precedent and must be followed by lower courts. Thus, even if Customary Law changes to reflect the evolving status of women, a common law court may still apply an older version of Customary Law based on precedent.

Post independent African countries face two challenges with regard to recognizing, incorporating and applying Customary Law. The first challenge comes when drafting constitution to provide for recognition of Customary Law; the second when a matter involving Customary Law comes before the common law courts. Below we will look at the constitutional provisions of several different African countries which reflect the different approaches that those countries have taken with regard to Customary Law.

---

7. Younger males in the family are also subjected to the guardianship of the male head of the family until they marry or leave home.

B. The South African Constitution — Recognition of Customary Law Subject to Guarantees of Equality in the Bill of Rights

The South African Constitution provides an example of recognizing Customary Law but subjecting it to the provisions of the Bill of Rights. Clearly some Customary Law practices are not compatible with individual based rights — particularly those practices which discriminate against women. The South African Constitution tries to balance the right to culture with the right to equality, but comes down in favor of equality. The relevant constitutional provisions are as follows:

Article 9. Equality

1. Everyone is equal before the law and has the right to equal protection and benefit of the law.

2. Equality includes the full and equal enjoyment of all rights and freedoms. To promote the achievement of equality, legislative and other measures designed to protect or advance persons, or categories of persons, disadvantaged by unfair discrimination may be taken.

3. The state may not unfairly discriminate directly or indirectly against anyone on one or more grounds, including race, gender, sex, pregnancy, marital status, ethnic or social origin, colour, sexual orientation, age, disability, religion, conscience, belief, culture, language and birth.

4. No person may unfairly discriminate directly or indirectly against anyone on one or more grounds in terms of subsection (3). National legislation must be enacted to prevent or prohibit unfair discrimination.

5. Discrimination on one or more of the grounds listed in subsection (3) is unfair unless it is established that the discrimination is fair.

Article 10. Human dignity

Everyone has inherent dignity and the right to have their dignity respected and protected. […]

Article 31. Cultural, religious and linguistic communities

(1) Persons belonging to a cultural, religious or linguistic community may not be denied the right:

[…]to enjoy their culture, practise their religion and … to form, join and maintain cultural, religious and linguistic associations …

(2) The rights in subsection (1) may not be exercised in a manner inconsistent with any provision of the Bill of Rights. […]

Article 211. Traditional Leadership

(1) The institution, status and role of traditional leadership, according to customary law, are recognised, subject to the Constitution.

(2) A traditional authority that observes a system of customary law may function subject to any applicable legislation and customs,

(3) The courts must apply customary law when that law is applicable, subject to the Constitution and any legislation that specifically deals with customary law.

C. The Zimbabwean Constitution — Subjugating Gender Equality to Customary Law

Zimbabwe specifically exempts Customary Law from its Bill of Rights, and its Supreme Court has enforced that approach.

Article 11 — Fundamental Rights and Freedoms of the Individual

Whereas persons in Zimbabwe are entitled, subject to the provisions of this Constitution, to the fundamental rights and freedoms of the individual specified in this Chapter, and whereas it is the duty of every person to respect and abide by the Constitution and the laws of Zimbabwe, the provisions of this Chapter shall have effect for the purpose of affording protection to those rights and freedoms subject to such limitations on that protection as are contained herein, being limitations designed to ensure that the enjoyment of the said rights and freedoms by any person does not prejudice the public interest or the rights and freedoms of other persons.

Article 23 — Protection from Discrimination on the Grounds of Race, etc.

(1) Subject to the provisions of this section —

(*a*) no law shall make any provision that is discriminatory either of itself or in its effect; and

(*b*) no person shall be treated in a discriminatory manner by any person acting by virtue of any written law or in the performance of the functions of any public office or any public authority.

(2) For the purposes of subsection (1), a law shall be regarded as making a provision that is discriminatory and a person shall be regarded as having been treated in a discriminatory manner if, as a result of that law or treatment, persons of a particular description by race, tribe, place of origin, political opinions, colour, creed, sex, gender, marital status or physical disability are prejudiced —

(*a*) by being subjected to a condition, restriction or disability to which other persons of another such description are not made subject; or

(*b*) by the according to persons of another such description of a privilege or advantage which is not accorded to persons of the first-mentioned description;

and the imposition of that condition, restriction or disability or the according of that privilege or advantage is wholly or mainly attributable to the description by race, tribe, place of origin, political opinions, colour, creed, sex, gender, marital status or physical disability of the persons concerned.

(3) Nothing contained in any law shall be held to be in contravention of subsection (1)(*a*) to the extent that the law in question relates to any of the following matters —

(*a*) matters of personal law;

(*b*) the application of African customary law in any case involving Africans or an African and one or more persons who are not Africans where such persons have consented to the application of African customary law in that case;

Article 89 — Law to be administered

Subject to the provisions of any law for the time being in force in Zimbabwe relating to the application of African customary law, the law to be administered by the Supreme Court, the High Court and by any courts in Zimbabwe subordinate to the High Court shall be the law in force in the Colony of the Cape of Good Hope on 10th June, 1891, as modified by subsequent legislation having in Zimbabwe the force of law.

D. The Botswana Constitution — Limited Constitutional Protection for Gender Equality with a Court that Affords Equal Protection

In its Constitution, Botswana appears to exempt Customary Law from the provisions of the Bill of Rights. The Constitution itself also does not prohibit discrimination on the basis of sex, although it does prohibit discrimination on other grounds such as race and tribe. The recent jurisprudence of the Botswana Supreme Court discussed below, suggests however, that the Court is taking it on itself to prevent discrimination on the basis of sex.

Art 15 (1)no law shall make any provision that is discriminatory either of itself or in its effect:

(2) Subject to the provisions of subsections (6), (7) and (8), no person shall be treated in a discriminatory manner by any person acting by virtue of any written law or in the performance of public office

(3) In this section, the expression "discriminatory" means affording different treatment to different persons, attributable wholly or mainly to their respective descriptions by race, tribe, place of origin, political opinions, colour or creed whereby persons of one such description are subjected to disabilities or restrictions to which persons of another such description are not made subject or are accorded privileges or advantages which are not accorded to persons of another such description.

(4) Subsection (1) of this section shall not apply to any law so far as that law makes provision — [...]

(c) with respect to adoption, marriage, divorce, burial, devolution of property on death or other matters of personal law;

(d) for the application in the case of members of a particular race, community or tribe of customary law with respect to any matter whether to the exclusion of any law in respect to that matter which is applicable in the case of other persons or not; or

(e) whereby persons of any such description as is mentioned in subsection (3) of this section may be subjected to any disability or restriction..., is reasonably justifiable in a democratic society.

Questions for Discussion

1. Customary Law poses particular problems for newly democratic states in that it appears to bring two different kinds of rights into conflict with each other: namely the right to culture and gender equality. Which of the three approaches described above seems the most equitable or best approach?

2. *Is it always possible to reconcile these two rights (culture and gender equality)? Is it justifiable to prefer one over another? On what basis?*

3. *If you were drafting a constitutional provision that afforded recognition to Customary Law, what limits, if any, would you place on the recognition of Customary Law, and how would you phrase these?*

4. *If you do subject customary law to the gender equality provisions of the Constitution (the South African approach), do you still have a valid system of Customary Law that is based on actual cultural practice? Or, by limiting the recognition of Customary Law, are you recognizing a legal system that is not actually based on "customs"?*

5. *Should a court or the legislature be responsible for determining which tenets of customary law will be recognized, and which will not?*

E. Customary Law as a System of Personal Law Applied by the Courts

Since many African countries formally recognize Customary Law as a valid parallel legal system in the area of "personal law"—marriage, succession/inheritance, adoption and other areas of personal law, we will look at how this system impacts women, and how the courts of these countries have interpreted and applied customary law in these areas.

1. Marriage

As noted, marriages in African society are often negotiated between families. Marriage in accordance with Customary Law may be problematic for women in a number of areas, specifically: brideprice (*lobolo*), property ownership and division of assets, polygamy, inheritance, and custody of children.

a. Brideprice (*Lobolo*)

One of the characteristics of traditional African marriage is the payment of bride price (or bridewealth) from the groom's family to the bride's father or male guardian. Bride price is sometimes referred to as *lobolo, lobola,* or *rovoro*. Its payment signifies the commencement of the marriage, and in the absence of proof of registration of a marriage, its payment was seen as proof of the actual existence of a marriage. Brideprice has long officially been recognized by statute in South Africa. Section 1(1) of the Law of Evidence Amendment Act 45 of 1988 recognizes the role and function of *lobolo* and defines it as "property in cash or kind ... which a prospective husband or head of his family undertakes to give to the head of a prospective wife's family in consideration of a customary marriage." In rural areas *lobolo* is commonly paid in cattle—the number may vary depending on the status and education of the bride, and on whether she is a virgin. In urban areas *lobolo* is commonly paid in cash or with gifts of furniture or other expensive items. It may take several years for *lobolo* to be fully paid off. The couple may still marry and live together while *lobolo* is being paid, but theoretically at least, the girl's father could demand her return until the *lobolo* is paid in full. The practice of paying *lobolo* is an important component of the marriage, as, if a marriage is not registered, it helps to determine whether such a marriage has in fact taken place, or whether a couple is merely cohabiting.

Critics of *lobolo* have contended that the practice is akin to the buying and selling of women, particularly since the price of *lobolo* may vary depending on the woman's education, and because it is paid to her guardian. However the South African Law of Evidence Amendment Act preserved the practice of *lobolo* when it provided that "it shall not be lawful for any court to declare that the custom of *lobolo* or *bogadi* or other similar custom is repugnant to [public policy or natural justice]."[8]

Among rural communities, *lobolo* or brideprice is seen as compensation for the loss of the woman's services to her family. It also may signify in part a union between the families, and compensation for any children born of the union, as children are generally seen as belonging to the husband's family, and if the marriage is dissolved, custody will generally go to the father. If the children are very young, the mother may raise them until such time as they are old enough to be turned over to the father's family.

If a marriage ends, the woman's father generally has to refund all or part of the *lobolo* to the husband's family. The woman's father may be entitled to retain a portion of the brideprice for children born of the marriage. In the event of a dissolution of the marriage, children are generally seen as belonging to the husband's family, although the wife may take care of them while they are young.

The following case from Uganda, where a women's organization sought to have the practice of brideprice declared unconstitutional, illustrates that brideprice is likely to continue to exist.

i. Constitutional Petition — *Mifumu v. Attorney General* (Uganda Constitutional Court)

Justice Mukasa-Kikonyogo:

The petitioners have an interest in the matters stated in the petition, which petitioners allege to be in violation of the Constitution of the Republic of Uganda. They also allege these matters to be in violation of the binding International Human Rights laws, conventions and treaties. For these violations, the petitioners seek the intervention of the Constitutional Court.

The first petitioner is a non-governmental Organization and women's rights agency. Its mission is to work with rural people to fight poverty, and to protect women and assist them to enforce their human rights. Other petitioners appear as individuals.

The petitioners challenge the constitutionality of the customary practice of demand for, and payment of bride price. They allege that bride price as a condition precedent to a marriage; and a demand for, and payment of, bride price as a condition precedent to dissolution of marriage should be declared unconstitutional....

---

8. This was confirmed by the (then) Transvaal Supreme Court in Thibela v. Minister van Wet en Orde en Andere, 1995 (3) SA 147 (T).

The meaning of the terms "bride price" and "dowry"

Before I proceed with the legal arguments advanced by both counsel in their submissions, I consider it necessary to determine the meaning of the terms 'bride price' and 'dowry' if you are to avoid confusion. This is because the two terms are sometimes used interchangeably, which is not correct. The two terms are different. The research carried out from the dictionaries, text books in those countries where the practices exist, the terms bride price and dowry, were described as stated below:

Firstly, the terms 'bride price' and 'dowry' refer to payments made at the time of marriage in many cultures, in Asia and Africa. Bride price is typically paid by the groom or the groom's family to the bride's family. Dowry is typically paid by the bride's family to the bride or to the wedded couple. Thus bride price and dowry are not necessarily the converse of each other. However, in the twentieth century, dowry payments in South Asia have increasingly been demanded by and paid to the groom's family (and not just to the bride or the wedded couple). This suggests a usage of the term dowry to mean a groom price, the reverse of a bride price.

Bride price and dowry need not be mutually exclusive. Marriage transfers in both directions can occur simultaneously. A complex set of norms may then govern the nature and the magnitude of payments in either direction.

Secondly, in Wikipedia, the term bride price sometimes known as bride wealth is described as—"an amount of money or property or wealth paid by the groom or his family to the parents of a woman upon the marriage of their daughter to the groom."

On the other hand, dowry is paid to the groom, or used by the bride to help establish the new household, and dower, which is property settled on the bride herself by the groom at the time of marriage. In the anthropological literature, bride price has often been explained in market terms; as payment made in exchange for loss to the family of the bride of the bride's labor and fertility within her kin group. The agreed bride price is generally intended to reflect the perceived value of the girl or young woman.

The same culture may simultaneously practice both dowry and bride price. Most traditional marriage ceremonies, to be valid, depend on the payment of the bride price.

Issues

Submissions by counsel for the parties

The petitioners first argue that the demand for a bride price by parents of the bride from prospective sons-in-law as a condition precedent to a valid customary marriage perpetuates conditions of inequality between the husband and wife. Article 31 of the Constitution mandates that "women shall have the right to equal treatment with men ..." As equals, the petitioners contend that a bride price, thus contravenes Article 21, which provides for equality and freedom from discrimination ("All persons are equal before and under the law in all spheres of ... economic, social and cultural life and in every other respect shall enjoy the equal protection of the law.").

Petitioners, further, argue that the practice of "bride price" "leads men to treat their women as mere possessions from whom maximum obedience is extracted ..." Under such a custom, the wife is not an equal in the realm of marriage vis-à-vis the husband, but rather she is simply a piece of his property.

1. Bride Price thwarts one's Constitutional right to freely consent to enter into marriage

Petitioners argue that the demand for and payment of bride price and dowry as a condition precedent to a customary marriage violates Article 31(3) of the Constitution, which states that: "marriage shall be entered into with the free consent of the man and woman intending to marry." Affidavits supplied by the petitioners illustrate the frequency with which the bride price is used either to force a woman to enter into a marriage against her consent, or to bar a man from entering into a marriage relationship. Additionally, a bride price or dowry may force a couple to cohabit due to not being able to raise funds sufficient to meet the obligation.

2. The cultural practice of bride price offends the Constitutional right to one's human dignity

The Constitution provides that "laws, cultures, customs or traditions which are against the dignity, welfare, or interest of women or which undermine their status, are prohibited by this Constitution." Art. 33(6). Additionally, Article 24 provides for "respect for human dignity and protection from inhuman treatment."

Accordingly, no person shall be subjected to "cruel, inhuman or degrading treatment or punishment." Art. 24. Petitioners state that, both the demand for a bride price and the demand for a refund of the bride price, amount to the buying and selling of a bride as an item for sale in a market. Such "haggling and pricing of young girls and women like commodities" is argued to be an affront to human dignity. (See Affidavit of Fr. Lawrence Ssendegeya, 3.)

Furthermore, according to the petitioners' affidavits, the use of bride price leads to social ills such as fathers forcing daughters to get married simply to collect a bride price and young women being removed from schools and forced into early marriages. Uneducated women may even fetch a higher bride price, or dowry, due to the assumption that women in a school setting are less likely to be undefiled.

Moreover, petitioners note that bride price can even lead to inhuman and degrading treatment of corpses. In her affidavit, Felicity Atuki Turner notes that she has come across several cases where a wife's corpse has been denied burial pending the refund of the applicable bride price to the husband.

III. Submissions in reply by counsel for the Respondents

On the other hand, Respondents argue that the term "Bride Price" means different things in different cultures of Uganda such that the Constitutional Court cannot make a uniform interpretation of such a practice. A declaration of bride price as *per se* unconstitutional would neglect the numerous forms of bride price. For example, in Kinyankore customary marriages, frequently the bride price, or "enjugano," takes the form of a gift from the groom to the bride. Moreover, such a gift is reciprocated from the bride to the groom (an "emihingiro"). It was contended by Mr. Kakuru that since payment of bride price is a customary practice that the Constitutional Court cannot decide the constitutionality of the alleged customary law of "bride price" before it is found to be applicable to a specific community.

In the same vein, respondents contend that even where bride price is practiced, it manifests itself in different ways. Respondents do note that the practice of bride price, both the initial demand for a bride price and a demand for refund of bride price as a condition *sine qua non* of a valid dissolution of marriage, occurs among tribes such as the Japadhola, the Langi, and the Banyankole. However, to them "there is no such thing as 'bride price' in Kinyankole culture or the culture of the Japadhola or the Langi ..." It was argued for 2nd respondent that "there is no culture in Uganda where a bride is sold or bought or where a married woman is not free and does not enjoy equal rights and protection of the Constitution and the law."

Additionally, Article 37 gives the right to "enjoy, practice, maintain and promote any culture, cultural institution ... [and] tradition ... in community with others." Respondents argue that the requirement to pay dowry or bride price does not contravene the Constitution because the practice of "bride price or dowry" is "intended to show appreciation to a woman's parents for taking care of the woman." Moreover, if such a practice does lead to isolated cases of men treating their wives as mere property, such a perversion of the purpose of bride price does not negate the noble aims of the practice, let alone render the custom unconstitutional. As contended by respondent, those men and women that appreciate the positive goals of a bride price agreement should not be denied their constitutional right to enter into such arrangements. Bride price being declared *per se* unconstitutional would thus deny a man and a woman one legitimate way to get married, which would contravene Article 33(1), which is a violation of the constitutional right to marry and begin a family....

Consideration of evidence by the Court

[...]I concede that the practice of bride price being customary, unwritten, diffuse, and varied may be difficult to ascertain. However, that alone cannot stop this Court from interpreting it. So the answer to issue No. 1 is in the affirmative.

Regarding the second issue whether the payment of bride price before marriage and its refund during divorce are customs judicially noticed and hence requiring no further proof in the instant petition, it was vehemently argued for the respondents that the practice of paying bride price being customary had to be proved in relation to a particular community where known or practiced. Besides, to the respondents the custom of bride price means different things in Uganda. I agree that custom must be proved where it is not judicially noticed in accordance with Section 55 of the Evidence Act ...

In the instant petition, it was incumbent upon the petitioners to establish the practice of bride price payment on marriage by, in the first instance, call witnesses or documentary evidence or any other satisfactory evidence to prove the practice. Although the court has got a wide discretion on this matter, the onus is on the party seeking to rely on the custom. Although many affidavits were filed alleging the suffering that might be caused or due to the practice of customary bride price, there was not a single affidavit to prove the custom. In the circumstances, I am unable to hold that the practice is so notorious that it should be judicially noticed by the court ...

As already noted, this matter is before this Court to determine the constitutionality of the custom and practice of demand and payment of bride price as requirement of customary marriage and or the refund of dowry as a requirement for its dissolution. As can be seen from the court record, many affidavits were filed in support of the arguments that the custom of bride price is unconstitutional. At the outset, it is important to note that the bride price encompasses two scenarios. First, the parents of a potential bride may require a bride price from their potential son-in-law as a condition precedent to their lawful customary marriage.

Secondly, in the event of a valid dissolution of marriage, the husband may demand refund of the bride price.

I wish to begin by acknowledging the significant rights and protections that the Constitution accords to women (See Article 31(1), (3) (rights to freely enter into marriage); Article 33 (rights of women to equality with men). Moreover, the Court is cognizant of the constitutional provisions intended to correct historical imbalances and an unequal playing field as between men and women (See Art. 33(6)). The Court, further, acknowledges the sentiment expressed by the petitioners that anytime a woman is equated with a sum of money or property, as occurs in any bride price agreement, such an agreement does, on its face, seem to undermine the status of the woman vis-à-vis the man. A potential bride price being discussed in terms of any quantity of money does, at first glance, seem to violate the constitutional prohibition against customs that undermine the status of a woman (See Art. 33(6)).

However, I accept the respondent's contention that in many situations, a bride price agreement is intended to show appreciation to the parents of a bride. In numerous instances, a bride price agreement may be entered into with joy by two parties seeking the felicities of a marriage relationship. Moreover, while Petitioners have produced affidavits suggesting that bride price can lead to social ills such as domestic abuse, the Court cannot state that such instances occur as a matter of course, or are definitively linked to a bride price arrangement. In any case, there are varied and numerous causes of spousal abuse, and the Court cannot say with certainty that bride price to be *per se* unconstitutional on such a ground. It is true bride price in some cases plays a factor in domestic abuse and women being treated as inferiors but that is no justification for the court to make a blanket prohibition of the practice of bride price.

In my opinion, therefore, the cultural practice of bride price, the payment of a sum of money or property by the prospective son-in-law to the parents of the prospective bride as a condition precedent to a lawful customary marriage, is not barred by the Constitution. It is not *per se* unconstitutional. The Constitution does not prohibit a voluntary, mutual agreement between a bride and a groom to enter into the bride price arrangement. A man and a woman have the constitutional right to so choose the bride price option as the way they wish to get married. In the premises, I would be declined to grant the petitioners' request for a declaration that bride price be declared *per se* unconstitutional.

The aforesaid notwithstanding, in the narrow instance where one or both of the man and woman wishing to get married is given no other alternative to customary marriage and a bride price agreement, such an arrangement contravenes one's constitutional right to freely and voluntarily enter into a marriage relationship (Articles 20, 31(3)). To be clear: "Marriage shall be entered into with the *free consent* of the man and woman intending to marry." Art. 31(3) (emphasis added). A man shall not be prevented from marrying the woman of his choice due to not being able to meet a bride price demand, nor shall a man or a woman be compelled to enter into a bride price marriage. A man and a woman's constitutional right to enter into a marriage relationship (Art. 31(1)) shall not be made contingent upon the demands of a third party, the parents of the bride, for the payment of a bride price or dowry. Any payment of a bride price or dowry must be conditioned upon voluntary consent of the two parties to the marriage.

Additionally, I am in agreement with the view that the customary practice of the husband demanding a refund of the bride price in the event of dissolution of the marriage demeans and undermines the dignity of a woman and is in violation of Article 33(6) of the Constitution. Moreover, the demand of a refund violates a woman's entitlement to equal rights with the man in marriage, during marriage, and at its dissolution (See Art. 31(1)).

Further, a refund demand fails to honor the wife's unique and valuable contributions to a marriage. A woman's contributions in a marriage cannot be equated to any sum of money or property, and any refund violates a woman's constitutional right to be an equal co-partner to the man. The aforesaid notwithstanding, in my view, the declaration sought; that is, to declare the practice unconstitutional is not essential. The Constitution itself, under Article 50 and others can adequately take care of her grievances. The aggrieved party would be at liberty to institute criminal proceedings or a civil action in a court of competent jurisdiction under the relevant law.

In the result, this petition must fail and it is accordingly dismissed.

Before I take leave of this judgment, I wish to comment further on the difference between 'bride price' and 'dowry'. In certain African societies, the custom of presenting a gift to the bride's family is practiced as a token of gratitude. This gratitude is for the part the bride's family has played in taking care of the potential bride. Under this view, the gift or gifts are, under no circumstances, to be considered payment. The groom's family is not the only one giving gifts; the bride's family may give gifts as well. This practice arises out of the value society attaches to virginity as the fountain of life that is valued as the proper form for any marriageable woman to be in. A woman is endowed with the spring of life, and the gifts in dowry sometimes express gratitude for preservation of this spring of life without using the spring wastefully.

Questions for Discussion

1. *Do you find the Court's reasoning in this case to be consistent? Look closely at the section where the Court finds itself unable to take judicial notice of the practice of bride price because no affidavit directly described the practice—yet later the Court defines the practice itself, and finds it to be not unconstitutional.*

2. *When the Court finds that demanding a refund of the bride price in the event of dissolution of the marriage "demeans and undermines the dignity of a woman" and is in violation of Article 33(6) and Article 31 of the Constitution, shouldn't the Court then have gone on to find bride price to be unconstitutional? Why didn't it?*

3. *What do you think of the Court's suggestion that a woman who believes her constitutional rights have been violated when a refund of bride price is demanded should file a civil claim under Article 50? (Article 50(1) of the Constitution provides that any person who claims that a fundamental or other right or freedom guaranteed under the constitution has been infringed or threatened, is entitled to apply to a competent court for redress which may include compensation.) Is it likely that women will file these kinds of claims?*

4. *Is the Court here really preferring a cultural practice over equality for women? Look at the last paragraph of the judgment. Does the Court appear to have a particular view on women and what they should bring to a marriage?*

2. Matrimonial Property

The concept of a marriage "in community of property" or "out of community of property" was unknown in Customary Law, since the male guardian held all property on behalf of the family unit. Under Customary Law, if a divorce occurred, women were often impoverished as they were not automatically entitled to half of the marital assets. Moreover, the woman's father often had to return the *lobolo*, thereby further impoverishing her family of origin to whom she might return for support. A woman also had limited options with regard to earning a living during her marriage, as not only did she have to care for the children, but because she was regarded as a minor by Customary Law, she could not enter into contracts in her own name, and would likely have to have her husband's permission to work. In 1998, the South African Parliament attempted to remedy this system by enacting the Recognition of Customary Marriages Act 120 of 1998. The Act recognizes Customary Law marriages as official marriages, and defines a Customary Law marriage as one:

> negotiated, celebrated or concluded according to any of the systems of indigenous African Customary Law which exist in South Africa and that this does not include marriages concluded in accordance with Hindu, Muslim or other religious rites.

Section 6 of the Act provides that:

> A wife in a Customary marriage has, on the basis of equality with her husband ... full status and capacity, including the capacity to acquire assets and dispose of them, to enter into contracts and to litigate, in addition to any rights and powers that she might have at Customary Law.

The Act also purported to regulate the marital property regime, but only among spouses married in accordance with African Customary Law after November 1, 2000. Section 7(2) of the Act provides that a Customary Law marriage entered into after November 1, 2000 shall be in community of property in the absence of a pre-nuptial agreement, while those married prior to that date are regulated by Customary Law. While the Act thus affords some degree of protection to women married under Customary Law after November, 2000, those married prior to November, 2000 may find themselves in an unenviable position as illustrated by the *Gumede* case decided by the South African Constitutional Court in 2008.

a. *Gumede v. President of the Republic of South Africa* (South African Constitutional Court)[9]

Moseneke DCJ. for a unanimous court

This case concerns a claim of unfair discrimination on the grounds of gender and race in relation to women who are married under customary law as codified in the province of KwaZulu-Natal. It brings into sharp focus the issues of ownership, including access to and control of family property by the affected women during and upon dissolution of their customary marriages. At one level, the case underlines the stubborn persistence of patriarchy and conversely, the vulnerability of many women during and upon termination of a customary marriage. At another level, the case poses intricate questions about the relative space occupied by pluralist legal systems under the umbrella of one supreme law, which lays down a common normative platform.

These issues arise in proceedings under section 167(5) of the Constitution in which Mrs. Elizabeth Gumede, a spouse in a customary marriage, seeks confirmation from this Court of an order of constitutional invalidity made in her favour by the High Court. The High Court found that the impugned provisions offend the equality protection afforded by sections 9(3) and (5) of the Constitution because they unfairly discriminate on the grounds of gender and race.

Section 167(5) provides:

> The Constitutional Court makes the final decision whether an Act of Parliament, a provincial Act or conduct of the President is constitutional, and must confirm any order of invalidity made by the Supreme Court of Appeal, a High Court, or a court of similar status, before that order has any force.

Section 9(3) provides:

---

9. *Available at* http://www.saflii.org/za/cases/ZACC/2008/23.html [last visited May 23, 2011].

The state may not unfairly discriminate directly or indirectly against anyone on one or more grounds, including race, gender, sex, pregnancy, marital status, ethnic or social origin, colour, sexual orientation, age, disability, religion, conscience, belief, culture, language and birth.

The High Court declared the following legislative provisions that regulate the proprietary consequences of a customary marriage as being inconsistent with the Constitution and invalid:

(a) Section 7(1) of the Recognition of Customary Marriages Act (Recognition Act). It provides that the proprietary consequences of a customary marriage entered into before the commencement of the Recognition Act continue to be governed by customary law.

(b) The inclusion of the words "entered into after the commencement of this Act" in section 7(2) of the Recognition Act. The inclusion provides that a customary marriage entered into after the commencement of the Recognition Act is a marriage in community of property subject to a number of exceptions which are not, for present purposes, relevant.

(c) Section 20 of the KwaZulu Act on the Code of Zulu Law (KwaZulu Act).

It provides that the family head is the owner of and has control over all family property in the family home.

(d) Section 20 of the Natal Code of Zulu Law (Natal Code) ... provides that the family head is the owner of and has control over all family property in the family home.

(e) Section 22 of the Natal Code. It provides that "inmates" of a kraal [tribal village] are in respect of all family matters under the control of and owe obedience to the family head.

Section 9(5) [of the Constitution] provides: "Discrimination on one or more of the grounds listed in subsection (3) is unfair unless it is established that the discrimination is fair."

On 29 May 1968, Mrs. Gumede and her husband entered into a customary marriage, the only marriage to which her husband was a party. Both Mr. and Mrs. Gumede reside permanently and are domiciled in the province of KwaZulu-Natal. Their marriage was of long duration. It has lasted for over 40 years and out of it four children were born, now all adults.

During the marriage, Mrs. Gumede was not in formal employment because her husband did not permit her to work. However, by whatever means she could garner, she maintained the family household and was the primary caregiver to the children. She had no means to contribute towards the purchase of the common home; her husband who was working did. Mrs. Gumede states that over time the family acquired two homes. She further explains, and the High Court accepted, that she acquired the furniture and appliances in the Umlazi Township home valued at approximately R40,000. For some time now, they have been living separately. Mrs. Gumede lives in the residence in Umlazi, eThekwini and Mr. Gumede lives in the house at Adams Mission, Amanzimtoti. He also receives a pension arising from his employment with Rennies Cargo, where he was a foreman until his retirement in April 2000. Mrs. Gumede has no other family who can care for her, no other residence or family home.

She is now an old-aged pensioner and lives off a government pension and the occasional financial support which she receives from her children. It should be added that she receives no maintenance contribution from Mr. Gumede. In January 2003, Mr. Gumede instituted court proceedings to end the marriage. The divorce proceedings are pending before the divorce court. Mrs. Gumede does not dispute that their marriage has broken down irreparably and that it cannot be salvaged.

Before a divorce was granted, she approached the High Court with a view to procuring an order invalidating the statutory provisions that regulate the proprietary consequences of her marriage. She sought to pre-empt the divorce court from relying on legislation she considers unfairly discriminatory to customary law wives on grounds of gender and race.

The Marriages Recognition Act provides that a customary marriage concluded after its commencement on 15 November, 2000 is ordinarily a marriage in community of property. For ease of reference, I refer to these customary marriages as 'new' marriages. The Recognition Act also provides that customary marriages concluded before the cut-off date of 15 November 2000 ('old' marriages) are governed by customary law. The Gumedes concluded their marriage in 1968. It follows that it is governed by customary law.

None of the parties has contended otherwise. In KwaZulu-Natal, where the Gumedes are domiciled, customary law has been codified in the KwaZulu Act and the Natal Code. These pieces of provincial legislation provide that in a customary marriage, the husband is the family head and owner of all family property, which he may use in his exclusive discretion. This plainly means that in terms of codified customary law in KwaZulu-Natal a wife to an 'old' customary marriage will not have any claim to the family property during or upon dissolution of the marriage. I make this observation mindful of the distinction that should properly be made between a particular version of 'official' or codified customary law, which should not be equated with living indigenous/customary law—a matter to which I revert later ...

[A] prominent feature of the law of customary marriage, as codified, is male domination of the family household and its property arrangements. Whilst patriarchy has always been a feature of indigenous society, the written or codified rules of customary unions fostered a particularly crude and gendered form of inequality, which left women and children singularly marginalised and vulnerable. It is so that patriarchy has worldwide prevalence, yet in our case it was nurtured by fossilised rules and codes that displayed little or no understanding of the value system that animated the customary law of marriage. As Professor Nhlapo poignantly points out:

> [L]egislating these misconstructions of African life had the affect of placing women 'outside the law'. The identification of the male head of the household as the only person with property-holding capacity, without acknowledging the strong rights of wives to security of tenure and use of land, for example, was a major distortion.

> Similarly, enacting the so-called perpetual minority of women as positive law when, in the pre-colonial context, everybody under the household head was a minor (including unmarried sons and even married sons who had not yet established a separate residence), had a profound and deleterious effect on the lives of African women. They were deprived of the opportunity to manipulate the rules to their advantage through the subtle interplay of social norms, and, at the same time, denied the protections of the formal legal order. Women became 'outlaws'.

In our pre-colonial past, marriage was always a bond between families and not between individual spouses. Whilst the two parties to the marriage were not unimportant, their marriage relationship had a collective or communal substance.

Procreation and survival were important goals of this type of marriage and indispensable for the well-being of the larger group. This imposed peer pressure and a culture of consultation in resolving marital disputes. Women, who had a great influence in the family, held a place of pride and respect within the family. Their influence was subtle although not lightly overridden. Their consent was indispensable to all crucial family decisions. Ownership of family property was never exclusive but resided in the collective and was meant to serve the familial good. After collecting authorities and reviewing ample ethnographic material, Aninka Claassens records the following about property rights, women and gender equity:

> There is a range of historical and ethnographic accounts that indicate that women, as producers, previously had primary rights to arable land, strong rights to the property of their married houses within the extended family, and that women, including single women, could be and were allocated land in their own right. Furthermore there are accounts of women inheriting land in their own right. However, Native Commissioners applying racially based laws such as the Black Land Areas Regulations and betterment regulations issued in terms of the South African Development Trust and Land Act repeatedly intervened in land allocation processes to prohibit land being allocated to women.

The Recognition Act is inspired by the dignity and equality rights that the Constitution entrenches and the normative value systems it establishes. It is also necessitated by our country's international treaty obligations, which require member states to do away with all laws and practices that discriminate against women. On the other hand, the Recognition Act gives effect to the explicit injunction of the Constitution that courts must apply customary law subject to the Constitution and legislation that deals with customary law. Courts are required not only to apply customary law but also to develop it. Section 39(2) of the Constitution makes plain that when a court embarks on the adaptation of customary law it must promote the spirit, purport and objects of the Bill of Rights.

The facial extent of the reform is apparent from the extended title of the Recognition Act. The legislation makes provision for recognition of customary marriages. Most importantly, it seeks to jettison gendered inequality within marriage and the marital power of the husband by providing for the equal status and capacity of spouses. It specifies the essential requirements for a valid customary marriage and regulates the registration of marriages. In this way, it introduces certainty and uniformity to the legal validity of customary marriages throughout the country. The Recognition Act regulates proprietary consequences and the capacity of spouses and governs the dissolution of the marriages, which now must occur under judicial supervision.

For purposes of the equality analysis in this case, a useful starting point is section 6 of the Recognition Act. It provides:

> A wife in a customary marriage has, on the basis of equality with her husband and *subject to the matrimonial property system governing the marriage*, full status and capacity, including the capacity to acquire assets and to dispose of them, to enter into contracts and to litigate, in addition to any rights and powers that she might have at customary law. (Emphasis added.)

On its terms it appears to usher in a remedial regime of equal worth and capacity of spouses in customary marriages. However, section 7(1) of the Recognition Act swiftly qualifies the equal dignity, status and capacity of the spouses by providing that the proprietary consequences of a customary marriage entered into before its commencement continue to be governed by customary law. This means that 'old' marriages are subject to the matrimonial system dictated by customary law. [I]t is necessary to note that section 20 of the KwaZulu Act and section 20 of the Natal Code provide that a family head is the owner and has control of all family property in the family home. In turn, section 22 of the Natal Code places all "inmates" of a kraal [home] in respect of all family matters "under the control" of the family head to whom they all "owe obedience" …

[T]he codified customary law, which is applicable in the province where Mrs. Gumede is domiciled, has the outcome that her husband is the exclusive owner of all the property that was acquired during the subsistence of the marriage.

These impugned provisions are self-evidently discriminatory on at least one listed ground: gender. The provisions are discriminatory as between wife and husband. Only women in a customary marriage are subject to these unequal proprietary consequences. This discrimination is on a listed ground and is therefore unfair unless it is established that it is fair. And within the class of women married under customary law, the legislation differentiates between a woman who is a party to an 'old' or pre-recognition customary marriage as against a woman who is a party to a 'new' or post-recognition customary marriage. This differentiation is unfairly discriminatory.

There can be no doubt that the marital property system contemplated by the KwaZulu Act and the Natal Code strikes at the very heart of the protection of equality and dignity our Constitution affords to all, and to women in particular. That marital property system renders women extremely vulnerable by not only denuding them of their dignity but also rendering them poor and dependent. This is unfair.

For the sake of completeness I restate the principal findings I have made:

(a) The order of constitutional invalidity made by the High Court in relation to certain legislation (sections 7(1) and (2) of the Recognition Act; section 20 of the KwaZulu Act; and sections 20 and 22 of the Natal Code) should be confirmed.

(b) The impugned legislative provisions unfairly discriminate against the applicant and other women similarly situated.

(c) The government has failed to furnish justification for the legislative discrimination on a listed ground, the discrimination is therefore unfair, and the provisions concerned are inconsistent with the Constitution and invalid.

(e) The order of constitutional invalidity in relation to section 7(1) of the Recognition Act is limited to monogamous marriages and should not concern polygamous relationships or their proprietary consequences.

(f) The order we are to make should not affect customary marriages that have been terminated by death or divorce before this order is made.

(g) Any exercise of marital power that is made before the date of the order should not be undone only as a result of this order.

Questions for Discussion

1. *Once a court changes the tenets of a legal system in the way that this court did, can this marriage still be regarded as a "Customary Law" marriage?*

2. *Does the approach taken by the South African Constitutional Court mean that many of the practices of Customary Law that discriminate against women are no longer valid?*

3. Are there circumstances under which the status of women under African Customary Law could be considered "fair"?

---

3. Polygamy

African Customary Law marriages may be polygamous or, more accurately, polygynous.[10] This was because procreation was such an important part of the marriage and polygamy ensured that children would be born of the marriage. It also enabled the man to offer protection to a group of women, which was important during tribal wars. Polygamy is still commonly practiced in rural areas in South Africa and Zimbabwe, as well as other African countries. In fact, the current President of South Africa recently concluded his fifth marriage. (One of his wives died and one marriage ended through divorce, so he currently has three wives.) Men do not have to seek the permission of their current wife to take another wife.

Polygamy is problematic for women. It often results in the impoverishment of women as polygamous marriages tend to produce more children and the family resources are thus shared among a larger family group. The proprietary consequences of such marriages are often unclear. Polygamous unions also potentially expose women to sexually transmitted diseases (including HIV/AIDs).

Affording recognition to polygamous or potentially polygamous, Customary Law marriages, while guaranteeing gender equality, has proven to be problematic for the post apartheid South African government. It attempted to deal with those marriages through the Recognition of Customary Marriages Act, by requiring parties to Customary Law marriages to register their marriages, and if entering a polygamous marriage, to provide for a matrimonial property regime that must be reviewed by a court. The Act also prohibits someone who is married under common law from entering a polygamous marriage, but someone married in accordance with Customary Law may marry multiple times, with no limit imposed on the number of marriages.

a. Recognition of Customary Marriages Act 120 of 1998 (South Africa)

Section 2:

(1) a marriage which is a valid marriage at customary law ... is for all purposes recognized as a marriage....

(3) If a person is a spouse in more than one customary marriage, all valid customary marriages entered into before the commencement of this Act are for all purposes recognized as marriages.

(4) If a person is a spouse in more than one customary marriage, all valid customary marriages entered into after the commencement of this Act, which comply with the provisions of this Act, are for all purposes recognized as marriages.

Section 4 provides that the spouses of a customary marriage have a duty to ensure that their marriage is registered.

---

10. Polygamy is the general term which refers to multiple partners in a marriage. Polygyny on the other hand, refers to the male partner having multiple wives.

Section 10 provides that no one who is a party to a marriage under the South African Law Marriage Act of 1961 (South African common law) may enter into a Customary Law marriage.

The Registration Act requires a Customary Law marriage to be registered within 3 months if the marriage was entered into after the Act came into effect. If the marriage was entered into before November, 2000, the parties have twelve months to register it. The Act requires both spouses, and at least one witness for each of the spouses' families, and/or the representative of each of the families to report for purposes of registration. The Act further provides that:

The prospective spouses must be above the age of 18 years.

Both prospective spouses must consent to the marriage.

The parents of a prospective spouse who is a minor must consent to the marriage. If either of the prospective spouses is a spouse in a civil marriage, a customary marriage cannot be entered into during the subsistence of the civil marriage.

Although there is no restriction on the number of customary marriages that a husband may enter into, no further customary marriage may be entered into unless an order of court regulating the future matrimonial property system of his marriages has been obtained.

b. The CEDAW Committee and Polygamy—
General Recommendation 21 of 1994

[...] 14. States parties' reports also disclose that polygamy is practised in a number of countries. Polygamous marriage contravenes a woman's right to equality with men, and can have such serious emotional and financial consequences for her and her dependants that such marriages ought to be discouraged and prohibited. The Committee notes with concern that some States parties, whose constitutions guarantee equal rights, permit polygamous marriage in accordance with personal or customary law. This violates the constitutional rights of women, and breaches the provisions of article 5 (a) of the Convention ...

16. A woman's right to choose a spouse and enter freely into marriage is central to her life and to her dignity and equality as a human being. An examination of States parties' reports discloses that there are countries which, on the basis of custom, religious beliefs or the ethnic origins of particular groups of people, permit forced marriages or remarriages. Other countries allow a woman's marriage to be arranged for payment or preferment and in others women's poverty forces them to marry foreign nationals for financial security. Subject to reasonable restrictions based for example on a woman's youth or consanguinity with her partner, a woman's right to choose when, if, and whom she will marry must be protected and enforced at law.[11]

Questions for Discussion

1. *What should African states do about polygamy? Even if they try to legislate it away, it is likely that the practice will still continue in the rural areas.*

---

11. *See* http://www.unhchr.ch/tbs/doc.nsf/(Symbol)/7030ccb2de3baae5c12563ee00648f1f?Open document [last visited May 22, 2011].

2. *Failure to register a Customary Law marriage in South Africa does not invalidate the marriage under the Registration Act. Should there be penalties for failing to register one's customary law marriage? Should the marriage be invalidated if it is not registered?*

3. *Does a registration requirement sufficiently protect women with regards to property distribution after the death of a spouse?*

---

4. Inheritance

Women cannot generally inherit under Customary Law, as an heir is regarded as someone who steps into the shoes of the deceased and assumes all of his liabilities and responsibilities as well as assets. The heir is generally obliged to maintain the deceased's wife or wives. The heir becomes head of the family group, thus in traditional Customary Law, the heir was always male. Countries in Africa have responded differently to the potential hardships the inability to inherit imposes on women. For example, in 2009 the South African Parliament enacted the Reform of Customary Law of Succession Act.[12] The Preamble of the Act acknowledged that "a widow in a customary marriage whose husband dies intestate does not enjoy adequate protection and benefit under the customary law of succession." Section 2 provides:

Modification of customary law of succession

2. (1) The estate or part of the estate of any person who is subject to customary law who dies after the commencement of this Act and whose estate does not devolve in terms of that person's will, must devolve in accordance with the law of intestate succession as regulated by the Intestate Succession Act, subject to subsection (2).

(2) In the application of the Intestate Succession Act—

(*a*) where the person referred to in subsection (1) is survived by a spouse, as well as a descendant, such a spouse must inherit a child's portion of the intestate estate or so much of the intestate estate as does not exceed in value the amount fixed from time to time by the Cabinet member responsible for the administration of justice by notice in the *Gazette*, whichever is the greater;

(*b*) a woman, other than the spouse of the deceased, with whom he had entered into a union in accordance with customary law for the purpose of providing children for his spouse's house must, if she survives him, be regarded as a descendant of the deceased;

(*c*) if the deceased was a woman who was married to another woman under customary law for the purpose of providing children for the deceased's house, that other woman must, if she survives the deceased, be regarded as a descendant of the deceased.

The union referred to in subsection 2(b) is known as the "sororate" union. If a man's wife cannot have children, her family may feel obliged to provide a woman (often the wife's sister) to the man so that children may be born of the union. The children are

---

12. Act No. 11 of 2009. *Available at* http://www.info.gov.za/view/DownloadFileAction?id=99544 [last visited May 22, 2011].

viewed as belonging to the infertile wife's "house." The Act also permits a woman married in accordance with Customary Law to dispose of property under a will.[13]

Zimbabwe has taken a different approach to the law of inheritance as seen in the much vilified case of *Magaya v. Magaya*.

a. *Magaya v. Magaya* — Zimbabwe Supreme Court (1999)[14]

Per Muchechetere JA (Gubbay CJ, Ebrahim and Sandura JJA concurring):

The Facts in the matter are that the deceased died intestate. He had two wives. The first wife was the mother of the appellant (born in 1941) and the second wife is the mother of the respondent (born in 1946). The first wife had only one child, the appellant, and it appears that the second wife had three children, the respondent and two other sons, namely Frank Shonhiwa Magaya (born in 1942) and Amidio Shonhiwa Magaya (born in 1950), The property in the deceased's estate included house number 767 Old Mahvuku in Harare (the said house) and some cattle at their communal home.

It is apparent from the above that the appellant is the eldest child of the deceased and is female, the respondent is not the eldest male child of the deceased. He, however, claimed the heirship because the eldest male child, Frank Shonhiwa Magaya, declined to claim the heirship on the ground that he was not able to look after the family.

Soon after the death of the deceased the appellant, with the support of her mother and three other relations, went to claim the heirship of the estate in the community court and it was granted to her. The respondent later discovered this and applied to the community court for the cancellation of the appointment on the ground that he and the other persons interested in the deceased's estate were not summoned to the hearing at which the appellant was appointed heir ... The appointment was duly cancelled and all interested parties were summoned to and did attend a new hearing on the matter on 14 October 1992. After hearing from the claimants, that is, the appellant and the respondent, and the other interested parties, the learned presiding magistrate awarded the heirship to the respondent. The learned magistrate stated the following in arriving at his decision:

> [...] The first claimant (the respondent) is not the first born son but the first born, Frank, refused to be appointed heir because he is not able to look after the family, and this is the view of all members of the family. There are only two Contestants, that is, (the respondent) and Venia. Venia is a lady [and] therefore cannot be appointed to (her) father's estate when *there is a man*. (emphasis per Muchechetere JA.)

The provisions of § 68(1) of the Act read as follows:

> 68(1) If any African who has contracted a marriage according to African law or custom or who, being unmarried, is the offspring of parents married according to African law or custom, dies intestate his estate shall be administered and distributed according to the customs and usages of the tribe or people to which he belonged. It was not in dispute that the deceased was an African who contracted his two marriages according to African law and custom. And it was taken for granted that the deceased belonged to the Shona tribal grouping in Zimbabwe.

---

13. Section 4.

14. Zimbabwe Supreme Court, February 16, 1999. *Available at* http://jurisafrica.org/docs/lawreports/Magaya%20v%20Magaya.judgment.pdf [last visited June 22, 2011].

It was also conceded that the Shona and Ndebele tribal groupings in Zimbabwe have broadly similar customs and usages on succession and inheritance. These, I gather, are similar to many tribal groupings in South Africa.

I therefore agree with what Bennett said at p 126 of his book entitled *Human Rights and African Customary Law* ...

> In customary law succession is intestate, universal and onerous. Upon the death of a family head his oldest son (if the deceased had more than one wife, it would normally be the oldest son of his first wife) succeeds to the status of the deceased. Emphasis on the term "status" implies that an heir inherits not only the deceased's property but also his responsibilities, in particular his duty to support surviving family dependants ...

What is common and clear from the above is that under the customary law of succession of the above tribes males are preferred to females as heirs. The said rule which prefers males to females as heir to the deceased's estates constitutes a prima facie discrimination against females and could therefore be a prima facie breach of the Constitution of Zimbabwe. See sub-§§ (1) and (2) of § 23 of the Constitution, which reads:

> *(1) Subject to the provisions of this section —*
>
> *(a) no law shall make any provision that is discriminatory either of itself or in. its effect; and*
>
> *(b) no person shall be treated in a discriminatory manner by any person acting by virtue of any written law or in the performance of the functions of any public office or any public authority.*
>
> *(2) For the purposes of subsection (1), a law shall be regarded as making a provision that is discriminatory and a person shall be regarded as having been treated in a discriminatory manner if, as a result of that law or treatment, persons of a particular description by race, tribe, place of origin, political opinions, colour or creed are prejudiced — (a) by being subjected to a condition, restriction or disability to which other persons of another such description are not made subject; — (b) by the according to persons of another such description of a privilege or advantage which is not accorded to persons of the first-mentioned description; and the imposition of that condition, restriction, or disability or the according of that privilege or advantage is wholly or mainly attributable to the description by race, tribe, place of origin, political opinions, colour or creed of the persons concerned.*

However, it seems to me that these provisions do not forbid discrimination based on sex. But even if they did on account of Zimbabwe's adherence to gender equality enshrined in international human rights instruments, there are exceptions to the provisions. The relevant exceptions are contained in sub-§ (3)(a) and (3)(b) of § 23 of the Constitution, which read as follows:

> *23(3) Nothing contained in any law shall be held to be in contravention of subsection (IX) to the extent that the law in question relates to any of the following matters — (a) adoption, marriage, divorce, burial, devolution of properly on death or other mailers of personal law; (b) the application of African customary law in any case involving Africans or an African and one or more persons who are not Africans where such persons have consented to the application of African customary law in that case ...' (emphasis per Muchechetere CJ.)*

In my understanding of the above provisions, matters involving succession are exempted from the discrimination provisions, firstly because they relate to 'devolution of property on death or other matters of personal law', and secondly in this case because they relate to customary law being applied between Africans, The application of customary law generally is sanctioned under s 89 of the Constitution....

[The court then went on to discuss the minority status of women under African Customary Law, and reviewed the provisions of the Legal Age of Majority Act which provided that everyone (even those subject to customary law) who attained the age of 18 should be considered a legal major.]

The question to consider is whether the 'disabilities' and 'discrimination' suffered by women under customary law were based on 'their perpetual minority', ... in a previous case, I came to the conclusion that they were not based on their perpetual minority but on the nature of African society, especially the patrilinial, matrilineal or bilateral nature of some of them, I reasoned that the concepts of 'minority' and 'majority' status were not known to African customary law but that they were common law concepts which, in my view, should only be used in customary law situations with great care. And I attempted to explain why allowing female children to inherit in a broadly patrilineal society, such as in the present case, would disrupt the African customary laws of that society ...

At the head of the family there was a patriarch, or a senior man, who exercised control over the property and lives of women and juniors. It is from this that the status of women is derived, ... The woman's status is therefore basically the same as that of any junior male in the family ...

In my understanding of African society, especially that of a patrilineal nature, the 'perpetual discrimination' against women stems mainly from the fact that women were always regarded as persons who would eventually leave their original family on marriage, after the payment of *roora/lobola*, to join the family of their husbands. It was reasoned that in their new situation—a member of the husband's family—they could not be heads of their original families as they were more likely to subject the interests of the original family to those of their new family. It was therefore reasoned that in their new situation they would not be able to look after the original family. It was also reasoned that the appointment of female heirs would be tantamount to diverting the property of the original family to that of her new family. This would most likely occur on the death, of a female heir. Then her property would be inherited by her children who would be members of her new family. This, in my view, would be a distortion of the principles underlying customary law of succession and inheritance ...

From the above it is clear that, in my view, the discrimination against women was not because of their 'minority' but mainly because of the consideration in African society which, amongst other factors, was to the effect that women were not able to look after their original family because of their commitment to the new family ...

[Allowing women to inherit would be] tantamount to giving them rights they never had under customary law. A woman, as is gathered from the above, had no rights under customary law to heirship, demanding payment of lobola (it never depended on her acceptance), or to contract a marriage under the Customary Marriages Act without the consent of her guardian and others ...

Whilst I am in total agreement with the submission that there is a need to advance gender equality in all spheres of society, I am of the view that great care must be taken when African customary law is under consideration. In the first instance, it must be recognized that customary law has long directed the way African people conducted their lives and the majority of Africans in Zimbabwe still live in rural areas and still conduct their lives in terms of customary law. In the circumstances, it will not readily be abandoned, especially by those such as senior males who stand to lose their positions of privilege ...

Despite having found that customary law obliged the heir to care for family members, within days of having been awarded his father's house by the Court, Amidio Magaya threw his sister into the street. She had purchased the house for her father and had been making the mortgage payments, yet she received no compensation for this and no support from her half brother. According to newspaper reports, she was left homeless and destitute.

Questions for Discussion

1. *Does the Customary Law system of succession/inheritance make sense in a society largely predicated on individual based rights? In a rural agricultural community, taking care of extended family members might be less costly, and there would be more social pressure in a small community to meet those kinds of obligations. Is it likely that if an heir fails to meet his Customary Law obligations of support to a woman, that the woman would bring a claim in court to enforce those obligations?*

2. *Justice Muchechetere noted that large numbers of people in rural areas still govern their lives in accordance with Customary Law. He thus felt it was not the role of the court to alter the tenets of Customary Law. What do you think of that argument? What should the role of the Court be in these kinds of cases?*

3. *What does it do for African women subject to Customary Law when the legislature enacts a law like the Age of Majority Act that purports to give women legal majority, and the Court finds that the Act does not apply to them? How would one determine whether the Act benefits one or not?*

Despite a Constitution that does not afford explicit protection from discrimination on the basis of sex, the Botswana High Court has chosen to advance the rights of women when confronted with gender discrimination in the form of citizenship laws favoring men:

b. *Unity Dow v. Attorney General Botswana* (1994)[15]

Per Amissah JP:

The Applicant Unity Dow is a citizen of Botswana having been born in Botswana of parents who are members of one of the indigenous tribes of Botswana. She is married to Peter Nathan Dow who although he has been in residence in Botswana for nearly 14 years is not a citizen of Botswana but a citizen of the United States of America.

Prior to their marriage on 7 March 1984 a child was born to them on 29 October, 1979 named Cheshe Maitumelo Dow and after the marriage two more children were born Tumisang Tad Dow born on 26 March 1985 and Natasha Selemo Dow born on 26 November 1987.

She states further in her founding affidavit that "my family and I have established our home in Raserura Ward in Mochudi and all the children regard that place and no other as their home."

---

15. Botswana Court of Appeals 1994 (6) BCLR 1. *Available at* http://www.elaw.org/node/2018 [last visited May 22, 2011].

In terms of the laws in force prior to the Citizenship Act of 1984 the daughter born before the marriage is a Botswana citizen and therefore a Motswana, whereas in terms of the Citizenship Act of 1984 the children born during the marriage are not citizens of Botswana (although children of the same parents), and are therefore aliens in the land of their birth. The respondent claimed that the provisions of the Citizenship Act of 1984 which denied citizenship to her two younger children were sections 4, 5. Those sections read as follows:

> 4(1) A person born in Botswana shall be a citizen of Botswana by birth and descent if, at the time of his birth: — (a) his father was a citizen of Botswana; or (b) in the case of a person born out of wedlock, his mother was a citizen of Botswana. (2) A person born before the commencement of this Act shall not be a citizen by virtue of this section unless he was a citizen at the time of such commencement.

> 5(1) A person born outside Botswana shall be a citizen of Botswana by descent if, at the time of his birth: (a) his father was a citizen of Botswana; (b) in the case of a person born out of wedlock, his mother was a citizen of Botswana. (2) A person born before the commencement of this Act shall not be a citizen by virtue of this section unless he was a citizen at the time of such commencement ...

The case which the respondent sought to establish and which was accepted by the Court a quo was captured by Paragraphs 13 to 15, and Paragraphs 18, 19, 21 and 22 of her founding affidavit. They read as follows:

> 13. I am prejudiced by the section 4(1) of the Citizenship Act by reason of my being female from passing citizenship to my two children Tumisang and Natasha.

> 14. I am precluded by the discriminatory effect of the said law in that my said children are aliens in the land of mine and their birth and thus enjoy limited rights and legal protections.

> 15. I verily believe that the discriminatory effect of the said sections, (4 and 5 supra) offend against section 3(a) of the Constitution of the Republic of Botswana. [...]

> 18. I am desirous of being afforded the same protection of the law as a male Botswana citizen and in this regard I am desirous that my children be accorded with Botswana citizenship ...

Since her children are only entitled to remain in Botswana if they are in possession of a residence permit and since they are not granted permits in their own right, their right to remain in Botswana is dependent upon their forming part of their father's residence permit....

[The Court went on to consider how the Constitution's guarantees of non discrimination should be interpreted.]

A written constitution is the legislation or compact which establishes the state itself. It paints in broad strokes on a large canvas the institutions of that state; allocating powers, defining relationships between such institutions and between the institutions and the people within the jurisdiction of the state, and between the people themselves. A constitution often provides for the protection of the rights and freedoms of the people, which rights and freedoms have thus to be respected in all further state action. The existence and powers of the institutions of state, therefore, depend on its terms. The rights and freedoms, where given by it, also depend on it. No institution can claim to be above the constitution; no person can make any such claim. The constitution contains not only the design and disposition of the powers of the state which is being established but embodies the hopes and aspirations of the people. It is a document of immense dimensions, portraying, as it does, the vision of the peoples' future. The makers of a constitution do not intend that it be amended as often as other legislation; indeed, it is not unusual for provisions of the constitution to be made amendable only by special procedures imposing more difficult forms and heavier majorities of the members of the legislature. By nature and definition, even when using ordinary prescriptions of statutory construction, it is impossible to consider a constitution of this nature on the same footing as any other legislation passed by a legislature which is itself established, with powers circumscribed, by the constitution ...

In Botswana, when the Constitution, in section 3, provides that 'every person ... is entitled to the fundamental rights and freedoms of the individual', and counts among these rights and freedoms 'the protection of the law', that fact must mean that, with all enjoying the rights and freedoms, the protection of the law given by the Constitution must be equal protection. Indeed, the appellant generously agreed that the provision in section 3 should be taken as conferring equal protection of the law on individuals. I see section 3 in that same light. That the word 'discrimination' is not mentioned in section 3, therefore, does not mean that discrimination, in the sense of unequal treatment, is not proscribed under the section....

If my reading of sections 3 to 16 of the Constitution is correct, and if section 3 provides, as I think, equal treatment to all save in so far as derogated from or limited by other sections, the question in this particular case is whether and how section 15 derogates from the rights and freedoms conferred by section 3(a) which requires equal protection of the law to all persons irrespective of sex.

The case made for the appellant in this respect is, to put it succinctly, that section 15 is the section of the Constitution which deals with discrimination; that, significantly, whereas section 3 confers rights and freedoms irrespective of sex, the word 'sex' is not mentioned among the identified categories in the definition of 'discriminatory' treatment in section 15(3); that the omission of sex is intentional and is made in order to permit legislation in Botswana which is discriminatory on grounds of sex; that discrimination on grounds of sex must be permitted in Botswana society as the society is patrilineal and, therefore, male oriented. The appellant accepts that the Citizenship Act 1984 is discriminatory, but this was intentionally made so in order to preserve the male orientation of the society; that Act, though discriminatory, was not actually intended to be so, it's real objective being to promote the male orientation of society and to avoid dual citizenship, the medium for achieving these ends being to make citizenship follow the descent of the child; and that even if the act were as a result discriminatory, it was not unconstitutional ...

It seems to me that the argument of the appellant was to some extent influenced by a premise that citizenship must necessarily follow the customary or traditional systems of the people. I do not think that view is supported by the development of the law relating to citizenship. Botswana as a sovereign republic dates from 30 September 1966. Before then persons who were within the territorial area which is now Botswana acquired their citizenship under British laws ...

By this, I understand that Botswana nationality in the sense of the identity of the Batswana people, which like the Poles would be a matter of descent, need not be the same as Botswana nationality in the sense of citizenship ...

As far as the present case is concerned, the more important prerequisite which each legislation must comply with is the requirement that the legislative formula chosen must not infringe the provisions of the Constitution. It cannot be correct that because the legislature is entitled to lay down the principles of citizenship, it should, in doing so, flout the provisions of the Constitution under which it operates. Where the legislature is confronted with passing a law on citizenship, its only course is to adopt a prescription which complies with the imperatives of the Constitution, especially those which confer fundamental rights to individuals in the State.

With those considerations in mind, I come now to deal with the central question, namely, whether section 15 of the Constitution allows discrimination on the ground of sex. The provisions of the section which are for the moment relevant to this issue are subsections (1), (2), (3) and (4). They state as follows:

15(1) Subject to the provisions of subsections (4), (5) and (7) of this section, no law shall make any provision that is discriminatory either of itself or in its effect.

(2) Subject to the provisions of subsections (6), (7) and (8) of this section, no person shall be treated in a discriminatory manner by any person acting by virtue of any written law or in the performance of the functions of any public office or any public authority.

(3) In this section, the expression 'discriminatory' means affording different treatment to different persons, attributable wholly or mainly to their respective descriptions by race, tribe, place of origin, political opinions, colour or creed whereby persons of one such description are subjected to disabilities or restrictions to which persons of another such description are not made subject or accorded privileges or advantages which are not accorded to persons of another such description.

(4) Subsection (1) of this section shall not apply to any law so far as that law makes provision—

a. for the appropriation of public revenues or other public funds;

b. with respect to persons who are not citizens of Botswana;

c. with respect to adoption, marriage, divorce, burial, devolution of property on death or other matters of personal law

d. for the application in the case of members of a particular race, community or tribe of customary law with respect to any matter whether to the exclusion of any law in respect to that matter which is applicable in the case of other persons or not; or

e. whereby persons of any such description as is mentioned in subsection (3) of this section may be subjected to any disability or restriction or may be accorded any privilege or advantage which, having regard to its nature and to special circumstances pertaining to these persons or to persons of any other such description, is reasonably justifiable in a democratic society.

Subsection (1) mandates that 'no law shall made any provision that is discriminatory either of itself or in its effect'. Subsection (2) mandates that 'no person shall be treated in a discriminatory manner by any person acting by virtue of any written law or in the performance of the functions of any public office or any public authority'. Subsection (3) then defines what discriminatory means in this section. It is 'affording different treatment to different persons, attributable wholly or mainly to their respective descriptions by race, tribe, place of origin, political opinions, colour or creed whereby persons of one such description are subjected to disabilities or restrictions to which persons of another such description are not made subject or accorded privileges or advantages which are not accorded to persons of another such description'. The word 'sex' is not included in the categories mentioned. According to the appellant, therefore, 'sex' had been intentionally omitted from the definition in section 15(3) of the Constitution so as to accommodate, subject to the fundamental rights protected by section 3 thereof, the patrilineal structure of Botswana society, in terms of the common law, the customary law, and statute law.

If that is so, the next question is whether the definition in section 15(3) in any way affects anything stated in section 3 of the Constitution. We must always bear in mind that section 3 confers on the individual the right to equal treatment of the law. That right is conferred irrespective of the person's sex. The definition in section 15(3) on the other hand is expressly stated to be valid 'in this section'. In that case, how can it be said that the right which is expressly conferred is abridged by a provision which in a definition for the purposes of another section of the Constitution merely omits to mention sex? I know of no principle of construction in law which says that a fundamental right conferred by the Constitution on an individual can be circumscribed by a definition in another section for the purposes of that other section. Giving the matter the most generous interpretation that I can muster, I find it surprising that such a limitation could be made, especially where the manner of limitation claimed is the omission of a word in a definition in that other section which is valid only for that section. What the legal position, however, is, is not that the Courts should give the matter a generous interpretation but that they should regard limitations to fundamental rights and freedoms strictly …

If the makers of the Constitution had intended that equal treatment of males and females be excepted from the application of subsections 15(1) or (2), I feel confident, after the examination of these provisions, that they would have adopted one of the express exclusion forms of words that they had used in this very same section and in the sister sections referred to. I would expect that, just as section 3 boldly states that every person is entitled to the protection of the law irrespective of sex, in other words giving a guarantee of equal protection, section 15 in some part would also say, again equally expressly, that for the purposes of maintaining the patrilineal structure of the society, or for whatever reason the framers of the Constitution thought necessary, discriminatory laws or treatment may be passed for or meted to men and women. Nowhere in the Constitution is this done …

I am fortified in this view by the fact that other classes or groups with respect to which discrimination would be unjust and inhuman and which, therefore, should have been included in the definition were not. A typical example is the disabled. Discrimination wholly or mainly attributable to them as a group as such would, in my view, offend as much against section 15 as discrimination against any group or class. Discrimination based wholly or mainly on language or geographical divisions within Botswana would similarly be offensive, although not mentioned.…

The upshot of this discourse is that in my judgment the Court a quo was right in holding that section 4 of the Citizenship Act infringes the fundamental rights and freedoms of the respondent conferred by sections 3 (on fundamental rights and freedoms of the individual), 14 (on protection of freedom of movement) and 15 (on protection from discrimination) of the Constitution.

F. The Approach Taken by the African Union

Member states of the African Union recently enacted *A Declaration of the Rights of Women* which encouraged member states to:

Article 2 — Elimination of Discrimination Against Women

1. States Parties shall combat all forms of discrimination against women through appropriate legislative, institutional and other measures. In this regard they shall:

a) include in their national constitutions and other legislative instruments, if not already done, the principle of equality between women and men and ensure its effective application;

b) enact and effectively implement appropriate legislative or regulatory measures, including those prohibiting and curbing all forms of discrimination particularly those harmful practices which endanger the health and general well-being of women;

c) integrate a gender perspective in their policy decisions, legislation, development plans, programmes and activities and in all other spheres of life;

d) take corrective and positive action in those areas where discrimination against women in law and in fact continues to exist;

e) support the local, national, regional and continental initiatives directed at eradicating all forms of discrimination against women.

2. States Parties shall commit themselves to modify the social and cultural patterns of conduct of women and men through public education, information, education and communication strategies, with a view to achieving the elimination of harmful cultural and traditional practices and all other practices which are based on the idea of the inferiority or the superiority of either of the sexes, or on stereotyped roles for women and men.

Article 6 — Marriage

States Parties shall ensure that women and men enjoy equal rights and are regarded as equal partners in marriage. They shall enact appropriate national legislative measures to guarantee that:

a) no marriage shall take place without the free and full consent of both parties;

b) the minimum age of marriage for women shall be 18 years;

c) monogamy is encouraged as the preferred form of marriage and that the rights of women in marriage and family, including in polygamous marital relationships are promoted and protected;

d) every marriage shall be recorded in writing and registered in accordance with national laws, in order to be legally recognised;

e) the husband and wife shall, by mutual agreement, choose their matrimonial regime and place of residence;

f) a married woman shall have the right to retain her maiden name, to use it as she pleases, jointly or separately with her husband's surname;

g) a woman shall have the right to retain her nationality or to acquire the nationality of her husband;

h) a woman and a man shall have equal rights, with respect to the nationality of their children except where this is contrary to a provision in national legislation or is contrary to national security interests;

i) a woman and a man shall jointly contribute to safeguarding the interests of the family, protecting and educating their children;

j) during her marriage, a woman shall have the right to acquire her own property and to administer and manage it freely.

Article 7 — Separation, Divorce and Annulment of Marriage

States Parties shall enact appropriate legislation to ensure that women and men enjoy the same rights in case of separation, divorce or annulment of marriage. In this regard, they shall ensure that:

a) separation, divorce or annulment of a marriage shall be effected by judicial order;

b) women and men shall have the same rights to seek separation, divorce or annulment of a marriage;

c) in case of separation, divorce or annulment of marriage, women and men shall have reciprocal rights and responsibilities towards their children. In any case, the interests of the children shall be given paramount importance;

d) in case of separation, divorce or annulment of marriage, women and men shall have the right to an equitable sharing of the joint property deriving from the marriage.

Chapter 13

Religious Practices and Women's Rights

Chapter Problem

Your client is a Muslim woman who dresses modestly and covers her hair in accordance with her interpretation of the tenets of her faith. She travels widely throughout Europe and the United States, and is concerned about the differing approaches to Islamic dress and veils that she has heard about. She wonders whether she might be prevented from wearing the veil, or alternatively be required to wear the veil in different parts of Europe, and has sought your counsel on what international human rights law has to say about religious practices—specifically the right to manifest one's religion—and women's rights.

Your client is also contemplating marriage to a Muslim man, who has urged that the two follow Shari'a (Islamic) law as their personal law, when they marry. Your client has sought your advice about what this means for her, specifically with regard to polygamy and divorce. She also wants to know if it is even an option to govern one's marriage in accordance with Shari'a law in parts of Europe and the U.S.

I. CEDAW and Religious Practices

Article 5

States Parties shall take all appropriate measures:

(a) To modify the social and cultural patterns of conduct of men and women, with a view to achieving the elimination of prejudices and customary and all other practices which are based on the idea of the inferiority or the superiority of either of the sexes or on stereotyped roles for men and women;

This problem involves two main issues, one relating to requirements of, and restrictions on dress—the other relating to personal law regulating marriage. Both issues require some knowledge of Islamic Law (*Shari'a*), as well as specific regulations related to Islamic dress and the enforcement of Islamic law in the United States and other countries.

II. The Islamic Requirement to Dress Modestly — Restrictions and Mandates

A. *Shari'a*

Shari'a literally means "the path." It is the body of Islamic law that regulates life for Muslims, who consider adherence to *Shari'a* to be a religious duty. *Shari'a* is derived from the Koran and the teachings of the prophet Mohammed found in the *Sunnah*. Sadiq Reza has argued:[1]

> Islam has no formal constitution or Bill of Rights; nor does its law, in theory at least, consist of a set of rules humans have devised to regulate their affairs. Rather, Islamic law — *sharia* ("path" or "way") — is God's law, set out by God for humans to acknowledge and obey in all matters and in His service. Some rules of government, civil society, and criminal law and procedure are within that law, but in no assigned place; they must instead be identified and extracted from a vast body of jurisprudence that is built upon the traditional sources, or "roots," of Islamic law. There are four such roots: the Quran, the Traditions, the consensus of scholars, and reasoning by analogy. The first two of these roots are textual and considered sacred: the *Quran*, seen as the divinely-revealed word of God, and the Traditions (*Sunna*), a record of authoritative sayings and actions of the prophet Muhammad. Also in the Traditions, but of lesser authority, are statements and actions of a revered group of Muhammad's contemporaries, the "Companions." The third and fourth sources of Islamic law constitute methods of adopting or articulating rules and norms that ostensibly find authority in the sacred texts; they operate much like precedent in common law, and gave rise in the early centuries of Islam to independent "schools" of law whose use and in-terpretations of the textual sources regularly differ. The result is a vast body of jurisprudence, articulated by individual scholar-jurists of one or another school of law and generally regarded by all schools as authoritative religious law.

One of the most contentious debates with regard to Islam is the question of whether women are required to veil. One of the verses in the *Qu'ran* that speaks to this issue states:

> Say to the believing men that they should lower their gaze and guard their modesty; that will make for greater purity for them; And Allah is well acquainted with all that they do. And say to the believing women that they should lower their gaze and guard their modesty and that they should not display their beauty and ornaments except what must ordinarily appear thereof; that they should draw their veils over their bosoms and do not display their beauty except to their husbands ...[2]

The verse has been interpreted in different ways. Some Muslims believe that it mandates that women veil, while others interpret as merely requiring both men and women to dress modestly. If one interprets the practice of Islam as requiring that women cover themselves, the question still remains of what kind of veil or head covering is required — one that covers the whole body (*burqa*), one that covers the face except for the eyes (*niqab*) or one

---

1. Sadiq Reza, *Islam's Fourth Amendment: Search and Seizure in Islamic Doctrine and Muslim Practice*, 40 GEO. J. INT'L L. 703, 710–11 (2009).

2. Qur'an 24:30–31.

that merely covers the hair (*hijab*). Aside from the fact that followers of Islam have to determine for themselves what is required by their religion, they must also determine what various laws say about the wearing of Islamic dress in public places.[3]

Hijab   Niqab   Burka

Generally the wearing of religious dress constitutes a manifestation of one's religion. When considering the legality of any restrictions on the right to practice and manifest one's religion, one must consider a number of international conventions, treaties, legislation and case law.

III. International Human Rights Law on the Manifestation of Religion

A. Article 9 of the European Convention on Human Rights

1. Everyone has the right to freedom of thought, conscience and religion; this right includes freedom to change his religion or belief, and freedom, either alone or in community with others and in public or private, to manifest his religion or belief, in worship, teaching, practice and observance.

2. Freedom to manifest one's religion or beliefs shall be subject only to such limitations as are prescribed by law and are necessary in a democratic society in the interests of public safety, for the protection of public order, health or morals, or the protection of the rights and freedoms of others

B. Article 18 of the International Covenant on Civil and Political Rights (ICCPR)

1. Everyone shall have the right to freedom of thought, conscience and religion. This right shall include freedom to have or to adopt a religion or belief of his

---

3. Drawings by Emma and Drew Venter. Used with permission.

choice, and freedom, either individually or in community with others and in public or private, to manifest his religion or belief in worship, observance, practice and teaching.

2. No one shall be subject to coercion which would impair his freedom to have or to adopt a religion or belief of his choice.

3. Freedom to manifest one's religion or beliefs may be subject only to such limitations as are prescribed by law and are necessary to protect public safety, order, health, or morals or the fundamental rights and freedoms of others....

Article 4

1. In time of public emergency which threatens the life of the nation and the existence of which is officially proclaimed, the States Parties to the present Covenant may take measures derogating from their obligations under the present Covenant to the extent strictly required by the exigencies of the situation, provided that such measures are not inconsistent with their other obligations under international law and do not involve discrimination solely on the ground of race, colour, sex, language, religion or social origin. No derogation from articles 6, 7, 8 (Paragraphs 1 and 2), 11, 15, 16 and 18 may be made under this provision. [...]

Article 27

In those States in which ethnic, religious or linguistic minorities exist, persons belonging to such minorities shall not be denied the right, in community with the other members of their group, to enjoy their own culture, to profess and practise their own religion, or to use their own language.

C. Article 15 of the International Covenant on Economic, Social and Cultural Rights (ICESCR)

1. The States Parties to the present Covenant recognize the right of everyone:

(a) To take part in cultural life; [...]

D. Article 5 of CEDAW

CEDAW does not deal directly with religious belief or manifestation, but requires that stereotyped roles for men and women be eliminated.[4]

E. Article 3(3) of the Arab Charter

Men and women are equal in respect of human dignity, rights and obligations within the framework of positive discrimination established in favour of women

---

4. Art. 5.

by the Islamic *Shari'ah*, other divine laws and by applicable laws and legal instruments.

Article 43:

Nothing in the Charter may be construed or interpreted as impairing the rights and freedoms protected by the domestic laws of the States parties or those set in force in international and regional human rights instruments which States parties have adopted or ratified, including the rights of women, the rights of the child and the rights of the persons belonging to minorities.

Questions for Discussion

1. *Consider the articles from the various Conventions set out above. Do they provide clear guidelines for states or individuals with regard to the right to manifest one's religious beliefs?*

2. *What do you think the Arab Charter means by "positive discrimination"?*

3. *Does the Arab Charter make* Shari'a *law subject to the provisions of treaties and Conventions like CEDAW?*

IV. The Headscarf Cases

A. *Leila Sahin v. Turkey*—European Court of Human Rights (2005)[5]

On 26 August 1997 the applicant, then in her fifth year at the Faculty of Medicine at Bursa University, enrolled at the Cerrahpaşa Faculty of Medicine at Istanbul University. She says that she wore the Islamic headscarf during the four years she spent studying medicine at the University of Bursa and continued to do so until February 1998.

On 23 February 1998 the Vice-Chancellor of Istanbul University issued a circular, the relevant part of which provides:

> By virtue of the Constitution, the law and regulations, and in accordance with the case-law of the Supreme Administrative Court and the European Commission of Human Rights and the resolutions adopted by the university administrative boards, students whose 'heads are covered' (who wear the Islamic headscarf) and students (including overseas students) with beards must not be admitted to lectures, courses or tutorials. Consequently, the name and number of any student with a beard or wearing the Islamic headscarf must not be added to the lists of registered students....

---

5. *Available at* http://portal.coe.ge/downloads/Judgments/LEYLA%20SAHIN%20v%20TURKEY.pdf [last visited May 17, 2011].

On 12 March 1998, in accordance with the aforementioned circular, the applicant was denied access by invigilators to a written examination on oncology because she was wearing the Islamic headscarf. On 20 March 1998 the secretariat of the chair of orthopaedic traumatology refused to allow her to enrol because she was wearing a headscarf. On 16 April 1998 she was refused admission to a neurology lecture and on 10 June 1998 to a written examination on public health, again for the same reason ...

In May 1998 disciplinary proceedings were brought against the applicant under Article 6(a) of the Students Disciplinary Procedure Rules (see Paragraph 50 below) as a result of her failure to comply with the rules on dress.

On 26 May 1998, in view of the fact that the applicant had shown by her actions that she intended to continue wearing the headscarf to lectures and/or tutorials, the dean of the faculty declared that her attitude and failure to comply with the rules on dress were not befitting of a student. He therefore decided to issue her with a warning.... On 13 April 1999, after hearing her representations, he suspended her from the university for a semester pursuant to Article 9(j) of the Students Disciplinary Procedure Rules ...

The relevant provisions of the Constitution provide:

Article 2

The Republic of Turkey is a democratic, secular (*laik*) and social State based on the rule of law that is respectful of human rights in a spirit of social peace, national solidarity and justice, adheres to the nationalism of Atatürk and is underpinned by the fundamental principles set out in the Preamble.

Article 10

All individuals shall be equal before the law without any distinction based on language, race, colour, sex, political opinion, philosophical belief, religion, membership of a religious sect or other similar grounds.

Men and women shall have equal rights. The State shall take action to achieve such equality in practice.

No privileges shall be granted to any individual, family, group or class.

State bodies and administrative authorities shall act in compliance with the principle of equality before the law in all circumstances ...

Article 13

Fundamental rights and freedoms may be restricted only by law and on the grounds set out in special provisions of the Constitution, provided always that the essence of such rights and freedoms must remain intact. Any such restriction shall not conflict with the letter or spirit of the Constitution or the requirements of a democratic, secular social order and shall comply with the principle of proportionality.

Article 14

The rights and freedoms set out in the Constitution may be not exercised with a view to undermining the territorial integrity of the State, the unity of the Nation or the democratic and secular Republic founded on human rights.

No provision of this Constitution shall be interpreted in a manner that would grant the State or individuals the right to engage in activities intended to destroy the fundamental rights and freedoms embodied in the Constitution or to restrict them beyond what is permitted by the Constitution....

Article 24

Everyone shall have the right to freedom of conscience, belief and religious conviction.

Prayers, worship and religious services shall be conducted freely, provided that they do not violate the provisions of Article 14.

No one shall be compelled to participate in prayers, worship or religious services or to reveal his or her religious beliefs and convictions; no one shall be censured or prosecuted for his religious beliefs or convictions....

Article 42

No one may be deprived of the right to instruction and education....

The Turkish Republic was founded on the principle that the State should be secular (*laik*)....

The defining feature of the Republican ideal was the presence of women in public life and their active participation in society. Consequently, the ideas that women should be freed from religious constraints and that society should be modernised had a common origin.

The first legislation to regulate dress was the Headgear Act of 28 November 1925 (Law no. 671), which treated dress as a modernity issue. Similarly, a ban was imposed on wearing religious attire other than in places of worship or at religious ceremonies, irrespective of the religion or belief concerned, by the Dress (Regulations) Act of 3 December 1934 (Law no. 2596). Under the Education Services (Merger) Act of 3 March 1924 (Law no. 430), religious schools were closed and all schools came under the control of the Ministry of Education. The Act is one of the laws with constitutional status that are protected by Article 174 of the Turkish Constitution.

In Turkey wearing the Islamic headscarf to school and university is a recent phenomenon which only really began to emerge in the 1980s. There has been extensive discussion on the issue and it continues to be the subject of lively debate in Turkish society. Those in favour of the headscarf see wearing it as a duty and/or a form of expression linked to religious identity. However, the supporters of secularism, who draw a distinction between the *başörtüsü* (traditional Anatolian headscarf, worn loosely) and the *türban* (tight, knotted headscarf hiding the hair and the throat), see the Islamic headscarf as a symbol of a political Islam.... The first piece of legislation on dress in institutions of higher education was a set of regulations issued by the Cabinet on 22 July 1981 requiring staff working for public organisations and institutions and personnel and female students at State institutions to wear ordinary, sober, modern dress. The regulations also provided that female members of staff and students should not wear veils in educational institutions.

On 20 December 1982 the Higher Education Authority issued a circular on the wearing of headscarves in institutions of higher education. The Islamic headscarf was banned in lecture theatres. In a judgment of 13 December 1984, the Supreme Administrative Court held that the regulations were lawful, noting: "Beyond being a mere innocent practice, wearing the headscarf is in the process of becoming the symbol of a vision that is contrary to the freedoms of women and the fundamental principles of the Republic." ... In a judgment of 7 March 1989 published in the Official Gazette of 5 July 1989, the Constitutional Court held that the aforementioned provision was contrary to Articles 2 (secularism), 10 (equality before the law) and 24 (freedom of religion) of the Constitution. It also found that it could not be reconciled with the principle of sexual equality implicit, *inter alia*, in republican and revolutionary values.

In their judgment, the Constitutional Court judges explained, firstly, that secularism had acquired constitutional status by reason of the historical experience of the country and the particularities of Islam compared to other religions; secularism was an essential condition for democracy and acted as a guarantor of freedom of religion and of equality before the law ...

[T]he Constitutional Court observed that freedom of religion, conscience and worship, which could not be equated with a right to wear any particular religious attire, guaranteed first and foremost the liberty to decide whether or not to follow a religion. It explained that, once outside the private sphere of individual conscience, freedom to manifest one's religion could be restricted on public-order grounds to defend the principle of secularism.

However, when a particular dress code was imposed on individuals by reference to a religion, the religion concerned was perceived and presented as a set of values that were incompatible with those of contemporary society. In addition, in Turkey, where the majority of the population were Muslims, presenting the wearing of the Islamic headscarf as a mandatory religious duty would result in discrimination between practising Muslims, non-practising Muslims and non-believers on grounds of dress with anyone who refused to wear the headscarf undoubtedly being regarded as opposed to religion or as non-religious.

Irrespective of whether the Islamic headscarf was a precept of Islam, granting legal recognition to a religious symbol of that type in institutions of higher education was not compatible with the principle that State education must be neutral, as it would be liable to generate conflicts between students with differing religious convictions or beliefs ...

For more than twenty years the place of the Islamic headscarf in State education has been the subject of debate across Europe. In Turkey, Azerbaijan and Albania it has concerned not just the question of individual liberty, but also the political meaning of the Islamic headscarf ...

[The Court then went on to consider headscarf laws in various European countries.]

In France, where secularism is regarded as one of the cornerstones of republican values, legislation was passed on 15 March 2004 regulating, in accordance with the principle of secularism, the wearing of signs or dress manifesting a religious affiliation in State primary and secondary schools ... In Germany, where the debate focused on whether teachers should be allowed to wear the Islamic headscarf, the Constitutional Court stated on 24 September 2003 in a case between a teacher and the *Land* of Baden-Württemberg that the lack of any express statutory prohibition meant that teachers were entitled to wear the headscarf. Consequently, it imposed a duty on the *Länder* to lay down rules on dress if they wished to prohibit the wearing of the Islamic headscarf in State schools.... In Sweden mandatory directives were issued in 2003 by the National Education Agency. These allow schools to prohibit the *burka* and *niqab*, provided they do so in a spirit of dialogue on the common values of equality of the sexes and respect for the democratic principle on which the education system is based.... In Austria there is no special legislation governing the wearing of the headscarf, turban or *kippa*. In general, it is considered that a ban on wearing the headscarf will only be justified if it poses a health or safety hazard for pupils.

In the United Kingdom a tolerant attitude is shown to pupils who wear religious signs. Difficulties with respect to the Islamic headscarf are rare.... In Finland and Sweden the veil can be worn at school. However, a distinction is made between the *burka* (the term used to describe the full veil covering the whole of the body and the face) and the *niqab* (a veil covering all the upper body with the exception of the eyes). In Sweden mandatory directives were issued in 2003 by the National Education Agency. These allow schools to prohibit the *burka* and *niqab*, provided they do so in a spirit of dialogue on the common values of equality of the sexes and respect for the democratic principle on which the education system is based.... In the Netherlands, where the question of the Islamic headscarf is considered from the standpoint of discrimination rather than of freedom of religion, it is generally tolerated. In 2003 a non-binding directive was issued. Schools may require pupils to wear a uniform provided that the rules are not discriminatory and are included in the school prospectus and that the punishment for transgressions is not disproportionate. A ban on the burka is regarded as justified by the need to be able to identify and communicate with pupils. In addition, the Equal Treatment Commission ruled in 1997 that a ban on wearing the veil during general lessons for safety reasons was not discriminatory.

THE LAW

I. ALLEGED VIOLATION OF ARTICLE 9 OF THE CONVENTION

The applicant submitted that the ban on wearing the Islamic headscarf in institutions of higher education constituted an unjustified interference with her right to freedom of religion, in particular, her right to manifest her religion.

She relied on Article 9 of the Convention, which provides:

> 1. Everyone has the right to freedom of thought, conscience and religion; this right includes freedom to change his religion or belief and freedom, either alone or in community with others and in public or private, to manifest his religion or belief, in worship, teaching, practice and observance.

Freedom to manifest one's religion or beliefs shall be subject only to such limitations as are prescribed by law and are necessary in a democratic society in the interests of public safety, for the protection of public order, health or morals, or for the protection of the rights and freedoms of others.

The Chamber judgment

The Chamber found that the Istanbul University regulations restricting the right to wear the Islamic headscarf and the measures taken thereunder had interfered with the applicant's right to manifest her religion. It went on to find that the interference was prescribed by law and pursued one of the legitimate aims set out in the second Paragraph of Article 9 of the Convention. It was justified in principle and proportionate to the aims pursued and could therefore be regarded as having been "necessary in a democratic society."

The Court's assessment

The Court must consider whether the applicant's right under Article 9 was interfered with and, if so, whether the interference was "prescribed by law", pursued a legitimate aim and was "necessary in a democratic society" within the meaning of Article 9 § 2 of the Convention.

The applicant said that her choice of dress had to be treated as obedience to a religious rule which she regarded as "recognised practice". She maintained that the restriction in issue, namely the rules on wearing the Islamic headscarf on university premises, was a clear interference with her right to freedom to manifest her religion.... The applicant said that, by wearing the headscarf, she was obeying a religious precept and thereby manifesting her desire to comply strictly with the duties imposed by the Islamic faith.

Accordingly, her decision to wear the headscarf may be regarded as motivated or inspired by a religion or belief and, without deciding whether such decisions are in every case taken to fulfil a religious duty, the Court proceeds on the assumption that the regulations in issue, which placed restrictions of place and manner on the right to wear the Islamic headscarf in universities, constituted an interference with the applicant's right to manifest her religion.

The Court reiterates its settled case-law that the expression "prescribed by law" requires firstly that the impugned measure should have a basis in domestic law....

[T]he Court finds that there was a legal basis for the interference in Turkish law, namely transitional section 17 of Law no. 2547 read in the light of the relevant case-law of the domestic courts. The law was also accessible and can be considered sufficiently precise in its terms to satisfy the requirement of foreseeability. It would have been clear to the applicant, from the moment she entered Istanbul University, that there were restrictions on wearing the Islamic headscarf on the university premises and, from 23 February 1998, that she was liable to be refused access to lectures and examinations if she continued to do so.

Legitimate aim

Having regard to the circumstances of the case and the terms of the domestic courts' decisions, the Court is able to accept that the impugned interference primarily pursued the legitimate aims of protecting the rights and freedoms of others and of protecting public order, a point which is not in issue between the parties.

"Necessary in a democratic society"

The Court reiterates that as enshrined in Article 9, freedom of thought, conscience and religion is one of the foundations of a "democratic society" within the meaning of the Convention ... That freedom entails, inter alia, freedom to hold or not to hold religious beliefs and to practise or not to practise a religion.... While religious freedom is primarily a matter of individual conscience, it also implies, inter alia, freedom to manifest one's religion, alone and in private, or in community with others, in public and within the circle of those whose faith one shares. Article 9 lists the various forms which manifestation of one's religion or belief may take, namely worship, teaching, practice and observance.

Article 9 does not protect every act motivated or inspired by a religion or belief (see, among many other authorities, *Kalaç v. Turkey*, judgment of 1 July 1997, ...)

In democratic societies, in which several religions coexist within one and the same population, it may be necessary to place restrictions on freedom to manifest one's religion or belief in order to reconcile the interests of the various groups and ensure that everyone's beliefs are respected ...

The Court has frequently emphasised the State's role as the neutral and impartial organiser of the exercise of various religions, faiths and beliefs, and stated that this role is conducive to public order, religious harmony and tolerance in a democratic society. It also considers that the State's duty of neutrality and impartiality is incompatible with any power on the State's part to assess the legitimacy of religious beliefs or the ways in which those beliefs are expressed ...

Where questions concerning the relationship between State and religions are at stake, on which opinion in a democratic society may reasonably differ widely, the role of the national decision-making body must be given special importance (see, *mutatis mutandis, Cha'are Shalom Ve Tsedek*, ...). This will notably be the case when it comes to regulating the wearing of religious symbols in educational institutions, especially ... in view of the diversity of the approaches taken by national authorities on the issue. It is not possible to discern throughout Europe a uniform conception of the significance of religion in … and the meaning or impact of the public expression of a religious belief will differ according to time and context (see, among other authorities, *Dahlab v. Switzerland*, no. 42393/98, ECHR 2001-V). Rules in this sphere will consequently vary from one country to another according to national traditions and the requirements imposed by the need to protect the rights and freedoms of others and to maintain public order (see, *mutatis mutandis*, *Wingrove*, cited above, p. 1957, § 57). Accordingly, the choice of the extent and form such regulations should take must inevitably be left up to a point to the State concerned, as it will depend on the specific domestic context …

This margin of appreciation goes hand in hand with a European supervision embracing both the law and the decisions applying it. The Court's task is to determine whether the measures taken at national level were justified in principle and proportionate … In delimiting the extent of the margin of appreciation in the present case, the Court must have regard to what is at stake, namely the need to protect the rights and freedoms of others, to preserve public order and to secure civil peace and true religious pluralism, which is vital to the survival of a democratic society … Consequently, it is established that institutions of higher education may regulate the manifestation of the rites and symbols of a religion by imposing restrictions as to the place and manner of such manifestation with the aim of ensuring peaceful coexistence between students of various faiths and thus protecting public order and the beliefs of others … the Court considers that, when examining the question of the Islamic headscarf in the Turkish context, it must be borne in mind the impact which wearing such a symbol, which is presented or perceived as a compulsory religious duty, may have on those who choose not to wear it.… The Court does not lose sight of the fact that there are extremist political movements in Turkey which seek to impose on society as a whole their religious symbols and conception of a society founded on religious precepts … It has previously said that *each Contracting State may, in accordance with the Convention provisions, take a stance against such political movements, based on its historical experience* … Having regard to the above background, it is the principle of secularism, as elucidated by the Constitutional Court … which is the paramount consideration underlying the ban on the wearing of religious symbols in universities. In such a context, where the values of pluralism, respect for the rights of others and, in particular, equality before the law of men and women are being taught and applied in practice, it is understandable that the relevant authorities should wish to preserve the secular nature of the institution concerned and so consider it contrary to such values to allow religious attire, including, as in the present case, the Islamic headscarf, to be worn. The Court must now determine whether in the instant case there was a reasonable relationship of proportionality between the means employed and the legitimate objectives pursued by the interference.

Like the Chamber … the Grand Chamber notes at the outset that it is common ground that practising Muslim students in Turkish universities are free, within the limits imposed by the constraints of educational organisation, to manifest their religion in accordance with habitual forms of Muslim observance.… Article 9 does not always guarantee the right to behave in a manner governed by a religious belief (see *Pichon and Sajous v. France* (dec.), no. 49853/99, ECHR 2001-X) and does not confer on people who do so the right to disregard rules that have proved to be justified.

Application of the foregoing principles to the present case

The interference in issue caused by the circular of 23 February 1998 imposing restrictions as to place and manner on the rights of students such as Ms. Şahin to wear the Islamic headscarf on university premises was, according to the Turkish courts ... based in particular on the two principles of secularism and equality.

In its judgment of 7 March 1989, the Constitutional Court stated that secularism, as the guarantor of democratic values, was the meeting point of liberty and equality. The principle prevented the State from manifesting a preference for a particular religion or belief; it thereby guided the State in its role of impartial arbiter, and necessarily entailed freedom of religion and conscience. It also served to protect the individual not only against arbitrary interference by the State but from external pressure from extremist movements. The Constitutional Court added that freedom to manifest one's religion could be restricted in order to defend those values and principles ...

As the Chamber rightly stated ... the Court considers this notion of secularism to be consistent with the values underpinning the Convention. It finds that upholding that principle, which is undoubtedly one of the fundamental principles of the Turkish State which are in harmony with the rule of law and respect for human rights, may be considered necessary to protect the democratic system in Turkey. An attitude which fails to respect that principle will not necessarily be accepted as being covered by the freedom to manifest one's religion and will not enjoy the protection of Article 9 of the Convention ...

After examining the parties' arguments, the Grand Chamber sees no good reason to depart from the approach taken by the Chamber ... as follows:

[...]The Court ... notes the emphasis placed in the Turkish constitutional system on the protection of the rights of women ... Gender equality—recognised by the European Court as one of the key principles underlying the Convention and a goal to be achieved by member States of the Council of Europe.

Consequently, the Court holds that there has been no violation of Articles 8, 10 or 14 of the Convention.

Dissenting Opinion of Judge Tulkens

As regards the general principles reiterated in the judgment there are points on which I strongly agree with the majority ... The right to freedom of religion guaranteed by Article 9 of the Convention is a "precious asset" not only for believers, but also for atheists, agnostics, sceptics and the unconcerned. It is true that Article 9 of the Convention does not protect every act motivated or inspired by a religion or belief and that in democratic societies, in which several religions co-exist, it may be necessary to place restrictions on freedom to manifest one's religion in order to reconcile the interests of the various groups and ensure that everyone's beliefs are respected ... Further, pluralism, tolerance and broadmindedness are hallmarks of a democratic society and this entails certain consequences. The first is that these ideals and values of a democratic society must also be based on dialogue and a spirit of compromise, which necessarily entails mutual concessions on the part of individuals. The second is that the role of the authorities in such circumstances is not to remove the cause of the tensions by eliminating pluralism, but, as the Court again reiterated only recently, to ensure that the competing groups tolerate each other.

Once the majority had accepted that the ban on wearing the Islamic headscarf on university premises constituted interference with the applicant's right under Article 9 of the Convention to manifest her religion, and that the ban was prescribed by law and pursued a legitimate aim—in this case the protection of the rights and freedom of others and of public order—the main issue became whether such interference was "necessary in a democratic society". Owing to its nature the Court's review must be conducted *in concreto*, in principle by reference to three criteria: firstly, whether the interference, which must be capable of *protecting the legitimate interest* that has been put at risk, was *appropriate*; secondly, whether the measure that has been chosen is the measure that is the *least restrictive* of the right or freedom concerned; and, lastly, whether the measure was *proportionate*, a question which entails a balancing of the competing interests. Underlying the majority's approach is the margin of appreciation which the national authorities are recognised as possessing and which reflects, inter alia, the notion that they are "better placed" to decide how best to discharge their Convention obligations in what is a sensitive area. I therefore entirely agree with the view that the Court must seek to reconcile universality and diversity and that it is not its role to express an opinion on any religious model whatsoever.

I would perhaps have been able to follow the margin-of-appreciation approach had two factors not drastically reduced its relevance in the instant case. The first concerns the argument the majority use to justify the width of the margin, namely the diversity of practice between the States on the issue of regulating the wearing of religious symbols in educational institutions and, thus, the lack of a European consensus in this sphere. The comparative-law materials do not allow of such a conclusion, as in none of the member States has the ban on wearing religious symbols extended to university education, which is intended for young adults, who are less amenable to pressure. The second factor concerns the European supervision that must accompany the margin of appreciation and which, even though less extensive than in cases in which the national authorities have no margin of appreciation, goes hand in hand with it. However, other than in connection with Turkey's specific historical background, European supervision seems quite simply to be absent from the judgment. However, the issue raised in the application, whose significance to the right to freedom of religion guaranteed by the Convention is evident, is not merely a "local" issue, but one of importance to all the member States. European supervision cannot, therefore, be escaped simply by invoking the margin of appreciation.

Religious freedom is, however, also a founding principle of democratic societies. Accordingly, the fact that the Grand Chamber recognised the force of the principle of secularism did not release it from its obligation to establish that the ban on wearing the Islamic headscarf to which the applicant was subject was necessary to secure compliance with that principle and, therefore, met a "pressing social need". Only indisputable facts and reasons whose legitimacy is beyond doubt — not mere worries or fears — are capable of satisfying that requirement and justifying interference with a right guaranteed by the Convention.... Merely wearing the headscarf cannot be associated with fundamentalism and it is vital to distinguish between those who wear the headscarf and "extremists" who seek to impose the headscarf as they do other religious symbols. Not all women who wear the headscarf are fundamentalists and there is nothing to suggest that the applicant held fundamentalist views. She is a young adult woman and a university student, and might reasonably be expected to have a heightened capacity to resist pressure, ...

The applicant's personal interest in exercising the right to freedom of religion and to manifest her religion by an external symbol cannot be wholly absorbed by the public interest in fighting extremism ...

The ban on wearing the headscarf is therefore seen as promoting equality between men and women. However, what, in fact, is the connection between the ban and sexual equality? The judgment does not say. Indeed, what is the signification of wearing the headscarf? As the German Constitutional Court noted in its judgment of 24 September 2003,[6] wearing the headscarf has no single meaning; it is a practice that is engaged in for

---

6. Federal Constitutional Court of Germany, judgment of the Second Division of 24 September 2003, 2BvR 1436/042.

a variety of reasons. It does not necessarily symbolise the submission of women to men and there are those who maintain that, in certain cases, it can even be a means of emancipating women. *What is lacking in this debate is the opinion of women, both those who wear the headscarf and those who choose not to.*

I fail to see how the principle of sexual equality can justify prohibiting a woman from following a practice which, in the absence of proof to the contrary, she must be taken to have freely adopted. *Equality and non-discrimination are subjective rights which must remain under the control of those who are entitled to benefit from them.* "Paternalism" of this sort runs counter to the case-law of the Court, which has developed a real right to personal autonomy on the basis of Article 8....

Questions for Discussion

1. *In this case the Court articulated the doctrine of the "margin of appreciation." The Court held that deference must be shown to a state in determining how to regulate manifestation of religion depending on the state's "particular domestic context." What is the likely outcome of the application of this doctrine in different states, given that states have differing domestic contexts?*

2. *The Court also took into account Turkey's commitment to* laik *(secularism). Does this mean that a country without an overt commitment to secularism would have to permit the wearing of a headscarf?*

3. *Is there necessarily a connection between what the Court termed "militant Islam" and the choice to wear a headscarf?*

4. *Does the headscarf signify the submission of women, or is an attempt to ban it "paternalistic," as Judge Tulkens suggested in her dissent?*

B. *Hudoyberganova v. Uzbekistan*— UN Human Rights Committee[7]

1. The author of the communication is Raihon Hudoyberganova, an Uzbek national born in 1978. She claims to be a victim of violations by Uzbekistan of her rights under articles 18 and 19 of the International Covenant on Civil and Political Rights. She is not represented by counsel.

The facts as presented by the author

2.1 Ms. Hudoyberganova was a student at the Farsi Department at the Faculty of languages of the Tashkent State Institute for Eastern Languages since 1995 and in 1996 she joined the newly created Islamic Affairs Department of the Institute. She explains that as a practicing Muslim, she dressed appropriately, in accordance with the tenets of her religion, and in her second year of studies started to wear a headscarf ("hijab"). According to her, since September 1997, the Institute administration began to seriously limit the right to freedom of belief of practicing Muslims. The existing prayer room was

---

7. *Available at* http://ap.ohchr.org/documents/dpage_e.aspx?m=86 [last visited May 11, 2011].

closed and when the students complained to the Institute's direction, the administration began to harass them. All students wearing the hijab were "invited" to leave the courses of the Institute and to study at the Tashkent Islamic Institute instead.

2.2 The author and the concerned students continued to attend the courses, but the teachers put more and more pressure on them. On 5 November 1997, following a new complaint to the Rector of the Institute alleging the infringement of their rights, the students' parents were convoked in Tashkent. Upon arrival, the author's father was told that Ms. Hudoyberganova was in touch with a dangerous religious group which could damage her and that she wore the hijab in the Institute and refused to leave her courses.... [O]n 1 December 1997 and the Deputy Dean on Ideological and Educational matters called her parents and complained about her attire; allegedly, following this she was threatened and there were attempts to prevent her from attending the lectures.

2.3 On 17 January 1998, she was informed that new regulations of the Institute have been adopted, under which students had no right to wear religious dress and she was requested to sign them. She signed them but wrote that she disagreed with the provisions which prohibited students from covering their faces. The next day, the Deputy Dean on Ideological and Educational matters called her to his office during a lecture and showed her the new regulations again and asked her to take off her headscarf. On 29 January the Deputy Dean called the author's parents and convoked them, allegedly because Ms. Hudoyberganova was excluded from the students' residence. On 20 February 1998, she was transferred from the Islamic Affairs Department to the Faculty of languages. She was told that the Islamic Department was closed, and that it was possible to re-open it only if the students concerned ceased wearing the hijab.

2.4 On 25 March 1998, the Dean of the Farsi Department informed the author of an Order by which the Rector had excluded her from the Institute. The decision was based on the author's alleged negative attitude towards the professors and on a violation of the provisions of the regulations of the Institute. She was told that if she changed her mind about the hijab, the order would be annulled.

2.5 As to the exhaustion of domestic remedies, the author explains that on 10 March 1998, she wrote to the Ministry of Education, with a request to stop the infringement of the law in the Institute; allegedly, the result was the loss of her student status on 15 March 1998. On 31 March 1998, she filed a complaint with the Rector, claiming that his decision was illegal. On 13 April 1998, she complained to the Chairman of the Committee of Religious Affairs (Cabinet of Ministers); on 22 April 1998, the Chairman advised her to respect the Institute's regulations. On 14 April 1998, she wrote to the Spiritual Directorate of the Muslims in Uzbekistan, but did not receive "any written reply". On 3 March and 13 and 15 April 1998, she wrote to the Minister of Education and on 11 May 1998, she was advised by the Deputy Minister to comply with the regulations of the Institute.

2.6 On 15 May 1998, a new law "On the Liberty of Conscience and Religious Organisations" entered into force. According to article 14, Uzbek nationals cannot wear religious dress in public places. The administration of the Institute informed the students that all those wearing the hijab would be expelled.

2.7 On 20 May 1998, the author filed a complaint with the Mirabadsky District Court (Tashkent), requesting to have her student rights restored. On 9 June 1998, the legal counsel of the Institute requested the court to order the author's arrest on the ground of the provisions of article 14 of the new law. Ms. Hudoyberganova's lawyer objected that this law violated human rights. According to the author, during the court's sitting on 16

June, her lawyer called on her behalf the lawyer of the Committee of Religious Affairs, who testified that the author's dresses did not constitute a cult dress.

2.8 On 30 June 1998, the Court dismissed the author's claim, allegedly on the ground of the provisions of article 14 of the Law on Freedom of Conscience and Religious Organizations.... The author then requested the General Prosecutor, the deputy Prime-Minister, and the Chairman of the Committee of Religious Affairs, to clarify the limits of the terms of "cult" (religious) dress, and was informed by the Committee that Islam does not prescribe a specific cult dress.

2.9 On 15 July 1998, the author filed an appeal against the District's court ... and on 10 September, the City Court upheld the decision. At the end of 1998 and in January 1999, she complained to the Parliament, to the President of the Republic, and to the Supreme Court; the Parliament and the President's administration transmitted her letters to the Supreme Court. On 3 February 1999 and on 23 March 1999, the Supreme Court informed her that it could find no reasons to challenge the courts' decisions in her case.

2.10 On 23 February 1999, she complained to the Ombudsman, and on 26 March 1999 received a copy of the reply to the Ombudsman of the Institute's Rector, where the Rector reiterated that Ms. Hudoyberganova constantly violated the Institute's regulations and behaved inappropriately with her professors, that her acts showed that she belonged to an extremist organisation of Wahabits, and that he had no reason to readmit her as student. On 12 April 1999, she complained to the Constitutional Court and was notified that it had no jurisdiction to deal with her case and that her claim had been channelled to the General Prosecutor's Office, which had forwarded it to the Tashkent Prosecutor's Office. On 30 June 1999, the Tashkent Prosecutor's Office informed her that there were no reasons to annul the court's rulings in her case. On 1 July 1999, she complained again to the General Prosecutor with a request to have her case examined. She received no reply.

The complaint

3. The author claims that she is a victim of violations of her rights under articles 18 and 19 of the Covenant, as she was excluded from University because she wore a headscarf for religious reasons and refused to remove it ...

The Human Rights Committee has considered the present communication in the light of all the information made available to it, as required under article 5, Paragraph 1, of the Optional Protocol.

6.2 The Committee has noted the author's claim that her right to freedom of thought, conscience and religion was violated as she was excluded from University because she refused to remove the headscarf that she wore in accordance with her beliefs. The Committee considers that the freedom to manifest one's religion encompasses the right to wear clothes or attire in public which is in conformity with the individual's faith or religion. Furthermore, it considers that to prevent a person from wearing religious clothing in public or private may constitute a violation of article 18, Paragraph 2, which prohibits any coercion that would impair the individual's freedom to have or adopt a religion. As reflected in the Committee's General Comment No. 22 (Para.5), policies or practices that have the same intention or effect as direct coercion, such as those restricting access to education, are inconsistent with article 18, Paragraph 2. It recalls, however, that the freedom to manifest one's religion or beliefs is not absolute and may be subject to limitations, which are prescribed by law and are necessary to protect public safety, order, health, or morals, or the fundamental rights and freedoms of others (article 18, Paragraph 3, of the Covenant). In the present case, the author's exclusion took place on 15 March 1998, and was based on the provisions of the Institute's new regulations. The

Committee notes that the State party has not invoked any specific ground for which the restriction imposed on the author would in its view be necessary in the meaning of article 18, Paragraph 3. Instead, the State party has sought to justify the expulsion of the author from University because of her refusal to comply with the ban. Neither the author nor the State party have specified what precise kind of attire the author wore and which was referred to as "hijab" by both parties. In the particular circumstances of the present case, and without either prejudging the right of a State party to limit expressions of religion and belief in the context of article 18 of the Covenant and duly taking into account the specifics of the context, or prejudging the right of academic institutions to adopt specific regulations relating to their own functioning, the Committee is led to conclude, in the absence of any justification provided by the State party, that there has been a violation of article 18, Paragraph 2.

7. The Human Rights Committee, acting under article 5, Paragraph 4, of the Optional Protocol to the Covenant, is of the view that the facts before it disclose a violation of article 18, Paragraph 2, of the Covenant.

8. In accordance with article 2, Paragraph 3 (a), of the Covenant, the State party is under an obligation to provide Ms. Hudoyberganova with an effective remedy. The State party is under an obligation to take measures to prevent similar violations in the future.

9. Bearing in mind that, by becoming a party to the Optional Protocol, the State party has recognized the competence of the Committee to determine whether there has been a violation of the Covenant or not and that, pursuant to article 2 of the Covenant, the State party has undertaken to ensure to all individuals within its territory or subject to its jurisdiction the rights recognized in the Covenant and to provide an effective and enforceable remedy in case a violation has been established, the Committee wishes to receive from the State party, within 90 days, information about the measures taken to give effect to the Committee's Views.

C. Report of the Special Rapporteur on Religious Freedom

In 2002, the Special Rapporteur on Religion produced a comprehensive report identifying the myriad ways in which religions and more precisely, the interpretation of religious tenets was used to rationalise and legitimise discrimination against women in both practice and law. The use of reservations played a key role in the legal disenfranchisement of women. The Special Rapporteur on Freedom of Religion and belief also noted that:

> varying interpretations of the same religion shows an urgent need for less ambiguous rules and principles. The issue is extremely delicate, but that should by no means deter us from confronting it. On the contrary, I believe that the longer we postpone tackling it, the greater the risk of embedding gender inequalities in the field of human rights.[8]

---

8. A. Jahangir, United Nations Special Rapporteur on Freedom of Religion or Belief, speech given at the Parliamentary Assembly of the Council of Europe. *Available at* http://assembly.coe.int/Main.asp?link=/Documents/Records/2005/E/0510041000E.htm#5t [last visited June 23, 2011].

Questions for Discussion

1. *The decision by the European Court of Human Rights in the* Sahin *case and the decision by the Human Rights Committee in* Hudoyberganova *seem to conflict. Can they be reconciled?*

2. *Does it matter what kind of head covering a person might wear? Should the courts distinguish between niqabs and hijabs?*

V. Current Efforts to Regulate Islamic Dress

A. Human Rights Watch Report— Enforcing Islamic Dress Code in Chechnya through Attacks and Harassment of Women[9]

In summer 2010 Human Rights Watch received reliable reports of attacks on and harassment of women in public places who did not dress according to the locally applied Islamic code. Coercion to force Chechen women to adhere to a compulsory Islamic dress code has manifested itself in a number of ways, including public shaming, threats, and even physical violence.

The incidents documented below took place from June through September 2010 in Grozny, Chechnya's capital.

June 2010: Paintball Attacks

In June 2010, Human Rights Watch received credible reports of individuals, including law enforcement agents, shooting pellets from paintball guns at women who were not wearing headscarves in the center of Grozny.... at least one of the victims was hospitalized as a result.

In September 2010, Human Rights Watch conducted interviews in Chechnya with two victims and three witnesses of paintball attacks.

A 25-year-old woman described her experience of being targeted in a paintball attack by men who, by their dress, appeared to be local security officials. She told a Human Rights Watch researcher:

I was walking down Putin Avenue [the main thoroughfare in Grozny] with a friend. It was a hot day in June—I don't remember the exact date. We were dressed modestly but not covered up—no headscarves, sleeves a little above the elbow, skirts a little below the knee. Suddenly a car with no license plates stops next to us. The side window rolls down and there is this gun barrel. I was paralyzed with fear and saw nothing but this

---

9. *Available at* http://www.hrw.org/en/node/97046/section/6 [last visited April 2, 2011]. (Internal citations omitted.)

barrel, this horrid black hole. I thought the gun was real and when I heard the shots I thought, "This is death." I felt something hitting me in the chest and was sort of thrown against the wall of a building. The sting was awful, as if my breasts were being pierced with a red-hot needle, but I wasn't fainting or anything and suddenly noticed some strange green splattering on the wall and this huge green stain was also expanding on my blouse. So, I understood it was paint.

[...] I was still trying to get myself together when a man's face appeared in the [car] window. He was laughing, then leaning out and pointing to us. He was dressed in this black uniform that Kadyrov's security people wear. And the men in the car with him— they also leaned out to snicker at us—also had those uniforms on ... It's only at home that I could examine the bruise and it was so huge and ugly. Since then, I don't dare leave home without a headscarf.

Another victim, a woman of 29, told a Human Rights Watch researcher that on June 6 she was walking down the same street in the afternoon with two other young women, all of them without headscarves, when two cars drove up to them. Bearded men in military-style black uniforms, who looked like law enforcement officials, shot at them from the cars' windows with pink and blue paint, screaming, "Cover your hair, harlots!" Male passersby applauded the attackers and yelled, "Serves you right for having no shame!"

[...] The woman also told Human Rights Watch that she personally knows 12 women who were subjected to paintball attacks that week in June. She also indicated that she wanted to make an official complaint to the prosecutor's office but her family and her work supervisor had talked her out of it, cautioning that such steps might result in serious repercussions for her and for her employer.

Another female resident of Grozny, aged 40, told Human Rights Watch that she witnessed two similar attacks against young girls without headscarves in the center of Grozny. Judging by the number of paintball attack stories that she personally heard from friends and relatives, she believed that "from 50 to 60" women fell victim to such attacks, although Human Rights Watch could not independently confirm this estimate. She also reported that after several days of frequent attacks, many of her friends who did not wear headscarves had put them on and ordered their daughters to do the same.

Concerns about personal security prompted the women we spoke with to wear headscarves. Threatening leaflets soon appeared in the streets of the Chechen capital, explaining to women that the paintball shootings were simply a preventive measure aimed at making them cover their hair—if they failed to cooperate, more "persuasive" means would be used. All of the women interviewed by Human Rights Watch unanimously interpreted this as a threat to use real weapons instead of paintball guns.

The leaflet, a copy of which Human Rights Watch examined, read as follows (bold and capital letters are reprinted as in the original document):

> Dear Sisters!
>
> We want to remind you that, in accordance with the rules and customs of Islam, every Chechen woman is **OBLIGED TO WEAR A HEADSCARF.**
>
> Are you not disgusted when you hear the indecent "compliments" and proposals that are addressed to you because you have dressed so provocatively and have not covered your head? **THINK ABOUT IT!!!**
>
> Today we have sprayed you with paint, but this is only a **WARNING!!! DON'T COMPEL US TO RESORT TO MORE PERSUASIVE MEASURES!!!"**

Numerous sources, including women's NGOs, reported to Human Rights Watch that the punitive paintball campaign ended in mid-June, likely due to the fact that its objective was achieved: for at least several weeks afterwards, women generally refrained from entering the city center without headscarves.

Commenting on the issue on the television station *Grozny* on July 3, 2010, Kadyrov expressed unambiguous approval of the lawless paintball attacks, claiming he was ready to "give an award" to the men who carried them out. He also stated that the targeted women deserved this treatment and that they should be so ashamed as to "disappear from the face of the earth." This comment amounts to open encouragement, at the highest level of the government of Chechnya, of the physical assault and public humiliation of women.

There is no evidence that federal authorities responded to Kadyrov's statement in any way.

Harassment and Additional Pressure during Ramadan and Beyond

Several weeks after the attacks subsided, some women cautiously began to appear in Grozny's center without headscarves. Around the start of Ramadan in mid-August, however, another punitive campaign began, targeting women not wearing headscarves and/or wearing clothes deemed too revealing.

In the first days of Ramadan, groups of men in traditional Islamic dress (consisting of loose pants and a tunic), claiming to represent the republic's Islamic High Council, started approaching women in the center of Grozny, publicly shaming them for violating Islamic modesty laws and handing out brochures with detailed description of appropriate Islamic dress for females. They instructed women to wear headscarves and to have their skirts well below the knee and sleeves well below the elbow. Chechen females were admonished:

> Dear sister in Islam! Today Chechnya wants to uphold decency and morality. Your dress, dear sister, should be a demonstration of your purity and your morality, but mainly of your faith. Your clothes and your morality preserve your honor and that of your relatives and parents!

The authors of the brochure, a copy of which was obtained by Human Rights Watch, also urged men to take charge of women's appearance:

> It has to be admitted, unfortunately, that a terrible picture is to be seen in the streets. We are not accusing women. The main fault belongs to the men. A woman won't lose her sense of reason if her husband doesn't [lose his]. Men, we need your help. Of all that we see, the worst is the way some women dress. But what is even more terrible is that the men folk allow their sisters, wives, and daughters to dress in this way and don't consider that it is wrong to do so.

The purported envoys from the Islamic High Council were soon joined in their efforts by aggressive young men who pulled on women's sleeves, skirts, and hair, touched the bare skin on their arms, accused them of being dressed like harlots, and made other humiliating remarks and gestures. This harassment persisted throughout the entire month of Ramadan, until mid-September. Dozens of victims and witnesses spoke about such incidents and confirmed this distinct pattern in their conversations with a Human Rights Watch researcher ...

In two cases reported to Human Rights Watch that occurred during Ramadan, law enforcement personnel harassed women for not adhering to the Islamic dress code. In the first case, a group of three police officers walked into a small grocery shop in Grozny and noticed that the woman behind the counter was not wearing a headscarf. They started screaming at her that she was a disgrace, and demanded the telephone number of her boss. They called the boss, demanded that she appear immediately, and instructed her to make sure her entire staff was "properly dressed" lest she face "serious problems."

In another case documented by Human Rights Watch, a 44-year-old woman, "Kheda" (not the woman's real name), described a humiliating attack that she witnessed in the center of Grozny at the end of August. Kheda was walking down Putin Avenue when she saw a group of seven to eight armed, bearded men in black uniforms drag a young woman towards a large garbage bin. The young woman, "Fatima" (not her real name), who had long, uncovered hair and wore a long, but clingy, dress, cried hysterically and tried to resist her attackers, flailing her arms and legs. The attackers were snickering and screaming that she was a slut and belonged in a garbage dump....

Several incidents that occurred after Ramadan indicate that the pressure to adhere to a strict Islamic code continued. For example, in mid-October 2010, a staff member from a local NGO working in the House of Print—a large building in the center of Grozny that houses numerous Chechen media outlets and organizations—called Human Rights Watch to report that on October 8, Ministry of Information officials had summoned all tenants to a meeting. During the meeting, women were specifically instructed that that they would not be allowed into the building unless their hair was fully covered with headscarves.

Several dozen women interviewed by Human Rights Watch in Chechnya told Human Rights Watch that they found the virtue campaign deeply offensive but could not protest openly, fearing for their own security as well as that of their relatives. One of them summed up the problem to a Human Rights Watch researcher in the following way:

It's so humiliating, but you have no other option—you have to put on the headscarf. If, say, they hit you, and that's not unlikely, then your brothers won't be able to leave it at that. They'll have to take action against the aggressors, who will just kill them. You dress according to their rules not so much out of fear for yourself, but to protect your family.

Response by Russia's Federal Authorities and Reaction of Chechen Officials

Federal authorities lodged a formal inquiry with the Chechen Ministry of Internal Affairs about the paintball attacks. However the response was to deny that such attacks had occurred and no further action was taken. Beyond this inquiry there is no publicly available evidence that Russia's federal authorities have taken any measures to respond to the unlawful polices regarding forced Islamic dress for women in Chechnya.

To his credit, on September 22, 2010, the Ombudsman of the Russian Federation, Vladimir Lukin, wrote to Russia's Deputy Prosecutor General, Ivan Sydoruk, demanding that he look into the reports of paintball attacks against women in Chechnya. The Ombudsman of Chechnya, Nurdi Nukhazhiev, denied that there had been any such attacks on women and stressed that his office had not received any complaints on the matter. Earlier, Ilias Matsiev, head of the Grozny mayor's press service, also denied any knowledge of these attacks.

However, in October 2010, the Federal Deputy Prosecutor General informed Lukin that in 2010 the Chechen law enforcement authorities had in fact received "three communications from citizens about women without traditional Islamic headdress being shot at by unknown men from paintball guns." However no criminal case was launched because a preliminary inquiry found the complaints lacked criminal content. According to Sydoruk, the Chechen Prosecutor's Office found the inquiry conducted by the Chechen Ministry of Internal Affairs to be incomplete and requested that the Minister look into the matter and discipline the servicemen responsible.

Sydoruk also assured Lukin that the Chechen prosecutor's office had examined a video of one of the attacks posted to the Internet and passed it on to the investigative authorities, instructing them to look into the possibility of opening a criminal investigation into hooliganism (Article 213 of Russia's Criminal Code). At this writing, Human Rights Watch is not aware of any criminal prosecutions for the attacks or disciplinary action against officials for failing to conduct a thorough inquiry into reports about the attacks.

B. The French *Burqa* Ban

France recently enacted a ban on wearing any garment in a public place which conceals the face (with limited exceptions). Although it is referred to in the press as the "*Burqa* Ban" its impact is directed at *niqabs* as well as *burqas.* The ban went into effect on April 11, 2011. France's President, Nicolas Sarkozy has said that the *burqa* is not a religious symbol, but rather a "sign of enslavement that is not welcome in the French Republic."[10]

> Article 1:
>
> No one may wear clothing designed to conceal one's face in public space.
>
> Article 2:
>
> Included in the definition of public space are public streets, places open to the public, and places offering public services.
>
> There are four exceptions to this prohibition:
>
> Covering prescribed by law;
>
> Covering authorized to protect the anonymity of the wearer (such as for people in the witness protection program);
>
> Covering justified by medical reasons;
>
> Coverings related to holiday purposes (disguises used for carnival, Santa Claus, etc.).

————————

Articles 3 prescribes that someone who covers his or her face in violation of this law is subject to a fine of 150 euros or community service, while Article 4 provides that someone who encourages or requires another person to cover her face may be subject to prison and a fine of 15,000 euros.

C. Other European Countries

Belgium's lower house of Parliament has passed a *burqa* ban, but the law must still go to the Senate. The city of Barcelona (Spain) has also passed such a ban. The Netherlands considered a *burqa* ban, but rejected the idea.

D. The United States

Although the freedom to manifest one's religion is an important constitutional right in the United States, it is not without its limitations as the following cases illustrate.

————————

10. Quoted in Alyssa Newcomb, *France to Become First European Country to Ban Burqa,* ABC News; *available at* http://abcnews.go.com/International/burqa-ban-effect-france/story?id=13344555 [last visited May 17, 2011].

1. *Freeman v. Florida DMV*

In 2003, the Florida Department of Motor Vehicles (DMV) refused to renew the driver's license of a woman, Sultaana Freeman, who refused to remove her niqab when having her picture taken for her license. The DMV had offered to take Freeman's picture in a private room so that she would not have to remove her niqab in public. She refused, and the DMV revoked her driver's license. Freeman then sued the DMV, asking the Court to declare the revocation of her driver's license unconstitutional, and ordering the DMV to reinstate it. The Court found that requiring the Plaintiff to lift her veil briefly in a private room did not impose a "substantial burden" on her right to exercise her religion, and moreover that the state had a "compelling state interest" of promoting public safety and security, and combating crime, in requiring picture identification documents.[11]

In a Michigan District Court case, a judge dismissed the small claims complaint of a woman disputing rental car charges when she refused to remove her niqab when testifying. Ginnah Muhammed's claim was dismissed because the judge felt that without seeing her face he could not make a determination about the veracity of her testimony.[12]

VI. *Shari'a* as Personal Law in Marriage

The idea of governing one's marriage in accordance with a personal law is not a new one. For example, many Catholics who wish to terminate their marriage seek annulments through the Catholic Church, as well as divorces in civil courts. Similarly, many Orthodox Jews regulate their marriages in accordance with Jewish laws and seek *Getts* from rabbis if they wish to divorce. Moreover, as we learned from the previous chapter, several countries specifically authorize in their Constitutions the use of personal law, such as African Customary Law.

In 2008, in Britain, the Archbishop of Canterbury caused a stir when he suggested that Muslims in Britain should be able to resolve disputes under *Shari'a* law before religious tribunals. Although lawmakers reacted with outrage, essentially that suggestion has gone into effect in England through the guise of *Shari'a* courts acting as arbitrators. Under the British Arbitration Act,[13] judgments rendered by *Shari'a* courts are enforced civilly as long as both parties agreed to binding arbitration.

The implementation of *Shari'a* law may be problematic. Nick Clegg, the leader of the Liberal Democratic Party in England has posited that "[e]quality before the law is part

---

11. *See* Freeman v. Florida Dept. of Highway Safety and Motor Vehicles, (2003) *available at* http://fl1.findlaw.com/news.findlaw.com/cnn/docs/religion/frmnfl60603opn.pdf [last visited May 16, 2011].

12. For a discussion of this case *see* Aaron J. Williams, *The Veiled Truth: Can the Credibility of Testimony of a Niqab Wearing Witness be Judged Without the Assistance of Facial Expressions?* 85 U. Detroit L. Rev. 273 (2008).

13. Arbitration Act 1996 c. 23 § 58 provides:

(1) Unless otherwise agreed by the parties, an award made by the tribunal pursuant to an arbitration agreement is final and binding both on the parties and on any persons claiming through or under them.

(2) This does not affect the right of a person to challenge the award by any available arbitral process of appeal or review or in accordance with the provisions of this Part.

of the glue that binds our society together. We cannot have a situation where there is one law for one person and different laws for another."[14] Many of the practices considered to be part of *Shari'a* are seen as discriminatory towards women. For example, polygyny[15] is generally recognized by *Shari'a*, which permits men to have up to four wives. Under some Islamic schools, the husband is entitled to custody of the children, and women face a greater hurdle in obtaining a divorce than men. Moreover, women do not receive an equitable distribution of the marital assets under *Shari'a*, although a woman is entitled to retain her *mahr* (dower), the amount paid by her husband on execution of the marriage contract. The wife is also generally only entitled to maintenance by the husband for a period after a few months after the divorce becomes final (this is known as the *iddat* period).

A. Polygamous Muslim Marriages

Polygamy appears to be permitted by the *Qu'ran*:

> If you fear that you shall not be able to deal justly with the orphans, marry women of your choice, two or three or four; but if you fear that you shall not be able to deal justly with them, then only one (*Qu'ran* 4:3).

Although polygamy is illegal in the United States, National Public Radio[16] recently aired a story describing how some Muslims practice polygamy in the United States by marrying one spouse under the civil law, and others in religious ceremonies that are not recognized by the state. Polygamy is generally banned in Europe, although de facto polygamous marriages exist, especially among immigrant communities. In contrast, several African countries recognize polygamous marriages. As noted in Chapter 12, the CEDAW Committee has urged an end to polygamy. Moreover, CEDAW Article 16 provides that:

> 1. States Parties shall take all appropriate measures to eliminate discrimination against women in all matters relating to marriage and family relations and in particular shall ensure, on a basis of equality of men and women:
>
> (a) The same right to enter into marriage;
>
> (b) The same right freely to choose a spouse and to enter into marriage only with their free and full consent;
>
> (c) The same rights and responsibilities during marriage and at its dissolution;
>
> (d) The same rights and responsibilities as parents, irrespective of their marital status, in matters relating to their children; in all cases the interests of the children shall be paramount;
>
> (e) The same rights to decide freely and responsibly on the number and spacing of their children and to have access to the information, education and means to enable them to exercise these rights;

---

14. *Quoted in* Ruth Gledhill & Phillip Webster, *Archbishop of Canterbury Argues for Islamic Law in Britain,* The Times (London) Feb. 8, 2008.

15. Although the word polygamy is commonly used to denote multiple partners in a marriage, the word polygyny more properly connotes the practice of one man having multiple wives.

16. NPR, Barbara Bradley Hagerty, *Some Muslims Quietly Engage in Polygamy. Available at* http://www.npr.org/templates/story/story.php?storyId=90857818 [last visited May 16, 2011].

(f) The same rights and responsibilities with regard to guardianship, wardship, trusteeship and adoption of children, or similar institutions where these concepts exist in national legislation; in all cases the interests of the children shall be paramount;

(g) The same personal rights as husband and wife, including the right to choose a family name, a profession and an occupation;

(h) The same rights for both spouses in respect of the ownership, acquisition, management, administration, enjoyment and disposition of property, whether free of charge or for a valuable consideration.

These rights are not always available to women under *Shari'a* law. The *Hassam* case, from the South African Constitutional Court, illustrates the precarious position that a woman who governs her marriage in accordance with *Shari'a* may find herself in, on termination of her marriage by death or dissolution.

1. *Hassam v. Jacobs (Master of the High Court) and Min. for Justice and Constitutional Development*[17] (South African Constitutional Court)

Nkabinde J.:

[T]he applicant was married to Mr. Ebrahim Hassam (the deceased) in accordance with Muslim rites. The deceased married a second wife, Mrs. Mariam Hassam, also according to Muslim rites without the applicant's knowledge or consent. The deceased died intestate in August 2001. His death certificate shows that he was "never married". The first respondent refused to regard the applicant as a spouse for the purposes of the [Intestate Succession] Act. The applicant approached the High Court and initially sought an order, among other things, entitling her to be recognised as a spouse and surviving spouse of the deceased for the purposes of the Act and the Maintenance of Surviving Spouses Act (Maintenance Act), respectively, and directing the executor of the deceased's estate to give effect to that recognition. The applicant also challenged the constitutional validity of section 1(4) of the Act. She maintained that the word "spouse" in that section should include a husband or wife married in terms of Muslim rites regardless of whether the marriage is monogamous or polygynous. By excluding her from the definition of "spouse" because she was party to a polygynous union, the applicant contended that the Act unfairly limits her right to religious freedom and equality before the law ...

The applicant's argument was largely devoted to the equality provisions in the Constitution. It was submitted that the facts clearly demonstrate unfair discrimination in respect of widows of polygynous Muslim marriages because a failure to include such widows within the ambit of the Act differentiates in three ways, ... [o]n the listed grounds of gender, marital status and religion ...

The applicant contended that there is no rational relationship between the differentiation in question and a legitimate governmental purpose proffered to validate it because the scheme in the Act confers benefits and imposes burdens unevenly ... The applicant further contended that the failure to interpret the word "spouse" so as to include widows whose marriages are celebrated in accordance with Muslim rites infringes the rights to freedom

---

17. South African Constitutional Court. *Available at* http://www.saflii.org/za/cases/ZACC/2009/19.pdf [last visited May 11, 2011].

of religion, conscience, belief and opinion, and to the enjoyment of culture under sections 15(1) and 31(1) of the Constitution, respectively.

This case, properly understood, is not concerned with the constitutional validity of polygynous marriages entered into in accordance with Muslim rites. The applicant advanced argument on sections 15, 30 and 31 of the Constitution. In the view I hold of the matter, it is not necessary to become entangled in the religious and cultural debates in this matter. It should also be emphasised that this judgment does not purport to incorporate any aspect of *Sharia* law into South African law....

The High Court found that the exclusion of spouses in polygynous Muslim marriages does not pass constitutional muster. I agree. The rights to equality before the law and to equal protection of the law are foundational. The Constitution, as the jurisprudence of this Court demonstrates, prohibits the breach of equality not by mere fact of difference but rather by that of discrimination. This nuance is of importance so that the concept of equality is not trivialised or reduced to a simple matter of difference.

The marriage between the applicant and the deceased, being polygynous, does not enjoy the status of a marriage under the Marriage Act. The Act differentiates between widows married in terms of the Marriage Act and those married in terms of Muslim rites; between widows in monogamous Muslim marriages and those in polygynous Muslim marriages; and between widows in polygynous customary marriages and those in polygynous Muslim marriages. The Act works to the detriment of Muslim women and not Muslim men.

I am satisfied that the Act differentiates between the groups outlined above.... [T]he question arises whether the differentiation amounts to discrimination on any of the listed grounds in section 9 of the Constitution. The answer is yes. As I have indicated above our jurisprudence on equality has made it clear that the nature of the discrimination must be analysed contextually and in the light of our history. It is clear that in the past, Muslim marriages, whether polygynous or not, were deprived of legal recognition for reasons which do not withstand constitutional scrutiny today. It bears emphasis that our Constitution not only tolerates but celebrates the diversity of our nation ...

The effect of the failure to afford the benefits of the Act to widows of polygynous Muslim marriages will generally cause widows significant and material disadvantage of the sort which it is the express purpose of our equality provision to avoid ... By discriminating against women in polygynous Muslim marriages on the grounds of religion, gender and marital status, the Act clearly reinforces a pattern of stereotyping and patriarchal practices that relegates women in these marriages to being unworthy of protection. Needless to say, by so discriminating against those women, the provisions in the Act conflict with the principle of gender equality which the Constitution strives to achieve. That cannot, and ought not, be countenanced in a society based on democratic values, social justice and fundamental human rights.

VII. *Shari'a* Law in the U.S.

A. *S.D. v. M.J.R.* (New Jersey Appellate Court 2010)

Plaintiff, S.D., appeals from the denial of a final restraining order following a finding of domestic violence. On appeal, she raises the following issues: ...

The Trial Court abused its discretion by finding that Defendant lacked the requisite intent to commit sexual assault based upon his religion. We reverse and remand for entry of a final restraining order.

I.

The record reflects that plaintiff, S.D., and defendant, M.J.R., are citizens of Morocco and adherents to the Muslim faith. They were wed in Morocco in an arranged marriage on July 31, 2008, when plaintiff was seventeen years old. The parties did not know each other prior to the marriage. On August 29, 2008, they came to New Jersey as the result of defendant's employment in this country as an accountant. They settled in Bayonne, where they were joined one month later by defendant's mother.

As plaintiff described it at trial, the acts of domestic abuse that underlie this action commenced on November 1, 2008, after three months of marriage. On that day, defendant requested that plaintiff, who did not know how to cook, prepare three Moroccan dishes for six guests to eat on the following morning. Plaintiff testified that she got up at 5:00 a.m. on the day of the visit and attempted to make two of the dishes, but neither was successful. She did not attempt the third. At 8:00 a.m., defendant arrived at the couple's apartment with his guests. He went into the kitchen, but nothing had been prepared. Defendant, angry, said to plaintiff, "I'm going to show you later on, not now, I'm not going to talk to you right now until the visitors leave." Approximately two hours later, the visitors departed. According to plaintiff:

> At that time I was sitting in my room. I was afraid. I was afraid, what is he going to do to me? ... and he said to me, now I'm going to start punishing you. So he started to pinch me all over my body. He would go — the pinching he would do it like a sensation with his fingers over circulation in my flesh, then he'd pull his fingers out.

> I felt he was enjoying hurting me.

When asked to describe specifically where defendant was pinching, plaintiff responded that the pinching took place on her breasts, under her arms, and around her thighs; that the pinches left bruises; and that some of the bruises remained at the time that a detective from the Hudson County Prosecutor's office took pictures of her body on November 22, 2008. The punishment continued for approximately one hour, during which time plaintiff was crying. Plaintiff testified that, while administering the punishment, defendant said "I am doing all that to correct you. You have to learn to do something." Nonetheless, plaintiff stated that she "kept all this inside of [her] and we started to live again together, normal life."

An additional incident took place on November 16, 2008. At approximately 3:00 p.m., defendant announced that he planned to have guests ... Plaintiff stated that the guests left at approximately midnight, and that defendant came into the bedroom between twelve and one.

> When he came in and he saw everything on the floor — so he entered and he came toward me and he took all my clothes off me. It was very cold day. I had two pants on. He said, what, you think you're going to escape my punishment to you? Let's see what we're going to do now.

> After that he took off all my clothes and he said the first — before we start punishing you, now you're nude. You have no clothes on. Even my underwear wasn't on. So I felt I was an animal, like an animal. So he said first of all, you

better go and pick [up] everything from the floor. Then he said, now we're going to start punishing you. Then he started to pinch my private area. And he was pinching ... my chest area. I was crying.

Additionally, plaintiff testified that defendant pulled her pubic hair.

Plaintiff stated that her vaginal area was very, very red and that it was hurting. Although she attempted to leave, defendant had locked the door. As a consequence, she attempted to lie on the other side of the bed. Plaintiff testified:

> He said to me, no, you can not go and sleep on the side of the bed. You're still my wife and you must do whatever I tell you to do. I want to hurt your flesh, I want to feel and know that you're still my wife. After that—he had sex with me and my vagina was very, very swollen and I was hurting so bad.

The judge then asked: "You told him that you did not wish to have ... intercourse, is that correct?" Plaintiff responded: "Of course because I was—I had so much pain down there." ... On the following morning, plaintiff asked defendant why he had done what he did. As she reported it, defendant responded

> [by] mak[ing] like a list and he would read the list and he started to say, okay, now you don't know how to cook, but there's other stuff you're going to do in the house, around the house. And when I come back from work, I will see—look at the list and see what you did and what you didn't do. Whatever you didn't do, I'm going to punish you the same way I punished you for the stuff that you didn't do before.

An additional incident occurred on November 22, 2008. Defendant, ... engaged in nonconsensual sex with plaintiff. Although plaintiff's mother-in-law and sister-in-law were in the apartment, and although plaintiff was crying throughout the episode, neither came to her assistance.

Defendant and his relatives then left the apartment,.... After defendant returned with his mother at approximately 4:00 p.m., plaintiff attempted to leave the apartment. However, defendant pulled her back into the bedroom and assaulted her by repeatedly slapping her face, causing her lip to swell and bleeding to occur. He then left the room, and plaintiff escaped without shoes or proper clothing through the ... window.

Once outside, plaintiff encountered a Pakistani woman from whom she requested shoes. Seeing plaintiff's condition, the woman called the police, who arrived shortly thereafter, along with an ambulance. Plaintiff was taken to Christ Hospital in Jersey City, where her injuries were treated, photographs were taken, and an attempt was made by detectives from the Hudson County Prosecutor's Office to interview her. However, she was too distraught to speak with them at length. Four of the photographs of plaintiff's body, introduced as exhibits at trial, appear in the appendix to defendant's brief. They depict bruising to both of plaintiff's breasts and to both of her thighs, as well as her swollen, bruised and abraded lips. Testimony of Detective Johanna Rak, the person who took the photographs, established that the remaining photographs disclosed injuries to plaintiff's left eye and right cheek. She testified that bruising appeared on plaintiff's breasts, thighs, and forearm. Additional police testimony established that there were stains on the pillow and sheets of plaintiff's and defendant's bed that appeared to be blood.

On the day of this episode, a domestic violence complaint was filed, and a temporary restraining order was issued. However, the action was later dismissed for lack of prosecution.

[T]he couple was persuaded to reconcile on the condition that defendant stop mistreating and cursing at plaintiff, that they move back to Morocco at the conclusion of defendant's employment, and that defendant obtain an apartment where the couple could live away from his mother. Plaintiff and defendant moved together into an apartment in Jersey City on January 15, 2009. Defendant's mother lived elsewhere.

However, on the night of the reconciliation, defendant again engaged in nonconsensual sex three times, and on succeeding days plaintiff stated that he engaged in further repeated instances of nonconsensual sex. According to plaintiff, during this period, she was deprived of food, she lacked a refrigerator and a phone, and she was left by her husband for many hours, alone.... On January 22, 2009, ... defendant forced plaintiff to have sex with him while she cried. Plaintiff testified that defendant always told her

> this is according to our religion. You are my wife, I c[an] do anything to you.
> The woman, she should submit and do anything I ask her to do.

After having sex, defendant took plaintiff to a travel agency to buy a ticket for her return to Morocco. However the ticket was not purchased, and the couple returned to the apartment. Once there, defendant threatened divorce, but nonetheless again engaged in nonconsensual sex while plaintiff cried. Later that day, defendant and his mother took plaintiff to the home of the Imam and, in the presence of the Imam, his wife, and defendant's mother, defendant verbally divorced plaintiff.[18]

Plaintiff remained at the Imam's house until January 25, 2009, at which time she filed a complaint in municipal court against defendant and obtained a temporary restraining order....

Plaintiff testified at the trial that she wanted a final restraining order because "I don't want anybody to interfere or push me back to him. So if I have the restraining order, that will protect me from him." Plaintiff testified additionally that she remained in fear of defendant. At the time of the domestic violence trial, a parallel criminal action was also pending ...

Testimony was additionally offered for the defense by the Imam ...

At the conclusion of this testimony, in response to the judge's questions, the Imam testified regarding Islamic law as it relates to sexual behavior. The Imam confirmed that a wife must comply with her husband's sexual demands, because the husband is prohibited from obtaining sexual satisfaction elsewhere. However, a husband was forbidden to approach his wife "like any animal." The Imam did not definitively answer whether, under Islamic law, a husband must stop his advances if his wife said "no." However, he acknowledged that New Jersey law considered coerced sex between married people to be rape.

On June 30, 2009, the judge rendered an oral opinion in the matter. He commenced his opinion by stating that plaintiff alleged that defendant engaged in conduct that constituted assault, criminal restraint, sexual assault, criminal sexual contact, and harassment under the Prevention of Domestic Violence Act. The judge found from his review of the evidence that plaintiff had proven by a preponderance of the evidence that defendant had engaged in harassment, pursuant to N.J.S.A. 2C:33-4b and c,[19] and assault.

---

18. The Imam testified that defendant divorced plaintiff on January 24, 2009, and called him to announce the fact shortly thereafter. Because plaintiff was pregnant, the divorce would not become effective until the child was delivered. If she had not been pregnant, the divorce would have become effective after three months if plaintiff's husband did not reconcile with her.

19. The statute provides in relevant part that:
   a person commits a petty disorderly persons offense if, with purpose to harass another, he: ...
      b. Subjects another to striking, kicking, shoving, or other offensive touching, or threatens

He found that plaintiff had not proven criminal restraint, sexual assault or criminal sexual contact. In finding assault to have occurred, the judge credited, as essentially uncontradicted, plaintiff's testimony regarding the events of November 1, 16 and 22, 2008. The judge based his findings of harassment on plaintiff's "clear proof" of the nonconsensual sex occurring during the three days in November and on the events of the night of January 15 to 16. He did not credit plaintiff's testimony of sexual assaults thereafter, since there was no corroboration in plaintiff's complaints to the police.[20] The judge also found no criminal restraint to have occurred.

While recognizing that defendant had engaged in sexual relations with plaintiff against her expressed wishes in November 2008 and on the night of January 15 to 16, 2009, the judge did not find sexual assault or criminal sexual conduct to have been proven. He stated:

> This court does not feel that, under the circumstances, that this defendant had a criminal desire to or intent to sexually assault or to sexually contact the plaintiff when he did. The court believes that he was operating under his belief that it is, as the husband, his desire to have sex when and whether he wanted to, was something that was consistent with his practices and it was something that was not prohibited.

After acknowledging that this was a case in which religious custom clashed with the law, and that under the law, plaintiff had a right to refuse defendant's advances, the judge found that defendant did not act with a criminal intent when he repeatedly insisted upon intercourse, despite plaintiff's contrary wishes.

Having found acts of domestic violence consisting of assault and harassment to have occurred, the judge turned to the issue of whether a final restraining order should be entered. He found such an order unnecessary, vacated the temporary restraints previously entered in the matter and dismissed plaintiff's domestic violence action. In doing so, the judge characterized November as a "bad patch" in the parties' marriage and plaintiff's injuries as "not severe." The judge then stated:

> [T]his is a case where there is no history of domestic violence. In fact, they have been—they were together for only three months. Then the bad patch was three weeks, and then another week.

> And then—and then, the record indicates that this defendant has filed for a divorce, he got divorced in—with the Imam, but the record indicates that he has filed for divorce in Morocco. This plaintiff has answered that complaint in Morocco. Divorce proceedings will occur in Morocco.

> The defendant has indicated that he is finished with the marriage. The parties are living separate and apart now. This defendant's visa expires in July, I believe.[21]

The judge therefore found that the parties had no reason to be together again, but immediately thereafter, he noted that their baby was expected in August and "[t]hat will require that the parties be in contact presumably." The judge then concluded:

---

to do so; or

    c. Engages in any other course of alarming conduct or of repeatedly committed acts with purpose to alarm or seriously annoy such other person.

20. In response to an objection by plaintiff's counsel, the judge later recognized that the police report upon which he relied in finding no corroboration for plaintiff's claims had not been admitted in evidence because of its hearsay nature. However, he declined to modify his ruling.

21. The judge indicated that plaintiff's visa status was unclear, because she was seeking to stay in the United States as a victim of domestic violence.

In this particular case, this court does not believe that a final restraining order is necessary under the circumstances. There's no need for the parties to be associated with one another. They are divorced now. They don't live together. They don't have to be together....

[T]his was a situation of a short-term marriage, a very brief period of physical assault by the defendant against the plaintiff and it's now a situation where the parties don't live together, won't be living together and won't have a need to be in contact with one another.

Nonetheless, the judge cautioned defendant not to have any contact with plaintiff and to instruct his family members and friends to have no further contact with plaintiff's family. Additionally, the judge acknowledged that the two would have to be involved in litigation over the baby and child support.

As a final matter, the judge recognized the pendency of a criminal action against defendant, and indicated its existence constituted an additional basis for the judge's ruling denying a final restraining order, since he assumed that a no-contact order had been entered as a condition of bail.

Plaintiff has appealed.

II.

The Supreme Court enunciated the standard of review for an appeal from a trial court's decision in a domestic violence case in *Cesare v. Cesare*, 154 N.J. 394 (1998). It stated:

The general rule is that findings by the trial court are binding on appeal when supported by adequate, substantial, credible evidence. Deference is especially appropriate "when the evidence is largely testimonial and involves questions of credibility." Because a trial court " 'hears the case, sees and observes the witnesses, [and] hears them testify,' it has a better perspective than a reviewing court in evaluating the veracity of witnesses." Therefore an appellate court should not disturb the "factual findings and legal conclusions of the trial judge unless [it is] convinced that they are so manifestly unsupported by or inconsistent with the competent, relevant and reasonably credible evidence as to offend the interests of justice." ...

Furthermore, matrimonial courts possess special expertise in the field of domestic relations.... Moreover, the [Prevention of Domestic Violence Act] specifically directs plaintiffs to file their domestic violence complaints with the Family Part of the Superior Court ...

Because of the family courts' special jurisdiction and expertise in family matters, appellate courts should accord deference to family court factfinding....

III.

[...] The New Jersey Prevention of Domestic Violence Act (PDVA), N.J.S.A. 2C:25-17-35, was enacted in its present form in 1991. In N.J.S.A. 2C:25-18, the Legislature set forth its findings and declaration, stating in relevant part:

The Legislature finds and declares that domestic violence is a serious crime against society; that there are thousands of persons in this State who are regularly beaten, tortured and in some cases even killed by their spouses or cohabitants;.... It is therefore, the intent of the Legislature to assure the victims of domestic violence the maximum protection from abuse the law can provide ...

> [I]t is the responsibility of the courts to protect victims of violence that occurs in a family or family-like setting by providing access to both emergent and long-term civil and criminal remedies and sanctions, and by ordering those remedies and sanctions that are available to assure the safety of the victims and the public.... It is further intended that the official response to domestic violence shall communicate the attitude that violent behavior will not be excused or tolerated, and shall make clear the fact that the existing criminal laws and civil remedies created under this act will be enforced without regard to the fact that the violence grows out of a domestic situation.

The PDVA defines "domestic violence" in N.J.S.A. 2C:25-19 to mean the infliction of one or more of an enumerated list of crimes upon a protected person. Among the crimes listed are assault, N.J.S.A. 2C:12-1; sexual assault, N.J.S.A. 2C:14-2; criminal sexual contact, N.J.S.A. 2C:14-3; and harassment, N.J.S.A. 2C:18-3.... [T]he judge shall consider, among other things, in making his dual decisions whether to find the occurrence of domestic violence and whether to issue a final restraining order, "(1) [t]he previous history of domestic violence between the plaintiff and defendant, including threats, harassment and physical abuse; (2) [t]he existence of immediate danger to person or property;" and other factors that are not relevant to the present proceeding. N.J.S.A. 2C:25-29a. The plaintiff must prove an act of domestic violence by a preponderance of the evidence ...

In the present matter, the judge found harassment and assault to have occurred, but declined to find sexual assault or criminal sexual contact, determining that the complained-of conduct occurred, but that defendant lacked the requisite criminal intent.

N.J.S.A. 2C:14-2c provides that "[a]n actor is guilty of sexual assault if he commits an act of sexual penetration with another person" under several circumstances, including when "[t]he actor uses physical force or coercion, but the victim does not sustain severe personal injury." N.J.S.A. 2C:14-2c(1). To establish physical force for the purposes of N.J.S.A. 2C:14-2, the plaintiff does not have to prove force in addition to "that necessary for penetration so long as the penetration was accomplished 'in the absence of what a reasonable person would believe to be affirmative and freely-given permission.'" *State v. Velasquez*, 391 *N.J. Super.* 291, 319 (App. Div. 2007) ... Testimony by plaintiff at trial adequately established the absence of freely given permission.

N.J.S.A. 2C:14-3b provides that "[a]n actor is guilty of criminal sexual contact if he commits an act of sexual contact with the victim under any of the circumstances set forth in section 2C:14-2c." "Sexual contact" is defined as "an intentional touching by the ... actor, either directly or through clothing, of the victim's ... intimate parts for the purpose of degrading or humiliating the victim or sexually arousing or sexually gratifying the actor." N.J.S.A. 2C:14-1. Neither the sexual assault statute nor the criminal sexual contact statute specifies the mental state that must be demonstrated in order to establish the defendant's criminal intent.

The trial judge found as a fact that defendant committed conduct that constituted a sexual assault and criminal sexual contact, but that defendant did not have the requisite criminal intent in doing so. His conclusion in this respect cannot be sustained. N.J.S.A. 2C:2-2c(3) establishes the principle that criminal statutes that do not designate a specific culpability requirement should be construed as requiring knowing conduct.

> A person acts knowingly with respect to the nature of his conduct or the attendant circumstances if he is aware that his conduct is of that nature, or that such circumstances exist ...

Defendant's conduct in engaging in nonconsensual sexual intercourse was unquestionably knowing, regardless of his view that his religion permitted him to act as he did.

[T]he case thus presents a conflict between the criminal law and religious precepts. In resolving this conflict, the judge determined to except defendant from the operation of the State's statutes as the result of his religious beliefs. In doing so, the judge was mistaken ...

Because it is doubtlessly true that the laws defining the crimes of sexual assault and criminal sexual contact are neutral laws of general application, and because defendant knowingly engaged in conduct that violated those laws, the judge erred when he refused to recognize those violations as a basis for a determination that defendant had committed acts of domestic violence.

In this context, we note, as well, the Legislature's recognition of the serious nature of domestic violence, the responsibility of the courts to protect victims of such violence and its directive that the remedies of the PDVA be broadly applied.... The Legislature's findings and declaration provide an additional basis for the rejection of the judge's view of defendant's acts as excused by his religious beliefs, and for a recognition of those acts as violative of New Jersey's laws.

IV.

Following a finding that a defendant has committed a predicate act of domestic violence, the judge is required to consider whether a restraining order should be entered that provides protection to the victim.

> Although this second determination—whether a domestic violence restraining order should be issued—is most often perfunctory and self-evident, the guiding standard is whether a restraining order is necessary, upon an evaluation of the factors set forth in N.J.S.A. 2C:25-29a(1) to -29a(6), to protect the victim from an immediate danger or to prevent further abuse....

In the present matter, the judge properly found that defendant had assaulted and harassed plaintiff in violation of the PDVA. However he declined to enter a final restraining order, determining that the domestic violence constituted merely a bad patch in a short-term marriage and did not result in serious injury to plaintiff, and that plaintiff and defendant had separated, a divorce proceeding was pending in Morocco, and the parties had no reason for further contact. Nonetheless, the judge recognized that contact between the parties would necessarily occur upon the birth of their child. The judge additionally appeared to be sufficiently concerned about the likelihood of renewed domestic violence to instruct defendant to have no contact with plaintiff. In this regard, he also relied upon the likelihood that a no contact order had been put in place as a condition of defendant's bail in the pending criminal proceedings against him arising from the acts of domestic violence that formed the basis for the civil action.

The judge's ruling raises several areas of concern that we regard as warranting reversal and a remand to permit the entry of a final restraining order. We construe the judge's characterization of the violence that took place as a bad patch in the parties' marriage and plaintiff's injuries as not severe as manifesting an unnecessarily dismissive view of defendant's acts of domestic violence. Although it is true that the November episodes spanned only three weeks, that period constituted approximately one-fourth of the parties' marriage. Moreover, we find it significant to the issue of whether a final restraining order should have been granted that the violence resumed on the very first night of the parties' reconciliation, and after defendant had assured the Imam that he would not engage in further such acts. We additionally note plaintiff's testimony that the significant bruising to her body shown on the photographs taken on November 22 merely represented the remnants of the bruising inflicted on November 1 and 16. In our view, the abuse that took place in this case was far removed from the domestic contretemps found not to constitute abuse in cases such as *Kamen v. Egan*, 322 N.J. Super. 222, 227–28 (App. Div. 1999).... We are also concerned that the judge's view of the facts of the matter may have been colored by his perception that, although defendant's sexual acts violated applicable criminal statutes, they were culturally acceptable and thus not actionable—a view that we have soundly rejected.

Viewing the evidence as a whole, we are satisfied that the judge was mistaken in determining not to issue a final restraining order in this matter in order to protect plaintiff from future abuse and in dismissing plaintiff's domestic violence complaint. We therefore reverse and remand the case for entry of such an order.

Reversed and remanded.

B. Efforts to Outlaw *Shari'a*

Intolerance towards *Shari'a* law appears to have grown in the United States in the wake of September 11. Tennessee and Oklahoma are examples of states that have proposed bans on *Shari'a* law in those states. The Tennessee Bill (Senate Bill 1028)[22] introduced in February, 2011 by State Senator Bill Ketron, defines *Shari'a* as a:

> legal-political-military doctrinal system combined with certain religious beliefs; ... (4) *Shari'a* as a political doctrine requires all its adherents to actively support the establishment of a political society based upon *Shari'a* as foundational or supreme law and the replacement of any political entity not governed by *Shari'a* with a *Shari'a* political order; (5) *Shari'a* requires all its adherents to actively and passively support the replacement of America's constitutional republic, including the representative government of this state with a political system based upon *Shari'a*; ... *Jihad* and *Shari'a* are inextricably linked, with *Shari'a* formulating and commanding *jihad*, and *jihad* being waged for the purpose of imposing and instituting *Shari'a*.

The Bill proposed that the Attorney General could designate organizations that support *Shari'a* as "*Shari'a* organizations." Anyone materially supporting such a designated *Shari'a* organization commits a class B felony punishable by up to fifteen years in prison.

C. State Question 755 (2010) — Oklahoma Ballot

On November 4, 2010, Oklahoma voters voted in favor of a legislatively referred constitutional amendment known as State Question 755, which purported to prohibit courts in Oklahoma from using international law or *Shari'a* law in their decisions. The ballot passed by a ratio of 7:3. On November 29, 2010 an injunction barring the law from taking effect was issued by the United States District Court. The ballot measure read as follows:

> This measure amends the State Constitution. It changes a section that deals with the courts of this state. It would amend Article 7, Section 1. It makes courts rely

---

22. *Available at* http://www.scribd.com/doc/49475739/SB1028-Outlawing-Sharia-law-in-Tennessee [last visited May 16, 2011].

on federal and state law when deciding cases. It forbids courts from considering or using international law. It forbids courts from considering or using *Shari'a* Law.

International law is also known as the law of nations. It deals with the conduct of international organizations and independent nations, such as countries, states and tribes. It deals with their relationship with each other. It also deals with some of their relationships with persons.

The law of nations is formed by the general assent of civilized nations. Sources of international law also include international agreements, as well as treaties.

Sharia Law is Islamic law. It is based on two principal sources, the Koran and the teaching of Mohammed.

Shall the proposal be approved?

For the proposal

Yes: _____

Against the proposal

No: _____

Questions for Discussion

1. Is there an appropriate role for using Shari'a *law as a personal law in marriage?*

2. Would outlawing Shari'a *violate one's religious freedom?*

3. Do the provisions of Shari'a *as described above violate the equality provisions of the Constitution? Is there any way that the courts could permit parties to use* Shari'a *as a personal law of marriage?*

Chapter 14

Obtaining Asylum on Gender Based Grounds

Chapter Problem

Imagine that you are a staff attorney in the Department of Justice's Office of Legal Counsel.[1] You have been asked to prepare a memorandum on policies related to granting women asylum status in the United States. In order to obtain asylum, applicants must be able to show that they face a well founded fear of being persecuted for reasons of race, religion, nationality, membership of a particular social group or political opinion. Because gender is not specifically listed as a protected category, many applicants with gender based claims file for asylum on the basis of their "membership in a social group." The Department would like you to explore the relationship between gender and this category in your Memorandum to obtain some clarity on how these categories may overlap.

Additionally, the Department has asked you to consider whether the United States' policies regarding gender-based claims provide adequate protection for women, and whether they are sufficiently gender sensitive.

I. CEDAW and Nationality

Article 9

1. States Parties shall grant women equal rights with men to acquire, change or retain their nationality. They shall ensure in particular that neither marriage to an alien nor change of nationality by the husband during marriage shall automatically change the nationality of the wife, render her stateless or force upon her the nationality of the husband.

2. States Parties shall grant women equal rights with men with respect to the nationality of their children.

---

1. The Office of Legal Counsel (OLC) exercises the Attorney General's authority under the Judiciary Act of 1789 to provide the President and executive agencies with advice on questions of law. *See* http://www.justice.gov/olc/preparation-opinions.html [last visited July 1, 2011].

II. International Human Rights Conventions Defining Refugees and Asylees

A determination whether someone qualifies as a refugee is made pursuant to the 1951 Convention Relating to the Status of Refugees, to which the United States is a party, subsequent treaties, and related U.S. legislation and case law. The Convention was drafted to address the plight of the many people displaced in the wake of World War II. It entered into force in 1954.

States and the international community have a great interest in ensuring that an individual does not become stateless. If an individual has been displaced from his or her own country, she becomes a refugee, and is entitled to protection under the 1951 Convention Relating to the Status of Refugees. If that individual flees to another state and seeks asylum from that state on the grounds that she is being persecuted on the basis of a criterion listed in the Convention, she is deemed an asylee. A refugee is an alien who is displaced abroad and his or her case is usually considered overseas. In contrast, an asylee is someone who enters a country of refuge, and once there applies for protection in the form of asylum.

A. The 1951 UN Convention Relating to the Status of Refugees

Article 1

Definition of the Term "Refugee"

A. For the purposes of the present Convention, the term "refugee" shall apply to any person who:

> (1) Has been considered a refugee under the Arrangements of 12 May 1926 and 30 June 1928 or under the Conventions of 28 October 1933 and 10 February 1938, the Protocol of 14 September 1939 or the Constitution of the International Refugee Organization;

> Decisions of non-eligibility taken by the International Refugee Organization during the period of its activities shall not prevent the status of refugee being accorded to persons who fulfil the conditions of Paragraph 2 of this section;

> (2) As a result of events occurring before 1 January 1951 and owing to well-founded fear of being persecuted for reasons of race, religion, nationality, membership of a particular social group or political opinion, is outside the country of his nationality and is unable or, owing to such fear, is unwilling to avail himself of the protection of that country; or who, not having a nationality and being outside the country of his former habitual residence as a result of such events, is unable or, owing to such fear, is unwilling to return to it.

> In the case of a person who has more than one nationality, the term "the country of his nationality" shall mean each of the countries of which he is a national, and a person shall not be deemed to be lacking the protection of

the country of his nationality if, without any valid reason based on well-founded fear, he has not availed himself of the protection of one of the countries of which he is a national.

B.(1) For the purposes of this Convention, the words "events occurring before 1 January 1951" in article 1, section A, shall be understood to mean either:

(a) "events occurring in Europe before 1 January 1951"; or

(b) "events occurring in Europe or elsewhere before 1 January 1951", and each Contracting State shall make a declaration at the time of signature, ratification or accession, specifying which of these meanings it applies for the purpose of its obligations under this Convention.

In 1967, the Convention was amended by a Protocol designed to extend the protections offered by the Convention to all refugees, not just those impacted by the Second World War. It thus removed the geographic and time limitations imposed by the original Convention. The Convention and Protocol have also been supplemented by various regional protections such as the Organization of African Unity Convention Governing the Specific Aspects of Refugee Problems in Africa (1969).[2]

B. The 1967 Protocol Relating to the Status of Refugees (the Refugee Protocol)

General Provision

1. The States Parties to the present Protocol undertake to apply articles 2 to 34 inclusive of the Convention to refugees as hereinafter defined.

2. For the purpose of the present Protocol, the term "refugee" shall, except as regards the application of Paragraph 3 of this article, mean any person within the definition of article 1 of the Convention as if the words "As a result of events occurring before 1 January 1951 and ..." "and the words" ..."a result of such events", in article 1 A (2) were omitted.

3. The present Protocol shall be applied by the States Parties hereto without any geographic limitation, save that existing declarations made by States already Parties to the Convention in accordance with article 1 B (1) (a) of the Convention, shall, unless extended under article 1 B (2) thereof, apply also under the present Protocol.

Co-operation of the National Authorities with the United Nations

1. The States Parties to the present Protocol undertake to co-operate with the Office of the United Nations High Commissioner for Refugees, or any other agency of the United Nations which may succeed it, in the exercise of its functions, and shall in particular facilitate its duty of supervising the application of the provisions of the present Protocol.

2. In order to enable the Office of the High Commissioner, or any other agency of the United Nations which may succeed it, to make reports to the competent organs of the United Nations, the States Parties to the present Protocol undertake

---

2. The Organization of African Unity is now known as the African Union.

to provide them with the information and statistical data requested, in the appropriate form, concerning:

(a) The condition of refugees;

(b) The implementation of the present Protocol;

I Laws, regulations and decrees which are, or may hereafter be, in force relating to refugees.

C. Reservation Filed by the United States to the 1967 Protocol

With the following reservations in respect of the application, in accordance with article I of the Protocol, of the Convention relating to the Status of Refugees, done at New York on 28 July 1951:

The United States of America construes Article 29 of the Convention as applying only to refugees who are resident in the United States and reserves the right to tax refugees who are not residents of the United States in accordance with its general rules relating to non-resident aliens.

The United States of America accepts the obligation of Paragraph 1 (b) of Article 24 of the Convention except insofar as that Paragraph may conflict in certain instances with any provisions of title II (old age, survivors' and disability insurance) or title XVIII (hospital and medical insurance for the aged) of the Social Security Act. As to any such provision, the United States will accord to refugees lawfully staying in its territory treatment no less favorable than is accorded aliens generally in the same circumstances.

———————

The United States went on to codify the provisions of the 1967 Protocol into U.S. law, by enacting the Refugee Act of 1980, which codified the definition of a refugee, and included provisions for asylum. The Act also instructed the Attorney General to establish uniform procedures for the treatment of asylum claims. It also created the possibility for asylees and refugees to be granted Legal Permanent Residence in the United States, provided that certain conditions were met.[3]

D. The Convention against Torture (CAT)

An asylee may also seek protection from deportation on the grounds that she or he faces torture should she be returned to her home country. This is known as a Convention Against Torture (CAT) claim, and is governed by CAT, to which the United States is a party. It is more of a temporary form of protection than the granting of asylum, as the removal of applicant may only be deferred until such time as the threat of torture ceases in the applicant's country, or if the applicant may be "removed" (deported) to a third country.

———————

3. The Immigration Act of 1999 amended the number of asylees that the United States would accept each year.

Article 1

1. For the purposes of this Convention, torture means any act by which severe pain or suffering, whether physical or mental, is intentionally inflicted on a person for such purposes as obtaining from him or a third person information or a confession, punishing him for an act he or a third person has committed or is suspected of having committed, or intimidating or coercing him or a third person, or for any reason based on discrimination of any kind, when such pain or suffering is inflicted by or at the instigation of or with the consent or acquiescence of a public official or other person acting in an official capacity. It does not include pain or suffering arising only from, inherent in or incidental to lawful sanctions....

Article 3

1. No State Party shall expel, return ("refouler") or extradite a person to another State where there are substantial grounds for believing that he would be in danger of being subjected to torture.

2. For the purpose of determining whether there are such grounds, the competent authorities shall take into account all relevant considerations including, where applicable, the existence in the State concerned of a consistent pattern of gross, flagrant or mass violations of human rights.

E. The UNHCR[4]

The United Nations Agency charged with monitoring and protecting refugees, is known as the Office of the United Nations High Commissioner for Refugees (UNHCR). The office was established in 1950, and it implements the Refugee Convention, and the Convention Relating to the Status of Stateless Persons (1954). It also periodically issues guidelines and reports on the state of the world's refugees, while offering practical assistance to displaced persons.

F. The Relationship and Agreement between the CEDAW Committee and UNHCR[5]

In June 2009, the UNHCR and CEDAW Committee held a joint seminar to examine the relevance of CEDAW to the protection of women of concern to the UNHCR. The two organizations agreed to strengthen their cooperation so that displaced women might avail themselves of the rights guaranteed by CEDAW. In the Summary of Proceedings, they noted:[6]

It was emphasized, however, that the obligations of States Parties to CEDAW encompassed all women within their territory, without distinction. Every State

---

4. For more information *see* http://www.unhcr.org/pages/49c3646c2.html [last visited May 31, 2011].

5. *See* the report *available at* http://www.unhcr.org/refworld/pdfid/4bac8e872.pdf [last visited July 20, 2011].

6. *Id.* at 14–15.

Party needs to be aware that they could be held responsible for the treatment of women within their jurisdiction, regardless of their origin or legal status. It was therefore noted that the Committee needed to remind States Parties of their obligation to comply with and implement the standards set out in the Convention.

Two groups were identified as particularly vulnerable, for whom effective State protection was often lacking. The first group was that of older women, who might have little or no knowledge as to how to claim their rights, especially if they were from rural areas. These women were also likely to face special hardship when fleeing to safety, and could confront additional challenges when presenting their asylum-claims. They were also often at risk of violence. The second group was that of trafficked women, who might not be recognized as such by the recipient country. They could, however, be in need of international protection, having a well-founded fear of returning to their country of origin. Women being trafficked were not always aware of the possibility of seeking asylum, and it was important that this option should be signaled to them as part of identification and referral systems. Trafficked women could also be at risk of becoming stateless if their documents were confiscated. It was reiterated that UNHCR needs to make efforts to reflect the statelessness dimension of trafficking in its confidential comments. It was also suggested to raise this in a General Recommendation.

G. Asylum and Gender

In the wake of the drafting of the Refugee Convention and the subsequent Protocol, it was often assumed by governments that the typical asylum seeker would be a male who had been imprisoned or tortured by the state for dissident acts. Thus policy makers drafted guidelines and formulated policies based on this assumption without much, if any consideration of gender concerns. Lawmakers and immigration officials were often slow to recognize gender based asylum claims. If a woman expressed political dissent, suffered persecution and then sought asylum, the woman's actions was often seen more as a form of personal rebellion— merely a woman chafing against societal conventions and strictures that were attempting to restrict her behavior; women were thus less likely to be granted asylum.

Moreover, women who had suffered torture at the hands of the state were often reluctant to testify against their accusers, especially if the torture they had suffered involved any acts that were of a sexual nature. Added to this, if a woman had suffered persecution at the hands of a private citizen or group, she often had little recourse under asylum or refugee laws, as chances of obtaining asylum are greatly increased if the country of origin of the asylum seeker is one known to perpetrate human rights violations against its citizens.

Considering that 80% of the world's displaced people are women and children, developing a gendered approach to asylum and refugee law became a necessity. In 1985, the Executive Committee of the UNHCR concluded that states:

> are free to adopt the interpretation that women asylum seekers who face harsh or inhuman treatment due to their having transgressed the social mores of the society in which they live may be considered as a 'particular social group' within the meaning of Article 1 A(2) of the 1951 United Nations Refugee Convention.[7]

---

7. United Nations High Commissioner for Refugees, *Executive Committee Conclusion No. 39 Refugee Women and International Protection*, 1985.

In 1993, the UNHCR Executive Committee adopted a further resolution on the evidentiary procedures used by states for determination purposes. The resolution noted that asylum seekers who had suffered sexual violence should be treated with particular sensitivity, and recommended the establishment of training programs designed to ensure that those involved in the determination process were adequately sensitized to issues of gender and culture. Canada became the first country to produce guidelines on the inclusion of gender as a "social group" in 1993. The *Beijing Declaration* and *Platform for Action*, urged representatives to:

> consider recognizing as refugees those women whose claim to refugee status is based upon the well-founded fear of persecution ... including persecution through sexual violence or other gender-related persecution.

In 1998, the UN Special Rapporteur on Violence against Women reiterated this call, urging parties to the Refugee Convention to "adopt guidelines with respect to gender-related asylum claims."

III. Asylum Law in the United States

As a party to the 1951 Convention, the U.S. has basically incorporated the definition from the Convention into its domestic law through the Immigration and Nationality Act.[8]

A. The Immigration and Nationality Act[9]

Section 101(a)(42)(A) of the Immigration and Nationality Act provides that: The term "refugee" means:

> (A) any person who is outside any country of such person's nationality or, in the case of a person having no nationality, is outside any country in which such person last habitually resided, and who is unable or unwilling to return to, and is unable or unwilling to avail himself or herself of the protection of, that country because of persecution or a well-founded fear of persecution on account of race, religion, nationality, membership in a particular social group, or political opinion, or

> (B) in such circumstances as the President after appropriate consultation (as defined in section 207(e) of this Act) may specify, any person who is within the country of such person's nationality or, in the case of a person having no nationality, within the country in which such person is habitually residing, and who is persecuted or who has a well-founded fear of persecution on account of race, religion, nationality, membership in a particular social group, or political opinion. The term "refugee" does not include any person who ordered, incited, assisted, or otherwise participated in the persecution of any person on account of race, religion, nationality, membership in a particular social group, or political opinion. For purposes of determinations under this Act, a person who has been

---

8. 8 U.S.C. § 1158.
9. 8 U.S.C. § 1158.

forced to abort a pregnancy or to undergo involuntary sterilization, or who has been persecuted for failure or refusal to undergo such a procedure or for other resistance to a coercive population control program, shall be deemed to have been persecuted on account of political opinion, and a person who has a well founded fear that he or she will be forced to undergo such a procedure or subject to persecution for such failure, refusal, or resistance shall be deemed to have a well founded fear of persecution on account of political opinion.[10]

The Statute has been supplemented by agency regulations. The Immigration and Nationality Act (INA) makes it clear that the Attorney General can exercise discretion in the granting of asylum.

Questions for Discussion

1. *The protections put in place for refugees and asylees are fairly old. Do you think that there are new circumstances and considerations which would justify a review of the Refugee Convention and Protocol, or are the criteria they articulate sufficiently flexible to permit the granting of asylum in varying circumstances?*

2. *How broad a discretion should the Attorney General have with respect to granting asylum?*

3. *One of the recent changes to Asylum law in the U.S. is that asylees are now required to petition for asylum within one year of entering the U.S. Do you think this is a reasonable requirement?*

B. Granting Asylum on the Basis of Forced Sterilization

The INA makes it clear that an asylee may be granted asylum based on her refusal to undergo forced sterilization. In a recent case, the Third Circuit Court of Appeals extended this form of protection to the spouse of an applicant.

1. *Chen v. Attorney General* (3d Circuit Court of Appeals 2007)[11]

This petition requires us to decide whether a husband may qualify for asylum on the well-founded fear that his wife may be persecuted under a coercive population control policy, a question of first impression in this Court. We hold that the husband may stand in his wife's shoes to bring such a claim. On the merits, we will grant the petition for review on Petitioner Chen's asylum claim ...

---

10. The Illegal Immigrant Reform and Responsibility Act of 1996 made some changes to the asylum process, including imposing time limitations on applying for asylum.

11. *Available at* http://caselaw.findlaw.com/us-3rd-circuit/1363503.html [last visited July 20, 2011].

The BIA's interpretation [in the *C-Y-Z-*case where it granted asylum to the spouse of an applicant who had been coercively sterilized] stems from its conclusion that, when one spouse is subjected to forced abortion or sterilization, it "naturally and predictably has a profound impact on both parties to the marriage." *Id.* The Board offers three principal explanations for this conclusion: First, that the forced abortion and sterilization "depriv[e] a couple of the natural fruits of conjugal life, and the society and comfort of the child or children that might eventually have been born to them." *Id.* (quoting *Matter of Y-T-L-*, 23 I. & N. Dec. 601, 607 (BIA 2003)). Second, that the husband "suffers emotional and sympathetic harm arising from his spouse's mistreatment and the infringement on their shared reproductive rights." *Id.* (citing our opinion in *Cai Luan Chen*, 381 F.3d at 225–226). And third, that in China, "such Government action is explicitly directed against both husband and wife for violation of the Government-imposed family planning law and amounts to persecution of both parties to the marriage." *Id.* As the BIA makes clear in *S-L-L-*, the *C-Y-Z-* rule would not apply in the hypothetical case where the spouse does not oppose the forced abortion or involuntary sterilization of his wife. *Id.* at 8. Where the *C-Y-Z-* rule does apply, it allows the forced abortion or involuntary sterilization of one spouse to be imputed to the other spouse.

We conclude that the BIA has exercised its delegated gap-filling authority reasonably. In a great many cases, forced abortion or involuntary sterilization of one spouse will directly affect the reproductive opportunities of the other spouse, and so the BIA is not unreasonable in considering the loss to the second spouse of the "natural fruits of conjugal life, and the society and comfort of the child or children that might eventually have been born to [him]." *S-L-L-*, 24 I. & N. Dec. at 7. And persecution of one spouse can be one of the most potent and cruel ways of hurting the other spouse-so the BIA's emphasis of "sympathetic harm" is not misplaced. *Id.* It also is not unreasonable for the BIA to consider evidence that China conceives its punishments for violations of its one-child policy as directed against married couples rather than just the party subject to forced abortion or sterilization. The BIA was not unreasonable in holding, based on these rationales, that the scope of the harm resulting from the enforcement of a population-control policy by forced abortion and involuntary sterilization extends to both spouses.

C. The United States' Gender Guidelines and Instructions to Asylum Officers[12]

In its training packets for asylum officers interviewing women, the U.S. government notes that:[13]

Types of Harm Directed at Women

The types of harm that women suffer vary across a broad range of countries, cultures, and classes. There are particular types of harm that will confront the asylum officer in the claims of women interviewed.

---

12. *Available at* http://www.asylumlaw.org/docs/united_states/guidelines/gender.pdf [last visited May 10, 2011].

13. *See* http://www.uscis.gov/USCIS/Humanitarian/Refugees%20&%20Asylum/Asylum/AOBTC %20Lesson%20Plans/Female-Asylum-Applicants-Gender-Related-Claims-31aug10.pdf [last visited May 10, 2011].

1. Rape

Rape and other forms of sexual assault are acts of violence serving non-sexual needs or aims. Rape is based on a desire to degrade, control, and/or terrorize a victim or her community. Rape of women civilians has long been an integral part of conflict, used as a tactical weapon to terrorize civilian communities.

2. Female Genital Mutilation (FGM)

Female genital mutilation (FGM) is a custom of unknown origins involving the cutting or removal of all or part of the female genitalia. This practice can have devastating and harmful consequences for a woman throughout her life.

3. Forced Marriage

Forced marriage is an arranged marriage against the victim's wishes and without the informed consent of both parties. The practice occurs throughout the world and may arise out of gender discrimination. Forced marriage constitutes a human rights violation.

4. Domestic Violence

Violence against women by relatives is related to the historically more powerful position of men in the family and society. In many societies, the police, the court system, and laws may condone the practice, allow for it, or at best may simply do nothing to prevent it or punish perpetrators. Although most battered women engage in various forms of resistance to abuse, there are many factors that make it difficult for a battered woman to leave her abuser.

Legal Analysis — Nexus

The "nexus" requirement applies equally to female and male applicants and to all claims, including those relating to gender.

When examining claims based on female applicants' political opinion, asylum officers must remember that in addition to expressing political opinions in the traditional sense of actively participating in political institutions within a country, women also express their political opinion in more non-traditional ways, such as cooking or providing food to rebel forces. Women also express political opinions when they oppose or challenge institutionalized discrimination or restrictive social norms.

The BIA has recognized gender as an immutable trait that could form the basis of a particular social group, as have a few federal courts. However, most courts analyzing gender-related social groups consider gender along with other characteristics shared by the groups, such as tribe and nationality.

Legal Analysis — Internal Relocation

Determinations regarding whether a female applicant could avoid future harm through internal relocation must take into consideration the legal restrictions and cultural or social norms governing women's behavior. This includes a woman's ability to travel, her economic circumstances, and her social circumstances.

Credibility

Cultural differences and norms governing women's behavior, as well as the effects of trauma, may present special difficulties in evaluating credibility of female asylum applicants. For example, social constraints controlling access to information, the effects of trauma, or customs of social interaction may limit a woman's ability to provide detailed testimony about certain aspects of her claim. Also, as women from certain countries are less likely to be literate than their male compatriots, they may not have the ability to review the asylum application for accuracy.

Questions for Discussion

1. *What do you think of the UNHCR's recommendation that states consider granting asylum to women who have "transgressed the social mores" of their country and now face a well founded fear of persecution? Does it offer sufficient protection to women?*

2. *One of the challenges inherent in seeking asylum is that women have to be able to leave the country where they are being persecuted in order to seek asylum in another state. Is the ability to leave particularly challenging for women in states which have repressive cultural rules for women? How might these challenges be overcome?*

D. Applying for Asylum in the U.S.

Within one year of entering the United States, an applicant for asylum must complete an I-589 form and file this with the United States Customs and Immigration Service's Regional Services Center. An asylum officer will then interview the applicant, and either grant asylum to applicants who meet the criteria set forth in the Refugee Convention, or refer the matter to an immigration judge if the potential asylee fails to meet the criteria. The asylum officer bases his or her decision on the information contained in the form, information that is brought forth during the interview, and information about country conditions.

Additionally, anyone subject to removal from the country for arriving in the United States without proper documentation should be asked the following questions by immigration officers:

1. Why did you leave your home country or country of last residence?

2. Do you have any fear or concern about being returned to your home country or being removed from the United States?

3. Would you be harmed if you were returned to your home country or country of last residence?

4. Do you have any questions or is there anything else you would like to add?

If any person expresses fear of return to his or her home country, he or she should be referred to an asylum officer. If an asylum officer and an immigration judge both deny the claim for asylum, the applicant may appeal to the Board of Immigration Appeals (BIA). Appeals from a decision of that Board may be taken to the Federal Court of Appeals.

Several notable cases regarding application for asylum by women have been decided in recent years.

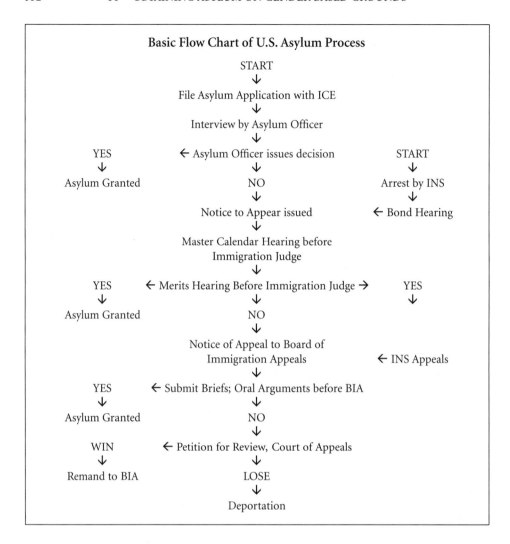

Basic Flow Chart of U.S. Asylum Process

START
↓
File Asylum Application with ICE
↓
Interview by Asylum Officer
↓

YES   ← Asylum Officer issues decision   START
↓   ↓   ↓
Asylum Granted   NO   Arrest by INS
↓   ↓
Notice to Appear issued   ← Bond Hearing
↓
Master Calendar Hearing before
Immigration Judge
↓

YES   ← Merits Hearing Before Immigration Judge →   YES
↓   ↓   ↓
Asylum Granted   NO
↓
Notice of Appeal to Board of
Immigration Appeals   ← INS Appeals
↓

YES   ← Submit Briefs; Oral Arguments before BIA
↓   ↓
Asylum Granted   NO
↓
WIN   ← Petition for Review, Court of Appeals
↓   ↓
Remand to BIA   LOSE
↓
Deportation

1. *In Re Fauziya Kasinga* (Board of Immigration Appeals 1996)[14]

A fundamental issue before us is whether the practice of female genital mutilation ("FGM") can be the basis for a grant of asylum under section 208 of the Immigration and Nationality Act, 8 U.S.C. § 1158 (1994). On appeal, the parties agree that FGM can be the basis for a grant of asylum. We find that FGM can be a basis for asylum.

Nevertheless, the parties disagree about 1) the parameters of FGM as a ground for asylum in future cases, and 2) whether the applicant is entitled to asylum on the basis of the record before us. In deciding this case, we decline to speculate on, or establish rules for, cases that are not before us. We make seven major findings in the applicant's case. Those findings are summarized below.

First, the record before us reflects that the applicant is a credible witness. Second, FGM, as practiced by the Tchamba-Kunsuntu Tribe of Togo and documented in the

---

14. File A73 476 695; *available at* http://www.justice.gov/eoir/vll/intdec/vol21/3278.pdf [last visited July 20, 2011].

record, constitutes persecution. Third, the applicant is a member of a social group consisting of young women of the Tchamba-Kunsuntu Tribe who have not had FGM, as practiced by that tribe, and who oppose the practice. Fourth, the applicant has a well-founded fear of persecution. Fifth, the persecution the applicant fears is "on account of" her social group. Sixth, the applicant's fear of persecution is country-wide. Seventh, and finally, the applicant is eligible for and should be granted asylum in the exercise of discretion. Each finding is explained below.

A. The Applicant's Testimony

The applicant is a 19-year-old native and citizen of Togo. She attended 2 years of high school. She is a member of the Tchamba-Kunsuntu Tribe of northern Togo. She testified that young women of her tribe normally undergo FGM at age 15. However, she did not because she initially was protected from FGM by her influential, but now deceased, father.

The applicant stated that upon her father's death in 1993, under tribal custom her aunt, her father's sister, became the primary authority figure in the family. The applicant's mother was driven from the family home, left Togo, and went to live with her family in Benin. The applicant testified that she does not currently know her mother's exact whereabouts.

The applicant further testified that her aunt forced her into a polygamous marriage in October 1994, when she was 17. The husband selected by her aunt was 45 years old and had three other wives at the time of marriage. The applicant testified that, under tribal custom, her aunt and her husband planned to force her to submit to FGM before the marriage was consummated. The applicant testified that she feared imminent mutilation. With the help of her older sister, she fled Togo for Ghana. However, she was afraid that her aunt and her husband would locate her there. Consequently, using money from her mother, the applicant embarked for Germany by airplane. Upon arrival in Germany, the applicant testified that she was somewhat disoriented and spent several hours wandering around the airport looking for fellow Africans who might help her. Finally, she struck up a conversation, in English, with a German woman. After hearing the applicant's story, the woman offered to give the applicant temporary shelter in her home until the applicant decided what to do next....

The applicant further stated that in December 1994, while on her way to a shopping center, she met a young Nigerian man. He was the first person from Africa she had spoken to since arriving in Germany. They struck up a conversation, during which the applicant told the man about her situation. He offered to sell the applicant his sister's British passport so that she could seek asylum in the United States, where she has an aunt, an uncle, and a cousin. The applicant followed the man's suggestion, purchasing the passport and the ticket with money given to her by her sister. The applicant did not attempt a fraudulent entry into the United States. Rather, upon arrival at Newark International Airport on December 17, 1994, she immediately requested asylum. She remained in detention by the Immigration and Naturalization Service ("INS") until April 1996.

The applicant testified that the Togolese police and the Government of Togo were aware of FGM and would take no steps to protect her from the practice. She further testified that her aunt had reported her to the Togolese police. Upon return, she would be taken back to her husband by the police and forced to undergo FGM. She testified at several points that there would be nobody to protect her from FGM in Togo.

In her testimony, the applicant referred to letters in the record from her mother ... Those letters confirmed that the Togolese police were looking for the applicant and that the applicant's father's family wanted her to undergo FGM.

The applicant testified that she could not find protection anywhere in Togo. She stated that Togo is a very small country and her husband and aunt, with the help of the police, could locate her anywhere she went. She also stated that her husband is well known in Togo and is a friend of the police. On cross-examination she stated that it would not be possible for her to live with another tribe in Togo. The applicant also testified that the Togolese police could locate her in Ghana. She indicated that she did not seek asylum in Germany because she could not speak German and therefore could not continue her education there. She stated that she did not have relatives in Germany as she does in the United State. According to the applicant's testimony, the FGM practiced by her tribe, the Tchamba-Kunsuntu, is of an extreme type involving cutting the genitalia with knives, extensive bleeding, and a 40-day recovery period ... The background materials confirm that the FGM practiced in some African countries, such as Togo, is of an extreme nature causing permanent damage, and not just a minor form of genital ritual....

The record material establishes that FGM in its extreme forms is a practice in which portions of the female genitalia are cut away. In some cases, the vagina is sutured partially closed. This practice clearly inflicts harm or suffering upon the girl or woman who undergoes it. FGM is extremely painful and at least temporarily incapacitating. It permanently disfigures the female genitalia. FGM exposes the girl or woman to the risk of serious, potentially life-threatening complications. These include, among others, bleeding, infection, urine retention, stress, shock, psychological trauma, and damage to the urethra and anus. It can result in permanent loss of genital sensation and can adversely affect sexual and erotic functions ...

The record also contains two reports compiled by the United States Department of State. The first of these, dated January 31, 1994, 1) confirms that FGM is practiced by some ethnic groups in Togo; 2) notes that while some reports indicate that the practice may be diminishing, an expert indicates that as many as 50% of Togolese females may have been mutilated; and 3) notes that various acts of violence against women occur in Togo with little police intervention....

For the purposes of this case, we adopt the description of FGM drawn from the record and summarized in Part I.B.4. of this opinion. We agree with the parties that this level of harm can constitute "persecution" within the meaning of section 101(a)(42)(A) of the Act, 8 U.S.C. § 1101(a)(42)(A) (1994).

While a number of descriptions of persecution have been formulated in our past decisions, we have recognized that persecution can consist of the infliction of harm or suffering by a government, or persons a government is unwilling or unable to control, to overcome a characteristic of the victim....

As observed by the INS, many of our past cases involved actors who had a subjective intent to punish their victims. However, this subjective "punitive" or "malignant" intent is not required for harm to constitute persecution....

To be a basis for a grant of asylum, persecution must relate to one of five categories described in section 101(a)(42)(A) of the Act. The parties agree that the relevant category in this case is "particular social group." Each party has advanced several formulations of the "particular social group" at issue in this case. However, each party urges the Board to adopt only that definition of social group necessary to decide this individual case.

In the context of this case, we find the particular social group to be the following: young women of the Tchamba-Kunsuntu Tribe who have not had FGM, as practiced by that tribe, and who oppose the practice....

In accordance with *Acosta*, the particular social group is defined by common characteristics that members of the group either cannot change, or should not be required to change because such characteristics are fundamental to their individual identities. The characteristics of being a "young woman" and a "member of the Tchamba-Kunsuntu Tribe" cannot be changed. The characteristic of having intact genitalia is one that is so fundamental to the individual identity of a young woman that she should not be required to change it. To be eligible for asylum, the applicant must establish that her well-founded fear of persecution is "on account of" one of the five grounds specified in the Act, here, her membership in a "particular social group." *See, e.g., Matter of H-, supra* (holding that harm or abuse because of clan membership constitutes persecution on account of social group).

Both parties have advanced, and the background materials support, the proposition that there is no legitimate reason for FGM. Group Exhibit 4 contains materials showing that the practice has been condemned by such groups as the United Nations, the International Federation of Gynecology and Obstetrics, the Council on Scientific Affairs, the World Health Organization, the International Medical Association, and the American Medical Association.

Record materials state that FGM "has been used to control woman's sexuality," *FGM Alert, supra*, at 4. It also is characterized as a form of "sexual oppression" that is "based on the manipulation of women's sexuality in order to assure male dominance and exploitation."

2. *Matter of S.A.* (Board of Immigration Appeals 2000)[15]

The respondent is a native and citizen of Morocco, who is either 20 or 21 years old. She testified that she was schooled for 3 years and knows how to write her name, but she is otherwise illiterate. The respondent claims that in Morocco she was a victim of her father's escalating physical and emotional abuse. According to the respondent, the abuse arose primarily out of religious differences between her and her father, i.e., the father's orthodox Muslim beliefs, particularly pertaining to women, and her liberal Muslim views. Her father beat her a minimum of once a week using his hands, his feet, or a belt. She notes that her father did not mistreat her two brothers. The respondent related that when she was about 14 years old, her maternal aunt, who is a United States citizen and resides in this country, sent her a somewhat short skirt. On one occasion the respondent wore the skirt outside her home. Upon returning home, her father verbally reprimanded her, heated a straight razor, and burned those portions of her thighs that had been exposed while she was wearing the skirt. He told her that he was taking this action to scar her thighs so that, in the future, she would not be tempted to wear what he considered improper attire. The respondent stated that she and her mother were afraid to go to the hospital after the incident, so her mother went to the local pharmacy and procured an ointment to treat the burns.

On another occasion, the respondent went to a pay phone to call her aunt in the United States. She explained that family members used a pay phone located near her parents' home because the family did not receive telephone service. On her way to the telephone, a young man stopped the respondent to ask for directions and she engaged in a short dialogue with the man. Upon observing this interchange, her father came into the street,

---

15. *Available at* http://www.justice.gov/eoir/vll/intdec/vol22/3433.pdf [last visited July 20, 2011].

shouted at her and the individual with whom she was conversing, and beat both of them. He used a ring he was wearing to beat the respondent in the face, particularly her forehead, the area between her eyebrows, and the bridge and top of her nose. She testified that she bled from the beating.

Thereafter, the respondent's father compelled her to remain in the house in order to prevent subsequent casual conversations with strangers. She was forbidden to attend school and was prohibited from other activities physically located outside her home. The respondent stated that her father believes that "a girl should stay at home and should be covered or veiled all the time." ... The respondent testified that during one of her aunt's visits to Morocco, she took a picture of the respondent. Her aunt later showed the picture to a man in the United States. A long-distance relationship developed, culminating in an offer of marriage. Although the respondent's fiancé died prior to their planned marriage, her prospective brother-in-law forwarded documents to her in an effort to assist her entry to the United States. The respondent stated that she understood such documents to be a valid Social Security card and resident alien card. The respondent claimed that after she received her passport and the above documents, her mother sold some of her jewelry and bought the respondent an airline ticket to the United States....

According to the aunt, going to the police would have been futile, because under Muslim law, particularly in Morocco, a father's power over his daughter is unfettered.

[The Immigration Judge denied asylum to the applicant because he found that the applicant's testimony was not credible and that the aunt's testimony was an attempt by the applicant to "embellish her claim." The BIA disagreed, finding that:]

Unlike the Immigration Judge, we place a great deal of weight on the testimony of the respondent's aunt and disagree that such testimony constituted mere embellishment of the respondent's claim. We find that the aunt's testimony was introduced to bolster the respondent's account and that the inclusion of such testimony was legitimate.... We find particularly significant the evidence of record regarding the respondent's fear of seeking governmental protection from her father's abuse. Both the respondent and her aunt testified that, in Moroccan society, such action would be not only unproductive but potentially dangerous. In addition, we find significant the aunt's testimony regarding the severity and frequency of the beatings suffered by the respondent and the futility of seeking governmental protection in such instances in light of societal religious mores. *See* Coven, U.S. Dep't of Justice, *Considerations for Asylum Officers Adjudicating Asylum Claims from Women* (1995). ("Breaching social mores (e.g., marrying outside of an arranged marriage, wearing lipstick or failing to comply with other cultural or religious norms) may result in harm, abuse or harsh treatment that is distinguishable from the treatment given the general population, frequently without meaningful recourse to state protection.") The report of the United States Department of State that is contained in the record confirms that "few women report abuse to authorities" because the judicial procedure is skewed against them, as even medical documentation is considered insufficient evidence of physical abuse, and women who do not prevail in court are returned to the abusive home.

In the instant case, the source of the respondent's repeated physical assaults, imposed isolation, and deprivation of education was not the government, but her own father. Although she did not request protection from the government, the evidence convinces us that even if the respondent had turned to the government for help, Moroccan authorities would have been unable or unwilling to control her father's conduct. The respondent would have been compelled to return to her domestic situation and her circumstances may well have worsened. *See, e.g., Matter of Chen, supra; Matter of D.V., supra.* In view of these facts, we conclude that the respondent established that she suffered past persecution in Morocco at the hands of her father and could not rely on the authorities to protect her. The Service has made no showing that conditions in Morocco have materially changed such that, upon her return, the respondent could reasonably expect governmental protection from her persecutor....

We find that the persecution suffered by the respondent was on account of her religious beliefs, as they differed from those of her father concerning the proper role of women in Moroccan society. The record clearly establishes that, because of his orthodox Muslim beliefs regarding women and his daughter's refusal to share or submit to his religion inspired restrictions and demands, the respondent's father treated her differently from her brothers. We conclude that the respondent is statutorily eligible for asylum. We further find that a favorable exercise of discretion is warranted in this case.

Accordingly, the respondent's appeal will be sustained and her asylum application will be granted.

3. *In re R.A. (Rodi Alvarado)*

Rodi Alvarado Pena, a Guatemalan woman, suffered brutal abuse at the hands of her husband over a ten year period. Fearing for her life, she fled to the United states, leaving her two children with relatives. She applied for asylum and was granted it by an asylum judge in 1996. However, the immigration service appealed, and the BIA reversed the asylum judge's decision in 1999, and ordered Alvarado Pena deported. Alvarado Pena appealed and in 2001, the Attorney General ordered Alvarado Pena's deportation stayed pending the issuance of new regulations on gender based asylum claims. These regulations never came. In 2004, the United Nations High Commissioner for Refugees wrote an Advisory Opinion on International Norms and Gender Related persecution.

E. UNHCR Advisory Opinion on International Norms: Gender Related Persecution and Relevance to Membership of a Particular Social Group and Political Opinion[16]

The facts of the case are undisputed. Both the Immigration Judge and the Board of Immigration Appeals (BIA) found Ms. Alvarado to be credible and recognized that the abuse she suffered at the hands of her husband amounted to persecution. Both decisions also recognized that Guatemalan authorities failed to provide protection from this abuse. For purposes of this Advisory Opinion, UNHCR relies on the record established in the Government's decisions, including the findings by both the Immigration Judge and the BIA that Ms. Alvarado's testimony was credible, as UNHCR cannot make a credibility determination based on the paper record before it. UNHCR, therefore, bases this Advisory Opinion on the assumption that the facts as set out in the decisions are accurate.

---

16. *Available at* http://www.unhcr.org/refworld/country,,,AMICUS,GTM,,43e9f6e64,0.html [last visited July 20, 2011].

As summarised by the BIA, Ms. Alvarado had been the victim of extreme spousal violence for over ten years, beginning when she married in 1984 and continuing and escalating as time went on until she fled to the U.S. in 1995 when he was working. He escorted the respondent to her workplace, and he would often wait to direct her home. To scare her, he would tell the respondent stories of having killed babies and the elderly while he served in the army. Oftentimes, he would take the respondent to cantinas where he would become inebriated. When the respondent would complain about his drinking, her husband would yell at her. On one occasion, he grasped her hand to the point of pain and continued to drink until he passed out. When she left a cantina before him, he would strike her. As their marriage proceeded, the level and frequency of his rage increased concomitantly with the seeming senselessness and irrationality of his motives. He dislocated the respondent's jaw bone when her menstrual period was 15 days late. When she refused to abort her 3- to 4-month-old fetus, he kicked her violently in her spine. He would hit or kick the respondent "whenever he felt like it, where he happened to be: in the house, on the street, on the bus." The respondent stated that "[a]s time went on, he hit me for no reason at all."

The respondent's husband raped her repeatedly. He would beat her before and during the unwanted sex. When the respondent resisted, he would accuse her of seeing other men and threaten her with death. The rapes occurred "almost daily," and they caused her severe pain. He passed on a sexually transmitted disease to the respondent from his sexual relations outside their marriage. Once, he kicked the respondent in her genitalia apparently for no reason, causing the respondent to bleed severely for 8 days. The respondent suffered the most severe pain when he forcefully sodomized her. When she protested, he responded, as he often did, "you're my woman, you do what I say."

Although Ms. Alvarado tried to run away, her husband always found her and the abuse continued: he beat and kicked her unconscious after she tried to escape; whipped her with an electrical cord; broke windows and a mirror with her head; pistol-whipped her; wielded a machete and threatened to deface her, cut off her arms and legs, and leave her in a wheelchair if she ever tried to leave him; and warned her that he would be able to find her wherever she was.

When she asked for his motivation, he would reply, "I can do it if I want to." He said he was "going to hunt her down and kill her if she comes back to Guatemala."

Her attempts to secure protection were futile: Ms. Alvarado's pleas to Guatemalan police did not gain her protection. On three occasions, the police issued summonses for her husband to appear, but he ignored them, and the police did not take further action. Twice, she called the police, but they never responded. When she appeared before a judge, the judge told her that he would not interfere in domestic disputes. Her husband told her that, because of his former military service, calling the police would be futile as he was familiar with law enforcement officials. Ms. Alvarado knew of no shelters or other organizations in Guatemala that could protect her.

Human rights reports covering the years during which Ms. Alvarado was abused describe a State that fails to protect women who suffer abuse at the hands of their husbands and an official policy of discrimination against women ...

[W]e agree with the Immigration Judge that the severe injuries sustained by the respondent rise to the level of harm sufficient (and more than sufficient) to constitute "persecution." We also credit the respondent's testimony in general and specifically her account of being unsuccessful in obtaining meaningful assistance from the authorities in Guatemala. Accordingly, we find that she has adequately established on this record that she was unable to avail herself of the protection of the Government of Guatemala in connection with the abuse inflicted by her husband …

States also generally rely in their practice on a number of other documents, including Executive Committee ("ExCom") Conclusions, and in particular UNHCR Guidelines on International Protection which are issued by UNHCR to complement and update the *Handbook*. Of specific relevance to this particular case are Guidelines that address gender-related persecution and "membership of a particular social group…." UNHCR's analysis and recommendations promote the adoption of a gender-sensitive interpretation of the international refugee instruments and national laws that incorporate the principles of these instruments and protect refugees. Historically, the refugee definition has been interpreted through a framework of male experiences; in the past decade, however, the analysis and understanding of sex and gender in the refugee context have advanced substantially in case law, in State practice, in academic writing and concomitantly in developments in international human rights law and standards.

Of utmost significance to gender-related claims in general, and specifically present in this case, is discrimination by the State in failing to extend protection to individuals against certain types of harm. "If the State, as a matter of policy or practice, does not accord certain rights or protection from serious abuse, then the discrimination in extending protection, which results in serious harm inflicted with impunity, could amount to persecution. Particular cases of domestic violence, or of abuse for reasons of one's differing sexual orientation, could, for example, be analysed in this context." Ms. Alvarado's attempts to seek protection from the police and the legal system were to no avail; and country conditions reports confirm the official tolerance of domestic violence in Guatemala. These facts and the need to analyse the persecution suffered by Ms. Alvarado in this context underscore how important it is to interpret the refugee definition—whether it be in the 1951 Convention or national laws—from a gender perspective, both to ensure that proper consideration is given to women claimants and that gender-related claims are recognized as such.

Sex can properly be within the ambit of the social group category, with women being a clear example of a social subset defined by innate and immutable characteristics, and who are frequently treated differently than men. Their characteristics also identify them as a group in society, subjecting them to different treatment and standards in some countries. Women asylum-seekers who face harsh or inhuman treatment due to their having transgressed the social mores of the society in which they live may be considered as "a particular social group."

The size of the group has sometimes been used as a basis for refusing to recognize "women" generally as a particular social group. This argument has no basis in fact or reason, as the other grounds are not bound by questions of size. There should equally be no requirement that the particular social group be cohesive or that members of it voluntarily associate, or that every member of the group be at risk of persecution. Though it is well-accepted that it should be possible to identify the group independently of the persecution, persecution, including in the form of discrimination, may be a relevant factor in determining the visibility of the group in a particular context.

In this case, therefore, Ms. Alvarado's particular social group can be defined by her sex, her marital status, and her position in a society that condones discrimination against women. In Guatemalan society, women are a social subset defined by innate and immutable characteristics (their sex) and they are treated differently than men. Their civil status (married) also identifies them as a group in society, subjecting them to different treatment and standards, both in the law and in practice. Their being married women in Guatemala makes them subject to particularly discriminatory treatment according to Guatemalan law, its implementation and societal norms.

That Ms. Alvarado protested against her husband's violence and sought the protection of State authorities also marks her as a person who has transgressed the social mores of her society, which condone and institutionalise discrimination against women. Women are expected to accept their "fate" without protest and without involving the authorities at all. This is another element identifying her as part of a particular social group.

Persecution often relates to acts by the authorities of a country. However, where serious discriminatory acts or human rights abuses are committed by segments of the population or private individuals, these acts will also amount to persecution if the government knowingly tolerates the behaviour, or if it is unwilling or unable to provide protection to the individuals affected. As noted above, the facts in Ms. Alvarado's case indicate that Guatemalan authorities knowingly tolerated the abuses that she suffered at the hands of her husband, and failed to provide legal remedies. With this in mind, it can be concluded that the Ms. Alvarado's "well-founded fear of persecution" was for persecutory acts that were a combination of abuse by her husband (a non-State actor) that he could inflict because she was his wife and that he could inflict with impunity because of State inaction and tolerance in a culture of discriminatory treatment of women and failure to protect them.

Ms. Alvarado clearly established a well-founded fear of being persecuted. This fear, however, must be related to one or more of the Convention grounds, *i.e.*, there must be a causal link to fulfil the "for reasons of" requirement in the refugee definition.... In cases where there is a risk of being persecuted at the hands of a non-State actor (e.g. husband, partner or other non-State actor) for reasons which are related to one of the Convention grounds, the causal link is established, whether or not the absence of State protection is Convention related. Alternatively, where the risk of being persecuted at the hands of a non-State actor is unrelated to a Convention ground, but the inability or unwillingness of the State to offer protection is for reasons of a Convention ground, the causal link is also established In Ms. Alvarado's case, though her husband may have been abusing her in part for purely personal reasons, because he was drunk or irrational or had been abused himself, the facts show that he also abused her because she was a woman, his wife (over whom he thought he had the right to exercise full power and control), and he knew that he could do so with impunity in Guatemala. He also escalated his attacks against her when she protested his treatment. When she went outside the home to seek protection, she showed her opposition to domination by her husband and to the social mores of Guatemalan society, which condones such domination. The Convention ground—her particular social group as defined above—was, therefore, a relevant contributing factor, sufficient to fulfil the causal link.

The persecution Ms. Alvarado suffered at the hands of her husband (the non-State actor) and the fear of being persecuted by him in the future are for reasons of her social group, thus establishing the causal link regardless of the absence of State protection.... In Ms. Alvarado's case, her opinion as to gender roles in Guatemala were evident through her numerous attempts to leave her husband, and to seek to have him punished or restrained. [Those] who face torture, or harsh or inhuman treatment due to their having transgressed the social mores of the society in which they live may also be considered to be demonstrating a political opinion.

In the context of Guatemalan society, which allows *de jure* and *de facto* discrimination against women, Ms. Alvarado's responses to her husband's attempts to dominate and abuse her could be seen as a transgression of social mores, in this case the socially—and legally—sanctioned domination of men over their wives. In Guatemala, these actions implicitly criticise State "policies, traditions or methods" and represent "opinions not tolerated by the authorities." ...

Ms. Alvarado lived in a society of official tolerance of domestic abuse. Neither the police nor the courts supported her or protected her or punished her abuser. The authorities—both official and in the person of her husband—were well aware of her views that she should not have to continue to be dominated and abused by her husband. In fact, she was criticised for complaining and protesting. Her husband was free to act with impunity.

Because it occurs in the privacy of the home it is not possible to know for certain the basis for domestic violence. Ms. Alvarado's opinion, which she manifested, that she should be free from her husband's dominance and abuse and that the State should protect her, may or may not have been at the root of, or contributed to, her husband's initial attacks. Once she protested, however, and sought outside help and tried to leave her husband, it is clear that subsequent attacks were exacerbated or provoked by these actions, actions which clearly demonstrated her refusal to acquiesce in society's acceptance of abuse. The facts indicate that some of her husband's attacks were meant to punish her for these actions, for example, he beat and kicked her unconscious after she tried to escape; threatened to maim her if she tried to leave him again and, after she left Guatemala, to kill her if she returned.

Given the power her husband had over her and would have over her in the future, and the continued lack of State protection in cases of domestic violence in Guatemala, it is clear that the consequences for Ms. Alvarado, should she be forced to return to Guatemala, would be extremely serious. This consideration, added to the facts surrounding the abuse she has suffered, support the conclusion that Ms. Alvarado has demonstrated a well-founded fear of persecution on account of her political opinion.

In 2004, Ms. Alvarado Pena's attorneys and the Department of Homeland Security (DHS) agreed to limit the outstanding issues to whether the "social group" that Ms. Alvarado Pena was a part of, met the requirements of particularity and visibility. The DHS filed a brief averring that it was in the process of determining a rule which would define and provide guidance in interpreting the term "particular social group" with respect to victims of domestic violence, because the case law developing that term had been uneven. The DHS conceded that under the rule that the DHS was in the process of developing, Ms. Alvarado would qualify for asylum, and the DHS therefore recommended that she be granted it.

1. Brief for the DHS[17]

The Board's analysis of the particular social group claim, however, is problematic. The Board rejected Alvarado's argument that the abuse she suffered and feared was on account of her membership in a particular social group defined as "Guatemalan women who have been intimately involved with Guatemalan male companions, who believe that women are to live under male domination." The Board found that this formulation did not qualify as a "particular social group."

---

17. *Available at* http://cgrs.uchastings.edu/documents/legal/dhs_brief_ra.pdf [last visited July 20, 2011].

The Board correctly concluded that this articulation of social group is faulty. By describing the group as "Guatemalan women who have been intimately involved with Guatemalan male companions, who believe that women are to live under male domination," the Immigration Judge essentially defined the group by the harm the applicant fears.... "We agree that under the statute a 'particular social group' must exist independently of the persecution suffered by the applicant for asylum.").

The facts of this case, however, give rise to other articulations that would both meet the requirements for a particular social group and accurately identify the reason Alvarado's husband harmed her. For example ... Alvarado asserted that it was because of her status as a married woman that she was harmed ... The record strongly supports such a conclusion. DHS argues that the social group in this case would more accurately be defined as "married women in Guatemala who are unable to leave the relationship" and that such formulation would meet the requirements for a particular social group.

2. *Perdomo v. Holder* (9th Circuit Court of Appeals, 2009)[18]

Lesly Yajayra Perdomo is a citizen and native of Guatemala. She left Guatemala at age fifteen to join her mother in the United States in April 1991. She requested asylum because she feared persecution as a member of a particular social group consisting of women between the ages of fourteen and forty. Perdomo testified that her fear was based on the high incidence of murder of women in Guatemala, and her own status as a Guatemalan woman. She provided the IJ with several reports by the Guatemala Human Rights Commission, which is based in the United States, documenting the torture and killing of women, the brutality of the killings, the non-responsiveness of the Guatemalan government to such atrocities, the countrywide prevalence of the killings, and the lack of explanation for the killings. Perdomo did not assert that she was the victim of past persecution; rather, she expressed a fear of future persecution if she were returned to Guatemala. Perdomo also testified that she would be targeted because she would not be accepted as a native citizen in Guatemala, but would be considered an American with financial resources due to the number of years that she has lived in the United States.

She further testified that she may be targeted because of her active involvement in the Pentecostal church as well as her lack of family and other personal contacts in Guatemala. Perdomo also testified that she would not be able to obtain employment in Guatemala because the secretarial positions listed in Guatemalan newspapers only accept female applicants between the ages of eighteen and twenty-five, and job applications must be submitted with photographs.

Although the IJ found Perdomo's testimony to be credible and truthful, she denied the applications for asylum, withholding of removal, and relief under CAT. The IJ noted that she was "sympathetic to the plight of the respondent," but declined to make the "finding that women between the ages of fourteen and forty who are Guatemalan and live in the United States form a particular social group which would entitle [Perdomo] to relief."

On appeal, the BIA agreed with the IJ's determination that Perdomo failed to establish a well-founded fear of future persecution in Guatemala on account of her membership in a particular social group. The BIA considered the group of "women between the ages

---

18. *Available at* http://cgrs.uchastings.edu/pdfs/9th%20Circuit%20Decision,%20Perdomo.pdf [last visited July 20, 2011].

of fourteen and forty who are Guatemalan and live in the United States" to be too broad to qualify as a protected social group. The INA does not provide a definition for the term "particular social group." *Hernandez-Montiel*, 225 F.3d at 1091. The BIA has interpreted the term to mean a group with members who "share a common, immutable characteristic" that "members of the group either cannot change, or should not be required to change because it is fundamental to their individual identities or consciences." *Matter of Acosta*, 19 I. & N. Dec. 211, 233 (BIA 1985); *In re C-A-*, 23 I. & N. Dec. 951, 955–56 (BIA 2006) (quoting the *Acosta* formulation and affirming continued adherence to it). The BIA has explained that "[t]he shared characteristic might be an innate one such as sex, color, or kinship ties," which would make the fact of membership "something comparable to the other four grounds of persecution under the Act, namely, something that is beyond the power of an individual to change or that is so fundamental to his identity or conscience that it ought not be required to be changed." *In re C-A-*, 23 I. & N. Dec. at 955 (quoting *Acosta*, 19 I. & N. Dec. at 233–34). The BIA also has clarified that a group must have "social visibility" and adequate "particularity" to constitute a protected social group....

The BIA, however, does not "generally require a 'voluntary associational relationship,' cohesiveness,' or strict 'homogeneity among group members.'" *Id.* at 74. The BIA has not yet specifically addressed in a precedential decision whether gender by itself could form the basis of a particular social group. It has, however, recognized as a "particular social group" women who belong to a particular tribe and who oppose female genital mutilation because that group is defined by characteristics that cannot be changed or should not be changed. *In re Fauziya Kasinga*, 21 I. & N. Dec. 357, 366 (BIA 1996). Whether females in a particular country, without any other defining characteristics, could constitute a protected social group remains an unresolved question for the BIA....

While we have not held expressly that females, without other defining characteristics, constitute a particular social group, we have concluded that females, or young girls of a particular clan, met our definition of a particular social group. *Mohammed v. Gonzales*, 400 F.3d 785, 798 (9th Cir. 2005). In *Mohammed*, we recognized that gender is an "innate characteristic" that is "fundamental to [one's] identit[y]." *Id.* at 797. We noted that the INS's (now U.S. Citizenship and Immigration Services') "'Gender Guidelines,' which provide Asylum Officers with guidance on adjudicating women's claims of asylum, state that gender is an immutable trait that can qualify under the rubric of 'particular social group.'" *Id.* at 797–98. We also considered the guidelines of the Office of the United Nations High Commissioner for Refugees, the United Nations agency responsible for refugee protection worldwide, which "ma[ke] clear that 'women may constitute a particular social group under certain circumstances based on the common characteristic of sex, whether or not they associate with one another based on that shared characteristic.'" *Id.* at 798.

After holding that female genital mutilation constitutes persecution and noting that genital mutilation clearly occurs on account of being female, we concluded that the petitioner's claim that "she was persecuted 'on account of' her membership in a social group, whether it be defined as the social group comprised of Somalian females, or a more narrowly circumscribed group, such as young girls in the Benadiri clan, not only reflects a plausible construction of our asylum law, *but the only plausible construction.*" *Id.* (emphasis added).

Thus, we clearly acknowledged that women in a particular country, regardless of ethnicity or clan membership, could form a particular social group. The Eighth Circuit has followed our reasoning in *Mohammed*, holding that "Somali females" constitute a particular social group. *Hassan v. Gonzales*, 484 F.3d 513, 518 (8th Cir. 2007)....

Perdomo argues that women in Guatemala comprise a "particular social group" at high risk of "femicide," and that as a woman she has an objectively well-founded fear of future persecution in Guatemala. The BIA dismissed Perdomo's appeal solely on the ground that "all women in Guatemala" could not constitute a cognizable social group, without reaching the question of whether Perdomo had demonstrated a nexus between her membership in that group and her fear of persecution. We therefore consider only whether the BIA erred in determining that women in Guatemala cannot be a cognizable social group.... To the extent we have rejected certain social groups as too broad, we have done so where "[t]here is no unifying relationship or *characteristic* to narrow th[e] diverse and disconnected group." *Ochoa v. Gonzales*, 406 F.3d 1166, 1171 (9th Cir. 2005) (emphasis added).... Because the BIA failed to apply both prongs of the *Hernandez-Montiel* definition to Perdomo's claim that women in Guatemala constitute a particular social group, and because the BIA's decision is inconsistent with its own opinions in *Matter of Acosta*, 19 I. & N. Dec. at 233–34, and *In re C-A-*, 23 I. & N. Dec. at 955, we grant Perdomo's petition for review. We are mindful that under the ordinary remand rule, the agency should be given an opportunity in the first instance to make legal determinations entrusted to it by Congress.

Questions for Discussion

1. *What other major human rights violations that impact women in particular might give rise to an application for asylum? Would any violation of the rights articulated in CEDAW give rise to such a claim?*

2. *One of the reasons that the definition of the term "membership in a social group" is so contested, is that if the group is too broadly defined the group will become too large, and countries like the United States may be overwhelmed by applications from women claiming membership in such group. Is this a valid fear? What role should gender play in these definitions and how broadly construed should these groups be?*

3. *The DSK case is a case that arose in May 2011, in New York, when a housekeeper in a hotel accused Dominique Strauss Kahn (then Director of the IMF) of sexually assaulting her while she was cleaning his room. While investigating the housekeeper's story, New York officials uncovered information that suggested that she lied on her application for asylum from Guinea. How damaging are claims of false asylum for future asylees? How might immigration officials ascertain whether claims for asylum are credible, while still being sensitive to the claims of asylees?*

Chapter 15

Women and Access to Resources — Land, Economic Resources, and Education

Chapter Problem

Imagine that you work as a special advisor to the director of UN Women. You have been asked to pick one area which, if changed, could have the most positive outcome in the lives of women. When reviewing relevant statistics and documents you note that women in Africa own approximately 2% of the land in that continent; this despite the fact that over 40% of women in Africa engage in agricultural activities. Worldwide the statistics are not much better.

You also conduct research on women and girls' access to education and resources in general, and find that women lag behind men in literacy rates and in access to economic resources and assets.

What sources and statistics would you use to advocate for ownership of land for women? What other resources do women need access to? How could you best bring about positive changes for women in this regard?

I. CEDAW and Access to Land and Resources

Article 13

States Parties shall take all appropriate measures to eliminate discrimination against women in other areas of economic and social life in order to ensure, on a basis of equality of men and women, the same rights, in particular: …

(b) The right to bank loans, mortgages and other forms of financial credit;

Article 14

1. States Parties shall take into account the particular problems faced by rural women and the significant roles which rural women play in the economic survival of their families, including their work in the non-monetized sectors of the economy, and shall take all appropriate measures to ensure the application of the provisions of the present Convention to women in rural areas.

2. States Parties shall take all appropriate measures to eliminate discrimination against women in rural areas in order to ensure, on a basis of equality of men and women, that they participate in and benefit from rural development and, in particular, shall ensure to such women the right:

(a) To participate in the elaboration and implementation of development planning at all levels; ...

(c) To benefit directly from social security programmes;

(d) To obtain all types of training and education, formal and non-formal, including that relating to functional literacy, as well as, inter alia, the benefit of all community and extension services, in order to increase their technical proficiency;

(e) To organize self-help groups and co-operatives in order to obtain equal access to economic opportunities through employment or self employment;

(f) To participate in all community activities;

(g) To have access to agricultural credit and loans, marketing facilities, appropriate technology and equal treatment in land and agrarian reform as well as in land resettlement schemes;

(h) To enjoy adequate living conditions, particularly in relation to housing, sanitation, electricity and water supply, transport and communications.

II. Documenting Inequality in Access to Resources

A. The Global Gender Gap—Introduction[1]

The Global Gender Gap Index, introduced by the World Economic Forum in 2006, is a framework for capturing the magnitude and scope of gender-based disparities and tracking their progress. The Index benchmarks national gender gaps on economic, political, education- and healthbased criteria, and provides country rankings that allow for effective comparisons across regions and income groups, and over time....

The Index is designed to measure gender-based gaps in access to resources and opportunities in individual countries rather than the actual levels of the available resources and opportunities in those countries. [This is done] in order to make the Global Gender Gap Index independent from countries' levels of development.

Nordic countries—Iceland, Sweden, Finland and Norway always place at or near the top of this Index.

---

1. *See* http://www3.weforum.org/docs/WEF_GenderGap_Report_2010.pdf [last visited July 10, 2011].

[In commenting on Iceland's top placing, the researchers noted:][2]

Iceland shows further gains in the area of political empowerment because of an increase in the number of women ministers, a near gender balanced parliament and the continued tenure of a female prime minister. Iceland continues to hold 1st position on both educational attainment and political empowerment, and women's labour force participation in Iceland is among the highest in the world. However, there is still a significant difference between men's and women's salaries in Iceland. The extensive preschool and day-care system provided by most municipalities, a legal right for parents to return to their jobs after childbirth and a generous parental leave system are major contributors to Iceland's ranking. In March 2010 the Icelandic parliament adopted a legislative reform to promote gender equality on the boards of publicly owned companies and public limited companies having at least 50 employees; these companies must have at least 40% of both genders represented on their boards by September 2013. Moreover, companies with 25 or more employees are required to disclose the number of men and women employed as well as the number of men and women in management positions.

[In evaluating the high placement of the Nordic countries, the researchers found that:]

This occurs because of a combination of factors: the labour force participation rates for women are among the highest in the world; salary gaps between women and men are among the lowest in the world, although not non-existent; and women have abundant opportunities to rise to positions of leadership. These patterns vary across the Nordic countries, but on the whole these economies have made it possible for parents to combine work and family, resulting in high female participation rates, more shared participation in childcare, more equitable distribution of labour at home, better work-life balance for both women and men and in some cases a boost to declining fertility rates. Policies applied in these countries include mandatory paternal leave in combination with maternity leave, generous federally mandated parental leave benefits provided by a combination of social insurance funds and employers, tax incentives and post-maternity re-entry programmes. Together these policies have also led to relatively higher and rising birth rates occurring simultaneously with high female workforce participation in the Nordic countries, as compared with the situation in other OECD economies such as Germany, Japan, Italy and Spain where both birth rates and participation are lower. The Nordic experience points to fewer problems with ageing in the future, as well as higher labour activity and a more robust economy. Finally there has also been success with a top-down approach to promoting women's leadership — in Norway, publicly listed companies are required to have 40% of each sex on their boards since 2008 and other countries are adopting similar measures.

The Nordic countries were early starters in providing women with the right to vote (Sweden in 1919, Norway in 1913, Iceland and Denmark in 1915, Finland in 1906).

In Denmark, Sweden and Norway, political parties introduced voluntary gender quotas in the 1970s, resulting in high levels of female political representatives over the years. In Denmark, in fact, this quota has since been abandoned as no further stimulus is required. Today, Sweden has among the highest percentage

---

2. *Id.* at 20.

of women in parliament in the world (47%) while the other Nordic countries are also successful in this respect. These countries have a similarly strong record on the percentage of women in ministerial level positions (Iceland 45%, Norway 53%, Finland 63%, Sweden 45% and Denmark 42%).[3]

Iceland, Norway, Finland and Sweden hold the top four spots, the United States ranks 19th, up from its previous placing of 31st.

B. Land Ownership in Africa

Land ownership, access to resources and assets and participation in the work place, thereby giving them income, all impact the equality of women. Many African countries rank particularly low on the Global Gender Gap report because of major inequalities between men and women. Customary Law plays a major role in determining whether women have access to land. In a study conducted by the International Land Coalition, an NGO, it found the following significant difference with regard to land ownership and control when comparing an African matrilineal tribe with a patrilineal one:

1. Summary of Comparison between Women's Land Access in Matrilineal and Patrilineal Communities[4]

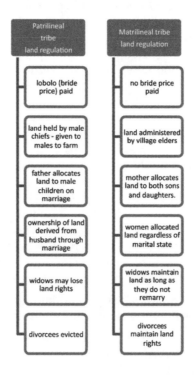

---

3. *Id.* at 23–24.

4. The research participants were drawn from Labani Chirwa, Mtezi, Zibande Ngwata and Joseph Mumba villages. The study was done by Land Coalition International, *available at* http://www.land-coalition.org/sites/default/files/publication/1119/WLR_15_Synthesis_Report_SA.pdf [last visited July 13, 2011].

2. Land Ownership among Patrilineal African Communities

Land Ownership by Gender (Africa)

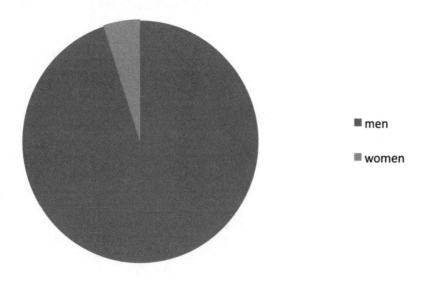

■ men

■ women

Questions for Discussion

1. *The difference in women's land security in a matrilineal tribe compared to a patrilineal tribe is startling. Yet most African tribes are patrilineal. How could one best advocate for some of the benefits enjoyed by women in matrilineal tribes to be extended to women in patrilineal tribes?*

2. *Access to, and ownership of land, and food security are closely intertwined. What might be some of the most effective methods to ensure that African women get and maintain secure access to land?*

3. *How does one go about transforming cultural practices that deny women access to land without being culturally imperialistic?*

C. The *Beijing Platform for Action*

We are determined to:

35. Ensure women's equal access to economic resources, including land, credit, science and technology, vocational training, information, communication and markets, as a means to further the advancement and empowerment of women and girls, including through the enhancement of their capacities to enjoy the benefits of equal access to these resources, inter alia, by means of international cooperation;

156. Although many women have advanced in economic structures, for the majority of women, particularly those who face additional barriers, continuing obstacles have hindered their ability to achieve economic autonomy and to ensure sustainable livelihoods for themselves and their dependants. Women are active in a variety of economic areas, which they often combine, ranging from wage labour and subsistence farming and fishing to the informal sector. However, legal and customary barriers to ownership of or access to land, natural resources, capital, credit, technology and other means of production, as well as wage differentials, contribute to impeding the economic progress of women.

Women contribute to development not only through remunerated work but also through a great deal of unremunerated work. On the one hand, women participate in the production of goods and services for the market and household consumption, in agriculture, food production or family enterprises. Though included in the United Nations System of National Accounts and therefore in international standards for labour statistics, this unremunerated work — particularly that related to agriculture — is often undervalued and under recorded.

On the other hand, women still also perform the great majority of unremunerated domestic work and community work, such as caring for children and older persons, preparing food for the family, protecting the environment and providing voluntary assistance to vulnerable and disadvantaged individuals and groups. This work is often not measured in quantitative terms and is not valued in national accounts. Women's contribution to development is seriously underestimated, and thus its social recognition is limited. The full visibility of the type, extent and distribution of this unremunerated work will also contribute to a better sharing of responsibilities.

D. The Gender Asset Gap

1. Human Rights Watch — *Report of the Task Force for the Review of Laws Relating to Women*, Nairobi (1998)[5]

Women's land ownership is miniscule despite their enormous contribution to agricultural production. Women account for only 5 percent of registered landholders nationally. The agricultural sector contributes over 80 percent of employment and 60 percent of national income. Women constitute over 80 percent of the agricultural labor force, often working on an unpaid basis, and 64 percent of subsistence farmers are women. Women provide approximately 60 percent of farm-derived income, yet female-headed households on average own less than half the amount of farm equipment owned by male-headed households. Rural women work an average of nearly three hours longer per day than rural men. With so many women working in the agricultural sector and so few in formal employment, it is all the more devastating when women lose their land. . . .

Wife Inheritance and Ritual Cleansing

The customary practices of wife inheritance and ritual cleansing continue in parts of Kenya with some permutations. The original practice of wife inheritance

---

5. *Available at* http://www.hrw.org/en/node/12352/section/3 [last visited July 3, 2011].

(known as *ter* in the Dholuo language spoken in western Kenya) was a communal way of providing widows economic and social protection. Since widows were not entitled to inherit property in their own right, being inherited was a way to access land. An inheritor was supposed to support the widow and her children. Although the terms "wife inheritance" and "cleansing" are sometimes used interchangeably, wife inheritance generally refers to the long-term union of a widow and a male relative of the deceased, and cleansing typically refers to a short-term or one-time sexual encounter with a man paid to have sex with the widow. These practices reflect the common belief that women cannot be trusted to own property and the belief that widows are contaminated with evil spirits when their husbands die.

Wife inheritance and cleansing practices take a number of different forms depending on the clan. First, there is non-sexual wife inheritance, whereby the coat of an inheritor is placed in a widow's house overnight to symbolically cleanse her. This generally applies to widows beyond childbearing age. Second, there is inheritance involving long-term sexual relations, typically with a brother of the deceased, in what amounts to a marriage. Third, there is a combination of cleansing and inheritance, whereby a widow first has sex with a social outcast (known as a *jater* in Dholuo) who is paid to have sex with her to cleanse her of her dead husband's spirits, and is then inherited by a male relative of the dead husband. Fourth, there is cleansing alone, where a widow has sex with a *jater* to cleanse her but is not inherited permanently.

Women's property rights closely relate to wife inheritance and cleansing rituals in that many women cannot stay in their homes or on their land unless they are inherited or cleansed. According to one women's rights advocate, "Women have to be inherited to keep any property after their husbands die. They have access to property because of their husband and lose that right when the husband dies." Women who experienced these practices told Human Rights Watch they had mixed feelings about them. Most said the cleansing and inheritance were not voluntary, but they succumbed so that they could keep their property and stay in their communities.

Wife inheritance is often portrayed as an act of generosity in that the widow will have a man to "look after" her and confer the legitimacy of being in a male-headed household. But men clearly benefit not just from their inherited wife's labor and childbearing potential, but also from the property the deceased husband leaves behind. A law professor observed, "Wife inheritance is a very common way to access property. If women resist, they are sent out of the household." Steven Oketch, a forty-three-year-old man from the Luhya ethnic group, told Human Rights Watch that he inherited his cousin's widow three months after his cousin died. Oketch initially moved into the widow's house and has since built a home and planted sugar cane on the land. As one widow told Human Rights Watch, a man who inherits a woman "inherits her home." A paralegal who works with widows added: "Men feel that if they stay with a woman, they will get the dead man's clothes and property. Younger brothers of a husband feel that since the husband died, now he can take the brother's belongings. They don't consider the wife of any consequence." Thus, even if wife inheritance was originally protective and if cleansing is supposed to be a benevolent way to "purify" widows, these practices are now in many ways predatory and exploitive.

Wife inheritance and cleansing practices also pose frightening health risks. These practices are common in western Kenya, home of Kenya's poorest province (Nyanza Province has an absolute poverty rate of 63 percent) and the most heavily AIDS-affected district (Kisumu district had a prevalence of 35 percent in 2000). According to one news report, one in three widows in western Kenya is forced to undergo the cleansing ritual. Condom use has lagged, in part because cleansing is not considered complete unless semen enters the widow and because women's inequality makes it difficult to demand condom use.

2. *Gender and the Distribution of Wealth in Developing Countries*— Carmen Diana Deere and Cheryl R. Doss (2006)[6]

Introduction: why the distribution of wealth by gender matters

It is well recognized that the ownership of assets improves the lives of the women and men who own and control them. The relationships between asset ownership and reduced poverty and enhanced security have been extensively researched, as has the relationship between asset accumulation and economic and political power. What has only recently garnered attention is that women may not share in the wealth of men, even within the same household or family. Women and men not only have significantly different access to wealth but also may use their assets and asset income differently, which may have consequences for household wellbeing as well as for the larger society. While the relationships are nuanced and complex, women's asset ownership is associated with their increased empowerment and individual wellbeing. To the extent that owning assets improves women's productivity and ability to earn a living, women's ownership of assets will contribute to economic growth and development. The evidence strongly supports the claim that the gender distribution of wealth is important.

The first reason that the gender distribution of wealth matters is related to equity. If women systematically have less access to wealth, then the equity issues are similar for the distribution of wealth by gender as by race and ethnicity. The patterns of wealth ownership by gender worldwide suggest that women face greater constraints than men in accumulating and keeping assets....

Lastly, asset ownership is related not only to wellbeing but also women's empowerment. Agarwal (1994, 1997) has argued forcefully that women's ownership of land leads to improvements in women's welfare, productivity, equality, and empowerment, a proposition that is gaining resonance among the international development community (World Bank 2001). Owning assets may give women additional bargaining power not just in the household, but also in their communities and other public arenas.

[M]en and women may use wealth in different ways. This discrepancy can have effects that originate in the household but permeate the larger society. A large body of evidence suggests that the outcomes of household decisions depend on who has more bargaining power within the household. Since bargaining power is often measured as access to income or ownership of wealth, this suggests that the gender patterns of wealth ownership are important, even within households.

---

6. United Nations University, Research Paper No. 2006/115; *available at* http://www.wider.unu.edu/stc/repec/pdfs/rp2006/rp2006-115.pdf [last visited July 20, 2011].

Studies have shown that household expenditures differ depending on the assets brought to marriage by each spouse (Quisumbing and Maluccio 2003) and that the current asset distribution by gender affects household expenditure patterns on food, health, education and household services (Thomas 1999; Katz and Chamorro 2003; Doss 2006a). Women's asset ownership may increase the anthropometric status of children (Duflo 2000) and the incidence of prenatal care (Beegle et al. 2001) and reduce domestic violence (Panda and Agarwal 2005; Friedemann-Sánchez 2006).

Questions for Discussion

1. *Owning assets would seem to benefit women in a multitude of ways—not only economically, but by giving them more status and bargaining power within the family. It also makes them more likely to be able to send their children to school. Do you think sufficient attention has been paid to the issue of women's ownership of land and other assets?*

2. *The lack of land and asset ownership makes women vulnerable in many ways as the example cited above regarding ritual cleansing of widows suggests. Is it more effective to focus on the larger issue—that of women's lack of land ownership— or should each violation be addressed in its own right?*

E. Customary Law Practices that Result in Women Being Disinherited

In many African countries under African Customary Law, women and girls may not inherit land and real property.

1. *Bhe v. Magistrate Khayalitsha* (South African Constitutional Court)[7]

Under the system of intestate succession flowing from §23 and the regulations, in particular reg 2*(e)*, the two minor children did not qualify to be the heirs in the intestate estate of their deceased father. According to these provisions, the estate of the deceased fell to be distributed according to 'Black law and custom'....

[17] The deceased's father made it clear that he intended to sell the immovable property to defray expenses incurred in connection with the funeral of the deceased. There is no indication that the deceased's father gave any thought to the dire consequences which would follow the sale of the immovable property. Fearing that Ms. Bhe and the two minor children would be rendered homeless, the applicants approached the Cape High Court and obtained two interdicts *pendente lite* to prevent *(a)* the selling of the immovable property for the purposes

---

7. (CCT 49/03) [2004] ZACC 17; 2005 (1) SA 580 (CC); 2005.

of off-setting funeral expenses; and *(b)* further harassment of Ms. Bhe by the father of the deceased.

[18] The applicants challenged the appointment of the deceased's father as heir and representative of the estate in the High Court. He opposed the application. The magistrate and the Minister, cited as respondents, did not oppose and chose to abide the decision of the High Court.

[19] The High Court concluded that the legislative provisions that had been challenged and on which the father of the deceased relied, were inconsistent with the Constitution and were therefore invalid. The order of the High Court, in relevant part, reads as follows:

> 1. It is declared that § 23(10)*(a)*, *(c)* and *(e)* of the Black Administration Act are unconstitutional and invalid and that reg 2*(e)* of the Regulations of the Administration and Distribution of the Estates of Deceased Blacks, ... is consequently also invalid.

> 2. It is declared that § 1(4)*(b)* of the Intestate Succession Act 81 of 1987 is unconstitutional and invalid insofar as it excludes from the application of § 1 any estate or part of any estate in respect of which § 23 of the Black Administration Act 38 of 1927 applies.

> 3. It is declared that until the aforegoing defects are corrected by competent Legislature, the distribution of intestate Black estates is governed by § 1 of the Intestate Succession Act 81 of 1987.

> 4. It is declared that the first and second applicants are the only heirs in the estate of the late Vuyu Elius Mgolombane. [...]

[21] The second matter is an application for the confirmation of the order of the Pretoria High Court. The applicant is Charlotte Shibi whose brother, Daniel Solomon Sithole (the deceased), died intestate in Pretoria in 1995. The deceased was not married nor was he a partner to a customary union. He had no children and, when he died, was not survived by a parent or grandparent. His nearest male relatives were his two cousins Mantabeni Sithole and Jerry Sithole, the first and second respondents respectively.

[22] Since the deceased was an African, his intestate estate fell to be administered under the provisions of § 23(10) of the Act. The magistrate of Wonderboom decided to institute an inquiry in terms of reg 3(2) in order to determine the person or persons entitled to succeed to the property of the deceased.... however, the magistrate abandoned the inquiry and, without further notice to Ms. Shibi, appointed Mantabeni Sithole as representative of the deceased estate. Mr. Sithole was not required to provide security because of the size of the estate and the fact that he did not have the means to do so. [...]

[24] The appointment of Mr. Sithole was not a happy one. There were complaints by his relatives, including his mother, that he was misappropriating the estate funds. The appointment was withdrawn by the magistrate who then appointed an attorney, Mr. Nkuna, to administer the estate and to distribute the assets according to customary law. In terms of the liquidation and distribution account the remaining asset in the deceased estate, an amount of R11 468,02, was awarded to Mr. Jerry Sithole, the second respondent, as the only heir to the estate.... Ms. Shibi was, ... precluded from being the heir to the intestate estate of her deceased brother. [...]

[26] Ms. Shibi ... sought an order declaring her to be the sole heir in the estate of the deceased.... The High Court set aside the decision of the magistrate and declared Ms. Shibi to be the sole heir....

For a proper understanding of the issues, it is necessary to set out in full the legislative provisions which are the subject of the constitutional challenge. Section 23 of the Act provides as follows:

> (1) All movable property belonging to a Black and allotted by him or accruing under Black law or custom to any woman with whom he lived in a customary union, or to any house, shall upon his death devolve and be administered under Black law and custom. (2) All land in a tribal settlement held in individual tenure upon quitrent conditions by a Black shall devolve upon his death upon one male person, to be determined in accordance with tables of succession to be prescribed under §§ (10). (3) All other property of whatsoever kind belonging to a Black shall be capable of being devised by will....

If the deceased, at the time of his death was—

> (i) a partner in a marriage in community of property or under ante nuptial contract; or

> (ii) a widower, widow or divorcee, as the case may be, of a marriage in community of property or under ante nuptial contract and was not survived by a partner to a customary union entered into subsequent to the dissolution of such marriage, the property shall devolve as if the deceased had been a European.

(d) When any deceased Black is survived by any partner—

> (i) with whom he had contracted a marriage which, in terms of §§ (6) of § 22 of the Act, had not produced the legal consequences of a marriage in community of property; or

> (ii) with whom he had entered into a customary union; or (iii) who was at the time of his death living with him as his putative spouse; or by any issue of himself and any such partner, and the circumstances are such as in the opinion of the Minister to render the application of Black law and custom to the devolution of the whole, or some part, of his property inequitable or inappropriate, the Minister may direct that the said property or the said part thereof, as the case may be, shall devolve as if the said Black and the said partner had been lawfully married out of community of property, whether or not such was in fact the case, and as if the said Black had been a European.

(e) If the deceased does not fall into any of the classes described in Paras *(b)*, *(c)* and *(d)*, the property shall be distributed according to Black law and custom....

The system that flows from the above legislative framework purports to give effect to customary law. It is a parallel system, different in concept and in effect, to that which flows from the Intestate Succession Act, ... Quite clearly the Constitution itself envisages a place for customary law in our legal system.

Certain provisions of the Constitution put it beyond doubt that our basic law specifically requires that customary law should be accommodated, not merely tolerated, as part of South African law, provided the particular rules or provisions are not in conflict with the Constitution. It should however not be inferred from the above that customary law can never change and that it cannot be amended or adjusted by legislation. In the first place, customary law is subject to the Constitution. Adjustments and development to bring its provisions in line with the Constitution or to accord with the 'spirit, purport and objects of the Bill of Rights' are mandated. Secondly, the legislative authority of the Republic vests in Parliament. Thirdly, the Constitution envisages a role for national legislation in the operation, implementation and/or changes effected to customary law ...

The prohibition of unfair discrimination on the ground of birth in § 9(3) of our Constitution should be interpreted to include a prohibition of differentiating between children on the basis of whether a child's biological parents were married either at the time the child was conceived or when the child was born.... The prohibition of unfair discrimination in our Constitution is aimed at removing such patterns of stigma from our society. Thus, when § 9(3) prohibits unfair discrimination on the ground of 'birth', it should be interpreted to include a prohibition of differentiation between children on the grounds of whether the children's parents were married at the time of conception or birth. Where differentiation is made on such grounds, it will be assumed to be unfair unless it is established that it is not....

Section 28 of the Constitution provides specific protection for the rights of children. Our constitutional obligations in relation to children are particularly important for we vest in our children our hopes for a better life for all....

A number of international instruments, to which South Africa is party, also underscore the need to protect the rights of women, and to abolish all rights violated are important rights, particularly in the South African context. The rights to equality and dignity are of the most valuable of rights in any open and democratic state. They assume special importance in South Africa because of our past history of inequality and hurtful discrimination on grounds that include race and gender.

It could be argued that despite its racist and sexist nature, § 23 gives recognition to customary law and acknowledges the pluralist nature of our society. This is however not its dominant purpose or effect. Section 23 was enacted as part of a racist programme intent on entrenching division and subordination. Its effect has been to ossify customary law. In the light of its destructive purpose and effect, it could not be justified in any open and democratic society. It is clear from what is stated above that the serious violation by the provisions of § 23 of the rights to equality and human dignity cannot be justified in our new constitutional order. In terms of § 172(1)(*a*) of the Constitution, § 23 must accordingly be struck down.

2. *Rono v. Rono* (Kenya Court of Appeal)[8]

The parties appealed to the Court of Appeal after a dispute arose as to the mode of distribution of the estate of the deceased. The main ground for appeal was that the superior court erred in taking into consideration the Keiyo customary law since the estate that fell

---

8. Civil Appeal No. 66 of 2002; *Available at* www.kenyalawreports.or.ke/family/case_download.php?go [last visited July 19, 2011].

for consideration had been governed by Law of Succession. The parties had agreed on the distribution of several properties but the bone of contention lay in the distribution of one of the 192 acres of land and the liabilities of the estate. The respondents/sons wanted the bigger portion of the property to go to the first house and specifically to the male children because the land was bought and improvements made on it before the existence of the second house. It was their contention their sisters had the option of getting married and moving away. Further, they submitted that under Keiyo traditions, the girls had no right to inherit their father's estate. The appellants/daughters claimed discrimination and stated that there was no proof that the respondents had worked harder on that property than they had. They also claimed that the deceased had also educated all his children without discriminating against the girls. In arriving at what it called "its own independent distribution", the Superior Court considered both customary and statutory laws on succession. It made a finding that ... the pattern of inheritance was patrilineal, and that in polygamous households distribution was by reference to the house of each wife irrespective of the number of children in it. Daughters receive no share of inheritance. The Superior Court also referred to the Law of Succession Act sections 27, 28, 40 (1) and (2) relating to distribution to dependants and division to houses according to the number of units, adding the widow as an additional unit. In the end, the learned judge took into consideration the wishes of the parties and of written law that the girls should also inherit. But she found that the possibility of the girls getting married and inheriting further property from their new families would give them an unfair advantage over the other family members. She held:

> The situation prevailing here is rather peculiar though not uncommon in that one house has sons while another has only daughters. Statute law recognizes both sexes to be eligible for inheritance. I also note that it is on record that the deceased treated his children equally. It follows that all the daughters will get equal shares and all the sons will get equal shares. However due to the fact that daughters have an option to marry, the daughters will not get equal shares to boys. As for the widows if they were to get equal shares then the second widow will be disadvantaged as she does not have sons. Her share should be slightly more than that of the first widow whose sons will have bigger shares than daughters of the second house."

The distribution of the land thus ended up as follows:

(a) Widows

Jane Rono—20 acres

Mary Rono—50 acres

Total—70 acres

(b) Daughters

Lina Rono—5 acres

Mary Chebii—5 acres

Cherutich Rono—5 acres

Grace Rono—5 acres

Chepkemboi Rono—5 acres

Rose Rono—5 acres

Total—30 acres

(c) Sons

William Rono—30 acres

Samuel Rono—30 acres

John Rono—30 acres

Total—92 acres (sic)

The main ground was that the superior court erred in taking into consideration the *Marakwet* customary law or any customary law, since the estate that fell for consideration was governed by the Law of Succession Act, cap 160 Laws of Kenya. Section 3(2) of that Act defines "child" without any discrimination on account of sex. The Constitution of Kenya also in section 82 outlaws discrimination on grounds, *inter alia*, of sex. Mr Gicheru thus submitted that section 40 of the Succession Act should have been applied in which case all the children and the widows would have been considered as units, entitling them to equal distribution of the land. It was erroneous therefore to entertain the consideration that the girls would have unfair advantage due to the possibility of their future marriage.

On the evidence the girls in both houses were advanced in age in 1994, and were still unmarried or divorced 10 years later when this appeal was argued. The speculation that they would marry had therefore no basis. As there was no special inquiry made to determine whether any of the heirs deserved more land than the others, there was no basis for discriminating against the girls. It did not matter, he submitted, that the appellant received 50 acres, which is 30 acres more than her co-widow. Such distribution would still be contrary to the law and the purpose of the appeal was to enforce compliance with the law of succession. The manner in which Courts apply the law in this country is spelt out in section 3 of the Judicature Act chapter 8, Laws of Kenya. The application of African customary laws takes pride of place in section 3(2) but it is circumscribed thus:

> [...]so far as it is applicable and is not repugnant to justice and morality or inconsistent with any written law, ...

The Constitution, which takes hierarchical primacy in the mode of exercise of jurisdiction, outlaws any law that is discriminatory in itself or in effect. That is section 82(1). In section 82(3), it defines discrimination as follows:

> Affording different treatment to different persons attributable wholly or mainly to their respective descriptions by race, tribe, place of origin or residence or other local connexion, political opinions, colour, creed, or sex whereby persons of one such description are subjected to disabilities or restrictions to which persons of another such description are not made subject or are accorded privileges or advantages which are not accorded to persons of another such description.

That provision has not always been the same with regard to discrimination on grounds of sex. "Or sex" was inserted in a relatively recent constitutional amendment by Act No. 9 of 1997. In the same section however, the protection is taken away by provisions in section 82 (4) which allow discriminatory laws, thus:

> Subsection (1) shall not apply to any law so far as the law makes provision—...
>
> (b) With respect to adoption, marriage, divorce, burial, devolution of property on death or other matters of personal law;

(c) For the application in the case of members of a particular race or tribe of customary law with respect to any matter to the exclusion of any law with respect to that matter which is applicable in the case of other persons; or

(d) Whereby persons of a description mentioned in subsection (3) may be subjected to a disability or restriction or may be accorded a privilege or advantage which, having regard to its nature and to special circumstances pertaining to those persons or to persons for any other description, is reasonably justifiable in a democratic society.

Is international law relevant for consideration in this matter? As a member of the international community, Kenya subscribes to international customary laws and has ratified various international covenants and treaties. In particular, it subscribes to the International Bill of Rights, which is the Universal Declaration of Human Rights (1948) and two International Human Rights Covenants: the Covenant on Economic, Social and Cultural Rights and the Covenant on Civil and Political Rights (both adopted by the UN General Assembly in 1966). In 1984 it also ratified, without reservations, the Convention on the Elimination of All Forms of Discrimination Against Women, in short, "CEDAW". Article 1 thereof defines discrimination against women as:—

Any distinction, exclusion or restriction made on the basis of sex which has the effect or purpose of impairing or nullifying the recognition, enjoyment or exercise by women irrespective of their marital status, on a basis of equality of men and women, of human rights and fundamental freedoms in the political, economic, social cultural, civil or any other field.

In the African context, Kenya subscribes to the African Charter of Human and Peoples' Rights, otherwise known as the Banjul Charter (1981), which it ratified in 1992 without reservations. In article 18, the Charter enjoins member states, *inter alia*, to:

[...]ensure the elimination of every discrimination against women and also ensure the protection of rights of the woman and the child as stipulated in international declarations and conventions.

It is in the context of those international laws that the 1997 amendment to section 82 of the Constitution becomes understandable. The country was moving in tandem with emerging global culture, particularly on gender issues. There has of course, for a long time, been raging debates in our jurisprudence about the application of international laws within our domestic context. Of the two theories on when international law should apply, Kenya subscribes to the common law view that international law is only part of domestic law where it has been specifically incorporated. In civil law jurisdictions, the adoption theory is that international law is automatically part of domestic law except where it is in conflict with domestic law. However, the current thinking on the common law theory is that both international customary law and treaty law can be applied by State Courts where there is no conflict with existing state law, even in the absence of implementing legislation. Principle 7 of the Bangalore Principles on the Domestic Application of International Human Rights Norms states:

It is within the proper nature of the judicial process and well established functions for national Courts to have regard to international obligations which a country undertakes—whether or not they have been incorporated into domestic law—for the purpose of removing ambiguity or uncertainty from national Constitutions, legislation or the common law.

While I do not doubt the discretion donated by the Act in matters where dependants seek a fair distribution of the deceased's net estate I think the discretion, like all discretions exercised by Courts, must be made judicially or to put it another way, on sound legal and factual basis. The possibility that girls in any particular family may be married is only one factor among others that may be considered in exercising the Court's discretion. It is not a determining factor. In this particular case however, I find no firm factual basis for making a finding that the daughters would be married. As shown by the undisputed facts above, all except one were unmarried or divorced in 1994 and were advanced in age. Eleven years later when this appeal was heard, there was no evidence that the situation had changed. It is also an undisputed fact that the deceased treated all his children equally and never discriminated between them on account of sex. It is a factor in my view that was not sufficiently considered although it resonates with the noble notions enunciated in our Constitution and international laws. The respondents themselves clearly recognized and honoured the wishes of the deceased when they proposed to give 14 acres of the land to each daughter of the deceased. I find no justification for the Superior Court whittling that proposal down to 5 acres to each daughter.

More importantly, section 40 of the Act which applies to the estate makes provision for distribution of the net estate to the "houses according to the number of children in each house, but also adding any wife surviving the deceased as an additional unit to the number of children." A "house" in a polygamous setting is defined in section 3 of the Act as a "family unit comprising a wife ... and the children of that wife". There is no discrimination of such children on account of their sex. I think, in the circumstances of this case there is considerable force in the argument by Mr Gicheru that the estate of the deceased ought to have been distributed more equitably taking into account all relevant factors and the available legal provisions. I now take all that into account, and come to the conclusion that the distribution of the land, which is the issue falling for determination, must be set aside and substituted with an order that the net estate of 192 acres of land be shared out as follows:

(a) Two (2) acres for the farm-house now commonly occupied by all members of the family to be held in trust by the joint administrators of the estate.

(b) Thirty (30) acres to the first widow, Jane Toroitich Rono.

(c) Thirty (30) acres to the second widow, Mary Toroitich Rono.

(d) Fourteen decimal four four (14.44) acres to each of the nine (9) children of the deceased.

Questions for Discussion

1. *The Courts in these two countries seem willing to alter customary practices in order to protect women's rights. Yet not all courts would be willing to do so. What are other ways of accomplishing changes for women in discriminatory customary practices?*

2. *Not all women have access to the legal system in order to bring their complaints before courts. What role might NGOs and other organizations play in assisting women who find themselves dispossessed? Could the CEDAW Committee play a role?*

3. *Would a customary law disinheritance case be a good case to bring to the CEDAW Committee if all domestic remedies had been exhausted?*

F. Access to Other Economic Resources

1. 2009 World Survey on the Role of Women in Development — Women's Control over Economic Resources and Access to Financial Resources, Including Microfinance[9]

Women's equal access to and control over economic and financial resources is critical for the achievement of gender equality and empowerment of women and for equitable and sustainable economic growth and development. Gender equality in the distribution of economic and financial resources has positive multiplier effects for a range of key development goals, including poverty reduction and the welfare of children....

Long-standing inequalities in the gender distribution of economic and financial resources have placed women at a disadvantage relative to men in their capability to participate in, contribute to and benefit from broader processes of development. Despite considerable progress on many aspects of women's economic empowerment through, inter alia, increases in educational attainment and share of paid work, deeply entrenched inequality persists as a result of discriminatory norms and practices, and the pace of change has been slow and uneven across regions. Women continue to be absent from key decision-making forums shaping the allocation of economic and financial resources and opportunities, which further perpetuates gender inequality....

Gender equality perspectives have, however, been largely ignored in formulation of macroeconomic policies. Development of gender-responsive policies requires an understanding of and attention to the distributional consequences of economic growth strategies and monetary, fiscal, trade and investment policies, as well as the specific constraints to women's economic empowerment, including in particular the unequal gender distribution of paid and unpaid work and its implications for access to economic resources and opportunities....

Access to full employment and decent work

Labour is the most widely available factor of production at the disposal of poor people around the world and the primary means through which they earn a living. Although women's share of employment has increased, a gender division of labour persists. The contraction of formal employment and decent work and proliferation of "atypical" or non-standard work, which is generally precarious, poorly paid and uncovered by labour legislation or social protection, has particularly affected women. Lack of access to decent work is a major cause of poverty among women.

Constraints faced by women in the labour market include their disproportionate concentration in vulnerable forms of work, occupational segregation — both horizontal and vertical, wage gaps and the unequal division of unpaid domestic work. These constraints reflect women's disadvantage in education; lack of organized voice and bargaining power; constraints on labour market mobility; relatively high involvement in part-time or temporary jobs; concentration in employment where pressures of global competition keep wages down; and direct discrimination.

---

9. *Available at* http://www.un.org/womenwatch/daw/public/WorldSurvey2009.pdf [last visited July 20, 2011].

Access to land, housing and other productive resources

Women in many parts of the world continue to face discrimination in access to land, housing, property and other productive resources and have limited access to technologies and services that could alleviate their work burdens. Unequal access to resources limits women's capacity to ensure agricultural productivity, security of livelihoods and food security and is increasingly linked to poverty, migration, urbanization and increased risk of violence. Population growth, climate change, the spread of markets and urbanization have created new opportunities and new challenges in women's access to land, housing and other productive resources.

Attention to the resource challenges women face in agriculture is essential for addressing the food and energy crises and climate change in both the short and long term.

Access to financial resources

Women's access to all financial services, including savings, insurance, remittance transfers and credit, is essential to allow them to benefit fully from economic opportunities. Legal, institutional and sociocultural barriers often, however, limit women's access to these services.

Microfinance, which emerged in response to the failure of the formal financial system to reach the poor, has been successful in reaching poor women through innovative measures to address gender-specific constraints. Some organizations seek to redress gender inequalities in access to finance and other work towards broader gender equality goals. Many combine financial services with a range of social services. Most organizations use group-based approaches to service provision, with variations around the basic principle. Some organizations combine group and individual lending since group lending, while useful for those starting up businesses, can act as a constraint on more successful entrepreneurs.

There is lack of consensus on the extent to which access to microfinance empowers women. While there is evidence that microfinance has a positive impact on income, there are limits to the income gains. Despite fewer studies on health, nutrition and education, positive impacts have been noted.

2. Report of the Special Rapporteur on the Right to Adequate Housing

The Special Rapporteur welcomes the adoption by consensus of Commission resolution 2001/34 on women's equal ownership of, access to and control over land and the equal rights to own property and to adequate housing, which, in its Paragraph 5, expressly reaffirmed women's right to adequate housing. It may be recalled that the International Covenant on Economic, Social and Cultural Rights guarantees in article 2 (2) the rights embodied in the Covenant without discrimination on account of "race, colour, sex, language, religion, political or other opinion, national or social origin, property, birth or other status", and in article 3 places an obligation on States to "ensure the equal rights of men and women."

Although discrimination on any of the prohibited grounds therefore constitutes a violation, discrimination often affects women disproportionately. For example, several States still retain legal systems that do not recognize or protect a woman's right to adequate housing, particularly regarding laws dealing with either home ownership or inheritance, or both. For States parties to the Covenant, the obligation to amend such laws so as to eliminate any discriminatory impact is an obligation of immediate effect and a failure to do so constitutes a human rights violation. The Maastricht Guidelines also recognize this point, and note that the Convention on the Elimination of All Forms of Discrimination against Women provides additional non-discriminatory protection to women with respect to economic, social and cultural rights.

3. Resolution 2001/34 on Women's Equal Ownership of, Access to, and Control over, Land and the Equal Rights to Own Property and to Adequate Housing

The Commission on Human Rights, ...

Recognizing that laws, policies, customs and traditions that restrict women's equal access to credit and loans also prevent women from owning and inheriting land, property and housing and exclude women from participating fully in development processes, are discriminatory and may contribute to the feminization of poverty,

Recognizing also that the full and equal participation of women in all spheres of life is essential for the full and complete development of a country,

Stressing that the impact of gender-based discrimination and violence against women on women's equal ownership of, access to and control over land and the equal rights to own property and to adequate housing is acute, particularly during complex emergency situations, reconstruction and rehabilitation,

Convinced that international, regional and local trade, finance and investment policies should be designed in such a way that they do not increase gender inequality in terms of ownership of, access to and control over land and the rights to own property and to adequate housing and other productive resources and do not undermine women's capacity to acquire and retain these resources,

Mindful of the fact that elimination of discrimination against women requires consideration of women's specific socio-economic context,

1. *Affirms* that discrimination in law against women with respect to having access to, acquiring and securing land, property and housing, as well as financing for land, property and housing, constitutes a violation of women's human right to protection against discrimination;

2. *Reaffirms* women's right to an adequate standard of living, including adequate housing as enshrined in the Universal Declaration of Human Rights and the International Covenant on Economic, Social and Cultural Rights;

3. *Also reaffirms* the obligation of States to take all appropriate measures to eliminate discrimination against women by any person, organization or enterprise;

4. *Urges* Governments to comply fully with their international and regional obligations and commitments concerning land tenure and the equal rights of women to own property and to an adequate standard of living, including adequate housing;

5. *Reaffirms* Commission on the Status of Women resolution 42/1, which, inter alia, urged States to design and revise laws to ensure that women are accorded full and equal rights to own land and other property, and the right to adequate housing, including through the right to inheritance, and to undertake administrative reforms and other necessary measures to give women the same right as men to credit, capital, appropriate technologies, access to markets and information;

6. *Encourages* Governments to support the transformation of customs and traditions that discriminate against women and deny women security of tenure and equal ownership of, access to and control over land and equal rights to own property and to adequate housing, to ensure the right of women to equal treatment in land and agrarian reform as well as in land resettlement schemes and in ownership of property and in adequate housing, and to take other measures to increase access to land and housing for women living in poverty, particularly female heads of household; ...

G. Access to Education

1. The *Beijing Declaration*[10]

Education and Training of Women

Education is a human right and an essential tool for achieving the goals of equality, development and peace. Non-discriminatory education benefits both girls and boys and thus ultimately contributes to more equal relationships between women and men. Equality of access to and attainment of educational qualifications is necessary if more women are to become agents of change. Literacy of women is an important key to improving health, nutrition and education in the family and to empowering women to participate in decision-making in society. Investing in formal and non-formal education and training for girls and women, with its exceptionally high social and economic return, has proved to be one of the best means of achieving sustainable development and economic growth that is both sustained and sustainable....

On a regional level, girls and boys have achieved equal access to primary education, except in some parts of Africa, in particular sub-Saharan Africa, and Central Asia, where access to education facilities is still inadequate. Progress has been made in secondary education, where equal access of girls and boys has been achieved in some countries.... Yet, more than five years after the World Conference on Education for All ... adopted the World Declaration on Education for All and the Framework for Action to Meet Basic Learning Needs, approximately 100 million children, including at least 60 million girls, are without access to primary schooling and more than two thirds of the world's 960 million illiterate adults are women. The high rate of illiteracy prevailing in most developing countries, in particular in sub-Saharan Africa and some Arab States, remains a severe impediment to the advancement of women and to development.

Discrimination in girls' access to education persists in many areas, owing to customary attitudes, early marriages and pregnancies, inadequate and gender-biased teaching and educational materials, sexual harassment and lack of adequate and physically and otherwise accessible schooling facilities. Girls undertake heavy domestic work at a very early age. Girls and young women are expected to manage both educational and domestic responsibilities, often resulting in poor scholastic performance and early drop-out from the educational system....

Creation of an educational and social environment, in which women and men, girls and boys, are treated equally and encouraged to achieve their full potential,

---

10. *Available at* http://www.un.org/womenwatch/daw/beijing15/ [last visited July 20, 2011].

respecting their freedom of thought, conscience, religion and belief, and where educational resources promote non-stereotyped images of women and men, would be effective in the elimination of the causes of discrimination against women and inequalities between women and men.

Women should be enabled to benefit from an ongoing acquisition of knowledge and skills beyond those acquired during youth....

Curricula and teaching materials remain gender-biased to a large degree, and are rarely sensitive to the specific needs of girls and women. This reinforces traditional female and male roles that deny women opportunities for full and equal partnership in society.... The lack of sexual and reproductive health education has a profound impact on women and men.

Science curricula in particular are gender-biased. Science textbooks do not relate to women's and girls' daily experience and fail to give recognition to women scientists. Girls are often deprived of basic education in mathematics and science and technical training, which provide knowledge they could apply to improve their daily lives and enhance their employment opportunities....

Actions to be taken

80. By Governments:

   a. Advance the goal of equal access to education by taking measures to eliminate discrimination in education at all levels on the basis of gender, race, language, religion, national origin, age or disability, or any other form of discrimination and, as appropriate, consider establishing procedures to address grievances;

   b. By the year 2000, provide universal access to basic education and ensure completion of primary education by at least 80 per cent of primary school-age children; close the gender gap in primary and secondary school education by the year 2005; provide universal primary education in all countries before the year 2015;

   c. Eliminate gender disparities in access to all areas of tertiary education by ensuring that women have equal access to career development, training, scholarships and fellowships, and by adopting positive action when appropriate;

   d. Create a gender-sensitive educational system in order to ensure equal educational and training opportunities and full and equal participation of women in educational administration and policy- and decision-making; ...

Strategic objective B.2.

Eradicate illiteracy among women

Actions to be taken

By Governments, national, regional and international bodies, bilateral and multilateral donors and non-governmental organizations:

   a. Reduce the female illiteracy rate to at least half its 1990 level, with emphasis on rural women, migrant, refugee and internally displaced women and women with disabilities;

   b. provide universal access to, and seek to ensure gender equality in the completion of, primary education for girls by the year 2000;

   c.   Eliminate the gender gap in basic and functional literacy, as recommended in the World Declaration on Education for All (Jomtien);

   d.   Narrow the disparities between developed and developing countries;

   e.   Encourage adult and family engagement in learning to promote total literacy for all people;

   f.   Promote, together with literacy, life skills and scientific and technological knowledge and work towards an expansion of the definition of literacy, taking into account current targets and benchmarks.

2. *Make it Right — Report on Ending the Crisis in Girls' Education*[11]

Education is central to developing a girl's capabilities, empowering her, promoting awareness and critical thinking, enabling her to claim all other human rights and make more informed decisions (Sen 1999). Education enables girls and women to demand their right to health for themselves and their families, promotes development of legal and policy frameworks that are in tune with gender equity, and advances other policies that promote the fulfilment of all their other rights. It can also increase awareness of legal and judicial mechanisms to protect women from rights violations, including exploitation and domestic violence. It furthermore fosters women's participation in countries' democratic life, increasing their participation in decisionmaking arenas and in formal power structures.

Education can transform the unequal power relations which consistently play out in the home and public sphere in the lived experience of women's oppression, for example by making it less likely that they will send their girl children away to work in domestic contexts or, worse, in commercial sexual exploitation. By providing the knowledge, skills and capabilities to make informed choices, protect and defend themselves from abuse and exploitation and achieve economic and social self-determination — education is an important catalyst to realize gender equality.

When a girl gets the opportunity to learn by accessing and remaining in good quality schooling it has a transformative effect not only on her own life chances and the realization of her human rights, but also on the wider social and economic environment (Herz and Sperling 2004, UNDP 1995, The Girl Effect 2010, ASPBAE 2010). Educating girls is the key to ensuring improved mother and child health, community development and economic growth.

3. UNICEF — *Report on the State of the World's Children* (2007)

Women must manage 3,000 days of menstruation in their lifetime, and 450 of those days coincide with the years of basic schooling. Each year, millions of girls and women do not attend fifty days of school or work because of their periods; many of them drop out of school or the workforce entirely. Education is key to solving many global issues such as gender-related injustices and economic inequalities. A report released by Goldman Sachs Economic Research states, "There

---

11. *See* http://www.ungei.org/files/MakeItRight_Report_07.pdf [last visited July 15, 2011].

may be no better investment for the health and development of poor countries around the world than investments to educate girls." Educated women are more likely to participate in the workforce, and there is a link between high education levels and low fertility rates. Statistics prove that female education correlates with higher national economic productivity and higher returns to investment.

Menstruation detrimentally impacts girls' schooling for a number of reasons; first, a poor girl in a developing country may not have access to the supplies she needs to deal with menstruation. Moreover, in a report conducted by UNICEF in Tanzania, researchers found that[12]

> Lack of sanitation, hand-washing facilities and hygiene education in schools makes it even more difficult for girls to handle menstruation. In a study of every school in 16 districts in Tanzania undertaken in 2009, it was identified that 52 per cent of all schools had no doors on their latrines, 92 per cent had no functional hand-washing facilities and 99 per cent had no soap, all of which would make it very difficult for a young girl to easily manage her menstrual period.

H. Women and Microfinancing

Microfinance is the practice of providing small loans to low-income people who are typically excluded from the formal banking sector because of their lack of credit history and lack of collateral. The recipients generally use these loans to start a business. Microfinance was largely pioneered by Muhammad Yunus, a Bangladeshi economist. It was seen as a way out of poverty for low income people, without merely providing them with a handout. Soon development specialist realized the potential microfinancing could offer to women, who are often excluded from access to loans through more traditional means.

Organizations like Kiva and Accion (www.kiva.org and www.accion.org) enable everyday donors to loan small amounts of money to individuals, who use the money to start small business such as selling produce and firewood. Borrowers pay the lenders back with interest. However, the initial enthusiasm for microfinancing has been somewhat tempered by the results of a recent case study conducted by Women's World Banking (WWB).

1. *Solutions for Financial Inclusion — Serving Rural Women — Report of Women's World Banking* (WWB) (2009)[13]

> Women in many rural households also struggle to maintain control over the use of microfinance loans, even when they are taken in their own name and intended for investment in a woman's income-generating activity. Because men generally control flows of money in and out of the household, it is often assumed that they can control the use of a loan, frequently resulting in men using all or some

---

12. *Available at* http://www.twesa.org/documents/Menstruation%20-%20UNICEF%20proposal.pdf [last visited July 20, 2011].

13. *Available at* http://www.swwb.org/sites/default/files/pubs/en/solutions_for_financial_inclusion _serving_rural_women.pdf [last visited July 20, 2011].

of the loan amount for their own use. This can leave women with an onerous loan repayment for money from which they have not (fully) benefitted. "After he has eaten that money, then he starts yelling 'Why can't you repay the loan?'" said a woman respondent. This pattern can prevent women from investing in agricultural improvements that matter to them—improvements to the types of livestock and crops and new labor-saving technologies that can help ease their workload and enhance productivity.

I. Women's Empowerment Principles— Empowering Women in Business[14]

The UN Global Compact drafted the following principles in 2009 as a means of empowering women in business:

1. Leadership Promotes Gender Equality

a. Affirm high-level support and direct top-level policies for gender equality and human rights.

b. Establish company-wide goals and targets for gender equality and include progress as a factor in managers' performance reviews.

c. Engage internal and external stakeholders in the development of company policies, programmes and implementation plans that advance equality.

d. Ensure that all policies are gender-sensitive—identifying factors that impact women and men differently—and that corporate culture advances equality and inclusion.

2. Equal Opportunity, Inclusion, and Nondiscrimination

a. Pay equal remuneration, including benefits, for work of equal value and strive to pay a living wage to all women and men.

b. Ensure that workplace policies and practices are free from gender-based discrimination.

c. Implement gender-sensitive recruitment and retention practices and proactively recruit and appoint women to managerial and executive positions and to the corporate board of directors.

d. Assure sufficient participation of women—30% or greater—in decision-making and governance at all levels and across all business areas.

e. Offer flexible work options, leave and re-entry opportunities to positions of equal pay and status.

f. Support access to child and dependent care by providing services, resources and information to both women and men.

---

14. Unifem-UN Global Compact; *Available at* http://www.unglobalcompact.org/Issues/human_rights/equality_means_business.html [last visited July 2011].

3. Health, Safety, and Freedom from Violence

a. Taking into account differential impacts on women and men, provide safe working conditions and protection from exposure to hazardous materials and disclose potential risks, including to reproductive health.

b. Establish a zero-tolerance policy towards all forms of violence at work, including verbal and/or physical abuse, and prevent sexual harassment.

c. Strive to offer health insurance or other needed services — including for survivors of domestic violence — and ensure equal access for all employees.

d. Respect women and men workers' rights to time off for medical care and counseling for themselves and their dependents.

e. In consultation with employees, identify and address security issues, including the safety of women traveling to and from work and on company-related business.

f. Train security staff and managers to recognize signs of violence against women and understand laws and company policies on human trafficking, labour and sexual exploitation.

4. Education and Training

a. Invest in workplace policies and programmes that open avenues for advancement of women at all levels and across all business areas, and encourage women to enter nontraditional job fields.

b. Ensure equal access to all company-supported education and training programmes, including literacy classes, vocational and information technology training.

c. Provide equal opportunities for formal and informal networking and mentoring.

d. Offer opportunities to promote the business case for women's empowerment and the positive impact of inclusion for men as well as women.

5. Enterprise Development, Supply Chain, and Marketing Practices

a. Expand business relationships with women-owned enterprises, including small businesses, and women entrepreneurs.

b. Support gender-sensitive solutions to credit and lending barriers.

c. Ask business partners and peers to respect the company's commitment to advancing equality and inclusion.

d. Respect the dignity of women in all marketing and other company materials.

e. Ensure that company products, services and facilities are not used for human trafficking and/or labour or sexual exploitation.

6. Community Leadership and Engagement

a. Lead by example — showcase company commitment to gender equality and women's empowerment.

b. Leverage influence, alone or in partnership, to advocate for gender equality and collaborate with business partners, suppliers and community leaders to promote inclusion.

c. Work with community stakeholders, officials and others to eliminate discrimination and exploitation and open opportunities for women and girls.

d. Promote and recognize women's leadership in, and contributions to, their communities and ensure sufficient representation of women in any community consultation.

e. Use philanthropy and grants programmes to support company commitment to inclusion, equality and human rights.

7. Transparency, Measuring and Reporting

a. Make public the company policies and implementation plan for promoting gender equality.

b. Establish benchmarks that quantify inclusion of women at all levels.

c. Measure and report on progress, both internally and externally, using data disaggregated by gender.

d. Incorporate gender markers into ongoing reporting obligations.

J. Calling Attention to the Special Needs of Vulnerable Women[15]

Secretary-General Ban Ki-moon today urged societies to ease the hardship that widows endure when their husbands die by respecting their rights to such social entitlements as access to inheritance, land tenure, employment and other means of livelihood.

"All widows should be protected by the rights enshrined in the Convention on the Elimination of All Forms of Discrimination against Women and other international human rights treaties," said Mr. Ban in a message to mark the first *International Widows Day*, which will be observed on 23 June every year.

"But in reality, interpretations of customary codes, as well as traditional mourning and burial rites, often deny widows virtually all of their universally recognized rights," said the Secretary-General.

The Day was created by the General Assembly last year in an effort to highlight violations of the rights of widowed women with a view to ensuring their protection under national and international law, empowering them and restoring their human dignity.

The Secretary-General noted that of the approximately 245 million widows in the world, more than 115 million live in extreme poverty, and that in countries affected by conflict, women are frequently widowed young, thrusting upon them

---

15. *See* http://www.un.org/en/events/widowsday/sgmessage.shtml [last visited June 2, 2011].

the heavy burden of caring for children, often in environments of unrest, displacement and lack of support.

"In places where a widow's status is linked to her husband, she may find herself suddenly shunned and isolated. Marriage—whether she desires it or not—may be the only way for a widow to regain her footing in society.

"Some of these widows are teenagers—or even younger. The death of their husbands can leave a terrible legacy these widows must endure throughout their remaining years," said Mr. Ban.

In many countries, widowhood is stigmatized and seen as a source of shame, with women whose husbands have died thought to be cursed in some cultures or even associated with witchcraft. Such misconceptions can lead to widows being ostracized and abused. Poverty among windows is often exacerbated by little or no access to credit or other economic resources, and by illiteracy or lack of education.

Mr. Ban said that despite the difficulties that widows face, many make valuable contributions to their communities, often taking on leadership roles at the highest levels. Others work in their families, taking in orphans, serving as caregivers and reaching across lines of conflict to mend tears in the social fabric.

"We must recognize the important contribution of widows, and we must ensure that they enjoy the rights and social protections they deserve.

"Death is inevitable, but we can reduce the suffering that widows endure by raising their status and helping them in their hour of need. This will contribute to promoting the full and equal participation of all women in society. And that will bring us closer to ending poverty and promoting peace around the world," the Secretary-General added.

Governments have the responsibility to adhere to their commitments to ensure the rights of widows as enshrined in international law are respected. Even when national laws exist to protect the rights of widows, weaknesses in the judicial systems may compromise the way widows' rights are defended. Lack of awareness and discrimination by judicial officials can also prevent widows from approaching the justice system to seek reparations.

Questions for Discussion

1. *Access to credit and microfinancing seems like one possible avenue to assist women in getting out of poverty. What gender based strategies could lenders offer women to enable them to take advantage of microfinancing? Could they travel to meet with women in their homes for example?*

2. *How could information about microfinancing best be made available to poor rural women?*

Chapter 16

Women and Employment

Chapter Problem

Your client is a young woman who has just graduated from college. She is as yet unmarried, but plans to marry, and hopes to start a family within the next few years. She is in the fortunate position of having been offered a position with a multinational firm, and has the choice of working either in the United States, or in the firm's offices in Sweden. She has consulted you for advice about gender-friendly policies in the workplace these two countries. She is particularly concerned with pay equity, opportunities for advancement, the commitment of each government towards advancing gender equitable policies, and a work environment that is respectful of women's rights, and that will enable her to spend time with her family too.

I. CEDAW and Employment

Article 11

1. States Parties shall take all appropriate measures to eliminate discrimination against women in the field of employment in order to ensure, on a basis of equality of men and women, the same rights, in particular:

(a) The right to work as an inalienable right of all human beings;

(b) The right to the same employment opportunities, including the application of the same criteria for selection in matters of employment;

(c) The right to free choice of profession and employment, the right to promotion, job security and all benefits and conditions of service and the right to receive vocational training and retraining, including apprenticeships, advanced vocational training and recurrent training;

(d) The right to equal remuneration, including benefits, and to equal treatment in respect of work of equal value, as well as equality of treatment in the evaluation of the quality of work;

(e) The right to social security, particularly in cases of retirement, unemployment, sickness, invalidity and old age and other incapacity to work, as well as the right to paid leave;

(f) The right to protection of health and to safety in working conditions, including the safeguarding of the function of reproduction.

2. In order to prevent discrimination against women on the grounds of marriage or maternity and to ensure their effective right to work, States Parties shall take appropriate measures:

(a) To prohibit, subject to the imposition of sanctions, dismissal on the grounds of pregnancy or of maternity leave and discrimination in dismissals on the basis of marital status;

(b) To introduce maternity leave with pay or with comparable social benefits without loss of former employment, seniority or social allowances;

(c) To encourage the provision of the necessary supporting social services to enable parents to combine family obligations with work responsibilities and participation in public life, in particular through promoting the establishment and development of a network of child-care facilities;

(d) To provide special protection to women during pregnancy in types of work proved to be harmful to them.

3. Protective legislation relating to matters covered in this article shall be reviewed periodically in the light of scientific and technological knowledge and shall be revised, repealed or extended as necessary.

II. International Conventions Guaranteeing Pay Equality

The International Labour Organization (ILO) has long been at the forefront of the battle for pay equality.

A. International Labor (ILO) Convention Concerning Equal Remuneration for Men and Women Workers for Work of Equal Value (1951)

For the purpose of this Convention —

[…]

2. The term equal renumeration means any renumeration paid without discrimination on the basis of sex.

Article 2

1. Each Member shall, by means appropriate to the methods in operation for determining rates of remuneration, promote and, in so far as is consistent with such methods, ensure the application to all workers of the principle of equal remuneration for men and women workers for work of equal value.

2. This principle may be applied by means of—

(a) national laws or regulations;

(b) legally established or recognised machinery for wage determination;

(c) collective agreements between employers and workers; or

(d) a combination of these various means.

Article 3

1. Where such action will assist in giving effect to the provisions of this Convention measures shall be taken to promote objective appraisal of jobs on the basis of the work to be performed.

2. The methods to be followed in this appraisal may be decided upon by the authorities responsible for the determination of rates of remuneration, or, where such rates are determined by collective agreements, by the parties thereto.

3. Differential rates between workers which correspond, without regard to sex, to differences, as determined by such objective appraisal, in the work to be performed shall not be considered as being contrary to the principle of equal remuneration for men and women workers for work of equal value.

Article 4

Each Member shall co-operate as appropriate with the employers' and workers' organizations concerned for the purpose of giving effect to the provisions of this Convention.

B. Recommendation Concerning Equal Remuneration for Men and Women Workers for Work of Equal Value (1951)

Whereas the Convention provides that the application of the principle of equal remuneration for men and women workers for work of equal value shall be promoted or ensured by means appropriate to the methods in operation for determining rates of remuneration in the countries concerned;

Whereas it is desirable to indicate certain procedures for the progressive application of the principles laid down in the Convention;

Whereas it is at the same time desirable that all Members should, in applying these principles, have regard to methods of application which have been found satisfactory in certain countries;

The Conference recommends that each Member should, subject to the provisions of Article 2 of the Convention, apply the following provisions and report to the International Labour Office as requested by the Governing Body concerning the measures taken to give effect thereto:

1. Appropriate action should be taken, after consultation with the workers' organizations concerned or, where such organisations do not exist, with the workers concerned—

(a) to ensure the application of the principle of equal remuneration for men and women workers for work of equal value to all employees of central government departments or agencies; and

(b) to encourage the application of the principle to employees of state, provincial or local government departments or agencies, where these have jurisdiction over rates of remuneration.

2. Appropriate action should be taken, after consultation with the employers' and workers' organisations concerned, to ensure, as rapidly as practicable, the application of the principle of equal remuneration for men and women workers for work of equal value in all occupations, other than those mentioned in Paragraph 1, in which rates of remuneration are subject to statutory regulation or public control, particularly as regards—

(a) the establishment of minimum or other wage rates in industries and services where such rates are determined under public authority;

(b) industries and undertakings operated under public ownership or control; and

(c) where appropriate, work executed under the terms of public contracts.

3. (1) Where appropriate in the light of the methods in operation for the determination of rates of remuneration, provision should be made by legal enactment for the general application of the principle of equal remuneration for men and w omen workers for work of equal value.

(2) The competent public authority should take all necessary and appropriate measures to ensure that employers and workers are fully informed as to such legal requirements and, where appropriate, advised on their application.

4. When, after consultation with the organisations of workers and employers concerned, where such exist, it is not deemed feasible to implement immediately the principle of equal remuneration for men and women workers for work of equal value, in respect of employment covered by Paragraph 1, 2 or 3, appropriate provision should be made or caused to be made, as soon as possible, for its progressive application, by such measures as—

(a) decreasing the differentials between rates of remuneration for men and rates of remuneration for women for work of equal value;

(b) where a system of increments is in force, providing equal increments for men and women workers performing work of equal value.

5. Where appropriate for the purpose of facilitating the determination of rates of remuneration in accordance with the principle of equal remuneration for men and women workers for work of equal value, each Member should, in agreement with the employers' and workers' organizations concerned, establish or encourage the establishment of methods for objective appraisal of the work to be performed, whether by job analysis or by other procedures, with a view to providing a classification of jobs without regard to sex; such methods should be applied in accordance with the provisions of Article 2 of the Convention.

6. In order to facilitate the application of the principle of equal remuneration for men and women workers for work of equal value, appropriate action should be taken, where necessary, to raise the productive efficiency of women workers by such measures as—

(a) ensuring that workers of both sexes have equal or equivalent facilities for vocational guidance or employment counselling, for vocational training and for placement;

(b) taking appropriate measures to encourage women to use facilities for vocational guidance or employment counselling, for vocational training and for placement;

(c) providing welfare and social services which meet the needs of women workers, particularly those with family responsibilities, and financing such services from general public funds or from social security or industrial welfare funds financed by payments made in respect of workers without regard to sex; and

(d) promoting equality of men and women workers as regards access to occupations and posts without prejudice to the provisions of international regulations and of national laws and regulations concerning the protection of the health and welfare of women.

7. Every effort should be made to promote public understanding of the grounds on which it is considered that the principle of equal remuneration for men and women workers for work of equal value should be implemented.

8. Such investigations as may be desirable to promote the application of the principle should be undertaken.

C. ILO Convention No. 111 — Convention Concerning Discrimination in Respect of Employment and Occupation (1958)

Article 1

1. For the purpose of this Convention the term "discrimination" includes

(a) any distinction, exclusion or preference made on the basis of race, colour, sex, religion, political opinion, national extraction or social origin, which has the effect of nullifying or impairing equality of opportunity or treatment in employment or occupation;

(b) such other distinction, exclusion or preference which has the effect of nullifying or impairing equality of opportunity or treatment in employment or occupation as may be determined by the Member concerned after consultation with representative employers' and workers' organisations, where such exist, and with other appropriate bodies.

2. Any distinction, exclusion or preference in respect of a particular job based on the inherent requirements thereof shall not be deemed to be discrimination.

3. For the purpose of this Convention the terms "employment" and occupation" include access to vocational training, access to employment and to particular occupations, and terms and conditions of employment.

Article 2

Each Member for which this Convention is in force undertakes to declare and pursue a national policy designed to promote, by methods appropriate to national conditions and practice, equality of opportunity and treatment in respect of employment and occupation, with a view to eliminating any discrimination in respect thereof.

Article 3

Each Member for which this Convention is in force undertakes, by methods appropriate to national conditions and practice —

(a) to seek the co-operation of employers' and workers' organisations and other appropriate bodies in promoting the acceptance and observance of this policy;

(b) to enact such legislation and to promote such educational programmes as may be calculated to secure the acceptance and observance of the policy;

(c) to repeal any statutory provisions and modify any administrative instructions or practices which are inconsistent with the policy;

(d) to pursue the policy in respect of employment under the direct control of a national authority;

(e) to ensure observance of the policy in the activities of vocational guidance, vocational training and placement services under the direction of a national authority;

(f) to indicate in its annual reports on the application of the Convention the action taken in pursuance of the policy and the results secured by such action.

Article 4

Any measures affecting an individual who is justifiably suspected of, or engaged in, activities prejudicial to the security of the State shall not be deemed to be discrimination....

Article 5

1. Special measures of protection or assistance provided for in other Conventions or Recommendations adopted by the International Labour Conference shall not be deemed to be discrimination.

2. Any Member may, after consultation with representative employers' and workers' organisations, where such exist, determine that other special measures designed to meet the particular requirements of persons who, for reasons such as sex, age, disablement, family responsibilities or social or cultural status, are generally recognised to require special protection or assistance, shall not be deemed to be discrimination.

D. CEDAW Committee *General Recommendation No. 13—Equal Remuneration for Work of Equal Value* (1989)

The Committee on the Elimination of Discrimination against Women,

Recalling International Labour Organization Convention No. 100 concerning Equal Remuneration for Men and Women Workers for Work of Equal Value, which has been ratified by a large majority of States parties to the Convention on the Elimination of All Forms of Discrimination against Women,

Recalling also that it has considered 51 initial and five second periodic reports of States parties since 1983,

Considering that although reports of States parties indicate that, even though the principle of equal remuneration for work of equal value has been accepted in the legislation of many countries, more remains to be done to ensure the application of that principle in practice, in order to overcome the gender-segregation in the labour market,

Recommends to the States parties to the Convention on the Elimination of All Forms of Discrimination against Women that:

1. In order to implement fully the Convention on the Elimination of All forms of Discrimination of against Women, those States parties that have not yet ratified ILO Convention No. 100 should be encouraged to do so;

2. They should consider the study, development and adoption of job evaluation systems based on gender-neutral criteria that would facilitate the comparison of the value of those jobs of a different nature, in which women presently predominate, with those jobs in which men presently predominate, and they should include the results achieved in their reports to the Committee on the Elimination of Discrimination against Women;

3. They should support, as far as practicable, the creation of implementation machinery and encourage the efforts of the parties to collective agreements, where they apply, to ensure the application of the principle of equal remuneration for work of equal value.

III. Employment Discrimination and Pay Equality in Europe

A. European Parliament Resolution on Equal Pay for Work of Equal Value[1]

A. whereas the wage gap between women and men in the EU is 28% on average and, after taking account of structural differences in relation to men and women on the labour market, including age, training, occupation and career pattern, women's pay is still 15% lower, on average, than that of men,

B. whereas this wage gap of 15% on average can only be explained by value discrimination mechanisms, which is unacceptable,

C. whereas legislation concerning equal pay for work of equal value has been laid down at both European and national level, which the two sides of industry are largely responsible for implementing; whereas, however, in many cases, the law has made only a partial contribution to equal treatment in terms of pay for female and male workers,

D. whereas, in particular, the undervaluing of characteristics associated with women in the wage formation process leads to direct discrimination, on the one hand, in cases of unequal pay for equal work, and to value discrimination, on the other, in cases of unequal pay for work of equal value, [...]

---

1. A5-0275/2001; *available at* http://eur-lex.europa.eu/LexUriServ/site/en/oj/2002/ce077/ce07720020328en01340138.pdf [last visited April 25, 2011].

N. whereas all work must be accorded the value which it merits, and whereas the employment segregation of men and women often results in lower wages in female-dominated sectors than in male dominated sectors and in less being paid for women's jobs than for men's jobs; whereas this is completely illegitimate, and female-dominated sectors and women's jobs need to be upgraded in order to narrow pay differentials between men and women, ...

Requests the Commission to examine how far the Member States have succeeded in: [...]

7.(a) forming an accurate, complete picture of the pay differentials existing between women and men;

(b) incorporating gender-neutral job rating systems into their national legislation;

(c) developing awareness-raising campaigns on equal pay for work of equal value; ...

(d) mobilising the two sides of industry to implement gender-neutral job evaluation and to make the elimination of pay differentials between men and women one of their priorities;

(e) themselves providing a model in the public sector and eliminating wage discrimination and differentials between men and women;

8. Calls on the Member States to further step up their efforts in all of these areas and to ensure that measures adopted are actually complied with: urges them, in this connection, to develop and exchange good practice with a view to closing the wage gap, and to draw up equal pay plans under their National Action Plans for Employment and present an annual report on progress made with regard to equal pay;

9. Considers that the gender pay gap is a core priority for adjustment in response to the conclusions of the Stockholm European Council and welcomes the proposal of the Advisory Committee on Equal Opportunities to include in the Employment Guidelines for 2002 the establishment of targets with timescales to reduce the gender pay gap; calls on the Commission, within the framework of the European employment strategy, in connection with the employment guidelines, to continue to devote itself to specific measures for combating the wage gap by introducing precise quantitative and timescale objectives; requests it, in monitoring National Action Plans for Employment, to draw up actual progress reports concerning equal pay;

10. Urges the Member States to facilitate training and access to jobs under optimum conditions, in particular by non-sexist vocational guidance in schools, and to eliminate current labour market segregation as well as to develop measures to narrow structural differences relating to men and women on the labour market and to enable both men and women to combine work and family commitments and to fulfill caring duties;

In accordance with Article 141(4) of the Treaty, with a view to ensuring full equality in practice between men and women in working life, the principle of equal treatment does not prevent Member States from maintaining or adopting measures providing for specific advantages in order to make it easier for the under-represented sex to pursue a vocational activity or to prevent or compensate for disadvantages in professional careers. Given the current situation and bearing in mind Declaration No. 28 to the Amsterdam

Treaty, Member States should, in the first instance, aim at improving the situation of women in working life.

It is clear from the case-law of the Court of Justice that unfavourable treatment of a woman related to pregnancy or maternity constitutes direct discrimination on grounds of sex. Such treatment should therefore be expressly covered by this Directive. [...]

(25) For reasons of clarity, it is also appropriate to make express provision for the protection of the employment rights of women on maternity leave and in particular their right to return to the same or an equivalent post, to suffer no detriment in their terms and conditions as a result of taking such leave and to benefit from any improvement in working conditions to which they would have been entitled during their absence.

(26) In the Resolution of the Council and of the Ministers for Employment and Social Policy, meeting within the Council, of 29 June 2000 on the balanced participation of women and men in family and working life (3), Member States were encouraged to consider examining the scope for their respective legal systems to grant working men an individual and non transferable right to paternity leave, while maintaining their rights relating to employment.

B. European Council Directive 2002/73/EC[2]

... (8) Harassment related to the sex of a person and sexual harassment are contrary to the principle of equal treatment between women and men; it is therefore appropriate to define such concepts and to prohibit such forms of discrimination. To this end it must be emphasised that these forms of discrimination occur not only in the workplace, but also in the context of access to employment and vocational training, during employment and occupation.

(9) In this context, employers and those responsible for vocational training should be encouraged to take measures to combat all forms of sexual discrimination and, in particular, to take preventive measures against harassment and sexual harassment in the workplace, in accordance with national legislation and practice.

(10) The appreciation of the facts from which it may be inferred that there has been direct or indirect discrimination is a matter for national judicial or other competent bodies, in accordance with rules of national law or practice. Such rules may provide in particular for indirect discrimination to be established by any means including on the basis of statistical evidence. According to the case-law of the Court of Justice, discrimination involves the application of different rules to a comparable situation or the application of the same rule to different situations.

(11) The occupational activities that Member States may exclude from the scope of Directive 76/207/EEC should be restricted to those which necessitate the employment of a person of one sex by reason of the nature of the particular occupational activities concerned, provided that the objective sought is legitimate, and subject to the principle of proportionality as laid down by the case-law of the Court of Justice.

---

2. *Available at* http://eur-lex.europa.eu/LexUriServ/LexUriServ.do?uri=CELEX:32002L0073: EN:HTML[last visited May 2, 2011].

(12) The Court of Justice has consistently recognised the legitimacy, in terms of the principle of equal treatment, of protecting a woman's biological condition during and after pregnancy. It has moreover consistently ruled that any unfavourable treatment of women related to pregnancy or maternity constitutes direct sex discrimination. This Directive is therefore without prejudice to Council Directive 92/85/EEC of 19 October 1992 on the introduction of measures to encourage improvements in the safety and health at work of pregnant workers and workers who have recently given birth or are breastfeeding (9) (tenth individual Directive within the meaning of Article 16(1) of Directive 89/391/EEC), which aims to ensure the protection of the physical and mental state of women who are pregnant, women who have recently given birth or women who are breastfeeding. The preamble to Directive 92/85/EEC provides that the protection of the safety and health of pregnant workers, workers who have recently given birth or workers who are breastfeeding should not involve treating women who are on the labour market unfavourably nor work to the detriment of Directives concerning equal treatment for men and women. The Court of Justice has recognised the protection of employment rights of women, in particular their right to return to the same or an equivalent job, with no less favourable working conditions, as well as to benefit from any improvement in working conditions to which they would be entitled during their absence.

(13) In the Resolution of the Council and of the Ministers for Employment and Social Policy meeting within the Council of 29 June 2000 on the balanced participation of women and men in family and working life (10), Member States were encouraged to consider examining the scope for their respective legal systems to grant working men an individual and untransferable right to paternity leave, while maintaining their rights relating to employment. In this context, it is important to stress that it is for the Member States to determine whether or not to grant such a right and also to determine any conditions, other than dismissal and return to work, which are outside the scope of this Directive.

IV. Employment Discrimination and Pay Equality in the United States

A. Title VII

42 U.S.C.A. § 2000e-2. Unlawful employment practices

(a) Employer practices

It shall be an unlawful employment practice for an employer—

(1) to fail or refuse to hire or to discharge any individual, or otherwise to discriminate against any individual with respect to his compensation, terms, conditions, or privileges of employment, because of such individual's race, color, religion, sex, or national origin; or

(2) to limit, segregate, or classify his employees or applicants for employment in any way which would deprive or tend to deprive any individual of employment opportunities or otherwise adversely affect his status as an employee, because of such individual's race, color, religion, sex, or national origin.

(b) Employment agency practices

It shall be an unlawful employment practice for an employment agency to fail or refuse to refer for employment, or otherwise to discriminate against, any individual because of his race, color, religion, sex, or national origin, or to classify or refer for employment any individual on the basis of his race, color, religion, sex, or national origin.

(c) Labor organization practices

It shall be an unlawful employment practice for a labor organization—

> (1) to exclude or to expel from its membership, or otherwise to discriminate against, any individual because of his race, color, religion, sex, or national origin;

> (2) to limit, segregate, or classify its membership or applicants for membership, or to classify or fail or refuse to refer for employment any individual, in any way which would deprive or tend to deprive any individual of employment opportunities, or would limit such employment opportunities or otherwise adversely affect his status as an employee or as an applicant for employment, because of such individual's race, color, religion, sex, or national origin; or

> (3) to cause or attempt to cause an employer to discriminate against an individual in violation of this section.

(d) Training programs

It shall be an unlawful employment practice for any employer, labor organization, or joint labor-management committee controlling apprenticeship or other training or retraining, including on-the-job training programs to discriminate against any individual because of his race, color, religion, sex, or national origin in admission to, or employment in, any program established to provide apprenticeship or other training

(e) Businesses or enterprises with personnel qualified on basis of religion, sex, or national origin; educational institutions with personnel of particular religion

> Notwithstanding any other provision of this subchapter, (1) it shall not be an unlawful employment practice for an employer to hire and employ employees, for an employment agency to classify, or refer for employment any individual, for a labor organization to classify its membership or to classify or refer for employment any individual, or for an employer, labor organization, or joint labor-management committee controlling apprenticeship or other training or retraining programs to admit or employ any individual in any such program, on the basis of his religion, sex, or national origin in those certain instances where religion, sex, or national origin is a bona fide occupational qualification reasonably necessary to the normal operation of that particular business or enterprise, and (2) it shall not be an unlawful employment practice for a school, college, university, or other educational institution or institution of learning to hire and employ employees of a particular religion if such school, college, university, or other educational institution or institution of learning is, in whole or in substantial part, owned, supported, controlled, or managed by a particular religion or by a particular religious corporation, association, or society, or if the curriculum of such school, college, university, or other educational institution or institution of learning is directed toward the propagation of a particular religion.

B. *Ledbetter v. Goodyear Tire & Rubber Co. Inc.*[3]

Petitioner Lilly Ledbetter worked for respondent Goodyear Tire and Rubber Company (Goodyear) at its Gadsden, Alabama, plant from 1979 until 1998. During much of this time, salaried employees at the plant were given or denied raises based on their supervisors' evaluation of their performance. In March 1998, Ledbetter submitted a questionnaire to the EEOC alleging certain acts of sex discrimination, and in July of that year she filed a formal EEOC charge. After taking early retirement in November 1998, Ledbetter commenced this action, in which she asserted, among other claims, a Title VII pay discrimination claim and a claim under the Equal Pay Act of 1963(EPA), 77 Stat. 56, 29 U.S.C. § 206(d).

[Ledbetter] introduced evidence that during the course of her employment several supervisors had given her poor evaluations because of her sex, that as a result of these evaluations her pay was not increased as much as it would have been if she had been evaluated fairly, and that these past pay decisions continued to affect the amount of her pay throughout her employment. Toward the end of her time with Goodyear, she was being paid significantly less than any of her male colleagues. Goodyear maintained that the evaluations had been nondiscriminatory, but the jury found for Ledbetter and awarded her backpay and damages. On appeal, Goodyear contended that Ledbetter's pay discrimination claim was time barred with respect to all pay decisions made prior to September 26, 1997 — that is, 180 days before the filing of her EEOC questionnaire. And Goodyear argued that no discriminatory act relating to Ledbetter's pay occurred after that date.

The Court of Appeals for the Eleventh Circuit reversed, holding that a Title VII pay discrimination claim cannot be based on any pay decision that occurred prior to the last pay decision that affected the employee's pay during the EEOC charging period.

Title VII of the Civil Rights Act of 1964 makes it an "unlawful employment practice" to discriminate "against any individual with respect to his compensation ... because of such individual's ... sex." 42 U.S.C. § 2000e-2(a)(1). An individual wishing to challenge an employment practice under this provision must first file a charge with the EEOC. § 2000e-5(e)(1). Such a charge must be filed within a specified period (either 180 or 300 days, depending on the State) "after the alleged unlawful employment practice occurred," *ibid.*, and if the employee does not submit a timely EEOC charge, the employee may not challenge that practice in court, § 2000e-5(f)(1).

Primarily, she [the Petitioner] urges us to focus on the paychecks that were issued to her during the EEOC charging period (the 180-day period preceding the filing of her EEOC questionnaire), each of which, she contends, was a separate act of discrimination. Alternatively, Ledbetter directs us to the 1998 decision denying her a raise, and she argues that this decision was "unlawful because it carried forward intentionally discriminatory disparities from prior years." Reply Brief for Petitioner 20. Both of these arguments fail because they would require us in effect to jettison the defining element of the legal claim on which her Title VII recovery was based.

Ledbetter asserted disparate treatment, the central element of which is discriminatory intent.... ("[A] disparate-treatment challenge focuses exclusively on the intent of the employer"). However, Ledbetter does not assert that the relevant Goodyear decisionmakers acted with actual discriminatory intent either when they issued her checks during the EEOC charging period or when they denied her a raise in 1998. Rather, she argues that

---

3. 550 U.S. 618 (2007).

the paychecks were unlawful because they would have been larger if she had been evaluated in a nondiscriminatory manner *prior to* the EEOC charging period. Brief for Petitioner 22. Similarly, she maintains that the 1998 decision was unlawful because it "carried forward" the effects of prior, uncharged discrimination decisions. Reply Brief for Petitioner 20. In essence, she suggests that it is sufficient that discriminatory acts that occurred prior to the charging period had continuing effects during that period. Brief for Petitioner 13 ("[E]ach paycheck that offers a woman less pay than a similarly situated man because of her sex is a separate violation of Title VII with its own limitations period, regardless of whether the paycheck simply implements a prior discriminatory decision made outside the limitations period"); see also Reply Brief for Petitioner 20. This argument is squarely foreclosed by our precedents.

In *United Air Lines, Inc. v. Evans*, 431 U.S. 553, 97 S.Ct. 1885, 52 L.Ed.2d 571 (1977), we rejected an argument that is basically the same as Ledbetter's. Evans was forced to resign because the airline refused to employ married flight attendants, but she did not file an EEOC charge regarding her termination. Some years later, the airline rehired her but treated her as a new employee for seniority purposes. *Id.*, at 554–555, 97 S.Ct. 1885. Evans then sued, arguing that, while any suit based on the original discrimination was time barred, the airline's refusal to give her credit for her prior service gave "present effect to [its] past illegal act and thereby perpetuate[d] the consequences of forbidden discrimination." *Id.*, at 557, 97 S.Ct. 1885.

We agreed with Evans that the airline's "seniority system [did] indeed have a continuing impact on her pay and fringe benefits," *id.*, at 558, 97 S.Ct. 1885, but we noted that "the critical question [was] whether any present *violation* exist[ed]." *Ibid.* (emphasis in original). We concluded that the continuing effects of the precharging period discrimination did not make out a present violation.

The instruction provided by *Evans, Ricks, Lorance,* and *Morgan* is clear. The EEOC charging period is triggered when a discrete unlawful practice takes place. A new violation does not occur, and a new charging period does not commence, upon the occurrence of subsequent nondiscriminatory acts that entail adverse effects resulting from the past discrimination. But of course, if an employer engages in a series of acts each of which is intentionally discriminatory, then a fresh violation takes place when each act is committed ...

Ledbetter's arguments here—that the paychecks that she received during the charging period and the 1998 raise denial each violated Title VII and triggered a new EEOC charging period—cannot be reconciled with *Evans, Ricks, Lorance,* and *Morgan.* Ledbetter as noted, makes no claim that intentionally discriminatory conduct occurred during the charging period or that discriminatory decisions that occurred prior to that period were not communicated to her. Instead, she argues simply that Goodyear's conduct during the charging period gave present effect to discriminatory conduct outside of that period. Brief for Petitioner 13. But current effects alone cannot breathe life into prior, uncharged discrimination; as we held in *Evans,* such effects in themselves have "no present legal consequences." 431 U.S., at 558, 97 S.Ct. 1885. Ledbetter should have filed an EEOC charge within 180 days after each allegedly discriminatory pay decision was made and communicated to her. She did not do so, and the paychecks that were issued to her during the 180 days prior to the filing of her EEOC charge do not provide a basis for overcoming that prior failure.

Justice GINSBURG, with whom Justice STEVENS, Justice SOUTER, and Justice BREYER join, dissenting.

Lilly Ledbetter was a supervisor at Goodyear Tire and Rubber's plant in Gadsden, Alabama, from 1979 until her retirement in 1998. For most of those years, she worked as an area manager, a position largely occupied by men. Initially, Ledbetter's salary was in line with the salaries of men performing substantially similar work. Over time, however, her pay slipped in comparison to the pay of male area managers with equal or less seniority. By the end of 1997, Ledbetter was the only woman working as an area manager and the pay discrepancy between Ledbetter and her 15 male counterparts was stark: Ledbetter was paid $3,727 per month; the lowest paid male area manager received $4,286 per month, the highest paid, $5,236. See 421 F.3d 1169, 1174 (C.A.11 2005); Brief for Petitioner 4.

Ledbetter launched charges of discrimination before the Equal Employment Opportunity Commission (EEOC) in March 1998. Her formal administrative complaint specified that, in violation of Title VII, Goodyear paid her a discriminatorily low salary because of her sex. See 42 U.S.C. § 2000e-2(a)(1) (rendering it unlawful for an employer "to discriminate against any individual with respect to [her] compensation ... because of such individual's ... sex"). That charge was eventually tried to a jury, which found it "more likely than not that [Goodyear] paid []Ledbetter a[n] unequal salary because of her sex." App. 102. In accord with the jury's liability determination, the District Court entered judgment for Ledbetter for backpay and damages, plus counsel fees and costs....

The Court's insistence on immediate contest overlooks common characteristics of pay discrimination. Pay disparities often occur, as they did in Ledbetter's case, in small increments; cause to suspect that discrimination is at work develops only over time. Comparative pay information, moreover, is often hidden from the employee's view. Employers may keep under wraps the pay differentials maintained among supervisors, no less the reasons for those differentials. Small initial discrepancies may not be seen as meet for a federal case, particularly when the employee, trying to succeed in a nontraditional environment, is averse to making waves.

Pay disparities are thus significantly different from adverse actions "such as termination, failure to promote, ... or refusal to hire," all involving fully communicated discrete acts, "easy to identify" as discriminatory.... It is only when the disparity becomes apparent and sizable, *e.g.*, through future raises calculated as a percentage of current salaries, that an employee in Ledbetter's situation is likely to comprehend her plight and, therefore, to complain. Her initial readiness to give her employer the benefit of the doubt should not preclude her from later challenging the then current and continuing payment of a wage depressed on account of her sex.

On questions of time under Title VII, we have identified as the critical inquiries: "What constitutes an 'unlawful employment practice' and when has that practice 'occurred'?" *Id.*, at 110, 122 S.Ct. 2061. Our precedent suggests, and lower courts have overwhelmingly held, that the unlawful practice is the *current payment* of salaries infected by gender-based (or race-based) discrimination—a practice that occurs whenever a paycheck delivers less to a woman than to a similarly situated man.

Title VII proscribes as an "unlawful employment practice" discrimination "against any individual with respect to his compensation ... because of such individual's race, color, religion, sex, or national origin." 42 U.S.C. § 2000e-2(a)(1). An individual seeking to challenge an employment practice under this proscription must file a charge with the EEOC within 180 days "after the alleged unlawful employment practice occurred." § 2000e-5(e)(1) ...

Ledbetter's petition presents a question important to the sound application of Title VII: What activity qualifies as an unlawful employment practice in cases of discrimination with respect to compensation. One answer identifies the pay-setting decision, and that decision alone, as the unlawful practice. Under this view, each particular salary-setting decision is discrete from prior and subsequent decisions, and must be challenged within 180 days on pain of forfeiture. Another response counts both the pay-setting decision and the actual payment of a discriminatory wage as unlawful practices. Under this approach, each payment of a wage or salary infected by sex-based discrimination constitutes an unlawful employment practice; prior decisions, outside the 180-day charge-filing period, are not themselves actionable, but they are relevant in determining the lawfulness of conduct within the period. The Court adopts the first view, see *ante*, at 2165, 2166–2167, 2169–2170, but the second is more faithful to precedent, more in tune with the realities of the workplace, and more respectful of Title VII's remedial purpose.

Pay disparities, of the kind Ledbetter experienced, have a closer kinship to hostile work environment claims than to charges of a single episode of discrimination. Ledbetter's claim, resembling Morgan's, rested not on one particular paycheck, but on "the cumulative effect of individual acts." ... She charged insidious discrimination building up slowly but steadily. See Brief for Petitioner 5–8. Initially in line with the salaries of men performing substantially the same work, Ledbetter's salary fell 15 to 40 percent behind her male counterparts only after successive evaluations and percentage-based pay adjustments. See *supra*, at 2178. Over time, she alleged and proved, the repetition of pay decisions undervaluing her work gave rise to the current discrimination of which she complained. Though component acts fell outside the charge-filing period, with each new paycheck, Goodyear contributed incrementally to the accumulating harm.

The realities of the workplace reveal why the discrimination with respect to compensation that Ledbetter suffered does not fit within the category of singular discrete acts "easy to identify." A worker knows immediately if she is denied a promotion or transfer, if she is fired or refused employment. And promotions, transfers, hirings, and firings are generally public events, known to co-workers. When an employer makes a decision of such open and definitive character, an employee can immediately seek out an explanation and evaluate it for pretext. Compensation disparities, in contrast, are often hidden from sight. It is not unusual, decisions in point illustrate, for management to decline to publish employee pay levels, or for employees to keep private their own salaries.

The problem of concealed pay discrimination is particularly acute where the disparity arises not because the female employee is flatly denied a raise but because male counterparts are given larger raises. Having received a pay increase, the female employee is unlikely to discern at once that she has experienced an adverse employment decision. She may have little reason even to suspect discrimination until a pattern develops incrementally and she ultimately becomes aware of the disparity. Even if an employee suspects that the reason for a comparatively low raise is not performance but sex (or another protected ground), the amount involved may seem too small, or the employer's intent too ambiguous, to make the issue immediately actionable—or winnable.

Further separating pay claims from the discrete employment actions identified in *Morgan*, an employer gains from sex-based pay disparities in a way it does not from a discriminatory denial of promotion, hiring, or transfer. When a male employee is selected over a female for a higher level position, someone still gets the promotion and is paid a higher salary; the employer is not enriched. But when a woman is paid less than a similarly situated man, the employer reduces its costs each time the pay differential is implemented.

The Court asserts that treating pay discrimination as a discrete act, limited to each particular pay-setting decision, is necessary to "protec[t] employers from the burden of defending claims arising from employment decisions that are long past." ... But the discrimination of which Ledbetter complained is *not* long past. As she alleged, and as the jury found, Goodyear continued to treat Ledbetter differently because of sex each pay period, with mounting harm. Allowing employees to challenge discrimination "that extend[s] over long periods of time," into the charge-filing period, we have previously explained, "does not leave employers defenseless" against unreasonable or prejudicial delay....

To show how far the Court has strayed from interpretation of Title VII with fidelity to the Act's core purpose, I return to the evidence Ledbetter presented at trial. Ledbetter proved to the jury the following: She was a member of a protected class; she performed work substantially equal to work of the dominant class (men); she was compensated less for that work; and the disparity was attributable to gender-based discrimination....

Specifically, Ledbetter's evidence demonstrated that her current pay was discriminatorily low due to a long series of decisions reflecting Goodyear's pervasive discrimination against women managers in general and Ledbetter in particular. Ledbetter's former supervisor, for example, admitted to the jury that Ledbetter's pay, during a particular one-year period, fell below Goodyear's minimum threshold for her position. App. 93–97. Although Goodyear claimed the pay disparity was due to poor performance, the supervisor acknowledged that Ledbetter received a "Top Performance Award" in 1996. *Id.*, at 90–93. The jury also heard testimony that another supervisor—who evaluated Ledbetter in 1997 and whose evaluation led to her most recent raise denial—was openly biased against women. *Id.*, at 46, 77–82. And two women who had previously worked as managers at the plant told the jury they had been subject to pervasive discrimination and were paid less than their male counterparts. One was paid less than the men she supervised. *Id.*, at 51–68. Ledbetter herself testified about the discriminatory animus conveyed to her by plant officials. Toward the end of her career, for instance, the plant manager told Ledbetter that the "plant did not need women, that [women] didn't help it, [and] caused problems." *Id.*, at 36. After weighing all the evidence, the jury found for Ledbetter, concluding that the pay disparity was due to intentional discrimination.

Yet, under the Court's decision, the discrimination Ledbetter proved is not redressable under Title VII. Each and every pay decision she did not immediately challenge wiped the slate clean. Consideration may not be given to the cumulative effect of a series of decisions that, together, set her pay well below that of every male area manager. Knowingly carrying past pay discrimination forward must be treated as lawful conduct. Ledbetter may not be compensated for the lower pay she was in fact receiving when she complained to the EEOC. Nor, were she still employed by Goodyear, could she gain, on the proof she presented at trial, injunctive relief requiring, prospectively, her receipt of the same compensation men receive for substantially similar work. The Court's approbation of these consequences is totally at odds with the robust protection against workplace discrimination Congress intended Title VII to secure.

Questions for Discussion

1. *What do you think of the majority decision in* Ledbetter? *Do you think that the court was giving effect to the purpose of Title VII in this decision?*

2. *Information about salaries is often kept private, therefore it is not surprising that Ledbetter did not know she was being paid less than her male peers for the same work. Should information about salaries be more public to prevent this kind of pay discrimination?*

3. *The Court seems to have give effect to a particularly narrow reading of Title VII. Note that the Justice who wrote the majority decision is male (Justice Scalia) while the Justice who wrote the dissenting opinion (and read the dissent aloud from the bench) is female (Justice Ginsburg). Do you think that the gender of the judges plays a role in these kinds of decisions? Should it? What kind of message does this decision send to the public about how serious society, or at least the Court, takes pay discrimination?*

4. *The U.S. seems to require discriminatory intent to establish pay discrimination. Should intent be a requirement of this type of claim? How difficult might this be to prove?*

C. Congress' Response to the Supreme Court's Decision in *Ledbetter*

Congress responded to the U.S. Supreme's Court's decision in *Ledbetter* by enacting the legislation set out below, which is known as the Lily Ledbetter Act.

1. The Lily Ledbetter Act — 42 U.S.C. § 2000e-5

SEC. 2. FINDINGS.

Congress finds the following:

(1) The Supreme Court in Ledbetter v. Goodyear Tire & Rubber Co., 550 U.S. 618 (2007), significantly impairs statutory protections against discrimination in compensation that Congress established and that have been bedrock principles of American law for decades. The Ledbetter decision undermines those statutory protections by unduly restricting the time period in which victims of discrimination can challenge and recover for discriminatory compensation decisions or other practices, contrary to the intent of Congress.

(2) The limitation imposed by the Court on the filing of discriminatory compensation claims ignores the reality of wage discrimination and is at odds with the robust application of the civil rights laws that Congress intended.

(3) With regard to any charge of discrimination under any law, nothing in this Act is intended to preclude or limit an aggrieved person's right to introduce evidence of an unlawful employment practice that has occurred outside the time for filing a charge of discrimination.

(4) Nothing in this Act is intended to change current law treatment of when pension distributions are considered paid.

SEC. 3. DISCRIMINATION IN COMPENSATION BECAUSE OF RACE, COLOR, RELIGION, SEX, OR NATIONAL ORIGIN.

Section 706(e) of the Civil Rights Act of 1964 (42 U.S.C. 2000e-5(e)) is amended by adding at the end the following:

(3)(A) For purposes of this section, an unlawful employment practice occurs, with respect to discrimination in compensation in violation of this title, when a discriminatory compensation decision or other practice is adopted, when an individual becomes subject to a discriminatory compensation decision or other practice, or when an individual is affected by application of a discriminatory compensation decision or other practice, including each time wages, benefits, or other compensation is paid, resulting in whole or in part from such a decision or other practice.

(B) In addition to any relief authorized by section 1977A of the Revised Statutes (42 U.S.C. 1981a), liability may accrue and an aggrieved person may obtain relief as provided in subsection (g)(1), including recovery of back pay for up to two years preceding the filing of the charge, where the unlawful employment practices that have occurred during the charge filing period are similar or related to unlawful employment practices with regard to discrimination in compensation that occurred outside the time for filing a charge.

Question for Discussion

1. *The speedy response of Congress to the* Ledbetter *decision, and the language of the amendment seems a rebuke to the Court. Is Congress' action a sign that the system is working, or a sign that the Court is removed from the reality of peoples' lives?*

V. Discrimination in Sweden

A. The Discrimination Act (2008)[4]

Section 1 The purpose of this Act is to combat discrimination and in other ways promote equal rights and opportunities regardless of sex, transgender identity or expression, ethnicity, religion or other belief, disability, sexual orientation or age....

Section 4 In this Act discrimination has the meaning set out in this Section.

1. Direct discrimination: that someone is disadvantaged by being treated less favourably than someone else is treated, has been treated or would have been treated in a comparable situation, if this disadvantaging is associated with sex, transgender identity or expression, ethnicity, religion or other belief, disability, sexual orientation or age.

2. Indirect discrimination: that someone is disadvantaged by the application of a provision, a criterion or a procedure that appears neutral but that may put people of a certain sex, a certain transgender identity or expression, a certain ethnicity, a certain religion or other belief, a certain disability, a certain sexual orientation or a certain age at a particular disadvantage, unless the provision, criterion or procedure has a legitimate purpose and the means that are used are appropriate and necessary to achieve that purpose.

---

4. Swedish Code of Statutes SFS 2008:567 (2008). *Available at* http://www.sweden.gov.se/content/1/c6/11/81/87/f6e1a2b8.pdf [last visited April 25, 2011].

3. Harassment: conduct that violates a person's dignity and that is associated with one of the grounds of discrimination sex, transgender identity or expression, ethnicity, religion or other belief, disability, sexual orientation or age.

4. Sexual harassment: conduct of a sexual nature that violates someone's dignity.

5. Instructions to discriminate: orders or instructions to discriminate against someone in a manner referred to in points 1–4 that are given to someone who is in a subordinate or dependent position relative to the person who gives the orders or instructions or to someone who has committed herself or himself to performing an assignment for that person....

Working life

Prohibition of discrimination

Section 1: An employer may not discriminate against a person who, with respect to the employer,

1. is an employee,

2. is enquiring about or applying for work,

3. is applying for or carrying out a traineeship, or

4. is available to perform work or is performing work as temporary or borrowed labourer.

The prohibition of discrimination also applies in cases where the employer, by taking reasonable support and adaptation measures, can see to it that an employee, a job applicant or a trainee with a disability is put in a comparable situation to people without such a disability.

Section 2: The prohibition in Section 1 does not prevent:

1. differential treatment based on a characteristic associated with one of the grounds of discrimination if, when a decision is made on employment, promotion or education or training for promotion, by reason of the nature of the work or the context in which the work is carried out, the characteristic constitutes a genuine and determining occupational requirement that has a legitimate purpose and the requirement is appropriate and necessary to achieve that purpose,

2. measures that contribute to efforts to promote equality between women and men and that concern matters other than pay or other terms of employment,

3. the application of age limits with regard to the right to pension, survivor's or invalidity benefits in individual contracts or collective agreements, or

4. differential treatment on grounds of age, if there is a legitimate purpose and the means that are used are appropriate and necessary to achieve that purpose.

Obligation to investigate and take measures against harassment

Section 3: If an employer becomes aware that an employee considers that he or she has been subjected in connection with work to harassment or sexual harassment by someone performing work or carrying out a traineeship at the employer's establishment, the employer is obliged to investigate the circumstances surrounding the alleged harassment and where appropriate take the measures that can reasonably be demanded to prevent harassment in the future.

This obligation also applies with respect to a person carrying out a traineeship or performing work as temporary or borrowed labour. [...]

Section 5: A natural or legal person conducting activities referred to in the Education Act (1985:1100) or other educational activities (an education provider) may not discriminate against any child, pupil or student participating in or applying for the activities. Employees and contractors engaged in the activities shall be equated with the education provider when they are acting within the context of their employment or contract.

The prohibition of discrimination also applies in cases where an education provider, by taking reasonable measures regarding the accessibility and usability of the premises, can see to it that a person with a disability who is applying or has been accepted for education under the Higher Education Act (1992:1434) or for education that can lead to a qualification under the Act concerning authority to award certain qualifications (1993:792), is put in a comparable situation to people without such a disability.

Section 6: The prohibition in Section 5 does not prevent:

1. measures that contribute to efforts to promote equality between women and men in admissions to education other than that referred to in the Education Act (1985:1100), [...]

Section 9: Discrimination against applicants or employees is prohibited with regard to labour market policy activities and employment services not under public contract.

However, this prohibition does not prevent measures that contribute to efforts to promote equality between women and men or equal rights and opportunities regardless of ethnicity, ...

Chapter 3. Active measures

Working life

Cooperation between employers and employees

Section 1: Employers and employees are to cooperate on active measures to bring about equal rights and opportunities in working life regardless of sex, ethnicity, religion or other belief, and in particular to combat discrimination in working life on such grounds.

Section 2: Employers and employees are in particular to endeavour to equalise and prevent differences in pay and other terms of employment between women and men who perform work which is to be regarded as equal or of equal value. They are also to promote equal pay growth opportunities for women and men.

Work is to be regarded as of equal value to other work if, on an overall assessment of the requirements and nature of the work, it can be deemed to be equal in value to the other work. The assessment of the requirements of the work is to take into account criteria such as knowledge and skills, responsibility and effort. In assessing the nature of the work, particular account is to be taken of working conditions. [...]

Section 5: Employers are to help enable both female and male employees to combine employment and parenthood....

Section 8: Employers are to promote an equal distribution of women and men in different types of work and in different employee categories, by means of education and training, skills development and other appropriate measures.

Section 9: When the distribution of women and men is not more or less equal in a certain type of work or in a certain employee category at a place of work, the employer is to make a special effort when recruiting new employees to attract applicants of the under-represented sex. The employer is to attempt to see to it that the proportion of employees from the under-represented sex gradually increases.

However, the first Paragraph shall not be applicable if there are special grounds not to take such measures or if the measures cannot reasonably be required in view of the employer's resources and other circumstances …

Section 10: In order to discover, remedy and prevent unfair gender differences in pay and other terms of employment, every three years the employer is to survey and analyse:

— provisions and practices regarding pay and other terms of employment that are used at the employer's establishment, and

— pay differences between women and men performing work that is to be regarded as equal or of equal value.

The employer is to assess whether existing pay differences are directly or indirectly associated with sex. The assessment is to refer in particular to differences between

— women and men performing work that is to be regarded as equal, and

— groups of employees performing work that is or is generally considered to be dominated by women and groups of employees performing work that is to be regarded as of equal value to such work but is not or is not generally considered to be dominated by women.

B. Swedish Government Statistics on Women in the Workforce

The Swedish government avers that gender equality is the "cornerstone of Swedish society."[5] The family is also important. Parents of an adopted or birth child are allowed 480 days of parental leave. Although Sweden ranks highly in the Global Gender Gap, it has been criticized for the fact that few women are represented on boards of listed companies (in 2006, women comprised only about 18% of directors on such boards). There is also pay disparity between women and men. The Swedish government accounts for that by claiming that many pay differences are based on:

> differences in their profession, sector, position, work experience and age. There are also pay differentials that cannot be explained in this way but may be attributable to gender. These are called unjustified pay differentials. On average, women's monthly salaries are 93 percent of men's when differences in choice of profession and sector are taken into account. Pay differentials are most pronounced in the private sector.[6]

In 2009, the government developed a strategy to promote gender equality in the labor market. The government will attempt to achieve its aims by working in four main areas to:

1. Combat gender divisions in the labor market and business sector

2. Promote equal conditions for entrepreneurship

---

5. *Available at* http://www.sweden.se/eng/Home/Society/Equality/Facts/Gender-equality-in-Sweden/ [last visited April 25, 2011].

6. *Available at* http://www.sweden.gov.se/sb/d/4096/a/130290 [last visited April 25, 2011].

3. Promote equal participation in working life
4. Create equal working conditions

VI. European Cases on Equal Pay

A. *De Frenne v. Sabena*[7] (European Court of Justice)

[…] 2. These questions arose within the context of an action between an air hostess and her employer, Sabena S. A., concerning compensation claimed by the applicant in the main action on the ground that, between 15 February 1963 and 1 February 1966, she suffered as a female worker discrimination in terms of pay as compared with male colleagues who were doing the same work as 'cabin steward'.

3. According to the judgment containing the reference, the parties agree that the work of an air hostess is identical to that of a cabin steward and in these circumstances the existence of discrimination in pay to the detriment of the air hostess during the period in question is not disputed.

4. The first question asks whether article 119 of the Treaty introduces 'directly into the national law of each Member State of the European Community the principle that men and women should receive equal pay for equal work and does it therefore, independently of any national provision, entitle workers to institute proceedings before national courts in order to ensure its observance?

Indeed, as the court has already found in other contexts, the fact that certain provisions of the Treaty are formally addressed to the Member States does not prevent rights from being conferred at the same time on any individual who has an interest in the performance of the duties thus laid down. […]

32. The very wording of article 119 shows that it imposes on states a duty to bring about a specific result to be mandatorily achieved within a fixed period.

33. The effectiveness of this provision cannot be affected by the fact that the duty imposed by the Treaty has not been discharged by certain Member States and that the joint institutions have not reacted sufficiently energetically against this failure to act.

34. To accept the contrary view would be to risk raising the violation of the right to the status of a principle of interpretation, a position the adoption of which would not be consistent with the task assigned to the court by article 164 of the Treaty. […]

39. In fact, since article 119 is mandatory in nature, the prohibition on discrimination between men and women applies not only to the action of public authorities, but also extends to all agreements which are intended to regulate paid labour collectively, as well as to contracts between individuals.

40. The reply to the first question must therefore be that the principle of equal pay contained in article 119 may be relied upon before the national courts and that these courts have a duty to ensure the protection of the rights which this provision vests in in-dividuals, in particular as regards those types of discrimination arising directly from

---

7. 1976 E.C.R. 455.

legislative provisions or collective labour agreements, as well as in cases in which men and women receive unequal pay for equal work which is carried out in the same establishment or service, whether private or public.

B. *Hill and Stapleton v. The Revenue Commissioners and Department of Finance*[8] (European Court of Justice)

A system of incremental credit based on the criterion of actual time worked which, where 98% of job-sharers are women, treats former job-sharers who have returned to full-time work in a manner less favourable than workers who have always worked full-time constitutes discrimination on the grounds of sex unless such unfavourable treatment can be objectively justified.

The purpose of the system of job-sharing, which was introduced into the Irish Civil Service in 1984, was to permit two civil servants to share one full-time job equally in such a way that both workers benefitted equally while the costs of the post for the national administration remained the same. Job-sharers work half the number of hours of full-time workers and are paid the same hourly rate. The scale of annual incremental salary increases for job-sharers are parallel to that for full-time workers with each point on the job-sharers scale representing 50% of the corresponding point on the full-time scale. 98% of job-sharers in the Irish Civil Service are women. According to the national referring tribunal a job-sharer can acquire the same experience as a full-time worker.

When Mrs. Hill and Mrs. Stapleton transferred from job-sharing to full-time work they were initially assimilated to the same point on the full-time incremental scale as that which they had occupied on the job-sharers' scale. They were both subsequently reclassified at a lower point on full-time scale on the grounds that two years on the job-sharers' scale represented one year on the full-time scale. The questions posed to the Court of Justice by the Labour Court in Ireland arose from the decision by Mrs. Hill and Mrs. Stapleton to contest their reclassification.

The Court of Justice took the view that workers who transferred from job-sharing, where they worked 50% of full-time hours and were paid 50% of full-time pay, to full-time work, were entitled to expect both the number of hours that they worked and the level of their pay to increase by 50%, in the same way as workers converting from full-time work to job-sharing would expect these factors to be reduced by 50%, unless a difference of treatment can be justified. Such development did not occur in this case, with the result that, as former job-shares are paid less than twice their job-sharing salary, their hourly rate of pay as full-time workers is reduced.

Within the category of full-time workers, therefore, there is unequal treatment, as regards pay, of employees who previously job-shared, and who regress in relation to the position which they already occupied on the pay scale.

In so finding, the Court observed that the use of the criterion of actual time worked during the period of job-sharing fails to take account, inter alia, of the fact that job-sharing is a unique category of work, given that it does not involve a break in service, or

---

8. *Available at* http://curia.europa.eu/en/actu/communiques/cp98/cp9839en.htm [last visited June 23, 2011]. Case 243/95.

of the fact that a job-sharer can acquire the same experience as a full-time worker. Furthermore, a disparity is retroactively introduced into the overall pay of employees performing the same functions so far as both the quality and quantity of the work performed is concerned.

In such a case, application of provisions of the kind at issue before the national tribunal result in discrimination against female workers which must be treated as contrary to Article 119 of the Treaty.

The Court of Justice concluded that it would be otherwise only if the difference of treatment which was found to exist between the two categories of worker were justified by objective factors unrelated to any discrimination on the grounds of sex. It added that it is for the national tribunal to decide if any such objective factors exist.

Questions for Discussion

1. *Since many women in the United States work in part-time jobs because they are primary caregivers for their children, what impact might an approach of this nature have on women's earning capacity and status at work if U.S. courts were to adopt it?*

2. *Compare the U.S. laws and regulations with the Swedish laws and regulations with regard to pay equality. Look closely at the language of the relevant U.S. and Swedish statutes. What differences do you see?*

3. *In particular, look at section 2 of the Swedish statute which provides that: "Employers and employees are in particular to endeavour to equalise and prevent differences in pay and other terms of employment between women and men who perform work which is to be regarded as equal or of equal value. They are also to promote equal pay growth opportunities for women and men."*

   Do you see this same commitment reflected in the language of the U.S. statute?

4. *Section 10 of the Swedish statute requires employers to survey and analyse:*

   — provisions and practices regarding pay and other terms of employment that are used at the employer's establishment, and

   — pay differences between women and men performing work that is to be regarded as equal or of equal value.

   The employer is to assess whether existing pay differences are directly or indirectly associated with sex.

   Would these kinds of regulations be tolerated in the United States? Does U.S. law have the concept of indirect discrimination?

5. *Sweden and the United States have different approaches with regard to how they classify and reward equal work. Sweden's approach is to broadly construe and demand equal pay for "work of equal value." The United States only guarantees equal pay for "equal work"—a narrower construction. How does this impact women?*

6. *Sweden, along with the other Nordic countries, is consistently ranked among the countries with the lowest gender inequalities. In contrast the United States attained its highest ranking in 2011—19th; prior to that it was ranked 31st. What role might statutes like the Discrimination Act play in this ranking?*

VII. CEDAW and Sexual Harassment

A. *CEDAW General Recommendation 19*

17. Equality in employment can be seriously impaired when women are subjected to gender-specific violence, such as sexual harassment in the workplace.

18. Sexual harassment includes such unwelcome sexually determined behaviour as physical contact and advances, sexually coloured remarks, showing pornography and sexual demand, whether by words or actions. Such conduct can be humiliating and may constitute a health and safety problem; it is discriminatory when the woman has reasonable grounds to believe that her objection would disadvantage her in connection with her employment, including recruitment or promotion, or when it creates a hostile working environment.

VIII. Sexual Harassment in Sweden

In Sweden, sexual harassment is defined as: "any type of conduct of a sexual nature in working life that violates the dignity of a job seeker or an employee."[9] Article 16(a) of the Equal Opportunities Act[10] defines "gender-related harassment" as "any type of conduct in working life that violates the integrity of a job seeker or employee and that is related to the person's sex."

IX. Sex Discrimination and Sexual Harassment in the United States

A. SEC. 2000e-2. [Section 703] of Title VII

(a) Employer practices

It shall be an unlawful employment practice for an employer—

(1) to fail or refuse to hire or to discharge any individual, or otherwise to discriminate against any individual with respect to his compensation, terms, conditions, or privileges of employment, because of such individual's race, color, religion, sex, or national origin; or

(2) to limit, segregate, or classify his employees or applicants for employment in any way which would deprive or tend to deprive any individual of employment opportunities or otherwise adversely affect his status as an employee, because of such individual's race, color, religion, sex, or national origin.

---

9. Equal Opportunity Act of 1991.
10. Equal Opportunity Act of 1991.

(b) Employment agency practices

It shall be an unlawful employment practice for an employment agency to fail or refuse to refer for employment, or otherwise to discriminate against, any individual because of his race, color, religion, sex, or national origin, or to classify or refer for employment any individual on the basis of his race, color, religion, sex, or national origin.

(1) (A) An unlawful employment practice based on disparate impact is established under this subchapter only if—

(i) a complaining party demonstrates that a respondent uses a particular employment practice that causes a disparate impact on the basis of race, color, religion, sex, or national origin and the respondent fails to demonstrate that the challenged practice is job related for the position in question and consistent with business necessity; or

(ii) the complaining party makes the demonstration described in sub-paragraph (C) with respect to an alternative employment practice and the respondent refuses to adopt such alternative employment practice.

(B) (i) With respect to demonstrating that a particular employment practice causes a disparate impact as described in sub-paragraph (A)(i), the complaining party shall demonstrate that each particular challenged employment practice causes a disparate impact, except that if the complaining party can demonstrate to the court that the elements of a respondent's decisionmaking process are not capable of separation for analysis, the decisionmaking process may be analyzed as one employment practice.

(ii) If the respondent demonstrates that a specific employment practice does not cause the disparate impact, the respondent shall not be required to demonstrate that such practice is required by business necessity …

(2) A demonstration that an employment practice is required by business necessity may not be used as a defense against a claim of intentional discrimination under this subchapter.

(d) Training programs

It shall be an unlawful employment practice for any employer, labor organization, or joint labor-management committee controlling apprenticeship or other training or retraining, including on-the-job training programs to discriminate against any individual because of his race, color, religion, sex, or national origin in admission to, or employment in, any program established to provide apprenticeship or other training …

B. Code of Federal Regulations — Sexual Harassment

§ 1604.11 29 CFR Ch. XIV

1 The principles involved here continue to apply to race, color, religion or national origin.

§ 1604.11 Sexual harassment.

(a) Harassment on the basis of sex is a violation of section 703 of title VII.

Unwelcome sexual advances, requests for sexual favors, and other verbal or physical conduct of a sexual nature constitute sexual harassment when

(1) submission to such conduct is made either explicitly or implicitly a term or condition of an individual's employment,

(2) submission to or rejection of such conduct by an individual is used as the basis for employment decisions affecting such individual, or

(3) such conduct has the purpose or effect of unreasonably interfering with an individual's work performance or creating an intimidating, hostile, or offensive working environment.

(b) In determining whether alleged conduct constitutes sexual harassment, the Commission will look at the record as a whole and at the totality of the circumstances, such as the nature of the sexual advances and the context in which the alleged incidents occurred. The determination of the legality of a particular action will be made from the facts, on a case by case basis. [...]

(d) With respect to conduct between fellow employees, an employer is responsible for acts of sexual harassment in the workplace where the employer (or its agents or supervisory employees) knows or should have known of the conduct, unless it can show that it took immediate and appropriate corrective action.

(e) An employer may also be responsible for the acts of non-employees, with respect to sexual harassment of employees in the workplace, where the employer (or its agents or supervisory employees) knows or should have known of the conduct and fails to take immediate and appropriate corrective action.

In reviewing these cases the Commission will consider the extent of the employer's control and any other legal responsibility which the employer may have with respect to the conduct of such non-employees.

(f) Prevention is the best tool for the elimination of sexual harassment. Employer should take all steps necessary to prevent sexual harassment from occurring, such as affirmatively raising the subject, expressing strong disapproval, developing appropriate sanctions, informing employees of their right to raise and how to raise the issue of harassment under title VII, and developing methods to sensitize all concerned.

(g) Other related practices: Where employment opportunities or benefits are granted because of an individual's submission to the employer's sexual advances or requests for sexual favors, the employer may be held liable for unlawful sex discrimination against other persons who were qualified for but denied that employment opportunity ...

Questions for Discussion

1. *The CEDAW Committee regards sexual harassment as a form of violence against women. Do you think it is regarded in that way in the United States? Should it be?*

2. *The Swedish approach seems to be to regard sexual harassment as a violation of the dignity or integrity of the worker or job seeker. The U.S. approach focuses on the hostile work environment that is created by the harasser's conduct. Are these essentially the same approach? Does the Swedish approach seem to provide more protection for the victim?*

X. Protections for Maternity in International Law

A. Convention No. 183 Convention Concerning the Revision of the Maternity Protection Convention (2000)

Article 1

For the purposes of this Convention, the term "woman" applies to any female person without discrimination whatsoever and the term "child" applies to any child without discrimination whatsoever.

Article 2

1. This Convention applies to all employed women, including those in atypical forms of dependent work.

2. However, each Member which ratifies this Convention may, after consulting the representative organizations of employers and workers concerned, exclude wholly or partly from the scope of the Convention limited categories of workers when its application to them would raise special problems of a substantial nature.

3. Each Member which avails itself of the possibility afforded in the preceding Paragraph shall, in its first report on the application of the Convention under article 22 of the Constitution of the International Labour Organization, list the categories of workers thus excluded and the reasons for their exclusion. In its subsequent reports, the Member shall describe the measures taken with a view to progressively extending the provisions of the Convention to these categories.

HEALTH PROTECTION

Article 3

Each Member shall, after consulting the representative organizations of employers and workers, adopt appropriate measures to ensure that pregnant or breastfeeding women are not obliged to perform work which has been determined by the competent authority to be prejudicial to the health of the mother or the child, or where an assessment has established a significant risk to the mother's health or that of her child.

MATERNITY LEAVE

Article 4

1. On production of a medical certificate or other appropriate certification, as determined by national law and practice, stating the presumed date of childbirth, a woman to whom this Convention applies shall be entitled to a period of maternity leave of not less than 14 weeks.

2. The length of the period of leave referred to above shall be specified by each Member in a declaration accompanying its ratification of this Convention.

3. Each Member may subsequently deposit with the Director-General of the International Labour Office a further declaration extending the period of maternity leave.

4. With due regard to the protection of the health of the mother and that of the child, maternity leave shall include a period of six weeks' compulsory leave after childbirth,

unless otherwise agreed at the national level by the government and the representative organizations of employers and workers.

5. The prenatal portion of maternity leave shall be extended by any period elapsing between the presumed date of childbirth and the actual date of childbirth, without reduction in any compulsory portion of postnatal leave.

LEAVE IN CASE OF ILLNESS OR COMPLICATIONS

Article 5

On production of a medical certificate, leave shall be provided before or after the maternity leave period in the case of illness, complications or risk of complications arising out of pregnancy or childbirth. The nature and the maximum duration of such leave may be specified in accordance with national law and practice.

BENEFITS

Article 6

1. Cash benefits shall be provided, in accordance with national laws and regulations, or in any other manner consistent with national practice, to women who are absent from work on leave referred to in Articles 4 or 5.

2. Cash benefits shall be at a level which ensures that the woman can maintain herself and her child in proper conditions of health and with a suitable standard of living.

3. Where, under national law or practice, cash benefits paid with respect to leave referred to in Article 4 are based on previous earnings, the amount of such benefits shall not be less than two thirds of the woman's previous earnings or of such of those earnings as are taken into account for the purpose of computing benefits.

4. Where, under national law or practice, other methods are used to determine the cash benefits paid with respect to leave referred to in Article 4, the amount of such benefits shall be comparable to the amount resulting on average from the application of the preceding Paragraph.

5. Each Member shall ensure that the conditions to qualify for cash benefits can be satisfied by a large majority of the women to whom this Convention applies.

6. Where a woman does not meet the conditions to qualify for cash benefits under national laws and regulations or in any other manner consistent with national practice, she shall be entitled to adequate benefits out of social assistance funds, subject to the means test required for such assistance.

7. Medical benefits shall be provided for the woman and her child in accordance with national laws and regulations or in any other manner consistent with national practice. Medical benefits shall include prenatal, childbirth and postnatal care, as well as hospitalization care when necessary.

8. In order to protect the situation of women in the labour market, benefits in respect of the leave referred to in Articles 4 and 5 shall be provided through compulsory social insurance or public funds, or in a manner determined by national law and practice. An employer shall not be individually liable for the direct cost of any such monetary benefit to a woman employed by him or her without that employer's specific agreement except where:

(a) such is provided for in national law or practice in a member State prior to the date of adoption of this Convention by the International Labour Conference; or

(b) it is subsequently agreed at the national level by the government and the representative organizations of employers and workers....

EMPLOYMENT PROTECTION AND NON-DISCRIMINATION

Article 8

1. It shall be unlawful for an employer to terminate the employment of a woman during her pregnancy or absence on leave referred to in Articles 4 or 5 or during a period following her return to work to be prescribed by national laws or regulations, except on grounds unrelated to the pregnancy or birth of the child and its consequences or nursing. The burden of proving that the reasons for dismissal are unrelated to pregnancy or childbirth and its consequences or nursing shall rest on the employer.

2. A woman is guaranteed the right to return to the same position or an equivalent position paid at the same rate at the end of her maternity leave.

Article 9

1. Each Member shall adopt appropriate measures to ensure that maternity does not constitute a source of discrimination in employment, including—notwithstanding Article 2, Paragraph 1—access to employment.

2. Measures referred to in the preceding Paragraph shall include a prohibition from requiring a test for pregnancy or a certificate of such a test when a woman is applying for employment, except where required by national laws or regulations in respect of work that is:

(a) prohibited or restricted for pregnant or nursing women under national laws or regulations; or

(b) where there is a recognized or significant risk to the health of the woman and child.

BREASTFEEDING MOTHERS

Article 10

1. A woman shall be provided with the right to one or more daily breaks or a daily reduction of hours of work to breastfeed her child.

2. The period during which nursing breaks or the reduction of daily hours of work are allowed, their number, the duration of nursing breaks and the procedures for the reduction of daily hours of work shall be determined by national law and practice. These breaks or the reduction of daily hours of work shall be counted as working time and remunerated accordingly.

B. *CEDAW General Recommendation 24*

...

Article 12 (2)

26. Reports should also include what measures States parties have taken to ensure women appropriate services *in connection with pregnancy, confinement and the post-natal period*. Information on the rates at which these measures have reduced maternal mortality and morbidity in their countries, in general, and in vulnerable groups, regions and communities, in particular, should also be included.

27. States parties should include in their reports how they supply *free services where necessary* to ensure safe pregnancies, childbirth and post-partum periods for women. Many women are at risk of death or disability from pregnancy-related causes because they lack the funds to obtain or access the necessary services, which include ante-natal,

maternity and post-natal services. The Committee notes that it is the duty of States parties to ensure women's right to safe motherhood and emergency obstetric services and they should allocate to these services the maximum extent of available resources.

C. European Council Directive (1992)[11]

[O]n the introduction of measures to encourage improvements in the safety and health at work of pregnant workers and workers who have recently given birth or are breastfeeding ...

Whereas pregnant workers and workers who are breastfeeding must not engage in activities which have been assessed as revealing a risk of exposure, jeopardising safety and health, to certain particularly dangerous agents or working conditions;

Whereas provision should be made for pregnant workers, workers who have recently given birth or workers who are breastfeeding not to be required to work at night where such provision is necessary from the point of view of their safety and health;

Whereas the vulnerability of pregnant workers, workers who have recently given birth or who are breastfeeding makes it necessary for them to be granted the right to maternity leave of at least 14 continuous weeks, allocated before and/or after confinement, and renders necessary the compulsory nature of maternity leave of at least two weeks, allocated before and/or after confinement;

Whereas the risk of dismissal for reasons associated with their condition may have harmful effects on the physical and mental state of pregnant workers, workers who have recently given birth or who are breastfeeding; whereas provision should be made for such dismissal to be prohibited; ...

XI. Protection for Maternity in Sweden

According to the Swedish government website,[12] parental leave allows parents to stay home with their children while keeping their job. Parents are entitled to 480 days of paid leave per child, with 60 days being reserved for each parent. This is mainly to encourage equality and shared responsibility. Fathers are also entitled to 10 extra paid days of leave when the child is born.

The Swedish parental leave system is quite flexible. Parents can choose to be off work for extended periods, single days or parts of days. Time off can even be saved and used at any time from 60 days before the expected delivery date until the child reaches the age of eight.

The New York Times reported that 85% of fathers in Sweden take paternity leave.[13]

---

11. 92/85/EEC of 19 October 1992.

12. *Available at* http://www.sweden.se/eng/Home/Work/The-Swedish-system/Employment_based_benefits/Parental-leave/ [last visited July 21, 2011].

13. *In Sweden Men Can Have it All, available at* http://www.nytimes.com/2010/06/10/world/europe/10iht-sweden.html [last visited July 21, 2011].

XII. Protection for Maternity Functions in the United States

A. The Pregnancy Discrimination Act

The Pregnancy Discrimination Act[14] amended Title VII of the Civil Rights Act of 1964. Discrimination on the basis of pregnancy, childbirth, or related medical conditions constitutes unlawful sex discrimination under Title VII, which covers employers with 15 or more employees, including state and local governments. Title VII also applies to employment agencies and to labor organizations, as well as to the federal government. Women who are pregnant or affected by pregnancy-related conditions must be treated in the same manner as other applicants or employees with similar abilities or limitations.

Title VII's pregnancy-related protections include:

- Hiring

   An employer cannot refuse to hire a pregnant woman because of her pregnancy, because of a pregnancy-related condition, or because of the prejudices of co-workers, clients, or customers.

- Pregnancy & Maternity Leave

   An employer may not single out pregnancy-related conditions for special procedures to determine an employee's ability to work. However, if an employer requires its employees to submit a doctor's statement concerning their inability to work before granting leave or paying sick benefits, the employer may require employees affected by pregnancy-related conditions to submit such statements.

   If an employee is temporarily unable to perform her job because of her pregnancy, the employer must treat her the same as any other temporarily disabled employee. For example, if the employer allows temporarily disabled employees to modify tasks, perform alternative assignments, or take disability leave or leave without pay, the employer also must allow an employee who is temporarily disabled because of pregnancy to do the same.

   Pregnant employees must be permitted to work as long as they are able to perform their jobs. If an employee has been absent from work as a result of a pregnancy-related condition and recovers, her employer may not require her to remain on leave until the baby's birth.

- Health Insurance

   Any health insurance provided by an employer must cover expenses for pregnancy-related conditions on the same basis as costs for other medical conditions. An employer need not provide health insurance for expenses arising from abortion, except where the life of the mother is endangered.

   Pregnancy-related expenses should be reimbursed exactly as those incurred for other medical conditions, whether payment is on a fixed basis or a percentage of reasonable-and-customary-charge basis.

---

14. Pregnancy Discrimination Act of 1978.

The amounts payable by the insurance provider can be limited only to the same extent as amounts payable for other conditions. No additional, increased, or larger deductible can be imposed.

B. The Family Medical Leave Act — FMLA

The FMLA guarantees that an eligible employee can have job protected time off work as follows:

A) Up to 12 work weeks of job protected time off work per year because of:

1. A serious health condition,

2. A family member's serious health condition,

3. Parental leave to care for a newborn or newly adopted or placed child. (NOTE: for birth mothers, any period of pregnancy related temporary disability is not deducted from the 12 week parental leave entitlement).

4. A qualifying exigency arising out of the fact that the employee's family member is on covered active duty (or has been notified of an impending call or order to covered active duty) in the regular Armed Forces Reserves or National Guard.

and/or

B) If the employee is an eligible family member or next of kin of a covered service member, the employee can have up to 26 workweeks of "Service Member Family Leave" during a single 12-month period to care for a covered service member who is:

- Undergoing medical treatment, recuperation, or therapy,

- Otherwise in outpatient status, or

- On the temporary disability retired list, for a serious injury or illness

  OR

- To care for veteran who is undergoing medical treatment, recuperation or therapy for serious injury or illness that occurred any time during the five years preceding the date of treatment.

C. Breastfeeding Mothers in the U.S. — The Patient Protection and Affordable Health Care Act[15]

SEC. 4207. REASONABLE BREAK TIME FOR NURSING MOTHERS.

Section 7 of the Fair Labor Standards Act of 1938 (29 U.S.C. 207) is amended by adding at the end the following:

(r)(1) An employer shall provide—

(A) a reasonable break time for an employee to express breast milk for her nursing child for 1 year after the child's birth each time such employee has need to express the milk;

---

15. Public Laws 111-148 & 111-152 (2010).

and

(B) a place, other than a bathroom, that is shielded from view and free from intrusion from coworkers and the public, which may be used by an employee to express breast milk.

(2) An employer shall not be required to compensate an employee receiving reasonable break time under Paragraph (1) for any work time spent for such purpose.

(3) An employer that employs less than 50 employees shall not be subject to the requirements of this subsection, if such requirements would impose an undue hardship by causing the employer significant difficulty or expense when considered in relation to the size, financial resources, nature, or structure of the employer's business.

(4) Nothing in this subsection shall preempt a State law that provides greater protections to employees than the protections provided for under this subsection."

Questions for Discussion

1. *The U.S. is an outlier among western democracies in terms of parental leave, in that it does not guarantee paid parental leave. What impact does this have on women and families?*

2. *In terms of promoting equal responsibility for the raising of children, does it make sense to offer men parental leave too? Does offering this type of leave help to erode gender stereotypes?*

Chapter 17

Women in the Public and Political Arena

Chapter Problem

NATO forces recently engaged in a campaign to protect civilians in Libya pursuant to UN Security Council Resolution 1973 of 2011. Now that the campaign is over, Gaddafi has been killed, and a new government has been formed. Now imagine that you have been consulted as an advisor on gender issues to the government of a post-Gaddafi Libya.

The new government wants to ensure gender equality in all fields, but specifically in the areas of public and political life. They ask you to come up with a strategy for increasing the participation of women in the political and public arena. To determine how this might best be accomplished, you start by reviewing various Libyan source documents to ascertain the status of women in the country, and then look to examples from other countries with substantial participation by women in political and public life. What strategies might be successful in accomplishing the goal of gender equality in the public arena?

I. CEDAW and the Equality of Women in Public and Political Life

A. CEDAW Article 7

States Parties shall take all appropriate measures to eliminate discrimination against women in the political and public life of the country and, in particular, shall ensure to women, on equal terms with men, the right:

(a) To vote in all elections and public referenda and to be eligible for election to all publicly elected bodies;

(b) To participate in the formulation of government policy and the implementation hereof and to hold public office and perform all public functions at all levels of government;

(c) To participate in non-governmental organizations and associations concerned with the public and political life of the country.

B. *CEDAW General Recommendation No. 23*

10. In all nations, the most significant factors inhibiting women's ability to participate in public life have been the cultural framework of values and religious beliefs, the lack of services and men's failure to share the tasks associated with the organization of the household and with the care and raising of children. In all nations, cultural traditions and religious beliefs have played a part in confining women to the private spheres of activity and excluding them from active participation in public life.

11. Relieving women of some of the burdens of domestic work would allow them to engage more fully in the life of their communities. Women's economic dependence on men often prevents them from making important political decisions and from participating actively in public life. Their double burden of work and their economic dependence, coupled with the long or inflexible hours of both public and political work, prevent women from being more active.

12. Stereotyping, including that perpetrated by the media, confines women in political life to issues such as the environment, children and health, and excludes them from responsibility for finance, budgetary control and conflict resolution. The low involvement of women in the professions from which politicians are recruited can create another obstacle. In countries where women leaders do assume power this can be the result of the influence of their fathers, husbands or male relatives rather than electoral success in their own right.

Political systems

13. The principle of equality of women and men has been affirmed in the constitutions and laws of most countries and in all international instruments. Nonetheless, in the last 50 years, women have not achieved equality, and their inequality has been reinforced by their low level of participation in public and political life. Policies developed and decisions made by men alone reflect only part of human experience and potential. The just and effective organization of society demands the inclusion and participation of all its members.

14. No political system has conferred on women both the right to and the benefit of full and equal participation. While democratic systems have improved women's opportunities for involvement in political life, the many economic, social and cultural barriers they continue to face have seriously limited their participation. Even historically stable democracies have failed to integrate fully and equally the opinions and interests of the female half of the population. Societies in which women are excluded from public life and decision-making cannot be described as democratic. The concept of democracy will have real and dynamic meaning and lasting effect only when political decision-making is shared by women and men and takes equal account of the interests of both. The examination of States parties' reports shows that where there is full and equal participation of women in public life and decision-making, the implementation of their rights and compliance with the Convention improves.

II. Current Libyan Laws Regulating Gender Equality

A. The Libyan Constitution (Relevant Articles on Gender Equality)[1]

… **Article 2** [State Religion, Language]

Islam is the religion of the State …[2]

Article 3 [Solidarity, Family]

Social solidarity constitutes the foundation of national unity. The family, based on religion, morality, and patriotism, is the foundation of society.

Article 5 [Equality]

All citizens are equal before the law.

B. The Green Charter for Human Rights of the Jamahiriyan Era[3]

… 7. The members of Jamahiriyan society are free in their private acts and their personal relationships. No one may interfere with their privacy, save in the event of a complaint from one of the partners involved, or if the act or the relationship are harmful or prejudicial to society or are conflicting with its values.[4] […]

21. The members of Jamahiriyan society, whether men or women, are equal in every human respect. The distinction of rights between men and women is a flagrant injustice that nothing whatsoever can justify.

They proclaim that marriage is an equitable association between two equal partners. No one may be coerced into a marriage contract, nor divorce except by mutual consent or after a fair judgment. It is unjust to deprive children of their mother and the mother of her home.

---

1. *Available at* http://unpan1.un.org/intradoc/groups/public/documents/cafrad/unpan004643.pdf [last visited April 11, 2011].
2. Refer back to Chapter12 to assess how the imposition of a state religion might impact the rights of women.
3. *Available at* http://www.ecoi.net/file_upload/1504_1217516548_great-green-charter-of-human-rights-of-the-jamahiriyan-era.pdf [last visited April 11, 2011].
4. *Available at* http://www.ecoi.net/file_upload/1504_1217516548_great-green-charter-of-human-rights-of-the-jamahiriyan-era.pdf [last visited April 11, 2011].

C. Libya and CEDAW

Libya signed onto CEDAW in 1989, but entered a reservation to Article 2 and Article 16 (c) and (d). In 1995 it modified its reservation as follows:

1. Libyan Arab Jamahiriya — Reservations[5]

Article 2 of the Convention shall be implemented with due regard for the peremptory norms of the Islamic *sharia* relating to determination of the inheritance portions of the estate of a deceased person, whether female or male. The implementation of article 16, Paragraph 1 (c) and (d), of the Convention shall be without prejudice to any of the rights guaranteed to women by the Islamic *sharia*.

In 2004, Libya signed the Optional Protocol to CEDAW.

D. U.S. State Department's 2010 Human Rights Report on Libya[6]

Women

The 1969 Constitutional Proclamation granted women equality under the law. In practice, however, traditional attitudes and practices continued to be used as reasons for discrimination against women. *Shari'a* governs inheritance, divorce, and the right to own property.

The law prohibits domestic violence, but there was no reliable information on the penalties. There was little detailed information regarding the extent of violence against women. Domestic abuse was rarely discussed publicly.

The law prohibits rape. The convicted rapist must marry the victim, with her agreement, or serve a prison term of up to 25 years.

The law does not distinguish between rape and spousal rape. According to government officials, spousal rape occurred and was resolved by "social solutions."

The law prohibits prostitution, but authorities tolerated it in practice.

The law does not prohibit female genital mutilation (FGM), which is foreign to the culture and society. There were reports that FGM occurred in remote areas of the country within African migrant communities.

Women and girls suspected of violating moral codes reportedly were detained indefinitely without being convicted or after having served a sentence and without the right to challenge their detention before a court. They were held in "social rehabilitation" homes, which provided social services, including education and health care. Many detained in these facilities had been raped and then ostracized by their families. The government stated that a woman was free to leave a rehabilitation home when she reached "legal age" (18 years), consented to marriage, or was taken into the custody of a male relative. According to HRW, most were transferred to these facilities against their will, and those who came

---

5. *Available at* http://daccess-dds-ny.un.org/doc/UNDOC/GEN/N06/309/97/PDF/N0630997.pdf? OpenElement [last visited April 10, 2011].

6. *Available at* http://www.state.gov/g/drl/rls/hrrpt/2010/nea/154467.htm [last visited April 11, 2011].

of their own volition did so because no genuine shelters for survivors of violence exist. HRW maintained that the government routinely violated women and girls' human rights in "social rehabilitation" homes, including violations of due process, freedom of movement, personal dignity, and privacy.

The law criminalizes sexual harassment, but there were no reports on how this law was enforced in practice.

The Department of Social Affairs under the General People's Committee secretariat collects data and oversees the integration of women into all spheres of public life. Women did not hold any cabinet-level offices in the government, though the General People's Congress has a representative for women's affairs.

The General Union of Women's Associations, which the government established as a network of quasi-nongovernmental organizations, addresses women's employment needs. According to a 2005 International Labor Organization (ILO) report, 32 percent of women older than 15 years were economically active. Traditional restrictions continue to discourage some women from playing an active role in the workplace.

The government is the country's largest employer. Civil service salaries are set by education and experience. Women and men with similar qualifications are paid at the same grade for positions that are substantially similar. The emerging private sector does not formally discriminate on the basis of gender for access to employment or credit, although cultural conceptions of gender roles reduce women's involvement in the economy.

Educational differences between men and women have narrowed, but a significant proportion of an older generation of rural women did not attend school and instilled in their children traditional beliefs, such as preserving women's subservient role in society.

Trafficking in Persons

The law does not specifically prohibit trafficking in persons, and there were reports that persons were trafficked to the country for commercial sexual exploitation and forced labor purposes.

The country was both a transit point for trafficked persons en route to Europe and a destination country for victims from sub-Saharan Africa and South Asia. International observers estimated that 1 to 2 percent of Libya's 1.5 to 2 million foreign residents may be victims of trafficking.

The law does not expressly criminalize trafficking for purposes of sexual exploitation or involuntary servitude, and the government provided no information on prosecutions related to trafficking offenses. On February 17, the government agreed to repatriate 26 Indian nationals whom an agent reportedly convinced to work for a local company, where they were paid low wages and locked up when they complained. The company agreed to pay five months' wages and airfare to India.

There were no reports of any government participation in, or facilitation of, trafficking in persons.

As in previous years, the government did not provide adequate protection to victims of trafficking. The government failed to screen vulnerable populations adequately to identify trafficking victims. Victims were susceptible to punishment for unlawful acts committed as a result of being trafficked, including unlawful presence in the country, working without a valid work permit, and engaging in prostitution. Trafficking victims, intermingled with economic migrants, may have been deported without receiving medical, psychological, or legal aid.

During the year the government took steps to prevent trafficking in persons by supporting a series of training workshops for members of the law enforcement community and select government-sponsored charity associations to raise awareness of trafficking.

Questions for Discussion

1. *The Libyan Constitution seems to guarantee equality for women, yet the State Department report suggests that de facto equality has not been achieved. What other means of fostering equality can you suggest since merely legislating equality has not achieved the desired goal?*

2. *Libya entered a reservation to CEDAW based on* Shari'a. *International human rights law enshrines protection for religion and culture in UN Conventions like the ICCPR and ICESCR. Should the CEDAW Committee permit reservations like the one entered by Libya? Should women's rights to equality take precedence over religious precepts?*

E. Excerpts from Concluding Observations of the Committee on the Elimination of Discrimination against Women: Libyan Arab Jamahiriya (6 February 2009)[7]

19. The Committee is concerned that a clear understanding of temporary special measures, as well as the reason for their application according to Paragraph 1 of article 4 of the Convention, which is directly applicable, seems to be lacking in the State party, in particular in the area of labour as well as political and public participation. It is further concerned that such measures are not systematically applied as a necessary instrument to accelerate the achievement of de facto equality between women and men in all areas of the Convention.

20. The Committee encourages the State party to enact specific legislation for the adoption of temporary special measures in accordance with article 4, Paragraph 1, of the Convention and the Committee's general recommendation No. 25 in order to accelerate the realization of women's de facto equality with men in areas where women are under-represented or in disadvantaged situations. The Committee recommends that the State party take measures to raise public awareness about the importance of temporary special measures in accelerating the process of achievement of gender equality.

Stereotypes, cultural practices

21. The Committee is concerned at the absence in the State party of a national strategy to promote the human rights of Libyan women and eliminate stereotypes about the role of women and men. The Committee remains concerned about the persistence of entrenched, traditional stereotypes regarding the roles and responsibilities of women and

---

7. CEDAW/C/LBY/CO/5, *available at* http://www.unhcr.org/refworld/docid/49c0ce7e2.html [last visited 11 April 2011].

men in the family and in society at large, which are reflected, in part, in women's educational choices, their situation in the labour market and their low participation in political and public life.

22. The Committee urges the State party to adopt a national strategic plan, in particular to bring about change in the widely accepted stereotypical roles of women and men, thereby promoting equal sharing of family responsibilities between women and men and the equal status and responsibilities of women and men in the private and public spheres. The Committee recommends that awareness-raising campaigns be addressed to both women and men and that the media be encouraged to project a positive image of women. [...]

Political participation and participation in public life

29. While noting with satisfaction that women's participation has risen to 32 per cent in the General People's Congress, and welcoming the information provided by the Libyan delegation on women's involvement in the Basic People's Congresses and positions held on these bodies, the Committee remains concerned that women continue to be under-represented in political and public life, particularly in decisionmaking bodies, including the executive branch of Government, and the diplomatic and public service.

30. The Committee urges the State party to take all appropriate measures, including temporary special measures under article 4, Paragraph 1, of the Convention, and in accordance with the Committee's general recommendations Nos. 23 and 25, and to establish concrete goals to accelerate the increase of women's representation in the executive branch of Government, Parliament and the diplomatic corps. It recommends that the application of such measures to increase women's political representation should include the establishment of benchmarks with timetables or increased quotas. The Committee recommends that the State party continue to undertake awareness-raising campaigns about the importance of women's participation in decision-making at all levels.

III. Advancing Political Representation by Women

A. CEDAW Committee's *General Recommendations on Measures to Advance Political Representation*[8]

The Convention on the Elimination of All Forms of Discrimination against Women places special importance on the participation of women in the public life of their countries. The preamble to the Convention states in part:

> *Recalling* that discrimination against women violates the principles of equality of rights and respect for human dignity, is an obstacle to the participation of

---

8. UN Committee on the Elimination of Discrimination Against Women (CEDAW) *CEDAW General Recommendation No. 23: Political and Public Life*, 1997, A/52/38, *available at* http://www.unhcr.org/refworld/docid/453882a622.html [last visited 11 April 2011].

women, on equal terms with men, in the political, social, economic and cultural life of their countries, hampers the growth of the prosperity of society and the family and makes more difficult the full development of the potentialities of women in the service of their countries and of humanity.

2. The Convention further reiterates in its preamble the importance of women's participation in decision-making as follows:

Convinced that the full and complete development of a country, the welfare of the world and the cause of peace require the maximum participation of women on equal terms with men in all fields....

The obligation specified in article 7 extends to all areas of public and political life and is not limited to those areas specified in sub-paragraphs (a), (b) and (c). The political and public life of a country is a broad concept. It refers to the exercise of political power, in particular the exercise of legislative, judicial, executive and administrative powers. The term covers all aspects of public administration and the formulation and implementation of policy at the international, national, regional and local levels. The concept also includes many aspects of civil society, including public boards and local councils and the activities of organizations such as political parties, trade unions, professional or industry associations, women's organizations, community-based organizations and other organizations concerned with public and political life.

The Convention envisages that, to be effective, this equality must be achieved within the framework of a political system in which each citizen enjoys the right to vote and be elected at genuine periodic elections held on the basis of universal suffrage and by secret ballot, in such a way as to guarantee the free expression of the will of the electorate, as provided for under international human rights instruments, such as article 21 of the Universal Declaration of Human Rights and article 25 of the International Covenant on Civil and Political Rights.

7. The Convention's emphasis on the importance of equality of opportunity and of participation in public life and decision-making has led the Committee to review article 7 and to suggest to States parties that in reviewing their laws and policies and in reporting under the Convention, they should take into account the comments and recommendations set out below.

Comments

8. Public and private spheres of human activity have always been considered distinct, and have been regulated accordingly. Invariably, women have been assigned to the private or domestic sphere, associated with reproduction and the raising of children, and in all societies these activities have been treated as inferior. By contrast, public life, which is respected and honoured, extends to a broad range of activity outside the private and domestic sphere. Men historically have both dominated public life and exercised the power to confine and subordinate women within the private sphere.

9. Despite women's central role in sustaining the family and society and their contribution to development, they have been excluded from political life and the decision-making process, which nonetheless determine the pattern of their daily lives and the future of societies. Particularly in times of crisis, this exclusion has silenced women's voices and rendered invisible their contribution and experiences.

10. In all nations, the most significant factors inhibiting women's ability to participate in public life have been the cultural framework of values and religious beliefs, the lack of services and men's failure to share the tasks associated with the organization of the

household and with the care and raising of children. In all nations, cultural traditions and religious beliefs have played a part in confining women to the private spheres of activity and excluding them from active participation in public life.

11. Relieving women of some of the burdens of domestic work would allow them to engage more fully in the life of their communities. Women's economic dependence on men often prevents them from making important political decisions and from participating actively in public life. Their double burden of work and their economic dependence, coupled with the long or inflexible hours of both public and political work, prevent women from being more active.

12. Stereotyping, including that perpetrated by the media, confines women in political life to issues such as the environment, children and health, and excludes them from responsibility for finance, budgetary control and conflict resolution. The low involvement of women in the professions from which politicians are recruited can create another obstacle. In countries where women leaders do assume power this can be the result of the influence of their fathers, husbands or male relatives rather than electoral success in their own right.

Political systems

13. The principle of equality of women and men has been affirmed in the constitutions and laws of most countries and in all international instruments. Nonetheless, in the last 50 years, women have not achieved equality, and their inequality has been reinforced by their low level of participation in public and political life. Policies developed and decisions made by men alone reflect only part of human experience and potential. The just and effective organization of society demands the inclusion and participation of all its members.

14. No political system has conferred on women both the right to and the benefit of full and equal participation. While democratic systems have improved women's opportunities for involvement in political life, the many economic, social and cultural barriers they continue to face have seriously limited their participation. Even historically stable democracies have failed to integrate fully and equally the opinions and interests of the female half of the population. Societies in which women are excluded from public life and decision-making cannot be described as democratic. The concept of democracy will have real and dynamic meaning and lasting effect only when political decision-making is shared by women and men and takes equal account of the interests of both. The examination of States parties' reports shows that where there is full and equal participation of women in public life and decision-making, the implementation of their rights and compliance with the Convention improves.

Temporary special measures

15. While removal of de jure barriers is necessary, it is not sufficient. Failure to achieve full and equal participation of women can be unintentional and the result of outmoded practices and procedures which inadvertently promote men. Under article 4, the Convention encourages the use of temporary special measures in order to give full effect to articles 7 and 8. Where countries have developed effective temporary strategies in an attempt to achieve equality of participation, a wide range of measures has been implemented, including recruiting, financially assisting and training women candidates, amending electoral procedures, developing campaigns directed at equal participation, setting numerical goals and quotas and targeting women for appointment to public positions such as the judiciary or other professional groups that play an essential part in the everyday life of all societies. The formal removal of barriers and the introduction of temporary

special measures to encourage the equal participation of both men and women in the public life of their societies are essential prerequisites to true equality in political life. In order, however, to overcome centuries of male domination of the public sphere, women also require the encouragement and support of all sectors of society to achieve full and effective participation, encouragement which must be led by States parties to the Convention, as well as by political parties and public officials. States parties have an obligation to ensure that temporary special measures are clearly designed to support the principle of equality and therefore comply with constitutional principles which guarantee equality to all citizens.

Summary […]

1. The critical issue, emphasized in the *Beijing Platform for Action*, is the gap between the de jure and de facto, or the right as against the reality of women's participation in politics and public life generally. Research demonstrates that if women's participation reaches 30 to 35 per cent (generally termed a "critical mass"), there is a real impact on political style and the content of decisions, and political life is revitalized.

Questions for Discussion

Consider the Observations made by the CEDAW Committee on the use of Special Temporary Measures (sometimes referred to as Affirmative Action or quotas — see Chapter 4). The Committee seems to consider that these kinds of measures are appropriate in ensuring women's political participation in the organs of government.

1. *Do you think it would make a difference in the everyday lives of women if a certain number of seats in the legislative body were reserved for women? Why or why not?*

2. *Consider countries like Rwanda and Afghanistan that do have reserved seats for women. Then consider the U.S. that does not have such a system, and has very low representation of women in Congress. Does the reserved seat system seem like an effective way to foster women's participation in the political system? Would it work in the U.S.?*

3. *Several academics argue that women's political participation will only make a difference in the lives of women when it reaches what they call a "critical mass" — usually defined as being when women hold about 30%–35% of the seats in a legislative body. Consider arguments for and against a critical mass when evaluating the success or failure of the systems in Rwanda, Afghanistan, and India.*

4. *Do you agree with the CEDAW Committee's finding that "Invariably, women have been assigned to the private or domestic sphere, associated with reproduction and the raising of children, and in all societies these activities have been treated as inferior. By contrast, public life, which is respected and honoured, extends to a broad range of activity outside the private and domestic sphere. Men historically have both dominated public life and exercised the power to confine and subordinate women within the private sphere"? Is guaranteeing women seats in parliament the only or best way to bring women effectively into public life?*

B. Women and Critical Mass Theory

1. Sarah Childs, Mona Krook — *Critical Mass Theory and Women's Political Representation*[9]

A central concept in research on women's political representation is the notion of 'critical mass'. It is frequently invoked to explain why women do not always appear to represent women once they are in political office. Gender and politics scholars and activists suggest that this pattern is due not to the inclinations of female office holders, but rather to the fact that there are fewer women than men in almost all elected assemblies. They argue that women are not likely to have a major impact on legislative outcomes until they grow from a few token individuals into a considerable minority of all legislators: only as their numbers increase will women be able to work more effectively together to promote women-friendly policy change and to influence their male colleagues to accept and approve legislation promoting women's concerns.

2. Karen Beckwith, Kimberly Cowell-Mayers — *Sheer Numbers: Critical Representation Thresholds and Women's Political Representation*[10]

Increasing the numbers of elected women in a legislature may even produce negative consequences. The possibility that an increase in women's descriptive representation might produce negative outcomes has not been considered in the literature. Sheer numbers of women might conceivably generate a backlash from male gate-keepers, impede cross-party legislative work among female legislators, or serve to advance individual women uninterested in (or hostile to) public policies concerning women. Furthermore, an increase in women's sheer numbers could increase the partisan, ethnic, and racial heterogeneity of elected women in a legislature, with potential concomitant increases in party discipline, dividing women by party, potentially provoking tensions involving the necessary constructions of cross-race, cross-ethnicity alliances among women. Electing more women could mean electing fewer women motivated by the absence of women in politics to "act for" other women or it may make no difference at all.

C. Legislating Political Representation — Examples from Other Countries

1. Rwanda

Several years after the 1994 genocide, a 12 member Constitutional Committee drafted a new Constitution for Rwanda. Three members of the Constitutional Committee were women. They were provided with advice, and input from several women's NGOs. Con-

---

9. Sarah Childs, Mona Krook, *Critical Mass Theory and Women's Political Representation*, 56 POLITICAL STUDIES 725 (2008).

10. Karen Beckwith, Kimberly Cowell-Mayers, *Sheer Numbers: Critical Representation Thresholds and Women's Political Representation*, 5 PERSPECTIVES ON POLITICS 553, 554 (2007).

sequently, the 2003 Rwandan Constitution espouses strong commitment to gender equality.[11] The Constitution affirms a commitment to "ensuring equal rights between Rwandans and between women and men without prejudice to the principles of gender equality and complementarity in national development."[12] Chapter 2 of the Constitution also establishes, as one of its "fundamental principles," the equality of Rwandans.[13] This respect for equality is to be ensured in part by granting women "at least 30 percent of posts 'in all decision-making organs."[14] The 24 seats that are reserved for women are contested in women-only elections; that is, only women can stand for election and only women can vote. In the 2008 election, women attained the majority of the seats in parliament, 56%, including the position as Speaker of the House. "Women also hold a third of all cabinet positions, including foreign minister, education minister, Supreme Court chief and Police Commissioner general."[15]

a. The Women's Councils

The Ministry of Gender and Women in Development first established a national system of women's councils shortly after the genocide, and their role has since been expanded. The women's councils are grass-roots structures elected at the cell level (the smallest administrative unit) by women only, and then through indirect election at each successive administrative levels (sector, district, province). They operate alongside general local councils and represent women's concerns.

2. Afghanistan

Article 22 of the Afghan Constitution[16] provides that "all discrimination or distinction between citizens of Afghanistan is forbidden. All citizens of Afghanistan, man and woman, have equal rights and duties before the law." Article 83 goes on to provide:

> Members of the *Wolesi Jirga* [lower house] are elected by the people through free, general, secret, and direct elections.
>
> Their mandate ends on the 1st of Saratan of the fifth year after the elections, and the new assembly starts its work.
>
> The number of members of the Wolesi Jirga, proportionate to the population of each region, shall be not more than two hundred and fifty.
>
> Electoral constituency and other related issues shall be determined by election laws.

---

11. Rwandan Constitution O.G. Special of 4 June 2003 P.119; *available at* http://www.mod.gov.rw/ ?Constitution-of-the-Republic-of: [last visited April 12, 2011]. *See* Art. 9 in particular.

12. Art. 54.

13. *See* Arts. 9 & 11.

14. Art. 9 provides that "The State of Rwanda commits itself to conform to the following fundamental principles and to promote and enforce the respect thereof: ... building a state governed by the rule of law, a pluralistic democratic government, equality of all Rwandans and between women and men reflected by ensuring that women are granted at least thirty per cent of posts in decision making organs."

15. *See* Stephanie McCrummen, *Women Run the Show in a Recovering Rwanda,* THE WASHINGTON POST, Monday, October 27, 2008; *available at* http://www.washingtonpost.com/wp-dyn/content/ article/2008/10/26/AR2008102602197.html [last visited April 11, 2011].

16. Afghan Constitution of 2004; *available at* http://www.afghan-web.com/politics/current_ constitution.html [last visited April 11, 2011].

In the election law, measures should be adopted for so the election system shall provide general and just representation for all the people of the country, and *at least two female delegates should be elected from each province.* (emphasis added).

This provision, guarantees at least 64 women representatives as there are currently 32 provinces. Moreover Article 84 permits the President to appoint one third of the members of the *Meshrano Jirga* (Senate/Upper House), and 50% of that one third are women.

Additionally in the 2009 elections, President Hamid Karzai undertook to appoint more women to positions of power. However, only one woman appeared on his list of Cabinet nominees. This lack of sustained commitment has raised serious doubts about his administration's commitment to ensuring gender equality. The lone woman among Karzai's ministerial picks, Husn Bano Ghazanfar, was nominated to hold on to her present post as Minister for Women's Affairs. But even this modest step towards women's rights was threatened when Ghazanfar failed to gain confirmation in Parliament—one of 17 nominees to be rejected by the legislature out of a field of 24.

Moreover, the new *Shia* Personal Law enacted in 2009 further circumscribes the position of women. The new law regulates marriage, divorce, and inheritance for the country's *Shia* population. It includes provisions that require a woman to ask permission to leave the house, except on urgent business; a duty to "make herself up" or "dress up" for her husband when demanded, and a duty not to refuse sex when her husband wants it.[17]

3. India

a. The Seventy Fourth Amendment to the Constitution (1992)[18]

The Seventy Fourth Amendment to the Indian Constitution provides that:

STATEMENT OF OBJECTS AND REASONS

In many States local bodies have become weak and ineffective on account of a variety of reasons, including the failure to hold regular elections, prolonged supersessions and inadequate devolution of powers and functions: […]

2. Having regard to these inadequacies, it is considered necessary that provisions relating to Urban Local Bodies are incorporated in the Constitution particularly for; […]

(iv) providing adequate representation for the weaker sections like Scheduled Castes, Scheduled Tribes and women. […]

(e) reservation of seats in every Municipality—

(i) for Scheduled Castes and Scheduled Tribes in proportion to their population of which not less than one-third shall be for women;

(ii) for women which shall not less than one-third of the total number of seats;

The 1992 Constitutional Amendment reserved seats for women in local councils. However, this move was seen as insufficient, and for the last several years, a Bill has been pending to guarantee women 30% of the seats in the National legislative bodies.

---

17. *See* Human Rights Watch Report, *Afghanistan: New Law Threatens Women's Freedom*; *available at* http://www.hrw.org/en/news/2009/04/14/afghanistan-new-law-threatens-women-s-freedom [last visited April 11, 2011].

18. *Available at* http://indiacode.nic.in/coiweb/amend/amend74.htm [last visited April 11, 2011].

b. The 108th Amendment to the Constitution—
The Women's Reservation Bill in India (2010)[19]

Article 3(2):

As nearly as may be, one third of the total number of seats reserved under clause (2) of article 330 shall be reserved for women belonging to the Scheduled Castes or Scheduled Tribes, as the case may be....

4. In article 331 of the Constitution, the following proviso shall be inserted at the end, namely:

> provided that where such nominations are made, in relation to every block comprising of three general elections to the House, one seat shall be reserved for nomination of a woman of Anglo-Indian community to every House constituted after the first two general elections and no seat shall be reserved for the women of that community in the House constituted after the third general elections.

5. After article 332 of the Constitution, the following article shall be inserted, namely:

332A.(1) Seats shall be reserved for women in the Legislative Assembly of every State.

After article 334 of the Constitution, the following article shall be inserted, namely:

334A. Notwithstanding anything in the foregoing provisions of this Part or Part VIII, the provisions of the Constitution relating to the reservation of seats for women in the House of the People, the Legislative Assembly of a State and the Legislative Assembly of the National Capital Territory of Delhi shall cease to have effect women on the expiration of a period of fifteen years from the Commencement of the ... Act.

The Bill has been criticized by some who fear that wealthy male patriarchs will put forward their wives or daughters as candidates but direct their wives on how to vote and what agenda to advance.

D. Women Holding Public Office in the United States

Ninety-one women currently serve in the 112th Congress: 74 in the House (50 Democrats and 24 Republicans) and 17 in the Senate (12 Democrats and 5 Republicans). Ninety-two women were initially sworn in to the 112th Congress, but one Democratic House Member has since resigned.[20] There are no reserved seats for women. Prior to the 2010 election, Nancy Pelosi, a woman, was the Speaker of the House. She is currently minority whip. Currently Hillary Clinton serves as Secretary of State, Hilda Solis as Secretary of Labor, Kathleen Sibelius as Secretary of Health and Human Services, Janet Napolitano as Secretary of Homeland Security, and Lisa Jackson as Head of the Environmental Protection Agency (EPA). Susan Rice is the United States Ambassador to the United Nations.

---

19. The Bill has been passed by one of the Houses of Parliament but has not yet entered into law, as of April, 2011.

20. *Available at* http://www.senate.gov/CRSReports/crs-publish.cfm?pid='0E%2C*PLS%3D%22% 40%20%20%0A [last visited April 11, 2011].

1. The Washington Post — *'Hillary Effect' Cited for Increase in Female Ambassadors to U.S.*[21]

In the gated Oman Embassy off Massachusetts Avenue, Washington's first female ambassador from an Arab country, Hunaina Sultan Al-Mughairy, sat at her desk looking over a speech aimed at erasing misconceptions about her Muslim nation.

A few blocks away inside a stately Dupont Circle mansion, India's first female ambassador in more than 50 years, Meera Shankar, huddled with top aides after her prime minister's state visit with President Obama.

Nearby, in a century-old residence with its own ballroom, Latin America's only female ambassador in Washington, Colombia's Carolina Barco, dashed back from talking up free trade on Capitol Hill to showcase her country's culture and food.

There are 25 female ambassadors posted in Washington—the highest number ever, according to the State Department.

"This is breaking precedent," said Selma "Lucky" Roosevelt, a former U.S. chief of protocol.

Women remain a distinct minority—there are 182 accredited ambassadors in Washington—but their rise from a cadre of five in the late 1990s to five times that is opening up what had been an elite's men club for more than a century.

A key reason is the increase in the number of top U.S. diplomats who are women, what some call the "Hillary effect."

"Hillary Clinton is so visible" as secretary of state, said Amelia Matos Sumbana, who just arrived as ambassador from Mozambique. "She makes it easier for presidents to pick a woman for Washington."

Three of the last four secretaries of state—the office that receives foreign ambassadors—have been women.

Madeleine Albright became the first female U.S. secretary of state in 1997. Condoleezza Rice served from 2005 to 2009.

Clinton, now in her second year, is especially well-known abroad because of her stint as first lady and her presidential run; she is seen by many as a globetrotting champion of women's rights.

"The pictures of U.S. diplomacy have been strongly dominated by photos of women recently," Shankar said. "That helps to broaden the acceptance of women in the field of diplomacy."

Claudia Fritsche, the ambassador from Liechtenstein, a principality that only gave women the right to vote in 1984, said the Albright-Rice-Clinton sequence has "a worldwide effect ... It's inspiring, motivating and certainly encouraging."

Albright said that when she spoke to foreign ministers around the world they told her governments had started thinking, "We need a Madeleine."

Some American diplomats said the appointment of a woman can be a visible way for a country to signal that is modernizing and in step with the United States.

---

21. Mary Jordan, *'Hillary Effect' Cited for Increase in Female Ambassadors to U.S.*, Washington Post, January 11, 2010; A01. [Used with permission.]

For many countries, a Potomac posting is prized, landed only by seasoned diplomats and influential political players. More women now have those credentials, a reflection of women's advancement in many parts of the world.

Eleven of the 25 female envoys in Washington are from Africa. Four are from Caribbean nations. The others are from Bahrain, the Netherlands, Croatia, Kyrgyzstan, Singapore, Oman, Colombia, India, Liechtenstein and Nauru, an eight-square-mile Pacific island with only 14,000 people.

Heng Chee Chan, the Singaporean ambassador and the longest-serving female envoy in Washington, said it has been a "quantum leap" for women in diplomacy since she arrived here in 1996.

In the beginning, she said people just assumed she was a man. When a table was booked under "Ambassador Chan" and she arrived asking for it, she was told, "'Oh, he is not here yet.'"

Many said they are still often bypassed in receiving lines and the male standing beside them is greeted as "Mr. Ambassador."

"Even when I say I am ambassador, people assume I am the spouse," said Shankar, who has represented India in Washington for nearly a year.

More than half of new recruits for the U.S. Foreign Service and 30 percent of the chiefs of mission are now women, according to the State Department. That is a seismic shift from the days, as late as the 1970s, when women in the Foreign Service had to quit when they married, a rule that did not apply to men.

"It was outrageous," said Susan Johnson, president of the American Foreign Service Association. "The idea was that a married woman could not be available for worldwide service. She would be having children and making a home."

That thinking is still alive in many parts of the world. But as the U.S. Foreign Service moves away from being "pale, male and Yale," the diplomatic ranks elsewhere are diversifying, too.

Johnson said the rise in female diplomats coincides with what she sees as a shift in investment away from diplomacy and toward defense. "Is the relative feminization of diplomacy indicative of its decline as a center of power and influence?" she wonders.

But she and others welcome the change and say it will have an impact.

Cathy Tinsley, executive director of Georgetown University's Women's Leadership Initiative, said gender diversity at the top of any organization leads to better decisions. When all the decision-makers have a similar background and mind-set, they can "amplify the error."

Barco, a mother of three who has served as Colombia's foreign minister, said capability and preparation—not gender—are what count. She held 630 meetings on Capitol Hill last year to lobby for a free trade agreement with the United States.

But several female ambassadors said they often bring a different perspective to discussions than their male counterparts and tend to focus more on certain issues such as poverty and lack of schooling for girls.

Shankar credited female leaders with turning the world's spotlight on the marginalization of Afghan women, and several U.S. diplomats said that since women have run the State Department, U.S. embassies have emphasized collecting information on rights abuses against women worldwide.

Several female ambassadors from developing countries said they are attentive to issues affecting families, such as health care and the lack of safe drinking water.

Albright said she guards against saying that women focus on "soft issues." "They are often the hardest issues: poverty, discrimination, education and health," she said.

Female envoys often pool their power to land meetings with busy U.S. senators or media personalities. A group recently met with Supreme Court Justice Ruth Bader Ginsburg.

E. Other Methods of Fostering Gender Equality — Appointing Women Judges

Consider another method of fostering equality for women — that of appointing women judges. Current Supreme Court Just Sotomayor caused a minor controversy when she suggested that "a wise Latina woman with the richness of her experiences would more often than not reach a better conclusion than a white male who hasn't lived that life."[22] Justice Sotomayor is not alone in her suggestion. Justice Ruth Bader Ginsburg supported the notion that women judges are often more sensitive to women's issues when she pointed out:

> As often as Justice O'Connor and I have disagreed, because she is truly a Republican from Arizona, we were together in all the gender discrimination cases.[23]

Judge Pillay, the South African judge, who has served as a judge on the International Criminal Tribunal for Yugoslavia (ICTY), and on the International Criminal Court (ICC), observed recently:[24]

> Who interprets the law is at least as important as who makes the law, if not more so … I cannot stress how critical I consider it to be that women are represented and a gender perspective integrated at all levels of the investigation, prosecution, defence, witness protection and judiciary.

Justice Sandra Day O'Connor similarly asserted that:[25]

> [W]omen's participation in the judiciary is important to establishing a judiciary that is reflective of the society of whose laws it interprets. People are more likely to put their trust and confidence in courts that represent all of the individuals that constitute a society. Furthermore, a judiciary comprised of judges with diverse experience may provide a more balanced and thus impartial perspective on matters before the court.

---

22. Sonia Sotomayor, *A Latina Judge's Voice.* Speech delivered at the UC Berkley School of Law in 2001. *Available at* http://www.nytimes.com/2009/05/15/us/politics/15judge.text.html?_r=1 [last visited April 12, 2011].

23. Justice Ginsburg in an interview with Joan Biskupic of USA Today. *Available at* http://topics.nytimes.com/top/reference/timestopics/people/g/ruth_bader_ginsburg/index.html?inline=nyt-per [last visited April 12, 2011].

24. Bendoit, B. and Hall Martinez, K., *Ending Impunity for Gender Crimes under the International Criminal Court,* 6 BROWN JOURNAL OF WORLD AFFAIRS, 65 (2008).

25. Sandra Day O'Connor & Kim Azarelli, *Sustainable Development, Rule of Law, and the Impact of Women Judges; available at* http://www.lawschool.cornell.edu/research/ILJ/Sustainable-Development-Rule-of-Law-and-the-Impact-of-Women-Judges.cfm [last visited April 12, 2011].

Women's participation in the judiciary may be of particular importance in the implementation and enforcement of laws that allow for women's full participation in society.

Questions for Discussion

1. *Is the gender of a judge important? Why or why not? Does it make a difference to how the judge views the facts of the case or the parties?*

2. *Should there be reserved "quotas" for judges as well as legislators?*

3. *Is it more important to have women legislators or judges, or are both equally important?*

4. *Should any "quota" measure for legislators or judges be temporary? In other words, can you envisage a time when these kinds of measures will not be considered necessary?*

5. *Given all this information, how would you best advise the new Libyan Government about attaining gender equality?*

Chapter 18

Women's Access to Healthcare, and Reproductive Rights

Chapter Problem

The Senate Subcommittee on Human Rights and the Law recently held hearings on CEDAW, and may be considering submitting CEDAW to the full Senate for a vote on ratification. (As you recall, CEDAW was signed by President Jimmy Carter in 1980. However, the treaty has never been submitted to the Senate for its advice and consent regarding ratification.) Before submitting the treaty, the Subcommittee wants some clarification on CEDAW's position on reproductive rights. In recent testimony before the Subcommittee, both proponents and opponents of CEDAW have used CEDAW's support of "reproductive rights" as reasons to ratify or not ratify the treaty. The Subcommittee wants to have some clarification about what the term "reproductive rights" actually means, and what CEDAW mandates in terms of so-called "reproductive rights." The Subcommittee is also interested in the development of the law in this area in other regional human rights systems. It has requested that you research this matter and write a memorandum detailing your findings.

I. CEDAW and Women's Health

Article 12

1. States Parties shall take all appropriate measures to eliminate discrimination against women in the field of health care in order to ensure, on a basis of equality of men and women, access to health care services, including those related to family planning.

2. Notwithstanding the provisions of Paragraph 1 of this article, States Parties shall ensure to women appropriate services in connection with pregnancy, confinement and the post-natal period, granting free services where necessary, as well as adequate nutrition during pregnancy and lactation.

Article 16

1. States Parties shall take all appropriate measures to eliminate discrimination against women in all matters relating to marriage and family relations and in particular shall ensure, on a basis of equality of men and women: […]

(e) The same rights to decide freely and responsibly on the number and spacing of their children and to have access to the information, education and means to enable them to exercise these rights;

II. Linking Maternal Health and Population Growth to Development

A. The Nairobi Conference (1985)

In 1985 the World Conference to Review and Appraise the Achievements of the United Nations Decade for Equality, Development and Peace was held in Nairobi, Kenya. There delegates discussed the alarming economic conditions that many countries were encountering, and the backward slide into poverty that was being experienced by many African and South American countries. Prevalent drought in Africa had caused extensive famine in Ethiopia, and the oil crisis had detrimentally impacted many developed and developing countries. UNICEF later assessed the situation thus in its 1988 State of the World's Children Report: "In many nations, development is being thrown in reverse.... After decades of steady economic advance, large areas of the world are sliding backwards into poverty."[1] Maurice Williams, President of the Society for International Development called the 1980s "a lost decade for most of the developing world."[2] Despite the economic crisis, many developing countries found themselves having to repay large interest laden loans that they had taken out from their wealthier neighbors or the World Bank during more prosperous economic times. Far more money was being spent on repaying these loans than on health care. As the populations expanded in poorer countries, citizens found themselves with less and less access to healthcare. Moreover, cultural practices like child marriages and the emphasis on having many children to ensure that one would be taken care of during old age, meant that women were not being afforded access to healthcare during their child bearing years. Add to this, the fact that AIDs was beginning to infect people in Africa at an alarming rate. All of these factors combined to create a situation where many women found their health at risk.

The emphasis on food shortages, as well as growing awareness about environmental degradation, had caused world leaders and researchers to take efforts to curb population growth. The delegates at the Nairobi Conference thus noted:

> During the period from 1986 to the year 2000, changes in the natural environment will be critical for women. One area of change is that of the role of women as intermediaries between the natural environment and society with respect to agro-ecosystems, as well as the provision of safe water and fuel supplies and the closely

---

1. *Available at* http://www.unicef.org/sowc/archive/ENGLISH/The%20State%20of%20the%20World%27s%20Children%201988.pdf [last visited April 18, 2011]. The report noted at p. 55 that: It is therefore the mothers who will normally be the focus of information and support ... At the moment that support is often weak or non-existent. And the everyday hardship and discrimination that women face—in food, in education, in health care ... is the single most important barrier to the improvement of their own and their children's health.

2. *Cited in* Donella H. Meadows, The Global Citizen; Island Press (1991) at 77.

associated question of sanitation. The problem will continue to be greatest where water resources are limited—in arid and semi-arid areas—and in areas experiencing increasing demographic pressure. In a general manner, an improvement in the situation of women could bring about a reduction in mortality and morbidity as well as better regulation of fertility and hence of population growth, which would be beneficial for the environment and, ultimately, for women, children and men.

29. The issues of fertility rates and population growth should be treated in a context that permits women to exercise effectively their rights in matters pertaining to population concerns, including the basic right to control their own fertility which forms an important basis for the enjoyment of other rights, as stated in the report of the International Population Conference held at Mexico City in 1984.[3]

B. The International Conference for Population and Development—Cairo (1994)

The theme of the impact of reproduction and population growth was reiterated in the Programme of Action of the United Nations' Conference on Population and Development held in Cairo in 1994. There the delegates agreed that:

4.1 The empowerment and autonomy of women and the improvement of their political, social, economic and health status is a highly important end in itself. In addition, it is essential for the achievement of sustainable development. The full participation and partnership of both women and men is required in productive and reproductive life, including shared responsibilities for the care and nurturing of children and maintenance of the household. In all parts of the world, women are facing threats to their lives, health and well-being as a result of being overburdened with work and of their lack of power and influence. In most regions of the world, women receive less formal education than men, and at the same time, women's own knowledge, abilities and coping mechanisms often go unrecognized. The power relations that impede women's attainment of healthy and fulfilling lives operate at many levels of society, from the most personal to the highly public. Achieving change requires policy and programme actions that will improve women's access to secure livelihoods and economic resources, alleviate their extreme responsibilities with regard to housework, remove legal impediments to their participation in public life, and raise social awareness through effective programmes of education and mass communication. In addition, improving the status of women also enhances their decision-making capacity at all levels in all spheres of life, especially in the area of sexuality and reproduction. This, in turn, is essential for the long-term success of population programmes. Experience shows that population and development programmes are most effective when steps have simultaneously been taken to improve the status of women.[4]

---

3. Articles 28–29, Third World Conference on Women, Nairobi (1985).

4. A/Conf. 171/13, Report of the ICPD (94/10/18); *Available at* http://www.un.org/popin/icpd/conference/offeng/poa.html [last visited April 25, 2011].

Debate ensued during the Conference about what providing for women's reproductive health required of countries. It became clear that the process of incorporating reproductive rights into the panoply of women's rights is a complicated and value-laden issue. The matter was particularly delicate for those societies and cultural groups where the role that women play in society is integrally related to their sexuality and/or fertility. For example, as we learned in Chapter 12, many societies such as rural societies in parts of Somalia value a woman's chastity and virginity, and resort to radical forms of Female Genital Mutilation (FGM) in part in order to preserve that virginity. Yet, while the practice of FGM has been widely condemned,[5] eradicating the practice has met with much resistance, and today about 90% of Somalian women still undergo FGM. Similarly, in parts of Africa where children are seen as economic resources, and having many children may give a woman additional status in her community, the idea that it might be prudent to limit one's family met with resistance.

Paragraph 8.25 of the Programme of Action provides that:

> In no case should abortion be promoted as a method of family planning. All Governments and relevant intergovernmental and non-governmental organizations are urged to strengthen their commitment to women's health, to deal with the health impact of unsafe abortion as a major public health concern and to reduce the recourse to abortion through expanded and improved family-planning services. Prevention of unwanted pregnancies must always be given the highest priority and every attempt should be made to eliminate the need for abortion. Women who have unwanted pregnancies should have ready access to reliable information and compassionate counselling. Any measures or changes related to abortion within the health system can only be determined at the national or local level according to the national legislative process. In circumstances where abortion is not against the law, such abortion should be safe. In all cases, women should have access to quality services for the management of complications arising from abortion. Post-abortion counselling, education and family-planning services should be offered promptly, which will also help to avoid repeat abortions", consider reviewing laws containing punitive measures against women who have undergone illegal abortions;

Because the term "reproductive rights" is so value laden, and often so closely identified solely with abortion, the term "reproductive health" better captures women's range of rights in this area. Reproductive health means the recognition of the basic right of all couples and individuals to decide freely and responsibly the number, spacing and timing of their children and to have the information and means to do so, and the right to attain the highest standard of sexual and reproductive health. They also include the right of all to make decisions concerning reproduction free of discrimination, coercion and violence. The Cairo Programme for Action described reproductive health as being:

> A state of complete physical, mental and social well-being and ... not merely the absence of disease or infirmity, in all matters relating to the reproductive system and to its functions and processes. Reproductive health therefore implies that people are able to have a satisfying and safe sex life and that they have the capability to reproduce and the freedom to decide if, when and how often to do so. Implicit in this last condition are the right of men and women to be informed and to have access to safe, effective, affordable and acceptable methods of family

---

5. *See* Art 4.22 of the Cairo Programme of Action.

planning of their choice, as well as other methods of their choice for regulation of fertility which are not against the law, and the right of access to appropriate health-care services that will enable women to go safely through pregnancy and childbirth and provide couples with the best chance of having a healthy infant.[6]

C. The Beijing Conference, *Declaration, and Platform for Action* (1995)

The *Beijing Declaration* and *Platform for Action*, which emanated from the Fourth World Conference on Women, held in Beijing in 1995, was one of the earliest documents to reference "reproductive rights" as part of the panoply of human rights.

One of the many demands that emerged from the Beijing Conference was a demand for access to healthcare, especially healthcare during pregnancy and childbirth. Access to health care for women was seen as inextricably linked with equality, development and peace which had been a focus of the Beijing Conference. Articles 93 and 94 of the *Beijing Declaration* noted that:[7]

> 93. Discrimination against girls, often resulting from son preference, in access to nutrition and health-care services endangers their current and future health and well-being. Conditions that force girls into early marriage, pregnancy and child-bearing and subject them to harmful practices, such as female genital mutilation, pose grave health risks. Adolescent girls need, but too often do not have, access to necessary health and nutrition services as they mature. Counselling and access to sexual and reproductive health information and services for adolescents are still inadequate or lacking completely, and a young woman's right to privacy, confidentiality, respect and informed consent is often not considered. Adolescent girls are both biologically and psychosocially more vulnerable than boys to sexual abuse, violence and prostitution, and to the consequences of unprotected and premature sexual relations. The trend towards early sexual experience, combined with a lack of information and services, increases the risk of unwanted and too early pregnancy, HIV infection and other sexually transmitted diseases, as well as unsafe abortions. Early child-bearing continues to be an impediment to improvements in the educational, economic and social status of women in all parts of the world. Overall, for young women early marriage and early motherhood can severely curtail educational and employment opportunities and are likely to have a long-term, adverse impact on the quality of their lives and the lives of their children. Young men are often not educated to respect women's self-determination and to share responsibility with women in matters of sexuality and reproduction.

> 94. Reproductive health is a state of complete physical mental and social wellbeing and not merely the absence of disease or infirmity, in all matters relating to the reproductive system and to its functions and processes. Reproductive

---

6. Principle 8 of the Cairo Programme for Action; this definition was incorporated in Article 94 of the Beijing Platform for Action, and has been adopted by the WHO, among other international groups.

7. *Available at* http://www.unesco.org/education/information/nfsunesco/pdf/BEIJIN_E.PDF at p33 [last visited April 18, 2011].

health therefore implies that people are able to have a satisfying and safe sex life and that they have the capability to reproduce and the freedom to decide if, when and how often to do so. Implicit in this last condition are the right of men and women to be informed and to have access to safe, effective, affordable and acceptable methods of family planning of their choice, as well as other methods of their choice for regulation of fertility which are not against the law, and the right of access to appropriate health-care services that will enable women to go safely through pregnancy and childbirth and provide couples with the best chance of having a healthy infant. In line with the above definition of reproductive health, reproductive health care is defined as the constellation of methods, techniques and services that contribute to reproductive health and wellbeing by preventing and solving reproductive health problems. It also includes sexual health, the purpose of which is the enhancement of life and personal relations, and not merely counselling and care related to reproduction and sexually transmitted diseases.

95. Bearing in mind the above definition, reproductive rights embrace certain human rights that are already recognized in national laws, international human rights documents and other consensus documents. These rights rest on the recognition of the basic right of all couples and individuals to decide freely and responsibly the number, spacing and timing of their children and to have the information and means to do so, and the right to attain the highest standard of sexual and reproductive health. It also includes their right to make decisions concerning reproduction free of discrimination, coercion and violence, as expressed in human rights documents. In the exercise of this right, they should take into account the needs of their living and future children and their responsibilities towards the community. The promotion of the responsible exercise of these rights for all people should be the fundamental basis for government — and community-supported policies and programmes in the area of reproductive health, including family planning. As part of their commitment, full attention should be given to the promotion of mutually respectful and equitable gender relations and particularly to meeting the educational and service needs of adolescents to enable them to deal in a positive and responsible way with their sexuality. Reproductive health eludes many of the world's people because of such factors as: inadequate levels of knowledge about human sexuality and inappropriate or poor-quality reproductive health information and services; the prevalence of high-risk sexual behaviour; discriminatory social practices; negative attitudes towards women and girls; and the limited power many women and girls have over their sexual and reproductive lives. Adolescents are particularly vulnerable because of their lack of information and access to relevant services in most countries. Older women and men have distinct reproductive and sexual health issues which are often inadequately addressed.

96. The human rights of women include their right to have control over and decide freely and responsibly on matters related to their sexuality, including sexual and reproductive health, free of coercion, discrimination and violence. Equal relationships between women and men in matters of sexual relations and reproduction, including full respect for the integrity of the person, require mutual respect, consent and shared responsibility for sexual behaviour and its consequences.

97. Further, women are subject to particular health risks due to inadequate responsiveness and lack of services to meet health needs related to sexuality and

reproduction. Complications related to pregnancy and childbirth are among the leading causes of mortality and morbidity of women of reproductive age in many parts of the developing world. Similar problems exist to a certain degree in some countries with economies in transition. Unsafe abortions threaten the lives of a large number of women, representing a grave public health problem as it is primarily the poorest and youngest who take the highest risk. Most of these deaths, health problems and injuries are preventable through improved access to adequate health-care services, including safe and effective family planning methods and emergency obstetric care, recognizing the right of women and men to be informed and to have access to safe, effective, affordable and acceptable methods of family planning of their choice, as well as other methods of their choice for regulation of fertility which are not against the law, and the right of access to appropriate health-care services that will enable women to go safely through pregnancy and childbirth and provide couples with the best chance of having a healthy infant. These problems and means should be addressed on the basis of the report of the International Conference on Population and Development, with particular reference to relevant paragraphs of the *Programme of Action* of the Conference. In most countries, the neglect of women's reproductive rights severely limits their opportunities in public and private life, including opportunities for education and economic and political empowerment. The ability of women to control their own fertility forms an important basis for the enjoyment of other rights. Shared responsibility between women and men in matters related to sexual and reproductive behaviour is also essential to improving women's health.

The *Beijing Platform for Action* also called for:

better regulation of fertility and hence of population growth, which would be beneficial for the environment and, ultimately, for women, children and men. The issues of fertility rates and population growth should be treated in a context that permits women to exercise effectively their rights in matters pertaining to population concerns, including the basic right to control their own fertility ...

The call for women to have the right to "control their own fertility" was not universally accepted by delegates to the Conference. Yet, the terminology made its way into the *Beijing Declaration* where Article 17 specifically provides that:

The explicit recognition and reaffirmation of the right of all women to control all aspects of their health, in particular their own fertility, is basic to their empowerment

Catholic countries, and some African countries where children are seen as a sign of wealth, and women are valued for their fertility, were quick to express concern over these new fertility or reproductive rights. Mary Ann Glendon, the delegate from the Holy See noted:

The Holy See shares the concerns of other delegations about efforts to represent the outcome documents of Beijing as creating new international rights. [...] Any attempt to do so would go beyond the scope of the authority of this Commission. With respect to the recently adopted declaration, the Holy See would have preferred a clearer statement emphasizing that the Beijing documents cannot be interpreted as creating new human rights, including a right to abortion.

The conference wants to oppose the abuses suffered by women? All right. Let's make a note of it. Among these abuses are programs for obligatory birth control, forced sterilizations, pressure to have abortions, and gender selection with the consequent destruction of female fetuses.

Many who promote abortion as a woman's right do not by any means have women's real interests at heart. The movement for abortion rights conceals irresponsible men, trafficking in prostitution, industries that make their profits from women's bodies.[8]

Questions for Discussion

1. *Maternal mortality rates are extremely high in developing countries. For example, in Afghanistan 1 in every 11 women dies in childbirth. Yet discussing "reproductive rights" is a highly value laden enterprise. Is there a way to focus the discussion on reducing the dire maternal mortality statistics in a way that does not offend countries that oppose abortion?*

2. *On several occasions the CEDAW Committee has cited with concern the number of deaths that occur each year from illegal abortions, as well as the punitive actions taken against women who have illegal abortions. If a state opposes abortion how could it better respond to women's needs?*

D. The Language of Responsibility — Art 95 of the *Beijing Platform for Action*[9]

[Reproductive rights are defined as:]

Includ[ing] their right to make decisions concerning reproduction free of discrimination, coercion and violence, as expressed in human rights documents. In the exercise of this right, they should take into account the needs of their living and future children and their responsibilities towards the community. The promotion of the responsible exercise of these rights for all people should be the fundamental basis for government- and community-supported policies and programmes in the area of reproductive health, including family planning. As part of their commitment, full attention should be given to the promotion of mutually respectful and equitable gender relations and particularly to meeting the educational and service needs of adolescents to enable them to deal in a positive and responsible way with their sexuality. Reproductive health eludes many of the world's people because of such factors as: inadequate levels of knowledge about human sexuality and inappropriate or poor-quality reproductive health information and services; the prevalence of high-risk sexual behaviour; discriminatory social practices; negative attitudes towards women and girls; and the limited power many women and girls have over their sexual and reproductive lives.

---

8. Statement of the representative of the Holy See made in explanation of position on the Declaration adopted by the Commission on the Status of Women at its forty ninth session in UNITED NATIONS COMMISSION ON THE STATUS OF WOMEN (28 February and 22 March 2005 e/2005/27; e/cn/6/2005/11 (Official records 2005 Supplement No. 7).

9. *Available at* http://www.un.org/womenwatch/daw/beijing/platform/health.htm [last visited April 25, 2011].

1. Comments of (then) U.S. First Lady Hillary Clinton at the Beijing Conference (1995)

On these issues, the U.S. supports the provisions in the *Beijing Platform for Action* that reaffirm consensus language that was agreed to at the Cairo Conference about a year ago. It declared that "in no case should abortion be promoted as a method of family planning." The Platform asks governments "to strengthen their commitment to women's health, to deal with the health impact of unsafe abortion as a major public health concern and to reduce the recourse to abortion through expanded and improved family planning services."[10]

E. Reservations to the *Beijing Declaration*

... 2. At the same meeting, the representative of the Philippines, on behalf of the States Members of the United Nations that are members of the Group of 77, introduced a draft resolution (A/CONF.177/L.9) whereby the Conference would adopt the *Beijing Declaration* and *Platform for Action* and recommend them to the General Assembly for endorsement at its fiftieth session. The Conference then adopted the draft resolution.

3. After the draft resolution was adopted, representatives of the following States made general and interpretative statements or expressed reservations on the *Beijing Declaration* and *Platform for Action*: Peru, Kuwait, Egypt, Philippines, Holy See, Malaysia, Iran (Islamic Republic of), Libyan Arab Jamahiriya, Ecuador, Indonesia, Mauritania, Oman, Malta, Argentina, Brunei Darussalam, France, Yemen, Sudan, Dominican Republic, Costa Rica, United Arab Emirates, Venezuela, Bahrain, Lebanon, Tunisia, Mali, Benin, Guatemala, India, Algeria, Iraq, Vanuatu, Ethiopia, Morocco, Djibouti, Qatar, Nicaragua, Togo, Liberia, Syrian Arab Republic, Pakistan, Nigeria, Comoros, Bolivia, Colombia, Bangladesh, Honduras, Jordan, Ghana, Central African Republic, Cambodia, Maldives, South Africa, United Republic of Tanzania, Brazil, Panama, El Salvador, Madagascar, Chad, Cameroon, Niger, Gabon, United States of America, and Canada. The observer for Palestine also made a statement.[11]

Argentina

No reference in these documents to the right to control matters related to sexuality, including sexual and reproductive health, may be interpreted as restricting the right to life or abrogating the condemnation of abortion as a method of birth control or an instrument of population policy (in accordance with article 75, Paragraph 23, of the Constitution of Argentina, article 16 of the Convention on the Elimination of All Forms of Discrimination against Women and Paragraph 42 of the Vienna Programme of Action, adopted by the World Conference on Human Rights). No proposal contained in the documents may be interpreted to justify programmes of female or male sterilization as an adjustment variable in eradicating poverty.

The Argentine delegation participated in the consensus on Paragraph 106 (k) of the Platform for Action, which recommends that Governments should consider

---

10. *Available at* http://www.columbia.edu/cu/augustine/a/beijing.html [last visited July 2, 2011].
11. *Available at* http://www.pogar.org/publications/other/un/conferences/women/beijing-95e.pdf [last visited June 21, 2011].

reviewing laws containing punitive measures against women who have undergone abortions.

Dominican Republic:

The Dominican Republic, as a signatory to the American Convention on Human Rights, and in accordance with the Constitution and laws of the Republic, confirms that every person has the right to life, and that life begins at the moment of conception. Consequently, it accepts the content of the terms "reproductive health", "sexual health", "maternity without risk", "reproductive rights", "sexual rights" and "regulation of fertility" in the Platform for Action, but it makes an express reservation to the content of these terms, or any others, if they include abortion or interruption of pregnancy as a component. We confirm the position taken by our country at the International Conference on Population and Development, and these reservations apply to all regional and international agreements referring to these concepts.

Holy See:

Surely we can do better than to address the health needs of girls and women by paying disproportionate attention to sexual and reproductive health. Moreover, ambiguous language concerning unqualified control over sexuality and fertility could be interpreted as including societal endorsement of abortion and homosexuality.

A document that respects women's dignity should address the health of the whole woman. A document that respects women's intelligence should devote at least as much attention to literacy as to fertility ...

With regard to the terms "family planning" or "widest range of family planning services" and other terms concerning family-planning services or regulation of fertility, the Holy See's actions during this Conference should in no way be interpreted as changing its well-known position concerning those family planning methods that the Catholic Church considers morally unacceptable or concerning family planning services that do not respect the liberty of spouses, the human dignity or the human rights of those concerned. The Holy See in no way endorses contraception or the use of condoms, either as a family planning measure or in HIV/AIDS prevention programmes.

F. Beijing + 10 United Nations Committee on the Status of Women — Speech by U.S. Ambassador Sauerbrey at the 49th Session of the Commission on the Status of Women (2005)[12]

As colleagues in this meeting know, the United States has had concerns about efforts to mischaracterize the outcome documents of Beijing and Beijing+5 in creation of new international rights. It is clear that there was no intent on the part of States supporting the Beijing documents to create new rights. While those documents express important

---

12. *Available at* http://www.un.int/usa/05_039.htm [last visited March 11, 2011].

political goals, they do not create rights or legally binding obligations on States under international law, including the right to abortion. The United States recognizes the International Conference on Population and Development principle that abortion policies are a matter of national sovereignty. And, we are pleased that so many other governments have indicated their agreement with this position, and we anticipate that we can now focus clearly on addressing the many urgent needs of women around the world.

Questions for Discussion

1. *With the number of reservations that have been filed to the* Beijing Declaration *with regard to reproductive rights, can it be said that a consensus has developed in the international community on this issue?*

2. *Should this be an issue that each state works out for itself, or must there be some level of consensus with regard to the protection of women's reproductive health?*

G. CEDAW and Abortion Rights

1. The Treaty Itself

CEDAW itself does not use the word abortion. The only articles to reference reproductive health are articles 10(h), which refers to "access to specific educational information to help and ensure the health and well-being of families, including information and advice on family planning"; as well as Articles 12 and 16 (set forth at the beginning of this chapter).[13] In a 2010 Congressional Research Service Report on CEDAW,[14] the author of that report noted that in 1994 the Clinton Administration determined that CEDAW was "abortion neutral."[15]

2. Overview of Some of the Concluding Observations Made by the CEDAW Committee to Various Countries in Respect of Their Policies on Abortion

In the United States, opponents of CEDAW are particularly concerned about Article 31(c) of CEDAW's *General Recommendation No. 24* that proposes that "legislation criminalizing abortion could be amended to remove punitive provisions imposed on women who undergo abortion." They point out that in recent Concluding Observations the CEDAW Committee has called on Mexico to review its abortion laws so that "where

---

13. Note that Article 14(2)(b) which pertains to the rights of rural women, essentially repeats the requirements of Article 12(1) by requiring that States parties take appropriate measures to ensure that rural women have access to adequate health care facilities, including information, counseling and services in family planning."

14. *Available at* http://fpc.state.gov/documents/organization/151974.pdf [last visited April 18, 2011].

15. *Id.* at 17.

necessary, women are granted access to rapid and easy abortion."[16] Additionally, in 2007, the Committee urged Poland "to ensure that women seeking legal abortion have access to it, and that their access is not limited by the use of the conscientious objection clause."[17] Much of the CEDAW Committee's concern emanates from the fact that in some countries, (Macedonia and Greece for example), abortion is used as a form of birth control.[18] Moreover, according to the 2009 UNICEF *Report on the State of the World's Children*, about 12% of the maternal deaths that occur in Latin America and the Caribbean between 1997–2002 occurred as a result of complications from illegal abortion.[19]

3. The Helms' Understanding on Abortion

In 2002, when then Senator Joe Biden was the Chair of the Senate Foreign Relations Committee, the Committee held hearings on ratifying CEDAW. The Committee ultimately voted 12:7 in favor of sending CEDAW to the Senate, subject to several Reservations, Understandings, and Declarations. The Helms' Understanding was a proposal made by Senator Jesse Helms that the United States sign CEDAW subject to an understanding that "nothing in this Convention shall be construed to reflect or create any right to abortion and in no case should abortion be promoted as a method of family planning."[20] The Senate has never voted on CEDAW, and some opponents have suggested that an understanding does not go far enough, and that the United States should in fact enter a reservation to Articles 12 and 16.

4. CEDAW Committee *General Recommendation 24* (1999)

Article 12: Women and Health

Introduction

1. The Committee on the Elimination of Discrimination against Women, affirming that access to health care, including reproductive health is a basic right under the Convention on the Elimination of Discrimination against Women, determined at its 20th session, pursuant to article 21, to elaborate a general recommendation on article 12 of the Convention.

Background

2. States parties' compliance with article 12 of the Convention is central to the health and well-being of women. It requires States to eliminate discrimination against women in their access to health care services, throughout the life cycle, particularly in the areas of family planning, pregnancy, confinement and during the post-natal period. The ex-

---

16. CEDAW Committee's Concluding Observations to Mexico; U.N. document, A/53/38/Rev.1, May 14, 1998, *available at* http://www.un.org/womenwatch/daw/cedaw/reports/18report.pdf [last visited June 23, 2011].

17. UN document, CEDAW/C/POL/CO/6, February 2, 2007.

18. UN document, CEDAW/C/GRC/CO/6, February 2, 2007, paragraph 2.

19. *Available at* http://www.unicef.org/sowc09/docs/SOWC09-FullReport-EN.pdf [last visited April 18, 2011].

20. U.S. Congress. Senate. Committee on Foreign Relations, "Convention on the Elimination of All Forms of Discrimination Against Women," Report, September 6, 2002. Washington, DC, Government Printing Office (Senate Exec. Rept. 107-9, 107th Congress, 2d Session), p. 7. The "The Helms Understanding" was originally proposed in 1994. (*See* Senate Exec. Rep. 103-38, 103rd Congress, 2d Session, p. 52).

amination of reports submitted by States parties pursuant to article 18 of the Convention demonstrates that women's health is an issue that is recognized as a central concern in promoting the health and well-being of women. For the benefit of States parties and those who have a particular interest in and concern with the issues surrounding women's health, the present general recommendation seeks to elaborate the Committee's understanding of article 12 and to address measures to eliminate discrimination in order to realize the right of women to the highest attainable standard of health.

3. Recent United Nations world conferences have also considered these objectives. In preparing this general recommendation, the Committee has taken into account relevant programmes of action adopted at United Nations world conferences and, in particular, those of the 1993 World Conference on Human Rights, the 1994 International Conference on Population and Development and the 1995 Fourth World Conference on Women. The Committee has also noted the work of the World Health Organization (WHO), the United Nations Population Fund (UNFPA) and other United Nations bodies. It has also collaborated with a large number of non-governmental organizations with a special expertise in women's health in preparing this general recommendation.

4. The Committee notes the emphasis which other United Nations instruments place on the right to health and to the conditions which enable good health to be achieved. Among such instruments are the Universal Declaration of Human Rights, the International Covenant on Economic, Social and Cultural Rights, the International Covenant on Civil and Political Rights, the Convention on the Rights of the Child and the Convention on the Elimination of All Forms of Racial Discrimination.

5. The Committee refers also to its earlier general recommendations on female circumcision, human immunodeficiency virus/acquired immunodeficiency syndrome (HIV/AIDS), disabled women, violence against women and equality in family relations, all of which refer to issues which are integral to full compliance with article 12 of the Convention.

6. While biological differences between women and men may lead to differences in health status, there are societal factors which are determinative of the health status of women and men and which can vary among women themselves. For that reason, special attention should be given to the health needs and rights of women belonging to vulnerable and disadvantaged groups, such as migrant women, refugee and internally displaced women, the girl child and older women, women in prostitution, indigenous women and women with physical or mental disabilities.

7. The Committee notes that the full realization of women's right to health can be achieved only when States parties fulfil their obligation to respect, protect and promote women's fundamental human right to nutritional well-being throughout their life span by means of a food supply that is safe, nutritious and adapted to local conditions. Towards this end, States parties should take steps to facilitate physical and economic access to productive resources especially for rural women, and to otherwise ensure that the special nutritional needs of all women within their jurisdiction are met.

8. States parties are encouraged to address the issue of women's health throughout the woman's lifespan. For the purposes of this general recommendation, therefore, *women* includes girls and adolescents. This general recommendation will set out the Committee's analysis of the key elements of article 12.

Key elements

9. States parties are in the best position to report on the most critical health issues affecting women in that country. Therefore, in order to enable the Committee to evaluate

whether *measures to eliminate discrimination against women in the field of health care* are *appropriate*, States parties must report on their health legislation, plans and policies for women with reliable data disaggregated by sex on the incidence and severity of diseases and conditions hazardous to women's health and nutrition and on the availability and cost-effectiveness of preventive and curative measures. Reports to the Committee must demonstrate that health legislation, plans and policies are based on scientific and ethical research and assessment of the health status and needs of women in that country and take into account any ethnic, regional or community variations or practices based on religion, tradition or culture.

10. States parties are encouraged to include in their reports information on diseases, health conditions and conditions hazardous to health that affect women or certain groups of women differently from men, as well as information on possible intervention in this regard.

11. Measures to eliminate discrimination against women are considered to be inappropriate if a health care system lacks services to prevent, detect and treat illnesses specific to women. It is discriminatory for a State party to refuse to legally provide for the performance of certain reproductive health services for women. For instance, if health service providers refuse to perform such services based on conscientious objection, measures should be introduced to ensure that women are referred to alternative health providers.

12. States parties should report on their understanding of how policies and measures on *health care* address the health rights of women from the perspective of women's needs and interests and how it addresses distinctive features and factors which differ for women in comparison to men, such as:

(a) Biological factors which differ for women in comparison with men, such as their menstrual cycle and their reproductive function and menopause. Another example is the higher risk of exposure to sexually transmitted diseases which women face;

(b) Socio-economic factors that vary for women in general and some groups of women in particular. For example, unequal power relationships between women and men in the home and workplace may negatively affect women's nutrition and health. They may also be exposed to different forms of violence which can affect their health. Girl children and adolescent girls are often vulnerable to sexual abuse by older men and family members, placing them at risk of physical and psychological harm and unwanted and early pregnancy. Some cultural or traditional practices such as female genital mutilation also carry a high risk of death and disability;

(c) Psychosocial factors which vary between women and men include depression in general and post-partum depression in particular as well as other psychological conditions, such as those that lead to eating disorders such as anorexia and bulimia;

(d) While lack of respect for the confidentiality of patients will affect both men and women, it may deter women from seeking advice and treatment and thereby adversely affect their health and well-being. Women will be less willing, for that reason, to seek medical care for diseases of the genital tract, for contraception or for incomplete abortion and in cases where they have suffered sexual or physical violence.

13. The duty of States parties to *ensure, on a basis of equality between men and women, access to health care* services, information and education implies an obligation to respect,

protect and fulfil women's rights to health care. States parties have the responsibility to ensure that legislation and executive action and policy comply with these three obligations. They must also put in place a system which ensures effective judicial action. Failure to do so will constitute a violation of article 12.

14. The obligation to *respect rights* requires States parties to refrain from obstructing action taken by women in pursuit of their health goals. States parties should report on how public and private health care providers meet their duties to respect women's rights to have access to health care. For example, States parties should not restrict women's access to health services or to the clinics that provide those services on the ground that women do not have the authorization of husbands, partners, parents or health authorities, because they are unmarried, or because they are women. Other barriers to women's access to appropriate health care include laws that criminalize medical procedures only needed by women and that punish women who undergo those procedures.

15. The obligation to *protect rights* relating to women's health requires States parties, their agents and officials to take action to prevent and impose sanctions for violations of rights by private persons and organizations. Since gender-based violence is a critical health issue for women, States parties should ensure:

(a) The enactment and effective enforcement of laws and the formulation of policies, including health care protocols and hospital procedures to address violence against women and abuse of girl children and the provision of appropriate health services;

(b) Gender-sensitive training to enable health care workers to detect and manage the health consequences of gender-based violence;

(c) Fair and protective procedures for hearing complaints and imposing appropriate sanctions on health care professionals guilty of sexual abuse of women patients;

(d) The enactment and effective enforcement of laws that prohibit female genital mutilation and marriage of girl children.

16. States parties should ensure that adequate protection and health services, including trauma treatment and counselling, are provided for women in especially difficult circumstances, such as those trapped in situations of armed conflict and women refugees.

17. The duty to *fulfil rights* places an obligation on States parties to take appropriate legislative, judicial, administrative, budgetary, economic and other measures to the maximum extent of their available resources to ensure that women realize their rights to health care. Studies such as those which emphasize the high maternal mortality and morbidity rates worldwide and the large numbers of couples who would like to limit their family size but lack access to or do not use any form of contraception provide an important indication for States parties of possible breaches of their duties to ensure women's access to health care. The Committee asks States parties to report on what they have done to address the magnitude of women's ill-health, in particular when it arises from preventable conditions, such as tuberculosis and HIV/AIDS. The Committee is concerned at the growing evidence that States are relinquishing these obligations as they transfer State health functions to private agencies. States parties cannot absolve themselves of responsibility in these areas by delegating or transferring these powers to private sector agencies. States parties should therefore report on what they have done to organize governmental processes and all structures through which public power is exercised to promote and protect women's health. They should include information on positive measures taken to curb violations of women's rights by third parties, to protect their health and the measures they have taken to ensure the provision of such services.

18. The issues of HIV/AIDS and other sexually transmitted disease are central to the rights of women and adolescent girls to sexual health. Adolescent girls and women in many countries lack adequate access to information and services necessary to ensure sexual health. As a consequence of unequal power relations based on gender, women and adolescent girls are often unable to refuse sex or insist on safe and responsible sex practices. Harmful traditional practices, such as female genital mutilation, polygamy, as well as marital rape, may also expose girls and women to the risk of contracting HIV/AIDS and other sexually transmitted diseases. Women in prostitution are also particularly vulnerable to these diseases. States parties should ensure, without prejudice and discrimination, the right to sexual health information, education and services for all women and girls, including those who have been trafficked, including those who have been trafficked, even if they are not legally resident in the country. In particular, States parties should ensure the rights of female and male adolescents to sexual and reproductive health education by properly trained personnel in specially designed programmes that respect their rights to privacy and confidentiality.

19. In their reports States parties should identify the test by which they assess whether women have access to health care *on a basis of equality of men and women* in order to demonstrate compliance with article 12. In applying these tests, States parties should bear in mind the provisions of article 1 of the Convention. Reports should therefore include comments on the impact that health policies, procedures, laws and protocols have on women when compared with men.

20. Women have the right to be fully informed, by properly trained personnel, of their options in agreeing to treatment or research, including likely benefits and potential adverse effects of proposed procedures and available alternatives.

21. States parties should report on measures taken to eliminate barriers that women face in gaining *access to health care services* and what measures they have taken to ensure women timely and affordable access to such services. Barriers include requirements or conditions that prejudice women's access such as high fees for health care services, the requirement for preliminary authorization by spouse, parent or hospital authorities, distance from health facilities and absence of convenient and affordable public transport.

22. States parties should also report on measures taken to ensure access to quality health care services, for example, by making them acceptable to women. Acceptable services are those which are delivered in a way that ensures that a woman gives her fully informed consent, respects her dignity, guarantees her confidentiality and is sensitive to her needs and perspectives. States parties should not permit forms of coercion, such as non-consensual sterilization, mandatory testing for sexually transmitted diseases or mandatory pregnancy testing as a condition of employment that violate women's rights to informed consent and dignity.

23. In their reports, States parties should state what measures they have taken to ensure timely access to the range of services which are *related to family planning*, in particular, and to sexual and reproductive health in general. Particular attention should be paid to the health education of adolescents, including information and counselling on all methods of family planning ...

Article 12 (2)

26. Reports should also include what measures States parties have taken to ensure women appropriate services *in connection with pregnancy, confinement and the post-natal period*. Information on the rates at which these measures have reduced maternal mortality and morbidity in their countries, in general, and in vulnerable groups, regions and communities, in particular, should also be included.

27. States parties should include in their reports how they supply *free services where necessary* to ensure safe pregnancies, childbirth and post-partum periods for women. Many women are at risk of death or disability from pregnancy-related causes because they lack the funds to obtain or access the necessary services, which include ante-natal, maternity and post-natal services. The Committee notes that it is the duty of States parties to ensure women's right to safe motherhood and emergency obstetric services and they should allocate to these services the maximum extent of available resources.

Other relevant articles in the Convention

28. When reporting on measures taken to comply with article 12, States parties are urged to recognize its interconnection with other articles in the Convention that have a bearing on women's health. Those articles include article 5 (b), which requires States parties to ensure that family education includes a proper understanding of maternity as a social function; article 10, which requires States parties to ensure equal access to education, thus enabling women to access health care more readily and reducing female students' drop-out rates, which are often due to premature pregnancy; article 10(h) which provides that States parties provide to women and girls specific educational information to help ensure the well-being of families, including information and advice on family planning; article 11, which is concerned, in part, with the protection of women's health and safety in working conditions, including the safeguarding of the reproductive function, special protection from harmful types of work during pregnancy and with the provision of paid maternity leave; article 14 (2) (b), which requires States parties to ensure access for rural women to adequate health care facilities, including information, counselling and services in family planning, and (h), which obliges States parties to take all appropriate measures to ensure adequate living conditions, particularly housing, sanitation, electricity and water supply, transport and communications, all of which are critical for the prevention of disease and the promotion of good health care; and article 16 (1) (e), which requires States parties to ensure that women have the same rights as men to decide freely and responsibly on the number and spacing of their children and to have access to information, education and means to enable them to exercise these rights. Article 16 (2) also proscribes the betrothal and marriage of children, an important factor in preventing the physical and emotional harm which arise from early childbirth ...

Recommendations for government action

29. States parties should implement a comprehensive national strategy to promote women's health throughout their lifespan. This will include interventions aimed at both the prevention and treatment of diseases and conditions affecting women, as well as responding to violence against women, and will ensure universal access for all women to a full range of high-quality and affordable health care, including sexual and reproductive health services.

30. States parties should allocate adequate budgetary, human and administrative resources to ensure that women's health receives a share of the overall health budget comparable with that for men's health, taking into account their different health needs.

31. States parties should also, in particular:

(a) Place a gender perspective at the centre of all policies and programmes affecting women's s health and should involve women in the planning, implementation and monitoring of such policies and programmes and in the provision of health services to women;

(b) Ensure the removal of all barriers to women's access to health services, education and information, including in the area of sexual and reproductive health, and, in particular, allocate resources for programmes directed at adolescents for the prevention and treatment of sexually transmitted diseases, including HIV/AIDS;

(c) Prioritize the prevention of unwanted pregnancy through family planning and sex education and reduce maternal mortality rates through safe motherhood services and prenatal assistance. When possible, legislation criminalizing abortion could be amended to remove punitive provisions imposed on women who undergo abortion;

(d) Monitor the provision of health services to women by public, non-governmental and private organizations, to ensure equal access and quality of care;

(e) Require all health services to be consistent with the human rights of women, including the rights to autonomy, privacy, confidentiality, informed consent and choice;

(f) Ensure that the training curricula of health workers includes comprehensive, mandatory, gender-sensitive courses on women's health and human rights, in particular gender-based violence.

Questions for Discussion

1. *One of the crucial issues for women is the rate at which women are being infected with HIV/AIDs, and the rate at which this disease is being transmitted to their children. Are states doing enough to help women with this crisis?*

2. *As evidenced from the Committee's observations above, women's health issues encompass a broad range of concerns, including access to clean water. Are these concerns being overshadowed in the debate about reproductive rights?*

III. CEDAW Commission Cases on Reproductive Rights

A. *A.S. v. Hungary*[21]

The first case to be heard under the Optional Protocol was *A.S. v. Hungary.* This case appears to illustrate that reproductive rights encompass more than just abortion-related rights, as the CEDAW Committee ordered Hungary to compensate a Roma woman who had consented to be sterilized without fully understanding the implications of the surgery.

2.1 The author is the mother of three children. On 30 May 2000, she was examined by a doctor and found to be pregnant, the delivery date estimated to be 20 December

---

21. Committee on the Elimination of Discrimination against Women Thirty-sixth session 7–25 August 2006; Views-Communication No. 4 of 2004; A.S. v. Hungary; *available at* http://www.un.org/womenwatch/daw/cedaw/protocol/decisions-views/Decision%204-2004%20-%20English.pdf [last visited April 18, 2011].

2000, during that time, she followed antenatal treatment and attended all the scheduled appointments with the district nurse and gynaecologist. On 20 December 2000, the author reported to the maternity ward of Fehérgyarmat Hospital. She was examined and found to be 36 to 37 weeks pregnant and was asked to return when she went into labour.

2.2 On 2 January 2001, the author went into labour pain and her amniotic fluid broke. This was accompanied by heavy bleeding. She was taken to Fehérgyarmat Hospital, one hour's drive by ambulance. While examining the author, the attending physician found that the foetus (the term "embryo" is used) had died in her womb and informed her that a caesarean section needed to be performed immediately in order to remove the dead foetus. While on the operating table, the author was asked to sign a form consenting to the caesarean section. She signed this as well as a barely legible note that had been hand-written by the doctor and added to the bottom of the form, which read:

> Having knowledge of the death of the embryo inside my womb I firmly request my sterilization [a Latin term unknown to the author was used]. I do not intend to give birth again; neither do I wish to become pregnant.

The attending physician and the midwife signed the same form. The author also signed statements of consent for a blood transfusion and for anaesthesia.

2.3 Hospital records show that within 17 minutes of the ambulance arriving at the hospital, the caesarean section was performed, the dead foetus and placenta were removed and the author's fallopian tubes were tied. Before leaving the hospital the author asked the doctor for information on her state of health and when she could try to have another baby. It was only then that she learned the meaning of the word "sterilization". The medical records also revealed the poor health condition of the author when she arrived at the hospital. She felt dizzy upon arrival, was bleeding more heavily than average and was in a state of shock.

2.4 The author states that the sterilization has had a profound impact on her life for which she and her partner have been treated medically for depression. She would never have agreed to the sterilization as she has strict Catholic religious beliefs that prohibit contraception of any kind, including sterilization. Furthermore, she and her partner live in accordance with traditional Roma customs—where having children is said to be a central element of the value system of Roma families.

2.5 On 15 October 2001, a lawyer with the Legal Defence Bureau for National and Ethnic Minorities, filed a civil claim on behalf of the author against Fehérgyarmat Hospital ...

2.6 On 22 November 2002, the Fehérgyarmat Town Court rejected the author's claim, ... The Court reasoned that the medical conditions for sterilization prevailed in the author's case and that she had been informed about her sterilization and given all relevant information in a way in which she could understand it. The Court also found that the author had given her consent accordingly. The Court further viewed as a "partial extenuating circumstance towards the defendant's negligence the fact that, with the author's consent, the doctors performed the sterilization with special dispatch simultaneously with the Caesarean section."

2.7 On 5 December 2002, the lawyer filed an appeal on behalf of the author before the Zabolcs-Szatmár-Bereg County Court....

2.8 On 12 May 2003, the author's appeal was rejected.... on the ground that the author had failed to prove a lasting handicap and its causal relationship with the conduct of the hospital. The appellate court reasoned that the performed sterilization was not a lasting and irreversible operation inasmuch as the tying of fallopian tubes can be terminated by plastic surgery ... and the likelihood of her becoming pregnant by artificial insemination could not be excluded....

The complaint

3.1 The author claims that Hungary has violated articles 10 (h), 12 and 16, Paragraph 1 (e) of the Convention....

The Committee has considered the present communication in light of all the information made available to it by the author and by the State party, as provided in article 7, Paragraph 1, of the Optional Protocol. [...]

11.2 *According to Article 10 (h) of the Convention:*

States Parties shall take all appropriate measures to eliminate discrimination against women in order to ensure to them equal rights with men in the field of education and in particular to ensure, on a basis of equality of men and women: [...]

(h) Access to specific educational information to help to ensure the health and well being of families, including information and advice on family planning.

With respect to the claim that the State party violated article 10 (h) of the Convention by failing to provide information and advice on family planning, the Committee recalls its general recommendation No. 21 on equality in marriage and family relations, which recognizes in the context of "coercive practices which have serious consequences for women, such as forced ... sterilization" that informed decision-making about safe and reliable contraceptive measures depends upon a woman having "information about contraceptive measures and their use, and guaranteed access to sex education and family planning services". The Committee notes the State party's arguments that the author was given correct and appropriate information at the time of the operation, during prenatal care and during her three previous pregnancies as well as its argument that, according to the decision of the lower court, the author had been in a condition in which she was able to understand the information provided. On the other hand, the Committee notes the author's reference to the judgement of the appellate court, which found that the author had not been provided with detailed information about the sterilization, including the risks and the consequences of the surgery, alternative procedures or contraceptive methods. The Committee considers that the author has a right protected by article 10 (h) of the Convention to specific information on sterilization and alternative procedures for family planning in order to guard against such an intervention being carried out without her having made a fully informed choice. Furthermore, the Committee notes the description given of the author's state of health on arrival at the hospital and observes that any counselling that she received must have been given under stressful and most inappropriate conditions. Considering all these factors, the Committee finds a failure of the State party, through the hospital personnel, to provide appropriate information and advice on family planning, which constitutes a violation of the author's right under article 10 (h) of the Convention.

11.3 *Article 12 of the Convention reads:*

1. States Parties shall take all appropriate measures to eliminate discrimination against women in the field of health care in order to ensure, on a basis of equality of men and women, access to healthcare services, including those related to family planning.

2. Notwithstanding the provisions of Paragraph 1 of this article, States Parties shall ensure to women appropriate services in connexion with pregnancy, confinement

*and the post-natal period, granting free services where necessary, as well as adequate
nutrition during pregnancy and lactation.*

With regard to the question of whether the State party violated the author's rights
under article 12 of the Convention by performing the sterilization surgery without obtaining
her informed consent, the Committee takes note of the author's description of the 17
minute timespan from her admission to the hospital up to the completion of two medical
procedures. Medical records revealed that the author was in a very poor state of health
upon arrival at the hospital; she was feeling dizzy, was bleeding more heavily than average
and was in a state of shock. During those 17 minutes, she was prepared for surgery, signed
the statements of consent for the caesarean section, the sterilization, a blood transfusion
and anaesthesia and underwent two medical procedures, namely, the caesarean section
to remove the remains of the dead foetus and the sterilization. The Committee further
takes note of the author's claim that she did not understand the Latin term for sterilization
that was used on the barely legible consent note that had been handwritten by the doctor
attending to her, which she signed.... The Committee finds that it is not plausible that
during that period of time hospital personnel provided the author with thorough enough
counseling and information about sterilization, as well as alternatives, risks and benefits,
to ensure that the author could make a well-considered and voluntary decision to be
sterilized. The Committee also takes note of the unchallenged fact that the author enquired
of the doctor when it would be safe to conceive again, clearly indicating that she was
unaware of the consequences of sterilization. According to article 12 of the Convention,
States parties shall "ensure to women appropriate services in connexion with pregnancy,
confinement, and the post-natal period". The Committee explained in its general recommendation No. 24 on women and health that "[A]cceptable services are those that are
delivered in a way that ensures that a woman gives her fully informed consent, respects
her dignity ..." The Committee further stated that "States parties should not permit forms
of coercion, such as non-consensual sterilization ... that violate women's rights to informed
consent and dignity". The Committee considers in the present case that the State party
has not ensured that the author gave her fully informed consent to be sterilized and that
consequently the rights of the author under article 12 were violated.

Article 16, Paragraph 1 (e) of the Convention states:

*States Parties shall take all appropriate measures to eliminate discrimination against
women in all matters relating to marriage and family relations and in particular
shall ensure, on a basis of equality of men and women: [...]*

*(e) The same rights to decide freely and responsibly on the number and spacing of
their children and to have access to the information, education and means to enable
them to exercise these rights;*

As to whether the State party violated the rights of the author under article 16, Paragraph
1 (e) of the Convention, the Committee recalls its general recommendation No. 19 on
violence against women in which it states that "[C]ompulsory sterilization ... adversely
affects women's physical and mental health, and infringes the right of women to decide
on the number and spacing of their children". The sterilization surgery was performed
on the author without her full and informed consent and must be considered to have
permanently deprived her of her natural reproductive capacity. Accordingly, the Committee
finds the author's rights under article 16, Paragraph 1 (e) to have been violated.

11.5 Acting under article 7, Paragraph 3 of the Optional Protocol to the Convention
on the Elimination of All Forms of Discrimination against Women, the Committee on
the Elimination of Discrimination against Women is of the view that the facts before it

reveal a violation of articles 10 (h), 12 and 16, Paragraph 1 (e) of the Convention and makes the following recommendations to the State party:

I. Concerning the author of the communication: provide appropriate compensation to Ms. A. S. commensurate with the gravity of the violations of her rights.

II. General:

• Take further measures to ensure that the relevant provisions of the Convention and the pertinent Paragraphs of the Committee's general recommendations Nos. 19, 21 and 24 in relation to women's reproductive health and rights are known and adhered to by all relevant personnel in public and private health centres, including hospitals and clinics.

• Review domestic legislation on the principle of informed consent in cases of sterilization and ensure its conformity with international human rights and medical standards, including the Convention of the Council of Europe on Human Rights and Biomedicine ("the Oviedo Convention") and World Health Organization guidelines. In that connection, consider amending the provision in the Public Health Act whereby a physician is allowed "to deliver the sterilization without the information procedure generally specified when it seems to be appropriate in given circumstances".

• Monitor public and private health centres, including hospitals and clinics, which perform sterilization procedures so as to ensure that fully informed consent is being given by the patient before any sterilization procedure is carried out, with appropriate sanctions in place in the event of a breach.

The State party is also requested to publish the Committee's views and recommendations and to have them translated into the Hungarian language and widely distributed in order to reach all relevant sectors of society.

Questions for Discussion

1. *Discrimination against the Roma people is rampant in Europe, and it is likely that the decision made to sterilize Ms. A.S. was made because she is Roma. Yet the Committee focused their decision narrowly on the violation of Ms. A.S.'s reproductive rights. Was this a missed opportunity to educate people about the "intersectionality" of rights—that a woman may suffer discrimination on multiple grounds through the same act?*

2. *Do you think that this decision complicates the reproductive rights discussion, particularly for those states opposed to abortion? If one accepts that a woman has autonomy to make an informed decision about reproduction in respect of sterilization, what implications does that have for reproductive rights in general?*

B. The Colombian Constitutional Court Abortion Case — *In Re Abortion Law Challenge in Colombia*[22]

The decision of the Colombian Constitutional Court which cited to CEDAW in finding that Articles 122 and 123 of the Colombian Penal Code were unconstitutional, bolsters the argument that CEDAW does provide support for abortion rights. Note that the Court referred to a "margin of discretion" afforded the legislature, in regulating access to abortion.

Honorable Justice JAIME ARAÚJO RENTERÍA; Honorable Justice CLARA INÉS VARGAS HERNÁNDEZ

[...]Colombian citizens Mónica del Pilar Roa López, Pablo Jaramillo Valencia, Marcela Abadía Cubillos, Juana Dávila Sáenz and Laura Porras Santillana ("the Plaintiffs") request in separate complaints that this Court declare unconstitutional Paragraph 7 of article 32, articles 122 and 124, as well as the expression "or on a woman of less than 14 years of age" contained in article 123 of Law 599, 2000 ... The Plaintiffs assert that the articles and Paragraphs in question violate the following constitutional rights: the right to dignity (Constitutional Preamble and article 1 of the Constitution); the right to life (article 11 of the Constitution); the right to bodily integrity (article 12 of the Constitution); the right to equality and the general right to liberty (article 13 of the Constitution); the right to the free development of the individual (article 16 of the Constitution); the right to reproductive autonomy (article 42 of the Constitution); the right to health (article 49 of the Constitution) and obligations under international human rights law (article 93 of the Constitution)....

In general, the arguments of the Plaintiffs revolve around the fact that the articles of the Penal Code that criminalize abortion (article 122) and abortion without consent (article 123), together with the mitigating circumstances therein (article 124), are unconstitutional because they disproportionately and unreasonably limit the rights and liberties of the pregnant woman, including when she is a minor of less than 14 years of age.

The Plaintiffs also assert that the articles in question violate various international human rights law treaties, which are part of the Constitutional bundle.... In particular, the challenge to Paragraph 7 of article 32 of the Penal Code revolves around the fact that the state of necessity prescribed therein breaches a woman's fundamental right to life and physical integrity because she is forced to resort to a clandestine abortion "which is humiliating and potentially dangerous to her integrity."

[...]The Preamble of the Constitution establishes "life" as one of the values that the constitutional legal system aims to protect ... Thus, it can be said that by virtue of the mentions of "life" in various constitutional articles, the Constitution of 1991 is inclined to a general protection of life. From this point of view, all of the state's actions must focus on protecting life ... Although it is Congress' role to determine and adopt ideal measures for complying with the duty to protect life, this does not mean that all norms aimed at

---

22. DECISION C-355/06.

that goal are justified, for, although "life" has constitutional relevance, it does not have an absolute value nor is it an absolute right; it must be weighed against other values and constitutional rights.... Even though the legal system protects the fetus, it does not grant it the same level or degree of protection it grants a human person....

These considerations must be taken into account by the legislature if it finds it appropriate to enact public policies regarding abortion, including imposing criminal penalties where the Constitution permits, while respecting the rights of women.

6. Life and international treaties on human rights; part of the Constitutional Bundle

[...] International treaties on human rights must be interpreted in harmony with one another, utilizing the decisions on said treaties by the international bodies charged with enforcing the rights and guarantees contained within them as a starting point.

In conclusion, it cannot be said that an absolute or unconditional duty to protect the life of the unborn fetus derives from the various international human rights treaties that form part of the Constitutional Bundle. A literal interpretation, just as a context-driven interpretation, requires weighing the unborn fetus' right to life against other rights, principles and values recognized in the 1991 Constitution and in other international human rights law instruments, an approach that has been followed by the Inter-American Court of Human Rights. This approach requires identifying and weighing the rights at issue in conjunction with the duty to protect life, while taking into account the constitutional importance of the bearer of the rights; in these cases, the pregnant woman.

7. Fundamental rights of women under the Colombian National Constitution and international law

[...] The 1991 Constitution expressly sets out the goal of recognizing and enhancing the rights of women, as well as of reinforcing these rights by protecting them in an effective and decisive manner. Thus, women are now entitled to special constitutional protection and their rights must be recognized and protected by government authorities, including those within the legal system, without exception ...

It is worth noting that there are situations that affect women differently and to a greater extent, like those that affect their lives and particularly those concerning their bodies, their sexuality and their reproduction.

Women's rights have achieved an important place in United Nations world conferences and the treaties that come out of these conferences. [T]he World Conference on Human Rights in Vienna in 1993, ... declared that "The human rights of women and of the girl-child are an inalienable, integral and indivisible part of universal human rights." The full and equal participation of women in political, civil, economic, social and cultural life and the eradication of all forms of discrimination on grounds of sex were also declared to be priority objectives for the international community.

The Programme of Action of the 1994 United Nations International Conference on Population and Development in Cairo ... recognized that "reproductive rights embrace certain human rights that are already recognized in national laws, international human rights documents and other consensus documents. These rights rest on the recognition of the basic right of all couples and individuals to decide freely and responsibly the number, spacing and timing of their children and to have the information and means to do so." This Programme also established that "Reproductive health therefore implies that people are able to have a satisfying and safe sex life and that they have the capability to reproduce and the freedom to decide if, when and how often to do so." It was also established that men, women and adolescents have the right "to be informed and to have access to safe, effective, affordable and acceptable methods of family planning of their choice," as well as "the right of access to appropriate health-care services that will enable women to go safely through pregnancy and childbirth."

The Fourth World Conference on Women (*Beijing Platform*) confirms the reproductive rights established in the Cairo's *Program of Action*. In effect, various international treaties form the basis for the recognition and protection of women's reproductive rights, which derive from the protection of other fundamental rights such as the right to life, health, equality, the right to be free from discrimination, the right to liberty, bodily integrity and the right to be free from violence—all of which constitute the essential core of reproductive rights. Other fundamental rights, such as the right to work and the right to education—which are also affected when women's reproductive rights are violated— serve as parameters to protect and guarantee sexual and reproductive rights.

It must be noted that ... special protection for the rights of Latin American women are found in the Convention on the Elimination of All Forms of Discrimination against Women (CEDAW), which entered into force in Colombia on February 19, 1982, ... and the Inter-American Convention on the Prevention, Punishment and Eradication of Violence Against Women (Convention of Belém do Pará).... These documents, ... are fundamental to the protection and guarantee of the rights of women as they form the point of reference for establishing concepts which contribute to their interpretation both in the national and international spheres. The right to health, which includes the right to reproductive health and family planning, has been interpreted by international bodies on the basis of international treaties, including CEDAW, to include the duty of all states to offer a wide range of high quality and accessible health services, which must include sexual and reproductive health services. Furthermore, these international bodies also recommend that a gender perspective be included in the design of public health policies and programs. These same international bodies have also expressed concern for the health of women living in poverty, women living in rural areas, indigenous women and adolescents, as well as with obstacles to access to contraceptive methods. In the area of health, all states should also eliminate all obstacles that impede women's access to services, education and information on sexual and reproductive health. CEDAW has emphasized that laws criminalizing medical interventions that specially affect women constitute a barrier to women's access to needed medical care, compromising women's right to gender equality in the area of health, and amounting to a violation of states' international obligations to respect those internationally recognized rights. The international community has also recognized that violence against women infringes on human rights and fundamental freedoms, and has established, specifically, the right of women to live free from violence based on sex or gender.

[....] CEDAW declared that "Gender-based violence is a form of discrimination that seriously inhibits women's ability to enjoy rights and freedoms on a basis of equality with men." The Convention of Belém do Pará, ... is one of the most important instruments for protecting women's rights against the various forms of violence faced by women in diverse spheres of their lives. The Convention ... defines violence against women both in the public and private spheres as a violation of women's human rights and fundamental freedoms. Second, the Convention establishes the state's responsibility for perpetrating or tolerating any such violence, regardless of where it occurs. It is also important to highlight that the Rome Statute establishes, among other things, that violence and other reproductive and sexual crimes are at the same level as the other most atrocious international crimes, and may amount to torture and genocide. The Rome Statute also recognizes for the first time that violations of women's right to reproductive autonomy, both by means of forced pregnancy and forced sterilization, are amongst the most serious crimes under international human rights law. One of the essential components of reproductive and sexual rights is women's right to choose freely the number and spacing of children. This is based on the principles of human dignity and the right to autonomy and intimacy, as has been recognized by various international conventions. CEDAW has established that a woman's right to reproductive autonomy is infringed upon by obstacles to her access to the means of controlling her fertility. Thus, non-consensual sterilization and imposed birth control methods constitute serious violations of this right.

Similarly, various committees have stated that the right to freely decide the number of children is directly linked to women's right to life when there are highly restrictive or prohibitive abortion laws that result in high maternal mortality rates. Other sexual and reproductive rights are based on the right of freedom to marry and start a family. The right to privacy is also connected to reproductive rights and is infringed upon when the state or private citizens interfere with a woman's right to make decisions about her body and her reproductive capacity. The right to privacy includes the right of a patient to have her confidentiality respected by her doctor. Therefore, the right to intimacy is infringed upon when the doctor is legally obliged to report a woman who has undergone an abortion.

With regard to the right to equality and to be free from discrimination, ... (CEDAW) establishes women's right to enjoy human rights in conditions of equality with men. It also prescribes the elimination of barriers impeding women's effective enjoyment of their internationally recognized rights, as well as of those found in national legislation....

Finally, the right to education is closely linked to reproductive rights at various levels. Having access to basic education empowers women within their families and their communities, ...

To conclude, women's sexual and reproductive rights have finally been recognized as human rights, and, as such, they have become part of constitutional rights, which are the fundamental basis of all democratic states. Sexual and reproductive rights also emerge from the recognition that equality in general, gender equality in particular, and the emancipation of women and girls are essential to society. Protecting sexual and reproductive rights is a direct path to promoting the dignity of all human beings and a step forward in humanity's advancement towards social justice.

Nonetheless, neither a mandate to decriminalize abortion nor a prohibition on the legislature's adoption of criminal abortion laws derives from international treaties or constitutional articles on the topic. Congress has a wide range of discretion to adopt public policies on abortion. However, this discretion is not unlimited, ... the legislature must respect two constitutional limits. First, the legislature cannot disproportionately encroach upon constitutional rights. Second, the legislature must not leave certain constitutional values unprotected. At the same time, the legislature must recognize the principle that criminal law, due to its potential to restrict liberties, must always be a measure of last resort.

8. Limits on legislative discretion over criminal matters

In summary, it is the legislature that must pass criminal laws for the protection of constitutional values such as life. However, fundamental rights and other constitutional principles establish limits on the legislature's discretion and it is the Constitutional Court that as guardian of the integrity and supremacy of the Constitution, must oversee the limits imposed by the Constitution on the legislature ...

8.1. The fundamental right to dignity as a limit on the legislature's discretion over criminal matters. As with "life," the concept of "dignity" has various functions in Colombian constitutional law, ... The sphere of protection for women's human dignity includes decisions related to their choice of life plan, among them decisions regarding reproductive autonomy.... According to constitutional jurisprudence, the concept of dignity, understood as protecting individual autonomy and the right to choose one's life plan, places a limit on the legislature's discretion over criminal matters.... In this way, the need to respect human dignity places a limit on the legislature's discretion with regard to criminal matters, even in circumstances where the legislature aims to protect other relevant constitutional values such as life....

8.2. The right to the free development of the individual as a limit on the legislature's discretion over criminal matters..., the state is "an instrument at the service of the citizens, as opposed to the citizen as a servant of the state." In this new light, individual autonomy—understood as the vital sphere of matters solely within the decisional ambit of the individual—becomes a constitutional principle, binding on public authorities, who are therefore prevented from infringing on this private sphere and making decisions on behalf of citizens because such infringement would amount to "a brutal usurpation of a citizen's ethical condition, reducing him/her to the condition of an object, converting him/her into a means to ends imposed from outside...."

The right to be a mother, or in other words, the right to opt for motherhood as a "life choice," is a decision of the utmost private nature for each woman. Therefore, the Constitution does not permit the state, the family, the employer or educational institutions to introduce any regulation or policy that infringes upon the right of a woman to choose to be a mother or that interferes with the rightful exercise of motherhood.... [T]he free development of the individual provides a clear limit on the legislature's discretion, not only in criminal matters but also in its general discretion regarding penalties and prohibitions. The Court has held that regardless of the constitutional values it is aiming to protect, the legislature cannot establish "perfectionist measures" that restrict the free development of the individual in a disproportionate manner....

8.3. Health, life and bodily integrity as limits on the discretion of the legislature over criminal matters.... [T]he right to health, even though it is not expressly found in the Constitution as a fundamental right, has a fundamental character when it is in close relation to the right to life.... The right to health is an integral right that includes mental and physical wellbeing. Furthermore, for women, it includes reproductive health, which is closely linked to both induced and spontaneous abortion. Induced abortions and miscarriages may in numerous circumstances put a woman's health or life at risk, or require medical intervention to preserve her reproductive capacity ... The constitutional right to health has a service provision dimension as well as an element of protection against government and third party intrusion or interference with this right. This latter dimension of protection from violation, or obligation on the state to not interfere, is closely related to the duty of every individual to be responsible for his or her own health. From this perspective, certain measures adopted by the legislature that disproportionately restrict the right to health are unconstitutional. This is so even when those measures are adopted in order to protect the constitutional rights of others.

Prima facie, it is not proportionate or reasonable for the Colombian state to obligate a person to sacrifice her or his health in the interest of protecting third parties, even when those interests are also constitutionally relevant.... The right to autonomy regarding one's own health encompasses other distinct rights, which are relevant here. These include the right to plan a family, the right to make free and non-coerced decisions regarding reproduction, and the right to be free from all forms of violence and coercion which affect sexual and reproductive health.... It implies the right to make decisions regarding reproduction without discrimination, coercion or violence, and therefore it is closely connected with the right to personal integrity. This right also requires the state to protect individuals, particularly women, from undue family, social and cultural pressures that diminish their ability to decide regarding sexual or reproductive matters. Such pressures include being forced into marriage at an early age without the full consent of both parties or the practice of female circumcision. The right also implies a prohibition of state-condoned practices such as forced sterilization, violence and sexual abuse....

8.4. The Constitutional Bundle as a limit on the legislature's discretion over criminal matters ... The legislature has a broad margin of discretion when it comes to defining social conduct that is so harmful to a greater protected good that it must become crime.... However, this discretion is not unlimited ... the legislature must take into account the entirety of the legal system, and in particular, it must respect the rights and dignity of others, ... [C]onstitutional rights and obligations must be interpreted in harmony with international human rights treaties to which Colombia is a signatory.... Accordingly, various articles of the International Covenant on Civil and Political Rights, the Convention on the Elimination of All Forms of Discrimination against Women, and the International Covenant on Economic, Social and Cultural Rights, while neither dispositive nor preemptive of the legislature's discretion, are relevant in the analysis of the constitutionality of the total ban on abortion ...

9. The Issue of Abortion in Comparative Law

[The court examined decisions from the constitutional courts of the United States, Germany and Spain] [...] When constitutional tribunals have examined the constitutionality of laws governing the termination of pregnancy, they have coincided in the need to balance the various interests at stake; on one hand, the life of the fetus, which is constitutionally relevant and therefore should be protected, and on the other hand, the rights of the pregnant woman. Even though the various tribunals have differed on which of those interests must prevail in particular cases, they have shared common ground in affirming that a total prohibition on abortion is unconstitutional because under certain circumstances it imposes an intolerable burden on the pregnant woman which infringes upon her constitutional rights ...

10.1. The unconstitutionality of a total prohibition of abortion

[...]In the case at hand, ... the life of the fetus is entitled to protection under constitutional law and therefore the decisions of the pregnant woman regarding the termination of her pregnancy go beyond the sphere of her private autonomy and implicate the interests of both the state and the legislature.... It is not the role of the constitutional judge to determine the character or the nature of the measures that the legislature should adopt in order to protect a particular state interest. [...]

If the legislature decides to serve legitimate ends by adopting criminal measures, its margin of discretion is limited due to the severity of such measures and their potential to seriously impair human dignity and individual liberties. In the case of abortion, the decision is extremely complex because the crime impacts various rights, principles and values, all of which are constitutionally relevant ...

Even though the protection of the fetus through criminal law is not in itself disproportionate and penalizing abortion may be constitutional, the criminalization of abortion in all circumstances entails the complete pre-eminence of the life of the fetus and the absolute sacrifice of the pregnant woman's fundamental rights. This result is, without a doubt, unconstitutional.

C. *A, B, & C v. Ireland*[23] (European Court of Human Rights)

The case originated in an application ... against Ireland lodged with the Court under Article 34 of the Convention for the Protection of Human Rights and Fundamental Freedoms ("the Convention") by two Irish nationals, Ms. A and Ms. B, and by a Lithuanian national, Ms. C, ("the applicants"), on 15 July 2005. The first two applicants principally complained under Article 8 about, *inter alia*, the prohibition of abortion for health and well-being reasons in Ireland and the third applicant's main complaint concerned the same Article and the alleged failure to implement the constitutional right to an abortion in Ireland in the case of a risk to the life of the woman.... On 7 July 2009 the Chamber relinquished jurisdiction in favour of the Grand Chamber ...

A. The first applicant (A)

On 28 February 2005 the first applicant travelled to England for an abortion as she believed that she was not entitled to an abortion in Ireland. She was 9½ weeks pregnant.

She had become pregnant unintentionally,.... At the time she was unmarried, unemployed and living in poverty. She had four young children. The youngest was disabled and all children were in foster care as a result of problems she had experienced as an alcoholic. She had a history of depression during her first four pregnancies, and was battling depression at the time of her fifth pregnancy....

B. The second applicant (B)

On 17 January 2005 the second applicant travelled to England for an abortion believing that she was not entitled to an abortion in Ireland. She was 7 weeks pregnant.

The second applicant became pregnant unintentionally. She had taken the "morning-after pill" and was advised by two different doctors that there was a substantial risk of an ectopic pregnancy ...

C. The third applicant (C)

On 3 March 2005 the third applicant had an abortion in England believing that she could not establish her right to an abortion in Ireland. She was in her first trimester of pregnancy at the time.

Prior to that, she had been treated for 3 years with chemotherapy for a rare form of cancer.... The cancer went into remission and the applicant unintentionally became pregnant. She was unaware of this fact when she underwent a series of tests for cancer, contraindicated during pregnancy. When she discovered she was pregnant, the first applicant consulted her General Practitioner ("GP") as well as several medical consultants. She alleged that, as a result of the chilling effect of the Irish legal framework, she received insufficient information as to the impact of the pregnancy on her health and life and of her prior tests for cancer on the foetus ...

Abortion is also prohibited under the criminal law by section 58 (as amended) of the Offences Against the Person Act 1861 ("the 1861 Act"): ... Section 10 of the Health (Family

---

23. *Available at* http://cmiskp.echr.coe.int/tkp197/view.asp?action=html&documentId=878721 &portal=hbkm&source=externalbydocnumber&table=F69A27FD8FB86142BF01C1166DEA398649 [last visited April 19, 2011].

Planning) Act 1979 re-affirms the statutory prohibition of abortion ... Article 50.1 of the Irish Constitution makes provision for the continuation of laws, such as the 1861 Act, which were in force on the adoption of the Constitution in 1937.

[The Court proceeded to examine the history of anti abortion law in Ireland noting that in 1992 two referenda were passed.]

The second proposal was accepted and became the Thirteenth Amendment to the Constitution ... It was designed to ensure that a woman could not be prevented from leaving the jurisdiction for an abortion abroad and it reads as follows:

> This subsection shall not limit freedom to travel between the State and another state.

The third proposal was also accepted and became the Fourteenth Amendment (also added to Article 40.3.3). It allows for the provision in Ireland of information on abortion services abroad and provides as follows:

> This subsection shall not limit freedom to obtain or make available, in the State, subject to such conditions as may be laid down by law, information relating to services lawfully available in another State ...

Efforts to preserve, *inter alia*, the existing Irish prohibition on abortion gave rise to Protocol No. 17 to the Maastricht Treaty on European Union which was signed in February 1992. It reads as follows:

> Nothing in the Treaty on European Union, or in the treaties establishing the European Communities, or in the Treaties or Acts modifying or supplementing those treaties, shall affect the application in Ireland of Article 40.3.3 of the Constitution of Ireland ...

> [...]Nothing in the Treaty of Lisbon attributing legal status to the charter of fundamental rights of the European Union, or in the provisions of that Treaty and the area freedom, security and justice, affects in any way the scope and applicability of the protection of the right to life in Article 40.3.1, 40.3.4 and 40.3.3 ... provided by the Constitution of Ireland ...

[The Court referred to various international and European jurisprudence and treaties on abortion including the 1994 Cairo Programme of Action, the *Beijing Platform for Action* and the *2008 European Pace Resolution* which provides in part that:]

> In most of the Council of Europe member states the law permits abortion in order to save the expectant mother's life. Abortion is permitted in the majority of European countries for a number of reasons, mainly to preserve the mother's physical and mental health, but also in cases of rape or incest, of foetal impairment or for economic and social reasons and, in some countries, on request. The Assembly is nonetheless concerned that, in many of these states, numerous conditions are imposed and restrict the effective access to safe, affordable, acceptable and appropriate abortion services. These restrictions have discriminatory effects, since women who are well informed and possess adequate financial means can often obtain legal and safe abortions more easily.

> 3. The Assembly also notes that, in member states where abortion is permitted for a number of reasons, conditions are not always such as to guarantee women effective access to this right: the lack of local health care facilities, the lack of doctors willing to carry out abortions, the repeated medical consultations required, the time allowed for changing one's mind and the waiting time for the abortion

all have the potential to make access to safe, affordable, acceptable and appropriate abortion services more difficult, or even impossible in practice.

4. The Assembly takes the view that abortion should not be banned within reasonable gestational limits. A ban on abortions does not result in fewer abortions but mainly leads to clandestine abortions, which are more traumatic and increase maternal mortality and/or lead to abortion "tourism" which is costly, and delays the timing of an abortion and results in social inequities. The lawfulness of abortion does not have an effect on a woman's need for an abortion, but only on her access to a safe abortion.

5. At the same time, evidence shows that appropriate sexual and reproductive health and rights strategies and policies, including compulsory age-appropriate, gender-sensitive sex and relationships education for young people, result in less recourse to abortion. This type of education should include teaching on self-esteem, healthy relationships, the freedom to delay sexual activity, avoiding peer pressure, contraceptive advice, and considering consequences and responsibilities.

6. The Assembly affirms the right of all human beings, in particular women, to respect for their physical integrity and to freedom to control their own bodies. In this context, the ultimate decision on whether or not to have an abortion should be a matter for the woman concerned, who should have the means of exercising this right in an effective way.

[The Court also noted the CEDAW Committee's Concluding Observations to Ireland in 2008 which included the comments that:]

While acknowledging positive developments ... the Committee reiterates its concern about the consequences of the very restrictive abortion laws, under which abortion is prohibited except where it is established as a matter of probability that there is a real and substantial risk to the life of the mother that can be averted only by the termination of her pregnancy.

397. The Committee urges the State party to continue to facilitate a national dialogue on women's right to reproductive health, including on the very restrictive abortion laws ...

[After finding that the applicants had exhausted domestic remedies, the Court held:]

The applicants complained of a violation of the positive and negative obligations in Article 3 of the Convention given the impact on them of the restrictions on abortion and of travelling for an abortion abroad. They maintained that the criminalisation of abortion was discriminatory (crude stereotyping and prejudice against women), caused an affront to women's dignity and stigmatised women, increasing feelings of anxiety. The applicants argued that the two options open to women—overcoming taboos to seek an abortion abroad and aftercare at home or maintaining the pregnancy in their situations—were degrading and a deliberate affront to their dignity. While the stigma and taboo effect of the criminalisation of abortion was denied by the Government, they submitted that there was much evidence confirming this effect on women. Indeed, the applicants contended that the State was under a positive obligation to protect the applicants from such hardship and degrading treatment.

The Court considers it evident, for the reasons set out at Paragraphs 124–127 above, that travelling abroad for an abortion was both psychologically and physically arduous for each of the applicants. It was also financially burdensome for the first applicant (Paragraph 128 above).

However, the Court reiterates its case-law to the effect that ill-treatment must attain a minimum level of severity if it is to fall within the scope of Article 3.... the Court considers that the facts alleged do not disclose a level of severity falling within the scope of Article 3 of the Convention....

The first and second applicants complained under Article 8 about the restrictions on lawful abortion in Ireland which meant that they could not obtain an abortion for health and/or well-being reasons in Ireland and the third applicant complained under the same Article about the absence of any legislative implementation of Article 40.3.3 of the Constitution.

They considered that it had not been shown that the restrictions were effective in achieving that aim: the abortion rate for women in Ireland was similar to States where abortion was legal since, *inter alia*, Irish women chose to travel abroad for abortions in any event.

Even if they were effective, the applicants questioned how the State could maintain the legitimacy of that aim given the opposite moral viewpoint espoused by human rights bodies worldwide.

While the State was entitled to a margin of appreciation to protect pre-natal life, it was not an absolute one. The Court could not give unqualified deference to the State's interest in protecting pre-natal life as that would allow a State to employ any means necessary to restrict abortion without any regard to the mother's life ... The ruling requested of this Court was not, as the Government suggested, to mandate a particular abortion law for all Contracting States: the proportionality exercise did not preclude variation between States and it did not require deciding when life began (States, courts, scientists, philosophers and religions had and would always disagree). However, this lack of agreement should not, of itself, deny women their Convention rights so that there was a need to express the minimum requirements to protect a woman's health and well-being under the Convention. Preserving pre-natal life was an acceptable goal only when the health and well-being of the mother were given proportionate value.

The restrictive nature of the legal regime in Ireland disproportionately harmed women. There was a medical risk due to a late, and therefore often surgical, abortion and an inevitable reduction in pre- and post-abortion medical support. The financial burden impacted more on poor women and, indirectly, on their families. Women experienced the stigma and psychological burden of doing something abroad which was a serious criminal offence in their own country.

The Court recalls that the notion of "private life" within the meaning of Article 8 of the Convention is a broad concept which encompasses, *inter alia*, the right to personal autonomy and personal development ... a person's physical and psychological integrity ... as well as decisions both to have and not to have a child ...

The Court has also previously found ... that legislation regulating the interruption of pregnancy touches upon the sphere of the private life of the woman, the Court emphasising that Article 8 cannot be interpreted as meaning that pregnancy and its termination pertain uniquely to the woman's private life as, whenever a woman is pregnant, her private life becomes closely connected with the developing foetus. The woman's right to respect for her private life must be weighed against other competing rights and freedoms invoked including those of the unborn child ...

While Article 8 cannot, accordingly, be interpreted as conferring a right to abortion, the Court finds that the prohibition in Ireland of abortion where sought for reasons of health and/or well-being about which the first and second applicants complained, and the third applicant's alleged inability to establish her qualification for a lawful abortion in Ireland, come within the scope of their right to respect for their private lives and accordingly Article 8....

Since the rights claimed on behalf of the foetus and those of the mother are inextricably interconnected ... the margin of appreciation accorded to a State's protection of the unborn necessarily translates into a margin of appreciation for that State as to how it balances the conflicting rights of the mother. It follows that, even if it appears from the national laws referred to that most Contracting Parties may in their legislation have resolved those conflicting rights and interests in favour of greater legal access to abortion, this consensus cannot be a decisive factor in the Court's examination of whether the impugned prohibition on abortion in Ireland for health and well-being reasons struck a fair balance between the conflicting rights and interests, notwithstanding an evolutive interpretation of the Convention ...

It is indeed the case that this margin of appreciation is not unlimited. The prohibition impugned by the first and second applicants must be compatible with a State's Convention obligations and, given the Court's responsibility under Article 19 of the Convention, the Court must supervise whether the interference constitutes a proportionate balancing of the competing interests involved.... A prohibition of abortion to protect unborn life is not therefore automatically justified under the Convention on the basis of unqualified deference to the protection of pre-natal life or on the basis that the expectant mother's right to respect for her private life is of a lesser stature. Nor is the regulation of abortion rights solely a matter for the Contracting States, as the Government maintained..., the Court must decide on the compatibility with Article 8 of the Convention of the Irish State's prohibition of abortion on health and well-being grounds on the basis of the above-described fair balance test to which a broad margin of appreciation is applicable.

From the lengthy, complex and sensitive debate in Ireland ... as regards the content of its abortion laws, a choice has emerged. Irish law prohibits abortion in Ireland for health and well-being reasons but allows women, in the first and second applicants' position who wish to have an abortion for those reasons ... the option of lawfully travelling to another State to do so.

Accordingly, having regard to the right to lawfully travel abroad for an abortion with access to appropriate information and medical care in Ireland, the Court does not consider that the prohibition in Ireland of abortion for health and well-being reasons, based as it is on the profound moral views of the Irish people as to the nature of life ... and as to the consequent protection to be accorded to the right to life of the unborn, exceeds the margin of appreciation accorded in that respect to the Irish State. In such circumstances, the Court finds that the impugned prohibition in Ireland struck a fair balance between the right of the first and second applicants to respect for their private lives and the rights invoked on behalf of the unborn ...

It concludes that there has been no violation of Article 8 of the Convention as regards the first and second applicants.

The third applicant's complaint concerns the failure by the Irish State to implement Article 40.3.3 of the Constitution by legislation and, notably, to introduce a procedure by which she could have established whether she qualified for a lawful abortion in Ireland on grounds of the risk to her life of her pregnancy.

The Court has found that the failure by the State to implement Article 40.3.3 constituted a failure to respect the third applicant's right to respect for her private life in violation of Article 8 of the Convention.

Questions for Discussion

1. In this case the Court used the doctrine of the "margin of appreciation"; a doctrine that permits a state some measure of discretion in determining, based on its own circumstances, the appropriate ways in which it will discharge its obligations under the European Convention on Human Rights. This doctrine permitted the Court to acknowledge the commitment of the Irish people to respect for life. Does this doctrine make the enforcement of rights somewhat contextual?

2. The Court also seems to use a balancing test to balance the right of a woman seeking an abortion to respect for her private life, with the right to life of the unborn. Is this an appropriate test for courts to use in this situation? How does one balance these two competing rights?

IV. Maternal Mortality

Maternal mortality is a major cause of death among women. In its 2008 Report, the World Health Organization[24] (WHO) estimates that in Afghanistan a woman has a one in eleven chance of dying from a maternal cause. In sub-Saharan Africa, the odds are slightly better — 1:31. The United Nations has also noted that:

- An estimated 1,600 women die every day from complications caused by pregnancy and child birth, 99 percent in developing countries

- Each year, approximately 2 million girls are at risk of female genital mutilation

- About 70,000 women die every year from unsafe abortions, and many more suffer infections and other consequences

- Women are more likely than men to contract HIV through sexual encounters and about 42 percent of all persons infected with HIV are women

- Fifty-one percent of all pregnant women suffer from iron-deficiency anemia

- In many countries of South Asia, Africa, Latin America, and the Middle East, one-third to one-half of women are mothers before the age of 20.

- Cancer of the cervix, the most common form of cancer in developing countries, is often linked to the sexually transmitted human papilloma virus

- Domestic violence, rape, and sexual abuse are a significant cause of disability among women[25]

---

24. The study, entitled Trends in Maternal Mortality was conducted and published by the World Health Organization, the United Nations Children's Fund (UNICEF) and the United Nations Population Fund, (UNFPA) along with the World Bank. It is *available at* http://whqlibdoc.who.int/publications/2010/9789241500265_eng.pdf [last visited November 30, 2010].

25. *Available at* http://www.un.org/ecosocdev/geninfo/women/womrepro.htm [last visited November 30, 2010].

Currently the CEDAW Committee is considering the case of *Alyne Da Silva Pimental v. Brazil.* Pimental died of complications from her pregnancy after her local health care center misdiagnosed her symptoms and then postponed providing her the emergency care that she needed. The Committee will also review another case, *L.C. v. Peru,* where a then 13-year-old girl, L.C., tried to kill herself by jumping off a roof when she learned that she was pregnant as a result of repeated rapes by a 34-year-old man. Although L.C. needed urgent spinal surgery after her fall from the roof, doctors in Peru refused to provide it, allegedly because it would cause the fetus to abort. L.C. subsequently miscarried due to her injuries, but did not receive the surgery until months later.

Chapter 19

Women's Rights, Development, Capabilities, Justice, and Equality

Chapter Problem

Imagine that you get to make a speech before the United Nations General Assembly on behalf of UN Women — the UN organization created in 2010 to promote gender equality and the empowerment of women.[1] *UN Women merged the following four UN entities into one:*

- *The Division for the Advancement of Women (DAW)*
- *International Research and Training Institute for the Advancement of Women (INSTRAW)*
- *Office of the Special Adviser on Gender Issues and Advancement of Women (OSAGI)*
- *United Nations Development Fund for Women (UNIFEM)*

Your speech to the General Assembly is a report on the progress of women with regard to gender equality, development, and empowerment. You have a multitude of development statistics, reports, recommendations, declarations, and conventions at your disposal. Much of the news is not good — women have made some progress but not enough. You are also aware that it has been 30 years since CEDAW entered into force. While you want to acknowledge the many challenges women still face, you also want your speech to be affirmative, and to go beyond a mere reiteration of the rights guaranteed by CEDAW. Beyond justice and equality, how might one want to advocate for women's "happiness"? To create a new era in women's development? For the right of women to live fulfilling and meaningful lives free from customs and practices which oppress them?

I. CEDAW, "Potentialities," and "Happiness"

CEDAW does not concern itself with happiness per se, but focuses instead on the principles of equality, non discrimination, (arts. 1 & 2), and human dignity. However, the Preamble to CEDAW notes that "States Parties to the International Covenants on Human Rights have the obligation to ensure the equal rights of men and women to enjoy

---

1. UN Women has now been in existence for a year and recently prepared its first report.

all economic, social, cultural, civil and political rights," and speaks to the "full development of the potentialities of women in the service of their countries and of humanity."

Much of the work of international organizations like the UN has been focused on asserting women's rights to equality and non discrimination. Alongside that, much of the work done by development organizations and NGOs has been in an effort to minimize the harsh effects of discrimination and poverty on women. Not much attention has been paid to happiness. The two most significant recent development documents, the *Millennium Declaration* and the *Millennium Development Goals*, have articulated some ambitious goals; principal among them is the goal of halving poverty by 2015.

II. Women's Progress in Equality and Development

A. Resolution Adopted by the General Assembly — United Nations *Millennium Declaration*[2]

19. We resolve further:

• To halve, by the year 2015, the proportion of the world's people whose income is less than one dollar a day and the proportion of people who suffer from hunger and, by the same date, to halve the proportion of people who are unable to reach or to afford safe drinking water

• To ensure that, by the same date, children everywhere, boys and girls alike, will be able to complete a full course of primary schooling and that girls and boys will have equal access to all levels of education

• By the same date, to have reduced maternal mortality by three quarters, and under-five child mortality by two thirds, of their current rates

• To have, by then, halted, and begun to reverse, the spread of HIV/AIDS, the scourge of malaria and other major diseases that afflict humanity

• To provide special assistance to children orphaned by HIV/AIDS

• By 2020, to have achieved a significant improvement in the lives of at least 100 million slum dwellers as proposed in the "Cities Without Slums" initiative

20. We also resolve:

• To promote gender equality and the empowerment of women as effective ways to combat poverty, hunger and disease and to stimulate development that is truly sustainable

• To develop and implement strategies that give young people everywhere a real chance to find decent and productive work

---

2. [(A/55/L.2)].

• To encourage the pharmaceutical industry to make essential drugs more widely available and affordable by all who need them in developing countries

• To develop strong partnerships with the private sector and with civil society organizations in pursuit of development and poverty eradication

• To ensure that the benefits of new technologies, especially information and communication technologies, in conformity with recommendations contained in the ECOSOC 2000 Ministerial Declaration, are available to all

IV. Protecting our common environment

21. We must spare no effort to free all of humanity, and above all our children and grandchildren, from the threat of living on a planet irredeemably spoilt by human activities, and whose resources would no longer be sufficient for their needs.

22. We reaffirm our support for the principles of sustainable development, including those set out in Agenda 21, agreed upon at the United Nations Conference on Environment and Development.

23. We resolve therefore to adopt in all our environmental actions a new ethic of conservation and stewardship and, as first steps, we resolve:

• To make every effort to ensure the entry into force of the Kyoto Protocol, preferably by the tenth anniversary of the United Nations Conference on Environment and Development in 2002, and to embark on the required reduction in emissions of greenhouse gases

• To intensify our collective efforts for the management, conservation and sustainable development of all types of forests

• To press for the full implementation of the Convention on Biological Diversity and the Convention to Combat Desertification in those Countries Experiencing Serious Drought and/or Desertification, particularly in Africa

• To stop the unsustainable exploitation of water resources by developing water management strategies at the regional, national and local levels, which promote both equitable access and adequate supplies

• To intensify cooperation to reduce the number and effects of natural and man-made disasters

• To ensure free access to information on the human genome sequence

V. Human Rights, Democracy and Good Governance

24. We will spare no effort to promote democracy and strengthen the rule of law, as well as respect for all internationally recognized human rights and fundamental freedoms, including the right to development.

25. We resolve therefore:

• To respect fully and uphold the Universal Declaration of Human Rights

• To strive for the full protection and promotion in all our countries of civil, political, economic, social and cultural rights for all

• To strengthen the capacity of all our countries to implement the principles and practices of democracy and respect for human rights, including minority rights

• To combat all forms of violence against women and to implement the Convention on the Elimination of All Forms of Discrimination against Women

• To take measures to ensure respect for and protection of the human rights of migrants, migrant workers and their families, to eliminate the increasing acts of racism and xenophobia in many societies and to promote greater harmony and tolerance in all societies

• To work collectively for more inclusive political processes, allowing genuine participation by all citizens in all our countries

• To ensure the freedom of the media to perform their essential role and the right of the public to have access to information

VI. Protecting the vulnerable

26. We will spare no effort to ensure that children and all civilian populations that suffer disproportionately the consequences of natural disasters, genocide, armed conflicts and other humanitarian emergencies are given every assistance and protection so that they can resume normal life as soon as possible.

We resolve therefore:

• To expand and strengthen the protection of civilians in complex emergencies, in conformity with international humanitarian law

• To strengthen international cooperation, including burden sharing in, and the coordination of humanitarian assistance to, countries hosting refugees and to help all refugees and displaced persons to return voluntarily to their homes, in safety and dignity and to be smoothly reintegrated into their societies

• To encourage the ratification and full implementation of the Convention on the Rights of the Child and its optional protocols on the involvement of children in armed conflict and on the sale of children, child prostitution and child pornography

VII. Meeting the special needs of Africa

27. We will support the consolidation of democracy in Africa and assist Africans in their struggle for lasting peace, poverty eradication and sustainable development, thereby bringing Africa into the mainstream of the world economy.

28. We resolve therefore:

• To give full support to the political and institutional structures of emerging democracies in Africa

• To encourage and sustain regional and sub regional mechanisms for preventing conflict and promoting political stability, and to ensure a reliable flow of resources for peacekeeping operations on the continent

• To take special measures to address the challenges of poverty eradication and sustainable development in Africa, including debt cancellation, improved market access, enhanced Official Development Assistance and increased flows of Foreign Direct Investment, as well as transfers of technology

• To help Africa build up its capacity to tackle the spread of the HIV/AIDS pandemic and other infectious diseases

---

Based on the Declaration, the UN articulated 8 *Millennium Development Goals* (MDGs) designed to half the rate of poverty by 2015.

B. *The Millennium Development Goals*

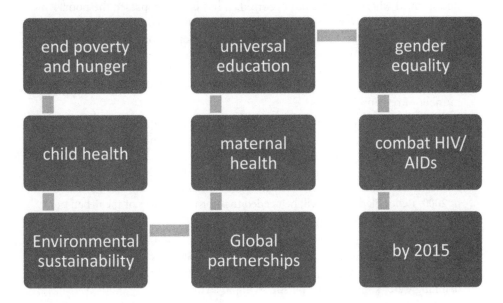

The Millennium Progress Report was issued in 2011.[3] Alongside that Report there are a number of development indices and statistics that track gender equality and the development of women. The Report illustrates that although significant strides have been made, reaching all the MDGs by 2015 remains challenging because progress has failed to reach the most vulnerable.

1. *The Millennium Goals Report 2011*[4]

Opportunities for full and productive employment remain particularly slim for women. Wide gaps remain in women's access to paid work in at least half of all regions. Following significant job losses in 2008–2009, the growth in employment during the economic recovery in 2010, especially in the developing world, was lower for women than for men. Women employed in manufacturing industries were especially hard hit.

Being poor, female or living in a conflict zone increases the probability that a child will be out of school. The net enrolment ratio of children in primary school has only gone up by 7 percentage points since 1999, reaching 89 per cent in 2009. More recently, progress has actually slowed, dimming prospects for reaching the MDG target of universal primary education by 2015. Children from the poorest households, those living in rural areas and girls are the most likely to be out of school. Worldwide, among children of primary school age not enrolled in school, 42 per cent—28 million—live in poor countries affected by conflict.

---

3. *Available at* http://mdgs.un.org/unsd/mdg/Resources/Static/Products/Progress2011/11-31339 %20(E)%20MDG%20Report%202011_Book%20LR.pdf [last visited July 11, 2011].

4. *Available at* http://www.un.org/millenniumgoals/pdf/(2011_E)%20MDG%20Report%202011_ Book%20LR.pdf [last visited July 11, 2011].

Advances in sanitation often bypass the poor and those living in rural areas. Over 2.6 billion people still lack access to flush toilets or other forms of improved sanitation. And where progress has occurred, it has largely bypassed the poor. An analysis of trends over the period 1995–2008 for three countries in Southern Asia shows that improvements in sanitation disproportionately benefited the better off, while sanitation coverage for the poorest 40 per cent of households hardly increased. Although gaps in sanitation coverage between urban and rural areas are narrowing, rural populations remain at a distinct disadvantage in a number of regions.

Improving the lives of a growing number of urban poor remains a monumental challenge. Progress in ameliorating slum conditions has not been sufficient to offset the growth of informal settlements throughout the developing world. In developing regions, the number of urban residents living in slum conditions is now estimated at 828 million, compared to 657 million in 1990 and 767 million in 2000. Redoubled efforts will be needed to improve the lives of the urban poor in cities and metropolises across the developing world.

Progress has been uneven in improving access to safe drinking water. In all regions, coverage in rural areas lags behind that of cities and towns. In sub-Saharan Africa, an urban dweller is 1.8 times more likely to use an improved drinking water source than a person living in a rural area.

At the 2010 High-level Plenary Meeting of the General Assembly on the *Millennium Development Goals*, world leaders reaffirmed their commitment to the MDGs and called for intensified collective action and the expansion of successful approaches. They acknowledged the challenges posed by multiple crises, increasing inequalities and persistent violent conflicts.

They called for action to ensure equal access by women and girls to education, basic services, health care, economic opportunities and decision-making at all levels, recognizing that achievement of the MDGs depends largely on women's empowerment. World leaders also stressed that accelerated action on the goals requires economic growth that is sustainable, inclusive and equitable — growth that enables everyone to benefit from progress and share in economic opportunities.

Finally, further and faster movement towards achievement of the MDGs will require a rejuvenated global partnership, expeditious delivery on commitments already made, and an agile transition to a more environmentally sustainable future.

Continued progress requires an active commitment to peace, equity, equality and sustainability.

C. The Gender Inequality Index[5]

The Gender Inequality Index (GII) reflects women's disadvantage in three dimensions — reproductive health, empowerment and the labour market — for as many countries

---

5. *Available at* http://hdr.undp.org/en/media/HDR_2010_EN_Table4_reprint.pdf [last visited July 13, 2011].

as data of reasonable quality allow. The index shows the loss in human development due to inequality between female and male achievements in these dimensions. In countries with low human development, the statistics tell a dressing tale in the areas of maternal mortality and adult female education.

The first UN Women Report was slightly more positive, and at least offered concrete suggestions for improving gender equality.

D. UN Women Report 2011–2012: *In Pursuit of Justice — Progress of the World's Women*[6]

The report called on countries to:

- *Repeal laws that discriminate against women*, and ensure that legislation protects women from violence and inequality in the home and the workplace

- *Support innovative justice services*, including one-stop shops, legal aid and specialized courts, to ensure women can access the justice to which they are entitled

- *Put women on the frontline of justice delivery*. As police, judges, legislators and activists, women in every region are making a difference and bringing about change

- *Invest in justice systems that can respond to women's needs*. Donors spend US$4.2 billion annually on aid for justice reform, but only 5 percent of this spending specifically targets women and girls

III. Progress in Domestic Jurisdictions

A. *The Magna Carta of Women in the Philippines* (2010)

SEC. 4. *Definitions.* — For purposes of this Act, the following terms shall mean:

(a) "Women Empowerment" refers to the provision, availability, and accessibility of opportunities, services, and observance of human rights which enable women to actively participate and contribute to the political, economic, social, and cultural development of the nation as well as those which shall provide them equal access to ownership, management, and control of production, and of material and informational resources and benefits in the family, community, and society.

(b) "Discrimination Against Women" refers to any gender-based distinction, exclusion, or restriction which has the effect or purpose of impairing or nullifying the recognition, enjoyment, or exercise by women, irrespective of their marital status, on a basis of equality of men and women, of human rights and fundamental freedoms in the political, economic, social, cultural, civil, or any other field.

---

6. *Available at* http://progress.unwomen.org/pdfs/EN-Report-Progress.pdf [last visited July 13, 2011].

It includes any act or omission, including by law, policy, administrative measure, or practice, that directly or indirectly excludes or restricts women in the recognition and promotion of their rights and their access to and enjoyment of opportunities, benefits, or privileges.

A measure or practice of general application is discrimination against women if it fails to provide for mechanisms to offset or address sex or gender-based disadvantages or limitations of women, as a result of which women are denied or restricted in the recognition and protection of their rights and in their access to and enjoyment of opportunities, benefits, or privileges; or women, more than men, are shown to have suffered the greater adverse effects of those measures or practices.

Provided, finally, That discrimination compounded by or intersecting with other grounds, status, or condition, such as ethnicity, age, poverty, or religion shall be considered discrimination against women under this Act.

(c) "Marginalization" refers to a condition where a whole category of people is excluded from useful and meaningful participation in political, economic, social, and cultural life.

(d) "Marginalized" refers to the basic, disadvantaged, or vulnerable persons or groups who are mostly living in poverty and have little or no access to land and other resources, basic social and economic services such as health care, education, water and sanitation, employment and livelihood opportunities, housing, social security, physical infrastructure, and the justice system.

(e) "Substantive Equality" refers to the full and equal enjoyment of rights and freedoms contemplated under this Act. It encompasses de jure and de facto equality and also equality in outcomes.

(f) "Gender Equality" refers to the principle asserting the equality of men and women and their right to enjoy equal conditions realizing their full human potentials to contribute to and benefit from the results of development, and with the State recognizing that all human beings are free and equal in dignity and rights.

(g) "Gender Equity" refers to the policies, instruments, programs, services, and actions that address the disadvantaged position of women in society by providing preferential treatment and affirmative action. Such temporary special measures aimed at accelerating de facto equality between men and women shall not be considered discriminatory but shall in no way entail as a consequence the maintenance of unequal or separate standards. These measures shall be discontinued when the objectives of equality of opportunity and treatment have been achieved.

(h) "Gender and Development (GAD)" refers to the development perspective and process that are participatory and empowering, equitable, sustainable, free from violence, respectful of human rights, supportive of self-determination and actualization of human potentials. It seeks to achieve gender equality as a fundamental value that should be reflected in development choices; seeks to transform society's social, economic, and political structures and questions they validity of the gender roles they ascribed to women and men; contends that women are active agents of development and not just passive recipients of development assistance; and stresses the need of women to organize themselves and participate in political processes to strengthen their legal rights.

(i) "Gender Mainstreaming" refers to the strategy for making women's as well as men's concerns and experiences an integral dimension of the design, implementation, monitoring, and evaluation of policies and programs in all political, economic, and societal spheres so that women and men benefit equally and inequality is not perpetuated. It is the process of assessing the implications for women and men of any planned action, including legislation, policies, or programs in all areas and at all levels.

The State, private sector, society in general, and all individuals shall contribute to the recognition, respect, and promotion of the rights of women defined and guaranteed under this Act.

SEC. 5. *The State as the Primary Duty-Bearer*—The State, as the primary duty-bearer, shall:

(a) Refrain from discriminating against women and violating their rights;

(b) Protect women against discrimination and from violation of their rights by private corporations, entities, and individuals; and

(c) Promote and fulfill the rights of women in all spheres, including their rights to substantive equality and non-discrimination.

The State shall fulfill these duties through law, policy, regulatory instruments, administrative guidelines, and other appropriate measures, including temporary special measures.

Recognizing the interrelation of the human rights of women, the State shall take measures and establish mechanisms to promote the coherent and integrated implementation and enforcement of this Act and related laws, policies, or other measures to effectively stop discrimination against and advance the rights of women.

RIGHTS AND EMPOWERMENT OF MARGINALIZED SECTORS

Women in marginalized sectors are hereby guaranteed all civil, political, social, and economic rights recognized, promoted, and protected under existing laws including, but not limited to, the Indigenous Peoples Rights Act, the Urban Development and Housing Act, the Comprehensive Agrarian Reform Law, the Fisheries Code, the Labor Code, the Migrant Workers Act, the Solo Parents Welfare Act, and the Social Reform and Poverty Alleviation Act.

SEC. 20. *Food Security and Productive Resources*—The State recognizes the contribution of women to food production and shall ensure its sustainability and sufficiency with the active participation of women.

Towards this end, the State shall guarantee, at all times, the availability in the market of safe and health-giving food to satisfy the dietary needs of the population, giving particular attention to the specific needs of poor girlchildren and marginalized women, especially pregnant and lactating mothers and their young children. To further address this, the state shall ensure:

(a) *Right to Food*—The State shall guarantee the availability of food in quantity and quality sufficient to satisfy the dietary needs of individuals, the physical and economic accessibility for everyone to adequate food that is culturally acceptable and free from unsafe substances and culturally accepted, and the accurate and substantial information to the availability of food, including the right to full, accurate, and truthful information about safe and health-giving foods and how to produce and have regular easy access to them;

(b) *Right to Resources for Food Production*—The State shall guarantee women a vital role in food production by giving priority to their rights to land, credit, and infrastructure support, technical training, and technological and marketing assistance. The State shall promote women friendly technology as a high priority activity in agriculture and shall promote the right to adequate food by proactively engaging in activities intended to strengthen access to, utilization of, and receipt of accurate and substantial information on resources and means to ensure women's livelihood, including food security:

(1) Equal status shall be given to women and men, whether married or not, in the titling of the land and issuance of stewardship contracts and patents;

(2) Equal treatment shall be given to women and men beneficiaries of the agrarian reform program, wherein the vested right of a woman agrarian reform beneficiary is defined by a woman's relationship to tillage, i.e., her direct and indirect contribution to the development of the land; ...

The Magna Carta articulated a vision of life that goes beyond basic rights and freedom from discrimination. Thirty years after the entry into force of CEDAW, is it now possible to articulate goals for women beyond the *Millennium Development Goals* and equality development statistics. The *Beijing Declaration* hinted at such a vision as long ago as 1995.

B. The *Beijing Declaration* — Article 12

The empowerment and advancement of women, including the right to freedom of thought, conscience, religion and belief, thus contributing to the moral, ethical, spiritual and intellectual needs of women and men, individually or in community with others and thereby guaranteeing them the possibility of realizing their full potential in society and shaping their lives in accordance with their own aspirations.

IV. Beyond Non Discrimination — Human Flourishing for Women?

Now that 2015 is almost here, and the *Millennium Development Goals* are in sight, philosophers and feminists are looking beyond basic rights for women, and positing the idea of human flourishing for women.

Aristotle is perhaps the most well known philosopher to posit an idea of human flourishing. His concept of *eudaimonia,* (human flourishing, well-being, or happiness) has profoundly impacted the scholarship of moral philosophy. Aristotle's *eudaimonia* presupposes a kind of happiness worth having, and lays down conditions which best support the attainment of that kind of happiness. More recently scholars from such diverse fields as economics, ethics, philosophy, and women's rights, have considered what those conditions might be for women to have optimal opportunities at happiness.

A. Philosophies of Human Needs — Doyal and Gough

Professors Doyal and Gough, two British researchers, have identified the most basic human needs as being physical health and autonomy.[7] They also identify four common social roles which exist in all societies, namely: production, reproduction, cultural

---

7. IAN GOUGH & LEN DOYAL, A THEORY OF HUMAN NEED (1991).

transmission and political authority. They note that one's personal autonomy is severely restricted if one is unable to participate in any of these roles. Beyond these basic requirements, Doyal and Gough urge the goal of critical participation—participating in a life form that is as far as possible of one's own choosing. They also claim that critical autonomy is a necessary good; that consists of "the ability to situate, criticize and, if necessary, challenge the rules and practices of the culture one is born into, or presently lives."[8]

Among the intermediate needs identified by Doyal and Gough are:

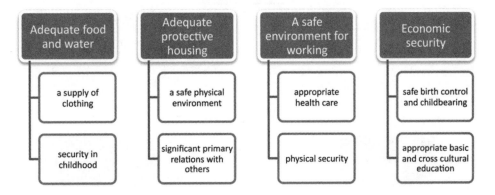

B. Human Development and Human Capability— Martha Nussbaum

Martha Nussbaum, an American philosopher and law professor, has also entered the debate and come up with her own terminology for human flourishing, which differs somewhat from that of Gough and Doyal. She uses the word "capabilities" rather than needs to describe the essentials for human flourishing in her seminal book *Frontiers of Justice*.

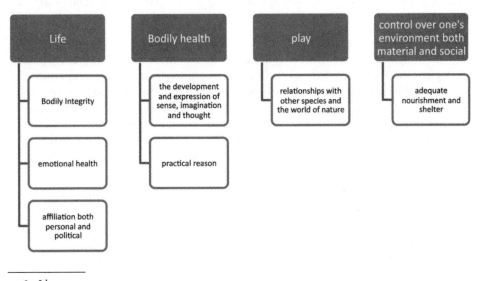

8. *Id.*

C. John Finnis — Basic Human Needs

Finnis, a noted proponent of Natural Law, uses the term "basic human needs"[9] to describe his prerequisites for a good life. His basic requirements are:

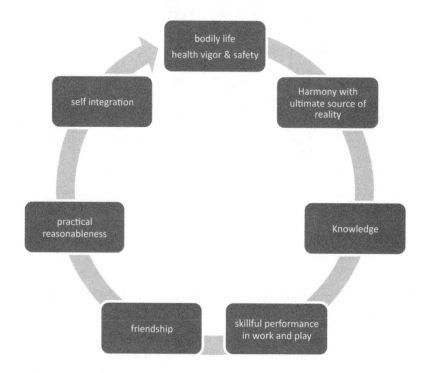

D. Amartya Sen — The Capabilities Approach

Economist, Amartya Sen, was largely responsible for pioneering the capabilities approach in the 1980s.

As Sabina Alkire has pointed out:[10]

> In this approach development is not defined as an increase in GNP per capita, or in consumption, health, and education measures alone, but as an expansion of capability. Capability refers to a person's or group's freedom to promote or achieve valuable functionings. "It represents the various combinations of functionings (beings and doings) that the person can achieve." Capabilities may relate to things near to survival (the capability to drink clean water) or those which are rather less central (the capability to visit one's aunt, the capability to eat rich sweets).
>
> The definition of capability does not delimit a certain subset of capabilities as of peculiar importance. Rather Sen argues that the selection of capabilities on

---

9. He uses this term in his book Natural Law and Natural Rights (1980).

10. Sabina Alkire, *Dimensions of Human Development,* Report for The World Bank, Washington, DC, USA; *available at* http://www.csun.edu/~sg61795/350/human_development.pdf [last visited July 13, 2011].

which to focus is a value judgement that is to be made explicitly, and in many cases by a process of public debate.

Together, Nussbaum and Sen started the *Human Development and Capability Association* in 2004. It focuses on economics, development, and human rights. The *Human Development and Capability Association* promotes research from many disciplines on key problems including poverty, justice, well-being, and economics. Frances Stewart is the president of the HDCA. Amartya Sen was the Founding President of HDCA 2004–2006; Martha Nussbaum was President of HDCA 2006–2008.

E. McGregor—3D Wellbeing[11]

British development economist, Professor Allister McGregor, has posited the theory of wellbeing on behalf of the poor. According to a Report entitled *After 2015—Promoting the Pro-Poor Policy After the MDGs,*[12] wellbeing arises from a combination of:

- what a person has
- what a person can do with what they have
- and how they think about what they have and can do.

It involves the interplay of:

- the resources that a person is able to command
- what they are able to achieve with those resources and what needs and goals they are able to meet
- the meaning that they give to the goals they achieve, and the processes in which they engage...

1. The Guardian Newspaper—*Poverty Matters*[13]

Taking a provocative approach Professor Allister McGregor, research fellow at the Institute of Development Studies, said in this week's debate that the MDGs were not fit for 2015. He argued for putting the notion of wellbeing into the next phase and for more sophisticated ways of looking at poverty. The MDGs, he said, had provided good momentum but the world needed to move beyond targets.

"Poor people are not just defined by poverty," he said. "They have aspirations ... we need to ask: what do you want to achieve and what are the obstacles that systematically frustrate you?"

Referring to the Arab spring, McGregor said the events in north Africa underlined the importance of trying to incorporate the concept of wellbeing, as prosperity without freedom had proved destabilising. He also cited the contrast between Bangkok and the poor rural northeast, where farmers were committing suicide because they had fallen into debt.

"It's basically about inequality, how we live well together and how we share wealth," said McGregor. "Let's get it on the agenda and have people work on wellbeing. We have to start coming up with new ideas on how we measure what we value."

---

11. *Available at* http://www.ids.ac.uk/files/dmfile/IF9.2.pdf McGregor 2007 [last visited July 20, 2011].

12. *Available at* http://www.ids.ac.uk/files/dmfile/IF9.2.pdf [last visited July 20, 2011].

13. *Available at* http://www.guardian.co.uk/global-development/poverty-matters/2011/jul/15/ millennium-development-goals-beyond-2015 [last visited July 18, 2011].

McGregor summed up wellbeing in an IDS report in 2009 as what a person has, what a person can do with what they have, and how they think about what they have and can do. It also involves the interplay of the resources a person is able to command: what they are able to achieve with those resources, what needs and goals they can meet, and the meaning they give to the goals they achieve and the processes in which they engage.

The notions of wellbeing and happiness are being taken increasingly seriously by governments, so it would not be surprising if they are taken into account in the post-MDG phase. The Stiglitz commission in France recommended in 2009 that statistical surveys should "incorporate questions to capture people's life evaluations, hedonic experiences, and priorities" and last year the British prime minister David Cameron started work with the Office for National Statistics on how to measure wellbeing.

But as former Scottish first minister Baron McConnell warned, there is a risk that the pursuit of more ambitious and nebulous goals will let governments off the hook.

"If you want to pin governments down, you need precise targets," he said.

Questions for Reflection

1. *This book has detailed many oppressive and harmful practices and situations endured by women. Obviously an end to those practices and situations is the ultimate goal. But beyond that, it seems important to speculate about the conditions that need to be met in order to have women flourish, and enjoy happy and productive lives—not just to focus on the elimination of negative practices, but to explore the need for a positive environment in which women will not only be free from discrimination but also be free to enjoy their lives. What do you consider to the pre requisites for happiness or wellbeing?*

2. *Are there conditions for happiness that transcend cultures and that could be considered universal? How could we determine what these are?*

3. *Will we be able to measure whether these conditions are present for women given how economists and statisticians measure development indices?*

Table of Cases

495

Index